Milfred Mast

HUNTS' HIGHLIGHTS

of

MICHIGAN

Mary and Don Hunt

D0916060

MIDWESTERN GUIDES
Waterloo, Michigan

A Midwestern Guides Book

**Printed in the United States of America
by
Malloy Lithographing Inc.,
Ann Arbor, Michigan**

Cover Designer & Design Consultant:
Chris Golus

Other Midwestern Guides titles:

Hunts' Guide to Southeast Michigan
Hunts' Guide to West Michigan
Michigan Fresh: A food-lover's guide to growers & bakeries
*Hunts' Getaways on the Upper Mississippi
between Chicago & the Twin Cities*

For a current catalog or purchasing information,
call (517) 629-4494, or write:

Midwestern Guides
504 1/2 Linden Avenue
Albion, Michigan 49224

Library of Congress Cataloging in Publication Data

Hunt, Mary. Hunt, Donald
Hunts' Highlights of Michigan.
Includes index.
1. Michigan — Description and travel — Guidebooks.
2. Outdoor recreation — Michigan — Guidebooks
917.74

Library of Congress Catalog Card Number: 91-062335

ISBN 0-9623499-2-5

Contents

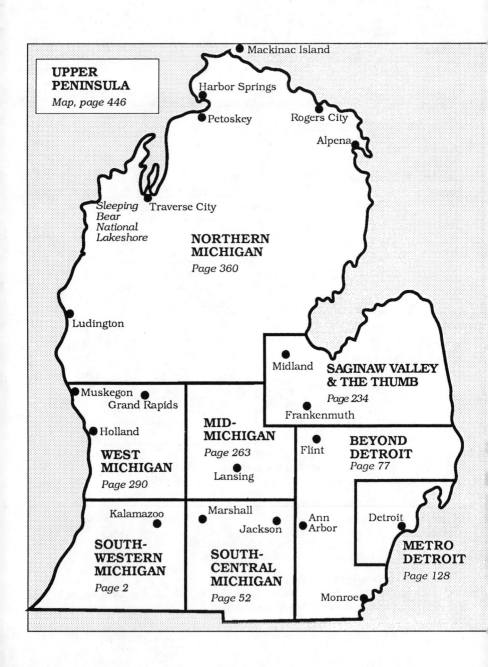

UPPER
PENINSULA
Map, page 446

Mackinac Island

Harbor Springs

Petoskey

Rogers City

Alpena

Sleeping
Bear
National
Lakeshore

Traverse City

**NORTHERN
MICHIGAN**
Page 360

Ludington

Midland

**SAGINAW VALLEY
& THE THUMB**
Page 234

Frankenmuth

Muskegon
Grand Rapids

Holland

**MID-
MICHIGAN**
Page 263

Lansing

Flint

**BEYOND
DETROIT**
Page 77

**WEST
MICHIGAN**
Page 290

Kalamazoo

Marshall

Jackson

Ann
Arbor

Detroit

**SOUTH-
WESTERN
MICHIGAN**
Page 2

**SOUTH-
CENTRAL
MICHIGAN**
Page 52

**METRO
DETROIT**
Page 128

Monroe

Introduction

Throughout the four years spent preparing this guidebook, our primary goal has been to evaluate the thousands of destinations in Michigan and report on ones that truly stand out. The over one thousand places recommended here are not just a long list of things we've seen, but represent the best of a much larger pool of places visited. Every entry included was carefully evaluated, often by multiple visits. Some well-known places were left out because we did not feel they measured up. On the other hand, some small, obscure places, such as Ed's Breads in Grand Rapids, were deemed outstanding enough to justify a major entry. Following many of the highlights are briefer comments (in smaller type) on other recommended attractions nearby. They help enrich a trip if you have the time or interest.

We have taken great pains to provide information which will make your visits more enjoyable. This includes helpful background information to give you more insight into a place you may want to visit. We also provide relatively detailed logistical information on how to get to a place, when it's open, how much things cost there, etc. Very few guidebooks provide so much helpful information to assist in planning a trip. Although we updated this information just before going to press, it's still a good idea to call ahead (every entry has a phone number) to check on the current situation. *Hunts' Highlights* is also full of hundreds of specific tips on such things as when it's best to visit a place, what's especially good there, what to avoid.

At the end of each region are recommended restaurants and lodgings. They range all the way from inexpensive to expensive. Selections for restaurants, as with all other entries in the book, are based on our own direct experience. We chose restaurants primarily on the basis of how good the food was. In most restaurant entries we note the atmosphere of a place, but it was usually a minor factor in selecting it. *Note:* lunch and dinner price ranges refer to a meal including entree plus appropriate side dishes. That price range doesn't include beverage or dessert.

Attractive, interesting locations played a big role in selecting lodgings. We tend to avoid busy motel strips at freeway interchanges and seek out places with views of water or town, places with their own beaches, or places within walking distance of shops, restaurants, and other attractions. We look for good owner-operated motels. Older facilities with smaller rooms often have the most interesting locations and lowest prices.

Finally, rest assured there is no charge for inclusion in our guidebooks. At a time when even many reputable-looking guides demand compensation for write-ups, we pride ourselves in providing readers with impartial assessments of the best Michigan has to offer.

Chapter 1
Southwestern Michigan

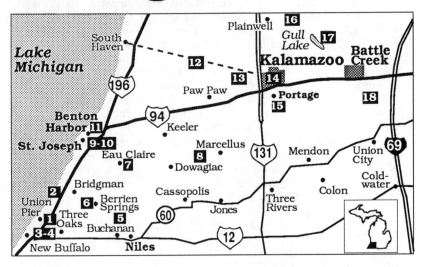

HIGHLIGHTS

Harbor Country Galleries and Shops

A beguiling mix of roadside nostalgia and challenging international art, Swedish cookies and country antiques.

In the mid-1980s the sleepy resort area around New Buffalo and Lakeside was discovered by overstressed Chicago media people seeking convenient weekend getaways. The ensuing PR they generated has transformed what was once a series of pokey resort communities frequented by southside Lithuanians, Bohemians, Jews, meat-packers, and professors. Today "Harbor Country" is Chicagoland's hot new playground, home of the largest marina-condo complex on Lake Michigan. *New York Times* lifestyle articles gush over the area's exciting new galleries and second homes.

All the exposure, plus all the new condos and renovated cottages to be decorated, have provided fertile soil for the galleries and shops strung out along and off the Red Arrow Highway from New Buffalo to Harbert, eight miles north. The four-lane road, predating interstate highways, now enjoys a growing reputation as a great place to drive, browse, and see art — great except on summer weekends, that is. Traffic then can be fierce.

Some of the galleries go beyond the light-hearted, decorative approach typical in resort areas. There's some provocative, unsettling art here as well. Harbor Country shops focusing on interior decor are unusually fresh and witty. Don't be surprised to find humble recent folk art like bottlecap figures and popsicle stick lamps enlivening the usual country mix. After all, these gallery owners are not self-conscious small-town folks who insist on proper English period looks, but sophisticated urban refugees, high-power if somewhat burned out, who are attempting to slow down and enjoy life.

The Red Arrow Highway itself is a nostalgic stretch of auto-age Americana, where roadhouses, drive-ins, and tourist courts of the 1920s and 1930s miraculously live on. Often they've been refurbished as monuments to the childhoods of war babies and aging baby boomers who vacationed here as kids, before interstates and cheap air fares made more exotic vacations widely possible.

A shop and gallery tour works best from north to south. Start at the Sawyer exit of I-94. After you pass through the town center of

Sawyer, which has an improbably urbane theater\storefront complex from the 1920s, turn left (south) upon reaching the Red Arrow Highway. Especially noteworthy places include:

◆ **Judith Racht Gallery.** The area's top gallery shows "young, up-coming artists — people who will rock and shake you," says co-owner Doug Stock. A quilt collector, he does an October quilt show augmented by tramp art and outsider art. Contemporary crafts and new folk art by naive painters are also big at this always interesting gallery in the old Harbert schoolhouse. It completely changes every three or four weeks. Racht is a protegée of John Wilson, who started the Lakeside Center for the Arts (see below). *Prairie Rd. just east of the Red Arrow Hwy. in Harbert. Turn at the Harbert Bakery. (616) 683-9527. Mem.-Labor Day open 10-5 daily. Otherwise, weekends only 10-5. Closed Jan.-March except by appointment.*

◆ **Harbert Swedish Bakery.** Full-line bakery spotlights traditional Swedish breads and cakes. Here since the days when Harbert was largely Swedish and Carl Sandburg had his goat farm nearby. Tables outside and in, coffee and milk. *Red Arrow Hwy. at Prairie Rd. (616) 469-1777. Open 7:30-6, Fri-Sun in spring and fall, Wed-Sun in July & Aug, closed Thanksgiving to Easter.*

◆ **The Silver Crane Gallery.** Claims to have the Midwest's largest collection of sterling silver — mostly jewelry, but with some striking vessels like the simple pitcher from Taxco's famed Los Castillo workshop, with a sinuous lizard handle inlaid with mala-chite. Prices range from $20-$40 for many pins and earrings imported direct from Mexico to $800 for turquoise and sterling necklaces by Navajos. The picturesque half-timber building was built as the store and post office of Lakeside, the area's old-money resort, long favored by southside meat packers and University of Chicago professors. *14950 Lakeside Rd. just west of Red Arrow Hwy. 7 days, 11-6.*

◆ **Lakeside Gallery.** Here in the sales gallery of the nearby Lake-side Center for the Arts, art comes alive as an exciting process of exploration and experiment. Both the center and gallery were started by John Wilson, the artist and print dealer who organized Chicago's influential Art Expo at Navy Pier. The center, in an old Lakeside summer hotel, is a working artists' retreat that furthers artistic and cultural exchange among artists from around the world, mainly the U.S., the Soviet Union, the Baltic republics, and China. Visitors are welcome to drop by and see the studios for printmaking, painting, ceramics, and sculpture. Ask for directions here at the gallery. Artists donate half the work they create there to support the center; it's sold in this gallery. Works are produced under conditions of unusual creative freedom. Gallery windows look out on a yard provocatively studded with sculptures. If most art galleries leave you feeling cynical and manipulated, this may be different. *15486 Red Arrow Hwy. at Warren Woods Rd. (616) 469-3022. Fri-Sun 10-6. Closed Jan & Feb.*

◆ **Lakeside Antiques.** Two barns are filled with quality pieces. Eight dealers offer some uncommon specialties: 1950s, folk art (both antique and by living artists), bamboo, wicker, and painted furniture, plus primitive and country. Different dealers run a shop and a mall next door. *14866 Red Arrow Hwy. just north of East Rd. in Lakeside. (616) 469-4467. Spring-Xmas: open Fri-Mon 11-6. Winter: Sat & Sun only.*

◆ **East Road Gallery.** Turning 1912 Craftsman-style resort into Lakeside's Pebble House bed and breakfast introduced Jean and Ed Lawrence to the Arts and Crafts furniture that the old place seemed to demand. Now they hold seminars on the Arts and Crafts movement and write guides to antiquing in Michigan. Their new shop features generic Mission and related styles never low-end, but seldom signed Stickley either. Room settings are fully accessorized with the likes of copper lamps, etchings, old Craftsman-style books, and some compatible paintings by living artists. *14906 Red Arrow Hwy. just south of East Rd. (616) 469-5995. Open year-round Sat & Sun 12-5, otherwise by chance or appointment.*

◆ **Filoni Vestimenti.** Owner-buyer Shari Filoni, who reps for Chicago designers, has assembled her favorites from their collections and elsewhere, along with interesting jewelry and accessories, including antique watches. Many outfits are as low as $100 or so. *15300 Red Arrow Hwy., Lakeside, next to Panozzo's. (616) 469-4944. Open 10-5 daily, year-round.*

◆ **Rabbit Run Antiques and Interiors.** Decorator Ken Gosh, an early Chicago emigré to Harbor Country, sets a relaxed, sophisticated, country tone. His quaintly situated old place is full of a constantly changing mix of Amish quilts, old and new folk art, dune country primitives, antique Irish scrubbed pine cupboards and tables ("scrubbed" really means chemically stripped and lightly refinished with wax), twig crafts, Turkish kilims, and new, often whimsical china and accessories from England and Brazil. The prices aren't out of sight. *15460 Red Arrow Hwy. north of Union Pier Rd. in Lakeside. Year-round, daily 10-6.*

◆ **Antique Mall and Village.** An appealingly fanciful "village" in the woods. 40 interesting dealers, mostly from Chicago — much higher quality than most malls. Plus, a produce market, gift shop, and outdoor cafe. *(616) 469-2555. 9300 Union Pier Rd. just west of the I-94 Union Pier exit and almost a mile east of* *the Red Arrow Highway. 10-6 daily, year-round.*

◆ **Local Color.** Works in many media by 80 artists and craftspeople from the area are attractively displayed in this consignment gallery. Some are whimsical, some serious, and all are contemporary in style. There's a good deal of hand-decorated wearable art. *16187 Red Arrow Hwy., south of Union Pier Rd. (616) 469-5332. Mem.-Labor Day: daily 12-5. Otherwise call.*

◆ **In downtown New Buffalo.** Whittaker Street, once a fairly humble place, now has some tony shops for home accessories and women's clothing in the old retail district, between the Red Arrow Highway and the lake. The **Whittaker House** at 26 North Whittaker stands out on account of its relaxed, contemporary classic clothing in beautiful fabrics of excellent quality, and also carries fashion and home accessories. It's open daily, year-round. On Whittaker south of the highway, houses have been converted to shops, mostly galleries and home accessory stores. It's also worth a look if you're in a browsing mood.

◆ **Hearthwoods.** Owner/craftsman Andy Brown has long been fascinated with rustic furniture made of tree trunks, branches, and twigs. A few years ago he quit his advertising job to start this workshop and store. Here he has gathered together all sorts of antique and contemporary rusticana — burl bowls, birchbark birdhouses, ornate chests decorated with geometric twig designs, Adirondack chairs, and his own simple board furniture handpainted by artists like Nancy Drew and Kris Hosbine. In his chunky four-poster bed ($1,600), the top canopy is formed by a lattice of thin branches that sprout directly from thick tree trunks. *116 1/2 N. Whittier, downtown, behind Lyssa. (616) 469-5551. Mem.-Labor Day: daily 10-6. Labor Day-Xmas and March 15-Mem.Day: Fri-Mon 10-6. Winter: weekends only.*

◆ **Country Mates.** The country look, complete with long skirts, geese, and teddy bears, still reigns supreme at this rambling, hugely successful gift and interiors shop. Classic country accessories stand out amid all the fads: simple painted furniture, wrought-iron lamps, handwoven rugs, salt-glazed pottery, and such. Some people come just for the dried flowers and herbs, color-keyed for customers' decor. In spring an unusual variety of **ornamental and culinary herbs** is sold on the patio. *120 W. Buffalo at Barton. 469-2890. Open 7 days year-round.*

Warren Dunes State Park

Crowded beaches and remote trails, hang-gliding and dune climbing at this splendid park

This remarkable park can handle huge crowds on its beach — up to 20,000 on hot holiday weekends — and still provide a remote, rugged getaway experience on hiking trails in the dunes. The northern two-thirds of the park is undeveloped except for hiking trails. The southern third contains Michigan's busiest state park facilities, planned to handle crowds of day-trippers from Chicago and South Bend. It makes for a stimulating contrast: people-watching and contemplative nature study.

The **beachfront** and parking area, though not exactly intimate, is far less overwhelming than most popular beaches within striking distance of urban areas. That's due to the outstanding site planning and design of three bathhouse and concession areas. (Food is much improved lately, incidentally.) By the closest parking area is **Tower Hill**, a big, bare dune kids love to climb and run down and climb again — exhilarating fun, and a high point of many outings. Hang-gliders soar from this hill on weekends, too — more often in the spring and fall, when wind is most likely to come out of the north-northwest. Angelo Mantis gives **hang-gliding lessons** here; $70 gets you a full-day introduction, including four or five short flights. Call (312) 929-1547, and have alternate weekend dates available.

Inland the huge dunes here are mostly covered with oak, beech, maple, and hickory woods. It's not hard to get away from the beach's crowds. Walk up the beach from the developed area — it's 2 1/2 miles long — or take your car to the deeply shady **picnic area,** along a creek in the relatively secluded back dunes. It has play equipment, grills, restrooms, and a new shelter. Come early on holiday weekends — it does fill up.

For the supremely fit and energetic, a foot trail climbs to the top of the **Great Warren Dune**, then descends to an uncrowded beach. Another shorter, 1 1/2-mile section climbs **Mount Randall**. On a clear day you can see the Sears Tower and Hancock Building in Chicago. There are **6 miles of cross-country skiing trails** (novice to intermediate difficulty). The trail head with maps is in the interpretive area, which has pit toilets, water, and a shelter. (Go right on the first drive past the entrance, past the park office.)

The 197 **modern campsites** have more privacy than many at state parks. Some back up to a wooded dune, and many are quite shady. Three-fourths are reservable; phone reservations recommended from mid-May through September.

Dune conditions fascinate scientists because they cover all possible extremes of moisture, from desert conditions to temporary ponds to constant wetness, in a geographically compact area with the same general climate. Dunes are home to plants uncommon in Michigan. Tasty wintergreen berries and cranberries grow in the interdunal wetlands of Warren Dunes and nearby Grand Mere state parks.

Preservation of this extensive area of high dunes is due to the foresight of E. K. Warren of Three Oaks, the serious-minded son of a Congregational minister who made a fortune by inventing a flexible corset stay made of turkey feathers. In the late 19th century, sand dunes were considered worthless, valued only for mining sand used in foundry molds and building materials. Warren realized the dunes' ecological value and bought 250 acres of these lakeshore dunes to preserve them for posterity. He gave them to the state as the nucleus of this park.

Dune Country: A Guide for Hikers and Naturalists ($8.95) by Glenda Daniels is the classic on becoming acquainted with the dunes' natural history. Based on the Indiana Dunes National Lakeshore, it's just as relevant for Michigan's dunes. Available at Brennen's Bookstore in The Roundhouse in New Buffalo.

On the Red Arrow Hwy. 3 miles south of Bridgman. From I-94, take Exit 16, follow the signs and go south. (616) 426-4013.

Open daily, year-round, at 8 a.m. Gates close at 10 p.m. from April 1 thru Labor Day; otherwise, gates close at dusk. Restroom facilities closed Oct. 15-April 15. $3/car/day ($4 for non-Michigan residents) or $15/year state parks sticker for residents and non-residents alike. **Camping:** *197 modern sites ($12/night) open all year. Half are available on a first-come, first-served basis. Phone reservations recommended from mid-May thru September.*

A SPECTACULAR INDUSTRIAL TOUR NEAR BRIDGMAN . . . . . on the shore of Lake Michigan is the **Cook Nuclear Power Center**, one of the largest in the country. Next to its plant, the Indiana & Michigan Electric Company has built a lavish tourist center. Visitors can also wander among multi-level terraces towards the lake, with expensive lighting, wrought-iron tables and chairs, and abundant, well-maintained shrubs and flowers. Upstairs is a large assortment of fancy **video games** where visitors can learn about energy and how electricity is made. Every few minutes visitors are taken by a professional guide on a **multi-stage presentation**, through three impressive auditoriums. In the first, the tour guide takes the stage to interact with a full-sized computer-driven robot. Next, the visitors file into a large circular amphitheater, where an elaborate model of the nuclear plant is explained. Finally, in a third and even larger auditorium, visitors see a wide-screen film about the Cook plant. One scene shows the churning area half a mile out in Lake Michigan where the plant gets its water to cool the steam which turns the giant turbines. A quarter of a mile out, the water is returned 3° F warmer. *On the Red Arrow Hwy. 3 miles north of Bridgman and I-94 exit 16. A traffic light is at the entrance. (616) 465-5901. June through Sept: Wed-Sat 10-5, Sun 11-5. Other times: Mon-Fri 10-5, plus special monthly weekend events. Closed mid-Dec to mid-Jan. Free.*

BLUEBERRY U-PICK . . . . . **Schmidt's Blueberries** near Bridgman is open daily from mid-July to Labor Day. Call (616) 465-5206 for directions and details.

A WILD DUNELAND BIRD-WATCHERS LOVE . . . . . is at **Grand Mere State Park**. Here bogs, ponds, and other wetlands among the dunes prevented cottage development and left the area remarkably wild, though within earshot of I-94. The Michigan Nature Conservancy gave the land to the state for a limited-development natural area. It's wonderful for spring wildflowers and migrating birds, and now it's much more accessible. A new entrance road leads to a parking lot, **picnic area**, 2,200-foot, handicapped-accessible **trail**, and 4 miles of hiking and cross-country ski trails circling a chain of small lakes, interdunal ponds, and cranberry and wintergreen bogs. Trails lead to Lake Michigan. No camping or swimming. *Take I-94 exit 22 (Stevensville) and follow the signs onto Thornton Rd. (under the freeway to the west). (616) 426-4013. $15 state park sticker or $3/day.*

Warren Woods Natural Area

*A primeval virgin woodland
an hour and a half from Chicago's Loop*

These 311 acres comprise one of Michigan's few remaining virgin beech-maple climax forests. The woods you see from the car off Elm Valley Road don't look different from a hundred other places. Off the road here, a drive leads to parking, a **picnic table**, and **restrooms.** But if you take the foot trail across the Galien River to the loop along the river, you'll come to some enormous, majestic beech trees, along with maples and hemlocks — the kind of woods the pioneers encountered. The damp soil here makes for a jungly, humid, environment that's sunnier and quite unlike the stand of virgin oaks and hickories at Russ Forest, another piece of southwest Michigan virgin forest not too far from here (p. 22). Warren Woods' location on the main Lake Michigan shoreline flyway, and the abundance of dead wood for woodpeckers and for nesting, make it an outstanding place for bird-watching. The gravel-surfaced **trails** (3 1/2 miles in all) are flat except for rolling terrain along the river. For **cross-country skiing**, they're rated novice.

That these woods were preserved at all is due to the remarkable foresight of E. K. Warren, the Three Oaks storekeeper who made a fortune by inventing a better, cheaper corset stay made of turkey feathers. Over a hundred years ago, when most good businessmen were figuring out how to exploit natural resources, he decided to buy this virgin timberland in order to preserve it.

Entrances on Elm Valley Rd. and Warren Woods Rd. (both go east from the Red Arrow Hwy.) about a mile west of Three Oaks Rd. (the north-south extension of Three Oaks' main street between U.S. 12 and the Red Arrow Hwy.). (616) 426-4013. Always open. State park sticker required ($3/day, $15/year.)

ANOTHER FAVORITE WOODLAND WALK . . . . . close to Harbor Country resort communities is the **Robinson Preserve** along the Galien River. When you leave the road and walk down into the valley, it's hard to believe you're just a mile from the Red Arrow Highway and Lakeside's shops and galleries. *Take East Rd. east from the center of Lakeside. The preserve is on the north side of the road just past Basswood Rd.*

Drier's Meat Market

Tasty ham and bologna, sold with old-fashioned
showmanship in a century-old shop in Three Oaks

They used to hold Chicago-bound trains at the Three Oaks depot so passengers could walk across to Drier's to buy some of its famous ring bologna and ham. Trains don't stop at little Three Oaks any more, but people still go out of their way to shop at Drier's. Drier's continues to make sausage and cure hams and bacon the old, careful, German way. The ancient frame building is an operating antique, listed on the prestigious National Register of Historic Places. Old tools and a fancy Victorian meat rack have been here over a hundred years. The four-paned windows predate the introduction of plate glass in the 1880s.

Despite the many old-fashioned touches — the sawdust on the floor, the corny signs like "This baloney cuts the mustard" — Drier's is actually one astute man's business response to changing times. Ed Drier has cleverly crafted his business to preserve quality of life — his own, and his employees' and customers'. Drier's today offers "a limited menu": hot dogs, Polish sausage, ring bologna at about $4 a pound ("all beef, less fat, no belching," a sign points out), liver sausage, and cheese that has been made elsewhere. Bologna, hams, and bacon is smoked on the premises. Choice meat justifies the premium prices.

Back in the 1930s, in pre-med classes at the University of Michigan, Drier says, a professor told him he'd be better off making baloney than pursuing a medical degree. After getting out of the service in 1945, he went back to work with his dad. "We always enjoyed our work," he says. Drier also enjoys living two minutes from his shop, playing tennis with old Kalamazoo College chums, and taking a vacation from January 1 to shortly before Easter.

Antiques and art make Drier's today a lot more interesting than the plain place it used to be. Now you'll find three massive marble butcher's tables from France, picked up on Drier's mid-winter travels around the world. There's a deer head, family memorabilia, signs like "Nicht auf den Boden spucken" ("no spitting on the floor" in German, a reminder that this place is quintessentially German in its earthy, unassuming style), and caricatures — frequently of Ed Drier, like the portrait of him as a grumpy-looking knight, done in magazine-cover style by a *Time* cover artist who was a customer.

All this stuff launches conversations with customers. "That's part of the deal — the dog and pony show," says Drier, who relishes the personal side of the business and the nice letters that come with orders for holiday hams.

Ed Drier has relied on his family, especially his daughter, Carolyn, and about a dozen young men from the area to help. Even after they've gone out into the work world to become teachers, dentists, engineers, and the like, some come back to the shop to help out on their vacations. "This hooey about what's the matter with young people is mostly what's the matter with the old people," comments Drier. "It's not how many mistakes are made, it's how they are corrected."

14 S. Elm (the main business street) in downtown Three Oaks, about a block north of the intersection with U.S. 12. (616) 756-3101. Closed Jan. 1 until 2 weeks before Easter. Mon-Sat 9-5:30. The comical branch store on U.S. 12 east of town is open Sat & Sun 9:30-5, but closed in winter.

MICHIGAN'S MOST UNUSUAL VISITOR INFORMATION OUTLET . . . . is two blocks north on Elm from Drier's. The remarkable **Three Oaks Bicycle Museum and Information Center** has loads of well organized free information on visiting southwest Michigan and on bicycling throughout the state. Unusual bicycles are on display. **Bike rentals** and a kids' bike cart are available. Videos feature bike safety and Three Oaks' Apple Cider Century Ride, the nation's largest 100-mile bike ride. It funds the museum and its enthusiastic creator, Brian Volstorf. Mayor of Three Oaks, he's a one-man economic development whirlwind. *110 N. Elm. (616) 3361. 9-5 daily, year-round. Call to confirm in winter.* **Free.** . . . . At the museum, get your free **Backroads Bikeways** map of marked bike routes radiating out from Three Oaks into the beautiful byways of Berrien County. . . . Across the street, take in the sprawling old brick factory buildings of the **Warren Featherbone Company**, where useless, one-sided turkey feathers were split and woven into improved, snap-proof corset stays. Three Oaks boomed with the widely marketed Featherbone. Founder E. K. Warren's restored headquarters and bank, the main office of **Harbor Country Bank** is worth a peek inside. *3. N. Elm. Open weekdays.*

Fernwood

One woman's enchanted gardens

Though Fernwood has grown into an impressive center for nature and arts education, its best part is a very personal garden. This serene, sensuous small universe of six acres is an inspiring example of what years of thinking about plants and working with them can create. Kay Boydston, a schoolteacher and a serious, self-taught horticulturist from Chicago, discovered this ravine and brookside area with her husband, Walter, in the 1930s. From upland fields the land descends 125 feet down to the St. Joseph River, creating an exceptional range of microclimates — perfect for a gardeners' and botanists' experiments with diversity. Soils vary from sand to clay, both wet and dry.

Boydston planted a **lilac garden** with lily pool; a **boxwood garden** with shady ground covers; a **perennial garden**; a **fern trail** leading to a rustic bridge by a corkscrew falls; and an enchanting **rock garden**, where dwarf conifers, primroses, heathers, and many little flowers from mountains, meadows, and bogs of the world bloom between April and May in the pockets of tufa stone.

Her gardens are a sensory delight. They are filled with the sounds of plashing water and birdsong and the smells of flowers, pines, and leaf mold in the air. They are a series of picturesque small spaces like outdoor rooms, arranged around the Boydstons' simple, shingled cottage homes. (They had one small house oriented for summer, one for winter.) Arbors, bridges, benches, stone walls, and pools accent the gardens and encourage visitors to stop and contemplate a small area. The planned and planted gardens are mixed with existing woodland trees and small plants for an enchantingly natural effect. Self-seeded wildflowers further blur the distinction between landscaping and nature.

Many famous American gardens are patterned on aristocratic European prototypes, requiring statuary, formidable garden architecture, and paid gardeners to maintain the grounds. Fernwood is more relaxed and natural; its purpose is to inspire home gardeners and show what can be grown in these climes by people of modest means. Any of the stone walls and benches could be built by an interested amateur — just as Kay Boydston built these, with some help from her gardener helper. Maintenance isn't fussy. Bulbs poke up through fall's leaves, and fallen branches remain in place in wilder areas.

Kay Boydston's method was to choose a plant type — ferns (her favorite) or Alpine flowers, for instance — study it intensely, landscape with it, and, years later, move on to another subject. Many of her gardens are impressive collections of a type of plant, and they do have instructive labels, but her part of Fernwood wears its learning lightly.

In 1964, the Boydstons turned their home into a nature center and garden open to the public. Since then Fernwood has expanded into a much bigger facility. Fernwood now offers a host of inexpensive and unusually wide-ranging gardening, nature and crafts **classes and workshops** for adults and children; ask for a catalog. Full-day, week-long summer nature classes for children and Japanese crafts classes for adults could be highlights of a summer vacation in the area.

The newer gardens don't yet have the special magic of Kay Boydston's gardens. They are so far only approached in effect by the Main Garden, planted in 1964. It showcases a fine viburnum collection and provides special winter twig and bark interest, complemented in summer by bedding plants.

There are many other attractions to draw visitors back to Fernwood: miles of **nature trails** with excellent trail guides; a youngish **arboretum** of 60 trees recommended for city lots, now coming into its own; and a **Japanese garden**, a **rose garden**, an **All-America test garden** (where new flower introductions are tested), and a **pioneer dooryard garden**.

The upland fields near the entrance have been replanted as a splendid **tallgrass prairie** — one of the very best prairie reconstructions around. A trail guide explains it; an overlook platform lets you survey it. The prairie blooms from May through August.

The new **Visitors' Center** has a big fern conservatory (especially nice in winter), space for changing exhibits, horticulture classroom space, and a **gift shop**, quite romantic and feminine in mood, with garden books and a wide selection of notecards, gifts, and china with botanical and bird motifs. A very reasonably priced **tea room** *(open Tues-Sat 11:30-2, April-Dec)* looks out onto the interesting **herb and sensory garden**.

*13988 Range Line Rd. between Berrien Springs and Buchanan. From Niles or Berrien Springs, take U.S. 31/33 to Walton Rd. turn west and follow the signs. From U.S. 12 and I-94, take Red Bud Trail (in Buchanan) to Walton, turn east (right), cross the river and turn north onto Range Line. Follow the signs. (616) 695-6491 or 683-8653. **Visitor center and gift shop:** Mon-Fri 9-5, Sat 9-6, Sun 12-6. Weekends in winter (Nov.-March) closing is 1 hour earlier. **Grounds** open to members sunrise to sunset. $3 adults, children 12 and younger free. Pick up a free **trail map** to plan your visit and see the highlights.*

IN NEARBY HISTORIC NILES. . . . . . the interesting **Fort St. Joseph Museum** has many remarkable Indian artifacts. Excavated from the late 17th-century French Fort St. Joseph just south of Niles there are glass and seed beads, silver crosses, merchants' seals, and pots. The outpost served to protect the Jesuit mission there, to advance French diplomatic interests with the neighboring Indians, and to supply them with trade goods in exchange for furs. The Smithsonian considers this collection of Plains Indian artwork among the very best in the U.S. In the late 19th century, Niles military officers and wives, stationed in forts on the Great Plains, became friendly with Indians, who gave them many beautiful and fascinating things, including a stunning Victorian-Indian beaded dress and large autobiographical pictographs done on cloth by Rain in the Face and Sitting Bull. If the director is available, he's happy to field questions. Also here: material on famous folks from Niles, including Ring Lardner, the Dodge brothers, and Montgomery Ward. *508 E. Main (U.S. 31/33) at Fifth (M-51), behind the ornate City Hall. (616) 683-4702. Tues-Sat 10-4, Sun 1-4. Donations appreciated. . . . .* Niles' City Hall next door occupies the super-ornate **Chapin Mansion**, a Queen Anne castle of a house in which each room has an elaborate fireplace made of a different imported wood. Visitors are welcome to look around during weekday business hours. Ask for the interesting book about it. *$1 Main at Fifth. Open weekdays. . . . . .* In the little shopping plaza across Main Street, at **Mamie's Jamaican BBQ** you can get tangy homemade ginger beer and, if you're lucky, Jamaican goat barbecue.

IN BUCHANAN. . . . . . the 1853 **Pears Mill** has been restored by gristmill enthusiasts, who have installed a wood waterwheel. The old mill stream now flows under an ugly parking lot, but the mill interior is being scrupulously restored. *Between Days and Oak just south of Front, downtown. Open 12-4 on summer weekends and holidays. $1. . . . . .* For $2.50 you can visit Michigan's only cave, **Bear Cave**, where springs formed unusual formations of tufa (a spongy limestone). Competent 20-minute audiotaped tour of the cave's interesting if unspectacular chambers, tunnels, and formations. *At the Bear Cave Campground, off Red Bud Trail 3 miles north of Buchanan. Open at most times, summers only. Kids under 12 free.*

Berrien County Wineries

*Where you can see it all — from fruit on the vine
to wine in the glass, in delightful rural settings*

If you want to understand what goes into making wine, focus on small, owner-operated wineries. There you can see vines in the vineyards and ask questions of the people responsible for the entire process, from growing and picking to fermentation and bottling. At St. Julian's big Paw Paw winery, grapes are trucked in from distant growers and paid public relations staff give tours. It's worthwhile but not as intimate.

This group of three close-together wineries in south central Berrien County provides an excellent introduction to winegrowing in Michigan — in a beautiful setting — hilly, pastoral, and remote in mood but convenient to big population centers. Tabor Hill, the pioneer in the Michigan's wine industry changeover to drier, more sophisticated wines, has become the state's second-biggest winery. It's a fancy, highly capitalized place that produces mid-priced wines. Lemon Creek, a simple, 150-year-old family fruit farm, has started producing many award-winning medium-priced wines. At Madron Lake Hills, a wine fanatic is determined to produce the first Michigan wine on a par with premium European wines — and he may be on the verge of success.

◆ **Lemon Creek Fruit Farms, Vineyards, & Winery.** Lemon Creek offers a rare opportunity to taste a good variety of medium-priced Michigan wines (including many award-winners), buy and pick fresh fruit, and see most phases of wine production, from grape growing to fermentation and bottling. (Pressing is done at St. Julian's.) Just outside, you can see the vines, neatly labeled by variety, and the tall mechanical picker that straddles the rows of vines and harvests the grapes. Visitors can **picnic** at tables outside the tasting room. Personable Cathy Lemon is happy to give visitors an informal tour of the winemaking facilities.

Home winemakers can purchase grapes already picked or pick them themselves. Varieties include Concord, Riesling (the premium variety that grows best in Michigan), and several French hybrids (Chamborsin, Baco, Vignole, and hardy Vidal, the Lemons' main stock). Fruits (sold packaged or **U-pick**) include raspberries, four kinds of sweet cherries, tart cherries, nectarines, pears, plums, three kinds of peaches, and eight apple varieties.

The three Lemon brothers grew up here. They were among the

first in the area to grow grapes for drier wines. In 1981, after years of falling fruit prices, many other southwest Michigan fruit farmers also replaced their orchards with French hybrid grapes. Prices fell dramatically as a result. The Lemons, like an increasing number of fruit and vegetable producers, realized they'd be more secure financially if they marketed their own produce. They decided to add value to it by producing wine.

Lemon Creek continued supplying Tabor Hill, St. Julian, and Good Harbor with wine grapes but also opened its own winery in 1984. For newcomers to the tricky business of winemaking, the Lemons have been extraordinarily successful, with 37 awards for their wines thus far. Wine prices start at $4.50 a bottle for Baco Rosé (a State Fair gold medal-winner). The three Vidal wines (dry, semi-sec, and semi-sweet) have won the most awards; they're $5.95. Sparkling juices are $3.50

533 Lemon Creek Rd. just east of Baroda, 5 miles east of Bridgman and 7 miles west of Berrien Springs. From I-94 exit 16 at Bridgman, go north on Red Arrow Hwy. 2 miles to Lemon Creek Rd., then east 5 miles. (616) 471-1321. Open May through Dec: Mon-Sat 9-6, Sun 12-6. Also by appt. A June festival each Father's Day weekend includes hayrides, games for kids, arts and crafts booths, and live music.

◆ **Tabor Hill Winery & Restaurant.** A spectacular view of vineyards, orchards, and the distant Lake Michigan dunes highlights a visit to this winery and restaurant, which serves up a glamorous, California-style country ambiance for city folks.

As a winery tour, this has some pluses and minuses. The weekend guides often don't know very much about winemaking. The restaurant is often so busy and bustling that you have to be aggressive in asking for samples of wine at the combined tasting area and bar. But the scenery is outstanding, and you can walk through the vineyards. The crusher-destemmer is right outside, and at harvest time in late summer, you can hang around and watch lugs of grapes being dumped into the hopper, where they are spun in a centrifuge and emerge as juice. Some fermenting tanks are outdoors, too, chilled for free by cold winter air. Inside are memorable oak wine barrels, beautifully hand-carved with scenes from each year of Tabor Hill's early crops. The shiny new German and Italian bottling equipment has a capacity of 600 to 800 cases a day — quite a contrast to the tiny hand bottle-capper at Lemon Creek.

It's all a far cry from the creative chaos of Tabor Hill's early days under wine visionary and pathfinder Len Olson. Brash and bold, Olson was convinced that Michigan could produce premium wines. When he founded Tabor Hill in 1972, he was the first in

Michigan to gamble and plant chardonnay and Riesling, two
varieties of vinifera or "noble grapes" used in fine European
wines. (Michigan winters, colder than Europe's, made them
chancy.) Olson's Tabor Hill "was like a commune," recalls
Michigan State wine professor Stan Howell. "A lot of people came
there to live and work. It was an interesting time. His wines were
so much better than any others being produced in Michigan."

Whirlpool heir David Upton rescued the financially shaky operation in the late 1970s. Today Tabor Hill is promotion-minded
and rather slick. Its mainstays have been middle-priced wines
using French hybrid grapes. Wine experts recommend its Vidal
Demi-Sec ($6.29), a semi-sweet, easy-drinking, summer picnic
kind of wine, as its best value.

*185 Mt. Tabor Rd. From I-94, take exit 16 at Bridgman, go north
about a mile to Lake St./Shawnee Rd., turn east and follow signs
to winery. (616) 422-1161. Winery open daily 11-6, year round,
summers to 9 p.m. Restaurant (see p. 45) open April through
Nov. April hours are Fri-Sun only. Otherwise Wed-Sat 11:30-3 &
5:30-9, Sun 11:30-3.*

◆ **Madron Lake Hills Winery.** What you see here is passionate,
intensely serious viticulture and winemaking, without any
trappings of tourism. Winemaker Jim Eschner lives in a mobile
home on the property. He and his partner, Franz-Bernard
Lickteig, whose family has been in the wine business for 200
years, have sunk their money into excellent custom-grafted vine
stock, a super-insulated winery, and the only overhead sprinkling
system in Michigan. (It protects the vines from early frost. The
site's only drawback is that it is in a frost-susceptible low
pocket.) Their office/reception room has all the romance of a
chemistry lab — which is what it also is.

At Madron Lake Hills, only vinifera grapes — classic European
"noble" grapes — are grown: Riesling, Gewürztraminer, Chardonnay, Pinot Noir, and 30 other varieties on a test basis. In
1988 the young winery's first production of Riesling and Gewürztraminer (currently priced at $12 to $14 a bottle) won raves
from leading Chicago wine lovers, including Chicago writer/chef
Michael Foley, the leading apostle of Midwest regional cuisine.

Eschner learned his winemaking lessons at nearby Tabor Hill,
where he was winemaker during its creative commune phase.
There he learned his first rule: you can't get rich quick making
premium wines. They require the best grapes possible, suited
specifically to the soil only through years of careful experimentation. State-of-the-art winemaking technology won't make up for
using grapes grown on contract by someone else, Eschner feels.
Low-wage hired help, traditionally paid by the bushel, can't be

depended upon to select the very best grapes and distinguish the "noble rot" mildew from the putrid stuff. Madron Lake Hills gets friends and relatives to camp here and pick their grapes, in return for tasting wine and a fabulous meal, often cooked by famous chefs who are friends.

Eschner and Lickteig expect to invest 10 years of sweat equity in developing outstanding wines and the reputation to go with them. In aiming for the top of the market, they avoid the fad-prone middle market of $6- to $8-a-bottle wines.

Some wine critics say Madron Lake Hills' much-praised wine is likely to become Michigan's first competitor on the world market for premium wines. It's exciting to see the early stages of this pioneering effort to find the best vinifera grapes for this southwest Michigan soil.

14387 Madron Lake Rd. 3 miles northwest of Buchanan. From U. S. 12 and the south, take Red Bud Trail north through Buchanan and turn west onto Miller Rd. about 2 miles from downtown. (616) 695-5660. **Winery tours** *Mem. Day through harvest in mid-Oct: Sat 12-5 or by appt.*

OTHER RECOMMENDED ATTRACTIONS IN NEARBY BERRIEN SPRINGS. . . . . .
From the wave of plain Greek Revival courthouses built shortly after Michigan statehood in 1837, only two survive. The dignified courtroom in the **1839 Courthouse Museum** in sleepy Berrien Springs has been carefully restored. An outstanding museum of Berrien County history is in the lower level. There's a restored sheriff's office, changing exhibits, a large log house, and a book and gift shop that's very good on regional history. *On U.S. 31 at Union, 3 blocks north of Shawnee/Ferry. (616) 471-1202. Tues-Fri 9-4, Sat & Sun 1-5. Closed holidays. No charge . . . . . .* **Wild Birds Unlimited** features a wonderful variety of bird feeding supplies and other bird-related stuff, from books and binoculars to jewelry and sweatshirts. Owner Richard Schinkel leads birdwatching trips here and around the world. *109 N. Main just north of Ferry in downtown Berrien Springs. Mon-Fri 9-5, Sat 9-1. . .* For picnics, nature hikes, and cross-country skiing through varied ecosystems, pretty **Love Creek County Park & Nature Center** is way above average. Two staff naturalists lead weekend programs. *From U.S. 31/33 just east of Berrien Springs, turn east onto Pokagon Rd. and follow signs to park on Huckleberry Rd. (616) 471-2617. Trails open daily dawn to dusk. Center open Wed-Sun 10-5. $3/car.*

Tree-Mendus Fruit

Informative orchard tours, antique apples,
exotic produce, and the pleasures of picking fruit
in a beautiful country setting near Eau Claire

Beginning in the 1960s, fruit farmers have found it difficult to make a profit selling their fruit wholesale. Trucking strikes, farm labor boycotts, and erratic prices led far-sighted growers to think about diversifying. In this challenging new economic environment, many successful growers have suc-ceeded by combining direct-to-consumer sales with recreation.

No one has done this better than Herb Teichman of Tree-Mendus Fruit. He has transformed his father's Skyline Orchards, tucked away on a scenic, hilly road west of Indian Lake, into a well-organized, attractive visitor destination, aggressively pro-moted while still personal and low-key.

Tree-Mendus Fruit artfully provides a pleasant day in the coun-try for a generation of Americans who no longer have relatives down on the farm. In addition to 560 acres of U-pick orchards, there's a big **picnic area** and 120-acre **nature park** with **hiking trails** through wooded wildlife areas with ponds. Visitors can fill **water jugs** at a deep well. On busy weekends ushers are on hand to direct visitors to all parts of the farm. The picking, picnicking, and bus tours are all very well organized, and the place has a nice, rural atmosphere. The **International Cherry Pit Spitting Championship** is held here each year on the first Saturday in July.

Teichman manages to focus on fruit and teach visitors a lot about it. He doesn't run a carnival, as some well-known cider mills and orchards do. He loves to talk to customers when time permits. His outstanding **orchard tours** cover the evolution of fruit varieties, samples of antique apples, and a first-hand look at cultivation techniques from grafting and pruning to harvesting, depending on the season. **One-hour tours** (from $3 to $5/person, depending on options, with a $40 minimum) are given by appointment, on short notice when possible. On the weekend of the Cherry Pit Spitting Championship, and on Saturdays and Sundays after Labor Day, musicians and comic characters circu-late in the orchard, and an orchard admission fee ($4/adult, $2/child) is charged, which includes a narrated orchard tour by wagon. The fee is credited toward purchase of fruit.

Teichman's **"old-time apple museum"** has grown from a few

dozen antique apple trees to a remarkable collection of over 300 varieties from around the world. Here you can taste the Spitzbergen (Thomas Jefferson's favorite), the Westfield Seek-No-Further, and the tasty, tart, crisp Calville Blanc, which goes back to 1627. Modern marketing demands apples that look uniform and attractive, ship well, and can be picked at once. Such requirements have eliminated many old favorites. About 50 antique varieties are for sale here. Much of the stock came from GM attorney Robert Nitschke, an avid fan who collected and propagated many kinds in his Birmingham back yard. To order scions of his trees, write for the catalog of **Southmeadow Fruit Gardens**, 15310 Red Arrow Highway, Lakeside, MI 49116.

Apples you pick yourself cost 38¢ a pound, while antique and unusual varieties are more like a dollar. Jams, apple butter, frozen peaches and cherries, homemade cherry topping, and the farm's distinctive varieties of cider and cherry cider are for sale in the **Tree House Country Store.** Waffle boat desserts, cooked while you wait, have peaches, cherries, or apples in season and lots of whipped cream. On crisp fall days, pickers and hikers can warm themselves by the big fireplace.

Cherries ripen in July, followed by apricots, peaches, plums, nectarines, apples, pears, and pumpkins. All are grown on the farm and sold U-pick or picked. Recently the Teichmans have gotten into experimental vegetables, traditional and exotic, for sale when available.

On E. Eureka Rd. east of M-140, 2 miles northeast of Eau Claire. Call first for Ripe-N-Ready report: (616) 782-7101. Open late June through 3rd week in Oct. Up to Labor Day: open daily except Tues 10-6. After Labor Day: Fri-Mon 10-6. Group tours by appt. any day, starting in blossomtime (early May). Free admission to orchard/park, except on Cherry Pit Fest and on Sat. & Sun. after Labor Day, when it's $4/adult, $2/child, including tour, fee credited toward fruit purchase.

🌳🌴🌳

MORE FRUIT AND LUNCH, TOO . . . . . Scenic Indian Lake Road leads north off M-62, passing the lake and **Sprague's Old Orchard** (a beautiful old farmstead and farm market) on the way to **Wicks Apple House**, another worthwhile destination. It has a good informal restaurant for breakfast and lunch. It's a glorified farm market, cider mill, gift shop, bustling and friendly. Glass walls give views of the bakery and, on October weekends, of the cider-making process. The Wicks family raises its own asparagus, tart cherries, Stanley plums, apples, and Concord grapes. Local produce is featured. *52281 Indian Lake Rd. (616) 782-6822. Open Mem. Day to Nov. 1, Tues-Sun 8-6.*

Russ Forest

Primeval oaks and giant tulip trees,
so old they were already huge in pioneer times

An awesome stand of huge virgin oaks makes the yard of the stately old Newton farmhouse dark and mysterious even on bright days. It's in an undeveloped part of developed Cass County. If you come Russ Forest from the west, it appears by surprise, unannounced by signs. All this contributes to the powerful, out-of-time feeling inspired by these great, primeval trees, a rare remnant of a virgin Eastern hardwood forest.

James Newton, builder of the **Newton House** farmhouse, was an English-born orphan who came to the U.S. as an indentured servant to a Quaker family. Many Quakers came to this part of Michigan; the escaped slaves they helped to settle here formed Cass County's old black communities. The house's older section dates from 1844; Newton's son erected the east wing in 1867. The unrestored house, finished with beautiful local hardwoods, displays historical memorabilia about Cass County and the Grange movement. To go up the unsettlingly narrow staircase to the house's cupola in the treetops is an adventure in itself. *Open Sundays from 1 to 4:30, April through October.*

White oak

Cassopolis businessman Fred Russ purchased the 580-acre Newton Woods Farm during the Depression and donated it to Michigan State University for use as a forestry research station. Such forests of sun-loving oaks and hickories cannot replenish themselves, since only shade-tolerant seedlings can survive here. This majestic stand must have established itself after a fire some 300 or 400 years ago, says forester Scott Newsom. Gradually the old oaks and hickories are being replaced by young beeches and maples.

Russ Forest's mixed hardwoods also include a stand of immense black walnuts, as big as any you'll ever see, and the biggest tulip poplar in Michigan, 180 feet high and 15' 6" in circumference. Its sister tree, perhaps 300 years old, was the tallest recorded tree in Michigan until a wind storm toppled it in 1984. The fallen giant and its sister can be seen from the trail on the east side of the parking lot. A spectacular **fall color display** is created by the varied trees: oak, hickory, hard maples, flame-orange sassafras, and the clear yellow of tulip trees.

Donor Fred Russ especially valued the property's huge tulip poplars, the giants of the Eastern forest, and wished to encourage research on them. In the 1930s standard forestry practice promoted planting cutover land with pines for timber and conservation. Russ was ahead of his time. He was convinced that tulip poplar plantations were a worthwhile idea. Unlike other softwoods of the poplar family, tulip poplar has a cell structure that keeps it from splintering or splitting when sawn or carved. It works and nails easily, like pine. It's naturally disease-resistant. Today the tulip trees Russ planted have reached usable size. A **tulip poplar log cabin** is less than 200 yards down the south trail leading from the parking lot.

Eighty acres of old-growth timber along the road has been set aside as a natural area. The only cutting done here was when some walnut trees were removed for gunstocks in World War I and some white oaks for PT boats in World War II. Tree-rustling of the valuable black walnuts presents no threat here; the area is thick with relatives of the pioneer Newton family who long owned this land. They regard the forest as their own and are quick to report any suspicious strangers with chain saws.

Cass County's adjacent **Russ Forest Park** provides parking, **picnic tables, play equipment, a small shelter, restrooms,** and access to **two miles of flat, scenic trails** that go through the research forest. They make two loops going over wooden footbridges and through virgin hardwoods and managed stands. **Cross-country skiing** on the flat, easy, ungroomed trails is encouraged. The area along Dowagiac Creek (a Class A **trout stream**) is quite open, with some low marshes.

*Park entrance and parking area is on Marcellus Hwy. just east of Newton House, 8 miles east of Marcellus and 5 miles west of Dowagiac. For **information and group tours** about forest ecology and management, contact the Michigan State University forestry research station, 20673 Marcellus Hwy., Decatur, MI 49045. (616) 782-5652. For **park information** or shelter reservations, contact: Cass County Parks Dept., 340 O'Keefe, Cassopolis, MI 49031. (616) 445-8611.*

OFF THE BEATEN TRACK NEAR RUSS FOREST . . . . . The main street of the remote town of **Marcellus** has lovely old homes, a quaint bank worth a visit, and the **Cozy Cupboard**, a homey restaurant where customers have assembled a collection of souvenir plates from around the world. . . . . . **Dowagiac's historic homes** are remarkable. The small city prospered with the phenomenal success of Round Oak stoves, once America's best-selling wood heater. Then it declined. Now Dowagiac is undergoing a modest downtown revival. Don't miss the 1926 vintage **Caruso's sweet shop and soda fountain** at 130 S. Front and **Olympia Books and Prints** at 208 S. Front, a delightful used book shop where you can pick up an interesting illustrated **walking tour** to historic houses west of Front along High, Indiana, and Green.

CASS COUNTY'S REMOTE STREAMS AND VIRGIN WOODLANDS are close to South Bend and Chicago. The book *Canoeing Michigan Rivers* calls **canoeing on the Dowagiac River** "one of the most interesting trips in southern Michigan." It's a short (4 hours or less), easy trip though varied, surprisingly remote terrain. Get an excellent **free pamphlet** on the canoe trip and the river's geology and history at the Dowagiac Chamber of Commerce (616-782-8212) or Olympia Books. **Doe-Wah-Jack's Canoe Livery** (616-782-9464) is 3 1/2 miles north of Dowagiac on M-51. . . . . . The canoe trip passes another majestic remnant of virgin hardwood forest, the Michigan Nature Association's **Dowagiac Woods**, known for its fabulous displays of spring wildflowers and fall color. It is likely Michigan's largest moist, virgin-soil woodland. Trees uncommon to Michigan, including the chinakapin oak, blue beech, and Ohio buckeye, can be seen here. From M-62 about 4 miles west of Dowagiac, turn south onto Sink Rd. In 1 mile turn east onto Frost. In about a mile you'll see a parking area on the north side of the road. Wear waterproof footgear. The short trail off Frost west of the parking area is the driest, with a good view of spring wildflowers.

Downtown St. Joseph

This quaint old place has a lively downtown,
band concerts, and an old-fashioned park
with a great view of Lake Michigan.

Other Michigan downtowns have more spectacular architecture or shops, but St. Joe is overall one of the most attractive. It has healthy small-town retailing, pleasant historic buildings, and a striking setting on a bluff overlooking Lake Michigan. Benches, sculptures, even a hot dog vendor and balloon-seller make State Street a nice place to linger.

Lake Bluff Park overlooks Lake Michigan and extends for seven blocks along Lake Boulevard around to the St. Joseph River on the north. It's a wonderful walk, with flower gardens, a century's worth of sculptures, and overlook benches. Get **walking tours** of public sculpture and downtown buildings from St. Joseph Today. *(616) 982-6739. 520 Pleasant, open weekdays 8:30-5.*

Takeout food for a **picnic in the park** is conveniently available at Clancy's Deli, half a block down Pleasant, or Mama Martorano's (p. 46). A stairway by Ship Street descends to the old Pere Marquette train station (now Zitta's Restaurant, p. 46), a few blocks' walk from **Silver Beach County Park** on Lake Michigan. The park has a big, sandy beach, some picnic tables, changing rooms, and access to the 1,000-foot **south pier**, a fine place for fishing and getting good view of the lake and shoreline.

Back on the bluff, the **Krasl Art Center** is just across from the Lake Bluff Park's south end. It's an outstanding example of how much a small art center can do with volunteers and well-chosen changing exhibits (three at a time), often organized around themes like product design, the water's edge, and contemporary Woodland Indian art. The **gallery shop** is strong on jewelry, scarves, ceramics, and other gifts hand-crafted by Michigan artists. *(616) 983-0271. 707 Lake. Mon-Thurs & Sat 10-4, Fri 10-1, Sun 1-4. Free admission.*

Going north, adjoining the park on Ship at Lake Bluff is the elegant **Whitcomb Tower**, now a retirement home. It's on the very site of **La Salle's 1679 fort**, a western outpost in the great French fur-trading empire. Visitors are welcome to peek in and see the mural of Marquette and Joliet's 1669 canoe journey down the St. Joseph River. Still farther north, the **bandshell**, below Port Street between State and Lake, is much used in summer. St.

❶❷ Two down-towns. Unsettling & dramatic contrast between trim white city and poor black one. **Benton Harbor's** downtown (❶) almost became a ghost town, while adjacent St. Joe (❷) thrives. Don't miss **St. Joe's** Krasl Art center, band concerts in Lake Bluff Park; Benton Harbor's Wolf's Marine.

❸ Curious Kids Museum. Outstanding small hands-on museum, more kid-centered and playful than most. Zany cartoon decor.

❸ Mama Martorano's. Real Italian home cooking, redolent of garlic and wine, shines at this simple spot. Excellent food for little money.

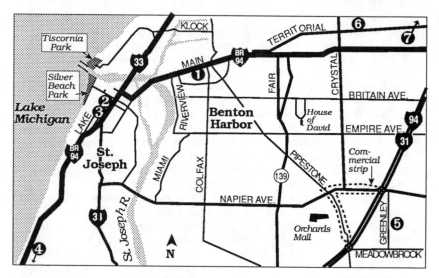

❹ Snowflake Motel. Frank Lloyd Wright conceived this once-luxurious motel which now caters to truckers and construction workers. Friendly staff, budget rates.

❺ The Herb Barn. A fragrant natural world a minute from I-94. Good prices on plants; lots of ideas for uses. Pretty display garden and dried arrangements.

❻ Benton Harbor Fruit Market. Watch the action at world's biggest cash-to-grower fruit & vegetable market. Good retail produce stand. Free posters, recipes.

❼ Sarett Nature Center. Bird-watcher's paradise, thanks to river wetlands, 5 miles of trails, boardwalks, and elevated viewing seats. Good gift shop, excellent talks & outings.

Highlights of
St. Joseph/
Benton Harbor

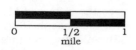

Joseph has the only tax-supported municipal band in Michigan. Evening audiences can enjoy musical sunsets over the lake. **Free band concerts** are from July through Labor Day, Sundays and holidays at 3:30 and 7:30 (with free horse-drawn wagon rides in between), Wednesdays at noon, and on August Fridays at 7.

State Street stores are mostly either small town standbys (including an old department store and a big dime store with a wonderfully creaky wood floor) or women's wear, gift, and accessory stores catering to fairly conservative, well-to-do women who expect good service and get it here. A more inventive exception is **Lou Lou's Leather and Lace** at 516 Pleasant, with an original mix of contemporary women's clothing, lingerie, and shoes.

Children are well served by **Hutchinson's** and **The Silver Balloon**, two large kids' clothing stores on State, and the inspired **Toy Company**, State at Pleasant. It offers well-chosen "amusements for all ages": colorful basics like Brio trains, dolls and stuffed animals, blocks, puzzles and "Brain Boosters," picture books, plus rubber stamps and nifty crafts supplies.

Shops are centered on State between Ship and Elm. Parking lots along Lake Blvd. and Elm. Typical shop hours: Mon-Sat 10-5:30, Fri until 8.

A THOUGHT-PROVOKING SIDE TRIP TO BENTON HARBOR. . . . . Across the Blossomland Bridge in downtown Benton Harbor, there's hardly a functioning store in sight, mainly a few lunch counters and bars. Benton Harbor (population 12,818) is still one of the most depressed cities in the U.S. How Benton Harbor went from being a prosperous city in 1960 to a 20th-century ghost town 20 years later is a story of America's post-World War II move to the suburbs at its most extreme. Mutual distrust between the white business establishment and leaders elected by increasingly poor black residents eventually made a shambles of the city and its government. Today, after decades of mistrust and dissension, moderate old-timers and some new urban pioneers are gaining political clout and moving the city in a pragmatic direction of rebuilding the local economy. Traffic signals now work, fewer streets are cratered, and vacant office buildings, which had reverted to city ownership for nonpayment of taxes, are being renovated.

A REAL FIND FOR BOATERS AND BARGAIN-HUNTERS . . . . . Savvy boaters detour through Benton Harbor to shop at **Wolf's Marine**, a cavernous marine accessory store that claims to be the Midwest's largest and offers to match or beat any advertised price. Wolf's makes a point to stock several kinds of most accessories, plus hard-to-find-parts and supplies, divers' supplies, and many kinds of smaller boats. Diving lessons are available. Even non-boaters will find lots of useful, fun stuff, like slickers, warm-up suits, seashells and netting, fishing poles, inner tubes, and inflatable boats. *250 W. Main between downtown Benton Harbor and the St. Joseph River. (616) 926-1068. Mon-Fri 9-6; Sat 9-5.*

Curious Kids' Museum

*Instead of only playing up to education-minded parents,
it taps into kids' own fantasies and curiosities —
like 'What happens when you flush the toilet?'*

This small but superior hands-on museum is more tuned
into kids and less out to impress their parents than many
bigger children's museums. More exhibits are in good
working order, and the captions are easier to understand. Bright,
fanciful lobby murals are by cartoonist Nancy Drew, who draws
and paints like a kid herself. They set a tone of playful messing-
around that's carried on inside by bubble-blowing, face-painting,
kaleidoscopes, a log cabin for make-believe pioneer living, and
musical instruments to play.

The mechanical section illuminates everyday mysteries with a
see-through toilet system and a transparent-fronted washing
machine (compliments of local giant Whirlpool). In the handicap
area, kids can learn what it's like to go up a ramp in a wheelchair
or wear leg braces. There are also time-tested hands-on favorites
like the giant bubble, the toaster-powered hot-air balloon, beehive, and tests of heart rate, blood pressure, and so forth

*415 Lake Blvd. between Broad and Elm in downtown St. Joseph.
Park next door. (616) 983-2543. Wed-Fri 10-5, Sat & Sun noon-
4. Adults $2.50, kids 2-18 $1.50. Kids 13 and under must be accompanied by an adult.*

THE BEST AREA BEACH . . . . . is **Tiscornia Park**, more scenic and secluded than
Silver Beach. The big old resort hotels are long gone, but there's some historic
flavor left, including a Shingle Style lifesaving station near the pier. The
thousand-foot **North Pier** is popular for perch fishing. The park is in two parts: a
quarter-mile of Lake Michigan **beachfront** with restrooms, and an area on the St.
Joseph River west of Ridgeway by the municipal marina, with **picnic tables**. *In St.
Joseph but north of the river. See map. $3/car.*

Sarett Nature Center

*An extraordinary place to watch birds
that even novices will enjoy*

What makes this Michigan Audubon Society sanctuary a
paradise for novice birdwatchers are its many benches
and elevated towers, strategically located in different
habitats. They are comfortable places where it's easy to sit and
stay still and quiet enough to observe birds at close range without
disturbing them. Excellent **trail booklets**, available at all hours at
the trailhead by the parking lot, are keyed to views you can often
enjoy while sitting. You could even buy a nature book at the top-
notch gift shop and read it comfortably sitting by an alder thicket, pond, or tamarack bog, observing the sights and sounds of
life around you. A tree house lets you observe from a tree canopy;
a bench overlooks a dogwood thicket.

These 350 acres along the Paw Paw River northeast of Benton
Harbor include many kinds of prime natural habitats. Here upland meadows and forests overlook lowland marshes and swamp
forests going down to the riverbank. In spring and fall the river
floods, attracting many migratory waterfowl. A sedge meadow
produces a fine fall wildflower display. Dead trees, created by
rising water levels in swamps, have created plenty of tree holes
for wood ducks, owls, woodpeckers, and the uncommon protho-
notary warbler. Shorebirds like the Virginia rail remain north in
winter if there is open water, provided here by the bayous of the
Paw Paw River.

Some five miles of **trails** include quite a bit of boardwalk for
good viewing of wetland habitats. The trails are planned as a
series of short loops, so you could plan hikes from 1/2 to 2 1/2
hours. **Cross-country skiers** are welcome in winter. Trails are not
handicapped-accessible because of occasional stairways, but they
are otherwise easy. Highway noise is occasionally distracting.
*Remember, birds are most active in the morning and evening,
when the sun is low in the sky. Plan your visit accordingly.*

Sarett's **gift shop** is among the very best for nature publications, notecards, bird feeders, seed, and the like. The adjoining
meeting/observation room has some well-done displays of
mounted birds, seeds, and antlers. A naturalist is usually on hand
to answer questions. The center sponsors a busy schedule of
talks, nature walks, demonstrations, outings, and adults' and

children's summer **classes.**

2300 Benton Center Rd. in Benton Township. Northeast of Benton Harbor/St. Joseph on the Paw Paw River, 1 mile north of the Red Arrow Hwy. From I-94, take I-196 north (toward South Haven), but get off in 1 mile at the Red Arrow Hwy. exit, go west to Benton Center Rd., then north. From St. Joseph and downtown Benton Harbor, take Main or Territorial 2 miles east to Crystal, north (left) on Crystal to Red Arrow Hwy. (616) 927-4832. **Interpretive center hours:** *Tues-Fri 9-5, Sat 10-5, Sun 1-5. Trails and parking lot open dawn to dusk.*

🌲🌳🌲

A SPLENDID INTRODUCTION TO BIRDWATCHING IN MICHIGAN . . . . . is a free **pamphlet** from the Michigan Audubon Society detailing 15 prime sites. Look for it at Michigan Visitor Information Centers on major interstates going into Michigan, or send a self-addressed, stamped envelope with 45¢ postage to: Michigan Audubon Society, 6011 W. St. Joseph #403, Lansing, MI 48917.

WORTHWHILE STOPS ON THE OLD TERRITORIAL ROAD . . . . . About two miles south on Benton Center Road you'll come to Territorial. Just east on Territorial is the big wholesale **Benton Harbor Fruit Market** and **Scott's Produce,** a sizable and very reasonable produce stand out front (open April through October). . . . . . Two miles east on Territorial and you come to the little hamlet of Millburg, with two affordable antique shops open weekend afternoons (Friday through Sunday) 12-5 and by chance other times: **Antique Exchange** (616-944-1987) and **Kountry Kubbard** (616-944-5227; closed Fridays from Jan. 1 to May). . . . . . During Michigan's main pioneering years in the 1830s, **Territorial Road** (C-352) was the federal "highway" (actually a rude dirt road) from Detroit to Chicago, the main route of western settlement and stagecoach line. Many orchards, old Greek Revival farmhouses from the 1830s and 1840s, and ancient big roadside maples and oaks make Territorial an interesting alternative to I-94.

ANTIQUES AND HERBS JUST OFF I-94 . . . . . It's a one-minute detour to **Bay Antiques,** an outstanding large shop south of Coloma, just east of Benton Harbor. It has lots of furniture, both rough and finished. Architectural artifacts, leaded glass, bisque dolls, and oriental rugs are other specialties. *From I-94, take exit 39 (Coloma), go south, turn onto Mountain Rd. in 1/8 mile, follow signs. (616) 468-3221. Open from April through September every day 12-5, Fri & Sat to 7. Otherwise Wed-Sun 12-5.* . . . . . Just a minute off the freeway you can enter the slow-paced, sensuous world of aromatic plants at **The Herb Barn.** The attractive display garden provides lots of ideas for landscaping with the 100 varieties of herbal plants sold here. Inside the sales room, a big selection of books, plus dried arrangements and wreaths, show how to use them. *Southeast of Benton Harbor. Take I-94 exit 30, head east on Napier Rd., then turn immediately south onto Greeley Ave. Stop behind the farmhouse at 1955 Greeley. (616) 927-2044. Mon-Fri 10-5, Sat 10-4, and May-Dec Sun 12-4.*

Kal-Haven Trail

*A 38-mile bike path from South Haven to Kalamazoo
passes scenic blueberry plantations and quaint old towns.*

This splendid 38-mile trail over a stretch of abandoned Penn Central railroad bed is a wonderful place for a bicycle trip. Hikers are also welcome. An adjacent equestrian trail is under development. The trail begins just north of South Haven and ends just west of Kalamazoo, passing through small towns which grew with the arrival of the railroad in the 1800s.

It goes through varied terrain and many wildlife habitats. It starts with the flat fields, blueberry farms, and lakes just east of South Haven and ends at the hilly Kalamazoo River valley. The extensive blueberry-growing region is a delight when the berries are ripe in July. Wetlands (great for bird-watching) are common between Grand Junction and Gobles. **Lake Eleven** east of Grand Junction has a public access fishing site.

At **Grandpa's Beehive Farm**, you can get sandwiches, drinks, baked goods, and free ice water and tour a funky farm animal zoo and nature preserve ($2). A primitive campground and a picnic spot is also here. This free-wheeling tourist stop is 10 1/2 miles west of the Kalamazoo entry point and just east of Gobles on County Road 388. *(616) 628-2854. Animal farm open April-Oct.*

In early May, **dogwood** bloom along the trail between Gobles and Kendall. The trail passes the village of Mentha, where an enormous barn and other buildings attest to the scope of the A. M. Todd spearmint-growing and distilling operation from the turn of the century. **Bicycle rentals** ($16/day) are available at Healy True Value Hardware in Gobles on the trail. *(616) 628-2584,*

South Haven trailhead: on the Blue Star Hwy. at the Black River just northeast of South Haven. Kalamazoo trailhead: in Orion Twp. 3/4 mile west of U.S. 131 on 10th St. between G and H Ave. Call (616) 637-2788 for an illustrated map/ brochure. Trail fee: $2/day individual, $5/family; annual pass $10/$25. Register at trailheads or access points.

Wolf Lake Hatchery

See millions of fish, from tiny fingerlings to huge
sturgeons, and learn a lot about Great Lakes fishing.

Each year millions of fish are grown annually at this state hatchery west of Kalamazoo. They stock the 11,000 lakes in Michigan, as well as its rivers, bays, and streams. Some years over 100 million walleye alone are hatched here, then transported to holding ponds around the state. Over one million chinook salmon are raised annually for six months until they are over three inches long, then released in rivers and streams in early spring. Three and one half years later they will return from the Great Lakes to their original stream to spawn.

Huge tanks also hold the enormous populations of northern pike, sturgeon, muskies and brown trout raised here. In the central visitors' area are plaques of Michigan's record fish, including a 26-pound rainbow trout, a 46-pound chinook salmon, an 193-pound lake sturgeon, and a 47-pound catfish.

Historical photos and captions tell how, in the late 19th century, Michigan commercial fishermen were taking 30 tons of whitefish a year, which led to an eventual collapse of the fish population. A slide show tells how the Welland Canal, which bypassed Niagara Falls, allowed the dreaded sea lamprey to enter the Great Lakes. The eel-shaped parasite killed off a huge portion of fish until a chemical was developed that reduced its numbers 90%. The tiny fish called alewives were similarly introduced through the St. Lawrence Seaway. Huge dieoffs threatened to ruin Michigan beaches until coho salmon were introduced to control their population.

A highlight here are the **outside ponds**, especially the show pond with its three enormous sturgeons swimming slowly along the bottom. They range from 55 to 65 inches and 30 to 50 years old. Visitors can get free bags of pellets to feed the big steelhead also in the ponds.

Ten miles west of Kalamazoo. From I-94, take U.S. 131 north to exit 38B (M-43), west 6 miles to Fish Hatchery Rd., left (south) to second drive. (616) 668-2696. Mem. Day to mid-Nov: Wed-Fri 9-4, Sat 9-5, Sun noon-5. Rest of year: Tues-Fri 9-4, Sat 9-5. Admission free.

Celery Flats
Interpretive Center

A nifty museum remembers the glory and hard work of Kalamazoo's most famous product.

Kalamazoo's bygone fame as America's Celery City is celebrated in the suburb of Portage's inspired little museum in a creekside park. Kalamazoo-area growers were the first to popularize celery as an important commercial vegetable. By the 1880s over 300 local growers were shipping huge quantities all over the U.S.A. A quarter of this region's entire populace earned its living from celery.

The Kalamazoo area's huge celery industry got its start in the 1860s, when one Cornelius DeBruyn developed and marketed a sweet but stringy yellow variety of celery. Within a decade other area celery growers were jointly marketing Kalamazoo celery as an appetizer — "fresh as the dew from Kalamazoo." Soon celery was touted as a relaxant in patent medicines, tonics, and sodas. At the train station and on street corners, many boys sold bunches of Kalamazoo's celebrated celery. At this entertaining museum, the celery story is told not only by gardening tools, tonic bottles, and the like, but by a demonstration greenhouse, celery beds, family photos, and retired celery farmers as weekend guides.

The museum vividly shows the very hard work of the "celery Dutch." Like almost all of West Michigan's Dutch, they were poor people from the rural Netherlands. Earlier settlers of Yankee stock had passed over the wetlands so plentiful in southern and western Michigan. For little money, poor Dutchmen, accustomed to farming wet soils, could buy swamplands and gradually clear them by laboriously grubbing out tamaracks and shrubs, then draining them by hand.

Profitable cultivation of celery depended on having large families (typical among Dutch immigrants) to do the tedious work: first harrowing the muck fine, then starting and coddling the

KALAMAZOO CELERY.

G. Van Bochove & Bro., Kalamazoo, Mich.

❶ Bronson Park. Its flowers alone are worth a special visit. Historic sculptures and imposing surroundings make this one of the Midwest's finest urban parks.

❷ Kalamazoo Mall. The country's 1st pedestrian mall hasn't thrived over the years, but see neat shops, ornate old theater, and lively midday scene in warm weather.

❸ Public Museum. Small, delightful Egyptian section highlights this local museum. Major emphasis is local history. Nice gift shop.

❹ Okuns Shoe Store. Big bustling warehouse of a place lets you bargain for good deals on a huge variety of shoes.

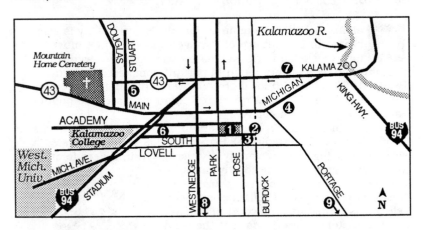

❺❻ Historic districts. On Stuart (5) and South (6) , see blocks of showy mansions built by wealthy Victorians. Most are well preserved; 4 are now bed & breakfast inns.

❼ Kalamazoo Brewery. Pick up tasty, potent stout in this small, funky brewery, and get an informal tour at the same time.

❽ Celery Flat Interpretive Center. Kalamazoo pioneered commercial celery growing. Fascinating museum shows the enormous work Dutch families did to grow this fussy vegetable.

❾ Air Zoo. Colorful group of World War II fighters, especially carrier planes like the legendary Corsair. Daily flights, films, and displays.

Highlights of
Kalamazoo

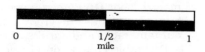

0   1/2   1
                                    mile

fussy seedlings, transplanting them, cultivating by hand, and picking off insects (chemicals injured the plants). Celery had to be irrigated in dry weather, then blanched by covering with boards in summer and dirt in fall, and watched for just the right time to harvest. Then came another round of intense family activity: harvesting before dawn (thought to bring fresher celery), cleaning, trimming, and neatly tying and packing each head, elaborately wrapped in paper and neatly packaged in crates. Kept in root cellars, celery lasted all winter — one of the few green vegetables reliably available in the 19th century.

World War II, smaller families, and scarce farm labor all hastened the demise of Michigan celery. Celery-growing shifted to California, with its reliable weather and cheaper labor. Today's Pascal celery replaced sweeter yellow varieties. Many of Kalamazoo's celery farms were sold for suburban development, but many greenhouses and family farmsteads continue as the basis for Kalamazoo's huge bedding plant industry today.

The celery museum is the centerpiece of a pretty (if unspectacular) linear park along Portage Creek. A two-mile, handicapped-accessible asphalt **path** along the stream forms a loop. There's an attractive **playground, picnic tables** and **shelter**, and, across the road, a one-room **country schoolhouse** (same hours as celery museum) and a grain elevator used for functions. For $6 you can take a 45-minute **canoe ride** from a dropoff point back to the center, through woods and marshland (good for seeing ducks and geese). **Special events** with live music include a crafts fair, a mid-July bluegrass festival, harvest day in late July (farmers demonstrate equipment), and mid-September's Celery Fest.

7335 Garden Lane in Portage. Easily reached from I-94 exit 76A (take S. Westnedge 2 mi. south, turn east — left — onto Garden La.) From U.S. 131, take exit 31, east on Centre, north on Westnedge, east on Garden Lane). (616) 329-4522. May 1-Sept. 30, Thurs-Sun & holidays noon-6. $2/adults, $1/children 5-15.

🌲🌴🌲

OLD WORLD WAR II FIGHTERS LOOKING LIKE NEW . . . . . can be seen at the **Kalamazoo Aviation History Museum (Air Zoo).** The emphasis of the 40,000-sqaure-foot museum is on carrier naval fighters. The classic Corsair fighter is joined by a Wildcat, Hellcat, Tigercat, Bearcat, Warhawk, Aircobra, and Skyraider, among others. In good weather one plane makes a daily flight. There are also murals, memorabilia, photos, film documentaries, and models, along with a gift shop. *Just south of Kalamazoo Airport. From I-94 exit 98, take Portage Rd. south to Milham, turn east. (616) 382-6555. 10-5 Mon-Sat, 1-5 Sun. $4 adults; $2.50 children.*

Bronson Park

*One of the Midwest's most delightful summertime
parks combines Kalamazoo history, fountains,
sculptures, and flowers.*

Even though a deadly 1980 tornado ripped out dozens of its
giant oak trees, Bronson Park is a most beautiful and interesting urban park. It's surrounded by imposing civic and
church buildings. Fountains and monuments immediately convey
to the visitor that this has long been an important focal point for
the citizens of Kalamazoo.

Once a cow pasture, the rectangular parcel became a park in
1876, part of a great era of American park-building commemorating the nation's centennial. In the southwest corner is the area's
only remaining **Indian mound**, a centuries-old Hopewell Indian
burial site. In the northeast corner an imposing 8-foot bronze
sculpture of an American footsoldier from 1923 commemorates
U.S. military campaigns. **Memorial plaques** sprinkled throughout
the park honor people as diverse as Adlai Stevenson and prominent feminist Lucinda Hinsdale Stone of Kalamazoo. The 1913
U.S.S. Maine Memorial Tablet was cast from parts of that famous
Navy ship which exploded in Havana harbor. Toward the east end
is a dramatic sculpture-fountain. Erected in 1939, it commemorates the sad removal of local Indians to the west in 1840.
Another fountain features sculptor Kirk Newman's lifelike playing
children. Both **fountains and pools** are favorite play spots for
nearby children on hot summer days.

What makes this park especially nice in summer is the abundance of well-maintained flowers, climaxing in a spectacular floral sculpture which changes every year. They are provided by the
region's huge bedding plant industry, successors of the once-
booming celery growers.

On the park's southern border is the city's distinctive 1931 Art
Deco **city hall** with lots of wonderful Egyptian-flavored embellishments outside and in. Along the tops of the four limestone exterior walls are bas-reliefs of events from the city's history. To city
hall's west is the **First Presbyterian Church**, a majestic Gothic-
inspired structure built in 1930. To city hall's east is the imposing **Park Club**, a Queen Anne made of Lake Superior sandstone in
1890. Once the home of a prominent local industrialist, it is now
a private club.

Half a block away across from the library at 120 West South is **Something's Brewing**, a good place to grab a fresh-ground cup of coffee (58¢) or tea, or any of five flavors of hot chocolate to take back and sip in the park.

Bronson Park is in downtown Kalamazoo, bounded by Rose, Park, South, and Academy streets. Best way to get downtown: avoid S. Westnedge. From west (Chicago), from I-94, go north on U.S. 131, follow Bus. Route I-94 (Mich Ave.), turn south onto Rose. From east (Detroit), from I-94, take exit 81, which is Bus. Route I-94 (Kalamazoo St.). Turn south onto Rose. Park on the street along Michigan, South, or Lovell.

INTERESTING EGYPTOLOGY AND INNOVATIVE LOCAL HISTORY . . . . . On the second floor of the city library at Rose and South is the **Public Museum**. It has a splendid Egyptian section, complete with mummy, lots of attractively displayed ancient artifacts, and good descriptions. And there's a very nice **gift shop** with educational toys. *Tues-Sat 9-5, Sun 1-5. Planetarium shows Wed 7 & 8, Sat & Sun 1:30, 2:30, 3:30. Free.* . . . . . Just two blocks west of Bronson Park are two remarkable blocks of fine old homes, the **South Street Historic District** (see map). They were built between 1847 and World War I in a wide variety of architectural styles, from Greek and Gothic Revival through Georgian and Tudor.

A PIONEERING DOWNTOWN MALL . . . . . The country's first downtown pedestrian mall was built in 1959 on a four-block-long car-free stretch along the main commercial avenue of Burdick, one block east of Rose and Bronson Park. The **Kalamazoo Mall** allows visitors to stroll or sit in what was once a busy thoroughfare but now has flowers, trees, and sculpture. For around $2, you can pick up an egg roll and a good-sized portion of fried rice from the **Dragon Inn**, 232 S. Kalamazoo Mall, and enjoy it at one of tables along the outdoor concourse. **Jacobson's** and **Gilmore's Department Store**, each with popular lunch rooms, anchor the southern end. The **Kalamazoo Center** with its newly revived Radisson Hotel anchors the north retail end at Michigan Avenue. Farther north, at 335 North Burdick at Kalamazoo, the **Sarkozy Bakery** is a very popular West Michigan outpost of European-style, made-from-scratch baking inspired by old-fashioned ethnic neighborhood bakeries in the owners' hometowns of Flint and Dearborn. Here you'll find danish, cookies, puff pastry, and a big variety of breads, including authentic French breads, sourdough rye and pumpernickel, Sicilian bread, oatmeal bread, and tomato-and-herb-garnished foccacia, all reasonably priced. It's closed Sunday and Monday.

The Mall is busy mainly on weekdays and closed evenings and Sunday, like so many Michigan downtowns. The department stores and some interesting shops make a visit worthwhile. At 223 S. Kalamazoo Mall, **Petal & Postings'** two stories are well stocked with cards and stationery. **Terrapins**, 245 S. Kalamazoo Mall, is a warm, pleasing shop with jewelry, scarves, beads and other accessories. The **Athena Book Shop**, 300 S. Kalamazoo Mall, is an inviting place to browse. Just off the south end of the Mall at 115 S. Lovell is **Woodrose Fine Imports**, featuring Guatemalan clothing ($20-$75), colorful painted wood masks ($48), Peruvian jewelry, and Ikat-dyed clothing from Indonesia. It's open Sunday afternoon. The 1927 **State Theater** at 404 S. Burdick has a fantasy world within. It's one of only 12 surviving "atmospheric theaters" designed by the famous John Eberson. Inside is a Spanish courtyard of long ago, complete with statues, fountain, and three-dimensional facades of picturesque buildings along the walls. Stars still twinkle in the ceiling-sky when the lights dim, and the cloud machine still works. The theater now books live music — rock, jazz, blues, country, and gospel music, plus comedy. Occasionally silent movie are shown, and the vintage Barton theater organ gets a workout. Call (616) 345-6500 for the schedule.

AN AMAZING DOWNTOWN SHOE EMPORIUM . . . . . Near the mall is **Okun Brothers Shoe Store**, one of the largest, most scruffily colorful shoe stores in the Midwest offers discount prices to boot. You can find everything from ballet slippers to firemen's boots, lizard cowboy boots to high-heeled sandals. This 70-year-old storeis from a bygone era of retailing — bustling and never fancy. The exterior walls plastered with painted signs of brand names. The 30 salespeople are willing to bargain even on discounted prices. *South St. at Edwards on the east edge of downtown. (616) 342-1536. Mon-Fri 8:30-9, Sat 8:30-7.*

A SHOW STREET OF THE GILDED AGE . . . . . The **Stuart Avenue Historic District** is just west of downtown (see map). See remarkably intact historic streetscapes of big, extravagant Victorian homes, mostly from the 1880s. When a horse-drawn streetcar came out this way in 1884, professional men and business owners built huge suburban homes to display the wealth they gained in the years after the Civil War. Today, the Casteel family's five carefully restored bed and breakfast inns have done much to promote this neighborhood.

A MICROBREWERY AT WORK . . . . . Housed in an old plumbing supply building, the small, informal **Kalamazoo Brewing Company** turns out about 1,000 barrels (32,000 gallons) of beer, ale, stout, and porter a year. Worthy of special notice is Bell's Double Cream Stout, with its hefty 8.7% alcohol. They don't have formal tours here, but somebody's usually around to give you a 10-minute lecture on how the brew is made plus a look at the interesting makeshift facilities. It's a friendly, funky ambience with lots of beer memorabilia on the walls and bottled brew for sale. You can also purchase their products right here. *315 E. Kalamazoo Ave. (Bus. Route I-94 east) downtown. (616) 382-2338. Mon-Fri 9-6, Sat 10-6.*

Gilmore Classic Car Museum

*On a splendid farm near Hickory Corners,
a choice collection shows how some
of the most impressive car models have evolved*

This superb collection of old cars is located north of Kalamazoo in immaculately maintained old barns moved from area farms. An Upjohn chairman and heir, Don Gilmore, clearly lavished money and attention on this remarkable collection of 125 cars. What's special here is the opportunity to see how various makes evolved over the years. Twenty pristine Packards, the largest such assembly in the world, show how that legendary car changed from 1905 through the last model in 1956. There are 15 Rolls Royces, from the 1910 Silver Ghost to the 1938 Pack Ward. Mark I and II Lincolns, from 1940 and 1956 show how old that sleek line is.

Most historically important is the fascinating evolution of Henry Ford's autos from his initial 1903 Ford Tonneau, to the 1906 Model N, and the record-breaking Model T (19 million sold from 1907-1928), to the 1928-31 Model A. You can see the humble 1903 Cadillac grow in nine models into the flashy, finny model of the 1960s. In addition there are fancy old fire engines, a series of Stanley Steamers, a full-scale replica of the Kitty Hawk, and even a narrow-gauge steam locomotive.

Although many exotic cars are here — specially made cars of various potentates and state officials — much emphasis is given to Kalamazoo cars. On display and still working are the first new car sold in the city, an 1899 Locomobile, and a variety of the popular and high quality Roamers, last made in Kalamazoo in 1930. Last but not least are three of Kalamazoo's legendary Checker cabs: one from 1922, one from 1935, and the last Checker that rolled off the line in 1982.

On M-43 at Hickory Rd. west of Hickory Corners and just north of Gull Lake, northeast of Kalamazoo. (616) 671-5089. Open mid-May-mid thru mid-Oct: daily 10-5. $5 admission, children under 12 free.

Kellogg Bird Sanctuary

*Where idyllic landscaping has created a paradise
of plentiful food for dramatic big birds*

Walking into the Kellogg Bird Sanctuary near dusk is like walking into a dream. It's a lush, romantic landscape. Peacocks amble freely on the lawn, langorously trailing tails of brilliant blue and green. Here a normally elusive Eastern wild turkey is so well socialized that it makes an excellent photo subject if you happen to meet it on its early-morning or late-afternoon foraging strolls. Inside the entrance gift shop, you pay a dollar to enter, plus 50¢ for a generous bucket of corn. Down a winding path through a wooded glade you come to lovely **Wintergreen Lake**. Birdsong fills the air. Squirrels are drawn by plentiful food from many nut trees, domestic and exotic. Arching bridges connect lagoons along the shore. Rare swans sail up majestically to you, hoping for corn. When emerge from the water, it's a surprise to see them plop along on huge, comical black feet. It's a terrific thrill to be able to feed the birds and see them up close in such a gorgeous setting.

These were barren, overgrazed hills in 1928. At that time cereal magnate W. K. Kellogg started the sanctuary as a refuge for Canada geese, threatened by loss of habitat to agriculture and urbanization. This and other conservation efforts proved so successful that Canada geese are now pests in many places.

Today the sanctuary offers the public a most dramatic opportunity to see birds up close and learn about them. It's a part of Michigan State University's Kellogg Biological Station. The excellent **book shop** has posters, clothing, gifts, and toys, plus an outstanding selection of publications geared to nature-lovers and teachers. Here you can find out how to transform your back yard into a paradise for birds, using the same landscaping principles and fruit-planting materials used in the refuge. Permanent residents among the free-flying waterfowl by the lagoon include seven of the world's nine varieties of swans (the rare Trumpeter among them) and 30 pairs of Canada geese. In spring through fall they are augmented by 20 varieties of migrating ducks, such as bufflehead, ruddy ducks, hooded mergansers, and northern shovelers. Canadas alone number 5,000 during fall migration.

Interpretive signs along the 1 1/2-mile asphalt loop tell about the waterfowl in some detail. In a secluded area, away from the lively hubbub of waterfowl at the lake, visitors have an unusual chance to see 14 **birds of prey** up close, including a threatened red-shouldered hawk, the endangered short-eared owl, and a bald eagle. Modern zoo practice ordinarily prohibits caging such big native birds. These are injured. Some are being rehabilitated; others are so badly hurt they couldn't survive in the wild.

The sanctuary's residents and their activities change with the seasons, so repeat visits are worthwhile. Spring means the return of winter migrants to pass through or nest here. Swans and geese nest in late March, ducks start in early April. Nesting structures have been built in public areas to be easily observed by visitors. The young are hatched in May and June. Summer residents include many ducks, geese, and swans, along with over two dozen species of backyard songbirds. (To see bobolinks and such, you'd have to go out into the fields of the Biological Station.)

Beginning in October, ducks and geese stop here on their way south. Early November usually brings the greatest numbers and most varieties. Winter isn't dull, either. Swans, some geese, and diving and dabbling ducks stay near the lake, which doesn't freeze. In warm, snowless winters, geese may linger by the thousands, thrown off-kilter by confusing weather signals.

12685 East C Ave. east of Gull Lake between Kalamazoo and Battle Creek. From M-89, turn north on 40th St. In a little over a mile, go west onto East C Ave. (616) 671-2510. May-Oct: daily 9-sunset. Nov.-April: 9-5. Early-morning bird-watching by special arrangement. $1/adult, 50¢/children 4-17. Wheelchairs available at the office; barrier-free trail.

SKIERS, HIKERS, AND PICNICKERS . . . . . enjoy the quiet, scenic **W. K. Kellogg Forest**, a Michigan State University forestry experiment station on the hills and valley formed by pretty Augusta Creek. It's about three miles southeast of the Kellogg Bird Sanctuary. Cereal king and philanthropist W. K. Kellogg started it as a demonstration project in reforesting cutover, overgrazed hills — marginal farmland typical of Michigan's many areas of glacial lakes and hills.

Today the forest's 740 acres are planted in a huge variety of trees, quite possibly the largest genetic archive of temperate plant tree species in the world. From the entrance a dirt road leads back behind the "Maple Manor" sugar shack (used for mid-March syrup-making demonstrations) to a series of rustic **picnic areas** beneath big pines along the creek. Artificial ponds and rapids have turned the creek into a designated **trout stream**. A 1/4-mile trail leads to a **scenic overlook** and **2 1/2-mile road loop**. (The trail is steep and unstable; you might prefer to use the road loop that circles around to the north.) You pass plantations of Scotch pines for Christmas trees in which the seedlings come from stock grown in different cold climates from around the world. Skiers, hikers, and bowhunters are all welcome to use the forest's 25 miles of ungroomed firebreaks separating experimental stands of trees. Stop for a **map and brochure** at the forest entrance off 42nd Street, 3/4 of a mile south of M-89 and two miles north of the quaint canal village of Augusta. Admission is free. Restrooms behind the office are always open. Call (616) 731-4597 for special, forest-related events.

VISIT A STATE-OF-THE-ART DAIRY. . . . . two miles north of the Kellogg Bird Sanctuary. A free, self-guided tour of Michigan State University's **Kellogg Dairy** starts in the milking parlor and ends with a chance to pet the calves in outdoor nursery hutches. Call (616) 671-2507 for current **milking times;** they're at dawn, around noon, and at dusk. If you miss seeing milking, you can watch an interesting nine-minute video on dairy farming practices. A **free booklet** explains the basics of milk production and nutrition.

This high-tech dairy has an automatic flush system that cleans out the barn in minutes. By hand that's a three-hour job. Dairy farms can be big polluters because of fertilizer runoff and manure. In this integrated waste management system, liquid manure and flushing water are stored in clay-lined ponds, then recycled as fertilizer and irrigation water for fields. Treated manure solids are used for bedding. A high-tech dairy like this could pay off for a herd of 150 or more, the size of a family farm with some hired help. It costs more in equipment but saves on time and fertilizer. *From M-89 east of Gull Lake and Richland, turn north on 40th St. The dairy is 2 1/2 miles north, past B Ave. (616) 671-2507. Free.*

STROLL THROUGH THE BEAUTIFUL GROUNDS OF W. K. KELLOGG'S LAKESIDE ESTATE. . . . . at the **Kellogg Biological Station** Manor House. It's on 3700 East Gull Lake Drive at B Avenue. (East Gull Lake Drive joins M-89 at the lake's southern tip.) In 1926 Battle Creek's cereal king built a simple, tasteful Tudor summer retreat, Eagle Heights, at the highest point overlooking Gull Lake. It became the core of a 3,500-acre, year-round Michigan State University center for biological research (birds, ecology, forestry, agriculture), conferences, and extension programs.

The **Manor House** itself is closed to the general public, but visitors are welcome to take the health-conscious Kellogg's favorite exercise **walk down to Gull Lake.** A picturesque stone and brick stairway zigzags down the steep, wooded hill to a pagoda and boat dock that juts out into the lake. This walk is especially lovely at sunset. For a dramatic, planned vista, look back up at the house from the pagoda. Just before the pagoda, there's a perennial garden with a rose arbor and sundial bearing the workaholic Kellogg's favorite saying, "The early bird catches the worm." Kellogg loved to take this walk with his friend and frequent guest, science writer Paul de Kruif. Kellogg ordinarily insisted on a smoke-free environment, but he let de Kruif smoke his omnipresent pipe on these walks.

FOR A SWIM IN GULL LAKE. . . . . there's the small, oak-shaded **Ross Township Park** on East Gull Lake Drive just north of the Kellogg estate. Parking is limited. The beach is stony, with a deep dropoff. The **Prairieville Township park** on M-43 at the north end of the lake is larger but less scenic, with an improved beach, bigger parking lot, and bathrooms. Both have modest fees per car, and both are often crowded on summer weekends.

Binder Park Zoo

*Emphasizing natural habitats, this small zoo is
a lot more satisfying than watching caged animals.*

This splendid small zoo is rapidly evolving into one of the
most interesting in the Midwest. You won't find caged lions
or tigers. The animals selected to live here have places
where they can feel at home. The gibbons live in a lush, spacious
area where they can swing through trees. The handsome zebras
have a long enough field to develop a full gallop. A 2/3-mile habitat trail takes you through fields, marshes and forests, adding to
the feeling that this is not an artificial environment. Elevated
boardwalks in parts of the zoo add to the feeling that most of the
zoo is the *animals'* turf with zoo visitors confined to smaller areas.
A special **children's section** has a dozen types of domestic animals, a place to feed goats, and a life-size replica of a dinosaur.
There is also a small **visitors' railroad**, snack bar, and picnic area.

Eleven years ago, when zoo director Greg Giese first arrived,
these 60 acres were mostly trees and grass. He credits a tremendous amount of planting over the past decade for creating the
animals' rich habitats. Geise carried the zoo's first animal with
him, a European ferret, when he accepted the challenge to start
this zoo. He began with a tiny budget, and it's been a bootstrap
operation, with no tax support. An animal behaviorist by training,
Geise thinks the zoo has ultimately profited from having to sustain
itself like a private business. No taxes means no political interfer-
ence, a problem in most city zoos. And depending on visitors for
revenues gives the staff a greater incentive to make the zoo
attractive. It has become so popular that attendance has grown to
a quarter million annually.

Your trip to the zoo will be more enjoyable if you come when
the animals are most active — in the morning or late afternoon,
preferably on a cooler day.

*7400 Division Drive at Beadle Lake Rd. 5 miles south of downtown
Battle Creek. From I-94 take exit 100, go south 2½ miles on
Beadle Lake Rd. (616) 979-1351. Open mid-April to mid-Oct.
weekdays 9-5; weekends & holidays 9-6 . Adults $2.50; children
3-12 $1.50*

Recommended Restaurants & Lodgings

Southwestern Michigan

See regional map, p. 2.

NEW BUFFALO

Rosie's. *128 N. Whittaker, downtown, 1 block n. of U.S. 12. (616) 469-4382. Open every day 7-2. Breakfast $2-$5 all day; lunch $2-$6 at 11. No alcohol, credit cards.* Super- popular family cafe, run by old-country Bohemians. Good homey fare: $5 roast pork w/ dumplings or potatoes and sauerkraut, red cabbage or applesauce. Fruit dumplings $4.50 w/ cottage cheese, soup, dessert. Breakfast hit: farmer's omelet.

Casey's Pub & BBQ. *136 N. Whittaker, downtown, 1 block n. of U.S. 12. (616) 469-9885. Open daily 11 a.m.-midnight. Dinners $5.50-$8 w/ 2 sides, dessert. Lunch specials. Sandwiches & fries $2.75-$4. Full bar. No credit cards.* Locals and Chicago people love this bar's worn wood floor, family atmosphere. Big draws: pork BBQribs ($6.25), smoked here; nongreasy broasted chicken dinner ($5.50).

Hannah's. *115 S. Whittaker, 1 block south of U. S. 12. (616) 469-1440. Sun-Thurs 11:30-10, Fri & Sat 11:30-11 (longer in summer). Lunch entrees $5-$6 served all day, dinner $10-$15 w/ salad, starch. Full bar. Visa, AmEx, MC.* Onetime Little Bohemia restaurant seats 250 in a remodeled house. Super-popular, more for convivial atmosphere than good,not great food. Favorite lunch picks: crab meat in wonton-like wrappers, deep fried ($6), crab salad ($5.25), Canadian jack chicken sandwich ($6). For dinner, duck and roast pork loin (both $12), prime rib. Pianist Friday & Saturday.

Redamak's. *616 E. Buffalo (U.S. 12), just east of downtown. (616) 469-4522. Closed Dec-Feb. Mon-Thurs 11-10:30, Fri 11-11, Sat & Sun 12-11. Full bar. No credit cards. Carryout burger hotline: 469-4522.* "The hamburger that made New Buffalo famous" started in 1950 as a convenient stop for vacationing Chicagoans. Dark, cool, oldtimey bar, now grown huge. Local tradesmen come for $2 burger and fries special (Mon-Fri 11-4). Very good, 5 oz. burgers normally $2.75, grilled onions 50¢ extra. Artificially thickened soups a disappointment. Expect a wait in summer despite new 130-seat patio.

Grand Beach Motel. *(616) 469-1555. US. 12 at Wilson Rd., 2 1/2 mi. w. of New Buffalo. 13 rooms, 1 floor. $40-$45 Mem.-Labor Day, $30-$35 otherwise. Open April 1-Nov. 15. Cable TV, a/c. No phones. Outdoor pool screened from highway. Cont. breakfast weekends.* *Friendly hosts; like a budget B&B.*

Sans Souci B&B. *(616) 756-3141. 19265 S. Lakeside Rd. 3 mi. e. of New Buffalo. 6 rooms with baths, 2 suites. $95-$160. Full breakfast. Suites & some rooms have phone, TV, VCR, whirlpool. On 50 acres w/ woods, lakes.* *Old farm decorated with German elegance*

UNION PIER

Miller's Country House *16409 Red Arrow Hwy. south of Union Pier Rd. (616) 469-5950. Open daily 12-10, to 11 Fri & Sat. Closed Tues, Labor Day thru June. Salads, sandwiches $4-$9 (served all day except Sat), dinners $9-$22 with starch, veg., Fr. bread. Full bar.Take-out deli. AmEx,Visa, Diners, MC.* 1920s dance hall/resort now a chic, casual 250-seat restaurant. Sophisticated, fun atmosphere draws Chicago celebrities. Good, fresh food, many Michigan wines. Rear garden, woods, deck. Dinner picks: grilled salmon ($17), fresh perch ($14), chicken breast ($12), rack of lamb ($19). Also: steaks, pasta. Espresso, capuccino, special desserts.

Pine Garth Inn. *(616) 469-1642.*
15790 Lakeshore Rd. 7 rooms with baths, all but 1 w/ lake views. 4 w/whirlpools, many w/ private decks. $105-$130. Lower off-season rates. Full breakfast, afternoon wine & cheese. TV &VCR (in armoires), good array of classic films. Library w/ fireplace, sun porch & patio overlook beach, private dock. 4 cottages across street, $195 night in season. *Only area B&B overlooking Lake Michigan; comfortable getaway with lovely grounds, beach, decks*

The Inn at Union Pier. *(616) 469-4700. 9708 Berrien St. 1/2 block from Lakeshore Dr. in Union Pier.* 15 rooms with baths in 3 bldgs of old resort. $85-$125. Full breakfast, afternoon snacks, evening wine. Swedish fireplaces in most rooms, 6 w/ balconies. 3 common rooms with large-screen TV. Outdoor hot tub, sauna. Beach access nearby. Light, unpretentious, Old Country Swedish decor. *Large inn, attractive grounds, friendly innkeeper*

LAKESIDE

Panozzo's Cafe. *15300 Red Arrow Hwy. at Sunset. (616) 469-2370. Summer hours: 9-3 daily, 9-2 Sun, plus Fri night pasta buffet 6-9. Open at least Fri-Sun from Easter to Dec 31. Closed Jan-Easter. Closing time varies; call ahead. Breakfast $4-$6, lunch soups, salads, sandwiches $3.50-$6. No credit cards or alcohol.* Overstressed Chicagoans rave over relaxing breakfasts at Patty Panozzo's woodsy 35-seat garden cafe. Engaging cookbook shares clever presentation ideas for pancakes with fruit, French toasts, egg dishes, cereals, muffins, breads. Cappuccino, espresso, desserts. Come before 10 to avoid a wait. Sunday brunch ($9), Friday-evening pasta buffet ($9) are very popular.

The Pebble House. *(616) 469-1416. 15093 Lake Shore Rd.* 7 rooms/suites in 3 Craftsman-style bldgs. 5 rooms with baths $90-$96, 2 suites w/ kitchen, wood-burning stove $106-$130. Scandinavian breakfast buffet. In quiet, shady area of large old summer homes. Tennis court, screen house, hammocks. Beach across the street. Several common rooms. Big art & arch. library, Craftsman furniture. *1912 resort with authentic, serene Arts & Crafts decor, lovely grounds*

BRIDGMAN AREA

Hyerdall's. *9673 Red Arrow Hwy. just north of light. (616) 465-5546. Tues-Sun 7-9 p.m. Breakfast $3-$7, lunch $2.75-$7, dinners $5.25-$10.45. No alcohol or credit cards. Since 1927.* The consummate diner despite a spiffy redo. Signature dish: stewed chicken & biscuits ($7 lunch/$8 dinner). Every full meal comes with salad, potato, terrific bread basket, often a vegetable. Homemade pie (2 fruit, 2 cream daily) $1.25/slice.

Golda's. *Red Arrow Highway near Warren Dunes State Park 4 miles south of downtown Bridgman. (616) 426-4114. 11-10 daily. No alcohol or credit cards.* Chicago-style hot dogs are main event at restored drive-in. Arty retro flair supplied by Golda, an ex-Chicago art student. Basic kosher frank ($2.40) comes with mustard, relish, hot pepper, tomatoes, cucumber, onions. Also: bratwurst, Polish sausage, chili dogs, grilled chicken, all with fresh, hand-cut fries. Ben & Jerry's ice cream, old-fashioned malts. Outside picnic tables, play area for children: sand box, yard toys, volleyball net. *Refreshing break.*

Tabor Hill Restaurant *185 Mt. Tabor Rd. Exit 16 from I-94 in Bridgman. Take Lake (which becomes Shawnee) 5 miles east, follow signs. (616) 422-1161. Open mid-April thru*

November. Lunch ($5-7) Wed-Sun 11:30-3. Dinner ($10-$16) Wed-Sat 5-9. Full bar. MC,Visa, AmEx. Sophisticated, vaguely California country restaurant amid Tabor Hill's vineyards. Stunning view looks out across vineyards and orchards to Lake Michigan dunes. Recommended: grilled shrimp ($8/lunch, $13/ dinner), raspberry pecan chicken ($7 lunch, $13.50 dinner). Stylish food, skimpy portions. Can get crowded with groups.

ST. JOSEPH AREA

Tosi's. 4337 Ridge Rd. between St. Joseph and Stevensville. From the Red Arrow Hwy. just north of I-94, turn west onto Glenlord Rd., then south onto Ridge. (616) 429-3689. Closed Jan & Feb. Mon-Sat. Dinner only March to mid-April. Lunch 11:30-2:30, dinner 5:30-10, Sat 5-10. Lunch entrees $5-$8 with side, dinner $10-$20 with 2 sides. Full bar. Visa, AmEx, Diners, MC. An area institution for 50 years. Northern Italian dishes are complex, aromatic, memorable and rich! Super service. Specialties: malfatti (spinach rolls with mushrooms; $10 dinner, $5 appetizer), chicken breast with pancetta and rosemary on fettucine ($12.50), babyback ribs ($15). Caesar salad $6 for two. Also:steaks, chops, prime rib ($15-$20), broiled fish, veal. Sharing pasta & oyster antipasti ($4.50 -$5.75) instead of ordering dinner is OK. Meals come with excellent minestrone, salad, bread.

Grand Mere Inn

5800 Red Arrow Hwy. less than 1 mi. south of I-94 exit 22 near Stevensville. 616) 429-3591. Tues-Fri 11-3 and 5-10. Sat 5-11. Lunch $4 (soup & salad)-$7.75. Dinners $8.50-$19 w/ 2 sides, good bread basket, liver paté. Full bar. Visa, MC, Diners, AmEx. Popular, lively resort-area restaurant. Parking mars lake view, sunset. Menu mixes traditional favorites (slow-cooked BBQ pork ribs $12/half slab, deep-fried perch $11, top-notch fresh seafood) with updates like roast duck-

ling & green peppercorn sauce ($12). Homemade desserts. Sandwiches ($4-$5), bar food available all day in bar. Reservations advised; expect a wait.

Mama Martorano's

422 State, 1 store north of Elm, downtown. (616) 982-0387. Mon-Sat 11:30-11, Sun 4-10. Dinners $4.50-$7. Daily pasta lunch special $4. No alcohol or credit cards. Simple, self-serve Italian pizzeria and carryout, perfumed with garlic. Mostaccioli ($4.50 small/$5.50 large, w/ salad, bread) a favorite. 25-minute wait for pizza; stroll around downtown. Mama's cooking shines in dishes like Chicken Vesuvius ($5.50), baked in butter-lemon-garlic-wine sauce, w/ roast potato, salad, bread. Delicious soups ($1.75). Italian ice 75¢.

Schu's Grill & Bar

501 Pleasant St. at Lake Blvd. across from YWCA downtown. (616) 983-7248. Mon-Thurs 11-10, Fri-Sat 11-midnight. Summer: open daily, longer hours. AmEx, Visa, MC, Disc. Full bar. New Win Schuler restaurant in informal grill format. Available all day: sandwiches ($5-$7), soup $1.50 bowl, salads $1.50-$7. Dinners from $7.65 for whitefish to $12 for a N.Y. strip.

Zitta's at the Depot

410 Vine near Silver Beach, below the bluff in St. Joe. Take Port St. (the street that parallels the river just north of downtown) west to Vine. (616) 983-6800. Open Mon-Fri 11 a.m Sat & Sun 8 a.m. Closing varies with season. Full bar. No credit cards. The Zittas of local burger fame renovated the 1914 train station as a combined bar/soda fountain (giant old-style malts are $3) with outdoor patio facing lake. Get there on foot from downtown via Ship St. stairway. Signature: good $1.75 burger. Other favorites: homemade soups, hot beef sandwich or Southern BBQpork sandwich (both $4.50), interesting salads (pasta crab salad and Bombay chicken salad are $6), fresh vegetable stir-fries ($5.50 and up), $8 fried chicken dinner.

Snow Flake Motel. *(616) 429-3261.
3822 Red Arrow Hwy. (Lake Shore Dr.),
about 4 mi. south of downtown St.
Joseph, less than 1 mi. north of I-94
exit 23.* 56 rooms. $30-$35 winter, $40-
$45 summer. Cable TV. Pool. Coffee
shop and bar. Some rooms still have
built-ins designed by Wright's office —
dresser-seats & desks. Star-shaped
motel looks on beautiful 2 1/2-acre
central court, long reflecting pool &
fountain leading to hexagonal heated
swimming pool. Snow sliding off roof
makes awful scraping noise.
*Designed in part by Frank Lloyd
Wright; budget rates, interesting rooms*

South Cliff Inn B&B. *(616)
984-4881. 1990 Lakeshore Dr., about
10 blocks south of downtown St.
Joseph.* 6 rooms w/ baths. Summer,
weekends year-round: $55-$95. Off-
season weekdays: $40-$60. Cont.
breakfast. A/C. Den with TV. Guests
use sunroom, living room, 2 decks
overlooking lake. Small beach down
and across RR tracks. Beautiful location in attractive neighborhood.
1920s lakeview house on bluff

Boulevard Hotel. *(616) 983-6600.
521 S. Lake Blvd. downtown.* 90 2-
room suites on 6 floors. May-Sept:
$76-$106. Winter: $70-$90, weekend
specials. Higher-price rooms have lake
view. Cable TV, phone, refrigerator,
wet bar, microwave. Cont. breakfast in
dining room with lake view. Romance,
golf , Star Clipper Dinner Train packages. Guest privileges at YWCA 2 blocks
away. Walk to Silver Beach.
*All-suite luxury hotel (good value),
great downtown site on lake bluff park*

St. Joseph Holiday Inn. *(616)
983-7341. 100 Main (U.S. 33) in downtown St. Joe, overlooking river.* 156
rooms on 6 floors. $66. Luxury level:
$83. Winter rates, suites. Packages for
charter boats, Amtrak,
x-c skiing. Cable TV, phones. Indoor
pool, whirlpool, sauna, steambaths.
Restaurant, lounge w/ dancing.
Downtown location, indoor pool

Ramada Inn. *(616) 927-1172. 798
Ferguson Rd. 3 mi. s. of downtown Ben-
ton Harbor, 5 mi. from downtown St.
Joseph. Take exit 28 (M-139) off I-94.*
117 rooms on 5 floors. $54-$59. Cable
TV. Indoor pool, whirlpool, game
room. Restaurant. Bar w/ DJ, comedy
night. On busy strip. Walk to park on
St. Jos River.
Indoor pool, activities, moderate rates

Red Roof Inn. *(616) 927-2484. At
The Orchards Mall on Pipestone, I-94
exit 29.* 109 rooms on 2 floors. $39-
$45. Package rates avail. TV w/movies,
ESPN. Phones. Vending room w/pop,
chips, ice.
Reasonable rates, at big regional mall

NILES

Golden Eagle Motel. *(616)
684-1000. On U.S. 33 on south side of
Niles.* Busy strip, but many rooms
don't face it. 38 rooms in 3 buildings, 1
with 2 floors. $30-$40. Cable TV,
phones. Outdoor pool. Adjoins good
family restaurant, Someplace Else.
Good budget choice with outdoor pool

SOUTH HAVEN

Jensen's Fishery. *On Dyckman at
harbor just over the drawbridge. (616)
637-2008. Spring & summer: open
daily 10-10. Shorter winter hours. No
credit cards. Takeout beer & wine.*
Basic, functional fish market with
fresh or cooked fish. Mostly takeout.
15 seats at 3 big tables overlook busy
harbor; screened-in deck has 15 more.
Known for shrimp: smoked, fried, or
fresh, $13.75/lb. cooked. Cooked lake
perch is $10.20/lb., whitefish $6.75/lb.
Dinners (w/fries, slaw,roll): shrimp
($7.50), BBQ pork ribs ($8.25), 1/2 BBQ
chicken ($5). Also: subs, sandwiches,
lunch specials.

Three Pelicans.
*At south end of North Shore Dr. (616)
637-5123. Lunch ($6-$8) Mon-Sat
11:30-2, dinner ($10-$26) Mon-Thurs
5:30-10, Fri & Sat 5:30-11, Sun 5:30-9.*

Longer summer hours, plus Sunday brunch. Pub w/ sandwich menu open 11:30- closing. Full bar. Visa, MC. Service at the former Ruppert's is good; food can be excellent. Nautical theme. Quiet main-level dining, noisy lower-level bar, decks all overlook busy harbor. Turkey, chicken, shrimp, fish, and ribs ($13/slab) smoked on the premises. Other picks: char-grilled honey-Dijon salmon ($13), prime rib with pepper, onions, BBQ sauce ($13 large, $11 medium). Tasty Pelican Pub Club smoked turkey sandwich ($6).

Sea Wolf. *Blue Star Hwy. 2 1/2 mi. n. of downtown , 2 blocks n. of end of North Shore Dr. and I-196/U.S. 31 exit 22. (616) 637-2007. Open May-Sept: daily 5:30-9:30, Sun brunch 10:30-2. (May-mid-June: closed Mon-Tues.) Full bar, extensive wine list. Visa, MC.* One of Western Michigan's very best restaurants. South Haven was long the Midwest's leading Jewish resort. Old World abundance lives on here at the former Weinstein's Resort, still in the family. Huge meals include matzoh ball soup, liver paté, rolls, salad, vegetables, wonderful desserts based on local fruits. "Petite" meals start at $10 for pork chop, lemon chicken. Fresh fish dependably excellent. Whitefish ($13-$15) comes broiled, fried, almondine, piccata, Veronique, Bernaise, or tropical. Other picks: live lobster, chicken Milanaise ($13), veal Oscar ($16). Feast of a Sunday brunch ($9): fresh shrimp, 30 salads, blintzes, ham, prime rib, desserts.

Yelton Manor B&B.*(616) 637-5220. 140 North Shore Dr., just south of Dyckman.* 11 rooms with baths. $85-$115. $115-$140 for large rooms w/jacuzzis. Full breakfast, hors d'oeuvres at 5:30 are almost a meal. Separate guest kitchen w/ cookies, drinks, homemade bedtime snack. Huge 3 story-Victorian house has 8 common areas including a new garden room w/ fireplace & TV/VCR. Beach access 1/2 block.
Rambling, updated North Beach B&B, lots of food and snacks

The Last Resort B&B. *(616) 637-8943. 86 North Shore Dr. just s. of Dyckman. Open mid-April thru Oct.* 15 rooms, all but one w/ water views. Shared baths, sinks in rooms. $48 for small rooms, $60 for large, $160 for suite w/ bath, kitchenette, fabulous view. 5th day free. Cont. brkfst. A/C. Big deck, attractively landscaped, large common areas, small TV room. At center of beach/resort/ restaurant area. Beach access 1/2 block away.
1883 North Beach inn, restored by artists with studio on premises

A Country Place. *(616) 637-5523. North Shore Dr. about 1 1/2 mi. n. of downtown.* 5 rooms w/baths. $55-$65. Greek Revival farmhouse. Large living room w/ TV, VCR, fireplace. Large screened-in gazebo, enc. porch, large deck. Less than 1 block to neighborhood beach. 3 cottages (1 on grounds, 2 on Lake Michigan). $400-$600/week. In spring & fall rented by the day: $70-$85.
B&B in pretty, quiet spot near Lake Michigan

Sun 'n' Sand Motel. *(616) 637- 2007. Blue Star Hwy., 2 1/2 mi. n. of downtown, 2 blks n. of U.S. 31 exit 22.* 30 units. Open May-Sept. $35 in 2-story main bldg. (no A/C). $45 in newer motel-like unit (A/C). Older rooms, clean and simple. No phones. TV. Lap-sized pool. Adjoins excellent Sea Wolf restaurant. Cool, rural location; orchard across road. No beach access.
Budget rates, pleasant setting

Friendship Inn. *(616) 637-5141. On M-140 (Blue Star Hwy.), just off I-196 exit 18 on strip.* 60 rooms on 2 floors). $58-$68, suites $95. Cable TV, phones. Suites w/ kitchenettes, whirlpool. Indoor pool, sauna, playground, health club. 2 racquetball courts, massage. Restaurant, bar.
South Haven's luxury facility

PAW PAW

Little River Cafe. *715 S. Kalamazoo across from St. Julian Winery. From I-94 take exit 60, north 1/4 mile. (616)*

657-6035. Sun-Thurs 11:30-8, Fri-Sat 11:30-9, open 1 hour longer in summer. Lunches $4-$9, dinners $11-$17. MC, Visa, AmEx, Disc. Full bar. Wine country decor, riverside patio dining. Casual. Features Michigan wines. Recommended: cashew chicken ($13 at dinner), shrimp & scallops Romano ($14), prime rib ($17). $9 early-bird specials. Sandwich menu all day in bar.

Annly's Chow

On Red Arrow Hwy. next to Morrison's huge produce stand. 2 1/2 mi. e. of Paw Paw, 3 mi. w. of Mattawan. (616) 657-2786. Open Feb-Dec, Tues-Sat 11:30-8, to 9 in summer. Lunch $4-$6, dinner $5-$10. No credit cards or alcohol. Checks OK. Simple, sunny family restaurant.Chinese w/some American standards. Based on fresh local produce in season. Light batters, little grease. Cashew chicken or beef in garlic-wine sauce a favorite. Pies.

Carrington's Country House

(616) 657-5321. 43799 60th Ave., next to State Police post, 1 blk from Lake Core swimming beach. 3 rooms on 2 floors. $35-$45. A/C. Full breakfast. TV in family room. 150-year-old farmhouse surrounded by orchards & vineyards.

Scenic farm/resort setting, big breakfast, budget rates

KALAMAZOO

Bravo Ristorante

5402 Portage Rd. across from airport. From I-94 take Portage south 1/2 mile. (616) 344-7700. Mon-Thurs 11:30-10, Fri-Sat 11:30-11, Sun 11-9. Lunches $6-$12, dinners $9-$15. AmEx, Visa, MC, Disc. Full bar & wine list. Popular new spot, bright and casual in crayons-and-white-paper-tablecloth vein. Dinner picks: shrimp scampi with linguine ($15) , pork chops ($13), eggplant parmesan or chicken pot pie ($9 each). Salads ($4 and up) avail. all day.

Mi Ranchito

Mexican family parlayed a former gas station into popular mini-chain, more Tex-Mex than authentic, good but not great. ***Downtown :*** *248 S. Kalamazoo Mall. (616) 343-7230.* Mon-Sat 11-3, lunch only. No credit cards or alcohol. Take-out available. Nothing over $5. Flauta $3.50, burrito or taco salad $3.75.***South Kalamazoo :*** *3806 S. Westnedge less than 1 mi. n. of I-94 exit 76. Across from Meijer and just n. of it. (616) 343-7262.* Mon-Sat 11-9, closed Sun. No credit cards or alcohol. Similar menu, nothing over $7.50.Take-out available. ***Oshtemo (west side) fine dining format:*** *3112 S. 9th St., just n. of Michigan Ave./ Stadium. From I-94, take U.S. 131 n. 2 miles to exit 36, go w. (616) 375-5861.* Mon-Sat 11-11, Sun 4-9. MC, Visa, AmEx, Disc. Full bar. Costs more than other Mi Ranchitos. Pleasant, whitewashed Southwest decor. Menu ranges from burritos and chimichangas ($4.75, or $6.75 with guacamole or cheese sauce and beans) to shrimp or seafood combos ($11).

Stuart Avenue Inns

(616) 342-0230. 405 Stuart Ave. at corner of Kalamazoo, 1 mi. west of downtown. Across from Kalamazoo College, near W.M.U. Includes Bartlett-Upjohn House (1886 Queen Anne), James Balch House (1889), Chappell House (1902). 20 rooms. $55-$75, VIP jacuzzi rooms $95-$120. A/C, cable TV, phones, full breakfast. In Stuart Ave. Historic District. Access to owners' McDuffee Gardens, 1 acre w/ 800' of lighted pathways. Gazebo, pavilion, pergola, goldfish ponds, swings. Also, Harris House w/ 4 apt. suites $65.
Pioneering B&Bs in splendid restored mansions with ornate interiors

Holiday Inn West

(616) 375-6000. 2747 S.11th. on w. side of U.S. 131 at Stadium Dr. 186 units on 4 floors. $85. Satellite TV, phones. Holidome: indoor pool, 2 whirlpools, sauna, game room, exercise room. Restaurant. Bar. Bowling adjacent.
Holidome, bowling, activities

Southgate Motor Inn

(616) 343-6143. 5630 S. Westnedge, just s. of I-94 (exit 76A) on busy strip. 124 rooms on 2 floors. $39. Cable TV, phones. Outdoor pool, picnic area, playground. Intense traffic. Breakfast-only restaurant. Near major malls. *Good budget choice*

PLAINWELL

Arie's Cafe

127 E. Bridge (M-89) in downtown Plainwell. (616) 685-9495. Mon-Sat 11-9, Sun 12-4. AmEx, Visa, MC. Full bar, extensive wine list. Kalamazoo's best, most popular restaurant is 12 miles north in pretty canal town of Plainwell. Refreshingly unpretentious cafe. Incredible value, considering the quality. Chalkboard menu changes daily. Lunch sandwiches ($3 or so), salads, soups, and unusual specials ($7 tops) draw big local clientele. Sample dinners: cheese tart with ratatouille ($7.25), roast pork, rosemary stuffing ($9.45), sea scallops, Dijon hollandaise ($12), prime rib $15 — all including soup or salad, vegetable, starch — couscous, fettucine, rice, new potatoes. Super-dedicated owner brothers cook from scratch in the tradition of their late father, Arie Van Ravensway. Peanut butter pie ($2.75) a specialty.

GULL LAKE AREA

Bayview Gardens

On M-89 at 38th St. at s.e. bay of Gull Lake, 3 miles east of Richland. (616) 629-9111 or (616) 731-4911. Mon-Thurs 11-10, Fri-Sat 11-11, Sun 8:30-9. Lunches around $5, dinners from $5 (steak sizzler) to $25 (steak & lobster), mostly around $11. MC, Visa, AmEx. Full bar. Big, friendly neighborhood tavern from 1920s. Wide mix of ages, incomes. Outdoor deck/patio with obstructed lake view. Good wet burrito ($7) easily feeds two. Sandwich menu ($4-$7) all day. Favorites: prime rib ($11 at dinner), BBQ ribs ($12), boiled shrimp in shell. Live band on Fri & Sat. (contemporary but not rock).

Gull Lake Cafe

12503 East D Ave. on s.e. bay of Gull Lake. From M-89, turn n. onto 38th St. (616) 731-2622. Mon-Thurs 11:30-9, Fri-Sat 11:30-10, Sun 11-9 (1 hour longer in summer). MC, Visa, AmEx. Full bar. Ambitious, California-style cafe from an owner-chef at Kalamazoo's late, lamented Oakley's. Airy, spare room designed to sound lively. Limited water view. Regular menu geared to conventional Gull Lakers. Sandwich menu ($5-$7) all day. Dinners (inc. salad, vegetable, starch) are $9-$18. Chicken, veg. lasagna, liver & onions, meat loaf on low end; ribs, steak, live lobster at top. Call for special theme weekends with coordinated meals, music, and decor; Wednesday gourmet nights; other events.

Gull Lake Motor Inn

(616) 731-4131. M-89 at 38th St., across from Bay View Gardens. 20 rooms on 1 floor. $65 mid May-mid Oct, $35-$42 off-season. A/C, fans, cable TV, refrigerators, coffeemakers. 2 whirlpools. Indoor pool for fall 1991. Picnic tables & grills in gazebos. Across street from 2 restaurants. Flanked by 2 top public golf courses. *Gorgeous golf course location, pleasant rooms, amenities*

BATTLE CREEK

Schrank's Cafeteria

85 W. Michigan Mall in downtown. (616) 964-7755. Mon-Fri 7-6:30, Sun 11-5, closed Saturday. No credit cards or alcohol. Pleasant cafeteria with good, inexpensive food. Everything a la carte. Breakfasts $1-$4, sandwiches $2.25-$4, dinners $5-$6 complete. Carryout.

Waterfront Seafood Company

315 W. Columbia on Goguac Lake, 2 mi. s. of downtown Battle Creek and 3 blks w. of Capitol. (From I-94, take Capital exit 97, go 2 1/2 miles n., left on Columbia. (616) 962-7622. Mon-Fri 11-10, Sat 5-10, Sun 11-8. Lunch $3-$9, dinners $6 - 25. AmEx, Visa, Disc, Din-

ers. Full bar. Pleasant lakefront setting, some of Battle Creek's best food. Prime rib ($10-$17), steaks plus the likes of pasta marinara ($6 at dinner), chicken stir-fry, whitefish ($9.50), coconut shrimp ($13). Sunday brunch $9 adults, $4 children.

Knights Inn South

(616) 964-2600. 2595 Capital Ave. north of I-94 (exit 97). On busy strip. 95 rooms on 1 floor. $30-$44. Cable TV. Kitchenettes avail.
Moderate rates, outdoor pool

Stouffer's Battle Creek Hotel

(616) 963-7050. Capital at Jackson,downtown. 244 rooms on 16 floors. $94-$164. Packages available. Cable TV. Indoor pool, sauna, jacuzzi, exercise room. McCamly's Roof restaurant on 16th floor. Casual pub, 2 bars w/ entertainment. Adjoins festival marketplace with shops, restaurants, Kellogg Arena.
Downtown luxury, lively location

The Old Lamp-Lighter's Homestay

(616) 963-2603. 276 Capital NE (M-66 North) in historical area. 10 min. walk to downtown. 7 rooms on 3 floors. $55, suites $75. Private baths, A/C. Phone on each floor. Full breakfast. 2 common rooms on main floor. Golf & ski pkgs. 1912 home w/ elaborate glass, light fixtures, murals, woodwork.
Friendly B&B in exceptional Arts & Crafts mansion

Greencrest Manor

(616) 962-8633. 6174 Halbert n.w .of Battle Creek on 10 1/2 acres. 5 rooms on 3 floors (11 rooms when fully renovated). $75-$150. Breakfast. 3 rooms w/ private bath, 2 rooms share bath w/sinks in rooms. Phone, TV available, hook-ups in each room. 3 levels of formal gardens. Not far from Kellogg Bird Sanctuary (p. 000).
B&B in Norman French chateau overlooking a lake

UNION CITY

Victorian Villa Guesthouse

(517) 741-7383. 601 N. Broadway, halfway between M-60 and downtown Union City. 10 rooms with baths on 3 floors of grand villa, 2 floors of carriage house on 2 acres w/gazebo, goldfish pond, gardens, full-size croquet court. $85, suites $125. A/C or ceiling fans in all rooms. Full breakfast. Afternoon tea. Victorian dinners avail. 7 common areas. 15-20 min to Battle Creek, Marshall.
B&B with opulent Victorian setting, furnishings, food

MENDON

Mendon Country Inn

(616) 496-8132. 440 W. Main St. (M-60) downtown . 18 rooms w/ baths in 3 bldgs. $45-$72. 7 jacuzzi suites w/ fireplaces $125. A/C in most rooms. TV, phone in large common room. Free canoeing, bicycles built for 2. 14 acres of woods and rapids on beautiful St. Joseph River. Some country decor pleasant, some corny. Self- guided restaurant and Amish tours. Across from quaint drive-in.
B&B, canoe livery well located for great canoe trips, bike rides

THREE RIVERS

Three Rivers Inn

(616) 273-9521. 1200 Broadway, 2 mi. sw of Three Rivers on U.S. 131 at M-60. 100 rooms on 2 floors. $50-$52. Packages avail. Cable TV. Indoor pool, whirlpool, rec.area, putting green. Restaurant, bar w/ entertainment.
Many activities, handy to Kalamazoo, South Bend, scenic St. Joseph Co.

Redwood Motel

(616) 278-1945. On U.S. 131 1 3/4 mi. sw of Three Rivers on busy strip near hospital. 15 units. Summer: $35. Winter: $28. Cable TV, phones.
Good budget choice with outdoor pool

Chapter 2
South Central Michigan

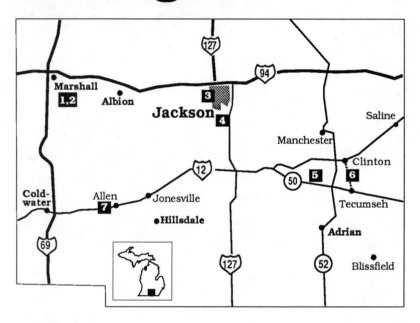

HIGHLIGHTS:

Marshall

Michigan's finest historic homes
in a picture-book small town

Peaceful and settled, this city of almost 7,000 retains the pleasant aura of its heyday in the 1850s. Big trees and attractive houses line its streets. Its September homes tour is famous. So is the original Win Schuler's restaurant (p. 74), which capitalized on an Old English theme and a remarkable host to become a favorite destination restaurant.

In the 1950s, Marshall boomed and grew rich in the mid-19th century, then went to sleep economically until antique-loving mayor Harold Brooks led a pioneering historic preservation crusade, beginning in the 1920s. It gained fame for Marshall as an unusually attractive version of the ideal American small town.

Marshall's quaint image belies both the aggressive real estate speculation launched by the town's founders and its present-day status as a small-scale industrial center and regional insurance headquarters. More people work here than live here.

The lovely big homes you'll see were built by Marshall's go-getting early settlers, unusually well-educated young people from wealthy New York State families. Frustrated by the lack of opportunity in the established and confining East, they went west — not to become farmers but to buy up large parcels of land, promote their area, and profit from it. They liked Marshall's strategic location on the Territorial Road, the major artery of Michigan settlement. At Marshall, a creek joined the Kalamazoo River, providing water power for future mills.

They were determined to build here the same kind of fine homes, good schools, and churches they had been accustomed to back east, and they had the money to build them. Marshall's state representative, John Pierce, devised Michigan's farsighted plan for a state education system. It laid the basis for the preeminence of the University of Michigan among public universities. Pierce unsuccessfully fought to win the state capitol for Marshall.

Financial incentives offered by Marshall men did succeed in wooing the Michigan Central Railroad's important machine shops and hotel restaurant in 1844. These machine shops led to three booming decades that ended after a 1872 fire destroyed the entire factory district. Weakened financially, town leaders couldn't come up with the new subsidy demanded by the railroad for improvements. In 1874 the railroad shops moved to Jackson, which boomed, while Marshall went to sleep for 50 years. Marshall was spared the stress and threats of an expanding industrial local economy.

Here's the basis for a satisfying, do-it-yourself tour of historic Marshall:

◆ **A walking tour map,** authoritative and free, is available from the Chamber of Commerce, 109 E. Michigan. Call 1-800-877-5163 for it and a helpful visitor packet. At the Chamber, *19th-century Homes of Marshall, Michigan* ($7.95) is an outstanding value for its interesting history and pictures of nearly every noteworthy historic house.

◆ **The Honolulu House,** a fabulously eccentric 1860 house with a pagoda-shaped observation deck, is on Michigan Avenue at Fountain Circle on the west edge of Marshall's attractive downtown. Its builder, state Supreme Court Judge Abner Pratt, fell in love with the Hawaiian Islands when he was U.S. consul there from 1857 to 1859. His wife's ill health forced him to return to Marshall. He built this authentic tropical home with Victorian trim to house their Polynesian treasures and replicate their relaxed lifestyle. His wife soon died, and so did he, reportedly of pneumonia contracted on a cold drive from Lansing on which he wore tropical clothing, as was his wont.

This most peculiar house is lavishly decorated, with beautiful fireplaces. The meticulously restored 1885-1888 murals are a knockout — a late-Victorian reinterpretation of Pratt's original tropical murals. Their lush Renaissance blend of leaf and vine patterns and classical motifs in rich, subtle greens, reds, purples, and pinks — 120 shades in all. The interesting furnishings assembled here by the Marshall Historical Society do not reflect the house as it was ever really lived in. There's an elaborate dining-room suite, sent to the 1876 Philadelphia Centennial to show off each kind of Michigan hardwood and help publicize the state's burgeoning furniture industry.

The basement rooms are arranged more like a typical house museum, with areas for quilts and needlework, toys, a kitchen, and a Marshall Folding Bathtub cleverly disguised as a cabinet. *Open daily from mid-May to October 31 from noon to 5. $2 admission. Park behind the house. You may learn more by reading the thorough 25¢ brochure than by asking the amiable volunteer guides.*

◆ **The Prospect Street hill,** two blocks north of Marshall's main street, offered the choicest building sites for Marshall's early elite. An easy hour's walk gives a good look at 29 fine Marshall homes and gardens. Take the time to look, and you'll be rewarded. (Look behind the houses, too. This area has some fabulous carriage houses.)

Two blocks north of the Honolulu House on Kalamazoo are two romantic Greek Revival temple-houses facing Prospect. The easterly one belonged to Mayor Harold Brooks for over 50 years, the west one to his brother, Louis, an authority on early chairs in the Middle West. North on Kalamazoo within the next half mile are 15 other noteworthy houses, including some picturesque Gothic Revival ones. Don't miss the square bracketed Italian Villa with the imposing setting at **603 North Kalamazoo.** William Wallace Cook, author of the Deadeye Dick, Buffalo Bill, and Frank Merriwell series, wrote up to a novel a week here between 1903 and 1933. East on Prospect at Grand, the Gothic Revival houses at **224 Prospect** and **311 North Grand** are straight out of influential romantic architect Andrew Jackson Downing's books. Finish your tour by continuing east on Prospect to Division, then going a block toward downtown and turning back on Mansion west toward the Honolulu House.

◆ **Ketchum Park**, a most pleasant riverside park and playground on Marshall's humbler south side, is at the millrace of Rice Creek, just behind the dam — a popular fishing spot. To get there, take Marshall Street south from the little park at downtown's north end. It's next to the Brooks Appliance Company, makers of abdominal corsets and source of the mayor's family fortune. **Picnic tables and grills** are at Ketchum Park, or you could take out a meal from Mancino's or Su Casa on Michigan Avenue.

◆ **Capitol Hill**, the land Marshall set aside for the state capitol, is on Marshall Street south of the Kalamazoo River. Today it's the Calhoun County Fairgrounds. The trim little 1839 **"Governor's Mansion"** at 612 S. Marshall at Washington is now a Daughters of the American Revolution clubhouse, *open Sundays in July and August from 2 to 4.* Also open then is the **Capitol Hill School**, a well-planned 1860 Gothic Revival schoolhouse, a block east of Marshall on Washington at Maple. Today it contains a nifty period schoolroom and a toy collection with a folk art masterpiece, Hinkle's Automatic Theater — a traveling marionette show with mechanical band.

◆ **Downtown Marshall** along several blocks of Michigan Avenue has an appealing mix of terrific Italianate architecture (look up to spot upper-floor details), upscale gift and antique shops, and wonderful small-town institutions like a good hardware store and dime store. Everybody in town, from top brass at leading firms to retirees and grandchildren, comes together at smoke-filled **Ken's Cafe.** Shopping standouts include **Kids' Place**, a small but choice children's bookstore at 106 N. Jefferson; **Williamson's Gift and Gourmet Shoppe** at 115 W. Michigan, lavish with laces and

fine chocolates; and an exceptionally interesting **Mole Hole** gift
shop at 150 W. Michigan. It has antique wood fixtures, a big selection of music boxes, and a seven-rank Barton theater organ.
You can ask to have it played and see the pipes operating through
a window.

MARSHALL'S BIG EVENT OF THE YEAR . . . . . is the **Marshall Historic Homes
Tour,** held the weekend after Labor Day. Almost everybody in town pitches in to
work on food, musical entertainment, arts and crafts displays, and tours of half
a dozen homes. For particulars on this year's tour, call the Chamber of Commerce, 1-800-877-5163.

AN INDUSTRIAL SMALL-TOWN COUNTERPART TO MARSHALL . . . . is right
next door in **Albion** (population 10,000), 11 miles to the east. Its Methodist
founders didn't quite have Marshall's money or style, but they did have energy
and brains. Their talent went into developing industry and making **Albion
College** (birthplace of both "The Old Rugged Cross" and "The Sweetheart of Sigma
Chi") into one of Michigan's best private colleges. The Gale Manufacturing Company, maker of a famous steel plow, grew into a giant iron foundry, now part of
Harvard Industries but still called the Malleable. Other foundries followed. Albion industries attracted workers from Germany, the Ukraine, Poland, Italy, Ser-
bo-Croatia, Hungary, south Texas, Kentucky, and Florida, creating a most eth-
nically and racially diverse population for a small town. Today all but one of the
foundries are closed, but the foundry workers and their descendants remain.
  Albion's prosperity in the late nineteenth century and its location at the **forks
of the Kalamazoo River** have resulted in a most **attractive townscape** — well
worth a visit. Take Business 94 to Superior, downtown's main street, and you'll
see some unusually elaborate Second Empire commercial buildings. You can
canoe *under* one downtown building. Also worth a look: the Chamber of Commerce in the beautifully restored **train station** on West Michigan and the neighborhood along East Erie. (It intersects with Superior just southwest of Albion
College). But downtown retailing is weak; shopping centers hurt it badly. Continue south on Superior and turn left onto River and you'll reach pretty **Victory
Park,** where the river's north and south forks join.
  An interesting **walking tour and map** can be obtained from the Gardner House
Museum (see below) or the Chamber (517-629-5533).

A TREAT FOR LOVERS OF QUALITY VICTORIANA . . . . . is the **Gardner House
Museum** in Albion, with its rich 1880s period rooms of choice furniture, paintings, and objects from local families. Exhibits on Albion's interesting history
are featured in upstairs and basement rooms. *509 S. Superior, just south of downtown. (517) 629-5100. Open last weekend April through last weekend October, Sat.
& Sun. 1-4 and by appointment.*

American Museum of Magic

A passionate fan's tribute to professional magicians, and to the sense of wonder they can create

The very best attractions are often little publicized, the products of dedicated amateurs in love with their subjects. A premiere example is the American Museum of Magic, which keeps no regular hours and distributes no brochures. Its fame extends mainly within the fraternity of magicians; many make annual pilgrimages here when they gather for the Magic Festival in nearby Colon.

You may arrange for a 1 1/2-hour museum tour at your convenience with proprietor and guide Robert Lund. A devotee of magic since the age of seven, he's not a magician himself. He is a most gracious and enlightening guide, provided you follow his rules. First, DO NOT BE LATE. (He won't wait.) Second, once he explains that all the magic props and artifacts you see are originals, NEVER ask again if they're the real thing. "I may throw a tantrum," he says sternly.

Even if you're altogether uninterested in magic, you may well be won over by the dazzling visuals in Lund's handsomely restored old storefront. It's full of posters, beautifully decorated antique magic props, collections of magic sets, and porcelain figures of magicians. Equally impressive are Lund's intelligence, wit, and commitment to his mission: the preservation of the artifacts and archives of many of the past century's magicians. Lund, who wrote for auto magazines and *Popular Mechanics*, retired to Marshall ("paradise," he calls it) and opened the museum in 1979 to house and display his collections.

Lund tells stories illustrated by his vast collection of old promotional posters from touring magicians. Obscure dead magicians come to life again. For example, "Here's one of my favorites, John C. Green, a crusty old coot and tough as the territory he played. Green worked the same small towns in Canada for 50 years. That indicated that he was a good magician, because you can only cheat the same people once. He left me his route books, with the towns he played and money he took in." A case contains Green's ledger, which shows the fate of most of the few full-time professional magicians: they gained little from a life of hard work and hard traveling.

To give a sense of the size and complexity of many props, there's a bulky 5' x 4' x 4' carrying case, one of scores that famed magician Harry Blackstone traveled with. They filled a 90-foot, double-size baggage car. Each piece, save one, was painted orange for quick identification at train stations. Lund points to the lone exception, a black tool chest with "Peter Bouton" stencilled on it. He opens it to show a neat array of the varied tools of the trade. Bouton was Blackstone's real name, and Pete, his brother, was his key offstage man, a gifted carpenter, chemist, painter, even a seamstress. Lund reckons the Blackstones, senior and junior, as the best all-round magicians he's seen. He knew Harry, Sr. well and Harry, Jr. is an occasional visitor to the museum. Many of their papers are in his extensive archives of magic.

Some highlights of the museum tour, which spans four centuries and six continents, include:

◆ Mandrake the Magician comics.

◆ an 18th-century book by Jean Eugene Robert-Houdin, the Frenchman who took magic out of the supernatural closet and promoted himself frankly as a performer.

◆ posters of magician Marjorie Waddell. They proclaim, "see a man sawed in half." Lund says she was one of several "very good lady magicians who didn't go anyplace because many men don't like to be challenged by women."

◆ a century's worth of sets of magic tricks for children.

◆ the original prop for the giant milk can stunt that rescued the young Harry Houdini's career. A St. Louis theater owner had threatened to book another act if he didn't draw more customers — soon. Houdini constructed it in a weekend. The audience filled the "milk can" with water, the lid was locked, but Houdini survived — thanks to a specially designed dome top

Poster of Fu Manchu, the inspiration for Robert Lund's lifelong interest in magic.

with air holes, so he could tip back his head to breathe.
Houdini, Lund says, "is one of my least favorites — a man of all-consuming ego, among other failings. It's a myth that Houdini's secrets died with him. He had no secrets. He was the greatest stunt man and daredevil of his day. But we can't confuse stunts with magic. He thrived on confrontation, as if he were saying, 'You dummies! How can you figure it out?'"

The tour ends with a touching tribute to David Bamberg, a. k. a. Fu Manchu. He was, Lund says, "the man who taught me what magic is all about — not tricks, but wonder and make-believe." Bamberg was the sixth and last of a six-generation family of magicians that began with a one-legged Jewish street magician in 18th-century Holland. The big names in magic in the early 20th century acted like their were geniuses and exploited a hostile, superior relationship with their audiences. Bamberg achieved a more marvelous effect with imagination and kindness, warmth and mystery. His magic lives on in a dazzling troupe of mostly volunteer performers, Le Grand David and His Own Spectacular Magic Company of Beverly, Massachusetts. Troupe members pay frequent visits to Lund's museum in Marshall.

107 E. Michigan between Madison and Jefferson, kitty-corner from the handsome sandstone post office. By appointment only. Call (616) 781-7674 at least a day or two ahead of time. $3/person, $2 for children under 16. Children must be accompanied by an adult.

A BEAUTIFUL RIVERSIDE REFUGE FOR BIRDS AND WILDLIFE . . . . . is part of Albion College's **Whitehouse Nature Center**. Over half a mile of Kalamazoo River frontage and an unusual variety of ecosystems make the 125-acre center special. In an hour you can visit a tallgrass prairie, marshes, ponds, a wildflower garden, upland and flood-plain woods, old fields, and an old gravel pit planted to encourage wildlife. The trails, not the interpretive building, make this place special. Best for first-time visitors are the half-mile **Marsh Trail** (a boardwalk path along the river; 20 minutes) and the one- mile **Prairie Trail** (40 minutes) along the river to the prairie and wildflower garden. Remember, the plentiful birds and rabbits are most active early and late in the day. Pick up free trail guides, engagingly written and illustrated, by the building. *Take Erie St. east from downtown Albion. Turn south on Hannah at the train tracks, and look for the signs for Farley Dr. and the nature center before you get to the football stadium. (517) 629-2030. Open year-round, dawn to dusk. Interpretive building open weekdays 8 a.m.-5 p.m., Sat & Sun noon-5. Free.*

Jackson Cascades

This huge artificial waterfall in a baroque
pleasure park is a nostalgic sight from the 1930s.

There's nothing subtle about Jackson's best-known sight —
an illuminated 500-foot artificial waterfall cascading down
a hill at 3,000 gallons a minute, in three pools and 16 falls.
After dark, shifting patterns of colored lights turn the Cascades
into a baroque fantasy in vivid Technicolor. Recorded show tunes
underscore its basic theatricality.

Every evening from Memorial Day to Labor Day the Cascades offer low-key summer entertainment for $2 a head. The falls, foun-
tains, and music are turned on at 7 o'clock. You can climb the
129 steps that flank the 30-foot-wide falls and watch the sun produce repeating rainbows in the spray. (Kids love this!) A hand
stamp lets you leave and reenter, so you can picnic, fish, feed
ducks, play, and enjoy the numerous facilities and scenic hills and
waterways of the surrounding **Cascades Park** (see below).

The Cascades are so grand and monumental, you'd expect them
to have been built only in a very large metropolitan area, not in a
small but enterprising city of 55,000. That was Jackson's population at its peak in 1930, two years before the Cascades were finished. (Today it has declined to 37,500.) In Jackson's glory years
of the 1920s, it prospered and made many local fortunes in auto
parts. "Little Detroit" was Jackson's nickname.

One especially forceful and enthusiastic local magnate was
Captain William Sparks. He had immigrated from England with
his family, grown up in Jackson, and became rich as a parts supplier. By 1920, the Sparks Withington Company, originally formed
to make buggy parts, employed over 7,000 people. They made
Sparton radios, electric auto horns (which Sparks pioneered),
and other automotive accessories.

Sparks's lifetime goal was to put Jackson on the map. Three
terms its mayor, he was once simultaneously the city manager and
Chamber of Commerce president. His Sparks-Withington Zouaves
(pronounced zoo-AHVS) were a kind of quick-stepping precision
drill team, patterned after a colorful Algerian infantry unit. Many
American towns had their own Zouaves units. "Cap" Sparks (the
title was honorary; he never served in the military) and his
Zouaves toured the world, bringing fame to their home town.

While in Barcelona, Sparks was so taken by the a grand, cascading waterfall that he later determined to build a version of it on

the marshland behind his magnificent Tudor home. Soon what began as a plan for a skating pond at the foot of the Cascades blossomed into 457 acres of lagoons, picnic areas, and an 18-hole PGA championship golf course and clubhouse.

The **Cascades-Sparks Museum**, just inside the entryway to the amphitheater, is a quirky, often amusing collection of old Sparton Electronics radios, colorful Zouaves costumes, recorded band music, and memorabilia, including photos of the Jackson Zouaves performing in *The Court Jester* with Danny Kaye, and scenes from the very successful concert Harry Chapin performed here shortly before his death.

The Cascades did succeed in putting Jackson on the national showbiz map during the 1930s and 1940s, as attested by press clippings from major U.S. cities about the seven-stage extravaganzas staged there. Today Sparks's mansion on West Street has been replaced by apartments after two feuding women's clubs torpedoed plans to reuse it. But its impressive Tudor garage and guest house can still be seen on Kibby Road, across from the matching Tudor Clubhouse at the entrance to the Sparks Foundation Park.

Air-conditioned movies and TV took their toll on Cascades attendance. The concrete crumbled, and the magnificent gift threatened to become an obsolete white elephant. But local construction workers restored the Cascades and built the amphitheater and museum building. (Seating came from Crosley Field, once home of the Cincinnati Reds.) In 1969 the county parks department fenced the Cascades and charged admission, causing an uproar that still occasionally flares up. The new sound system is excellent.

Today the Cascades are an entertainment anachronism. Some Jacksonians consider them irredeemably tacky and dumb. To others, their status is secure as a wonderful, nostalgic period extravaganza with a direct, childlike charm.

S. Brown at Denton Rd. in the Cascade County Park, Jackson. From I-94, take West Ave. exit 138 at Jackson Crossing mall and follow the signs south. (517) 788-4320. Memorial Day through Labor Day, 7:30-11 p.m. daily. $2 per person.

BY THE CASCADES, A BIG PARK WITH ACTIVITIES AND GREAT GOLF . . . . .
Inspired by his dream of creating a magnificent landscaped waterfall on his estate, industrialist William Sparks went on to create **Cascades Park**, where meadows and wetlands meet rolling hills. Adjoining the Cascades are a fanciful **playground** with cast concrete animals and a moonwalker, and an 18-hole miniature golf course ($2, open daily in summer 11-11). Across Denton, behind the Tudor-style Cascades clubhouse is a **duck pond**, a **parcours/jogging track** with 21

exercise stations on a 2.2 mile trail, and two miles of **lagoons** for fishing and
boating with a **handicapped-accessible fishing pier.** Here paddleboats can be
rented for $3.75/ half-hour.

Golf is a an obsession in Jackson. Its high-quality of its public and municipal
courses make it available to virtually everybody. Two courses are in Cascades
Park. **Hill Brothers Golf Course** is a 9 holes, par 3 "executive course" with shorter
holes; $3.75 ($1.75 before 11 weekdays.) Call (517) 782-2855 for reservations. The
Cascades Golf Course is an 18-hole PGA championship course, and quite challenging. Its front 9 are longer and easier, the back 9 shorter and more difficult.
Weekdays $6 for 9 holes, $11 for 18; weekends $13 for 18. Call (517)
788-4323 for reservations.

In winter, the park's glacial hills lends themselves to **cross-country-skiing**
(trails begin south of the Clubhouse), **sledding** down the Cascades hill, and **skating**
on the duck pond behind the Clubhouse (warming house open weekends 11-7).

THE BIRTHPLACE OF THE REPUBLICAN PARTY . . . . . is Jackson's biggest claim
to fame. A meeting of Free Soilers, abolitionists, anti-slavery Whigs and Democrats, men concerned about the growing power of the railroads, and others was
organized in Jackson by local attorney Austin Blair and other dissidents. It
proved so large it had to be held outdoors, **"under the oaks"** in a grove just west of
town. Blair went on to become Michigan's beloved Civil War governor, a staunch
backer of Lincoln, before being thwarted by Michigan big-money interests who
came to dominate the party he helped found. The oak grove was later subdivided
and built up, but two city lots now make up a small **park** commemorating the
historic site. Some big oaks remain, and the park is within blocks of fine homes
along old Jackson's residential show streets: Michigan Avenue, Washington, and
Franklin to the north and Fourth going south to Ella Sharp Park. *On Franklin at
Second. Take West Ave. from I-94 exit 38 to 2 blocks south of Michigan Ave., turn
east onto Franklin for 4 blocks.*

FAMOUS FOR ITS GIANT SUNDAES . . . . . the **Parlour** soda fountain at the
Jackson All-Star Dairy is the most popular spot in town. No super-premium ice
cream here, just the basics — chocolate syrup, nuts, whipped cream, good ice
cream made at the ice cream plant right next door, and lots of it. (A single scoop
here is closer to two normal scoops.) The $4.25 banana split (6 scoops, piled in a
foot-high pyramid) is more than three people can comfortably eat. "Dare to Be
Great" ($14.45) is a 21-scoop monster. Typical three-scoop sundaes are under $3.
Obliging counter girls will honor requests for extra sides of whipped cream and
toppings (you do pay for them) and for special fountain treats — lemon malts, or
hot fudge malts, for instance. (Malts are made with soft ice cream unless you spec-
ify extra rich.) Expect a wait in summer, longer on weekends or after the malls
close and movies are out. The entire fountain menu, plus big $1 cones in 31 fla-
vors, is available at the faster **takeout** line. Its prices and portions are less. A few
picnic tables are outside. *On Higby at Daniel, just east of Brown and the Westwood
Mall. From I-94 exit 138, take West Ave. to Michigan Ave., turn west; in 7 blocks
turn north on Higby. (Brown Street runs from the Dairy to the Cascades.) (517)
782-7141. Open daily 10-10, to 11 in summer.*

Michigan Space Center

A fascinating, up-close view of America's great leap to dominance in space exploration

Housed in a big geodesic dome south of Jackson, the Michigan Space Center manages to take a complex topic — America's space ventures of the 1960s and 1970s — and illuminate it in a way that entertains rather than overwhelms the visitor. There are background displays on the Solar System and the evolution of rocketry. But most of the displays pertain to that amazing era when the U.S. moved from far behind the Soviets in rocket design to become the first and only country to land humans on the moon.

Liberally scattered throughout the Center are historically important space equipment, such as a prototype of the Mariner IV spacecraft which flew close to Mars in 1964 and a Lunar Rover Vehicle. Most spectacular is the actual Apollo 9 command module used to link up in space with a test Lunar Excursion Module three months before the first moon landing. You get to look right inside the module to see the cramped quarters. An array of spacesuits shows their rapid evolution from the stiff early Mercury suits (1958-1963) through Gemini to the flexible Apollo suits of the 1970s. Especially fascinating for children is the detailed explanation of how astronauts go to the bathroom. Also interesting are displays of the food eaten in space. Get on a big digital scale and compare your weight on earth with what it would be on any of the other planets. The large but primitive-looking computer console which guided John Glenn's historic first Earth orbit in 1962 shows how much more sophisticated today's space electronics is compared with a quarter century ago. There are **films** on space topics, a **gift shop**, and a self-guided tour.

2111 Emmons Road. Take exit 142 from I-94 to 127. Take 127 to the Monroe and M-50 exit. Turn left onto McDevitt Ave. Turn left onto Hague at the first traffic light on McDevitt. Take Hague to Emmons Road and follow the signs. (517) 787-4425. Mon-Sat, 10-5. Sun 11-5 during summer. Shorter hours thereafter. Adults $3, Students $2, children under 5 free.

AN OUTSTANDING VICTORIAN HOUSE MUSEUM AND MORE . . . . . is a short, scenic drive from the Space Center. The multifaceted **Ella Sharp Museum** consists of an especially elegant 1857 farmhouse, an authentically furnished settlers' log cabin, circa 1840, a schoolhouse, several 19th-century businesses, and **changing exhibits on arts and local history**, plus the hands-on **Discovery Gallery** for children. "Settlement 1829-1859" shows how the area developed within only 13 years from the rudest initial settlement to having a railroad and the state prison by 1842.

Tours of the house, given every half hour and customized to each small group's interests, go way beyond Victorian decorating to point out things like how quickly industrialization changed people's everyday lives in the late 19th century, and how fascinated the Victorian middle class was with nature and its spiritual power. Ella Sharp's mother was a wealthy Easterner who invested in Western land and actually came out to live on it (most investors were absentee landlords). With her husband she developed Hillside Farm into a showplace of progressive agriculture. Ella herself was a successful reformer. Her causes were good government, improving town and rural life through women's clubs, and conservation. She wrote lots of letters, never threw anything out, and left her intact household to the city, so the museum benefits from having an interesting, especially well documented history, intelligently used to good effect. Don't miss a trip to the house's treetop cupola.

The Granary restaurant (see p. 75) is most attractive, and there are two good **gift shops**, one in the country store (more informal, with some cheap things for kids) and a fairly upscale shop in the main exhibit building. *The museum is in Ella Sharp Park on Fourth just south of Horton Rd. From the Space Center take Browns Lake Rd. past the Jackson Community College Campus. It turns into Stonewall and leads to the museum. Enter the park and park behind the museum. From I-94, take M-50/Business 127, exit 138 at Jackson Crossing, go south on West and follow the signs. (517) 787-2320. Tues-Fri 10-5, Sat & Sun 12-5. $2.50/person, $1 child, $5 family.*

Hidden Lake Gardens

A lovely spot in the Irish Hills pairs picturesque landscape gardens with woodland trails.

For nature-lovers from Ann Arbor to Toledo, Hidden Lake Gardens is a very special place year-round. It's primarily a landscape arboretum, first planted by Harry Fee of Adrian, who sold his electric company to Consumers' Power. His interest was in creating pictures and scenes with plants, and in sharing the benefits of horticulture with the general public. He assembled a property that took advantage of the unusually varied glacial landscape in this band of hills and lakes known as the Irish Hills. Here huge ice chunks from the last Ice Age left a crazy-quilt landscape of round kettle-hole lakes, steep-sided valleys, and dramatic vistas interspersed with sweeping meadows and marshes.

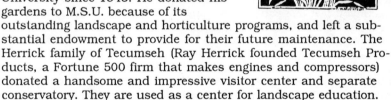

Fee's plantings, begun in 1926, provide a mature backdrop for later collections and gardens planted by Michigan State University since 1945. He donated his gardens to M.S.U. because of its outstanding landscape and horticulture programs, and left a substantial endowment to provide for their future maintenance. The Herrick family of Tecumseh (Ray Herrick founded Tecumseh Products, a Fortune 500 firm that makes engines and compressors) donated a handsome and impressive visitor center and separate conservatory. They are used as a center for landscape education.

The front part of Hidden Lake Gardens has been landscaped for maximum picturesqueness, while the back oak uplands, laced with **five miles of hiking trails**, remain in their natural state. (Get a **trail guide** at the visitor center.) Six miles of one-way drives wind through the front part so close to branches of flowering magnolias, crabs, and cherries that even from the car you notice individual flowers. A bike drive through this part lets you stop and smell the flowers, but bikes are prohibited on Sundays. You can also park your car on one of many pullovers, and get out and walk.

It all makes for an especially nice blend of the cultivated and wild. You can go for a vigorous hike (a good mix of hardwoods makes **fall colors** gorgeous), then learn about Michigan forest communities in the visitor center, or take in the damp, fragrant atmosphere of the tropical house, or see rare dwarf conifers in a special garden. Everywhere you can glean ideas for your own yard from the many identified plantings. Lists of commercial nursery sources for plants are provided whenever possible.

Here are some highlights not to miss:

◆ The **front road system** artfully invites you into a special world and manipulates the views to give a fresh, intimate perspective on the trees and shrubs you see. Lilacs, flowering crabs, and cherries are wonderful in May. At the far west end is a choice collection of evergreens.

◆ There's **Hidden Lake** itself, beneath overarching willows next to the visitor center. A pair of swans, often with baby cygnets, will come up to the pullover area and eagerly eat bread visitors bring. (No moldy bread, please! It makes them sick.)

◆ Naturalized **primroses and daffodils** bloom in the last two weeks of April. The primroses are at the lake's north end; daffodils are all over.

◆ **Exhibits in the visitor center** cover topics like the development of plant aristocrats through hybridization, the life and death of a glacial lake, forest communities in southern Michigan, conifer classifications, and Michigan geology. They're dense yet satisfying to the inquiring lay mind. Take one or two topics on a visit, and you could learn a lot of botany and horticulture basics fast.

◆ The large **conservatory** is unusually enjoyable, especially in winter. Some very large, luxuriant specimens in the **tropical house** make you feel like you're in a rain forest; it's fun to see grapefruit, figs, guava, and tangerines growing on trees. There's also an **arid house** and a **temperate house**, where you can see **orchids, ferns, fuchsia,** and some remarkable **bonsai,** artistically pruned trees up to 25 years old but only a foot high. Well-written signs about plants' culture and uses in food and ornament are good reading. After a thoughtful visit to the temperate house, you'd see familiar house plants in a new way.

◆ **The Harper Collection of Rare and Dwarf Conifers** behind the conservatory. Some are bluish or gold, some weep or lie flat on the ground. Many come from genetic mutations or witch's brooms: small, thick growths on the limbs of a tree that grow true to form when propagated by cuttings.

A **picnic area** with restrooms has been provided behind the Harper Conifer collection. The excellent visitor center **gift shop** has many books and pamphlets on nature and gardening, plus nature-related notecards, T-shirts and sweatshirts, rock samples, and bird feeders and houses.

The Gardens are on M-50 8 miles west of Tecumseh and 7 miles east of Cambridge Junction, the historic crossroads where M-50 joins U.S.12. From Adrian or Chelsea, take M-52 to M-50, turn west. (517) 431-2060. Grounds and conservatory open 365 days/ year, April thru Oct. 8 a.m.-dusk, Nov. thru March 8 a.m.-4 p.m. Visitor center open 8-4:30 weekdays, 12-6 weekends; in winter 8-4 weekdays, 10-4 weekends. $1/person weekdays, $3/person weekends, children under 2 free.

BEEKEEPING SUPPLIES, HONEY, AND CANDLE MOLDS . . . . . along with a **working beehive** (cut away so you can see inside) and all sorts of gifts and books pertaining to bees, are sold a few miles west of Hidden Lake Gardens at **Hubbard Apiaries.** $120 buys you everything needed to get started in beekeeping, including a bee suit. Pick up a free catalog. *On M-50 at Springville Rd., east of U.S. 12. (517) 467-2051. Open weekdays only, 7-4:30.*

SIGHTSEEING ALONG U.S. 12, THE OLD CHICAGO TURNPIKE . . . . . through the Irish Hills, can be fun. Along the road is a weird blend of early Michigan history and 20th-century tourism: 1920s gas stations and lookout towers, the Prehistoric Forest, Mystery Hill, water slides, bumper boats, go-cart raceways, and the Michigan International Speedway. Many farmhouses and some taverns date to the old Indian trail's first round of improvements in the 1830s.

Here's a short list of recommended sights (all free or inexpensive) for a pleasant drive along U.S. 12 between M-52 on the east and M-50 on the west:

◆ **Ike's Presidential railroad car.** Original interiors, memorabilia.

◆ **Irish Hills Towers.** Corny, fun lookout is best in fall.

◆ **Shrine of St. Joseph.** Inspired folk art. The Stations of the Cross behind the parking lot leading down the hill to the lake were made of colored tile and cement by an out-of-work Italian tile-setter during the Depression.

◆ **Walker Tavern Historic Complex.** Fine state historical museum tells the story of pioneer settlers here on the Chicago Road.

Stagecoach Stop, a make-believe 19th-century village theme park just west of Ike's railroad car, is more of an all-day attraction. It successfully blends soap opera, nostalgia, museum-quality antiques and coin-operated musical devices, arcade games, wild game park, and crafts demonstrations. *Most sights are open daily in summer and on fall weekends. List reads from east to west. Call (517) 592-8907 weekdays for more Irish Hills information.*

OVER TWO DOZEN ANTIQUE SHOPS . . . . . are in or near the Irish Hills. Among the best are the **Manchester Antique Mall** in delightful downtown Manchester, the **Hitching Post Antiques Mall** on M-50 near M-52, two miles west of Tecumseh, the **Brick Walker Tavern** on U.S. 12 at M-50 (closed Mon & Tues), and the **Town & Country Mall** in Saline, in the 1830s Weller Mill on U.S. 12 just west of downtown. *Ask for a helpful shop guide and map to other area dealers.*

Southern Michigan Railroad

*A scenic trip between two attractive small towns
on old cabooses and work cars*

This short train ride is a low-key delight. The 45-minute trip between the picturesque towns of Clinton and Tecumseh passes through woods, marshes full of wildlife, and farm fields, by some terrific vegetable gardens. It seems like a real event when you arrive at Tecumseh's handsomely restored downtown — much more than when you come by car. You can make the return trip immediately, but many passengers prefer to spend two hours browsing in Tecumseh's downtown gift shops, restaurants, and antique malls. Ask for a **walking/ driving tour** of Tecumseh's handsome historic homes at the depot where you begin your trip.

This is a real stretch of railroad, with real, workaday equipment, not a scaled-down steam engine and cute open-air cars. The 1942 switch engine pushes the train the Tecumseh and pulls it back to Clinton. The passenger cars aren't fancy, but they do offer adventure. One train consists of an engine, an open-air

Evan Garrett

gondola, and one or two cabooses. A panoramic view of the countryside can be had from the open-air passenger gondola. Or you can survey the tracks from a caboose's bay window or the rear platform. (Since the train is pushed to Tecumseh, the platform is in front of the train.)

The alternate train, occasionally used, has four has open-air work cars used for carrying gandy dancers out to work on track. These minimally cushioned cars make for a bumpy ride. Two of the cars have no sides or guard rails — a definite hazard for small children. But it is thrilling when the train crosses a trestle and you look down past your feet at a pond of the dammed Raisin River below. Call ahead to find out the schedule if you prefer both kinds of train. Several days a year, both types run.

On the train, look for informational handouts on the track and railroad. In the typical style of true rail fans, the line's equipment and history is minutely detailed. The Southern Michigan Railroad is in operation because of a small group of high school students. For generations of Tecumseh boys, a favorite pastime was to hitch rides on the slow-moving train as it carried wheel and brake assemblies to and from the Budd factory in Clinton. In 1982 the plant closed, and the line folded. But a group of high school juniors, aided by a lawyer father, formed a nonprofit corporation, raised a down payment, and bought 13 1/2 miles of track for $100,000. Now local kids still ride the rails as staff of the popular weekend train.

Plan to spend some time in the Clinton depot, actually built as part of a municipal power plant. Its **gift shop** is full of nifty railroad insignia items on mugs, patches, and T-shirts, plus trainmen's caps, postcards, and other memorabilia. There's also an informal **museum**, and you can go downstairs to see work in progress restoring hand cars, baggage trucks, and the like.

Station and museum at 320 S. Division at Clark in Clinton. (517) 456-7677. From U.S. 12 in downtown Clinton, turn at Manufactuers' Bank and take Division three blocks south to the depot. Runs weekends and holidays, June through Sept., plus weekend color tours in Oct. (leave from Tecumseh). Trains leave Clinton at 11, 1, and 3. Tecumseh stopover and loading point at downtown light, M-50 and Evans. Trains leave Tecumseh 12 and 2. Arrive 15 minutes before departure; limited seating. $5 adults, $2.50 children 2-12.

Green Top County Village and Antique Mall

In Michigan's "antique capital" of Allen,
a whimsical group of orphaned historic buildings

This celebrated spot just west of Allen on U.S. 12 thankfully makes no pretense at being a real country village. It's a fanciful collection of some 30 old buildings — country stores and schools, granaries and barns, a root beer stand and a work-crew trolley car. The effect looks as if pieces of Midwestern towns were sucked up in a tornado, transported to Oz, and rearranged and painted by Munchkins in combinations of soft earthtones and dulled pastels. Woodchip paths wind through a grove of shady young maples to courtyard groupings of the orphaned buildings. It's a much more diverting way to look at a lot of antiques than the usual warehouse-like malls. When looking at stuff gets to be too much, you can stroll through the grounds. They are accented with benches and various ornaments, including an elaborate Italianate outhouse. Pick up a **flyer on the buildings' origins** at the front sales desk in the main building.

The original Green Top Lodge and Cabins (the name comes from their green roofs) are the core of this inspired confection. The onetime roadhouse opened in 1925, the year the Chicago Road out front was paved. Motor touring was fast becoming a popular middle-class pastime. Green Top, one of the favorite stops between Detroit and Chicago, hosted salesmen, truckers, and tourists. The cabins were among the first to have their own toilets. Jim Klein, a native of nearby Adrian, and his wife, Beth, bought the old place as their own antique shop in 1982, when the village of Allen was far less lively than it is today. Soon after that, their friend Norma Kaetzel despaired of being able to fix up a dilapidated historic building on her property, a plain little Greek Revival schoolhouse from 1840. Her dilemma inspired Klein to expand Green Top by moving such endangered buildings onto the five-acre site. Since then Green Top has become "a home of last resort for orphaned buildings," says Klein.

There's a consciously laissez-faire approach to quality control among Green Top's dealers. New country crafts are allowed, but they don't overwhelm. If some dealer finds a good buy on irregular socks, they're perfectly welcome at Green Top. Most dealers here are above average for Michigan antique malls, but most of the merchandise isn't especially refined, and it seldom dates before the Civil War. It's also considerably less expensive than in big metropolitan areas. In some ways the place *is* like a real village, with a friendly atmosphere and some real characters among the dealers. If malls full of slicked-up, overcategorized antiques and collectibles turn you off, Green Top may be a place you'll like a lot. Its 70 dealers cover a lot of territory, mostly moderately priced: Victoriana, oak, walnut, and a good deal of furniture in the rough to balance the small things and collectibles. The Kleins' own stock consists mostly of primitives and unusual pieces in the Victorian schoolhouse with the bell tower.

Green Top is a natural for Hillsdale County. As is common in Michigan's southern tier of counties, many of its towns are hardly bigger today than they were in their prime in the 1870s. Some, like Allen, almost became ghost towns. Derelict buildings are in good supply here. The land is variously too gravelly, hilly, or wet to pay off for large-scale, mechanized agriculture, but it is well suited to Amish methods of small-scale, general, self-sufficient farming. Several Amish communities have moved into the area. Amish men are excellent house-movers. To move the new 1,100-square-foot Methodist church to Green Top, teams of Amish workmen carefully pried the walls apart (a crane then lifted them onto a truck), dug the new foundation by hand, and put the building back together.

Green Top is on U.S. 12, 12 miles east of I-69 and half a mile west of Allen. (517) 869-2100. Open daily including most holidays, year-round 10:30-5.

"THE ANTIQUE CAPITAL OF MICHIGAN" . . . . . is what the village of **Allen** calls itself. Allen consists of a four-corners and a strip of 19th-century stores and houses along U.S. 12, the old Chicago Road.

Founded in 1827, Allen had 500 people in 1880, but has dwindled to little more than half that today. Moribund by 1960, it was revived by an explosion of antique shops. Today it numbers three antiques malls and many freestanding antique shops (nearly 90 dealers in all), plus an in-town herb shop and greenhouse/produce stand.

The very first antique shops, here and elsewhere along the Chicago Road, date from the road's paving in 1925, which spawned tourists courts, gas stations, and curio shops. Many Allen shops, especially the older ones like **Poor Richard's Antiques and Books** and **Michiana Antiques**, have room after room of stuff piled high, not overly categorized or showcased. For people who like to paw through stuff, there's the alluring hope of hidden treasures. Specialities range form services (such as upholstery and chair caning) to plants. **Andy's Antiques** is another old shop in the onetime general store and post office. At the **Little Farm Herb**

Shop, Susan Betz offers over 250 kinds of herbs, everlastings, and cottage flowers in season (from Mother's Day through early summer). There's a good-sized display garden behind the shop, which is in an old chicken coop. **Simple Treasures Antiques** also has classes and supplies for porcelain dolls. **Lakeview Antiques** specializes in Depression glass, china, and pottery. **Chesney's Antiques** in the Olde Chicago Mall sells refinished furniture and cane chairs. **Poor Richard's** has a vast stock of framed popular pictures.

In the **Old Township Hall Mall**, John Alward and his wife Janice Fentiman have created in the former town hall an attractive two-level space for appealingly presented booths. Their own eclectic merchandise includes masks from Nepal, rocks and minerals, trade beads, and African crafts. At the **Quilt Lady**, Fentiman produces traditionally styled Amish quilts and wall hangings, pieced and quilted by 60 area Amish women. Quilts are sold here retail for much less than in shops on the coasts.When you get to town, look for the bold black-and-white **brochure and map** to plan your visit. *Malls and larger shops open daily from 10 or 11 to 5 throughout the year. Some shops open weekends only. Summer festivals have open-air antiques, flea market stalls, and barbecues put on by the volunteer firefighters. They are held on Memorial Day, Independence Day, and Labor Day.*

A SPRINGTIME DELIGHT . . . . . is the **Slayton Arboretum** at nearby Hillsdale College. Even in winter, this arboretum is exceedingly picturesque — the epitome of that informal rock-garden romanticism so popular in the 1920s. In May and June it is spectacular with displays of flowering crabs and peonies. Clumps of white birch and Norway and white spruce, planted in 1929 in this former gravel pit, now loom tall above fieldstone walls and gazebos, rustic footbridges and goldfish ponds. Lagoons and nearby lakes attract many birds. Paths wind up a steep slope form the gazebo and outdoor amphitheater. An overlook terrace permits views of a landscape studded with specimen plantings and quaint little structures like the English cottage-style horticultural laboratory. *On Barber at Union, east of the college. From U.S. 12 at Jonesville, take M-99 almost into downtown Hillsdale, but turn east at Fayette. In about 1/2 mile turn north onto Union.*

A RICH BANKER'S PALATIAL HOME . . . . . designed by Elijah Myers, the architect of Michigan's state capitol, has been splendidly restored as the **Grosvenor House Museum** in Jonesville, 5 miles east of Allen on U.S. 12. Jonesville banker E.O. Grosvenor's 1870s house is full of elaborate details and the then-latest tricks in modern engineering and planning. It has that rich layering of exotic objets d'art, patterned motifs, and wood surfaces that gives high Victorian style its eclectic, opulent effect. An upstairs **museum room** presents ordinary Jonesville history well, featuring local products from Jonesville's old cigar factory and dairy to recent plastic dollhouse play sets from Kiddie Brush and Toy — "toys that mold character," says the ad, like Susy's Superette and the Friendly Folks Motel. *From U.S. 12 at the park in downtown Jonesville, take Maumee south 3 blocks to 211 Maumee. (517) 849-9596. Open the first full weekend in June through September, Sat. & Sun 2-5. Holidays open house 1st full weekend in Dec. $2.*

Recommended Restaurants & Lodgings

South Central Michigan

To locate cities, see regional map p. 52.

COLDWATER

Little King Motel. *(517) 278-6660. 847 E .Chicago (U.S. 12), 2 blocks e. of I-69.* 18 rooms on 1 floor. $36. Cable TV. Outdoor pool. Rustic trails, play area on 7 acres. Picnic tables. *Budget choice with outdoor amenities*

Quality Inn. *(517) 278-2017. N.w. of jct. I-69 & U.S. 12, exit 13.* 123 units, inc. 28 suites, 6 jacuzzi suites. $62-$110. Cable TV. Cont. breakfast. Indoor courtyard w/ pool, whirlpool, sauna, game room. Driving range, running track. Restaurant, bar w/live entertainment weekends. *Well run, new, back from highway, lots of activities.*

HILLSDALE

The Great Wall. *122 N. Broad , downtown. (517) 439-1924.* Mon-Thurs 11:30-9:30, Fri-Sat 11:30-10, Sun noon-9. Visa, MC, Disc. Very good Chinese restaurant, rare in small towns. Fresh ingredients, not overcooked. Szechuan, sweet & sour dishes. Lunch $2.60-$4.30w/ fried rice. Dinners (w/ eggroll, fried rice) $6 to $10 (for a crab meat, shrimp, scallop combo).

A. J. Wedge. *77 N. Howell at Broad downtown. (517) 437-2888.* Mon-Sat 9-3. No credit cards or alcohol. Deli with excellent coffee, pastries, good food. Sandwiches from $3.75 (Herb's herb, smoked turkey) to $4.25 (chutney chicken). $4 turkey club a favorite. For breakfast, muffins, ham & cheese croissant. Cinnamon rolls on Sat. Dessert cookies, brownies .70-.90. Seating for 24 upstairs in wedge-shaped building with view of downtown Hillsdale, one of Mich.'s liveliest, most small attractive towns.

Bavarian Inn Motel. *(517) 437-3367. (800) 779-8033 (MI only). On M-34) just south of downtown, fairgrounds.* 18 rooms on 1 floor. $30-$34. Cable TV. Basketball court. Some rooms knotty pine. Clean. Some shabby furniture. Serene view of private golf course & lake. Restaurant for breakfast, lunch only. *Cozy, old -fashioned budget choice in outstanding scenic location*

Dow Conference Center/ Hillsdale College. *(517) 437-3311. 22 E. Galloway Dr .on north edge of main campus quadrangle.* 36 rooms on 2 floors. $53. Cable TV. $3 extra to use campus pool, racquetball, outdoor tennis. Good college cafeteria during school session. *Nice rooms, interesting setting on campus famed for not accepting a penny of federal aid*

JONESVILLE

Munro House B&B. *(517) 849-9292. 202 Maumee St. 2 blocks s. of downtown & U.S. 12.* In lovely residential area across from Grosvenor House Museum. 5 rooms with baths on 2 floors, some with fireplaces. Sun-Thurs $50, Fri, Sat $63. A/C. Full breakfast. Living room & library w/coffee, teas, cookies. 2 phone areas. TV avail. Ask about package dinner at Billingsgate w/ limo service. Station on Underground RR. *1840 Greek Revival B&B with outstanding antiques*

MARSHALL

Mancino's Pizza. *113 E. Michigan, downtown. (616) 781-0018.* Mon-Thurs 11-10, Fri-Sat 11-11. No credit cards or alcohol. Better than average, family-run small pizza chain. Eat in or take out. Pizza $6.50-$14; subs $5.50, $2.50

chain. Eat in or take out. Pizza
$6.50-$14; subs $5.50, $2.50 for half.
Meatball sub stands out. Italian
dinners $3-$4, pizza salads.

Schuler's. *115 S. Eagle downtown.*
I-94 exit 110, south to the fountain,
3/4 around to Michigan Ave. turn right
at the 1st light. (616) 781-0600. Mon-
Thurs 11-10, Fri-Sat 11-11, Sun 10-10.
Major credit cards. Full bar. Family-
owned 82 years. A Michigan pioneer
of destination dining. Old English
decor remains, but updated, like
mainstream menu, changing season-
ally. Famous Bar Scheeze still comes
with dinner. Lighter menu all day in
Winston's Pub. Lunch $5.45-$8.
Dinner w/salad, starch, vegetable
from $13.45 (London broil). Known
for prime rib ($17.25), fresh seafood.
Sunday brunch ($10.25) 10 a.m.-2
p.m.

Su Casa. *307 E. Michigan*
downtown. (616) 781-7770.Mon-Thurs
11-9, Fri & Sat to 10. No credit cards
or alcohol. Cheerful, simple spot with
all the familiar Tex-Mex standards.

Arborgate Inn. (616) 781-7772.
Michigan Ave at I-69 (exit 36), west
edge of Marshall. 48 rooms on 1 floor.
$37-$43. Packages avail. Cable TV.
New, pleasant, outdoor pool

National House Inn. (616)
781-7374. *On Fountain Circle down-*
town. 16 rooms with baths on 2
floors. $58-$95. Cont. breakfast, cable
TV, phones. Road noise heard in
rooms facing street. Large common
room.
B&B in 1835 Greek Revival stagecoach
stop with antique furnishings

McCarthy's Bear Creek Inn.
(616) 781-8383. 15230 C Drive N., 1 mi.
w. of downtown in rural setting. 14
rooms with baths on 2 floors. $63-
$93. Full breakfast, A/C. 1940s brick
Cape Cod house , plus renovated stone
& wood barn. Each has 7 guest rooms,
most w/balconies. 2 common rooms.
Overlooks Bear Creek. Beautifully
landscaped estate. Host's furniture-

making studio/ showroom here.
Country B&B close to town, highway

Howard's Motel. (616) 781-4201.
14884 W. Michigan, 1/2 mi. w. of I-69
exit 36. 1 1/2 mi. to downtown. Not on
busy strip. 23 rooms on 1 floor.
Summer: $34-$40. Off-season: $30. 2
2-bedroom units $50. Satellite TV.
Attractive older budget choice
with outdoor pool

HOMER

Grist Mill Inn. (517) 568-4063.
310 E. Main, 1 block off M-60. 6 rooms
w/baths on 3 floors. $50 weekdays,
$65 Fri & Sat. Some A/C. Deluxe
cont. breakfast weekdays, champagne
brunch weekends. Biking, canoeing
packages avail. Large brick Victorian
home of gristmill owner. Eclectic mix
of antique and contemporary. A
favorite with cyclists. New: guest
house with Jacuzzi suites, all A/C.
Convival B&B
on pretty small-town street

ALBION

Charlie's Tavern. *111 W. Porter.*
Take Bus. I-94 downtown to Superior
St., turn west one block south of the
theater. (517) 629-9582. Mon-Sat 9:30
a.m.-[1 a.m., Sun noon-11. Full bar. No
credit cards. Terrific vintage 1940s-
1950s atmosphere and surprisingly
good food. Excellent soups. Huge
salads with mozzarella and pepperoni
or turkey are more than a meal in
themselves.

Best Western Adams Arms. (517)
629-3966. *On service road just s.e. of*
main Albion exit at 28 Mile Rd. 32
rooms on 1 floor. $40-$43 (some weekends to $58). Cable TV. Next to Big Boy.
Moderate prices, outdoor pool,
handy location between strip, farm

JACKSON

Gilbert's Steak House. *2323 Shirley Dr. Near junction of I-94 & US. 127 exit 138 n. From I-94, go n.on U.S.127 to to Springport exit, then e. (517) 782-7135. Mon-Thurs 11-10, Fri-Sat 11-11, Sun noon-7. AmEx, MC, Visa. Full bar.* Most famous steakhouse in a town that loves its meat. 80 antique Tiffany-style lamps. Best atmosphere is old log barroom at center. Big, updated menu, but iceberg lettuce mentality still reigns. At lunch, $5 sandwiches & salads; $9 sizzler w/ salad, bread, side. Dinners from $10 (sweet & sour cherry chicken, stir-fry veggies). Known for prime rib ($15 & $18), cheesecake.

Todoroff's. *211 E. Ganson at Cooper, across from St. John's Church just n.e. of downtown. I-94, Cooper St. exit, turn south. (517) 787-6168. Sun-Thurs 10:30-10, Fri-Sat 10:30-11. Eat in or take out. No credit cards or alcohol.* Jackson loves Coneys, and these (80¢ each) are considered tops. Todoroff's chili sold by the pound here and in supermarkets. $3.50 Poor Richard's sub is top of the line. Sandwich plates $4-$5.25, dinners from $5.50 (chicken strips) to $10.45 (12 oz. rib eye). Desserts. See massive sandstone walls of original state prison across the way.

International Dog House. *800 Lansing Ave. not too far from Cascades, All-Star Dairy. I-94 exit 138 (West Ave.) ,s. to North St. e. to Lansing (first light) ,turn s. Bright yellow building on right. (517) 783-1031. Mon-Fri 11-7, Sat 11-3. No credit cards, alcohol, or smoking.* 14 dogs with international fixings on homemade buns. Mexican, Italian stand out. Regular chili dog $1.20. Polish sausage & kraut or Cajun sausage $2. Eat-in, take out, drive thru. Clever and clean.

Giglio's. *On Airline Dr. (M-50) about 1/2 mi. s. of South St. From U.S. 127, take B.R. 127/M-50 exit north, look for green awning & greenhouse. From anywhere else, ask directions. (517)*

787-5025. *Mon-Thurs 11-10, Fri & Sat to 11. Visa, MC.* Popular new Italian restaurant w/ old favorites (spaghetti w/ meatballs $6.50; fettucine Alfredo $7.25, lasagne ($7.75), served w/ salad, bread. homemade sauce. Big servings, half portions available. Crisp, thick-crusted pizza in red and white (no sauce!): $8/full tray plus 90¢/ item. Good meal-size salads ($3.50-$6), sandwiches ($3-$4.50). Daily specials. Convenient take-out to Sharp Park.

The Granary. *Inside Ella Sharp Museum (p. 000). (517) 787-2320.Tues-Fri 11-2:30, Sat noon-4. Visa, MC, checks. No alcohol.* A la carte menu changes often. Cooking from scratch. May be Jackson's best for non-carnivores. Cup of soup, 1/2 sandwich ($4-$4.50), bread pudding ($1.50) are favorites. Salads come w/very good cornbread, honey butter: house salad w/ marinated turkey $5, pasta $4. Lasagna $6.25.

Holiday Inn. *(517) 783-6404. Just n.w. of U.S. 127/I-94 interchange. Take Springport Rd. exit w.* 182 rooms on 2 floors. $67. Satellite TV. Holidome: small indoor pool, whirlpool, sauna, game room, exercise room, putting green, mini golf. Mediocre restaurant. Bar. Busy strip, near mall. *Top-of-the-line in Jackson with Holidome*

Motel Jackson. *(517) 784-0517. 2500 Spring Arbor Rd. W. side of Jackson in residential/ business area, 3 blocks from Cascades.* 12 units. $26. 3 kitchenettes $2 extra. Cable TV. *Quiet budget choice near Cascades*

Days Inn. *(517) 787-1111. N. of I-94 at Elm Rd exit just n.e. of Jackson. Not on a strip.* 100 rooms on 2 floors. $30-$45. Cont. breakfast. Satellite TV. Restaurant, bar. Near golf, Waterloo Rec. Area. *Budget rates, outdoor pool, easy access to country for golf, biking*

BROOKLYN

Chicago Street Inn. *(517) 592-3888. 219 Chicago, 1 block from downtown.* 3 story Queen Anne, 4 rooms with baths. $65. A/C. Cont. breakfast. Guests use front room & parlor w/ fireplace, TV, phone. Package dinners at Billingsgate.
B&B in Irish Hills' prettiest town

TECUMSEH

Harvey House Motel. *(517) 423-7401. On M-50, 1 1/2 mi. w. of downtown on busy strip.* 60 rooms on 2 floors. $38-$45. TV w/ movie channel. ESPN, phones. *Convenient to antiquing, Irish Hills, pretty historic Tecumseh*

ADRIAN

El Chapulin/The Grasshopper. *116/118 S. Winter (M-52) downtown. (517) 265-6670. Sun-Thurs11-11, Fri-Sat 11-midnight.* MC, Visa. Full bar. Imported beers, good margaritas. Oldest, biggest Mexican restaurant in town. Taco $1. Dinners from $3.85 (single-item plate) to $7.75 (combination). $2.25 apple or cherry fried burrito a favorite. Same menu all day. Daily specials. Menudo (tripe soup)

other uncommon dishes for Mexican diners. Adrian and Holland have Mich.'s biggest Mexican populations — over 15% — attracted by jobs picking and processing vegetable. Pool table, occasional live music. More good Mexican food: Sunnyside Cafe on east side.

BLISSFIELD

Hathaway House. *424 W. Adrian (U.S. 223) on west edge of town. (517) 486-2141. Tues-Thurs 11:30-9, Fri-Sat 11:30-10, Sun 12-8.* Visa, MC. Full bar. Big, old house. Long tradition of ample fare (country version of elegant), good service. Antique furnishings. Shoppes outside. $8 lunch buffet (Tues-Sat), dinner salad bar are huge. Dinner favorites: fried chicken,country baked ham in brandy-raisin sauce (both $13), prime rib ($16 & $18), fresh fish & seafood. Children's menu. Not dressy.

Main Street Stable & Tavern.
116 N. Main, in old stable behind Hathaway House. (517) 486-2144. Mon-Thurs 11:30-10, Fri-Sat 11:30 - midnight, Sun 11-10 (brunch 11-2). Visa, MC. Full bar. Lighter, more casual adjunct of Hathaway House. Same menu all day. Sandwiches, burgers $4-$5.50. Dinners from $5.75 (fish & chips, vegetable lasagna) to $12 (steak & shrimp).

Chapter 3
Beyond Detroit

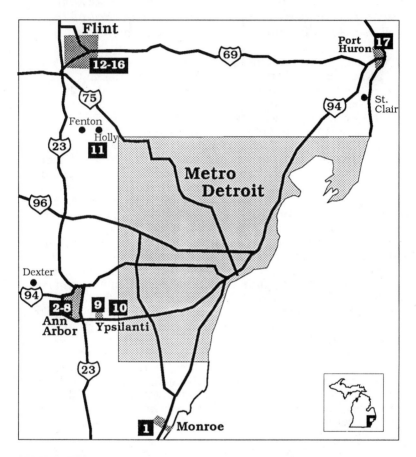

HIGHLIGHTS

Monroe

It boomed well before the Civil War. Now it's a backwater where you can see a battlefield site from the War of 1812, well preserved old homes, and Custer memorabilia.

Just up the beautiful River Raisin from the marshes along Lake Erie, Monroe is a settled old industrial city, originally French. For centuries Indians harvested wild rice in these marshes downriver. Lotuses blossom here every August, giving a spectacular view to visitors who head east out Dunbar Road just south of town. Hunters and bird-watchers are attracted by the huge flocks of migrating waterfowl which come to the marshes, home of some of the state's best bird-watching.

Monroe is one of Michigan's most historic cities. Only Detroit was incorporated earlier. But relative to the Motor City, Monroe has stagnated over the decades. Today the historic city center seems curiously remote from the busy highways that go past it from Toledo to Detroit.

Monroe was founded by Detroit French who grew disenchanted with life there under the British after France lost control in 1760. Some natives still speak in the area's distinctive French accent. The Indians taught Monroe's French the custom of eating muskrat (pronounced "mushrat" in these parts), and it is still considered a delicacy here. Trapped before the spring thaw, muskrat is often featured at late winter dinners of Monroe fraternal orders and charitable organizations.

The most colorful and exciting era in the city's history occurred between 1825 and 1837 when thousands of Easterners landed here on their way to settle Michigan, Indiana, and Illinois. The Erie Canal, opened in 1825, brought settlers to Buffalo, where they boarded sailing ships or steamers to make the sometimes dangerous and usually uncomfortable 10-day voyage to Monroe.

St. Mary's Park, just north of downtown, is a pleasant riverside picnic spot. You can pick up a coney island at downtown's most popular and quaintest eatery, **Coney Island Lunch** (4 W. Front) and saunter across the pedestrian bridge to the park.

Highlights of the Monroe area:

◆ **Monroe County Historical Museum.** Housed in the old post office, this interesting general museum of local history has many memorabilia about General George Armstrong Custer, the most

famous person associated with Monroe. Custer spent much of his
youth in Monroe and visited it often afterwards. Before his famous
end at Little Big Horn in 1876, Custer had been a heroic Civil War
officer, promoted to general at the unheard-of age of 23 because
of his aggressive, courageous leadership.

Here you can see Custer's swords and beloved rifles, a map he
made of a Confederate camp while he was held aloft by balloon,
and his big buffalo robe worn during the Washita Campaign of
1868 when he defeated a bigger band of Sioux. People come from
around the world to visit the museum and the Custer collection of
the Monroe County Library. The museum, outstanding for a town
of Monroe's size, has much more than Custer memorabilia of
interest. A sequence of dioramas shows what it looked like at
Frenchtown (Monroe's former name) looked like in 1813 when
American troops were surprised by the British and disastrously
surrendered, leading to the famous massacre of some 60
wounded soldiers by Indians. A display about the pride of Monroe,
Kaye Lani Rae Rafko, Miss America 1988, features the revealing
green sequined Hawaiian costume she made for her hula dance in
the pageant's talent competition. *126 S. Monroe St. (313) 243-
7137. May-Sept: Tues-Sun 10-5. Oct-April: Wed-Sun 10-5. Free.*

◆ **Downtown.** The most interesting part of this faded commercial
and civic area is **Loranger Square**, at the intersection of First and
Washington. This New England-type square, unique in Michigan,
shows how much older Monroe is than other cities in the state.
The unusual, impressively ornate 1880 **County Courthouse** is on
the square's southeast corner. In front is a cannon that dates to
the reign of George II of England. Across First Street is the site
of the **First Presbyterian Church,** built in 1846. Next to the
church on First is the **Dorsch Memorial Library**, located in the
former home of Dr. Eduard Dorsch, a Bavarian physician who fled
after the failed 1848 German revolution. On the square's northwest corner, a plaque commemorates the spot where a **whipping
post** once stood. Whipping posts were a rarity in the Midwest.

Along Washington Street (one street over from Monroe) are
some attractively restored commercial buildings north of the
courthouse. The **Monroe Bank & Trust** is a fine example of early
20th-century Beaux Arts architecture. It's worth a peek inside to
see the imposing interior. A map on the kiosk outside orients
visitors to major Monroe sights. At **Paul's Bakery** across the
street, you can buy tasty fresh pastries and coffee to go.

North of the river across the Monroe Street bridge is the impressive **Custer Monument** at Elm and Monroe. It was unveiled in
1910 by his widow, by then a well-known New York writer, with
President Taft at her side.

South on Monroe Street are several noteworthy establishments. The tidy, well-organized **Thrift Shop** at 119 S. Monroe sells its merchandise (used clothes, furniture, dishes, etc.) at amazingly cheap prices. *Open Monday through Saturday from 9:30 to 3:30, except for closing at 11:30 on Tuesday and opening at 11:30 Saturday.* At **Spainhower's Auction House** is a wild variety of antique items for sale. *(Open 9-5 Monday-Saturday. Call 313-242-5411 about upcoming auctions held every three weeks or so.)*

Finally, if you walk west on Front Street past Monroe Street, you'll soon see the home of the ***Monroe Evening News*** at 201 W. First. Giant glass windows let the passing public see its big web presses in action. Around 2:30 on weekday afternoons, you can see that day's edition roaring off the presses. *Centered at the intersection of Front St. with Monroe and Washington, extending south from the River Raisin.* A **walking tour brochure** available at the museum takes you on an interesting walk through Old Monroe's historic commercial and residential district.

◆ **River Raisin Battlefields and Massacre Site.** The War of 1812 again pitted the British and Indians against the Americans. At stake was the extent of American holdings on the continent. One of the major battles in that often ineptly led war occurred on the River Raisin between Dixie Highway and Detroit Street. In 1813 an American army was badly mauled here in an early-morning surprise attack by British and Canadian soldiers. Nearly 280 Americans were killed, and a brigade of 600 militiamen surrendered. Wounded Americans, left in the homes of Monroe settlers, were set upon by Indians a day later. Over 60 were murdered. This famous "River Raisin Massacre" later ignited the American troops. A series of metal markers along the river explains its the major incidents. *Along the River Raisin on E. Elm St. just west of the I-75 exit. The new battlefield interpretive museum and park, at E. Elm just west of Detroit St. (between M-50 and I-75), is due to open in May, 1990. Call (313) 243-7137 for hours.*

◆ **Navarre-Anderson Trading Post.** The centerpiece of this three-building complex is the plain house built in central Monroe in 1789 by fur trader François Navarre. It's believed to be the oldest surviving house in Michigan, and it has been restored and furnished with simple French-Canadian furniture to look as it might have when the Navarres lived there between 1789 and 1802. The brick schoolhouse built on this site in 1860 has been interpreted as a **country store** from between 1910 and 1920. *N. Custer Rd. at Raisinville Rd., 4 miles west of downtown Monroe. From M-50 (S. Custer Rd.) turn north onto Raisinville Rd. and cross the river. (313) 243-7137. Open Memorial Day-Labor Day, weekends 1-5; other times, by appointment for groups. Free.*

◆ **Sterling State Park.** Sterling State Park, just north of Monroe, is western Lake Erie's only park with camping and swimming. From the beach, swimmers and sunbathers get a stark view of the giant cooling towers of the Fermi Nuclear Plant four miles north. Half of this 1,000-acre park consists of water — lagoons that are excellent habitats for migrating and nesting shore birds. A 2.6-mile loop along the **Marsh View Nature Trail** surrounds the park's largest lagoon. (It's open for cross-country skiing in winter.) A mile-long walk leads to its observation tower. A causeway leads to the large **beach**, beach house, parking area and, behind it, the partly shaded **picnic area** and **playground** on a rise offering a panorama of Lake Erie. The park has **288 modern campsites** without privacy or shade, overlooking the boat basin. *On State Park Rd., off Dixie Hwy. 1 mile northeast of I-75 exit 15. (313) 289-2715. 8 a.m.-10 p.m. $3/day , or $15 annual state park sticker.*

◆ **Fermi 2 Power Plant & Visitors Center.** These tours of Detroit Edison's only nuclear power plant get high marks from radiation experts for straightforward information about nuclear power and about the much-publicized delays and cost overruns in starting up Fermi 2. The visitor center tours combine a film on how nuclear energy is produced, a tour of the facility (some adults-only tours include the protected area where the turbine generator produces electricity), and lots of chances for questions-and-answers. Not surprisingly, the tour emphasizes safety and environmental issues. There's a scale model of Fermi 2's drywell or primary containment system. *On Enrico Fermi Drive off Dixie Hwy., 7 miles north of downtown Monroe. (313) 586-5228. 3-5 weeks advance reservations required for free group tours conducted Mon-Sat between 9 and 5. Individuals may join scheduled group tours.*

◆ **Manufacturers Market Place.** There aren't nearly as many bargains here as you might think. Its discounts of 30% to 70% seem almost standard these days. Tenant stores here include **Harve Benard, Van Heusen, Maidenform, Leggs/Hanes/Bali, Bass** and **Mushrooms** shoes, **Sneakers 'n Cleats, American Tourister, Toy Liquidators, Corning/Revere, Sportsland USA,** and **Salem China Factory Outlet.** Places with especially good deals are **Carter's Childrenswear, Wearever's Kitchen Collection** (great on kitchen gadgets), **Socks Galore, The Paper Factory** (giftwrap and school supplies), and the large **Westpoint Pepperell** store (which opens at 9 a.m. and is the only one in Michigan). *14500 La Plaisance at I-75 (exit 11), 2 1/2 miles southeast of downtown Monroe. Mon-Sat 10-9, Sun 11-7. For information: (616) 728-5170.*

❶ Huron St. historic buildings. Impressive 19th-century mansions line bluff overlookin Huron River. Evokes more scenic, preindustrial Ypsilanti.

❷ Historical Museum. Humdrum Victorian rooms, but great display of underwear which made Ypsi mills famous. Wonderful arrowhead collection, eccentric items.

❸ Depot Town. Old, once-bustling commercial district fueled by two train depots. District now home to bars and antique shops, highlighted by the Side Track with great hamburgers and ornate big bar.

❹ Miller Motors. Long after the beloved Hudson auto ceased production, this Hudson dealership keeps trading both parts and cars and retains its 1940s look.

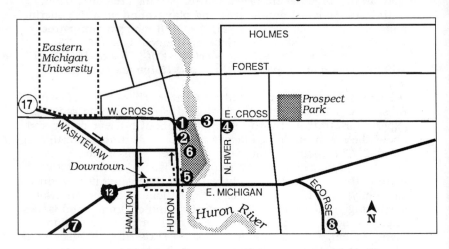

❺ Materials Unlimited. Extraordinarily big selection of vintage architectural items, both antiques and repros. Many ornate fixtures, including stained glass, columns, and hardware, make it good for browsing.

❻ Riverside & Frog Island Parks. Scenic Huron River parks host great events—June's Frog Island Blues/Jazz Festival, August's big Heritage Festival, and cheery holiday light display at Riverside in December.

❼ Schmidt's Antiques. One of country's best places to get English antique furniture. The monthly auction is a comic treat just to watch. 5138 W. Michigan. (313) 434-2660.

❽ Yankee Air Museum/ Willow Run Airport. Interesting collection of old military aircraft at the historic and now crumbling Willow Run Airport, where Ford built bombers during WWII.

Highlights of
Ypsilanti

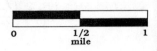

Miller Motors

Take a trip back in time at this Hudson auto dealership, little changed from the 1940s.

In front of this old Hudson dealership is a vintage HUDSON sign, and in the show window is a spiffy-looking Hudson coupe. This isn't a mirage — or a museum. It's the business of Jack Miller, whose father started selling Hudsons here in 1933. Though production ceased in 1957, Miller still trades in Hudsons. His place is probably the best in the world to get Hudson parts, still in their original cartons, some half a century old. They have been bought up from old warehouses around the country.

In the service area behind the sales room are an array of Hudson cars, part of Miller's private collection. These include a 1953 Hudson Hornet, the 1946 Hudson pickup Miller drives to work in the summer, a 1946 Hudson convertible, and 1956 pink and grey Hudson which Miller says "could be bought." In an adjoining area Miller repairs old Hudsons. He also sells Hudson memorabilia as well as die cast scale models of vintage cars and tractors ($5.75 and up).

Hudson aficionados often stop by to chat. Miller affably shares his wealth of knowledge about Hudsons with visitors. He explains that they were first manufactured in 1909 and named after financial backer J. L. Hudson, the Detroit department store magnate. The Hudson name was sullied in the mid-1950s when Nash took over the firm and turned out what some consider gaudy imitations of the real thing. But the Hudsons of the 1940s were extraordinary automobiles, Miller points out, fast but stable highway cars engineered and built extremely well.

Looking around the showroom is a treat. The walls are covered with old Hudson promotional posters, as well as with photos and other antique artifacts. Visitors are welcome to browse. And you can also kick the tires of what a *Car and Driver* article called the "vaguely eccentric" array of old cars other than Hudsons.

100 E. Cross Street at River just east of Depot Town. From I-94, take Huron St. exit 183 north about 1 $^1/_4$ miles, then east on Cross. (313) 482-5200. Wed-Sat 9-5:30 (except for lunchtime). Call first to make sure it's open.

INTERESTING ARCHITECTURE AND ANTIQUE SHOPS . . . . . are in the 19th-century commercial district along East Cross is called **Depot Town**. It features some popular bars, several antique and resale shops, a food co-op, and other attractions. Depot Town actually became the city's main downtown for awhile after the railroad arrived in 1838 from Detroit. The passenger and freight depots are still here. The **Michigan Central passenger station** on North River Street, now one story high, is a pale shadow of the ornate three-story building and tower built here in 1863. A fire and train collision have reduced it to its present humble state. Across the tracks, the **freight depot** is a long Italianate structure from 1875. It is now headquarters for the **Ypsilanti Farmers' Market**, open Wednesdays and Saturdays from 8 a.m. to 3 p.m. Many of the upper stories of the 1850s and 1860s brick storefronts along Cross are now apartments, and the area, with its own sprightly neighborhood publication, has a sense of camaraderie. The 1859 **Follett House** at 17-25 E. Cross was known as one of the finest hotels on the Michigan Central line. The third-floor ballroom hosted Buffalo Bill, Tom Thumb, and other 19th-century celebrities. The **Side Track** at 56 East Cross is a very popular watering place, with excellent hamburgers and a massive back bar. The **Old Town Restaurant** at 38 East Cross is a lively breakfast spot. Around the corner of North River Street is the **Ypsilanti Food Co-op**. Yet to be renovated on the very east end of Depot Town is **Thompson Block**. Built around 1860, it was a barracks during the Civil War. *East Cross St. between the Huron River and River St. Many stores open Sundays 11-5; some antique shops are closed Mondays and Tuesdays.*

OTHER YPSI STANDOUTS FOR ANTIQUERS . . . . . **Materials Unlimited** is one of the biggest and best places in the Midwest to find attractive architectural artifacts, new and old: stained glass windows, ornate brass door hinges, carved oak column capitals, 19th-century building ornaments, etc. Also: some antique furniture here, eccentric items like wooden masks and cigar-store Indians. *2 W. Michigan Ave. between Huron St. and the river. (313) 483-6980. 7 days a week 10-5.* . . . . . **Schmidt's Antique Shop** is widely known for its entertainingly funny monthly auctions that often have high quality furniture. For decades Schmidt's imported mostly middle-quality English antiques by the container load, but shifting exchange rates have diminished that trade. Still, the gallery sales room makes for interesting browsing. *5138 Michigan Ave., 4 miles west of Ypsilanti. (313) 434-2660. Mon-Sat 9-5, Sun 11-5. Auction: first Sat of month, 11 a.m.*

IN AN IMPRESSIVE MANSION . . . . . perched on a bank of the Huron River, the **Ypsilanti Historical Museum** has an amusing assortment of local artifacts.. You can see the famous long underwear that gave the city a national reputation in the 19th century. A poster touts the woolen garments as "the perfect underwear for progressive people" with the jingle: "*Never rip and never tear/ Ypsilanti underwear.*" A back room is full of old dolls. Kids are said to be most intrigued by the large dollhouse made from crates during the Depression. *220 N. Huron St. near Cross. (313) 482-4990. Thurs, Sat, Sun 2-4. Free.*

Yankee Air Museum/ Willow Run Airport

At a legendary, aging airport, an imposing collection of famous American fighting planes

Part of the fun of visiting this military air museum is roaming around Willow Run Airport, a remarkable place built in the early 1940s to test the long-range B-24 bombers built in the huge adjacent factory. Today the airport has a rather seedy, almost disreputable look to it. The carcasses of old planes are strewn around the fringes of the giant field, some partially devoured for spare parts. Big old four-engine propeller-powered cargo planes still lumber into the air from the long runways. Many rush critically needed parts to keep auto plants around the country in production.

Just west of the field is the gigantic **GM Hydra-Matic Plant**, so big that specially-made superhighways funnel workers in and out of the complex. This was initially the famous **Willow Run Bomber Plant**. Erected by Ford Motor in 1941, it was the largest building ever built. The monster covers 70 acres and sprawls over 3/4 of a mile. Architect Albert Kahn built it in an L-shape to keep it from spilling into Wayne County, which Ford considered un-friendly Democratic territory with higher taxes. The big plant proved to be a big boost to American morale after Pearl Harbor.

When the giant facility was planned, it wasn't clear whether or not the Allies would lose Great Britain to the Nazis, so Willow Run had to make quickly thousands of bombers big enough to fly missions across the Atlantic to reach Germany. Between 1942 and 1945, some 42,000 women and men worked in the plant. Midgets were hired to fit parts in the nose section and other hard-to-reach areas. By the time the bomber plant closed in June of 1945, it had produced 8,685 B-24 Liberators.

GM purchased the plant in 1953 to make automatic transmissions. The big Hydra-Matic plant has actually been expanded over the years to 4.8 million square feet. It now employs about 9,300 workers. Next door is a Chevrolet assembly plant which makes Caprices.

On the airport's other side, off Beck Road, is the **Yankee Air Museum**, housed in a cavernous 1941 hangar. It has the interest-ingly scruffy atmosphere of a bootstrap creation by dedicated fans. Although the museum was only organized in 1981, the huge hangar is already crowded with aging military aircraft. Some are in the process of being renovated. On weekends you'll often see an elderly volunteer mechanic working on an engine.

Some of the 28 planes here already fly. One is a 1945 C-47, the cargo version of the classic DC-3. Another is a 1943 B-25 gunship that saw action in Europe, providing close ground support and flying 90 bombing missions. This is the same model used in the Doolittle raid of Japan. Museum members are hard at work on a classic B-17 "Flying Fortress," the Allies' largest heavy bomber during most of World War II. Also on display in the hangar is another classic military aircraft: the F-86 Sabre jet, a major fighter during the Korean War.

On the second floor of the hangar complex are rooms with memorabilia on display: Air Force patches and medals, old newspaper clippings, paintings and photos of planes in action, engines, shells, radios, flights suits, goggles, and so on. Just outside the hangar are even more planes, highlighted by the hulking, rather ominous presence of a camouflaged B-52 bomber. The **gift shop** is well stocked with books on aviation, model airplanes, postcards, T-shirts, and other souvenirs.

Willow Run Airport, off Beck Rd. Take exit 190 from I-94. (313) 483-4030. Tues-Sat 10-4, Sun 12-4. $3.50/adult, $2.50 seniors & students, $1.50 children 3-12.

Downtown Ann Arbor Shopping

Michigan's liveliest downtown has an unequaled mix of unusually specialized shops, from pop culture of the 1950s to Chinese art.

Ann Arbor has one of the most interestingly diverse downtowns in the Midwest. Within just a few square blocks there are lots of noteworthy shops, lively nightspots, and very good restaurants. Restaurant competition has become so fierce, most of the food is pretty good or better. Many traditional old German businesses such as Ehnis & Son work clothes shop and Schlenker Hardware remain downtown, giving unusual historical continuity to the area. Remnants of Ann Arbor's once-lively counterculture lives on at the Del Rio Bar at 120 West Washington, the Old Town at 120 West Liberty, and upstairs over the Heidelberg Restaurant, 214 North Main, where monthly "poetry slams" are held.

But gradually the old Ann Arbor has given way to the new, most tellingly, perhaps, in the case of the transformation of the beloved old Quality Bakery into the hip Quality Bar, geared to a Yuppie crowd, with an upper-level deck costing $250,000. On evenings in good weather, Main Street sidewalk cafes make for a street life almost like European cities. Even in winter, a bit of that ambiance remains at the Espresso Royale coffeehouse, 214 South Main.

What sets Ann Arbor apart form other downtowns that experienced rampant gentrification in the 1980s is that many — maybe even most — stores haven't simply jumped onto the latest hot trend. Stores here are usually owned and run by knowledgeable people with longstanding interests in what they sell, whether it be backpacking gear or Chinese art. Upscale specialty chains, which threaten to overwhelm Birmingham and Grosse Pointe, have made few inroads here.

Here are some standouts, arranged from west (on Ashley Street, west of Main) toward the University of Michigan campus to the east:

◆ **16 Hands.** Attractively displayed contemporary crafts at a wide range of prices — jewelry, furniture and wood accessories, leather goods, weaving, blown glass, and other media by talented artists, mostly from the region. *119 W. Washington. Mon-Fri 11-6, Sat*

❶ Downtown. Michigan's most interesting concentration of restaurants & shops. Lively street scene on into the evening with plenty of good open-air summer cafes.

❷ Kerrytown. Lively restaurant/ shop complex. Popular bistro, large farmers' market, outstanding kitchenware shop, Nearby Treasure Mart is must visit for bargain-hunters.

❸ Zingerman's. Extraordinary deli and fancy food shop. Delicious huge sandwiches, outstanding bread & interesting selection of cheeses, meats, and ethnic dishes.

❹ State-Liberty shopping area. Anchored by Jacobsons & Borders' Books. Good record & book shops, other interesting stores & coffee house.

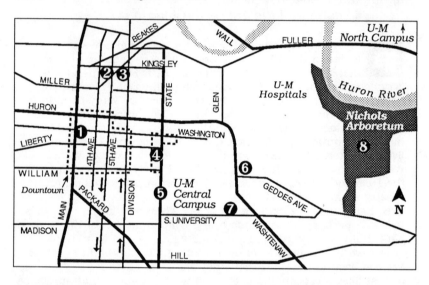

❺ Two U-M museums on State St. At the **Kelsey,** priceless ancient Egyptian, Greek, and Roman pieces. **Museum of Art** has important paintings, medieval to modern.

❻ U-M Exhibit Museum. Extraordinary natural science displays with prehistoric scenes, dramatic dinosaur skeletons, many rare specimens.

❼ Middle Earth. Entertaining shop in student-oriented commercial strip. Full of all sorts of amusing items, many outrageous. Nearby Village Corner has one of state's best selections of wines.

❽ Nichols Arboretum. Delightful hilly 126 acres. Paths down to Huron River. Over 2,000 kinds of plants, many exotic. Beautiful Forest Hills Cemetery is next door to west.

Highlights of
Ann Arbor

0   1/2   1
           mile

10-6, also Fri evening 8:30-10.

◆ **Ann Arbor Art Association.** The gallery shop in this one-time carriage factory presents an interesting mix of accomplished local artists — largely painters, weavers, jewelers, printmakers. Quality is high. Some work retains a refreshingly uncommercial sincerity; much is sophisticated in both positive and negative senses. Changing exhibits always worth checking out. *117 W. Liberty at Ashley. Mon noon-5:30, Tues-Sat 10-5:30.*

◆ **Rider's Hobby.** Among Michigan's best hobby shops: trains, radio-control planes, adventure games, kits. *115 W. Liberty. Mon-Fri 10-8, Sat 10-6.*

◆ **West Side Books.** See p. 100. *113 W. Liberty.*

◆ **The Conservatory.** Products of good design, not fads, are the focus of this delightfully serene gift shop run by an architect and his jeweler wife. The eclectic assemblage ranges from crisply contemporary to ethnic and antique. Unusual blank books, baskets, playing cards. *111 W. Liberty. Mon-Sat 10-6, Fri to 9 or later.*

◆ **Ehnis & Son.** A genuine working man's clothes store, descended from a harnessmaker whose sideline was shoes. Quality overalls, work shirts, and boots. Old-time interior. *116 W. Liberty. Mon-Sat 8-6.*

◆ **Selo/Shevel Gallery.** Stunning new corner space at Liberty and Main has a fascinating mix of ethnic art and contemporary crafts from leading American craftspeople. Hanging wood mermaids and dragons from Bali ($65), Japanese chests, kimono-style jackets ($125), old silver belts and necklaces from India ($400), Pat Garrett's wonderful gold and rose quartz jewelry with bird and leaf embellishments, African masks and giant bird figures, Turkish kilims. Contrasting to this earthy, rich mix is the colorful, clear, shimmering mood of a second gallery down the street, where back-lit blown glass and more jewelry is displayed. *301 and 335 S. Main. Mon-Thurs 10-6, Fri & Sat 10-10.*

◆ **Collected Works.** Popular natural-fibers clothing shop, mostly for women but with some sweaters, shirts, and pants for men. Relaxed, comfortably sophisticated look plays off ethnic prints and textures against basic solid colors in unstructured clothing, often knit. Prices from inexpensive to moderate. Known for ethnic classics like Peruvian sweaters, Indonesian print skirts, and colorful knit caps. *317 S. Main. Mon-Sat 10-6, Fri to 9, Sun 12-5.*

◆ **After Words.** See p. 100. *219 S. Main.*

◆ **The Peaceable Kingdom.** Warm, clever, personal shop has become an Ann Arbor institution with its potpourri of imaginatively displayed things, from small inexpensive toys and gadgets to imported and contemporary American folk art. Don't be so distracted by the novelties that you forget to look up on the walls and see Mexican and African masks and Ann Arbor artist Charla Khanna's compelling one-of-a-kind dolls. *210 S. Main. Mon-Sat 10-6, Fri 'til 9.*

◆ **Lotus Gallery.** Art and furniture of China and Japan, including Chinese jades, Japanese netsuke and simple 19th-century wood chests with many drawers, unusual things like an opium scale. Look downstairs for old and new kimonos, prints, tasteful mass-produced souvenirs. Also, outstanding Southwest Indian pottery. Owner-collector Les Werbel is available after 5 and on many Saturdays. *119 E. Liberty. Tues-Sat 11-6.*

◆ **Rage of the Age.** The Fifties revisited, from furniture classics by Charles Eames and Arne Jacobson to squeeze bottles of mustard. Good prices, fun atmosphere. Lots of vintage clothes. *220 S. Fourth. Tues-Fri 12-6, Sat to 5.*

◆ **Common Language.** Books, cards, posters, T-shirts about subgroups of the human rainbow: gays, lesbians, African-Americans, and more. See p. 100. More of a sense of humor than you might expect. *214 S. Fourth. Tues-Fri 12-8, Sat 11-8, Sun 12-4.*

◆ **Whole Cloth.** Fabrics from around the world, including Austrian lodencloth, Nigerian cottons, Liberty prints, basic high-quality wools, cotton sheeting, 100% cotton knits, many expensive silks and crepes you'd expect to see at English tea parties. Unusual buttons: wood, shell, antiques. *206 S. Fourth. Mon-Sat 10-6.*

◆ **Art Deco Design.** Nine-tenths of the artfully displayed Art Deco furniture, accessories, and jewelry here was made between 1925 and 1939, but 1950s designer classics add extra zing. Prices are reasonable, and reproductions are few and far between. Owner Constance Basil is knowledgeable and enthusiastic about the style. *207 E. Washington. Tues-Sat 11-6.*

◆ **The Artful Exchange.** An eclectic variety of fine art — paintings, sculpture, drawings, ethnic art, and prints — sold on consignment. Prices start as low as $5 and go up into the thousands, for "investment art" by the likes of Chagall, Dali, and Calder. A good place to find works by retired U-M art school faculty. *215 E. Washington. Wed-Thurs 11-5, Fri 'til 6:30, Sat 10-5.*

◆ **The Bead Gallery.** A fabulous array of beads is enough to inspire you to make your own creations. Ceramic beads from Thailand, old glass beads, antique jade buttons, gemstones, Ethiopian silver beads, millefiore Venetian beads, glass and wood beads of all colors and kinds. Books, instructional sheets, and sample necklaces show what you can do. *309 E. Liberty between Fifth and Division (lower level). Mon-Fri 10-6, Sat 10-4.*

Just upstairs, at **Creative Tattoo**, a degree-holding artist and former art teacher, Suzanne Fauser, has won national awards with her beautiful tattoos and relieved a lot of embarrassment by modifying ill-advised body ornament.

DOWNTOWN PARKING HINTS . . . . . Two big parking structures are your best bet for avoiding frustration. The new structure entered from **Ann and Ashley** just west of Main at Miller has a glass-faced elevator with an interesting view and plenty of space. The huge structure entered on **William at Fourth** is conveniently located at downtown's south edge. Hourly parking at both is metered (50¢/hour). Bring lots of quarters.

THE ANN ARBOR ART SCENE . . . . . is lively, but more oriented to showcasing the area's unusual number of productive artists than to an art-hungry market. There are dozens of places that exhibit visual art, but no single gallery guide. The cultural smorgasbord of **performances, lectures,** etc. is similarly rich. Your best bet for an overview of what's going on is to pick up a copy of the *Ann Arbor Observer* monthly magazine, with a calendar of events and exhibits that's easy to use and virtually complete. The current day's main events are on the Observer's calendar information line, (313) 665-6155.

GOOD MOVIES DOWNTOWN . . . . . are shown at the small, easy-to-miss **Ann Arbor Theater,** 210 S. Fifth between Liberty and Washington. (313) 761-9700. Tuesday matinees and weekday shows at 4:40 are a fine alternative to fighting rush-hour traffic.

FUN WITH SCIENCE . . . . is the mission of the popular **Ann Arbor Hands-On Museum** downtown. The 150 science exhibits for children get mixed reviews; some are tedious, and old standbys can become tiresome. Others are repeat winners. Educational computer games for kids. Good gift shop. It's in a landmark 1879 fire station. Call (313) 995-KIDS for info on one-day workshops and free demo topics. *Huron at N. Fifth. Tues-Fri 10-5:30, Sat 10-5, Sun 1-5. Adults $3, children and students $2, families $7.50.*

Zingerman's Delicatessen

This fantastic deli also showcases
choice foods from around the world.

Depending on who you talk to, this is the best deli in Michigan or in the entire Midwest. Sandwiches (over 100 in all) are huge and delicious; the $7 corned beef Reuben is the best-seller. The extensive takeout counter offers tempting salads and favorites, from deli classics like coleslaw ($1.90/side), chicken soup, and noodle kugel ($1.75/slice) to inventive potato salads, the popular Thai noodle salad, and salmon-dill pasta salad ($4.50/side) made with Irish smoked salmon. With Bruce Aidell's sausages from San Francisco and unusual hand-made cheeses, domestic and imported, the deli counter is absolutely top-of-the-line. The selection of olive oils, vinegars, and mustards is outstanding. The owners do a great job of searching out unusual jams, relishes, and goodies of all kinds. The fun, information-packed free handouts are a short course in food. Call (313) 663-0974 to subscribe to their **newsletter** ($6/year).

This feels like a real deli and not a gourmet shop, especially if you stop by in the leisurely morning hours, when it's favored by various tradesmen, downtown workers, and academic types. The main way it differs from New York delis is the astounding politeness and patience of the knowledgeable staff, which prides itself on providing advice and samples to sometimes obnoxiously fussy customers. For shopping and sampling, it's best to time your visit during a lull — mornings, mid-afternoons, or early in the week.

For awhile, Zingerman's was so crowded it was a pain to enter the place, but expansion has streamlined the service, quickening it appreciably. The eating area, in the deli and a separate converted house, is now positively spacious. It's nice to see an enormously successful establishment like Zingerman's that continues to put its energy into improving what it offers rather than starting up clones elsewhere.

422 Detroit at Kingsley. (313) 663-3354. Mon-Sat 7 a.m.-
9 p.m., Sun 9 a.m.-9 p.m.

TRASH OR TREASURE? . . . . . Ann Arbor's legendary resale shop, the **Treasure Mart**, has a sprawling array of home furnishings at all price levels. (The Treasure

TRASH OR TREASURE? . . . . . Ann Arbor's legendary resale shop, the
Treasure Mart, has a sprawling array of home furnishings at all price levels.
(The Treasure Mart's clothing counterpart, **The Tree,** is at Detroit at Kingsley,
across from Zingerman's.) It's like going to dozens of garage sales at once.
Some terrific bargains are here, due to occasionally erratic pricing and a
monthly mark-down system. With a large and fast-moving stock, this place is
truly addictive. Some customers stop by daily; more than a few local dealers
have launched successful businesses by buying and selling here. *529 Detroit St.
between Kingsley and Division. (313) 662-1363. Mon-Sat 9 a.m-5:30 p.m., Mon &
Fri 'til 8:30.*

GOOD FOOD AND MORE . . . . . Specialty shops near Zingerman's are
centered in the **Kerrytown** complex of some 30 shops in a converted lumber
yard. These include purveyors of premium vegetables, seafood at Monahan's
outstanding market, meat, breads and pastries at The **Moveable Feast Bakery**
(tucked away in a front corner), and good mid-priced wine. Of the gift and
specialty shops upstairs, **Vintage to Vogue** is a standout. Kerrytown anchors
are **Workbench** contemporary furniture on the Fourth Street side (**Dragon's
Lair Futons** is in the basement) and **Kitchen Port,** a very large and complete
cooking and table top shop. *Kerrytown is between North Fourth and Fifth just
south of Kingsley. Park in lot at Kingsley and Fourth, or Catherine at Fourth.
Typical hours: Mon-Fri 10-6, Sat 9-5, Sun 12-4. Food shops open earlier, and
they're closed on Sunday.*
   Ann Arbor is a town that has long taken food quite seriously, and
Kerrytown was a logical outgrowth of the popular **Farmers' Market** next door.
The market runs between Detroit and North Fourth; it's open Saturdays year-
round, plus Wednesdays from spring through fall.

ALTERNATIVE BUSINESSES have suffered from Ann Arbor's yuppification in
the 1980s, but they thrive on North Fourth between Catherine and Ann, a block
south of Kerrytown and the Farmers' Market. The **People's Food Co-op** has
long hours and an impressive variety of unusual ingredients. Its neighbors
include **Wildflour** whole-grain bakery, **Birkenstock** shoes, and **Crazy
Wisdom** bookstore, strong on wholistic health, mysticism, Eastern religions,
and accoutrements from tarot cards and incense to crystals and jewelry.

CORRECTIONS AND UPDATES AS OF FALL 1992. . . . . . Though Ann Arbor
retailing isn't as volatile as Birmingham's, a fair amount of change is to be
expected. Since most of this book went to press, **Sixteen Hands** has moved to
216 S. Main. The **Lotus Gallery** has moved to 207 E. Washington. Prager Indonesian imports has become **Kioti** on Liberty just east of the Michigan Theater
and added Southwest Indian things to its stock. **Dawn Treader Books** has
moved aboveground and across the street next to Harry's Army Surplus on
Liberty at Thompson. Yet another big, crowded coffeehouse, **Gratzi's,** has
replaced the **Collected Works** branch at Liberty and State. And a scaled-down
version of the East Coast **Tower Records** chain is now on South University.

Campus-area shopping

The colorful U-M district mixes expensive clothing, exceptional book shops, inviting coffee and snack shops

Just a few blocks east of downtown lies a lively, cosmopolitan commercial district spawned by its proximity to the U-M central campus. On the often-crowded sidewalks around State and Liberty are a colorful mixture of college students, street people, professors, expensively dressed shoppers, and punks. The best vantage point for enjoying the passing scene is the outdoor tables or front windows of Espresse Royale, the popular Italian coffee bar on State opposite North University.

During the 1980s the State Street area changed from a focus on undergraduates to a more sophisticated, affluent clientele, with a growing concentration of specialty shops in some slick new buildings. At the same time, the area has become a nationally known center of book and record stores.

Retailing is anchored by **Jacobson's** department store and **Borders Book Shop**. Prominent historic landmarks include **Nickels Arcade**, an unusual 1915 arcade of elegant little shopfronts that runs through to Maynard from State Street opposite North University, and two movie theaters, the restored 1928 **Michigan Theater** (see p. 97) and the jazzy 1940 **State Theater** on State at Liberty. The State was recently converted into **Urban Outfitters**, featuring youth-oriented clothes and lifestyle accessories with retro looks. (Right now it's the 60s, with love beads and daisies.) Though first-run movies have vanished from the campus, the State's landmark neon sign is again fully operational.

Though much has changed from the memories of hundreds of thousands of Michigan graduates, a few things have stayed remarkably the same. The windows of the Caravan Shop in Nickels Arcade still have tiny china miniatures and the "All is vanity" picture seen two ways: a lovely turn-of-the-century woman primping at her mirror, or a skull. Moe Sport Shop at 711 North University is the same Go Blue bastion with vintage wood showcases. And next door, Drake's Sandwich Shop has the same 1930s soda-shoppe booths, same complicated ordering system, and similarly devoted fans among the current generation.

The intensity of foot traffic has enabled upper stories along State Street to be used for retailing. Venture upstairs, and you may find yourself in any of several different worlds: Ann Arbor's most civilized and scholarly bookstore (Shaman Drum, p. 98), a richly stocked comic shop (Dave's Comics at 623 E. William), an outstanding used recordings store full of intent pop music lovers seeking rarities and bargains (Wazoo Records, p. 102), or a haven for Grateful Dead fans, the Stairway to Heaven poster shop at 340 S. State. Rock tour T-shirts are another of its specialties.

STATE STREET AREA

State Street is a splendid place for browsing. See **Ann Arbor bookstores,** p. 98, and **Ann Arbor record stores,** p. 101. Among its other more unusual stores, arranged from west to east, are:

◆ **Harry's Army Surplus.** Big new campus location for a longtime student favorite. Everything from paint guns and throwing stars to genuine surplus East German border guards' coats. Good collection of discounted boots and camping equipment. *500 E. Liberty at Thompson. Mon-Fri 9-8, Sat 9-6, Sun 11-5.*

◆ **Collected Works.** Natural-fiber clothes and colorful imports. See p. 89. *222 S. State at Liberty. Mon-Sat 9:30-6, Fri to 8:30.*

◆ **Renaissance.** The costly European men's and women's clothing here, largely Italian, has a stylishly classic, contemporary look. *336 Maynard. Mon-Sat 10-6, Fri 'til 7.*

◆ **Matthew Hoffmann.** Expensive custom jewelry. Hoffmann, a self-taught phenomenon, has parlayed winning personal charm and enthusiasm into classy shops here and in Chicago and New York, supported by a base of loyal customer-friends.

◆ **Inside Nickels Arcade.** New additions have made browsing here more interesting than it's been in decades. For a glimpse of bygone Ann Arbor landmarks, check out Milt Kemnitz's paintings displayed in the **post office** at the Maynard Street end. Across the way, the **Caravan Shop** remains chock-full of choice imports like Chinese bowls, Russian lacquer boxes, baskets, Swiss music boxes, and Italian porcelains. **The Clay Gallery** is a cooperative of several area ceramics artists. **The Hundred-Acre Wood** is a tiny, charming children's bookshop, with well-chosen picture books and some toys. **The Arcadian** antique shop has loads of glassware and antique jewelry, most appealingly displayed. Cameos alone take up one case. Big basement space has furniture and quilts. Antique lamps cast a golden glow over all. **Van Boven's** fine men's shop, a longtime Ann Arbor fixture, specializes in traditional, classic quality. Its shoe store (for men and women) is just inside the arcade. *The arcade extends from Maynard south of Jacobson's to State. Store hours are typically Mon-Sat 9 or 10 to 5:30 or 6.*

◆ **Espresso Royale.** A dollar buys a delicious cup of cappucino and 80¢ a cup of espresso. Also, muffins, bagels, croissants, and European treats like poppyseed bread. This college-town chain has

recreated slick, high-tech Italian cafes without being offensively
cute or self-conscious about it. The State Street location is phenomenally popular; be prepared to stand in line. *324 S. State.
Mon-Fri 7 a.m.-midnight, Sat & Sun 9 a.m.-midnight.*

◆ **Steve's Ice Cream.** Popular spot has the best super-premium
ice cream in town, with a many toppings. New Englanders take
their ice cream very seriously; this is Michigan's only store in the
Boston-based chain. *State and William. 7 days noon-midnight.*

◆ **Drake Sandwich Shop.** Legendary campus sweet shoppe looks
much as it did when owner Truman Tibbals remodeled it in the
1930s. The pressed metal ceiling, pale green booths, and cluttered, darkened atmosphere are just as generations of Michigan
students remember them. Here you can get a wonderful glass of
fresh-squeezed limeade in the summer or hot chocolate in the
winter, plus sandwiches, cakes, and pies. Impulse items include
packaged teas and teapots and novelty candies like sea shells.
Another specialty is good chocolates, searched out by chocolate-
lover Tibbals. The butter almond toffee (2 oz. for $1.10) is
outstanding. *709 North University near State. Mon-Thurs 10 a.m. -
10:45 p.m., Fri & Sat to 11:45, Sun 3 p.m.-10:45 p.m.*

SOUTH UNIVERSITY COMMERCIAL DISTRICT

Three blocks of stores and restaurants along South University
connect the central campus with the fraternity and sorority area
along Washtenaw and Hill. Over the past ten years, the area's
character has come to be almost exclusively oriented to undergraduates, with a proliferation of fast-food chains. If you are unfor-
tunate enough to arrive by car at the top of the hour when classes
are getting out, you'll just have to wait, as there is no doubt in
these students' minds that pedestrians have the right of way.

◆ **Middle Earth.** One of the most entertaining shops in the entire
state. Nostalgia candy and novelties competes for space with a
striking display of beautiful jewelry, some quite expensive, including thousands of earrings. You'll find a wild and outrageous variety
of constantly changing "cheap thrills": life-size cardboard
standups of Michael Jordan, Magic Johnson, and George and Barbara Bush, Elvis troll dolls, inflatable pink Cadillacs. T-shirts are
also a big deal here — both funny and arty. Current favorite
imprints include "Pink Freud," "Homeboy Shopping Network"
from In Living Color, and a picture of the Milky Way captioned
"You are here." The first shop in town to sell bawdy greeting
cards, Middle Earth still has the most ribald selection, though
there are plenty of lovely, artistic cards any mother would love to
get. Over 20,000 offbeat post cards. *1209 South University. Mon-
Sat 10-7, Thurs & Fri 'til 9, Sun noon-5.*

◆ **Village Corner.** The VC obstinately keeps its scruffy, vaguely counter-culture ambience in the face of Ann Arbor's rampant gentrification. Clerks, often outlandishly clad, wait on you in amusingly surly fashion. You'd never realize a nationally known wine shop is in the back. The VC has one of Michigan's most sophisticated and wide-ranging selections of wine, from inexpensive to very fine — 4,000 kinds, along with 600 kinds of spirits. In the wine section, sales people are knowledgeable and willing to take the time to advise customers on their selections, even if it's a $5 bottle to accompany spaghetti and meatballs. Prices are reasonable, and deals on cases of wine are especially good. Masterfully clear and informative shelf descriptions of wines are likely written by Village Corner owner Dick Scheer, a well-known wine authority and judge. Ask for the free annotated catalog and newsletter. For picnics, the VC has a good selection of convenience and takeout food (fresh fruit, sandwiches, good bread and cheese) and groceries. *SE corner South University and Forest. (313) 995-1818. 7 days 8 a.m.-1 a.m.*

PARKING HINTS . . . . . On **State Street**, the best place to find a space is the staffed city structure entered off Maynard (by Jacobson's) or Thompson near Liberty. The metered Tally Hall garage off Washington between Division and State is another good choice, but you can't tell it's full until you get to the top, and you must have change. Both are 50¢/hr. . . . . . On **South University**,the metered 50¢/hour city structure on Forest just south of South University is your best bet.

A 1928 PICTURE PALACE . . . . . the **Michigan Theater** was bought by the city in the 1980s for use as a community venue rentable to any group. Splendidly restored to all its gilded grandeur, it has blossomed by filling in gaps in the city's formidable array of entertainment. The **drama series** features big-time productions from Broadway and leading regional theater companies. **Not Just For Kids** offers big-name family entertainment. The **Serious Fun** series consists of commercially tested avant-garde performers such as Laurie Anderson, Sankai Juku, and frequently Philip Glass. **Revival films** ($4.50) fill in the off-nights. Music on the big Barton theater organ frequently precedes movies. *Call (313) 668-8397, or stop by the theater entrance on Liberty at Maynard for a schedule.*

INTENSE STREET LIFE . . . . . comes to Ann Arbor each July during the **Art Fair** — actually three big fairs with a thousand artists, stretching from South University to Main Street. There's too much of everything — bargain-priced merchandise, art, food , hot weather — but people come back year after year. Two fairs include art of the highest caliber found at street fairs anywhere, while a third is more pedestrian but continually being upgraded. Some terrific area musicians perform on several stages. Wednesday through Saturday, in the last part of July. (313) 994-5260.

Bookstores in Ann Arbor

*The bookstore mecca of the Midwest is centered
at Liberty & State, near the U-M campus.*

Few places in the country have as lively, high-quality concentration of bookstores, both new and used, as does central Ann Arbor. Its anchor is the fabulously successful Borders. Ann Arborites buy more books per person than any other city in the United States, according to some surveys. Increasingly the town has become a magnet attracting book-lovers from distant cities.

Connoisseurs of antiquarian books would do well to pick up a listing of area dealers at any used-book store. It will direct them to several distinguished home book shops, such as Jan Longone's internationally known **Wine and Food Library**, which deals exclusively in out-of-print and rare publications on wine, food, and gastronomy. It's by appointment only; call (313) 663-4894.

♦ **Borders Book Shop.** Ann Arbor was a virtual trade book wasteland in 1971 when the two Borders brothers, former grad students, started their store in an obscure second-story retail space on William. It has become one of the very finest U. S. bookstores; now it's the flagship of a rapidly-growing, high-quality chain. Secrets of its success: knowledgeable, helpful clerks; a relentlessly attentive manager, Joe Gable; pleasing ambience; and outstanding back list. Over 90,000 titles. Quality remainders. Big children's and young adult section, with tables. An impressive selection of maps and better posters. *303 S. State at Liberty. (313) 668-7652. Mon-Sat 9-9, Sun 11-6.*

♦ **Shaman Drum Bookshop.** This serene, intimate, second-story shop, a few doors south of Borders, specializes in serious books in the humanities, chosen by its highly knowledgeable staff. Important books in religious studies, classical studies, literature and literary studies, poetry, Native American culture (owner Karl Pohrt's specialty), and anthropology. Frequent book signings. Table of free publications. Trade manager Keith Taylor, winner of a major poetry award, is most helpful at recommending good books for many tastes. A fine place to connect up with area book people. *313 1/2 S. State. (313) 662-662-7407. Mon-Fri 10-5:30, Sat 'til 4:30.*

♦ **Kaleidoscope.** Big space full of oddball old stuff: lots of books, also cameras, toys, magazines, sheet music, posters, and more. A knack for presentation makes it look great. Book condition isn't choice (some are library discards), but ample room means you can find things smaller stores couldn't afford to keep around. Stories for kids Sundays at 3. *217 S. State. (313) 995-9887. Mon-Wed 10-6, Thurs-Sat 10-8, Sun 1-5.*

◆ **David's Books.** Legendary, somewhat scruffy upstairs store, crowded with some 50,000 used books at quite reasonable prices. Good collection of new books on chess. *622 E. Liberty at State. (313) 665-8017. Mon-Sat 9:30 to 9 or 9:30, Sun 12-9.*

◆ **Dawn Treader.** Rambling spaces with general line, specialties in sci-fi, mysteries, natural history, math, science, philosophy, art, Americana, exploration. Some rare and early printing books in Liberty store. *525 E. Liberty near State (downstairs). (313) 995-1008. May-Oct: Mon-Sat 10-9, Sun 1-6. Winter: closes at 8. 1202 South University (downstairs). Mon-Sat 11-10, Sun 1-6.*

◆ **State Street Book Shop.** The fanciest of Ann Arbor's used bookstores, State Stre~~et~~ ~~spe~~cializes in angling books, first editions, and old ~~p~~ ~~pri~~nts (portraits, botanicals, views, medieval man ~~uscripts, Engl~~ish), in addition to its general-line stock. *31 ~~S.~~ State. (313) 994-4041. Mon-Sat 10-5:45, Sun 12-4.*

◆ **Books in General.** Big, airy, loft-like space. A large, round table makes this a pleasant place to sit down and browse through a huge stock of used books in literature, science, humanities. General line, better than usual sections in science and technology, foreign languages. *332 S. State (upstairs). (313) 769-1250. Mon-Sat 9:30-9, Sun 12-8.*

◆ **The Hundred-Acre Wood.** Children's picture books. See p. 95.

◆ **Barnes & Noble Bookstore.** Spiffy big textbook store also has, among its general reading books, a special section with English and American paperback editions of the classics. *In the basement of the Michigan Union, on State at South University. (313) 995-8877. Mon-Thurs 9-6, Fri 9-5, Sat 10-4, Sun 12-4. Shorter summer hours.*

◆ **Ulrich's Book Store.** The oldest textbook store in town, Ulrich's also has a good art supplies department and a big selection of U-M insignia items and inexpensive posters. *East University at South University. (313) 662-3201. Mon-Fri 8:30-5:30, Sat 9:30-5.*

◆ **Logos.** Large, attractive book and gift shop features mainly Christian, inspirational, self-help titles. General and religious gifts, cheerful greeting cards. Started decades ago by the Intervarsity Christian Fellowship to insure availability of religious books on campus. Store philosophy mixes religious and secular. *1205 South University. (313) 761-7177. Mon-Thurs 9:30-6, Fri & Sat to 9, Sun 12-5. Shorter Sunday hours in summer.*

◆ **Community Newscenters.** Both Ann Arbor stores of this Lansing-based chain have an outstanding magazine section, as well as a selection of paperback and hardcover books that's surprising for newsstands. The extraordinarily long hours of these lower-level stores are an impulse browser's delight. *330 E. Liberty west of Division. (313) 663-6168. 7 days 7:30 a.m.-11 p.m. Second location: 1301 South University at Forest. (313) 662-6150. 7 days 8:30 a.m.-11 p.m.*

◆ **Common Language.** "For women and their friends." Feminist and gay studies, erotica, also mainstream books like detective series where the detective is not a white man. Kids' books stress positives of being different, having a gay parent, etc. *214 S. Fourth. (313) 663-0036. Tues-Fri 12-8, Sat 11-8, Sun 12-4.*

◆ **Falling Water Books and Collectables.** New Age books, plus crystals, other minerals, gifts. *213 S. Main. (313) 747-9810. Mon-Sat 10-10, Sun 12-6.*

◆ **After Words.** Attractively laid out and good for browsing, this good-sized store carries drastically discounted new books. A third are remainders, two-thirds are still in print but at least 40% off. *219 S. Main. (313) 996-2808. Mon-Sat 10-10, Sun 12-8.*

◆ **West Side Book Shop.** This delightful shop fits the traditional image of a used bookstore: antique in a comfortable way, cluttered, accented with old prints, and personal — conducive to browsing and chatting. Space constraints make for higher quality. General-line, with nautical topics, exploration, and photography as specialties. Edward Curtis Indian photographs, other old photographs in antique-filled back room. *113 W. Liberty just west of Main. (313) 995-1891. Mon-Fri 11-6, Sat 10-5.*

◆ **Wooden Spoon.** The Wooden Spoon is in the very spot where the legendary Joe's saloon once was. Its many rooms have a distinctly dusty, well-worn aura. Specialities include cookbooks, books on gardening, literary criticism, history, regional Americana, and arts and crafts. Unusually low prices. *200 N. Fourth Ave. at Ann. (313) 769-4775. Mon, Tues & Thurs 9:30-4, Wed & Fri 9:30-6, Sat 7:30-5, Sun 1-5.*

◆ **Crazy Wisdom.** A new owner has expanded and deepened titles in metaphysical and holistic subjects, including holistic health, bodywork, Jungian and transpersonal psychology, Buddhism, and women's spirituality. Also, audiotapes, jewelry, and interesting objects. *206 N. Fourth Ave. (313) 665-2757. Mon & Tues 10-6, Wed-Fri 10-8, Sat 10-6, Sun 12-6.*

Ann Arbor record stores

*For CDs, tapes, and even discs,
the selection is vast in the State and Liberty area.*

Music-lovers from across the U.S. consider Ann Arbor the
best place to shop for recordings because of the outstanding comparison-shopping permitted by the concentration
of high-quality stores. In its 15 years here, Schoolkids has grown
into the musical equivalent of Borders Books. The 1991 opening
of a branch of Tower Records on South University will certainly
affect the local marketing scene. That monster store, known for
selection, could take away a good deal of the mainstream market
from existing stores.

Most record stores are open evenings and Sunday afternoons.

◆ **Schoolkids Records & Tapes.** Early on, Schoolkids learned
that having a great back list in the right town can build a market
dramatically. Its strength is its breadth and depth in everything
from rock and jazz to country, folk, blues, and new age, including
esoteric labels and foreign pressings. Some CDs it imports direct.
Vinyl, which held on longer here, is being phased out. Prices are
below that of most big U.S. chains. No returns. Good place to pick
up information; the staff is knowledgeable and helpful. *523 E. Liberty. (313) 994-8031. Mon-Sat 100-9:30, Sun noon-8.*

◆ **SKR Classical.** SKR's relatively recent classical music store is a
Schoolkids' subsidiary, managed by Jim Leonard. Passionately
opinionated when he was a music critic, he's a most approachable
advisor for people who are intimidated by classical music and
their ignorance of it. He strives for a user-friendly, anti-snobbish
store, started a **newsletter,** and instituted Sunday **music appreciation classes** from 1 to 2 p.m. SKR has the state's biggest collection of classical compact disks, and a great many tapes. It also has
scores and many pirate tapes of live performances. *539 E. Liberty.
(313) 995-5051. Mon-Thurs 10-8, Fri & Sat 10-9, Sun 12-6.*

◆ **Liberty Music.** The granddaddy of Ann Arbor's great record
stores, Liberty was one of North America's best-known classical
music shops for decades. Now it deals only in used CDs and LPs.
Other specialties are show tunes, band music, spoken word,
children's, and international. Its tradition of almost incredible
personal service, including mail order, continues. *417 E. Liberty
at Thompson. (313) 662-0675. Mon-Sat 10-5:30.*

◆ **Discount Records.** Discount covers all the pop, jazz, and classical bases and keeps local prices competitive. *State and Liberty. (313) 665-3679. Mon-Thurs 9-9, Fri & Sat 9-10, Sun 12-8.*

◆ **State Discount.** A campus general store, State is known by music buffs not as a source of shampoo and snacks but as the cheapest place in town to buy just-released, mass-volume CDs. *309 S. State. (313) 994-1262. Mon-Fri 8:30-9, Sat 10-7, Sun 12-6.*

◆ **Wazoo Records.** This upstairs store has a well-organized stock of used vinyl and CD records and tapes (mostly rock, but with big sections of jazz, country, folk, classical). Reasonable prices ($4.50 for most vinyl records, $5-10 for used CDs). A stock of newly released CDs encourages trade-ins. Used CDs run $5-$10. Everything is guaranteed. The only scratchy records you'll find here are rare ones. Good prices paid for used records. *336 1/2 S. State (upstairs) (313) 761-8686. Mon-Fri 10-8, Sat 10-6, Sun 12-6.*

◆ **PJ's Used Records and CDs.** PJ's is an interesting used record store run by knowledgeable jazz, R&B, and blues enthusiasts. "Opinions rendered on all subjects," they advertise. *617B (upstairs) Packard between Hill and State. (313) 663-3441. Mon-Thurs 10-9, Fri & Sat 10-10, Sun noon-8.*

◆ **Earth Wisdom Music.** A purveyor of New Age music for meditation, relaxation, guided imagery, "creative ambiance," and dance, Earth Wisdom has been around since before the genre became a Muzak for the 80s. *Inside Seva Restaurant, 314 E. Liberty. 769-0969. Mon & Tues 11-7, Wed-Sat 11-8:30, Sun 11-2:30.*

RARE BOOKS IN A STATELY SETTING . . . . . Next door to the President's House on South University across from Tappan, the **Clements Library** has one of the country's leading collections of rare books, manuscripts, and maps on America through the 19th century. The library is patterned on an Italian Renaissance villa. The style was chosen to reflect the age of great explorers and cartographers who opened up the Americas. Beyond the ornate bronze grilles on the entrance doors is the grand main reading room. Antiques are on display throughout. A grandfather clock comes from George Washington's 1782-83 headquarters at New Windsor, New York, a gift from Carl Van Doren, who used the library to write his *Secret History of the Revolution.* A collection of Amberina glassware, fashionable in the 1880s, was made by the New England firm which eventually moved to Toledo, Ohio, and became Libbey Glass. At the west end of the room is one of the most popular paintings of 18th-century England, Benjamin West's *The Death of General Wolfe.* The painting shows British General Wolfe, fatally wounded, surrounded by his staff. The year was 1759, just after Wolfe had completed a victory over the French at Quebec, sealing British control over North America *909 S. University at Tappan. (313) 764-2347. Mon-Fri 10:30-12, 1-5.*

U-M Museums

In a small campus area are
three of the state's finest museums.

O ne of the country's top research universities for a over a century, the U-M has developed over the decades three exceptional museums. They are:

◆ **U-M Exhibit Museum.** Not many other natural science museums in the country match the rarity and breadth of items on display here. The very number of displays can be overwhelming, however, and most of the explanatory signs are beyond most visitors' interest and knowledge levels.

Still, there's much here to interest most visitors. Over the decades the staff has meticulously constructed dozens of dioramas — miniature three-dimensional scenes which vividly show life on Earth in the distant past. View a lush scene from a Pennsylvania forest 300 million years ago when giant insects abounded, dragonflies had 30-inch wingspans, and huge roaches crawled among gigantic palm trees. Another diorama shows what New England looked like 10 million years ago when populated with camels, primitive elephants, short rhinoceroses, and rodents the size of woodchucks. You can see Los Angeles 15 millions ago when sabertooth tigers roamed the region.

A series of seven dioramas reveals the evolution of life, beginning way back in the Cambrian age 575 million years ago when crab-like creatures were the most sophisticated beasts around. You also get an intriguing glimpse into the villages of the various Indian tribes who inhabited Michigan before Europeans arrived.

An area of special interest to children is the dinosaur section, seven skeletons strong, highlighted by the looming remains of a big allosaurus that roamed Utah 140 million years ago. The flesh-eating giant had forbiddingly long claws and sharp, menacing teeth. More subtle but also evocative are the various fossil footprints made by dinosaurs millions of years ago.

The museum has a nifty **gift shop** on the ground floor, full of all sorts of small items to delight kids, along with some interesting jewelry, nature publications, and folk art.

The 4th-floor **planetarium** has changing shows ($1/person, no children under 5) on Saturday mornings at 10:30 and 11:30 and weekend afternoons at 2, 3, and 4. Weekday showings are by advance reservation only. *1109 Geddes Ave. where it intersects with N. University. (313) 764-0478. Tues-Sat 9-5, Sun 1-5. Free.*

◆ **Kelsey Museum of Archaeology.** This small but important museum has two special attractions. The first is the 1891 building itself, made of local fieldstone in the Richardsonian Romanesque style. Originally called Newberry Hall, it was built to house the private Student Christian Association. Great pains were taken in choosing beautiful stones for the structure. The decorative glass and woodwork, blue slate roof, and imposing front turret combine to make this a memorable campus landmark.

Inside is stored one of the most important collections of ancient Greek, Egyptian, Roman, and Near Eastern artifacts. Only a fraction of the 90,000-piece collection is on permanent display, and what you see is very choice indeed. Colorful Egyptian mummy masks, exquisite Greek black-and-red-figured vase paintings, rare and amazingly intact Roman glass are all presented in a comfortable, intimate setting which encourages close study. Most surprising of all, perhaps, are the early Egyptian sculptures, dating from 2400 to 200 B.C.. They reveal remarkable artistic skill. *434 S. State, across from Angell Hall. Sept-Apr: Mon-Fri 9-4, Sat & Sun 1-4. May-Aug: Tues-Fri 11-4, Sat & Sun 1-4. Call (313) 764-9304 for general information and special exhibits.*

◆ **U-M Museum of Art.** This is considered among the top ten university art museums in the country. The permanent collection of over 20,000 includes works by Dürer, Delacroix, Rodin, Picasso, Rembrandt, Corot, Millet, Monet, Cezanne, Miro, and Klee. Well-known paintings on permanent display include Expressionist Max Beckman's *Begin the Beguine,* the Italian Baroque painter Guercino's *Esther before Ahasuerus,* and Carl Wimar's dramatic portrayal of the American West, *Attack on an Emigrant Train.*

Collections of Whistler prints and German Expressionist paintings are outstanding, and there is a large collection from China and Japan. One remarkable work is "Autumn Colors At Jushan." Drawn about the year 1700, it shows in detail a walled town and fishing villages in front of mountains along a river bank.

The small **gift shop** has a choice assortment of cards, art publications, posters, handmade and ethnic jewelry, folk art and craft collectibles. An enthusiastic, high-caliber staff of volunteer docents conducts regularly scheduled free tours. Each Sunday at 2 pm., a different adult-oriented **gallery tour** focuses on one part of the collection. Lunchtime **art breaks** (Tues & Thurs at 12:10 and 12:30) explain one object or part of a show. For free group tours, call (313) 747-2067. *525 S. State at South University. (313) 764-0395. Sept-May: Tues-Fri 10-4, Sat-Sun 1-5. June-Aug: Tues-Fri 11-4, Sat-Sun 1-5. Free.*

THE HEART OF THE CAMPUS . . . . . is the **Diag**, the diagonal walk crossing the original 40-acre campus between the retail districts on State and North University and on South University at East University. Many major classroom buildings are clustered here, backing up to a plaza in front of the Graduate Library. Countless rallies and demonstrations have been held here. On pleasant days, this is a good place to see students and their myriad organizations and causes set up here to garner support. The action spills over into the adjacent **Fishbowl**, a large-windowed connecting hall between classroom buildings to the west.

THE FIRST STUDENT UNION . . . . . was the venerable **Michigan Union** on State at the head of South University, built in 1920. On its front steps President Kennedy first announced the Peace Corps, saying "Ask not what your country can do for you, but what you can do for your country." For many years women were only allowed entrance to the Union through a side door, and then only for special events. The second-floor **billiard room** was the last male bastion to fall, in the late 1960s. It remains one the Union's most interesting areas. With oak paneling and quality tables, the room retains the atmosphere of gentlemen's gaming rooms in decades past. Some of the country's best players still drop in to play here. In the slickly remodeled Union basement is a a big **Barnes and Noble student book store** and large **food court**.

CARILLON CONCERTS BY A PLAYFUL FOUNTAIN . . . . . . The Union's female counterpart as a student center was the 1929 **Michigan League** on North University at the Ingalls Mall, a rather grand axis between the graduate library and the monumental Art Deco/neoclassical Rackham Building on Washington Street. Smaller than the Union, the League has long been popular for its well-stocked newsstand at the front desk, its large and excellent **cafeteria**, and its basement grill. The League also houses the 700-seat **Lydia Mendelssohn Theater**, Ann Arbor's most congenial space for theatrical performances. . . . . . Between the League and tall Burton Tower is the delightful **Cooley Fountain** created by Swedish sculptor Carl Milles in 1940, when he was on the Cranbrook faculty. It shows Triton, the Greek god of the sea, frolicking with his children. . . . . . Across from the League is **Burton Tower**, a campus landmark. At its top is the **Baird Carillon**. Its 53 bronze bells weigh from 12 pounds to 12 tons. **Half-hour concerts** begin weekdays at noon when school is in session. During that time you can go up to the top and see the single player pound hand and foot levers in quick succession to ring the bells. The tower offers a fine view of the campus. On the eighth floor is the **Japanese music room**, with tatami mats. Its instruments can be heard when School of Music students practice there Tuesdays between noon and 9 p.m., September through April. Likewise, the **gamelan** or Indonesian orchestra can be heard in practice on the fourth floor Thursday afternoons and evenings.

A BIT OF OXFORD AND CAMBRIDGE IN THE MIDDLE WEST . . . . . Right across State Street from the Union is the **Law Quadrangle**, home of the U-M's highly ranked law school. This picturesque court of Gothic buildings was built between 1923 and 1933 and largely modeled on Cambridge. The Law Quad's quality of workmanship was rare even in the 1920s. The striking reading room of the **old Law Library** at the south side of the quadrangle has richly ornamented blue and gold plaster medallions decorating the ceiling.

North Campus

Visitor attractions at the U-M's newer Ann Arbor campus range from a nuclear reactor to a presidential library.

This outlying 800-acre campus across the Huron River northeast of the Central Campus was planned in the 1940s, when residential neighborhoods blocked future growth of the university in central Ann Arbor. Famous architect Eero Saarinen planned the new campus, which includes the College of Engineering, School of Music, and the combined School of Art and College of Architecture and Urban Planning. The **Art School snack bar**, open from 8 a.m. to 10 p.m. weekdays, Saturdays 8 to 5, may well be the most interesting place to eat out here, with a good selection of deli sandwiches, fresh bagels and donuts, trail mix, and the like.

Major attractions are:

◆ **Phoenix Memorial Laboratory.** The two-megawatt experimental nuclear reactor built here in 1954 was one of the first university reactors in the postwar surge of research interest in peaceful applications of atomic energy. Half-hour tours are available by appointment Monday through Friday. *Bonisteel Blvd. near Beal. (313) 764-6220.*

◆ **Gerald R. Ford Presidential Library.** This is one of only eight presidential libraries in the country. It's here because Ford was a 1935 graduate of the U-M. Scholars from around the world come here to delve into myriad issues affected by the Ford presidency. The library's 15 million pages of documents brought from Washington include all of Ford's White House papers as well as the papers of certain key advisors such as economist Arthur Burns and energy chief Frank Zarb. Some papers remain classified and are kept in locked vaults, but most are available for public scrutiny. *1000 Beal south of Bonisteel Blvd. (313) 668-2218. Mon-Fri 9-4:30.*

◆ **Stearns Collection of Musical Instruments.** The core of this unusual collection is 1,400 instruments collected by wealthy Detroit drug manufacturer Frederick Stearns and donated to the university in 1899. They include some extremely rare Asian and African instruments along with European instruments like a Baroque cello in almost-original condition and a recorder from Leipzig at the time of Bach.

The collection, now over 2,000 and growing, is intended to be encyclopedic, representing instruments of all sorts from throughout the world. New additions, including the first Moog synthesizer to be sold, reflect an effort to collect 20th-century materials. Interesting lecture-demonstrations are held at 2 o'clock on the second Sundays of September, October, January, and February. *In the new Dow Towsley south wing of the Moore Building, the main part of the School of Music, at the end of Baits Dr. (Baits is off Broadway at the top of the hill, about 1/4 mile west of Plymouth Rd. Or, from Murfin on North Campus, take Duffield to Baits.) (313) 763-4389. Thurs & Fri 10-5, Sat & Sun 1-6. Free.*

THE BIGGEST COLLEGIATE STADIUM IN THE U.S. . . . . is **Michigan Stadium** on Stadium at Main. It seats over 101,000, but they're packed in mighty tight. The stadium is dug into the side of a valley wall; the football field lies directly over Allen's Creek. If you could put your ear down on the 50-yard line when the stands are empty, you could hear the creek running. Next door is **Crisler Arena**, which seats 13,60. It hosts concerts, NCAA wrestling and gymnastics matches, as well as U-M basketball and gymnastics.

HEADQUARTERS OF TOM MONAGHAN'S PIZZA EMPIRE . . . . . **Domino's Farms** is intended to be a major tourist attraction, but things at the complex are in constant flux. The almost-new car museum has already shrunk to half its original size, and the impressive architecture bookshop has been combined with other shops. Still, it can be a worthwhile place if you're interested classic cars, Eskimo art, the Detroit Tigers, Frank Lloyd Wright, or Monaghan himself and the drama of how a very wealthy, enthusiastic, grandiose, and religious man chooses to spend his dough.

The long, low Prairie House was inspired by the work of Monaghan hero Frank Lloyd Wright. It's planned to be over half a mile long when finished, topped by the world's longest copper roof. As you enter just behind the 23 international flags (one flag for each country where Domino's operates), the building looks like a parody of the serene, organic spirit of Wright, ominously out of scale in a Brave New World sort of way.

Attractions include:

◆ **Monaghan's office.** Two stories of luxury, with leather-tiled floor and gold bathroom fixtures. He prefers to work in an adjacent, austere cubicle, reflecting his conflicting ascetic, priestly side. Weekend tours include the office, board room, fitness center, and in-house Pizza Store. Inquire at Exhibition Hall.

◆ **Domino's Center for Architecture and Design.** Museum featuring the world's largest collection of decorative designs created by Wright, plus works by designers who worked with him: art glass, ceramics, and furniture. Taken out of context, the emotional impact of his total interiors is drained. Huge photos of complete interiors try to fill that gap. Best attraction: Wright's drawings of the exteriors and interiors of many projects. Wright's subtle draftsmanship was renowned.

◆ **Domino's Classic Cars.** Though the collection is smaller, the sophisticated setting remains, and the cars look great. Hundreds of small spotlights highlight their special features, and visitors can get up close to the cars. The centerpiece remains the 1931 Bugatti Royale, the personal car of the luxury carmaker, which cost $8.1 million in 1986. Old jukeboxes, classic bikes, toys and kiddie cars, and dune buggies add to the fun.

◆ **Domino's Detroit Tigers Museum.** Artifacts, photos, and more about the venerable team owned by Monaghan.

◆ **Eskimo Art.** Soapstone, ivory, and bone carvings by the seminomadic Eskimos of Canada's eastern Arctic. Their art, often fashioned from the animals they hunt, shows life through the keenly observant eyes of hunters. Forms are smooth, round, and simple. Ann Arbor microfilm pioneer Eugene Powers has been among the collectors and artist to encourage the Inuit people to continue their traditional art and to help find new markets for it. Prices range from around $40 for small carvings to over $4,000, with most between $100 and $200. The popular $15 calendar has reproductions of stone block prints, stencils, and lithographs. *Tues, Wed, Fri 10-2 or by appt. 668-7319.*

◆ **Petting Farm.** The authentic farmy atmosphere in this fine old barn has been jazzed up by a farmer-entertainer who squirts milk at kids and tells corny jokes at Farmer John's Barnyard Show on weekends (12:30, 2:30, 4:30). Some people love it, others find it grotesque. The animals — some four dozen — are the best part. They don't try to be funny. *Look for the big red barn at the end of the entry road. $2/adults, $1/ children 6-12.*

◆ **Artifacts.** Gift shop/book store relating to Domino's, classic cars, architecture, and Detroit Tigers.

◆ **Four restaurants. Prairie Cafe** in Exhibition Hall has hot dogs, sandwiches, snacks. Inquire on how to get to employee dining (open to public, weekdays only) at **Pizza Store, EBA** (Everything but anchovies) general cafeteria. $7 buffet at **Mario's Executive Dining Room**, prepared by top-notch catering staff, must be reserved in advance (665-9663).

Domino's Farms is just east of U.S. 23 (take exit 41) off Plymouth Rd. Except for the petting farm, Domino's activities are headquartered at Exhibition Hall, the farthest main building from the entrance, with the flags in front. (313) 995-4258 (tour info), (313) 930-3033 (special events info). Passport includes separate tickets to all museums: adults $6, kids 6-12 and seniors $4, family (up to 5 members) $15.

Holly

A brawling saloon town long ago,
Holly now draws antiquers and tourists.

This town of about 5,600 nestles in the low hills and lakes at Oakland County's very northwestern corner. It's a pastoral contrast to the densely populated suburbs to the southeast. The well-preserved downtown is a tourist attraction, highlighted by the infamous **Battle Alley** between Saginaw and Broad, a block southeast of the center of town. Brawls among taverngoers were once common here, hence the name. A well deserved Battle Alley attraction is the **Holly Hotel**, now a restaurant (see p. 125). Built in the mid-19th century, it combines very good food with an exceptional Victorian decor that feels authentic without becoming a silly parody of that era.

Stimulated by a number of festivals each year, Holly has developed a number of tourist attractions. A festival on the weekend after Labor Day celebrates the time axe-wielding temperance crusader Carry Nation staged her felonious assault on Battle Alley taverns, smashing whiskey bottles right and left. The Michigan Renaissance Festival recreates a medieval fair and joust on weekends in August and September. Weekends in December, Dickens characters perform on the streets.

Of special interest to visitors are:

◆ **Battle Alley.** Holly's 19th-century prominence as a rail and lumber center resulted in a big concentration of saloons between here and the nearby depot. Today these buildings house shops ranging from kitschy to unusual and even outstanding. They carry women's fashions, old coins, decorative and kitchen accessories, Hawaiian clothing and accessories, and Hong Kong imports. *South end of downtown, off Saginaw St. Open Sundays.*

◆ **Balcony Row Antiques.** In some ways this place is more like a museum than a store. The name commemorates the old opera house, replaced by a plain block post office now completely covered over with an assemblage of architectural artifacts. Globetrotting proprietors Evelyn Raskin and Jim Hilty, who developed Battle Alley, don't buy anything they don't like. As a result, this rambling 14-room store is filled with some choice furniture, china, and art objects from Europe and the U.S. (going back to the 18th century and even much earlier) and ancient Egypt. *216 S. Broad. (313) 634-1400. Thurs-Sun 1-5.*

◆ **Water Tower Antique Mall.** Sixty or so dealers in three inter-connected buildings offer a great variety of merchandise, from primitives to Art Deco. *310 Broad St., around the corner from Battle Alley. (313) 634-3500. Mon-Sat 10-5, Sun 12-5.*

◆ **Detroit Model Railroad Club.** Since it bought the old Holly Theater here in the early 1970s, the Detroit Model Railroad Club has been working on a huge layout in "O" gauge, twice the size of the usual HO model trains, and correspondingly more realistic in detailing. Every Tuesday evening, club members come to work on the scenery, which is a cross-section of the U.S., with valleys, countryside and cities, and lots of switchyards for plenty of switching action. Visitors are welcome to drop by then or Sundays and see what they're up to. Radio controls guide trains on 2,000 feet of track. *104 N. Saginaw, just north of Maple St. (Holly Rd.) in downtown Holly. Call (313) 634-9167. 2nd Sunday of month, noon-5.*

◆ **Holly Recreation Area.** This spread-out recreation area east of Holly includes nearly all the wonderfully diverse terrains and habitats that go with Michigan's belts of glacial landscapes: lakes (over 20, good for fishing, with no motors allowed), high hills with mature woods and big trees, wetlands, and open fields. It makes for very good nature observation.

There's a good mix of trees for fine fall colors. Off the drive from the Grange Hall Road park entrance to Wildwood Beach is a **scenic overlook.** Three **hiking trails** total 25 miles; a short one circles two heavily used lakes, while the others extend into more remote areas. Ask for a map at the headquarters. In winter there are 10 miles of **cross-country ski trails** around the beach and campground areas (parts are easy and parts are challenging) and 15 miles of **snowmobile trails** in a separate area west of I-75.

Heron Beach is on Heron Lake close to the day-use park entrance on Grange Hall Road. It is big, often very crowded, and treeless. Boats and canoes can be rented here. At the end of a road that winds alongside Heron and Wildwood lakes is the much nicer **Wildwood Beach**, small, quiet, and shady. Picnic areas along this road either offer hilltop views or wooded shoreline settings.

Near a third interconnected lake is the **McGinniss Lake Camp-ground**, with 160 large lots made unusually private by many trees and shrubs. It seldom fills up, even on summer weekends, and it has all the amenities of a modern campground — showers, flush toilets, a dump station, and 80 year-round sites with electrical hookups — without cramped conditions. *Headquarters and maps: 8100 Grange Hall Rd. just east of Dixie Hwy. From I-75 north of Pontiac, take Grange Hall Rd. exit 101 and go east about 2.5 miles. (313) 634-8811. State park sticker required: $3/day or*

$15/year.

◆ **Mt. Holly.** Seventeen trails at this ski lodge are served by five rope tows and seven chairlifts, including a slow, easy-to-ride beginner's lift. Lessons include Kinder-Sparks Ski Instruction for 4-10-year-olds. Mt. Holly claims to have the area's largest, most efficient rental system. Three lounges include one with live entertainment and drinks. *13536 S. Dixie Hwy. north of Grange Hall Rd. From I-75 and U.S. 23.*

Fenton maps and information: *For maps of Fenton and nearby Seven Lakes State Park, plus brochures about events and visitor destinations, contact the Chamber of Commerce, 207 Silver Lake Rd., Fenton, MI 48430. (313) 629-5447. A helpful map on the entire Holly, Fenton, and Linden area including golf courses, recreation areas, local beaches, & ski areas is $2.*

IN NEARBY FENTON . . . . . the **Fenton Museum** has the quaint, informal ambience of a true small-town historical museum with a wide assortment of local artifacts. *301 S. Leroy St., Fenton, Michigan. (313) 629-0549. Open Mon-Fri 12-4, Sun 1-4.* . . . . . Also in Fenton, next to the noisily rushing waters of the Shiawassee River, is a big, old-fashioned **gazebo**, dramatically situated just below the serene mill pond. Built in 1980, the gazebo has quickly become a Fenton focal point and a favorite spot for weddings. It is a great place for a picnic. Just south on LeRoy you can pick up a tasty takeout lunch or snack at **Brick's Oven Bakery** or at the **Fenton House Carryout.** *Leroy at Mill streets.*

SOUTHEAST MICHIGAN'S ONLY COMMERCIAL VINEYARD . . . . is the **Seven Lakes Vineyard Orchard & Cider Mill**, just northeast of Fenton. 100 hilly acres include 35 acres of woods and 15 acres of apple trees. Visitors are invited to taste the wine. Vignoles and their Cady Lake blended white wine have done especially well. Home winemakers may buy bottles and fresh grape juice by the jug or barrel in September and October. Eight varieties of apples are also for sale. You can pick your own. From late September to Thanksgiving a very good apple cider is available on weekends, along with doughnuts. You are welcome to **picnic** at the tables here. Maps of the **walking trails** are available. *1111 Tinsman Rd near Eddy Lake Rd., northeast of Fenton and near Seven Lakes State Park. (313) 629-5686. Mon-Sat 10-5, Sun noon to 5. In winter by appointment.*

Sloan Museum

*One of the state's top museums skillfully illuminates
Flint's fascinating lumbering and auto history.*

Vivid displays show how lumbering turned the small city of
Flint into a 19th-century boom town, generating more
money than the Gold Rush out West. Other exhibits show
how Flint went on to become a leading manufacturing center,
first for carriages and then for autos. There is also a choice selection of splendid old American automobiles.

The centerpiece of the section on Flint's lumbering era is a
vast miniature model of a Michigan lumber company, from the
lumberjacks' camp to the big mill which cut the logs into boards.
"Michigan's lumbering era lasted slightly over four decades,"
concludes one of the unusually well-written captions. "Thousands
of square miles of fine-grained white pine were cut. It had been
the largest virgin white pine forest in the world when the lumbermen moved in. When they left, there remained only miles and
miles of stumps."

Two memorable full-scale displays depict scenes from Flint's
early auto years. One is the ornate dining room of Flint banker
A.G. Bishop, showing a manikin of Bishop with that amazing
entrepreneur, Billy Durant, the Flint resident who founded General Motors. The time was 1905, and the men signing the
agreement insuring that Buicks would continue to be manufactured in Flint rather than Jackson. Durant had already helped
make Flint the country's leading carriage-making center. Just
three years after he took over Buick, it had become the country's
leading auto manufacturer, producing more cars than Ford and
Cadillac combined.

A full-scale tarpaper shack symbolizes the desperate housing
shortage in Flint as its auto industry boomed. In 1910, Flint's
population had jumped in just six years from 15,000 to 39,000,
making it America's most congested city. A thousand homeless
workers camped on the banks of the Flint River, unable to buy or
rent a place to stay. Tarpaper shacks, tents, and empty piano
crates were common housing, even in winter. Inside the museum's shack panoramic photos reveal these squalid scenes.

The **display of historic autos** here is a delight even for nonen-
thusiasts. The gleaming cars are shown against an appealing
background of advertising signs and enlarged photos of old gas
stations. The sporty, bright red 1910 Buick "Bug," Buick's racing

car, reached 106 mph. One of its racing team members was none other than Louis Chevrolet. After the banker-dominated GM board of directors shoved Durant aside, he teamed up with Chevrolet to create Chevrolet Motors, eventually earning enough to buy back control of GM.

The oldest production-model Chevrolet in existence, the unsuccessful 1912 Classic Six, looks like it just came out of the factory. More historically significant is the famous Chevy "490," which became the world's top-selling line by 1918. Most eye-catching of all is the futuristic 1959 Cadillac Cyclone, a non-production concept car which still looks modern today. In its nose-cone, radar devices signal the driver as objects approach the vehicle.

1221 E. Kearsley in Flint's Cultural Center. From I-75 and the south, take I-475 north to Exit 8A (Longway Blvd.), turn right at 1st light, turn right at next street (Forest). Park on your right. (313) 760-1169. Tues-Fri 10-5, Sat & Sun 12-5. Open Mon in July & August. $3 adults, $2 children 5-12.

A SCENIC PICNIC SPOT IN DOWNTOWN FLINT . . . . Riverbank Park along the Flint River is an unusually elaborate urban park, the outgrowth of needed flood-control measures. Four and one half blocks long, it has flower gardens, picnic sites, a playground, a large amphitheater, and a fish ladder for the big salmon migrating upriver in the fall. There is even a water-powered Archimedes screw which lifts water to create multiple waterfalls. In the fall it's exciting to see the **fish ladder** and watch for giant coho and chinook salmon swimming upriver from Lake Huron to spawn. The greatest migration is usually from late September through October. A nifty pictorial **monument** commemorates the 50th anniversary of the UAW Flint Sitdown Strike. It's across the river from the University of Michigan Flint, at the park's east end. The handsome display features big, rather primitive mural paintings on Pewabic tiles. One shows the great Flint Sitdown strike of 1936-37 at Fisher Body Plants 1 & 2. The other shows workers in an automobile plant. An amusing touch is the benches in front of the displays: tan concrete car seats.

BEST PIPE SHOP IN THE MIDWEST . . . . . Paul's Pipe Shop at 647 S. Saginaw in downtown Flint stocks over a million pipes ranging from a $1.49 corncob to a $5,000 Dunhill. Pipes cram the shop; even more are stored on the second story. Owner Paul Spaniola's best selling tobacco is his "58th Anniversary" blend — $2.25 for 2 ounces. Cigars fill another climate-controlled room. Paul boils his own Cayuga pipes in a special South American nut oil and claims flatly is "the best pipe you ever smoked." Paul himself is a five-time winner of the world pipe-smoking title. (The person who can smoke his pipe the longest wins.) Mon-Sat 9-7.

Flint Institute of Arts

Splendid 19th-century French paintings help make this a leading Midwestern art museum.

Generous donations from wealthy Flint citizens have built this into the state's second most prominent art museum, behind only the Detroit Institute of Arts. An exceptional collection of **19th-century French paintings**, mostly landscapes, includes worksby Corot, Courbet, Renoir, and Toulouse-Lautrec.

The **Bray Renaissance Gallery** is a Renaissance-style hall, with an ornate coffered ceiling and marble floor. It houses an impressive collection of 15th- to 17th-century European works of art, including furniture, paintings, and tapestries. The museum's collection of Oriental vases and sculptures is also noteworthy.

Another highlight is the stunning **paperweight collection** donated by a wealthy local patron. In the 19th century paperweights were popular collectors' items, and some are true works of art. Here many exceptional French mid-19th century pieces are beautifully displayed in special illuminated wall cases.

The **gift shop** includes decorator items, handmade contemporary jewelry, scarves, art books, toys, cards, and souvenirs.

1120 E. Kearsley, in Flint's Cultural Center. From I-475 from the south, get off at the Court St. exit, turn right, go to 2nd light, turn left onto Crapo. At the next light, turn right onto Kearsley. (313) 234-1695. Tues-Sat 10-5, Sun 1-5. Oct-May 7 p.m.-9 p.m.

MICHIGAN'S LARGEST PLANETARIUM . . . . . is the state's **Longway Planetarium**, with a 60-foot domed screen for an especially realistic depiction of the skies. It's the same size as the big planetaria in Chicago and New York. Entertaining multi-media shows change every three to five months and explore the skies, ancient mythology and the constellations, science fiction, and space travel, in addition to a regular show about the current season's sky. An excellent **gift counter** has astronomy- and space-related T-shirts, stickers, books, posters, and hard-to-find educational items. Gift and **exhibit areas** are open 9-5 weekdays. Individuals are welcome to tag along with any school group coming to see shows during the week. *1310 E. Kearsley in the Cultural Center. From I-475 from the south, take Longway Blvd. exit, go 2 blocks east to Walnut and turn right. (313) 760-1181. Regular astronomy shows ($3/adults, $2/kids and seniors) are scheduled Thurs-Sun, with weekend matinees.*

Buick City Tour

Robots make Buicks in one of the country's most sophisticated factories.

Buick City is one of the country's most interesting industrial tours. You can see Buick LeSabres built from scratch in the U.S.'s most totally integrated auto assembly plant. The operation's very size is impressive. Buick City's 123-acres, part of the 450-acre, two-mile-long Buick complex north of downtown Flint. The main plant turns out 480 cars per daily shift. This most modern of auto factories is located on the very site of Flint's first Buick plant, which Billy Durant quickly turned it into a national giant beginning in 1904.

Most of the difficult operations are performed by robots, some of the most sophisticated in the industry. The robots' intense activity contrasts with the workers' leisurely pace. Some have time to read a newspaper between their repetitious duties. Humans do the simple tasks like placing windshields on a conveyor belt one after another, while a vision-guided robot does the sensitive job of attaching the windshield to the frame. Few young workers are in evidence, as there has been virtually no hiring since 1979, when the dramatic decline in the American auto industry began.

The labyrinthine multi-layer conveyor belt is another wonder to behold. It's a far cry from Henry Ford's straightforward original assembly line. A part manufactured in one section of the plant will be automatically elevated to an overhead line and carried in timely fashion to another spot. All this automation seems to be paying off. Defects are dramatically down and Buick is regaining its image as one of the country's best built automobiles.

3 miles north of downtown Flint between Industrial Ave. and I-475. (313) 236-4494. Free tours, 1 to 1 1/2 hours, are Tues & Thurs at 9:30 a.m. and noon. Make reservations well in advance. No children under 6, no cameras.

Tour of GM Truck & Bus Flint Assembly Plant

At this old auto plant,
fancy pickups are assembled the old-fashioned way.

GM's popular Blazer and Suburban pickup trucks are made here. They are so much in demand that each one being built (at the rate of 38 an hour) has already been sold. At up to $30,000, the trucks all comes with V-8 engines and plush interiors. In Texas they're called "Texas Cadillacs." Indeed, Texas is the biggest customer for these fancy trucks, followed by Saudi Arabia.

The tour of the huge three million-square-foot assembly plant is conducted by two affable plant veterans who know their way around. It's a pleasantly informal tour. Questions are encouraged. Here you get to see the classic assembly line manned by 5,000 workers in action. It starts with a bare frame that crawls steadily along at about half mile an hour as workers put more and more parts on it. Unlike the heavily roboticized Buick City, workers do most of the procedures at this old-fashioned plant, one of the last in the country to use the old "body drop" way of construction. The completed body is lowered onto the chassis from a second level about 30 feet above. It takes about 14 hours to make one truck.

Van Slyke at Atherton, southeast of town. From I-75, take the Bristol Rd. exit, go east to Van Slyke, turn north to plant. (313) 236-4978. Free one-hour tours 9:30 & 11:30, Tues and Thurs. Reservations required.

Crossroads Village and Huckleberry Railroad

*Charming 19th-century settings
and the grit, noise, and smoke that went with them*

This museum village is an outstanding destination for families and history-lovers, but with certain caveats. Crossroads Village is the only place in Michigan where you can see a big variety of 19th-century industries in action every day: a pre-Civil War **gristmill**, a **sawmill**, and a **cider mill**, along with more common things like a **print shop**, **blacksmith shop**, and **toy-maker's shop**, outside of which kids can roll hoops and play with other old-fashioned toys. Some longtime demonstrators are experts in their fields. Generally competent costumed workers make simple tools, cornmeal, and cider, which visitors can purchase:

A special attraction is a 45-minute ride on the **Huckleberry Railroad,** a narrow-gauge steam engine, similar to those built for logging campus and mines, with a train of open-air cars. The train ride's grit and jolts do much to de-romanticize 19th-century train travel, and watching the old mechanical technologies in action sheds a perspective on how hard people had to work under noisy, dangerous conditions to make basic products.

Bees swarm around the apple pulp at the cider mill. Belts whir overhead in the grist mill. The smell of coal smoke and sawdust irritate your eyes. Most historic recreations are only for looking, and never confront all your senses with these realities.

Other things at Crossroads Village, however, can be so annoying that they can threaten to spoil the whole visit. The general store is full of contemporary gifts and Christmas ornaments made in the Far East. Suburban landscaping near the train station is bright and cheery but completely inauthentic. The staged train robbery melodrama is corny, even for some children. If things like this bother you, plan to concentrate on the buildings and activities on the periphery first, and save the downtown and train trip for later. Bring a picnic for the flavor of an old-fashioned outing, or go to the **chicken broil** (about $5) weekends from noon to closing. That way you'll avoid the mediocre snack shop.

Crossroads Village highlights include:

◆ **Atlas Mill.** A pre-Civil War grist mill sits on a splendidly lazy "mill pond" that's actually part of Mott Lake. The whole building shakes when the watergate is opened up to move the grindstones and make cornmeal.

◆ **Carousel.** Music from an antique organ that imitates a whole band accompanies the chariots and 36 horses of this 1912 carousel. It was manufactured by Charles Parker, "America's Amusement King." Rides are 50¢. Tucked away beyond the chapel and sawmill, it's easy to miss.

◆ **Ferris wheel.** A new addition manufactured in 1910. 50¢ a ride.

◆ **Sawmill** with demonstration.

◆ **Cider mill** with demonstration.

◆ **Restored, 19th-century buildings** authentically furnished with antiques includes a lawyer's office and home, a church, a school, and a recreated doctor's office. (These are quite well done, unlike the historic buildings which conceal souvenir and snack shops.)

◆ **Durant barn** with toymaking demonstrations.

◆ **Print shop** in the Manwaring Building downtown. The Crossroads Chronicle is a good read in the lively, folksy style of small-town journalism.

For a **daily schedule** of hourly demonstrations and special performances such as band concerts and magic shows, consult the map given to you on arrival. **Weekends** have more activities. Most summer weekends feature a **special show** of some sort at no extra charge. Annual events include the Michigan Storytellers Festival; an antique machine show; a special for rail fans; an old-fashioned Fourth of July (no fireworks); Capt'n Fogg's Balloon Classic; and Labor Day's Suffragette March.

If you plan to spend a half day or more, Crossroads Village is an excellent entertainment value.

Bray Rd. north of Coldwater Rd. east of I-475. From I-475, take Carpenter Rd. (exit 11) and follow signs. (313) 763-7100. **Summer season:** *mid-May through Labor Day. Mon-Fri 10-5:30, weekends & holidays 11-6:30.* **Fall:** *open weekends through mid-October. Halloween ghost train, trick or treat. Rates: adults $7.50, children 4-12 $5.25, seniors over 60 $6.50.* **Holiday lights,** *train ride, gift shopping (Thurs-Sun 3:30-9:30): from day after Thanksgiving to Sunday before New Year's.) $1.50 off regular rates.*

MORE FAMILY SUMMER ATTRACTIONS NEARBY. . . . . make Crossroads Village an ideal low-cost summer destination. (All, including the village itself, are operated by Genesee County Parks and Rec.) There's nearby scenic camping on the Flint River at the **Timberwolf Campground.** . . . . **Pennywhistle Place** is a spiffy, creative play environment with 10 activities aimed at toddlers to pre-teens — easy, fun ones like the Ball Crawl, Cloud Bounce, and Music Machine (a sort of giant calliope with keys you step on), or challenging, scary ones like climbing high on a net, or swinging from platform to platform on a gliding cable. A real hit with kids. **Bluebell Beach,** using the same parking area, provides a convenient place to swim, but without much shade. *Pennywhistle Place and beach are on Bray Road just south of Crossroads Village. Open Memorial Day to Labor Day, daily 12-8. (517) 785-8066. $2.50/person.* . . . . . **Stepping Stone Falls** has wooded picnic spots, especially nice near dusk, when the man-made falls at the outlet of Mott Lake are illuminated with changing colored lights. The water flows over rectilinear platforms with stepping stones across the shallow parts. *From Crossroads Village and Pennywhistle Place, take Bray south to Carpenter, then east, north on Branch. From I-475, take Carpenter exit 11, go east 1 1/2 miles to Branch, north briefly on Branch to falls. Open daily from Memorial Day to Labor Day, noon-11. Free.*

Port Huron

*Striking views of freighters and water
in one of America's earliest interior outposts*

Strategically sited where Lake Huron pours into the St.
Clair River, this city of 34,000 offers several striking
scenic and historic sights. It became one of the earliest
outposts in the American interior when the French built Fort St.
Joseph here in 1686 to seal off the upper Great Lakes from the
English. Later the Americans built Fort Gratiot in 1814 on the
same site as Fort St. Joseph, also to keep the British out of Lake
Huron and beyond. American friction with British-controlled
Canada had changed to cooperation by 1891 when the two-mile-
long underground St. Clair Railroad Tunnel was built beneath the
St. Clair River to join Sarnia with Port Huron. Located just south
of John Street, the tunnel is still quite active. For the high railroad cars which can't fit through the tunnel, ferry service is in
operation 24 hours a day to get them across the St. Clair River.
The line's owner, Grand Trunk, has its big railroad car repair
shops at 25th and Minnie streets.

Despite its strategic position, Port Huron has been something
of a pleasant backwater in this century. Military concerns disappeared after the Civil War, and no industrial giants sprang up
here as they did in Midland or Battle Creek or Kalamazoo. For
environmental reasons the city rejected the bids of chemical
companies to build plants here; they settled on the laxer Canadian side of the river instead. It's main claim to fame is as the
hometown of Thomas Edison. The one big event, which attracts
thousands, is the **Mackinac Race Day** in late July, when a flotilla
of sailing boats races to Mackinac Island.

Highlights of Port Huron are:

◆ **1858 Grand Trunk Depot.** Port Huron's strategic location
where Lake Huron flows into the St. Clair River provides an
exceptional visual setting in this new park by the historic train
station. To the left, facing Canada, looms the enormous **Blue
Water Bridge**, and beyond that, the great expanse of **Lake Huron**.
Directly ahead, the river is quite narrow, less than a quarter mile
wide. It therefore runs quite swiftly, seven or eight miles an hour.
The river's narrow width brings the big freighters up close.

Standing starkly near the railroad tracks is the recently
restored 1858 **Grand Trunk Depot**. From here in 1859 Thomas
Edison, a Port Huron boy of 12, embarked to sell fruits, nuts,

magazines, and newspapers on the train to Detroit and back. He used much of his earnings to buy chemicals for the small laboratory he set up in the train's baggage car. Just south of the old depot is the new Thomas Edison Inn, a pricey 150-suite dining/hotel complex built by the owners of the popular St. Clair Inn downriver. Just south of the inn's parking lot is where **Fort Gratiot** (1814-1879) stood. *Just south of the Blue Water Bridge. From Pine Grove Ave. take Thomas Edison Parkway just north of the tracks. Parking spaces and boardwalk by the river.*

◆ **Blue Water Bridge.** This imposing structure rises 152 feet over the St. Clair River to allow freighters to pass underneath. It is 1.4 miles long, with a main span of 871 feet. Completed in 1938, it connects Port Huron with Sarnia, Ontario. Its height gives you a splendid view of Lake Huron to the north and the St. Clair River to the south. Also interesting are the bird's-eye views of Port Huron neighborhoods. Just to the north you see the Dunn Paper facilities. You can also walk across the bridge. *U.S. entrance is the northern terminus of I-94. Toll: 75¢ per car.*

◆ **Sarnia, Canada.** Port Huron's neighbor across the St. Clair River is a pleasant, if rather unexciting, place to visit. No longer are there great buys on Commonwealth products to lure Americans across the border. The flow is now reversed, and Canadians flock to Port Huron's malls for good deals. The economy of Sarnia (population 80,000) is based on the petrochemical industry, whose fascinating-looking plants sprawl for some 20 miles below the city along the St. Clair River. At night, the spaghetti-like complex of lights and tubing are quite a sight from the American side.   An elaborate government-run information center is just to the south of the Canadian side of the bridge. *Take I-94 to the Blue Water Bridge. No passport necessary for American citizens.*

◆ **Lighthouse Park** This park is next to the oldest surviving lighthouse in Michigan, this park is another good vantage point from which to enjoy the splendid view of Lake Huron as it enters the St. Clair River. Lights illuminate an asphalt path leading to the sandy beach. On foggy days, it's an eerie sight to see giant northbound freighters quietly churning past and becoming quickly engulfed in the mist on the Lake. On the short path to the beach, you pass a small Coast Guard complex, complete with an 1874 lightkeeper's dwelling of red brick and a white clapboard Coast Guard station. Also in the complex is the 86-foot-tall **Fort Gratiot Light**. It still flashes a warning to freighters coming south into the river, a tricky maneuver because of the river's narrow width and swift current. *Off Omar St. between Robinson and Riverview 5 blocks north of the Blue Water Bridge. From Pine Grove north of I-94, take Garfield east to the park.*

◆ **Pinegrove Park.** This city park also fronts the St. Clair River
and provides a wonderful view of the big bridge, the Canadian
shoreline, and boat traffic. On the concrete walk right at the
riverbank, fishermen with big landing nets fish for walleye and
steelhead. At the park's northeastern edge, perched strangely on
the riverbank, is the **Lightship Huron,** a retired floating lighthouse whose light could be seen for 14 miles. The 97-foot-long
ship served six miles north of Port Huron from 1935 until 1970.
North of the lightship you can see a red **pilot house,** quarters for
the American freighter pilots who take the wheels of foreign vessels heading into U.S. waters. The vacant lot behind the pilot
house was where Thomas Edison's family home stood.

Looking south across the river, you can see the beginning of
Canada's 20-mile-long **"chemical valley,"** Canada's greatest concentration of chemical factories and a spectacular nightime sight
reflected in the water. They are responsible for creating most of
the pollution in the lower St. Clair River. *East off Pine Grove
between Prospect and Lincoln, north of downtown.*

◆ **Diana Sweet Shop.** Fine woodwork abounds in this beautifully
preserved 1926 sweet shop. The ornate wallpaper, the lighting,
the pressed metal ceiling, the pictures — all combine to create
an extraordinary atmosphere. It is still owned and operated by
the sons of the founder. Sweet shops flourished in the 1920s as
the tempo of American urban life sped up and people stopped
going home for lunch. Elegant interiors were a mark of success.
Diana's preserves not only the decor but the menu: sandwiches,
ice cream, pastries, and fudge. Don't miss the original 1926
"Violino Virtuoso" up front as you enter. For 25¢ it will play five
tunes, plucking at a violin and hammering on strings. *307 Huron
between Grand River and McMorran downtown. (313) 985-6933.
Mon-Sat 5:45 a.m.-6 p.m. Fri to 8 p.m. Sat 7:30-6. MC, Visa, Am
Ex. No alcohol.*

◆ **Museum of Arts & History.** This sizable museum in the
impressive 1904 Carnegie library building. It has a little bit of
everything, from 7,000 B.C. Indian artifacts to recent paintings
for sale by local artists. There is a remarkable array of Indian
stone points and tools from the region, and small-scale models of
old Fort St. Joseph and Fort Gratiot. Most haunting are the
objects brought up by divers from wrecks. *1115 Sixth St. between
Wall and Court, south of the Black River and downtown. Sixth is
one block west of M-25, the main artery. (313) 982-0891. Wed-
Sun 1-4:30. Free admission, donations welcome.*

▲🌲▲

Recommended Restaurants & Lodgings

Beyond Detroit

To locate cities, see regional map, p. 77

MONROE

Detroit Beach Restaurant. *2630 N. Dixie Hwy. (2 mi. n.of I-75 exit 15, past Sterling State Park. (313) 289-9865. Tues-Sun 11 a.m.-1 a.m., Fri & Sat to 3 a.m. Beer & wine. No credit cards.* "A genuine find," says the *Free Press*'s Molly Abraham. Plain Italian family spot. Big servings of good home cooking at remarkably low prices. Pizza with homemade sauce is a mainstay, starting at $2.70 for a 12" plain cheese pizza. Also recommended: mostaccioli casserole ($5), veal ($9 for veal parmesan, $10 for pan-fried scallopini in mushroom-wine sauce). All entrees include salad, crusty homemade bread, bread sticks, plus spuds or pasta w/ meat entrees.

Arborgate Inn. *(313) 289-1080. Dixie Hwy. at I-75 exit 15. Busy strip n.e. of downtown.* 89 units on 1 floor. $31 for 1-4 people. Kitchenettes avail. Cable TV.
Pleasant budget choice

Holiday Inn. *(313) 242-6000. Dixie Hwy. s.w. of I-75 exit 15. Busy strip n.e of downtown.* 127 units on 4 floors. $58-$65. Satellite TV, phones. Large indoor pool, sauna, game room. Mediocre restaurant, bar w/weekend entertainment.
Best for kids, activities in Monroe

DUNDEE

Comfort Inn. *(313) 529-5505. At U.S. 23 & M-50, Dundee exit, 3 blocks e. of downtown on busy strip.* 64 units. $46-$49. Suites w/ whirlpool or

jacuzzi: $72-$125. Cable TV. 1/2 hour to Ann Arbor.
Easy-on, easy-off stopover on U.S. 23 near Ann Arbor, Monroe, Tecumseh

YPSILANTI

Haab's. *18 W. Michigan between Huron St. and river downtown. From I-94, take exit 183 n. (313) 483-8200. Sun-Thurs 11-9, Fri & Sat 11-10. Full bar. Major credit cards. Lunch $3-$8 w/ 1 side; dinner $6-$17 w/ 2 sides.* Longtime reputation based on beef, service. Specialties: prime rib ($9 at lunch, $15 at dinner), New York strip (12 oz. $14). Also: 18 seafood dishes, fresh catch. "Chicken in the rough" w/ fries, biscuit, slaw $7.45.

Old China. *505 W. Cross, just s.of Eastern Michigan U. campus. (313) 482-8333. Tues-Thurs 11:30-9:30, Fri 11:30-11, Sat 4:30-11, Sun 4:30-9:30. No alcohol; bring your own. Visa, MC, AmEx. $3-$5 (lunch); $7-$10(dinner).* Plain place still draws Ann Arbor diners despite many newer Chinese spots. Peking duck $25 with pancakes, soup, dessert. Sizzling rice soup ($7.55), moo shi pork always good.

Radisson Resort on the Lake. *(313) 487-2000. On Huron at Whittaker Rd. just s. of I-94 (exit 183).* .236 rooms on 7 floors. $85-$95 for 2-4 people. Suites, packages avail. Cable TV. Indoor pool, sauna, jacuzzi, steam room, game room, exercise room w/Nautilus. Restaurant. Sports bar w/ shuffleboard, pool, fooze ball. Ice-skating, ski trails, golf on site.
Full-service resort on Ford Lake

ANN ARBOR

The Earle *121 W. Washington at First downtown. (313) 994-0211. Mon-Thurs 5:30-10, Fri 5:30-12, Sat 6-12. Sun 5-9 except May-August. Full bar, outstanding wine list. Major credit cards. A la carte entrees (including a starch)* $10-16. Earthy French and

Italian provincial cooking, served up for demanding, well-traveled clientele. Changing menu with specialties like fresh salmon fillet in puffed pastry with a spinach-dill mousse ($16), changing veal, duck, and lamb dishes. Budget-conscious diners order the $10-$11 pastas or cheaper appetizers to allow for noteworthy desserts. Many wines by the glass at wine bar; sometimes free mussels until 6:30.

Gratzi. *326 S. Main downtown. (313) 663-5555. Mon-Sat 11:30-11, Fri-Sat to 12, Sun 4-9. A la carte entrees: $6-$13 lunch, $6-$15 dinner. Full bar. Visa, AmEx, MC.* Loud, convivial bistro still a hot spot. Theatrical decor in old theater. Northern Italian specialties are not for the hungry: thin-crust pizzas ($6-$7); shrimp, mussels, scallops in pesto ($11), sauteed chicken breast w/ mushrooms ($12). Strolling accordionist Thurs-Sat.

Old German. *120 W. Washington. (313) 662-0737. Mon-Wed, Sat 11-8:30, closed Thurs, Fri 11-9, Sun 11-8. All major credit cards. Full bar.* A living link to the longtime German community that once dominated Ann Arbor's west side. The big round table by the cashier is a *Stammtisch* (communal table) for hometown regulars from many walks of life. Menu does include vegetarian sides, including good dilled cucumbers, spatzen (homemade, bumpy-looking noodles, a specialty of Swabia, local Germans' southwest German homeland), Zwiebelkuchen (onion quiche), red cabbage. But meat is the main show (smoked pork loin is tops), and the daily specials are often the stars — such as pork loin with sauerkraut ($4.75 at lunch, $7.75 dinner, Tuesdays only), veal-stuffed noodle w/ good German potato salad ($4.50/$6.75). Don't overlook the sandwich menu w/ goodies like grilled bratwurst w/ pan-fried onions ($2.75). Rebuilt because of a fire. Note owner Bud Metzger's outstanding collection of antique beer steins and plates. German-language newspaper in sidewalk box out front.

Moveable Feast. *326 W. Liberty just w. of downtown. (313) 663-3278. Full bar. Major credit cards. Lunch 11:30-2 Mon-Fri; dinner 6-9:30 Mon-Sat; desserts only Mon-Thurs to 11 p.m., Fri-Sat to 12. Reservations suggested. A la carte entrees $4.50-$8.75 (lunch); $16.50-$23.50 (dinner). Prix fixe dinners $23-30.* Consistently among the very best in a town with lots of high-caliber competition. Locally famous for sourdough baguettes, perfect croissants, rich butter cakes like super-chocolaty gateau Nancy ($4/slice), sold here to go and at Kerrytown shop. In elegant Italianate house; local artists exhibited. French-accented international menu, changed frequently. Simple lunches a bargain: fritatta omelet ($4.50), beef tenderloin with wild rice pilaf ($8.50). Prix fixe dinners under $30 with appetizer, wonderful soup, entrees like medallions of lamb with goat cheese, fresh basil; grilled chicken in rosemary cream sauce; choice of dessert.

Fuji Restaurant. *327 Braun Court, off N. 4th Ave. between Catherine and Kingsley near Kerrytown. (313) 663-3111. Tues-Sat 11-2 & 5110. Visa, AmEx, MC. Full bar.* Food and setting here are well thought out and serene, for a calm and happy feeling. Sake, Japanese beer, a sushi bar, but no karaoke machine or Japanese-style big screen w/ singalongs. Tempura, made w/ salmon, chicken, fish, pork, lobster, or vegetables, is excellent. Dinners from $8 for some noodle dishes to about $20 (for a lobster combination, w/ most between $10 and $12. Lunches average $6 or so. All meals w/ soup, salad, rice.

Other good Braun Court restaurants include **The Blue Nile** (see p. 224, **La Casita de Lupe**, and **Bangkok 2**.

Zingerman's. *Detroit at Kingsley, e. of Kerrytown. (313) 663-3354. Mon-Sat 7 a.m.-8:30 p.m., Sun 9-8:30. No credit cards; checks OK. No alcohol.* Fabulous, high-energy deli (see p. 92) covers the basics (chicken soup, bagels, lox), adds cross-cultural home cooking, desserts. Top-quality ingredients; working with local organic farmers on produce. Main attraction: 60 huge sandwiches from $3.50 to $8. Most popular: grilled Reuben, followed by Georgia Reuben with turkey breast, coleslaw; #55 (fresh mozzarella, pesto, tomatoes). All $6.50. Much shorter waits thanks to seating in neighboring house, terrace. Neat workaday ambiance in mornings.

Cottage Inn. *512 E. William between Thompson & Maynard, 1 block w. of State & U-M Campus. (313) 663-3379. Mon-Sat 11 a.m.-1 a.m., Fri & Sat to 1:30, Sun noon 1 a.m. Visa, MC,AmEx. Full bar.* Not just a popular campus meeting spot, also one of the few places in town where parents on a budget can relax with their kids and have a beer. The pizza is #1 in Domino's home town. Comfortable booths, warm atmosphere. A big bowl of Greek or antipasto salad and a half tray of Sicilian pizza makes a meal for 2 for $12.75; for 4, w/ a full tray, it's $15.25. Dinner dishes like lasagna, chicken stir-fry Alfredo, or chicken Florentine are around $8 or under, w/ pasta & soup or salad.

Cousins Heritage Inn. *7954 Ann Arbor St. just east of downtown Dexter. From Ann Arbor, take Huron to forks, west on Dexter Rd. 8 miles; look for inn on your right. (313) 426-3020. Lunch 11-2 Mon-Fri; dinner 6-9 Tues-Sat. 90 -item wine list.Visa, MC, Diners, checks.* Perfectionist couple and chef trained at Golden Mushroom run outstanding little restaurant in pleasant 1850s house. Wild game a specialty, super-sweet flown-in corn and unusual grains like hi-protein quinoa a point of pride. Changing dinner menu runs from $17 (leg of lamb) and $18 (yellowfin tuna saute with scallops, shrimp, and lobster sauce) to $23 (venison loin w/ wild rice pancakes, cabbage, cranberry relish); dinner includes salad, starch, vegetables. $8 lunches: tenderloin tips with wild mushrooms, or seafood pasta, with salad. Wonderful soups, desserts, not necessarily rich.

Hampton Inn North. *(313) 996-4414. Green Rd. at Plymouth Rd. w. side of U.S. 23 exit 41.* 130 rooms on 4 floors. $55-$59. Cable TV. Small indoor pool, whirlpool, exercise room. *Moderate rates, indoor pool, near North Campus, Domino's*

Red Roof Inn. *(313) 996-5800. Plymouth Rd. w. of U.S. 23 exit 41.* 108 rooms on 2 floors. Cable TV. $44-$49, higher on busy weekends. *Best budget motel, near Domino's and North Campus*

Wood's Inn B&B. *(313) 665-8394. 2887 Newport Rd. off Miller, 1 1/2 mi. w. of downtown.* 4 rooms (2 with baths, 2 share). $45-$50. 1859 home on 2 acres, large glassed-in porch w/ wicker overlooks gardens. *B&B has country in the city*

Regency Campus Inn. *(313) 769-2200. E. Huron at State.* 202 rooms on 15 floors. $99, suites avail. TV. Outdoor pool, sauna. Restaurant. Bar. Valet parking. Being renovated. *Campus location, good views, especially of historic area to north*

Bell Tower Hotel. *(313) 769-3010. 300 S. Thayer next to U-M campus, shopping.* 66 rooms on 4 floors. $99, suites avail. Cont. breakfast. Valet parking. Cable TV. Haute cuisine restaurant, bar. European inn w/traditional furnishings. *Luxury close to U-M campus, State St.*

Holiday Inn West. *(313) 665-4444. Jackson Rd. just w. of I-94 exit 172 , 2 mi. w. of downtown on busy strip.* 223 rooms on 5 floors. $84-$89. Suites $125-$225. Cable TV. Holidome: indoor & outdoor pools, whirlpool, sauna, game & exercise rooms, playground. Restaurant, bar w/ live entertainment, snack shop. *Best Ann Arbor choice for activities*

<u>**HOLLY**</u>

Historic Holly Hotel.*Battle Alley at Broad downtown. (313) 634-5208. Mon-Sat lunch 11-3, dinner 5-10, to 11 Fri & Sat; Sun noon-8. Full bar, good wine list. Visa, MC AmEx,*

Diners. Splendid Victorian decor, very good food. Dinner picks: Beef Wellington ($19.50), roast chicken breast w/ red bell peppers ($15), poached salmon with champagne sauce ($18.50) — all w/ bread, soup, salad, vegetable. At lunch: chicken strudel ($5.50), onion soup w/cheese and puff pastry ($3.50). Also, big salads ($4), fresh fish ($8), croissants, soup.

FLINT

Top of the Park. *432 N. Saginaw (Northbank Center), 12th floor. (313) 232-8888. Mon-Fri 11-10:30, Sat 5:30-10:30. Lunch $6-$13; dinner $16-$30 w/ salad, sorbet, veg., starch. Full bar, 80-bottle wine list (longest in the area).* MC, Visa, Diners. Excellent food (terrific bread) in pleasing setting. Fine view of Flint River from s. windows. Changing menu. Lunch picks: chicken & broccoli in filo pastry w/ hollandaise ($7), grilled duckling breast sauced w/ strawberries, coconut milk, Grand Marnier ($9.50). At dinner, Filet of Waronoff (marinated tenderloin w/ sauce Bordelaise; $25, paupiettes of swordfish w/carrots, fennel ($19).

Bill Thomas' Haloburger. *14 locations; see below. Typical hours: Mon-Sat 7 a.m.-10 p.m., to 11 Fri & Sat. Sun 7:30-8 p.m. 24 hours at 800 S. Saginaw downtown. No alcohol, no credit cards.* Family-owned alternative to franchised fast food offers good burgers at good prices, also breakfasts, grilled & fried chicken, chef salad (large is under $3). Haloburgers (the name is tied in with the logo, a cow with a halo) are made w/ fresh beef & your choice of fixings, in 3 sizes. The half-pound is $2.75. What a deal!

The downtown Haloburger at 800 S. Saginaw at Court is a vintage late 1920s building, once a Vernor's ginger ale outlet. The wonderful outdoor mural, showing Vernor's gnomes rolling barrels in front of a castle, has been carefully preserved.

Windmill Place. *877 E. Fifth at N. Saginaw, n. of the river downtown. (313) 234-2640. Mon-Thurs 10-8, Fri & Sat 10-9, Sun 12-9.* Pleasant, popular food court originally intended to go w/ Autoworld. Eateries include Chinese, Greek, Italian, Hungarian, Middle Eastern (very good), southern BBQ, a deli w/ corned beef & pastrami, and coney dogs.

Riverfront Center. *(313) 239-1234. On Saginaw St. just s. of Flint R. downtown.* 369 rooms on 16 floors. $48. Former Hyatt being renovated. Cable TV/ Whirlpool. Pool, restaurant, bar temporarily closed.
On beautiful Riverfront Park. Reasonable rates, good views

Holiday Inn. *(313) 232-5300. U.S. 23 at Hill Rd. 10 min. s. of downtown on busy strip.* 165 rooms on 4 floors. $78-$84. Suites, kitchenettes avail. Satellite TV. Holidome: indoor pool, Jacuzzi, sauna, whirlpool, game room, exercise room. Restaurant, bar, nightclub.
Lots of amenities, Holidome

Walli's Motor Lodge West. *(313) 789-0400. I-75 at Pierson Rd (exit 122), n.w. of downtown.* 67 rooms on 2 floors. $36-$40. Cable TV, phones. Walli's restaurant open 24 hours. Bar.
Budget choice w/24 hour restaurant

Country Inn of Grand Blanc. *(313) 694-6749. 6136 S. Belsay on n. outskirts of Grand Blanc.* 3 rooms on 2 floors. $45-$75. Private or shared baths. Country setting, furnished w/ antiques. Picnic baskets avail.
Turn-of-century B&B in Flint's poshest suburb

PORT HURON

Victorian Inn. *1229 7th at Union, 2 blocks w. of M-25, s. of downtown. (313) 984-1437. Tues-Sat lunch 11:30-1:30, dinner 5:30-8:30.* Lunch entrees $5.50-$7 w/ salad, starch. Dinners

$15-$24 w/ salad, starch, veg. Full bar.
Basement pub to 11 weekdays, 1 a.m.
Fri & Sat. . White linen service in elaborate, restored Queen Anne house. Very
good soups, desserts. Grilled rack of
lamb w/ wine ($24) a dinner hit on
changing American menu. Omelets,
strudels, crepes, sandwich menu at
lunch.

Thomas Edison Inn. *(800)
451-7991, (313) 984-8000. Just s. of
Blue Water Bridge on St. Clair River.*
149 rooms on 3 floors. $85 double,
$115 suite. Cable TV. Full-service
health club, indoor pool, sauna,
whirlpool. Access to golf, tennis.
Restaurant w/ Sun. brunch. Bar w/
dancing, entertainment.
Indoor spa with river & bridge views

Knights Inn. *(313) 982-1022. 2160
Water St. (I-94, exit 274) on w. side of
Port Huron 1 mi. from downtown.* 105
units on 1 floor. $42-$43. Kitchenettes
avail. Cable TV.
Budget choice with pool

Colonial Motor Inn. *(313)
984-1522. 2908 Pine Grove (M-25)
about 1 1/2 mi. n. of downtown. Take
I-94 almost to the Blue Water Bridge,
go north onto M-25.* 107 rooms on 2
floors (30 kitchenettes). $54-$59 May-
Sept, lower prices off-season. Cable
TV. Indoor pool, whirlpool, game
room, playground, 1 tennis court.
Short drive to Lighthouse Park, bridge.
*Many activities, moderate rates,
some kitchenettes*

Victorian Inn B&B. *(313)
984-1437. 1229 7th in Port Huron.* 4

rooms. $55 shared bath, $65 private
bath. Cont. breakfast. TV in Pub.
Restaurant on 1st floor. 1 blk from
Museum of Arts & History.
*Elegantly redone Queen Anne house
with excellent restaurant*

ST. CLAIR

St. Clair Inn. *(800) 482-8327 (MI
only), (313) 329-2222. In downtown St.
Clair, which was leveled for a shopping center.* 97 rooms on 2 floors. $70,
$110 suite. Packages avail. Cable TV.
Beautiful indoor pool, whirlpool, game
room. Access to golf, tennis, fitness
center. Improved restaurant. Bar
w/dancing, entertainment. Boat dock.
Long boardwalk for lovely evening
strolls with lights reflected in river.
1920s Tudor inn on St. Clair river

MARINE CITY

Port Seaway Inn. *(313) 765-4033.
On M-29/S. River Rd. 3 1/2 mi. s. of
Marine City.* 18 rooms on 2 floors.
$40-$45. VIP 2-level suite: $62. Cable
TV, phones. 2 fishing docks.
Riverside location in pleasant town

Chapter 4
Metro Detroit

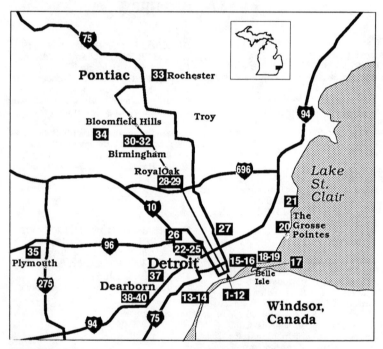

Pontiac

33 Rochester

Troy

94

Bloomfield Hills
34
30-32
Birmingham
RoyalOak
28-29

696

Lake
St.
Clair

10

21

The
Grosse
Pointes

26
27
20

96
22-25

35
Plymouth

Detroit

15-16 18-19 17

37
Dearborn
38-40

13-14 1-12

Belle
Isle

275

94

75

Windsor,
Canada

Hart Plaza

Where music, people, and riverfront scenery
come together on a fine summer's day

Highlights of the past and present converge at this popular riverfront gathering place. Eight acres of multi-level paved park lead down from Jefferson Avenue to the Detroit River and the very spot on which Cadillac built Fort Pontchartrain in 1701. One side of the plaza looks out onto the river, with views of the **Ambassador Bridge** and **Windsor**, Ontario. On the other side is a view of Detroit's impressive **skyline**. The bright-painted antique **trolley cars** wait on Jefferson at the side of **Mariners' Church** (p. 133) between regular runs to **Grand Circus Park** (p. 142) from 10 a.m. to 6 p.m. The giant sculptural fist at Woodward and Jefferson memorializes Joe Louis, Detroit's famous Brown Bomber, who became the world heavyweight boxing champion in 1938.

Hart Plaza is a splendid place to be in nice weather. On weekdays at lunchtime it's crowded with downtown workers. Regulars play chess at concrete tables near the Dodge Fountain, by famed sculptor Isamu Noguchi. It's easy to be mesmerized by the fountain's changing water patterns.

Visitors flock to the free Riverfront Festivals held each weekend (Friday through Sunday) all summer long. These include **ethnic festivals** with music, dance, and food. Five of the best-organized festivals also include national talent: the Irish Festival (late May/early June), the German Festival (early June), the Italian Festival (early July), the Polish Festival (early August) and the African World Festival (mid-August). The free **Montreux-Detroit Jazz Festival** on Labor Day weekend elicits raves from critics. Other big, free events are the mid-May **Downtown Hoedown**, the world's largest free country music festival, and the **Detroit-Windsor International Freedom Festival** with fireworks just before the July 4 weekend.

*Hart Plaza is at the foot of Woodward between Jefferson and the Detroit River. People Mover stop: exit at Millender Center and walk across Jefferson or the RenCen skywalk. Call (313) 224-1184 weekdays 9-6 for a **Riverfront Festivals schedule** and parking information.*

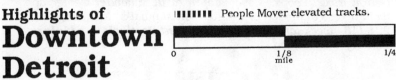

Highlights of
Downtown Detroit

IIIIIIII People Mover elevated tracks.

0   1/8   1/4
                    mile

❶ Fox Theater. Restored "Siamese Byzantine" extravaganza, one of the most lavish U.S. picture palaces, has become nation's top-grossing venue for big-name acts. Nearby **Gem** presents clever revues.

❷ Grand Circus Park. Once a 19th-century jewel, this old park has many important historic statues. The heart of Detroit's grand Theater District now coming to life again.

❸ People Mover. A must for visitors, this 2.9 mile elevated train gives a spectacular view of the entire downtown. Terrific public art in the 12 stations. Despite ailing finances, not likely to close.

❹ Silver's. Interesting office supply/gift store has an excellent cafeteria in the basement, Britt's Cafe. Old bank an architectural gem designed by Stanford White.

❺ Guardian Building. One of the country's great skyscrapers. Flamboyant 1929 Art Deco building has a stunning main lobby and adjacent banking room.

❻ John King Books. Big old glove factory now houses one of country's biggest used book stores. 750,000 books plus collectibles like postcards and framed pictures.

❼ Hart Plaza. Views of river, city, fountain-sculpture. Good free weekend entertainment from mid-May to Labor Day's great Montreux-Detroit Jazz Festival.

❽ Renaissance Center. Huge & disorienting modern landmark includes large hotel, shops, and restaurants. Catch great view from the 72nd-floor steak house.

❾ DuMouchelle Gallery. Michigan's premiere auction gallery, featuring expensive possessions of the rich and sometimes famous. Known to sell architectural fixtures stripped by scam artists.

❿ Greektown & Trappers Alley. Downtown's liveliest, most colorful spot. Authentic old Greek shops and restaurant next to a beautiful 4-level festival marketplace.

⓫ Harmonie Park. Hidden potential oasis with art galleries, creative shops, facing park and one Grand River.

⓬ Eastern Market. Hard-to-match mix of shops for cheese, meat, fish, poultry, spices, nuts, produce, wine plus open-air market Bargains, selection, earthy atmosphere. New: coffeehouse inside Rocky Peanut Co.

INFO SOURCES

◆ For a **downtown Detroit map** and metro Detroit **visitor packet**, or for information on attractions and events, call the What's Line, (313) 567-1170.

◆ For a **People Mover map** and attractive **Art in the Stations guide**, call (800) 541-RAIL.

◆ For a **Detroit parking guide** to lower-cost city-operated parking, call (313) 224-0300, or write Municipal Parking Department, 200 Civic Center, Detroit, MI 48226.

Renaissance Center

A symbol of Detroit's attempt to bounce back,
this confusing complex has a stunning view
from the world's third tallest hotel.

Huge and controversial, the RenCen includes a towering hotel (73 stories high), over two million square feet of office space, and dozens of shops and restaurants. The RenCen sits behind a massive concrete wall next to the tunnel to Canada. It looks like a fortress intended to protect its occupants from neighboring vandals. The project was spurred by the 1967 Detroit riot, which accelerated the exodus of whites from the city's center. Henry Ford II pushed through this formidable project, cajoling Ford suppliers and other major area businesses to invest the hundreds of millions to build the riverside complex.

After opening in 1977, the RenCen quickly became notorious as a bewildering circular maze for casual visitors. Without memorable landmarks, the space connecting four look-alike round towers surrounding the Westin Hotel proved disorienting. Monied suburbanites were not drawn to the forbidding, confusing place. Many luxury retailers, intended to be a big draw, pulled out, while the huge hotel suffered from a low occupancy rate. By 1983, the original investors had defaulted on their loans.

The revamped RenCen is better but still confusing, and it still doesn't draw many suburbanites downtown. Nonetheless, the massive complex is credited with helping to launch the succeeding wave of riverfront office and residential projects. The RenCen's 50-odd shops and service businesses and 25 or so eateries have achieved a stable presence, due mainly to the 12,000 people who work for the 140 companies with offices here. The restaurants range from numerous fast-food outlets (some open for breakfast) to the spectacular, 72nd-story **Summit Steak House & Lounge**, with Tex-Mex, Japanese, Greek, and seafood sit-down restaurants in-between.

The shops, which close at 6 and on Sundays, include Anton's menswear, Gantos, Alvin's, Winkelman's, and five other women's wear stores, and a small assortment of typical mall outlets for cookies, books, cards and gifts, plus a complete range of office and visitor services.

One remarkable RenCen attraction is the **view** from the revolving **Summit Steak House** on the hotel's 72nd floor. You're up so high it's like looking at a living map of the Detroit River and its islands, up to Lake St. Clair and down almost to Lake Erie. Just a trip on the elevator to the lounge, without a meal or drink, isn't cheap ($3/adult, $1 for kids 5-12, free for seniors and pre-schoolers). But lunches begin at just $7 and let you take in the view at your leisure. Sunday brunch (10:30-2:30) is $7 to $17. For a quick, **free view** from not quite so high up, take one of the glass-sided elevators attached to each office tower. From the 400 Tower you can see Hart Plaza, downtown, and downriver. *E. Jefferson at Brush on the Detroit River. Open 7 a.m.-11 p.m.* **Shops** *open 10-9, Sun.10-9. Second-story* **bridges across Jefferson** *connect with the Millender Center and People Mover Station.* **Information kiosk** *in Jefferson Ave. lobby.* **Park** *in "A" transient lot off Beaubien east of Jefferson. Rates encourage short-term and off-hours parking: $1 for 3 hours weekdays 10-6, $2 week nights after 6, 12 hours for $2 weekends. Rates for over 3 hours start at $7.50. To get a helpful* **directory and map,** *call (313) 568-5600 weekdays, write Renaissance Center Venture, 100 RenCen #1400, Detroit 48243, or stop at the information kiosk in the Jefferson Ave. lobby.*

UNDER THE RIVER TO CANADA . . . . . It's a bit eerie taking the dark, damp **Detroit-Windsor Tunnel** to Canada under the Detroit River — certainly not as scenic as the Ambassador Bridge downstream. The 5,135-foot-long tunnel was finished in 1930. The center 2000-foot section was created by sinking nine steel tubes, each 31 feet wide, in a trench 45 feet under the riverbed. At times there are considerable delays waiting to get through customs on either side. Weekday mornings are least busy. *Foot of Randolph St., just west of the Renaissance Center. Fare: $1.50 per car (one way).*

AN ANCIENT DETROIT CHURCH ON THE RIVER . . . . . Across Jefferson Avenue from the RenCen **Mariners' Church** served the crews of the Great Lakes ships, many of whom were laid up in Detroit for the winter. It was donated by Julia Anderson, who came to Detroit with her husband in 1819 on the Lakes' first steamboat, *Walk-in-the-Water.* The first services were held Christmas Eve, 1849. Mariners' Church uses the old Episcopal liturgy and maintains its historical independence from the Episcopal diocese, which claims to own it and has long tried to oust the minister. At the Blessing of the Fleet on the second Sunday of every March, dozens of captains bring the flags of their ships to be blessed. The closest Sunday to November 10 is a memorial service for the crew of the sunken Edmund Fitzgerald. *170 E. Jefferson east of Woodward. (313) 259-2206. Open for casual visitors Tues, Thurs, Fri 10-4. Services Thurs noon, Sun 8:30 & 11.*

DuMouchelle Art Galleries

Detroit's premiere auction house handles the likes of $49,000 Tiffany lamps and $60,000 carpets from a shah's palace.

The region's premier auction spot, this is where the furniture, art, jewelry, and bibelots of the very rich are put on the block. Once Detroit's first Cadillac dealership, the building has big display windows today full of things like chandeliers (over 60 are typically on hand), porcelain, paintings, cut crystal, silver, rugs, and furniture. These are priced items for sale right from the floor.

Auctions take place once a month, usually the second or third week. The event attracts collectors from all over the world. Items may be inspected the week before the auction from 9:30 to 5:30. The auction lasts three days, beginning Friday at 7 p.m., Saturday at 11 a.m., and Sunday at noon. Items go for anywhere from $10 to $200,000. A Tiffany lamp recently sold for $49,000. A silk Oriental rug from the Shah of Iran's palace was picked up for $60,000. And the high bid for an Andy Warhol "slipper collage" was $10,000.

409 E. Jefferson at Brush across from the RenCen. (313) 963-6255. Mon-Sat 9:30-5:30. Free valet parking on auction dates. Pick up a free illustrated brochure for the upcoming auction here or at the Hart Plaza visitor information booth.

OF INTEREST NEAR DuMOUCHELLE . . . . . A beautifully renovated Italianate townhouse, the **Beaubien House**, is a good first stop for people interested in making their own tour of downtown and Rivertown historic architecture. The historic home is now headquarters of the Michigan Society of Architects, and several **free pamphlets and maps on area architecture** are available. In the elegant front parlor are worthwhile changing exhibits related to architecture or people involved in architecture in Michigan *553 E. Jefferson just east of Beaubien. (313) 965-4100. Mon-Fri 8-5.*

Greektown

*Long a Greek commercial district,
this is Detroit's liveliest block.*

With its many Greek restaurants, this bustling, busy block of Monroe Street has long been one of Detroit's most popular tourist attractions. It's one of the few areas in Detroit where the 19th-century city holds its own. With the addition of adjacent **Trappers Alley** festival marketplace, there's even more to see and do.

This is the core of a Greek neighborhood going back to 1915, with its bakeries, grocery stores, and coffee houses where old-timers drink coffee and play cards. The coffee houses are now tucked behind profitable video arcades.

Greektown, wrote *Detroit News* editor Martin Fischhoff "is a success story right out of some urban planner's dream (though planning had nothing to do with it). It's about the only place in Detroit that's alive around the clock."

Overpopulation caused hard times that drove over a fourth of the Greek labor force off their native rocky farmlands between 1890 and 1920. Greek men found their way to then-booming industrial towns throughout Michigan, from Detroit and Flint to Dowagiac and Calumet. They parlayed earnings from factory and construction work into small business opportunities opening up in a rapidly urbanizing America: shoe repair, groceries, rooming houses and downtown commercial property, and above all, confectioneries and restaurants. They did it so quickly and successfully that it's hard to believe that they were mostly farmers thrust into a totally unfamiliar environment, who hailed from remote rural villages that first got electricity well after World War II.

Greektown families have long since moved onward and upward. They are scattered throughout the metro area. But many Greek-Americans still patronize Greektown establishments. Restaurant menus feature gyros, shish kebob, spinach pie, Greek salads, egg-lemon soup, rice pudding, baklava, and the like. Locals joke that it's really all prepared in one kitchen.

For restaurants, see p. 224. Additional Greektown points of interest in addition to restaurants are:

◆ **Trappers Alley.** A spectacular, four-level festival marketplace Trappers Alley is a pleasant place to wander around. The rich brick facades of old buildings are juxtaposed with crisp, colorful tiles and lush foliage. These buildings once were part of the huge tannery operations of Traugott Schmidt and Sons, one of the country's largest tanneries in the late 19th century. A leading attraction here is the **Blue Nile**, an outstanding Ethiopian restaurant. (**Fishbone's Rhythm Kitchen** down the street, a wildly popular New Orleans-style restaurant, is the other big culinary draw.) Noteworthy Trappers Alley stores include several fashion boutiques (the most interesting is **Plum Street**, named in memory of Detroit's locus of Sixties-era flower power), the **Jill Perette Gallery**, with attractive African-inspired gifts, and **Made In Michigan**, with Up North sweatshirts and regional books, oven mitts and cutting boards shaped like Michigan's mitten, and long-lasting fragrant candles made by the proprietors. *Beaubien between Lafayette and Monroe. 963-5445. Mon-Thurs 10-9, Fri & Sat 10-11, Sun noon-7.*

◆ **Astoria Pastry Shop.** The spiffy new location of this old Greek pastry shop has been expanded to appeal to strolling Greektown crowds, with ice cream, cappucino, and quite a few tables. The spinach pie ($1) is a nice snack if you don't feel like buying an entire meal at nearby restaurants. Crusty yet soft Greek breads ($1 a loaf) are made for sopping up salad oils and pan juices. All the traditional Greek and Middle Eastern filo-honey-nut pastries are here, some with a new twist, like chocolate baklava. Prices are better at Arab pastry shops in east Dearborn (pp. 215-216). But Astoria offers a much wider range, including American favorites and Italian standards like toasted biscotti (some dipped in chocolate and walnut) and cannoli. *541 Monroe. (313) 963-9603. Mon-Sat 8 a.m.-11:30 p.m., Sun 9 a.m.-11 p.m.*

◆ **Athens Bookstore.** *The* place to find Greek-language publications, cassettes of Greek music, ornate coffee urns, gaudy religious icons, along with lots of tacky Detroit souvenirs. *520 Monroe (also entered from Trappers Alley). (313) 963-4490.*

◆ **Athens Grocery and Bakery.** Both Greektown groceries enjoy good reputations among Greek-Americans, and they smell wonderfully of fresh bread (in the morning) and spices. The crusty loaves, soft in the middle, sell for under a dollar apiece. The Athens' old-fashioned front window, filled with neatly arranged produce, nicely balances Greektown's neon glitz. *527 Monroe. (313) 961-1149. Mon-Thurs 9-9, Fri & Sat 9-11, Sun 9-7.*

◆ **Monroe Grocery and Bakery.** Open the beat-up wood screen door, and you feel you're in a time warp. Ornate, shiny tins of olive oil and imports have a turn-of-the-century look, while pistachios, Greek cheeses, olives, pastas, and filo dough are sold in bulk at the counter. *573 Monroe. (313) 964-9642. Sun-Thurs 9:30-8:30, Fri & Sat until 10 or 11.*

tables, or you can eat on benches by the parking structure out-
side. *1219 St. Antoine just north of Monroe. (313) 965-1692.
7:30 a.m.-6 p.m., Fri until midnight.*.
*Greektown is on Monroe St. between St. Antoine & Beaubien.
Most restaurants open 11 a.m.- 2 a.m. or later, 7 days a week.*
Park *at large, 24-hour city structure just east of Greektown, en-
tered off Monroe or Macomb.* ***People Mover Stations:*** *Greektown
(Monroe and Beaubien), Bricktown (Beaubien and Fort).*

GROCERIES IN GREEKTOWN . . . . . . Hours at Greektown's two old-world grocery
stores are so long ('til 9 p.m. at the earliest) that you can both dine and shop for
groceries. Greek bread, cheese, and wine can be the center of simple, delicious
meals.Greek feta cheese, made from sheep's milk, is richer and quite unlike the
domestic variety. Creamy white Kasseri cheese is like a mild cheddar. It can be
cut into cubes, dredged in seasoned flour, and pan-fried 'til it's soft. Greeks serve
it with lemon, crusty Greek bread, and a red wine like the dry red from the highly
recommended Nemea (pronounced "nuh-MAY-uh") region. An excellent, very
light white wine is made by Boutari. Both are about $7 a bottle. Retsina wine, fla-
vored with rosin, is admittedly an acquired taste even when served correctly
(very, very cold). Greeks like to drink it with fish, or with olives, bread, and fresh
tomatoes.

THE CRIMINAL JUSTICE SYSTEM AT WORK. . . . . Criminal mystique has been
one of Detroit's hottest cultural exports lately, thanks to area detective writers
Elmore Leonard and Loren Estleman, who set many of their stories here. **Detroit
Recorder's Court** is where Leonard and Estleman get much of their material, and
where Harrison Ford hung out to pick up atmosphere for the movie *Presumed
Innocent*. A model of efficiency under difficult conditions, the court recently
won a prestigious national award for its operation. "Watching criminal investigations in Recorder's Court is better than going to the movies, and it's free," says
a Leonard character. *Frank Murphy Hall of Justice, 1441 St. Antoine south of
Gratiot, a block northwest of Greektown.*

Detroit People Mover

*Get a spectacular bird's-eye view of downtown Detroit
on one of the country's most lavish
public transportation systems.*

T his elevated rail system runs in a 2.9-mile loop around
downtown. It offers extraordinary views of the central
city, the river, and Windsor. Even in winter, it's a memorable ride. As a bonus, big, colorful works of art make it an adventure to pass the platforms in each of the 12 stations. Call the
People Mover for a splendid brochure on "Art in the Stations."

The People Mover is the most expensive public transport in
history. The 2.9 miles cost federal and state taxpayers a whopping $200 million, vastly more than initial projections. Unfortunately, there are one-third fewer riders than projected (about
11,500 a day), requiring the financially strapped city to subsidize
it to the tune of over $9 million a year.

Still, the People Mover is a visitor's delight: beautifully
designed, clean, safe, and frequently patrolled. It's a smooth-working system which gives the rider an unparalleled view of the
glories and desolations of downtown Detroit. The entire loop
takes only 15 minutes. You may want to make several trips to
take it all in: the beauty of the aqua Detroit River on a sunny day,
the ornate 1920s skyscrapers, the VIPs' cars double-parked for
lunch at the elite Detroit Club, historic Grand Circus Park, the
once proud and now sadly abandoned hotels and office buildings
on the north part of the loop, the towering Renaissance Center,
lively Bricktown and Greektown. Special highlights: the swing
out over the Detroit River by the Joe Louis Arena and the up-close glimpse of City-County Building employees at their desks.

*Downtown Detroit (See map for route.) 1-800-541-7245 ; from
Detroit, 962-RAIL. Current operating hours: Mon-Thurs 7 a.m.-
11p.m., Fri 7 a.m.-midnight, Sat 9 a.m.-midnight, Sun noon-8
p.m. Fare: 50¢, children 5 and under free. Call to confirm; budget
cuts may necessitate changes.)*

Guardian Building

One of the country's most remarkable Art Deco skyscrapers, the Guardian is a visual feast.

This ornate Art Deco skyscraper, finished in 1929, is a flamboyant banking tribute to the go-go years of the 1920s. It also symbolizes the financial excesses of that time, for its occupant and owner, Guardian National Bank, was the very first in a nationwide domino-like chain of banks to close in 1933, greatly intensifying the national Depression.

The notched Aztec facade is unusual in itself. The 535-foot-high building is faced with specially made bricks, which bands of colored tiles enliven. The bricks, less costly than the granite or limestone exteriors of most skyscrapers of the era, allowed architect Wirt Rowland to use the savings on a variety of spectacular visual effects.

Most stunning are the **main lobby** and the adjacent **banking room** half a story up. Over the main entrance is a half dome cov-

ered in colorful tiles from Detroit's famous Pewabic Pottery (p. 139). Concealed in the 1950s, the dome has since been restored by the Guardian's present owner-occupant, Michigan Consolidated Gas. The walls of the main lobby are blood-red Numibian marble. Rowland had to reopen an African mine to get such a vivid natural hue. The lobby's mosaic mural was designed by noted artist Ezra Winter. The ceiling of the main banking room to the south is painted on canvas, behind which is a horsehair mat to mute sound in the vast room. Ask at

the information desk in the lobby for an interesting historical **brochure** on the building.

Ernest Kanzler, brother-in-law and close friend of Edsel Ford, built the Guardian Building. His Guardian Group became the major banking power in Detroit. Edsel Ford put millions of his and Ford Motor Company's money into Kanzler's banking syndicate, So successful was this group that there was even talk that Detroit would overtake Chicago as the financial center of the Midwest. Then the 1929 stock market crash put increasing strain on the overextended bank. Despite a personal plea from President Hoover, Henry Ford refused to bail the bank out at a critical juncture, even though his son lost up to $20 million with its failure.

500 Griswold at Congress. (313) 965-2430. Mon-Fri 9-5.

OTHER FINE DOWNTOWN ARCHITECTURE FROM THE EARLY 20TH CENTURY . . . . . The 1925 **Buhl Building** feels like a church, a true temple of commerce, with the dark, enclosed, rich effect of heavy medieval masonry and Romanesque decorative embellishments. The marble lobby with its Italian bronzes is a splendid setting for the dark, richly decorated **Buhl Cafe and Bar** and the elegantly simple little corner cafeteria, **Quattro Punti.** *Southwest corner, Griswold at Congress. Open Mon-Fri.* . . . . In the 47-story **Penobscot Building,** finished in 1928, architect Wirt Rowland designed one of Detroit's most endearingly appealing buildings. Setbacks above the 30th floor form an interesting cubistic pattern topped by an observation deck (now closed) and a big, illuminated ball, once a hallmark of the city. Inside, the warm-colored marble floors feature geometric designs, with Indian eagles on the elevator doors and mailboxes. The interior shops include a large **Doubleday** bookstore (the oldest in that big chain), the **Epicurean Cafe,** and **John T. Woodhouse Sons** tobacconist, whose wood-inlaid interior is a period delight. *Corner of Griswold and Fort. (313) 961-8800. Mon-Fri 8 a.m.-6 p.m.* . . . . . The former People's State Bank is Detroit's only building designed by the famous Beaux Arts architects McKim, Mead and White. It dates from 1900 and is now occupied by **Silver's,** a stylish office supply firm. Balustrades, allegorical sculpture, and two Ionic columns make it appropriately bank-like, but huge arched windows let in lots of light. Today the dignified banking floor showcases gifts and accessories, plus room arrangements of office furniture. It feels a little like a museum of serious good design. The gifty, impulse-oriented lower level (opening onto Congress) is jazzy, with trendier items and good sales on glassware, dishes, cards, candies, and the excellent and very popular cafeteria-style **Britt's Cafe** . *151 W. Fort at Shelby. (313) 963-0000. Mon-Fri 8:30-3 p.m..*

Fox Theatre

*Peacocks and Buddhas and unabashed excess
in a Siamese-Byzantine-Indian picture palace,
lavish with fake jewels and gilt*

Detroit's extraordinary boom decade of the 1920s resulted in many palatial homes and some flamboyant office buildings, Art Deco storefronts, and, especially, theaters. Detroit's auto boom and explosive population growth had coincided with the era of palatial movie theaters put up across America by Hollywood studio owners. Detroit's Grand Circus Park area developed an unusual concentration of opulent theaters, each designed to outdo the last. None was more utterly and unabashedly gaudy than the 5,000-seat Fox Theatre on Woodward, opened in 1928 and restored in 1988. Part of the nationwide 250-theater Fox chain, this $6 million picture palace was the flagship of the empire, the pinnacle of Detroit architect C. Howard Crane's successful career as a movie theater designer. (It was later duplicated by St. Louis's Fox Theatre.)

The eclectic Asian interior was designed by owner William Fox's wife, Eve Leo. She humorously called it "Siamese Byzantine." The six-story lobby was designed to look like an ancient temple in India. In the main auditorium you can see a two-ton stained-glass chandelier. Walls feature peacocks, serpents, Buddhas, Chinese tomb guardians, Greek masks, Egyptian lions, and other motifs from Hindu, Persian, Indian, Chinese, and southeast Asian art. This era of unbridled opulence was not to last long. Fox lost control of his theaters during the Depression, which left him $91 million in debt.

The Fox was designed for both movies and live performances. Thanks to hometown booster Mike Ilitch, owner of Little Caesar's Pizza and the Detroit Red Wings hockey team, a careful $15 million restoration has been completed. The Fox is packing in crowds with over 250 acts a year — a heartening boon for a troubled downtown abandoned by major retailers. New restaurants have opened nearby, and energy for a theater district revival is gaining steam. The 1925 State Theater, a block toward downtown from the Fox, has been transformed into **ClubLand**, one of entrepreneur Steve Jarvis's razzle-dazzle, multi-screen dance clubs in spectacular old picture palaces.

For its first full year the Fox was the top-grossing venue anywhere in the U.S. Wide-ranging attractions have included Bill Cosby, Chuck Berry and Jerry Lee Lewis, Bonnie Raitt, The Red Army Chorus, Donald O'Connor, and Mickey Rooney, Barbara Mandrell, the Eurythmics, and an occasional movie. Ilitch has renovated the 10-story office building attached to the Fox as the new world headquarters of Little Caesar's, the first major firm to move to Detroit in over 30 years.

If you go, don't miss **"Peacock Alley,"** a hallway above the Fox's main lobby. It displays paintings, furniture, and artifacts assembled by Eve Leo from around the world.

2211 Woodward between Montcalm and Columbia. Parking directly across Woodward. (313) 567-6000 .

MORE EXCITEMENT FOR THE THEATER DISTRICT. . . . . 1992 saw the smashing success of **"The All Night Strut"** and **"Forbidden Broadway"** in the intimate, stunningly restored 1927 **Gem Theater**, a half block from the Fox. It was the realization of real estate executive/investor Chuck Forbes's dream to engineer the revival of the grand theater district he had loved growing up in Detroit. First he bought numerous threatened theaters, including the Fox, and made deals to assure their preservation and reuse. Now the two sassy, smartly produced cabaret-style musical revues (with a cast of four and one piano) are bringing people into the city for the first time in years. "Strut" has been called "a time-tunnel express back to the 1930s and 40s," while "Broadway" satirizes the pretensions of recent musicals like "Les Miz" and "Cats." Shows are daily, and tickets fun from about $15 (groups) to $25 (individuals on Fri/Sat evenings). Two-year runs are expected. Call (313) 645-6666.

THE MUSIC HALL Center for the Performing Arts . . . . . , another elegant theater being restored, is on Madison facing Grand Circus Park. The Music Hall is the new home of the very popular **Detroit Youtheatre**, offering children's programs on Saturdays at 11 and 2 and the Wiggle Club on Sundays at 2 (October-May). Call (313) 963-7663 for Youtheatre, (313) 963-7680 for the Music Hall special events. . . . . Around the corner on Broadway, the **Michigan Opera Theater** is restoring the lovely and large Grand Circus Theater, a massive project not ready for years.

THE GRAYSTONE JAZZ MUSEUM . . . . . has moved downtown to 1521 Broadway, just down from Grand Circus Park. Founder/director James Jenkins is enthusiastically devoted to keeping Detroit's great jazz tradition alive with concerts, book signings, a film series, and the videos, memorabilia,and instruments you can see here. Named after the celebrated Graystone Ballroom. Detroit jazz greats include Betty Carter, Donald Burrd, Sonny Stitts, Milt Jackson, and Barry Harris. *Open Tues-Fri 10-5, Sat 11-4. (313) 963-3813. $2 ,*

A STATELY DOWNTOWN PARK . . . . . is **Grand Circus Park** on Woodward and Adams, a block southeast of the Fox. Its semi-circular shape was created

Downtown Detroit shops and galleries

*Tucked away in quaint, odd corners —
established galleries and creative new shops*

Contrary to the popular impression, quality retailing in downtown Detroit isn't completely dead. It's just scattered in pockets that can be hard for outsiders to find. Seeking them out can be a tonic to the jaded, because doing business in the city, much more than in malls, is still about personal relationships. This is true at the sturdy old survivors around the Eastern Market (p. 152) and downtown, and at creative new shops and galleries.

It comes as a surprise to many outsiders to notice that in Detroit people on the street are, on the whole, friendlier and more open than in upscale suburbs and resorts. They even smile! Crime in Detroit is what outsiders worry most about. But downtown Detroit, Rivertown, and the New Center are frequently patrolled. The People Mover has been virtually incident-free. Normal discretion about avoiding deserted places is advisable, of course. And lighted, guarded parking at night should be the rule. The biggest danger in Detroit at night, insiders say, is car theft, not muggings. The attended city garage under Grand Circus Park is inexpensive, safe, never full, and close to the People Mover route. Try to avoid being on the freeways at rush hour (3:30-6 p.m.). Instead, stay for dinner, or see a movie.

Here's a selection of shops and galleries well worth a look:

◆ In the **Harmonie Park** area, two blocks east of the Broadway People Mover station. A fountain and park occupies one of the odd triangles created by Judge Woodward's circle-and-spokes street layout after the 1805 Detroit fire. Street people sit in the park; creative shops are scattered nearby. A longtime Harmonie Park gallery, the interesting, respected **Detroit Artists' Market**, has been lured away to Stroh River Place, page 161. But architects Schervish Vogel Merz, who helped orchestrate the successful revival of Rivertown (p. 159), have moved to the old Harmonie Hall and acquired rights to much area property. They may pull off Harmonie Park's long-anticipated rebirth. Watch this space!

On Randolph just down from the park, **Cluttered Corners** *(313-963-5977; Tues-Sat 11-5)* displays unusual, reasonably priced antiques and some contemporary crafts in striking room settings. Also on hand: interesting estate and modern jewelry, including African-face cameos. **Preston Burke Galleries** on Randolph and Grand River *(313-963-2350; Mon-Sat 11-5)* has diversified to include not only "corporate art" — big, abstract pieces to enliven office walls) — but a lively assortment of jewelry, pottery, bright painted furniture, and posters and original art by African-American artists.

A walkout basement at 297 East Grand River, across from the park, is shared by two friendly shops with extremely well-made women's clothes that are classic without being traditional, presented with a subdued ethnic/African flair. **Spirit in the Park** *(313-965-4919)* features owner-designer Joie Coelho's simple, flowing capes, jackets, hand-painted sweatshirts, and dresses in wool and various ethnic fabrics (patchwork, mudcloth, batik), along with Japanese kimonos ($100), African artifacts, and jewelry. The motto of adjoining **Baseline Boutique** *(313-965-2542)* is "if you want to dress for the boardroom but your budget says mailroom." It specializes in choice resale career clothes. *Hours for both stores, usually Mon-Sat 11-5, can be irregular; call first.*

Half a block down from the park at 230 E. Grand River, **Spectacles** (313-963-6886) is the quintessence of cool, Spike Lee-style urban hip. It features Ts, sweats, jackets, and caps with designs from his movies. (It may be the only store outside Lee's native Brooklyn to carry his pricey gear.) Other sportswear, jewelry, accessories, leather goods, and shades are also on hand. Mon-Sat *11-5:30 except Thurs & Sat to 6 and Fri to 7.*

On Grand River at Library two blocks toward Woodward from Harmonie Park are two interesting galleries just behind the old Hudson's. The **Sherry Washington Gallery** *(313-961-4500, open Tues-Sat noon-6)* represents two internationally acclaimed African-American painters, Benny Andrews and Richard Mayhew, as well as Shirley Woodson, Charles Burwell, and David Fludd, all with national reputations and all of African descent. Big windows and a splendidly restored Beaux Arts building make this a fine place to look at art. Kitty-corner from it at 35 East Grand River, **Gallery Biagas** showcases works mostly by Latin American artists and Americans of Latin extraction in a striking modernistic former bank building. *(313) 961-0634, Mon-Fri 11-7, Sat 12-5. Call to confirm.*

◆ **Broadway at Gratiot** has long been a center of men's clothing. **The Broadway** at 1241 Broadway is loaded with designer names, leather coats, and beautifully accessorized displays — the GQ look. It's favored by style-conscious men, including famous rock and sports stars and occasional drug dealers like the one assassinated in the store itself.

Notwithstanding, it's a friendly place, and the sales are terrific. *Mon-Thurs 9:30-6 p.m., to 6:30 on Fri & Sat.* Across Gratiot at 1307 Broadway, **Henry the Hatter** is in its 99th year. "Everything that's made, we carry," claims its owner, including $8 wool berets, British silk hats, Western hats, and the flat-top black hat with a snap brim ($65) favored by jazz great Dexter Gordon. *(313) 962-0970. Mon-Sat 9-6.*

◆ **Beaubien near Congress**, near Greektown. In an elegantly renovated townhouse at 511 Beaubien, the **Muccioli Studio Gallery** downstairs offers owner-created jewelry and art. You have to look carefully to find the entrance to 743 Beaubien and the third-floor **Detroit Focus Gallery**. This respected, artist-run nonprofit gallery shows the work of established and new artists in juried and curated shows. *(313) 962-9025. Wed-Sat 12-6.*

◆ **Woodward Avenue**, once Detroit's equivalent of Fifth Avenue, isn't just wig shoppes and discount stores, though it can seem like it. There's a big, bustling **Winkelman's** at 1448 Woodward, much appreciated by those Detroiters determined to support the city by shopping Detroit despite the blandishments of encircling suburban malls. *(313) 961-3252. Mon-Sat 10-5:45.*

◆ **John R at Elizabeth**, two blocks northeast of the Fox. **Twenty One Ten Elizabeth's** is a tucked-away downtown treasure charmingly cluttered with interesting jewelry, baskets, pottery, stationery, and cards — multi-ethnic in origin, arranged with a gentle sort of nouveau Victorian flair. There's so much to see, you might easily miss the nifty rubber stamps and beads for necklaces and earrings. A friendly, savvy staff makes this a good stop for scoping out downtown happenings. *(313) 964-2649. Mon-Sat 11-5.*

🌲🎄🌲

MOVIES IN THE CENTRAL CITY . . . . . For standard first-run fare, **Renaissance One Two Three & Four** in the RenCen, Tower 200, level 2. Weekday shows start at 5:15, weekends from 1 p.m. (313) 259-2370 . . . . . . The **Detroit Film Theater** shows high-caliber films that haven't often been seen locally. The plush auditorium in the Detroit Institute of Arts boasts excellent acoustics and technical equipment, and there's even a bar with wine, cappucino, and pastries. Call (313) 833-2323.

JAZZ FOR EARLY BIRDS . . . . . . Clean, well-run, not too smoky, no cover, and good, reasonably-priced down-home food like pork chop sandwiches and macaroni. The crowd is mixed — young and old, black and white, suburban and urban — and the atmosphere is wonderfully friendly. Most music clubs are never as organized as **Bo-Mac's Lounge** at 281 Gratiot between Broadway and Randolph, around the corner from Harmonie Park. It's open from 11 a.m. to 2 a.m., and Thursday through Sunday the live music starts at 8 p.m. (313) 961-5152.

John King Books

*In an old glove factory near downtown Detroit,
one of the biggest used book stores in the country*

Housed in a big old former work glove factory just west of downtown, John King Books has quickly become a national leader in used and rare books. Its workaholic owner, John King, flies all around the country in search of big lots of used and remaindered books to fill his store's over 30,000 square feet. (A separate warehouse has another 20,000 square feet.) At 750,000 volumes, his may be the biggest book store in the country. The stock is well organized, and browsing is comfortable. The store also sells a fascinating variety of framed pictures, printed ephemera, postcards, and collectibles, artfully displayed in several rooms of this pleasant catacomb. The store will search for hard-to-find titles for a dollar. There's always a box of free books out front.

John King in his store.

King's philosophy for acquiring books is to stay general, partly because he finds it "too boring" to specialize. He keeps the prices reasonable, and he and his staff do a good job weeding out the drivel.

901 W. Lafayette just west of the Lodge Expressway (U.S. 10) at Sixth St. Park on expressway side of building. (313) 961-0622. Mon-Sat 9:30-5:30.

Tiger Stadium

One of very last of the legendary old ball parks, it's got atmosphere the new ones can't beat.

This glorious old ball park may have only a few more years before it is replaced. The exploits of Tigers past — Ty Cobb, Charlie Gehringer, Mickey Cochran, Al Kaline, plus Lou Gehrig's last game and Reggie Jackson's 1971 All-Star home run onto the upper-deck roof — all these resonate in the minds of knowledgeable visitors to the venerable park, where the cast-iron supports of the old seats are embellished with tiger heads. Tiger Stadium has several hundred seats behind pillars, and more cheap seats than any other ball park. That jeopardizes it in the new economics of baseball.

The Tigers were already playing at this site (then called Bennett Park, capacity 8,500) when a 23,000-seat stadium was built in 1912. It is the core of today's Tiger Stadium. In 1924 double decks were constructed from first to third base. They extend all the way out over the lower deck, providing some of baseball's best upper-level seats, right on top of the action. In 1936 more double decks in the right field pavilion and bleachers were added, and still more seats in 1938, bringing the capacity to 53,000.

Aficionados of surviving old ball parks rate Tiger Stadium at the top, right up with Forbes Field. Tiger fans are ecstatic now that Mike Ilitch of Little Caesar's Pizza has bought the club from fellow pizza baron Tom Monaghan, whose flair for alienating diverse groups of people may be unmatched. Ilitch's renovated Fox Theater has been the best thing for downtown in years; now he's committed to keeping the Tigers in the city, and bringing back the organ and maybe beloved announcer Ernie Harwell, too. The old ball park's fate remains uncertain, so it's best to see it while you can.

Michigan Ave. at Trumbull, one mile west of downtown Detroit. Call (313) 962-4000 for schedule and ticket reservations.

A TASTE OF MEXICO NEAR TIGER STADIUM . . . . . Just half a mile southwest of the stadium on Bagley is **Mexican Town**, with several popular Mexican restaurants and an interesting Mexican import shop. Businesses here and on Vernor between Grand River and Livernois serve southwest Detroit's sizable Hispanic population of over 30,000. A wide selection of Mexican groceries and beers is at **La Colmena** grocery to the east, on 2443 Bagley at 17th. It stays open until 8.

Boblo Island

An especially delightful amusement park,
Boblo makes up for its lack of terrifying rides
with a scenic boat ride and great atmosphere.

A trip to Boblo Island makes for a splendid outing. The
Detroit River cruise between Detroit and the island is an
exceptional treat by itself. And the amusement park,
dating back to 1898, has enough amusing spectacles to entertain
adults as well as children.

By far the best boat ride is on the big, old original Boblo steamers from the Detroit dock at the foot of Clark Street. Both the
Columbia and the *Ste. Claire* offer game rooms for kids, concession stands, and superb river views from the top deck. The
boats themselves are the last remaining steam-pwered passenger
vessels in North America, and passengers can see the engines.
The scenery is also much more interesting when you leave from
Detroit. There's a great view of the Ambassador Bridge and
downtown Detroit. As you sail downriver, the 90-minute trip
takes you past the dock area, once bustling and now mostly quiet.
You pass river traffic, big old steel mills, chemical factories, Zug
Island, Grosse Ile, impressive riverfront estates, Amherstburg,
and the open expanse of Lake Erie. As long as you're not being
lashed by a chilly wind, it's an exhilarating outing.

Boblo Island is in the Canadian half of the Detroit River. Last
century the 272-
acre island was
militarily strategic
because it faced
out toward the
opening of Lake
Erie. You can still
see a blockhouse
built by the British

in 1837, and the first lighthouse built on the Great Lakes. The
great Indian chief Tecumseh held a war council on Boblo during
the War of 1812.

Though Boblo rides don't compare with the nation's major
amusement parks, there are enough here to amuse all but quite
demanding thrill-seekers. Over 75 rides and attractions include
all the stock classics. The **Ferris wheel** and **sky tower** offer fine

views of the surroundings. Small kids enjoy Fort Fun, complete with ball crawl, rope climb, punching bag forest, and other exhausting activities.

The Nightmare **enclosed roller coaster** is a 90-second ride in the dark, punctuated by special sound effects and lighting. It's the centerpiece of the **International Pavilion** (built as the dance pavilion in 1913, recently renovated for $1.9 million), with food booths, shops, and a games arcade. Admission to Boblo also covers several shows, including animated singing characters and water-skiing.

Boblo can be uncomforttable on cool, windy days and there can be long waits for rides on weekends and holidays.

By boat only, from docks at Amherstburg (Canada), or Gibraltar. **Gibraltar dock** *is just north of the foot of Gibraltar Rd. east of Jefferson and about a mile east of I-75 exit 29A (Gibraltar Rd.). Amherstburg dock is at Front Rd. and Simcoe St., 16 1/2 miles south of Windsor.* **Park open** *Memorial Day weekend-Labor Day. Weekdays through mid-June 11 a.m. until 5:30 until 8:30 weekends through mid-June, until 8:30; after mid-June, open to 8:30 weekdays, to 10:30 on weekends.* **For departure times**, *call (313) 843-0700.* **Cost**, *including boat trip and all rides and shows: $17.50 ($8.75 after 3 p.m.) for ages 7-50, $14.50 for 51 and over, and $11.50 (ages 3-6). Call for lower group prices.* **Moonlight cruises**: *11 p.m.-1 a.m. Fri & Sat, $10.95.*

1992 UPDATE: The old steamers have been sold and the Detroit docks closed. That move, lamented by all who love the city and its heritage, destroyed a good deal of the charm of a trip to Boblo.

DETROIT'S MAIL BOAT AND HOW TO SEE IT . . . . . Detroit is an eagerly-awaited port for most Great Lakes sailors, because it is the only place in the world where ships in motion regularly receive deliveries of mail, passengers, and packages. The service is provided by the J.W. Westcott Company. Its little 45-foot boat pulls up beside each passing freighter, looking alarmingly fragile next to the giant it is servicing. The freighter's crew drops down a line with a bucket at its end to receive shipments. Mail going to these passing freighters even has a special zip code, 48222. The best place to see this interesting spectacle is at **Riverside Park** on W. Jefferson at the foot of West Grand, one block south of Fort. To find out if a freighter is coming, you can call the Westcott Company at (313) 496-0555.

Historic Fort Wayne

Built to defend Detroit from the British,
this fort now dramatizes Detroit's military history.

This old U.S. Army fort, now a Detroit museum, has been connected with a good deal of important U.S. military history. Though it was built in the 1840s and 1850s, its design was based on principles of warfare developed in the 17th century. The fort is closer to a medieval fortress than a 20th-century military base. It's a reminder of how rapidly warfare has changed in the past century, compared with the previous six centuries.

Like a castle, Fort Wayne depends on an encircling moat, thick walls, and heavy, studded doors. Its star shape allowed cannon to fire grapeshot out of embrasures to repel attackers who approach the 22-foot-high outer walls. Fort Wayne also harks back to the time when the U.S. was still in conflict with Great Britain. It was built on a narrow bend in the Detroit River three miles south of downtown Detroit in order to stop enemy vessels from heading up the river.

Visitors can explore the tunnels and casemates (chambers for guns) within the outer walls and walk through the handsome three-story barracks near the fort's parade ground. The fort's first two floors house exhibits telling the story of Detroit's military history, from the coming of the French in 1701 through the Indian Wars of the 1890s.

Smaller museums are housed in the separate buildings of officers' row, outside the old star fort. The **commanding officer's house** has been restored to an authentically furnished 1880 Victorian residence. In the **guardhouse**, furnished as it was during the Spanish-American War in 1898, a costumed soldier usually talks about his life as a guard.

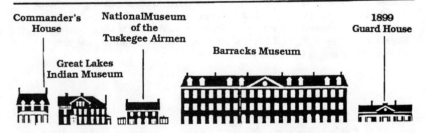

| Commander's House | NationalMuseum of the Tuskegee Airmen | | 1899 Guard House |
| Great Lakes Indian Museum | | Barracks Museum | |

6325 W. Jefferson at Livernois. (313) 297-9360. Usual season: first week in May through Labor Day, Wed-Sun 9:30-5. Tours of the **National Museum of the Tuskegee Airmen** and the **Great Lakes Indian Museum** can sometimes be arranged throughout the year. <u>Budget constraints during 1991 have eliminated regular hours, but the fort and museums are open during eight special events; call for information.</u>

BLACK FLIERS AND WOODLAND INDIANS AT FORT WAYNE . . . . . The **National Museum of the Tuskegee Airmen** tells the story of American black servicemen's struggle to achieve equality during World War II. The Airmen were an all-black Air Force unit, formed in 1942 at the instigation of civil rights leaders, and stationed at Tuskegee, Alabama. In the North African and Italian campaigns, the Airmen proved their skill as pilots, bombardiers, navigators, and ground crew. . . . . . The **Great Lakes Indian Museum** has one of the finest collections of Woodland Indian artifacts, including beautiful quillwork, beaded moccasins and ceremonial clothing, and early trade goods. *Both museums open same hours as Fort Wayne.*

OUTSTANDING SPECIAL EVENTS AT HISTORIC FORT WAYNE . . . . . include informal weekend concerts and events like the Maytime antique car show. For **Civil War Day** (first weekend in May), hundreds of people depict life at the fort during the Civil War and demonstrate tactical weapons. On **Fort Night** (same night as the big Detroit River fireworks display at the pre-July 4 International Freedom Festival) there is patriotic band music and a good view of the fireworks. The **Highland Games** (first weekend in August) is the oldest continuous Highland games in North America, sponsored by Detroit's St. Andrew's Society. It features bagpipes and athletics. Call (313) 297-9360 for information.

Eastern Market

A colorful, earthy vestige of old Detroit,
with wonderful food appealing to the city's diverse peoples

Since the 1890s, this colorful, bustling market has been where Detroiters come to buy produce from local farmers and to find meats, fish, coffee, nuts, produce, fruit, spices, wine, and cheese from the stores around the market. Surrounding the large open-air stall area called "the sheds," where up to 800 farmers can sell their produce, are wholesale-retail specialty shops. The entire area has an earthy atmosphere.

The Market is a genuine vestige of old Detroit: a great medley of smells and sounds and colorful sights, and a vast variety of food appealing to the city's diverse populations and cultures. Much of the market's color comes from the old wholesale/retail businesses clustered around the square (used for parking) in front of the main market sheds. In front of **Ciaramitaro's**, the third-generation Italian produce business on Market and Winder, you'll see dozens of crates of onions being unloaded, followed  by piles of burlap bags of potatoes, as customers buy grapefruit and celery from the stand that's in front of the store, winter and summer. Next to the **Gratiot Central Market,** southeast of the Eastern Market sheds across the recessed Fisher Freeway, the aroma of nuts pervades the air at **Germack's**, the oldest pistachio importer in the U.S. Pungent spices greet you in several Middle Eastern shops; an Islamic slaughterhouse is a few blocks away. Nearby at **Capital Poultry**, live ducks (a favorite with Detroit's many Poles) and chickens cackle away. Feathers are mixed in the dirt in the gutter outside.

Wholesalers at the market today are likely to be descended from Belgian, German, and Polish farmers who sold at the market generations ago, or from Italian and Lebanese produce peddlers who first catered to Detroit's booming population of industrial workers beginning about 1910. In a city that's known great ups and downs, people love the Eastern Market because it's still the same.

The market changes with the time and day of the week.

◆ **Saturday mornings.** The market is a madhouse, especially from 7 to 10, when the crowds are largest. Food-lovers from far and wide converge here for weekend shopping.

◆ **Early weekday mornings.** The wholesalers' weekday work is mostly done before sun-up. Around 1 a.m. trucks from the South and Southwest arrive to be unloaded. Throughout the early-morning hours, trucks of all sizes are coming and going, unloading and loading. Some produce is already destined for distributors like I.G.A., Spartan, and Abner Wolf, and some is sold at the market. By the time restaurants open around 6 or 7 a.m., the main part of the work day is over, and it's time for a break.

Farmers in market stalls compete with these out-of-state producers for retail buyers, and a lot of bargaining takes place. Farmers at the market are prepared to sell wholesale to distributors, retailers, and restaurants, and retail to the general public, but consumers can try their hand at bargaining down to wholesale prices, especially if they buy in quantity.

◆ **Weekdays in the mid-morning and afternoon.** Now the atmosphere is leisurely — a good time to get the undivided attention of the knowledgeable clerks at market shops. The farmers are gone by late morning, but wholesale/retail produce places remain well stocked.

The thickest concentration of retail stores is on Russell just north of the market. There, low new buildings house a variety of retail stores, including the venerable and highly recommended **Al's Fish and Seafood** (2929 Russell, 313-393-1722) and **B & S Produce** (3111 Russell, 313-833-6133), where you can get big bags of onions and potatoes, 5 pounds of raw peanuts for under $5, fresh-roasted peanuts for little over a dollar, or choose from five kinds of watermelon in season.

North of the market between Gratiot and Mack are several more blocks of wholesalers and meat packers, who cut up and package carcasses for retailers. Every odd turn reveals something else: **Rudy's New and Used Restaurant Equipment, Berry & Sons Islamic Slaughterhouse, Amrine's** Middle Eastern grocery near the Gratiot Central Market, the **Jenuwine Candy & Tobacco** wholesale/retailers on Russell (pun intended), **Fuchs Religious Goods** across Gratiot from the Gratiot Central Market (where you'll find jinx-removing incense and herbal remedies), the **Farmers' Restaurant** on Market and Division, and the **Meat Cutters Inn** at 2638 Orleans ("Fine Food, open 7 a.m.-7 p.m., Hires Root Beer").

Here are some of the Eastern Market's most notable shops.

◆ **Cost Plus Wine Warehouse.** It's a real pleasure to deal with Irishman Tim McCarthy. Knowledgeable without being condescending or snobbish, he is a great guide to wines. He puts his own label (Tara Hills) on a very good Michigan Riesling produced by Chateau Grand Traverse and sells it for only $5 a bottle. *2448 Market. (313) 259-3845. Mon-Fri 8:30-6, Sat 7-4:30.*

◆ **R. Hirt Jr. Company.** This century-old Detroit grocery has a great range of merchandise: cheese, sausage and ham products, crackers, bottled waters, beans and rice, coffees and teas, mustards and condiments, chocolates and cookies, and all sorts of imported pastas, jams, sparkling waters, olives, and fancy foods. As at many Eastern Market wholesale/retailers, prices are somewhere between wholesale and normal retail prices.

Hirt's is big-hearted and resolutely old-fashioned, even when old-fashioned means somewhat inefficient. You take a basket, load up on shelved merchandise, then go to the counterperson. He or she gets your cheese from the ancient, walk-in wood refrigerator, cuts it straight from the wheel (you can often get samples), wraps your purchases, and writes up a bill. This you pay at the separate cashier's, then return to pick up your purchases. Saturdays are crazy, what with the big, convivial crowds who seem to enjoy the opportunity to socialize in line and pick up food ideas. On weekdays, it's quiet, and the service is attentive, prompt, and knowledgeable.

Hirt's non-food treasure trove is the third-floor wicker and basket department, where you can find classics ($5 laundry baskets, $2 door mats, tomato, bushel, and berry baskets, covered picnic baskets), decorator items (including decorative tins, hampers, $55 Adirondack chairs), and a huge variety of shapes and sizes of all kinds of baskets. *2468 Market at Windsor. (313) 567-1173. Mon-Fri 8-5, Sat 7-2.*

◆ **Ciaramitaro Brothers Produce.** Ciaramitaro's (pronounced "SHERM-uh-ta-ro's) and many other market old-timers started as "commission houses" that took farm produce and resold it at a percentage. Today Ciarmitaro's is mainly a wholesale food purveyor. The colorful, year-round produce stand on the sidewalk is more of a sideline run by retirees. The ancient-looking frame building was used as a tavern and inn going back to the 1840s. Slaves fleeing to Canada were housed in its basement. *2506 Market at Winder. (313) 567-9064. Mon-Sat 5:30 a.m.-2 p.m.*

◆ **Joe's Wine and Liquor.** Known for its extensive collection of beers. *2933 Russell. (313) 393-3125. Mon-Sat 7-6, Fri until 7.*

◆ **Rafal Spice Company.** Even if you don't need any spices, be sure to stop in here just to smell the 400 herbs and spices on hand. It's a visual treat, too, to see row upon row crammed with everything from asafoetida powder to burdock root. Rafal also carries 85 kinds of coffee beans (at attractive prices), 60 kinds of bulk teas, and a large assortment of hot sauces, plus potpourri, oils, and books with recipes for concocting your own scents. Pick up a mail-order catalog, and you can conveniently inventory and restock your spice rack from home. *2521 Russell. (313) 259-6373. Mon-Fri 7-4, Sat 7-2.*

◆ **Gratiot Central Market.** This colorful amalgam of butchers and other shops is in the white building with the terra cotta cow heads over the entrances. **Ronnie's Meats** (313-567-3226) offers a wide range of meats, including portions of a sheep's or cow's anatomy most Americans never consider edible. *Detroit Monthly* has called its baby back ribs the best in town. Goat is butchered to Islamic halal standards. **Joe Wigley Meats** (313-567-2857) is famous for its lamb and kosher-style corned beef. *1429 Gratiot. It faces Gratiot on one side and the Fisher Freeway Service Drive on the other. Mon-Fri 8-5, Fri until 6, Sat 7-7.* **Park** *on the service drive or Gratiot, or take the pedestrian walkway over the Fisher Freeway from market square parking.*

◆ **Capital Poultry.** Here you can actually pick out a live chicken to be dressed and picked up later. Free-range chickens grown by northern Indiana Amish are sold for very reasonable prices. Other poultry is also available, including guineas, pigeons, and wild game in season. *1466 E. Fisher Freeway next to the Gratiot Central Market. Tues-Sat 7:30-5.*

◆ **Germack Pistachio Company.** America's oldest pistachio processor (since 1924) offers natural and red pistachios and many kinds of nuts, seeds, and dried fruits. Roasting is done on the premises. *1416 E. Fisher Freeway, near the Gratiot Market. (313) 393-0219. Mon-Fri 8:30-4:30, Sat until 2.*

The Eastern Market is just north of Gratiot 1 mile east of downtown. From Gratiot, take Russell north over the Chrysler Freeway. Signs clearly direct visitors from Gratiot to the market. Eastern Market Central Administration: (313) 833-1560. **Market hours:** *Mon-Fri 5 a.m.-noon (but most farmers are gone by mid-morning), Sat 5 a.m.-6 p.m.* **Retail store hours:** *typically 8 a.m. (earlier on Saturday) until 4 p.m. or 2 p.m. Sat.*

EASTERN MARKET RESTAURANTS . . . . . There are a variety of popular eating places in the Market to pick up a cheap breakfast or lunch. The new **Russell Street Deli** (2465 Russell, 313-567-2900; current hours Mon-Fri 11-2:30, Sat 8:30-2) stands out above the rest with its excellent homemade soups, changing daily, and fresh-roasted turkey sandwiches. Classic deli sandwiches mostly around $4. Also in the vicinity: the venerable **Roma Cafe** , **Joe Muer's** outstanding fish restaurant on Gratiot at Vernor (see p. OOO), and, on the inexpensive, takeout end, the highly regarded **Louisiana Creole Jambalaya** just north of Joe Muer's on the opposite side of Gratiot .

Heidelberg Street Project

Color and castoffs turned a decaying neighborhood into a fantasy environment.

Tour busses stop regularly on Heidelberg Street, in the oldest and most decrepit part of Detroit, the near east side. Here are street after street of modest worker homes from the 1880s. Most are older and run-down. A few look well-maintained. More are boarded up. There are so many vacant lots that pheasants are known to thrive in these parts.

Artist Tyree Guyton grew up on Heidelberg Street, and here he started creating a remarkable piece of inner-city environmental art. His first work was "Fun House," an abandoned house next to his grandfather's neat, grey and green home. He splashed the weathered frame house with color and covered it with old toys, dollhouses, pictures, signs, plastic bottled and the like.

Guyton's Heidelberg Project grew beyond individual buildings. Now the pavement of Heidelberg Street sports a tangle of colored lines. Bright shoes march up a tree trunk. A crowd of stately pedestal drinking fountains gathers in the vacant lot across the street. Black and white splotches decorate the dead tree behind them. New discards arrive regularly, dropped off by Guyton's many fans, and the project is always evolving with new ideas and new material. Smiling faces painted on Naugahyde-type chairs enhance the party atmosphere of a vacant lot.

For Guyton, the project has been both a way to stabilize the neighborhood, now turned into a tourist attraction, and to work out his own personal demons. As a child he lived in poverty on this street. His mother was overwhelmed by family responsibilities. He was abused by a family acquaintance and teased for his interest in art. Only his grandfather encouraged his art.

As an adult, Guyton studied at Detroit's Center for Creative Studies and has pursued art as a career. "Fun House" got him started using color, imagination, and cast-off toys to transform a depressing environment into a wild and appealing fantasy of the childhood he never enjoyed. The effect is loose and not conventionally cute. It evokes strong reactions — pro and con.

Photos can't convey the magical, powerful feeling of this place. Coming here is a very special experience, especially if you have a talk with Guyton's grandfather, Sam Mackey. Mackey has lived in the neat, green house next to the Fun House for 40 years. He has seen the neighborhood become spotted with abandoned homes that invite arson, drugs, and other crimes. He's a philosopher and preacher, and he's often out on the park bench installed for the steady stream of visitors.

UPDATE: In spring, 1992 the city of Detroit, responding to unidentified neighbors' complaints, gave Tyree Guyton 15 minutes to salvage bits of his assemblages before demolishing Fun House and several other city-owned buildings he had decorated. His outdoor arrangements of pedestal sinks, shoes marching up spotted trees, assemblages of doors, and embellished environments not attached to houses remain and continue to grow. In June Sam Mackey died; hundreds of people who loved the Heidelberg Project attended his funeral. His house has now been decorated with multicolored designs. Tyree Guyton's work has been exhibited at the Detroit Institute of Arts and elsewhere; his career as an artist seems on its way.

On Heidelberg between Mt. Elliott and Ellery. From downtown, take Gratiot to Mount Elliott, turn right. Three blocks past Mack, turn right onto Heidelberg Street. Or, go east on Jefferson, turn left onto Mt. Elliott, and turn left onto Heidelberg in about a mile.

IN THE VICINITY AND WORTH A LOOK. . . . . The well-known **Capuchin monastery and soup kitchen** is a few blocks southeast on Mt. Elliott. . . . . For almost two centuries Detroit notables have been buried at picturesque **Elmwood Cemetery,** entered off Elmwood just north of Lafayette. . . . . . If you take Mt. Elliott all the way southeast to the river, you'll be at **Mt. Elliott Park,** one of the new riverfront parks. It's a good place to fish and watch river traffic and activities at the Coast Guard's station for ice-breaking, rescue, buoy-tending, and policing operations. Pick up a snack or deli food at the upscale Harbortown Market on Jefferson at Mt. Elliott.

Detroit River

*One of the world's major freighter highways
is beautiful on a sunny day.*

This wide, deep river connects the upper Great Lakes (Huron, Superior, and Michigan) with the lower Great Lakes of Erie and Ontario. Three centuries ago, when French fur-trading interests dominated this region, the river's almost half-mile width made it difficult in wartime for shore batteries to stop ship traffic. So in 1701 the French set up a fort at the relatively narrow point now marked by downtown Detroit. They perched cannon on the high northern bank to repel enemy English ships.

For Detroit's first two hundred years, shipping from the downtown wharfs was central to its economy, connecting the city with New York to the east and Chicago to the west. The river still carries the world's largest tonnage of cargo, but Detroit is no longer a significant port. Today the old industries that once separated the river from the city are gone. The riverfront from downtown to Belle Isle emerged in the 1980s as the magnet for the only new office and residential development in Detroit. Three attractive new riverfront parks are at the feet of St. Aubin, Chene, and Mt. Elliott, all within two miles of downtown.

On a warm, not-too-windy day, the banks of this attractive aqua river are a wonderful place to watch the big boats go by. Belle Isle is the best place to see the river traffic. In the 1960s, freighters passed an average of once every 12 minutes. Today only about 25 to 35 a day pass by Detroit. One reason is the giant thousand-foot-long Great Lakes freighters, which can do the job of six conventional freighters. It's a thrill to see these massive boats pass by. Some have up to 60,000 tons of cargo. It adds to the mystique that a freighter may be coming from any port in the world.

SPLENDID RIVERFRONT LODGING . . . . . An especially good overnight place to watch the freighters go by as well as get a dramatic view of downtown Detroit is the **Holiday Inn** of Windsor. Be sure to ask for a room on the Detroit River side, and you'll get your own personal outdoor porch overhanging the water. Call ahead for reservations at (519) 963-7590. Rooms are about $60 a night and up.

Rivertown

History, good music, and striking riverfront scenery

In 1980 this three-mile stretch of riverfront between the RenCen and Belle Isle bridge was industrial. Old warehouses and factories, and remnants of docks and ship yards blocked off the river from public use. Today the departure of most industry has paved the way for the Rivertown entertainment/office/apartment district of the most expensive land in Detroit. Scattered nightspots and restaurants range from the Woodbridge Tavern, an old speakeasy with a nifty terrace, and the earthily casual and eclectic Soup Kitchen Saloon blues and jazz club to famed chef Jimmy Schmidt's Rattlesnake Club restaurant (p. 226). Ample parking and safe streets are plusses.

The city's three new riverfront parks at the feet of St. Aubin, Chene, and Mt. Elliott streets have proven aesthetic and popular successes. Chene Park outdoor jazz and pop music concerts at sunset are a don't-miss attraction worth a visit to Detroit.

Harbortown and Stroh River Place, two large mixed-use luxury developments, have proven popular with upper-income empty-nesters and young professionals. But enough old buildings and businesses like Medusa Cement remain to give the place a kind of gritty, real-world visual atmosphere.

Here are Rivertown highlights, arranged from west (the Ren-Cen end) to east, toward Belle Isle.

♦ **Jefferson Avenue historic buildings.** Pre-Civil War Detroit, with its gentle Federal-style and Gothic Revival townhouses and churches, has largely been erased by the industrialization spurred by the war between the states. But pieces of antebellum Detroit can still be seeen on Jefferson, especially on the two blocks east of the Chrysler Freeway (I-75/I-375). The parade of old houses is occasionally interrupted by turn-of-the-century apartment buildings and clubhouses built by the wealthy before they left the city for the suburbs. For an interesting brochure on historic Rivertown architecture, stop by the Beaubien House (p. 134).

Two fine old buildings are regularly open to the public.

♦ **Christ Episcopal Church** is a beautiful 1863 Gothic Revival church designed by Gordon Lloyd, a star of 19th-century Michigan architecture. Weekdays ask at the office to look inside and see the beautiful stained glass windows. A Tiffany window depicts the legend of St. Elizabeth of Hungary. A portrait window honors the family of the church's first rector, Willliam Lyster. As a missionary in pioneer Michigan, he coined the name "Irish Hills" for the glacial hills of Jackson and Lenawee counties. *On Jefferson just east of I-75.*

◆ The 1840s **Moross House**, Detroit's oldest existing brick dwelling, is the headquarters of the Detroit Garden Club. Portions of it have been furnished with mid-19th-century antiques from old Detroit families. Its walled rear garden is a lush, vine-clad oasis planted with favorites from the mid-19th century: peonies, lilacs, spring bults, and wisteria. *1460 Jefferson west of Riopelle. (313) 259-6363. Open Tues-Thurs 9:30-3:30.*

◆ **St. Aubin Park.** This new park features two fishing shelters, a grassy picnic area, and two river overlooks, plus a 67-slip transient marina handy to downtown. New in summer, 1991, are a series of creative **outdoor exhibits** that interpret Detroit riverfront and its history. A coalition of government agencies and civic groups funded them. History plus riverfront scenery make the park a fine place for a leisurely stroll.

Many exhibits are on the river's edge buffer between the river and the marina. A path to it starts at St. Aubin and Atwater. Along the riverwalk on the north end of the river's edge buffer, are inscriptions with a dozen moments in the riverfront's history. Some of the largest marine steam engines ever made were built across the street at the Detroit Drydock Company. A seven-foot model of a drydock shows an 1892 freighter being worked on.

By the marina office and restrooms, is **Vito Acconci's Concrete Boatyard**, the first play sculpture designed by the internationally known sculptor. On a curved wall on the north end of the park, three markers give a historical overview of African-Americans in Detroit. *On Atwater between Orleans and St. Aubin about a mile north of the RenCen. Open for fishing during daylight hours. (313) 259-4677 or 1-800-338-6424. Moorage fees: $15-$40 overnight. Reservations $25 extra. For a fee, a costumed guide from the Rec. Dept. offers group tours (313-224-1184).*

◆ **Chene Park.** Chene Park combines low-key fishing and riverfront access with an expanded, 6,500-seat riverfront amphitheater that promises to become a major regional concert venue for top performers in blues, jazz, classical, and adult contemporary music. Concert-goers can get up during concerts and walk along the river and small pond. At sunset and after dark, the effect of lights reflected in the water is fabulous. And during a concert, the combination of spectacular scenery, good music, and mellow crowds along the river is hard to equal.

Every 10 days or do, the Medusa Challenger, a boat as long as two football fields, unloads cement from Charlevoix to the Medusa silos next to the park. Call (313) 496-0555 to find out when it is coming. *On Atwater at the foot of Chene and Dubois, between St. Aubin Park and Stroh River Place. For specific information on concerts, call (313) 224-1184 between 8:30 and 5:30, or the 24-hour Leisure Line at (313) 224-2732.*

◆ **Stroh River Place.** The giant Parke-Davis pharmaceutical company began here in 1873. Today the handsome brick buildings have been stylishly renovated and developed by the Stroh Brewery. River Place has offices (including Stroh corporate headquarters), apartments and townhouses, the **River Place Inn** luxury hotel (p. 228), and Jimmy Schmidt's **Rattlesnake Club**, with innovative American regional food at surprisingly moderate prices. *At the foot of Joseph Campau, corner of Atwater. Valet parking, or park on a nearby street and walk.*

The Detroiter paddle wheel riverboat is docked here. It offers two-hour river cruises with three-course meals and live entertainment daily in good weather ($21-$32). Call (313) 567-1400.

◆ **Mt. Elliott Park.** Coast Guard operations for ice-breaking, rescue, policing, and buoy-tending are headquartered at the foot of Mt. Elliott, readily observable from the park, which is under construction in 1991. Coming: an interpretive center on Detroit riverfront history in the 19th-century Coast Guard depot. *On Atwater at the feet of Mt. Elliott, Iron, and Meldrum.*

Chene Park at dusk.

Belle Isle

A top Michigan attraction, this 3-mile-long island features great views, a splendid zoo and aquarium, along with deer, hiking, canoe rides, and much more.

Belle Isle is one of the most interesting and beautiful urban parks in the world. Here you can get a dramatic **view of downtown Detroit**, a panoramic **view of the Detroit River** with its international freighter traffic, and an equally sweeping **view of Canada** and the big Prohibition-spawned distillery right across the river. On the 981-acre island itself, you can find waterfront **picnic areas** throughout, two long **fishing piers**, and an elaborate **playground** for kids along with a **giant slide**. There's a delightful **zoo**, an extraordinarily beautiful **aquarium**, a fascinating **Great Lakes museum**, a sizable plant **conservatory** and formal gardens, and a **nature center** with nature trails through forests filled with deer. A quaint **floral clock** still graces the entrance in summer. Even if you don't get out of your car, it's pleasant to drive around the park with its antique cast-iron street lights, fanciful old picnic pavilions, and frequent monuments.

The crush of visitors (10 million a year) creates problems on this attractive island. At times maintenance personnel cannot keep up with the accumulation of trash. Some areas are scarred and need upgrading. On warm evenings teenagers cruising with loud portable stereos can create so much congestion that this is one of the last places you would want to be. Evenings and weekends in early and midsummer are best avoided.

There is a quaint **police station** on the island, at Inselruhe and Central Avenue, with enough patrols to make it safe for visitors day or night. (The island is never closed.) By big-city standards, Belle Isle is quite safe.

The city bought Belle Isle in 1879 for $200,000. A century earlier, it had been a common grazing ground for the French farmers whose narrow ribbon farms fronted on the river. Today the major thoroughfare is around the island's perimeter. Originally swampy throughout, most of the park has been elevated with fill. Only the eastern wooded area looks the way it did a century ago. Canals allow canoeists to traverse the length of the island.

The one-way perimeter road goes counter-clockwise. Sights are arranged in the order in which you come to them. Of special

Scott Fountain and the downtown skyline.

interest on Belle Isle are:

◆ **Scott Fountain.** To make room for this huge and ornate foun
tain, Belle Isle's western end was extended a thousand yards.
From that western tip you can see not only the fountain but its
reflection in the specially constructed lagoon. Italian white marble — some 20,000 square feet of it — was used to create the
monument, which the city was at first reluctant to build. The half
million dollars were supplied in the bequest of James Scott
when he died in 1910. But Scott was viewed as such a scoundrel
that the city at first refused to honor his request to spend the
donation on an imposing monument in his honor.   Eventually
the city held an international competition, won by the eminent
Beaux-Arts architect Cass Gilbert. (The following year he also was
hired to design Detroit's Public Library.) For the fountain, Gilbert
came up with a complex series of bowls, basins, and fountains,
complete with spewing turtles, dolphins, lionesses, Neptunes,
and animal horns. Sculptor Herbert Adams created the required
bronze statue of Scott. It graces the fountain's west side. Some
say the spot was chosen so that prevailing winds keep him wet

much of the time. For the first time in decades, all four pumps
work, and the central spray reaches a height of over 75 feet.

◆ **Dossin Great Lakes Museum.** Overlooking the Detroit River,
this is one of the niftiest museums in Michigan. Outside you'll
find two big cannons from Commodore Perry's key naval victory
in the Battle of Lake Erie, the turning point of the War of 1812.

Just beyond the entrance is a splendid carved oak and stained
glass interior from the 1912 steamer, the *City of Detroit*. This
was the Gothic Room, where male passengers came to smoke
and talk. The ornate room suggests that vanished era when passengers could cruise the Great Lakes in luxurious comfort.

In the next room leading toward the river, a giant three-
dimensional relief map of the Great Lakes shows the relative
depths of the five lakes, from shallow Lake Erie (only 210 feet at
its deepest) to Lake Superior (1,333 feet).

Among models of Great Lakes ships and large photos of boat
christenings and spectacular wrecks, a display promotes Great
Lakes shipping, which today takes a back seat to railroads and
trucks. It points out that a boat delivering 15 million tons of ore
to Chicago from the East Coast takes just 24 million gallons of
fuel, compared with 35 million gallons by rail and 123 million
gallons by truck.

At the end of the room, a reconstruction of a steamer's pilot
house allows the visitor to look right out over the river through
the pilot house's windows. Above it is an observation deck, a
splendid place to look at passing steamers. Their radio messages
can be heard from a nearby speaker. On the river's near bank are
signs showing the distance and direction to frequent freighter
destinations:

> < Marquette 481 miles
> < Green Bay 507 miles
> < Alpena 219 miles
> < Duluth 728 miles
> Montreal 618 miles>
> Toronto 299 miles>

Next to the pilot house and observation deck is the most popular museum item of all: a working submarine periscope. It gives a
great view of what's coming up and down the river as well as a
full 360° view of the island. *(313) 267-6440. Wed-Sun 10-5:30.
Closed holidays. $1 donation requested.*

◆ **Aquarium.** Not only is this the oldest public aquarium in the
U.S. but one of the most visually striking. It was built in 1904,
designed by Albert Kahn, the architect who shaped much of
Detroit. Carved dolphins, now mostly covered by vines, grace the
entrance. The interior, with muted, indirect lighting, has a

delightful aura created by the serene green-tiled ceiling contrasted with the black-tiled lower level. The effect, augmented by the many strange fish in crystal-clear aquaria, is that of entering a fantastic new world.

Over 100 species of fish are here. The rarest is the tiny and endangered desert pupfish from the southwestern U.S., where rampant development is dangerously lowering the water table. Most popular is the huge, ugly electric eel, which delivers a hefty 650 volts to stun prey. Through a speaker visitors can hear the big eel's electric output when it is fed at 10:30, 12:30, and 2:30 daily (and at 4:30 Sunday). Often big crowds gather to experience the noisy performance.

Informational signs in this striking aquarium are excellent. Neither frustratingly brief nor overly long, they provide interesting nuggets of information. The sign next to the piranha exhibit reads: "Outside of the movies, piranhas have never been known to kill a person. In fact, people swim and bathe in rivers where piranhas live. Piranhas use their razor-sharp teeth and strong jaws to feed on fish. An injured animal that falls into piranha-infested waters may be reduced to bones in minutes."

Because of corrosive vapors from salt water, the aquarium no longer keeps saltwater fish. But you can see most major groups of freshwater fish, including a big 2,800-gallon tank of Great Lakes fish: largemouth bass, lake sturgeon, spotted gar, and long-nose gar. 10,000 gallons of refrigerated water is used to keep muskies, trout, and salmon. *Inland from Dossin Museum. (313) 267-7159. 10-5 daily, including holidays. Free.*

◆ **Whitcomb Conservatory.** Capped by an imposing 85-foot glass dome, this 1904 building was made of parts from an exhibit at the St. Louis World's Fair. The giant palms in the central space are spectacular. Adjoining rooms feature cacti, ferns, tropical plants, a large collection of orchids, and seasonal displays. In front are formal gardens and a delightful fountain capped by a **bronze gazelle**, created by Marshall Fredericks in 1936. At the base are four animals native to the island: a hawk, rabbit, otter, and grouse. *Inland from Dossin Museum. (313) 267-7134. Open 9-5, every day of the year. Free.*

◆ **Belle Isle Zoo.** Set amid splendid, shady trees, this small, 13-acre zoo is an exceptionally pleasant place to spend a warm summer day. The key to its charm is the 3/4-mile-long elevated walkway from which most of the animals are viewed. Looking down into the animals' settings gives a more three-dimensional, interesting view. The naturalistic settings are ample enough to allow most of the 30 species to roam freely. Especially for brief visits or people with small children, a visit to the Belle Isle Zoo may well be more satisfying than seeing the much larger and more expensive Detroit Zoo.

Among the rarer animals on display are endangered maned wolves from South America. They are known as "foxes on stilts" because their long legs enable them to see over tall vegetation. New to the zoo are a pair of siamangs, primates of the gibbon family which have extraordinary leaping and acrobatic skills. They live in mountainous forests of Indo-China. Siamangs make terrific zoo exhibits because they are such active and noisy creatures. *On Vista, just south of Central Avenue in center of island. (313) 398-0900. Open May 1-Oct 31, 10-5 daily. Admission: 13 and older, $2, seniors $1, ages 2-12 50¢. ,*

◆ **Nature Center.** Belle Isle's nature center is on the eastern side of the island where the forest and marsh remain in their natural state. Two self-guided nature trails, one 3/4 of a mile long, the other 1/4 mile, give good views of the native wildlife in the 200-acre natural area. For wheelchair users there's a short paved trail as well. Here you can also see the now tame and abundant European fallow deer, brought to the island in 1937. In April the trails are likely to be underwater.

Most of the snakes, birds, turtles, and mammals inside are temporarily held injured animals or illegal confiscated pets such as ferrets and foxes. *North end of island on Oakway. (313) 267-7157. 10-5, closed Mondays. Free.*

◆ **The Livingstone Memorial Lighthouse,** made of Georgian marble, is topped by a bronze lantern cap. It's almost 70 feet tall; its light can be seen 15 miles away in the middle of Lake St. Clair.

FISHING ON BELLE ISLE . . . . . The island has four special fishing spots. The two long piers at either end of Inselruhe are especially interesting. Fishing bulkheads are at the island's east end, one on the south side (just west of the Coast Guard Station) and one on the north, across a channel from the Detroit Yacht Club. Sizable catches are common. Among the fish caught are silver bass, bluegill, perch, sheephead, catfish, salmon, pickerel and pike. A bait shop is four blocks west of the MacArthur Bridge: **Jefferson & Meldrum Service** (6220 E. Jefferson, 259-1176). It can fix you up with a pole, hook, line, and sinker for under $10. Don't forget a fishing license. Minnow and worms are $1.50 a dozen. Worms are used in summer, while minnows are used in the winter for pike and pickerel.

A BROCHURE WITH MAP . . . . . "Detroit's Beautiful Belle Isle Park," describes the full range of activities and sights. It is available weekdays 8-3:30 at the park office, which is in the White House on Inselruhe, or by writing Detroit Recreation Dept., 735 Randolph #2006, Detroit, MI 48226.

Pewabic Pottery

*Since 1903, some of the world's finest pottery and tile
has been made at this quaint studio.*

The pottery made here since the early 20th century is
famous for its beautiful, subtle glazes. Pewabic's founder,
Mary Chase Perry Stratton, is best known for her
six iridescent glazes, which were used extensively on both vessels and tile. She had been prompted by a local industrialist who
was also one of the world's foremost connoisseurs of Oriental art,
Charles Freer. He showed Stratton a piece of Babylonian pottery
which had a mysteriously beautiful patina, and eventually, after
years of experimentation, she found a way to emulate it.

Stratton was an important part of the Arts and Crafts movement that flourished in Detroit at the turn of the century. It
promoted a return to simple, pre-industrial handcraftsmanship.
Stratton never attempted to exploit her glaze formulations by
mass-producing her art. It was critical to her that her work
maintain its artistic integrity; for her, this meant the freedom of
constant experimentation and change. She encouraged other
potters to conduct their own lifelong experiments and quests,
rather than following in others' footsteps. Some of her most
striking work was in architectural tiles, which can be found from
the Nebraska State Capitol to the Shrine of the Immaculate Conception in Washington, D.C. Pewabic tiles can be seen all over
Detroit,including the entrance of the Guardian Building in
downtown Detroit and Christ Church in Bloomfield Hills.

Stratton named the fledgling pottery "Pewabic" after a copper
mine near Hancock, Michigan, her home-
town. Her work was so well received that
she was able to build this pleasant gallery
and workshop built in the style of an
old English country inn. She later
married its architect, William
Stratton. The pottery declined
after her death in 1961.

But since 1981 there has been
a revival under the auspices of the
non-profit Pewabic Society. Production is once again underway, in the spirit of Stratton's

work. All architectural commissions are produced to order by a team of designers and craftspeople. With a staff of 25 professional artists, Pewabic is again a national center for the design and production of architectural tile. Homeowners can commission custom-made tiles for as little as $300 — enough for a fireplace. Contemporary designs in Pewabic tiles adorn four People Mover stations downtown. There are classes for beginners, residencies for experienced craftspeople, and a **gallery** which shows both new works and some of Perry's original ceramics.

Visitors can wander freely throughout the two-story building, which looks much as it did decades ago. In the rear **studios** downstairs, artists shape Pewabic's pieces and fire the big kilns. For sale in the **gift shop** at quite reasonable prices are some beautiful pieces including bowls, ceramic jewelry, and a big variety of charming early Pewabic tile designs, used largely on fireplaces of homes and libraries. Motifs include animals and themes from fairy tales and fables. For as little as $4 you can buy a small Buddha or pony. The upstairs **consignment gallery** features works for sale by potters throughout the country, chosen in part to illustrate the vast variety of shapes, sensual effects, and creative ideas possible with ceramics. Its quality and variety is impressive.

10125 E. Jefferson between Cadillac and Hurlbut, across from Waterworks Park and about 1 1/2 miles east of the Belle Isle bridge. Park in courtyard in front of the building. (313) 822-0954. Tues-Sat 10-5. Free admission; donations welcome.

AN ENDURINGLY ELEGANT NEIGHBORHOOD . . . . . is **Indian Village**, between the Belle Isle bridge and Pewabic Pottery. The large mansions on three long streets were built between 1895 and the mid-1920s on land that used to be 18th-century French ribbon farms. *Indian Village is on Burns, Seminole, and Iroquois between Jefferson and Mack.*

Fisher Mansion

*Amusingly lavish, this auto baron's mansion
recalls the excesses of the Roaring Twenties.*

This fancifully lavish mansion is one of the extraordinary
sights of Detroit. It was built in the 1920s by the playboy
head of Cadillac Motors. Its style has been described
as "glitz bordering on garish." Neglected after owner Lawrence
Fisher's death, the mansion has been purchased, restored, and
maintained by an improbable team of Hare Krishna converts —
Alfred Brush Ford, great-grandson of Henry Ford, and Elisabeth
Reuther Dickmeyer, daughter of legendary UAW chief Walter
Reuther. Today it serves a small community of Hare Krishna followers, who use the ballroom for their chanting hall. On the second floor is the excellent **Govinda's** vegetarian restaurant, also
run by the Hare Krishnas.

Lawrence Fisher was one of the seven Fisher Brothers who
helped revolutionize the auto industry in the early 20th century
by building enclosed bodies for cars. Lawrence was a big, beefy
bachelor who squired the likes of Jean Harlow and threw opulent
parties. No elitist, he invited local tradespeople as well as celebrities to these events. Champagne flowed continuously during
parties from the mouth of a solid silver head of Neptune in the
entryway.

The home of publishing magnate William Randolph Hearst,
Fisher's good friend, inspired this mansion on the Detroit River.
Hearst's San Simeon then set the standard for California opulence, mixing a dazzling array of florid architectural styles. Fisher's 50-room mansion follows in this grandiose tradition. The
entranceway has black Majorcan tiles on the floor with gold
insets. Art Deco tiling surrounds the silver head of Neptune. Long
Roman tiles alternate with Pewabic tile. The marble columns are
Corinthian Greek. In all, 75 ounces of golf leaf and 140 ounces of
silver were used on the mansion's ceilings and moldings.

Always impeccably dressed, Fisher remained a bachelor until,
at 62, he married his childhood sweetheart, then 67. One of his
great loves was his dogs. He frequently dined alone with his
cocker spaniel, who ate out of a silver bowl. When the dog suddenly disappeared one day, the disconsolate auto baron personally went door to door in the neighborhood, offering a $10,000
reward for its return, to no avail. When another dog drowned in
the adjacent swimming pool, he had the pool filled in. He buried

two of his beloved pooches in signed, silver Tiffany caskets on the mansion's grounds. One of the first things a subsequent owner did was to dig up the caskets, dump the bones in the trash, and sell the silver.

Sailing was another of Lawrence Fisher's passions. Hence, the mansion is strategically situated on the Detroit River. Fisher had a wide canal built up to the house, with large enclosed boat houses on each side. The larger held his 106-foot yacht. The smaller housed the vessel which later became President Kennedy's presidential yacht.

The ballroom emulates a Spanish courtyard, complete with Venetian parapet and delicate white clouds painted on the blue ceiling. During Fisher's festive parties, a machine projected stars on this ceiling, and lighting was adjusted to simulate dusk or dawn, whichever time it might be. Some of the world's top wood-carvers were brought to work on detailing. In some cases a carver would spend over a year on a single door. Not much of a reader, Fisher ordered the hand-tooled leather books in the library by color rather than title.

Amazingly, this splendid mansion was sold by a bank in the early 1960s for just $80,000. The Hare Krishnas have for the most part respected the historical integrity of the place. Their own colorful religious paintings hang on some walls, but they don't obscure the feel of the place when Fisher lived there. One startling exception is an upstairs room in which sits a full-sized, bluish seated statue of their deceased guru.

383 Lenox. Take Jefferson to Dickerson, turn south at Golightly Vocational School. Dickerson becomes Lenox. (313) 331-6740. Tours Fri & Sat 12:30, 2, 3:30, & 6; Sun 12, 1:30, 3, & 6. $4 admission ($3 seniors and children)

Grosse Pointe

A haven for Detroit's old money,
the Pointes offer lovely views of Lake St. Clair,
lavish early 20th-century estates, and great used stuff.

This famous string of five affluent suburbs is a splendid place to tour by car or bicycle, thanks to beautiful Lake St. Clair and the handsomely landscaped estates. "Grosse Pointe" is actually five separate municipalities stretching along the lake just east of Detroit. Driving out Jefferson from Detroit into Grosse Pointe Park has always been a dramatic change. As you cross Alter Road, you enter a green, kempt domain of big trees and beautiful homes. In recent decades, much of Detroit's east side has become blighted, so the contrast is even more striking.

The prominent old families of Grosse Pointe, Grosse Pointe Shores, and Grosse Pointe Farms are about as close as Metro Detroit comes to having an aristocracy. Many scions of the founding auto barons still live in the Pointes. This is definitely George and Barbara Bush territory, with the tone set by low-key people with inherited money.

Property on the lake is always expensive — often over a million dollars per home. Some of the choicest streets are Vendome, Provençal (overlooking the Country Club of Detroit), and Lake Shore Road. There still aren't many Jews or Democrats or blacks in the Pointes, though their numbers are gradually increasing. For years through the 1950s, prospective Grosse Pointe home buyers were screened by the Grosse Pointe Realtors' infamous point system. Private detectives hired to fill out reports didn't even bother to rate blacks or Asians. Other prospective home buyers were secretly rated on such issues as:

1. Is their way of living typically American?
2. Appearances—swarthy, slightly swarthy, or not at all?
3. Accents—pronounced, medium, slight, not at all?
4. Dress—neat, sloppy, flashy, or conservative?

Actually, there's more diversity of income and ethnicity here than the WASP stereotype suggests. Away from the lake, especially toward Detroit in the planned buffer suburb of Grosse Pointe Park, there's a good deal of modest, middle-class 1920s housing. The Grosse Pointes offer better housing deals on comparable houses than Ann Arbor. Grosse Pointers reflect the ethnic mix of

Detroit's old east side: Italians, Belgians, Poles, and Lebanese, plus a few old French families — and lots of executive transfers. The shoreline of these affluent communities was first settled by Detroit French who left the city after England took it over in 1760. The French established distinctive ribbon farms along Lake St. Clair. Only 300 to 600 feet wide, they extended a mile or more inland, permitting each farmer crucial access to Lake St. Clair for transportation.

Wealthy Detroiters began building summer homes in the Grosse Pointe area as early as the 1840s, but few who worked in Detroit dared live year-round so far out. Wealthy businessmen often commuted by yacht to Detroit from their summer residences. A few of these fine old Victorian mansions still stand, such as the 1895 Queen Anne house at 365 Lake Shore.

Beginning around 1910, wealthy Detroiters withdrew from the city, with its booming factories they themselves built and the masses of immigrants who came to work there. Grosse Pointe became famous for its magnificent lakeshore estates that imitated elegant country houses in England, France, and Italy. Some of the most spectacular mansions have been razed to make way for more modest half-million-dollar homes. But many remain.

A trip out Jefferson and Lake Shore Road from Detroit to Grosse Pointe Shores is a fine drive, especially when the sun is shining on the stunning turquoise blue of Lake St. Clair. The wonderful Art Deco storefronts on Jefferson remind you just how urban these close-in suburbs of the 1920s really are. They were laid out along streetcar lines, in fact. Where Jefferson becomes Lake Shore Road, no houses obscure motorists' views of the lake. You could park on a side street and walk along here. But don't venture into the public parks. They're for card-carrying residents only — and always have been. (Suburbs like these throughout the U.S. were developed with the explicit intention of keeping the growing cities and their exotic populations at bay.)

Stop in at the **Grosse Pointe War Memorial** at 32 Lake Shore Road in Grosse Pointe farms. Originally the home of a Packard Motor Company founder, it is now the hub of recreational and cultural activities in the Pointes. Visitors are welcome to look inside the meeting rooms, provided they don't disturb a function, and see the stunning views of the lake, framed by elegant, formal interiors in 15th-century Florentine, 16th-century Venetian, and Italian Baroque styles.

A particularly striking sight is the private **Grosse Pointe Yacht Club** off Lake Shore at the foot of Vernier Road. What began as a ice boating club in 1914 had, by 1929, become an Art Deco version of Venetian splendor. The picturesque 187-foot tower has ship bells which strike the hours during sailing season. This

28   41   4   19   8   (30)

Mrs Norman
Nevenger

1-616-223-7770

Old Mission

The Grosse Pointe Memorial, an Italian Renaissance villa from 1910.

remarkable yacht club, finished just before the Depression, was to be Grosse Pointe's last gasp of gilded grandeur. The Thirties ushered in a sober Georgian neoclassicism, which set the tasteful, albeit dull, tone for most Grosse Pointe construction ever since. A visit to the Cotswold-inspired **estate of Edsel and Eleanor Ford** (p. 175) is a worthwhile end to this drive.

To get from Jefferson to Kercheval, Grosse Pointe's main shopping street, is tricky. You have to go west on a street going in from Lake St. Clair that is south of the Country Club of Detroit. In Grosse Pointe Farms to the north, Moran is a good cross street. So is Maryland, in Grosse Pointe Park to the south.

Shopping in the Pointes is famously dull, compared to glitzy, trendy Birmingham in the heart of Oakland County's new-money affluence. The Pointes' pervasively preppy look — traditional good taste, little makeup — barely changes form one generation to another. **The Village**, Kercheval's chief shopping area, is between Cadieux and Neff in Grosse Pointe. It's almost completely dominated by chains: Talbot's, Laura Ashley, Jacobson's, Winkelman's, etc. The wonderful old **Sanders Confectionery** at 17043 Kercheval has a popular soda fountain and lunch counter in the vintage 1935 interior. **The Hill,** on Kercheval in Grosse Pointe Farms between Fisher and Muir, has non-chain shops and upscale services.

Grosse Pointe's most interesting browsing is on **Kercheval in the Park**, between Wayburn and Beaconsfield, just across from the Detroit line. The popular Sparky Herbert's restaurant (p. 227) inspired its revival. Noteworthy stores include:

◆ **Grosse Pointe Reliques.** Crowded consignment shop full of quality antiques and used furniture at reasonable prices. *(313) 822-0111. 14932 Kercheval. Mon-Sat 11-5.*

◆ **Third Coast Booksellers.** Self-described as "Detroit's literary bookstore." Owner/novelist Michael Goodell decided to borrow some money and open a first-class bookstore on the east side modeled on personal European bookshops when his chosen calling of writing fiction failed to take off. The result is a beautiful, service-oriented store that aspires to be a Borders in a tenth the size — strong on literature, women's studies, art and architecture, travel, and children's books. (Don't miss the specially commissioned stained-glass versions of "Goodnight Moon" and "Peter Pan.") It's "a Danielle Steele-free zone" — no romances; no sports, sci fi, New Age, or westerns, either; and no trash in biographies, self-help or business sections, Goodell says. *15129 Kercheval. (313) 822-1559. Mon-Fri 9-7, Sat 9-6, Sun 10-4.*

◆ **James Monnig, Bookseller.** Satisfyingly cluttered used book shop, strong in biography, mysteries, history, art, and children's books. A few hundred vintage videos are for sale ($5-$15). Customers can look through books in the delightful back courtyard. *15133 Kercheval. (313) 331-2238. Tues-Sat 11-6, Fri 'til 9.*

◆ **Rustic Cabins Bar.** In the early 1930s, when this onetime blind pig went legit, the "cabins" were applied to the façade — two northwoods cabins outlined in round log slabs. Inside, this favorite hangout has barely changed. It has original booths and beat-up old tables, a moose head and mounted fish on the knotty-pine walls, and an Art Deco bar. There's pool, foosball, pinball, but no food. Old-timers stop by in the afternoon, a young crowd comes in the evening. *15209 Kercheval. Mon-Sat 11 a.m.-2 a.m.*

◆ **Mulier's Omer Market.** Fourth-generation grocer-butcher has evolved from a neighborhood store geared to nearby Belgians into a gourmet grocery, without losing any of its character. They make liver paté, meat loaf, sausage, and Rose Mulier's famous potato salad. *15215 Kercheval. Mon-Sat 8-6.*

🌲🌳🌲

LAKE ST. CLAIR . . . . . named by La Salle in 1679, is a heart-shaped body of water 400 square miles, sandwiched between Lake Erie and Lake Huron. It separates the Detroit River from the St. Clair River above. The lake is shallow, averaging just 10 feet in depth. A 700-foot-wide shipping channel has been dredged for 18 1/2 miles, giving freighters the needed 27 feet of water.

A USEFUL GUIDE TO THE POINTES . . . . . . For a fuller account of the fine homes and other sights along East Jefferson and Lake Shore Road, be sure to get *Pointe to Pointe*, an informative booklet available at local bookstores.

Edsel & Eleanor Ford Home

The best Cotswold manor money could buy,
just as it looked when the Fords lived there

Built on 87 acres overlooking Lake St. Clair, this splendid mansion takes the prize for formal good taste among the Detroit auto barons' abodes. A large, rambling house, it mimics on a grander scale those in the Cotswolds 100 miles west of London. Much of the interior paneling and furniture comes from distinguished old English manors. The roof is of imported English stones expertly laid by Cotswold roof-makers. Many interior hallways are of limestone, which gives you the feeling of entering a centuries-old manor, though the house was actually completed in 1929.

The one-hour tours, led by a professional staff member of the estate, are informative and entertaining. What makes this house especially interesting is that it remains as it was when the Fords lived here. Edsel, Henry Ford's son and the president of Ford Motor, died in 1943. His wife, Eleanor, left the estate virtually untouched. Only some of the priceless paintings — by Renoir, Degas, Titian, Van Gogh — have been replaced by copies. Originals by Cezanne, Matisse, Hals, and others remain here. And the original furniture and carpeting is intact.

Most rooms have a stately, formal feel. A striking exception is what the Fords called the "Modern Room," executed in harmonious Art Deco style in 1938 by Walter Dorwin Teague. This casual gathering place is a stylishly sophisticated yet comfortable room.

Eleanor left Edsel's personal study unchanged after his early death from stomach cancer. It was here that he was reportedly seen bent over his desk, weeping in frustration from the abuses heaped on him by his father. Edsel, an intelligent, modest, gentle person with a genuine flair for automobile design, was Henry and Clara Ford's only child. President of Ford Motor since he was 25 years old, Edsel was widely respected by Ford workers and managers. But as the years went by, he was at times sadistically treated by his increasingly curmudgeonly father. More than once Henry publicly demolished badly needed auto innovations that his son had spearheaded. Edsel and his co-workers had to watch helplessly as Henry refused to upgrade his Model T while Chevrolet surged into the lead as the nation's best-selling automobile. Ford Motor didn't begin to rebuild until Edsel's son, Henry II, with Eleanor's backing, wrested control of the company from Henry's thugs after Henry died.

The estate's lakefront setting is as remarkable as the manor. It was planted in native Michigan trees and shrubs by the famous landscape architect Jens Jensen, an influential proponent of loose, natural landscaping using only native species. Now his plantings are mature, and the effect is hauntingly serene.

Another treat is daughter Josephine's playhouse, given to her on her sixth birthday. It is carefully crafted in a similar Cotswold style but executed in 3/4 scale so that the ceiling is only six feet high. The furniture is similarly smaller. Boys weren't permitted in the playhouse, the tour guide says, but Josephine sometimes spent the night there, alone except for her two bodyguards.

1100 Lake Shore Rd. at the north end of Grosse Pointe Shores. (313) 884-4222. Tours Wed-Sun 1, 2, 3, 4 p.m. Adults $4, seniors $3, under 12 $2.

The Cotswold-style gatehouse to the Edsel and Eleanor Ford estate.

Detroit Institute of Arts

*One of the nation's most extraordinary collections
of great art, from modern to prehistoric*

Detroit is blessed with a truly great art museum. Only four or five others in this country surpass the DIA. It gives a dazzling view of masterpieces from Mesopotamian through modern eras. The museum's huge size and disorienting labyrinth of halls and corridors present the visitor with the problem of excess. You need to be careful not to become numbed by the thousands of pieces on display. One helpful antidote is free a one-hour **guided tour** *(given Wed-Sat 12:15, Sun at 1 & 2:30)*. It gives a quick view of the highlights.

The museum's greatest strengths are in American, Italian Renaissance, Dutch-Flemish, and German Expressionist art. While there are dozens of masterpieces throughout, the following are considered the museum's most important:

The Wedding Dance (Pieter Bruegel the Elder), ca. 1566. Colorful, realistic view of a peasant wedding. **Detroit Industry** (Diego Rivera), 1932-33. An enormous series of frescoes focusing on Detroit's auto industry. **Cotopaxi** (Frederic Church), 1862. Grand, mystical oil painting of an active volcano in the Andes. **Self Portrait** (Vincent van Gogh), 1887. One of the great artist's sunnier self-portraits. **Reclining Figure** (Henry Moore), 1939. Large sculpture in elm wood of a female. **Nail Figure** (from the Western Kongo), ca. 1875-1900. 46-inch wooden icon which served an African community's mystical needs. **Early Autumn** (Qian Xuan), 13th or 14th century. Delicate handscroll in ink and color of insects in autumn. **Seated Bather** (Pierre-Auguste Renoir), 1903-6. Sensuous, languid nude painted when the artist was in his sixties. **Saint Jerome in His Study** (Jan van Eyck), ca. 1390-1441. Small, richly symbolic oil painting by the great Flemish painter. **The Visitation** (Rembrandt), 1640. Dramatic presentation of the Biblical scene in which Mary and Elizabeth encounter God. **Gudea of Lagash** (Mesopotamian), ca. 2141-2122 B.C. Superb stone sculpture of the ruler of a city-state.

Many other important works are worth mentioning— major pieces by Whistler, Picasso, Miro, Kokoschka, Gauguin, Seurat, Degas, Cezanne, and Matisse, among others.

Don't miss the striking **Kresge Court** (Wed-Sat 11-4, Sun 1-4). It's a vast, open dining area inspired in part by the courtyard of the Bargello Palace in Florence. Here you can eat cafeteria-style, sip coffee, or drink beer and wine. There is also a popular sit-

-down restaurant with full bar and nouvelle cuisine, **La Palette** (11:30-2, reservations recommended).

The **Museum Shop** by the Farnsworth entrance carries a sophisticated selection of art books, cards, reproductions, jewelry, and gift items, but is weak on inexpensive things for kids.

Compared to similar art museums in large cities with more old money, the DIA is way underendowed and far more dependent on subsidies. So Governor John Engler's budget 1991 cutbacks forced a dramatic curtailment of hours and virtually all special exhibits not based on the museum's own extensive collections.

5200 Woodward between Kirby and Farnsworth, 1/4 mile southeast of I-94. From I-94, take service drive exit just past Woodward, go right on John R to Science Center lot or Farnsworth. (313) 833-7900. Wed-Sun 11-4. Pay what you can but you must pay something. Suggested admission: adults $4, students $1. Occasional charge (typically $3) for special exhibitions. **Parking** *surface Science Center lot at John R and Farnsworth, $3 (benefits Science Center). In a secure, lighted parking garage on Farnsworth: $3 maximum. On-street parking: be sure to keep meters fed!* **Guided tours:** *Wed-Sat 12:15; Sun 1 & 2:30 (call to confirm).*

THE DETROIT FILM THEATER at the DIA . . . . . shows high-caliber films that haven't often been seen locally. The plush auditorium boasts excellent acoustics and technical equipment. There's even a bar for socializing before shows. (Wine, cappucino, great pastries, and sandwiches are the order of the day.) $5 admission. Call (313) 833-2323 for program information.

TWO OTHER NEARBY MUSEUMS OF NOTE . . . . . The handsome **Museum of African-American History** documents the history and culture of African-Americans from pre-slavery life in African villages through the dreaded Middle Passage to life in the U.S. under slavery. Also featured: famous revolts and escapes to "free" life in the northern U.S. and Canada. The museum's most dramatic display is a full-scale mock-up of part of a slave ship below deck, complete with sound effects. *301 Frederick Douglass between John R and Brush. From Woodward, take Kirby to John R, turn right, then left. (313) 833-9800. Wed-Sat 9:30-5; Sun 1-5. Free.* . . . . . The newly reopened **Detroit Science Center** has items now familiar in hands-on museums. The big draw is the **Omni-Max Theater**, a huge tilted screen which conveys a sense of motion in specially filmed movies. Science-related films are shown every hour on the half hour from 10:30 until 3:30. *5020 John R. (313) 577-8400. Mon-Fri 10-2, Sat-Sun 12-6. Adults $6.50, ages 4-12 and seniors $4.50.*

SHOWTIME CLOTHING. . . . . . is a huge, hidden treasure at 5708 Woodward at Palmer between the DIA and I-94. New and vintage clothing geared to Wayne students, plus jewelry , postcards, comics, boots. Expect to find vintage after 5, peace ties, floppy hats, 1960s leather, lots of sterling silver. *875-9280. Closed Mon.*

Detroit Historical Museum

*From fort to Motor City, Detroit's past
is illuminated with bold, insightful exhibits.*

Detroit has had an especially rich, eventful history.
Founded in 1701, it has changed sovereignty five times.
Its strategic location at a narrow point on the Detroit
River made the fort town a keenly fought-over prize, ruled by
France and then England before joining the U.S. in 1796. This
museum, one of the best in the state, captures much of that his-
tory quite well. The new **Furs to Factories** exhibit of Detroit
history to 1901 may add needed zing to permanent exhibits. The
changing shows can be compelling. The **Tavi Stone Fashion
Library** (limited hours) is a rare resource for fashion historians.

A longtime highlight is **The Streets of Detroit** exhibit in the
basement. It's a three-quarters-scale, realistic nighttime recreation of Detroit commercial streetfronts in the 1840s, 1870s,
and at the turn of the century. Along cobblestone and then brick
streets you walk by banks, a printing shop, a drug store, a bicycle
shop, and a grocery store, among others. The darkened ambience makes the settings seem lifelike. It's a rich step back into
the past, no doubt magical for many children. Particularly wonderful is the old Kresge & Wilson Big 5 and 10¢ Store, which
once occupied the spot where the National Bank of Detroit now
stands across from Kennedy Square. "Nothing over 10¢ in this
store" was its motto. S.S. Kresge went on to establish dime
stores across the nation, building the giant company which
evolved into today's K Mart Corporation, now headquartered in
nearby Troy.

Behind the Streets of Detroit is the new **National Toy
Gallery**, with changing exhibits from one of the world's largest
collections of toys, including the notable Glancy Trains.

In the Round Hall near the entry is a 15-foot-high carved mahogany **clock** from the turn of the century. At noon a procession
of figures from around the world marches in native costume
around a globe while a music box plays. The attractive first-floor
gift shop features a wide assortment of antique reproductions,
posters of Detroit scenes, books, toys, and souvenirs.

*5401 Woodward at Kirby (across from Detroit Institute of Arts).
Park free behind museum off Kirby. (313) 833-1805. Wed-Fri
9:30-4, Sat & Sun 10-5. Freewill donation: adults $4, others $1.*

Fisher Building

1920s-style Persian grandeur,
thanks to the brothers who started Fisher Body

The Fisher Building ranks with the Guardian Building downtown as the most fantastic of Detroit's remarkable collection of 1920s office buildings. The seven Fisher brothers had become enormously rich by developing the enclosed auto body and then selling Fisher Body to GM. They planned the New Center complex across from the General Motors headquarters as a second major commercial center in the city, to rival the increasingly congested downtown area. Here the brothers set out to create the world's most beautiful office building. The architect was Albert Kahn, famed for his factories. Plans called for erecting another identical 26-story building, with a 60-story tower between them. But the Depression stopped them cold.

When the Fisher Building opened in 1928, it sported one of the most fabulous interiors of any office building in the world. It's full of what architectural historian Hawkins Ferry called "pagan splendors" — mosaics and inlaid marbles patterned in geometric and stylized naturalistic motifs. "Upon the walls gleam 40 different varieties of marble that would dazzle even the most jaded Roman emperor," remarked Ferry. Cherubs and muses, orange trees and hemlocks, eagles, vines, and folk art motifs adorn the ceiling and walls of the three-story arcade. Rich greens and oranges, lavishly gilded with gold leaf, make ztoric Central American art, rivalled those of the fabulous Fox. They were removed in 1961, at the end of the theater's moving picture days, when it was transformed into Detroit's preeminent legitimate theater. Its acoustics, stage, and orchestra pit make it superb for even the biggest and most elaborate musicals. Hits including *Hello, Dolly* and *Fiddler on the Roof* originated here before moving to Broadway.

As in most status office towers of the 1920s, elevator

The Depression curtailed the Fisher brothers' grand plan to build a duplicate of the existing Fisher Building and connect them with a 60-floor tower.

doors and mailboxes are treated as works of art. Unusual
amenities here included free babysitting in a richly decorated
nursery, white-dressed parking attendants, and, in the theater
lobby, banana trees, a pond of goldfish and turtles, and
wandering macaws fed by moviegoers.

A bank's sumptuous Aztec plaster decoration and ornate vault
are now part of the affordably priced **Pegasus in the Fisher** restaurant. Shops line the main arcade and elevator wing. Two
standouts toward the Lothrop entrance of the main arcade are
open Mondays through Saturdays 10-6 and on theater nights.
The **Detroit Gallery of Contemporary Crafts** offers a select and
beguiling array of American contemporary crafts by top craftspeople, priced from $25 to $500 and up. Displays mix media to
good effect: jewelry, ceramics, rugs, toys, a little furniture,
clothing, quilts, and dolls. Don't miss the sunburst of tiles from
Detroit's famous Pewabic Pottery (p. 167) on the floor in the
rear. The **Poster Gallery** includes an outstanding selection of
quality posters with African-American themes, along with a general poster line. Also on hand: interesting musical chimes for

wall or table. **Jacques Patisserie**, in the elevator wing, is a good spot for pastry and coffee.

W. Grand Blvd. at Second Ave. Rear entrance on Lothrop. Open Mon-Fri 8 a.m.-9 p.m., Sat 9-6. Freeway directions: take the Lodge (U.S. 10) to Pallister exit, turn left onto Lothrop. 3 hours free parking in New Center One lot, Lothrop between Second and Woodward. Ask for yellow tag from any New Center store.

THE REST OF THE NEW CENTER IS ALSO WORTH A LOOK. . . . . The lobby of the massive, sprawling **General Motors world headquarters** (1922; Albert Kahn, architect) across the street is loaded with a sense of both Renaissance grandeur and high-stakes corporate drama. Will the brisk-paced, blue-suited executives seen at work here regain market share for the automotive giant and help stabilize Michigan's economy? Displayed on the lobby's east hall (toward Woodward) are its current-model cars, plus historical displays. . . . . . **Free summer concerts** with top local musicians are held at the park across Second from the GM Building. *Times: Wed 11:30-1, Thurs 5:50-8:30.* . . . . **New Center One** is an attractive small shopping center anchored by Crowley's department store, with Winkelman's, Gantos, and Waldenbooks. It's across from the Fisher Building on Grand at Second. For dedicated Detroiters committed to keeping their dollars in the city, it's a godsend. (Hudson's, having debilitated the city by leading the way in suburban retail and housing development, closed its flagship Detroit store in 1982, then prevented competing retailers from leasing the space.) . . . . . North of the Fisher Building, **New Center Commons**, a mix of new and renovated housing, is a successful GM project to gentrify the neighborhood around it.

NEW CENTER ENTERTAINMENT IS FIRST-CLASS. . . . . . For program and ticket information about the **Fisher Theater**, where most major Broadway road shows perform, call (313) 872-1000. The **Attic Theater**, Detroit's resident professional theater company — artistically respected, fiscally plagued — is across Third from the Fisher Building, near Grand. Call (313) 875-8284. **Club Penta**, in the Fisher Building lower level, presents first-rate soul music of the sleek, sophisticated variety, in an atmosphere of quiet elegance. Wed-Sat at 9. (313) 972-3760.

Motown Museum

*In a simple neighborhood home, hit after hit
was churned out with assembly-line regularity.*

Top music legends — scores of them — were made during
the Sixties in these two adjacent homes. The genius
behind Motown's amazing hit factory was Berry Gordy
Jr. a former boxer and autoworker. His father, a Georgia farm
worker who came to Detroit in 1922, was a part of the Great
Migration from the agricultural South to the industrial North.

Under Gordy, Motown Records launched stars whose music is
part of American life today: Michael Jackson, Stevie Wonder,
Diana Ross and the Supremes, Marvin Gaye, Martha Reeves and
the Vandellas, Smokey Robinson and the Miracles, the Four
Tops, the Temptations, Lionel Richie, Gladys Knight and the
Pips, the Isley Brothers, Junior Walker, and more.

Records produced in the small, crudely fashioned rear studio
were among the first 45s by black artists to break out of the R&B
charts. Within a few years of its founding in 1959, Motown became America's biggest black-owned company.

In 1972 Gordy left Detroit for Los Angeles to pursue movie and
television projects. Music industry analysts date the decline of
Motown Records to its departure from Detroit and its inability to
develop new talent in Los Angeles to replace its increasingly
independent stars and songwriters from the Motor City. In 1988
Motown sold its recording arm to MCA-linked investors for $61
million.

The Motown Museum takes you back to an earlier, much simpler era. By the early 1960s, so many local kids flocked here that
traffic on West Grand was jammed for blocks. Some wanted to
glimpse the stars who recorded there. Others hoped to audition
informally on the front porch, an approach that had succeeded
for more than one Motown star.

Gordy grew up in the neighborhood behind the Detroit Institute of Arts. Each member of his hard-working family contributed $10 a month to build an enterprise fund from which any
family member could draw. After his jazz-oriented record shop
went bankrupt, Gordy began focusing on writing and producing
rhythm and blues songs for local groups. At a critical juncture,
Gordy borrowed $800 from the family fund to start his own
record production company. "Shop Around," written by Smokey
Robinson, was the first big hit he produced.

A talented manager and an autocratic disciplinarian, Gordy perfected the assembly-line style of hit production. He hired teams of writers who, as one critic describes it, put out "a wholly mechanical style and sound that roared and purred like a well-tuned Porsche." The Supremes recorded 12 #1 pop hits in five years, all written by the great songwriting team of Lamont Dozier and Eddie and Brian Holland. Gordy so carefully orchestrated Motown affairs that charm coaches were hired to polish the manners and dress of Motown recruits.

In the museum, rooms are crowded with Motown memorabilia. On display are publicity photos and scrapbook shots, letters, album jackets, newspaper clippings, plaques and gold records. Highlights include the recording studio, with original sheet music on the music stands just as it was, and the modest four-track board from which most of Motown's greatest hits were engineered.

This isn't a slick, professional museum. But it is the real thing — run by Gordy's own sister Esther Edwards, a Motown executive who saw it all happen right here.

2648 W. Grand Blvd., west of the Lodge Freeway (U.S. 10) and 1 1/2 blocks west of Henry Ford Hospitals. From the Lodge, take W. Grand Blvd. exit, head west. (313) 875-2264. Mon-Sat 10-5, Sun 2-5. Admission adults $3, 12 and under $2.

Shrine of the Black Madonna Bookstore

*A terrific selection of books on Africa
and African-Americans, plus African fabrics and artifacts*

The attractive cultural centers/bookstores of the Shrine of the Black Madonna present the largest selection of books on Africans and African-Americans anywhere in the U.S., according to jobbers and well-traveled book buyers. The Detroit store, though not as big as the Shrine's Houston facility, is most impressive: spiffy, well-organized, and serene in mood. The staff is knowledgeable and friendly to customers of all races.

The Shrine is a black church founded in Detroit over 40 years ago to promote African-American self-sufficiency and to stress black Americans' connectedness with African culture. It describes itself as a Pan-African orthodox (i.e., traditional) Christian church; today it's part of the United Church of Christ and has churches in Detroit, Atlanta, and Houston.

The large bookstore and import shop is also a gallery (on the second floor) with space for occasional lectures and readings by visiting authors and others. Here you can find an unparalleled range of books on Africans and African-Americans, from mainstream bestsellers like Taylor Branch's biography of Martin Luther King, to obscure publications by small political and literary presses here and abroad. This is the place to find the complete works in print of Langston Hughes, Zora Neale Hurston, and James Baldwin, as well as a passel of biographies of Motown stars and numerous scholarly and popular histories by black and white historians. Egyptology is another specialty. The children's book section is large and especially inviting. It's a surprise to find Scott Nearing's 1930s classic on subsistence farming until you realize that self-sufficient agriculture is what the Shrine's Beulahland project is all about. Beulahland is an 5,000-acre farm planned for the South, where young black boys can grow up off the streets and help feed the poor in American cities.

Other sections of the store feature jewelry, imported fabrics, and handcrafted objects from Africa. Prices are lower than what you'd expect to pay at gift shops. Fabrics, mostly $7 to $12 a yard, include woven kente cloth strips, once worn only by Ghanaian royalty; vivid aso-oke from Nigeria, accented with metallic threads; heavy cotton mudcloth in bold patterns and muted, neu

Adrian Wylie

Bookstore manager Ayele Bennet in the shop.

tral colors; long pieces of khorogo cloth, with designs of animals, birds, and village life; and batiks from Nigeria and Ghana. For inspiration on how to use these beautiful fabrics, there's a book on 101 ways to wrap kanga cloth.

The shop offers quite a range of African artifacts: little thumb pianos, wonderful wood elephants for $6, copies of Ashanti kings' stools, and carved stone chess sets for $96 to $110. Considering the craftsmanship, prices are low. Kissi stone plates, incised with etched designs of plants and fish, are $35. Handpainted papyri in beautiful golds and bronzes are copies of ancient pictures of Egyptian deities.

13535 Livernois at Davison in Detroit. From I-96, get off at the Davison ramp and go east. Turn left at Livernois and immediately look for the parking lot and sign. This is a rough part of town but OK in daytime. (313) 491-0777. Mon-Sat 11-6.

Hamtramck

*This Polish autoworkers' enclave has
a bustling, nostalgic, 1940s-era commercial district
with some outstanding shops and markets.*

This city of just two square miles, totally surrounded by
Detroit, has been a Polish stronghold since the First
World War. Drive along its bustling main street of Joseph
Campau and you'll see Polish bakeries, Polish meat shops, Polish
bookstores, Polish clubs. At the corner of Belmont and Joseph
Campau is a tribute to the Polish Pope, a large statue of Pope
John Paul.

For years now, Detroiters have been discovering the gritty
charm of a trip to Hamtramck: eating heartily in its good, cheap
restaurants; browsing in the small, budget-oriented shops, bakeries, and meat markets; and, more recently, dancing to some of
the area's most innovative rock at Lilli's Bar. Joseph Campau's
long retail blocks have the vintage appeal of a living, thriving
blue-collar relic from the 1930s or 1940s, before chains came to
depersonalize retailing and before malls had sucked the vitality
out of most American downtowns. Hamtramck's downtown today
presents an amazing contrast with the boarded-up bleakness of
similar 1920s shopping strips in nearby Detroit.

Hamtramck's Polish population is declining, from a high of
60% to 40% today. Taking up the slack are Albanians from Yu-
goslavia. They are now 20% of the population and growing.

The dense workers' neighborhoods here were built for autoworkers' families in one amazing gush between 1914 and 1920,
when the village's population skyrocketed from 3,589 to 45,615,
the largest such increase in that decade anywhere in the U.S.
The sudden growth occurred because in 1910 the Dodge Brothers built Dodge Main, a huge auto factory on the south edge of
what was then an old German farming village.

Today, even with the declining Polish presence in Hamtramck, its commercial district has a distinct Polish feel to it.
But city services are suffering as the population, which peaked in
1930 at 56,000, has dropped to just 18,400 today. A major blow
to the community was the closing of Dodge Main in 1979. The
GM Poletown plant, built on some of the same land, sits two-
thirds over the Detroit border. Its 3,000 jobs, half of what GM
anticipated, haven't come close to replacing the 11,000 Dodge

workers. Dana Corporation's departure in 1986 cost the city hundreds more jobs.

Hamtramck highlights include:

◆ **Monument to Pope John Paul II.** It's not surprising that this distinctively Polish city would want to do something special to commemorate the installation of the first Polish pope. Much of the funding has come from the proceeds of an annual festival held for four days around Labor Day, when over 700,000 visitors flock to the city. The austere little park is enlivened by the colorful and well-executed mural of costumed folk dancers in a historic Polish street scene. The fence is formed by the original entrance gates to the late, lamented Dodge Main plant, Hamtramck's reason for being. *Corner Belmont and Joseph Campau.*

◆ **New Palace Bakery.** Hamtramck is known for its Polish bakeries, and the New Palace is a favorite among the locals. One Polish specialty is angel wings, a very light dough fried with a powdering of sugar. Another favorite is paczki, or jelly-filled doughnuts. On the day before Lent, lines form by 7 a.m. to buy them. Lemon tortes, cinnamon-raisin breakfast rolls, and pumpernickel and rye breads are other standbys. *9833 Joseph Campau between Yemans and Evaline. (313) 875-1334. Mon-Sat 5 a.m.-7 p.m., Fri 'til 8.*

◆ **Ciemniak Meat Market.** Lots of people around Hamtramck think this is the best meat market in town. Ciemniak's own smokehouse is in back, where they make such things as hunter's sausage ($4.59/lb.) and smoked kielbasa (with veal and pork, $3.59/lb.). Their fresh pork kielbasa is $2.99 a pound. Kiszka ($1.98/lb.) is made with buckwheat, beef blood, liver, and pork. *9629 Joseph Campau between Norwalk and Edwin. (313) 871-0773. Mon-Fri 9-6, Sat 9-6.*

◆ **Polish Art Center.** This delightful shop has such an attractive array of Polish arts and crafts that people visit it from all over the U.S. Here you can find Polish folk art rugs ($35 to $300). Beautiful wooden plates inlaid with metal ($8 to $50), Polish leaded glass ($11.50 to $500), costume dolls ($7.50 and up), and brightly painted Russian nesting dolls starting at just $12 a set. Sparkling and intricate tinfoil nativities, called *szopka*, are $75.

Colorful Easter eggs, including Ukrainian goose and ostrich eggs, are on hand, as are egg-decorating supplies (dyes, wax, tools, unfinished eggs). There are inexpensive paper cuttings (and books on creating this cheery Polish folk art), amber jewelry, replicas of antique Polish swords, and Polish greeting cards. *9539 Joseph Campau at Norwalk. (313) 874-2242. Mon 9:30-7, Tues-Thur 9:30-5, Fri-Sat 9:30-5.*

◆ **St. Florian Church.** This magnificent Gothic church, completed in 1926, is on the scale of a great European cathedral. Serving one of the region's largest parishes, it holds 1,800. The church was designed by Ralph Adams Cram, America's high priest of the 20th-century Gothic Revival. The interior is awesome, with an enormously high ceiling. Massive stained glass windows fill the high walls. *2626 Poland. Faces Florian St. one block west of Joseph Campau. (313) 871-2778. Church is open to visitors 8:30 a.m.-6 p.m.; enter from back door on Poland St.*

◆ **Cadillac Detroit-Hamtramck Assembly Center.** The highly roboticized new Poletown plant makes Cadillac Sevilles, Buick Rivieras, and Oldsmobile Toronados. The 1 1/2-hour tour begins with a 12-minute slide show. An extended, wrenching controversy and much pain was created when the city of Detroit condemned and tore down a whole neighborhood and the Immaculate Conception church so GM could build its big new Poletown plant here in the city, incorporating the site of the old Dodge Main plant. A vital retail district along Chene Street was turned into a ghost town in the process. *Just north of I-94 between Mt. Elliot and I-75. (313) 972-6000. Tours by reservation only (booked up months in advance) Tues-Thur 9 a.m., Thurs noon.*

NEIGHBORHOOD TAVERNS . . . . . off the main drag are enduringly popular Hamtramck institutions best observed after work. Many have inexpensive food and/or entertainment. They include **Artie's Locker Room** (31421 Caniff at Charest), **G's Place** (2764 Florian), **Dr. Dave's Waiting Room Lounge** (3216 Carpenter), and **Paycheck's Lounge** (2932 Caniff). **The Attic** (11667 Joseph Campau) is a popular hangout for blues musicians who drop by to play and listen.

Detroit Zoo

Long a pioneer in creating natural settings, it now has a spectacular new chimp compound

The world's finest zoo chimpanzee exhibit is the highlight in this big zoo. Its four acres are enough to provide a natural habitat for over a dozen chimps. The $8 million setting allows the chimps to establish a natural social order, so that visitors can see them acting as they would in their indigenous habitats. Creating natural settings was a major focus of former zoo director Steve Graham, who avoided naming the zoo's animals and treating them like pets. No more cute chimps in jackets doing tricks!

Several good viewing points encircle the exhibit Visitors can see the chimps in three different settings: forest clearing, meadow, and and rock outcropping. The chimps will stay outside a good 300 days a year, but when the weather is too severe, they can be viewed in two large indoor rooms behind one-way glass.

As many people actually come to ride on the **zoo railroad** as to see the animals. The free train carries visitors from the Main Station 1 1/4 miles to the African Station. There are also tractor-pulled 45-minute narrated tours of the zoo ($2 adults, $1 children).

FEEDING TIMES
Penguins: daily 10:30, 11:30, 1:30.
Polar bears: May to mid-Oct. 1:30.
Sea lions: late May-mid-Oct. 11-2
Lemurs: early June-mid-Oct. 2:30.

Another popular exhibit is the **Holden Museum of Living Reptiles**, constructed in 1960. The **Penguinarium** houses four species of penguins (blue, king, macaroni, and rockhopper) in three different habitats. The outer, triangular ring of the exhibit is water. The penguins can swim around continuously, giving visitors a wonderfully intimate underwater view of the birds.

The **Wilson Aviary Wing** provides a big free-flight space for birds as large as the rare Andean condor, with a 10-foot wingspan. In this horseshoe-shaped space are a waterfall, stream, pond, and hundreds of tropical plants. The birds have unrestricted use of this scenic space, which visitors traverse on a walkway.

This pioneering zoo opened in 1928 to huge and wildly enthusiastic crowds. Detroit's was the first American zoo to emphasize barless exhibits rather than more confining and jail-like cages typical of the day. This is perhaps most dramatically seen in one of the zoo's first displays, the dramatic, enormous **polar bear exhibit**. Instead of fences, large moats protect visitors from the huge bears. A moat proved ineffective on opening day in 1928. A bear leaped the moat and approached Detroit's mayor, who affably — and foolishly — reached out to shake its paw.

Ten Mile at Woodward in Royal Oak just north of I-696 (take Woodward exit). Enter from Woodward. (313) 398-0900. Open Wed-Sun 10-4; Nov. through April. May through Oct. open daily 10-5. Adults and teens 13 and over $5.75; 2-12 $2.50; under 2 free.

Royal Oak shops and galleries

The hippest, most idiosyncratic retailing in Metro Detroit

A decade ago, Royal Oak's twin commercial boulevards, Main Street and Washington Avenue, were in decline, like most aging American downtowns upstaged by shopping malls. That trend began to reverse itself in 1980 when energetic Patti Smith started her vintage clothing shop on Washington. Hip and affordable, Patti Smith Collectibles attracted customers from far and wide with both its interesting vintage clothing and its inexpensive original designs. Smith set a successful example, and her Sixties-style, community-minded spirit has been infectious. There has been an extraordinary influx of interesting shops, many started by entrepreneurs who can afford the district's relatively low rents.

ON AND OFF WASINGTON

◆ **Swidler Gallery.** This young gallery has quickly become one of the Midwest's most impressive ceramics galleries. Prices range from $30 to over $1,000 for one-of-a-kind pieces. Most of the works are functional and in earth tones. Also, a large range of art jewelry. *308 W. Fourth at Washington in Washington Square. (313) 542-4880. Tues-Sat 11-5.*

◆ **LA Express.** The takeout arm of the popular Les Auteurs bistro offers an inviting variety of inventive food, from chicken and beef chili ($3.50) to California pizza ($13.50 large). Popular dishes include chicken salad ($3.50/half-pound) and vegetarian lasagna ($4.25). *222 Sherman Dr. at the rear of Washington Square. (313) 544-2372. Mon-Sat 10-9.*

◆ **The Sybaris Gallery.** One of a kind pieces in clay, fiber, wood, glass, and metal, plus art furniture. "The work showcased pushes the limits of technology, material, and concept," say directors Linda Ross and Arlene Selik. *301 W. Fourth at Washington. (313) 544-3388. Tues-Sat 11-5.*

◆**Patti Smith Collectibles.** This very popular women's apparel and jewelry shop carries one-third vintage and two-thirds small company and local artists' designs. Many come here especially for the Twenties and Thirties vintage clothing. *407 S. Washing-*

ton. *(313) 399-0756. Mon-Wed 11-6, Thurs-Fri 11-9, Sat 10-6.*

◆ **Dave's Comics and Collectibles.** New and used comics plus antique toys, from the 30s through 60s. A colorful display of vintage kids' lunchboxes is at the back. *407 S. Washington. (313) 548-1230. Mon-Wed 11-8, Thurs-Fri 11-9, Sat 11-7, Sun 11-4. In winter, Mon & Tues until 6 only.*

◆**Gayle's Chocolates.** Gayle's is a jewel of a shop, one of the most pleasing Art Deco makeovers to be found. Noted area designer Ron Rea also helped renovate the interesting Washington Square Building up the block. Outstanding chocolate truffles ($1.10 each) are the main attraction. Some say Gayle's are the best available. You can also buy excellent espresso and cappuccino, hot chocolate, or steamed milk and honey. A front area with tables lets you sit back and enjoy the decor and people on the street. *417 S. Washington. (313) 398-0001. Mon-Sat 10-6, open later in summer.*

◆ **Lotus Import Co.** Ethnic jewelry, clothing, and decorative accessories from all continents, with quite a few Asian selections — all appealingly displayed in this visually rich shop. The Indonesian clothing, made from old sarongs of ikat fabrics, includes patchwork coats, dresses, shirts, blouses, jumpers ($50-$200). Also a good selection of African masks ($20-$600). *204 W. Fifth. (313) 546-8820. Mon-Tues 10-6, Wed 10-7, Thurs-Fri 10-9, Sat 10-6.*

◆ **Vertu.** Vertu is known for its interesting collection of Art Deco-influenced small appliances (toasters, waffle irons, mixers, etc.) and chrome furniture from the 1930s and 1940s. More generally, it deals in objects of modern design (largely furniture and ceramics) from 1900 to 1960. The owner is quite knowledgeable about mid-20th-century design. *511 S. Washington. (313) 545-6050. Tues-Sat noon-6.*

◆ **World of Kites.** Here you'll find over 250 varieties of kites and an amazing array of accessories: kite ferries which go up and down the kite string ($13), kite parachutes ($4.50), and even kite strobe lights ($30-$50) to light up your kite in the night sky. *525 S. Washington at Sixth. (313) 398-5900. Tues-Fri 11-5, Sat 10-6.*

◆ **Dos Manos.** Well-chosen, affordable handcrafts from Latin America exclusively. Oaxaca rugs ($65-$250), wall hangings from Mexico, Mexican pottery, copper decorative pieces, jewelry, and cotton placemats. Terra cotta planters in the shapes of frogs and turtles are $15 to $50. *210 W. Sixth. (313) 542-5856. Mon-Wed 11-6, Thurs 11-9, Fri 11-6, Sat 11-5.*

◆ **Deco Doug.** Radios, clocks, lamps, and some furniture, exclu-

sively Art Deco from the 1920s into the 1950s. *106 W. Fourth.*
(313) 547-3330. Mon-Sat 12-6 unless at a show.

◆ **Neon Images.** Owner Darcy Salbert searches far and wide for
old neon clocks, then refurbishes them to like-new condition
and sells them for $250-$775. You can also find old gum ball machines ($65-$275), slot machines ($1,100 and up), and new
small neon advertising signs ($125 and up). *108 W. Fourth. (313)*
543-5063. Mon-Fri 11-5, Sat 12-5.

◆ **Stamping Grounds.** Rubber stamps here are taken as serious
fun, a means for inspired creative expression, and not just a
passing fad or cute gift item. There are plenty of nifty examples
and idea books to get you started, and special inks for stamping
on fabrics and special purposes. The selection of rubber stamp
designs goes way beyond the usual lines to include offbeat new
releases and lots of alphabets. *228 W. Fourth. (313) 543-2190.*
Mon-Sat 10-5.

◆ **Chosen Books.** Metro Detroit's only gay bookstore in metro
Detroit. The shop is well-stocked with books, magazines, cards,
novelties, gifts, videos, and various paraphernalia. *120 W. Fourth.*
(313) 543-5758. Noon-10 daily.

ON MAIN BETWEEN THIRD AND LINCOLN

◆ **Bright Ideas.** The Midwest doesn't have many contemporary
home furnishings stores featuring original new Italian, Swedish,
and German furniture designs. Bright Ideas has them, plus accessories like halogen lighting. *220 S. Main at Third. (313)*
541-9940. Mon, Thurs, Fri 10-9; Tues, Wed, Sat 10-6; Sun 12-5.

◆ **Carol/James Gallery.** An exceptionally pleasing contemporary
arts and crafts gallery, Carol/James carries glass, decorative and
functional ceramics, wood, jewelry, and fiber by 75 craftspeople.
The blown glass paperweights and perfume bottles ($55-$365)
stand out. *301 S. Main. (313) 541-6216. Tues-Wed 10:30-5:30,*
Thurs 10:30-9, Fri 10:30-5:30, Sat 10-5:30.

◆ **Incognito.** Rock 'n' roll clothing takes up most of the space in
this shop, but there is also an extraordinary selection of sun-
glasses in over 300 styles. *323 S. Main (at Fourth). (313)*
548-2980. Mon-Sat 11-7, Sun 12-5.

◆ **Noir Leather.** Downtown Royal Oak can boast of some genuinely eccentric shops. Noir Leather is the most notorious. "It is
certainly one of the few places in the Midwest where you can buy
how-to videos on body piercing and tattooing, underwear that
glows in the dark, and a range of political buttons fit for everyone
from peacenik to storm trooper," writes *Detroit Free Press*
reporter Lewis Beale. "Where else could you see in-store signs

that read "Absolutely no return on Bondage items for sanitation reasons."? Most Noir customers are punks interested in fairly conventional things like its big selection of leather motorcycle caps and leather sheath skirts, but there's an ample supply of handcuffs, ominous-looking leather masks, and crops for customers with kinky sexual tastes. Owner Keith Howarth is no punk himself but an art historian and former art conservator with exceedingly polite manners. *415 S. Main. (313) 541-3979. Mon-Fri 11-8, Sat 11-7. Sun 1-5.*

GOOD FRESH FOODS AND GOOD STUFF . . . . . Many discriminating cooks shop for in-season produce and fruit at the year-round, 110-stall **Royal Oak Farmers' Market**. Most stalls are indoors, and there's a big parking lot. *Open May through October on Tues, Fri, Sat 7 a.m. -1 p.m. Open year-round on Saturday.*

Sundays year-round from 10-5 the market changes into a highly regarded **flea market** that's better than the name implies. A number of the 75 dealers have permanent booths set up, from which they sell everything from dried flowers and crafts to precious metals and coins. Lots of clothes (both old and new) and antiques and collectibles are always on hand. Patti Smith got her start selling vintage clothing here. *316 East 11 Mile Rd., 1 1/2 blocks east of Main St. (313) 548-8822.*

THE RADIO PRIEST'S LEGACY . . . . . The impressive **Shrine of the Little Flower** Catholic Church at Woodward and Roseland just north of 12 Mile Rd. was built by the famous radio priest Charles Coughlin. The genial, theatrical priest sympathized with the Depression-era plight of his autoworker parishioners and became an influential New Deal backer. But by 1935 Coughlin had become a blatant anti-Semite and almost a fascist. He denounced Roosevelt as a tool of Jewish bankers. His admirers contributed to the church, completed in 1933. Stones from each state are inscribed with that state's flower.

Birmingham galleries

In an intensely fashion-conscious downtown, one of the most important concentrations of art galleries in the Midwest

During the Eighties, Birmingham has become a major Midwestern center of important art galleries. They focus on everything from museum-quality ancient artifacts to contemporary art by internationally known artists. Catalyst for this convenient concentration was the prestigious Donald Morris Gallery on Townsend, which moved from Detroit in 1975. Now a number of galleries are near him, and some are scattered along Woodward in downtown Birmingham. So many galleries have come to occupy a charming strip of small shops on Woodward north of downtown that it's now known as "gallery row."

Disappointingly, Birmingham gallery owners do not cooperate with joint maps and directories for customers, the way most dealers in books, antiques, and other fields typically do. Rather, they tend to operate in self-absorbed vacuums, as if theirs is the only gallery worthy of consideration. They often aren't very friendly, either, so don't take it personally if you're ignored. Birmingham retailing is famous for being in a constant state of flux, driven by high rents. Shops are always opening and closing. So if you're planning an expedition to Birmingham, window-shopping may uncover new galleries.

ON TOWNSEND STREET

◆ **Donald Morris Gallery.** Morris primarily sells the established 20th-century American and European masters: Picasso, Miro, Leger, Dubuffet, and Calder, to name a few. The gallery also handles classic African art and turn-of-the-century decorative arts. This is the state's most expensive gallery, with prices often into the hundreds of thousands of dollars. *105 Townsend. (313) 642-8812. Tues-Sat 10:30-5:30.*

◆ **G. R. N'Namdi Gallery.** Paintings, sculpture, and a good number of collages, all characteristically vibrant and colorful, by contemporary artists with national and international reputations, including many African-American and Latin American artists. *161 Townsend. (313) 642-2700. Tues-Sat 11-5:30.*

◆ **Hill Gallery.** Building on its longtime base of museum-quality American folk art (mostly historic, some contemporary) and interesting regional artists, Hill has become a leading Michigan gallery. It now also shows contemporary paintings and, especially, sculptures by nationally well-known artists. *163 Townsend. (313) 540-9288. Tues-Sat 11:30-5:30.*

WOODWARD NEAR MAPLE

◆ **K. C. Larson Gallery.** Room-like settings of small antique objects, leather-bound books, colorful rugs, and Biedermeier and other neo-classically inspired furniture, plus pieces by designers Josef Hoffmann and other Wiener Werkstätte artists in early 20th-century Vienna. The stimulating, eclectic mix of folk art, sculpture, old pine and oak furniture, and Art Deco wrought iron from France — which used to be the gallery's stock in trade — is now in the rear warehouse. *209 N. Woodward (upstairs). (313) 647-0135. Tues-Sat 11-6.*

◆ **Duke Gallery.** Largest selection of Arts & Crafts furniture, lighting, pottery, and art glass in the state. Other distinctive 20th-century design movements are also represented: Art Nouveau, Art Deco, and Art Moderne. The work of Frank Lloyd Wright, Gustav Stickley, Charles Eames, and Louis Comfort Tiffany is often found here. An energetic collector of art glass praises the quality and taste but comments that the prices are "outstandingly high." *209 N. Woodward (upstairs, to the rear). (313) 258-6848. Tues-Sat 11-6 and by appt.*

GALLERY ROW ON NORTH WOODWARD

Don't overlook second-story shops on the upper end. Salvatore Scallopini across the street is a fine spot for a quick meal or snack. *N. Woodward between Harmon & Oak, a few blocks north of downtown.*

◆ **D. & J. Bittker Gallery.** Antique Chinese furniture. *536 N. Woodward. (313) 258-1670. Tues-Fri 12-5.*

◆ **Lemberg Gallery.** Contemporary paintings, drawings, and graphics by artists who are locally and nationally prominent. A $30,000 Frank Stella work may hang on one wall, and on another a $2,000 mixed media work by Steve Murakishi, Cranbrook's graphic arts department head. *538 N. Woodward. (313) 642-6623. Tues-Sat 11-5:30.*

◆ **Halsted Gallery.** This gallery has a national reputation for its 19th- and 20th-century photography. It also carries out-of-print and rare books on photography. *560 N. Woodward. (313) 644-8284. Tues-Sat 10-5:30.*

◆ **Xochipilli.** Pronounced "ZO-sha-pee-lee," it's named after the Aztec god of the arts. Director Mary Wright gets raves from area artists as one of the most interesting, committed, supportive, and discriminating gallery directors around. She shows paintings and sculpture by contemporary artists from in and around Michigan. *568 N. Woodward. (313) 645-1905. Tues-Sat 11-5.*

◆ **Artspace.** Consignment sale gallery carries quality 19th- and 20th-century paintings, drawings, sculpture, prints, and decorative arts. Prices start at $200 and go up as high $20,000. Almost all works are below market price, many brought to market after divorces or moves. *574 N. Woodward. (313) 258-1540.*

◆ **Donna Jacobs.** This fascinating gallery specializes in ancient art: Greek, Roman, Egyptian, Etruscan, Near Eastern, and Pre-Columbian objects. These include pottery, glass, bronzes, stone, textiles, and custom-designed jewelry using ethnic, contemporary, and ancient elements. These museum-quality pieces sell for as little as $50, for a small, 2,000-year-old terra-cotta oil lamp from the Holy Land or a 2,300-year-old Egyptian *ushabti,* a little figure set in tombs to serve the dead. *574 N. Woodward. (313) 540-1600. Tues-Sat 11-5:30.*

◆ **Elizabeth Stone Gallery.** Original paintings and drawings by book illustrators — mostly contemporary, and some old masters of the genre — assembled by a longtime children's librarian at Cranbrook's elementary school. Media range from large oils to pastels to very detailed watercolors. Prices from $100 for spot illustrations to $7,500, with most from $800 to $3,500. *Tues-Sat 11-5:30.*

◆ **Artful Domain.** Attractive gallery-shop of American contemporary crafts owned by the owner of 16 Hands in Ann Arbor. Wide range of prices, but with more furniture and other higher-ticket items than the Ann Arbor store. *700 N. Woodward. (313) 646-2030. Tues-Sat 11-5.*

◆ **Feigenson-Preston Gallery.** The late Jackie Feigenson won widespread respect as the first commercial gallery director to focus primarily on Michigan artists, rather than just as additions to a stable of New York or European artists. A major emphasis has been on the exciting Cass Corridor group. Now her longtime associate Mary Preston says, "After all these years in business [since 1976], the majority of our artists who started in Detroit are living in New York. Staying in the Midwest, artists don't put the right pieces in the career puzzle together. I'd like to help change that." Of her Detroit artists, only Brad Iverson remains in the area; Tom Bills, James Chatelain, and Ruth Leonard are in New York. The gallery now shows works by contemporary American artists regardless of Michigan connections, including Ursula von Rydingsvard, Jane Hammond, and David Kapp. *796 N. Wood-*

ward (rear). (313) 644-3955.

◆ **Mettal Studio.** Highly original sculptural art jewelry by Center for Creative Studies alums Patrick Irla and Cary Stefani. *798 N. Woodward. (313) 258-8818. Tues-Fri 10-6, Sat 10-4.*

◆ **In Situ/Arkitektura.** Reproductions of classic 20th-century modern design. It was started in 1984 by the grandson of Eliel Saarinen and two other alums of nearby Cranbrook, where the great Swedish designer lived and worked for many years. In addition to Saarinen designs, In Situ (formerly Arkitektura) sells authorized reproductions of classic furniture by late, great architect/designers like Le Corbusier, Mies van der Rohe, and Charles Rennie Macintosh, and current names like Robert Venturi, Stanley Tigerman, Michael McCoy, and Joe D'Urso. Prices range from $10 to over $10,000, but few of these careful reproductions are cheap. A Saarinen dining chair is $1,700, a table by Le Corbusier $1,500, and a Tizio lamp $300. In Situ also carries the Swid Powell line of architect-designed china, crystal, and silver by the likes of Venturi, Charles Gwathmey, Robert Siegel, Richard Meier, and Michael Graves. *800 N. Woodward (upstairs). (313) 646-0097. Mon-Fri 9:30-5, Sat 1-5.*

MICHIGAN'S MOST FASHION-CONSCIOUS, GLITZIEST DOWNTOWN . . . . . is in **Birmingham**, centered at Woodward and Maple. Blessed with virtually the only functioning downtown in this booming suburban region of central Oakland County, the prestigious residential suburb of 20,000 has assumed a new role, unwelcome by many longtime residents, as the shopping mecca for one of the 10 wealthiest counties in the U.S. Twenty years ago downtown Birmingham wasn't all that different from Grosse Pointe: somewhat clubby and preppy, and fairly traditional and sedate in tone. Today it is alive with the latest upscale trends and creative ideas, with cafes and unusual shops, prestigious offices, even a luxury hotel and legitimate theater. Stylish people come to see and be seen. Attitude is everything for these self-conscious fashionplates, adolescent and adult, and you don't see many smiles on the street on bustling Saturdays. The place is mellower, less crowded, and more pleasant in summer. **Shain Park**, two blocks west of Woodward and a block south of Maple, is a lovely place for a relaxing takeout meal from the Merchant of Vino **(see below)**.

Turnover is continual in this high-rent area, and upscale national chains with deep pockets are driving out independent merchants. *Store hours are generally from 10 to 5:30 or 6, Monday through Saturday, Thursday to 8.* Easiest parking is in city ramps; look for signs. Distinctive standouts include:

◆ **Linda Dresner.** Featuring leading high-fashion designers for women who are both thin and rich. *99 W. Maple.*

◆ **It's the Ritz.** Crazy, high-impact clothes for men and women. *193 W. Maple.*

◆ **The Merchant of Vino.** The area's leading deli/wine shop/fancy food store. A visual delight in the robust style of updated Italian groceries. Competitive prices. *254 West Maple.*

◆ **Jacobson's.** Flagship of the upper-end department store chain. *336 W. Maple.*

◆ **Birmingham Bookstore.** Pleasant browsing. The first part of the store is devoted to decorating and lifestyle, a good indication of local tastes. *263 Pierce.*

◆ **Marley's Boutique.** A creative melange of handmade clothes (denim jackets appliqued with rhinestones, rainbow cocoons of knit coats, fanciful sweaters), in a magical arbor-like environment. Folk art, costume jewelry, and a soft-edged, witty sensibility that's sometimes romantic, sometimes outrageous. *Inside the Townsend Hotel, 100 Townsend. Open daily 10-9, Sun to 5.*

◆ **Expressions.** Uncommon national chain with wildly eclectic furniture (country, Deco, painted folk), upholstery fabrics. Good prices. *950 S. Woodward.*

◆ **Garys Flowers and Antiques.** The ebullient Gary Kalm (known as "Gary Flowers") has created a delightfully luxurious if somewhat disheveled space where ornate antiques and crystal chandeliers coexist with soft, natural, uncontrived bouquets of flowers. *415 E. Frank at Ann, just east of Woodward. (313) 642-2612. Usually open Tues-Sat 10-5; call to confirm.*

◆ **Russell Hardware.** Unusual hardware, from basic builders' lines to exclusive and hard-to-find brass fittings and door knockers, reproduction antique doorknobs, unusual door locks, contemporary architect-designed handles, and such, has long been the specialty of **Russell Hardware.** Renovators and designers who are fussy about details travel way out of their way to find things like the right doorbell or replacement knobs and custom address plaques. *1036 N. Hunter at Woodward, 1/4 mi. south of Big Beaver. (313) 644-0100. Mon-Fri 8-5, Thurs 'til 8. Closed Sat.*

AN INVITING PARK FOR A CHANGE OF PACE. . . . . Long, narrow **Quarton Lake** is created by a small dam on the Rouge River, once used to power a mill. Kids like to fish at the dam. The lake is the focus of a shady, informal park just a few blocks west of downtown Birmingham. Visitors are welcome to sit on a bench and eat a bag lunch while enjoying the huge trees reflected in the water. *North of W. Maple 1/4 mile west of downtown Birmingham. North from W. Maple onto Baldwin, bear left onto Lakeside. Park along the lake.*

Bloomfield Hills

*Lushly landscaped estates and hilly terrain
mark Michigan's wealthiest town.*

This beautiful suburb of 2,000 homes (average price over $400,000) is the second wealthiest community in the U.S. Long the preferred residence of Detroit's elite business executives and "new money," Bloomfield Hills is the home of the heads of the Big Three automakers, along with various celebrities such as Pistons' star Isiah Thomas, soul queen Aretha Franklin, and WJR's popular deejay, J. P. McCarthy.

Privacy, prestige, and service is what living in Bloomfield Hills is all about. Residents receive fabulous services. Three-fourths of all homes are connected with the city's emergency dispatch system. The entire area is served by old-fashioned milkmen who walk right into residents' kitchens to fill orders for Borden dairy products, top-rated Guernsey Farms ice cream, and Amish poultry and eggs.

The famous Cranbrook schools occupy 315 stunningly landscaped acres in the very heart of Bloomfield Hills. While most of the terrain in the Detroit area is boring and flat, it starts to get hilly in Bloomfield Hills.

The interesting terrain and lush landscaping make for pleasant drives on Bloomfield Hills' winding streets. Ivy grows up many trees, and woodsy thickets frame many houses. A bike ride would be better yet, to let you stop and admire architectural details.

Not surprisingly, some of the most outstanding domestic architecture in Michigan is here. 1920s-era houses around Cranbrook and Christ Church Cranbrook are especially striking. Occasional iron gates and stone or brick walls make for an English country look that's engaging rather than forbidding. Frank Lloyd Wright designed the house at 5045 Pon Valley Road (off Lone Pine Road in Bloomfield Township), finished in 1951.

A few of the oldest remaining houses, mostly along Woodward, date from 1896, when the interurban railway to Birmingham first allowed wealthy commuters to establish estates in these scenic hills. Before that it had been a farming village founded in 1810 by Amasa Bagley. He followed an Indian trail to an opening where he established a farm.

Cranbrook

Here famed architect Eliel Saarinen created
an extraordinarily beautiful environment
for artists and students.

T his educational complex on 315 rolling acres has several claims to renown. Internationally, Cranbrook is known for its Academy of Art, a graduate school of art, design, and architecture. Locally it is known for its distinguished private elementary, middle, and upper schools, as well as for its popular art and science museums.

Finally, Cranbrook is also known throughout the world for the total aesthetics of its environment — a careful integration of buildings, gardens, sculpture, and interiors. The noted architectural photographer Balthazar Korab, who lives nearby, expressed this nicely. "Cranbrook is my place of recreation. Walking there, you find yourself in a different atmosphere. It's like a large private estate that has been opened to us pedestrians, where you can inhale a time past, an era of great patrons and great ideas. There is a great unity there — not like on a university campus, where you have just groups of diversified buildings. The gardens, the grounds, and the buildings have a definite, luxurious cohesiveness."

Two remarkable men, a patron and an artist, joined their energies to create this special place. The patron was newspaper magnate George Booth. The artist was Eliel Saarinen. In 1904 Booth bought a rundown Bloomfield Hills farm and commissioned Albert Kahn to build a large, Tudor-style mansion there. Booth, the grandson of a Kent coppersmith, was a leading proponent of the Arts and Crafts movement, which stressed a greater unification of life and art through handcrafted artistic production by individual craftspeople. Before he married into a newspaper family, Booth had owned a successful ornamental ironwork factory in Windsor. A trip Booth took to Rome in 1922 was the catalyst for the Cranbrook schools which would gain worldwide attention. There he saw the American Academy and decided to create a school of architecture and design. He persuaded the well-known Finnish architect, Eliel Saarinen, along with Saarinen's wife and children, to move to Bloomfield Hills in 1925 to lay the groundwork for the Cranbrook community.

The Brookside elementary school, built up close to Cranbrook

Road, shows the rustic charm of the cottage style. It has a wonderful iron gate, Scandinavian-style brickwork, and numerous sculptural accents. Saarinen's first designs were for an Academy of Art and Cranbrook School for boys in 1925. In 1928 he designed his own house and a second along Academy Way off Lone Pine Road. Saarinen and Booth had begun to bring distinguished artists to assist in creating the many designs within the complex and to teach at the Academy, which opened in 1931.

The Cranbrook Academy quickly gained a reputation as one of the world's top artistic communities. It continues today to be an important advanced art institute, with internationally known artists in residence in nine departments: architecture, ceramics, design, fiber, metalsmithing, painting, photography, printmaking, and sculpture. A high point of Cranbrook was just before World War II, when Saarinen's son, famed architect Eero Saarinen, together with Charles Eames, created a new, leaner interior design look in frankly machine-made furniture. By the 1950s, alumi Eames, Florence Knoll, and Harry Bertoia had popularized the look so much that it has become the very essence of International-style "modern" design.

Cranbrook is a wonderful place to take walks at every time of year. Covered with fresh snow, it's a magical place. In spring and summer the formal gardens at Cranbrook House are a special delight. The outstanding buildings, many with engaging decorative details, combine with the hilly terrain and mature landscaping to create a memorable environment. Throughout the grounds are 60 sculptures by the prominent Swedish sculptor Carl Milles, who headed the sculpture department for 20 years. Marshall Fredericks was Milles' protegé. His "Spirit of Detroit" and other sculptures are familiar Detroit-area landmarks, was Milles' protegé.

Three Cranbrook buildings are open to the public:

◆ **Cranbrook House & Gardens.** The 1908 mansion designed by Albert Kahn is now the Cranbrook community's administrative office. It features leaded-glass windows and tapestries and art objects collected by Cranbrook founders George and Ellen Booth. The stunning, impeccably maintained gardens around the house are marked by dramatic vistas, fountains and cascades, sculptures and architectural fragments. *380 Lone Pine Road. (313) 645-3149. Gardens open: May-Aug. daily 10-5., Sun 11-5. Sept. daily 1-5, Sun 1-5. Oct. weekends only, 1-5. $2. House open Thursdays May -Sept. Combined house and garden tour: $6. Call (313) 645-3149 by Tues. for Thurs. lunch reservations. Park at Christ Church Cranbrook.*

◆ **Academy of Art Museum.** On permanent view are works by the Cranbrook Academy's many prominent faculty and students, including Carl Milles, Florence Knoll, Charles and Ray Eames, and Marshall Fredericks. Many examples of Eliel Saarinen's decorative work and architectural drawings are here. *Enter on Academy Way, 500 Lone Pine Rd. (313) 645-3312. Turn right and park behind the museum. Daily except Monday 1-5. Adults $2.50; $1.50 students and seniors. Call for information on frequent lecture series and special exhibits by noted artists.*

◆ **Institute of Science.** This exhibit museum is filled with displays illuminating key aspects of the physical sciences, botany, biology, anthropology, and archeology. Here you can find one of the most extensive and well arranged **mineral collections** in the country. One room is devoted to hands-on exhibits, mostly demonstrating scientific principles. The **hall on American Indian culture** is especially noteworthy. Full-scale teepees are on display, along with many artifacts and dioramas showing what life was like in Indian villages of various tribes. The **observatory** is open to the public Saturday evenings after dark. Planetarium and laser shows are held on weekends. Two **gift shops** are here, one especially for children. *Enter on Academy Way, 500 Lone Pine Rd., and proceed straight back to Institute Way. Park in the lot by the entrance. (313) 645-3200. Mon-Thurs 10-5; Fri-Sat 10-10, Sun 1-5. Adults $4, students and seniors $3.*

Cranbrook is off Lone Pine and Cranbrook roads just west of Woodward. See individual sights for particulars. A map of the grounds and general brochure about the Cranbrook Educational Community is available from the Public Relations office in Cranbrook House, or call (313) 645-3142.

NEAR CRANBROOK . . . . . **Christ Church Cranbrook** is an imposing English Gothic-style Episcopal church donated by Cranbrook founder George Booth. The 118-foot tower holds a large **carillon** whose 62 English-made bells range from 48 to 9,408 pounds. Hour-long **concerts** are every Sunday at 4 p.m. beginning the last Sunday in June and ending the first Sunday in September. Visitors can listen from their cars or loll on the pleasant, park-like grassy space in front of the church. On selected Sundays there are tours of the tower, from which you can get a spectacular view of Bloomfield Hills and a particularly nice view of Cranbrook next door. *Lone Pine Rd. at Church St. and Cranbrook Rd. (across from Cranbrook House). (313) 644-5210. Main sanctuary open to visitors 8:30-5 daily. Call church to find out which Sundays bell tower is open. Summer carillon concerts Sundays at 4 p.m.*

Meadow Brook Hall

Built by the widow of automaker John Dodge,
this 100-room mansion is a joy to visit.

Of the major auto magnate mansions in the Detroit area, this is the warmest and most pleasing. It's a remarkable feat to make a 100-room Tudor mansion feel comfortable and inviting. The credit goes to Matilda Dodge Wilson, the daughter of a German immigrant from Canada who ran the Dry Dock Saloon on Detroit's riverfront. Second wife of the great automaker John Dodge, she was left over $150 million after he died in 1921. At age 41 she married Alfred Wilson, a wealthy lumber broker. In 1926 she began building the long planned Tudor home at Meadow Brook. Industrious, warmhearted, and strong-willed, Matilda was closely involved in Meadow Brook's design, construction, and decor.

Happily, the interior of this magnificent home is still quite close to what it was when Matilda Dodge Wilson lived here. Although she ultimately spent $4 million on the home, she resisted overpowering effects. In a very natural way, priceless works of art occupy the same rooms as works of purely personal interest. Most of the rooms, big and small, pleasingly combine fine works of art (including paintings by Van Dyke, Reynolds, and Rosa Bonheur), ornate carved wood and plaster architectural detailing, carpeting, and furniture.

Matilda Dodge Wilson donated her estate and $2 million to help start Oakland University on these grounds. Its five schools now enroll 12,000. The well-known **Meadowbrook Theatre** on campus offers eight professional performances between October and May. The outdoor **Meadow Brook Music Festival**, just over the hill from Meadow Brook Hall, runs June through August, that includes pop, classics, rock, and jazz. Call (313) 377-3300 for information.

On the Oakland University campus off Walton Rd. on Adams Rd. 3 miles northeast of downtown Pontiac. From I-75, take Exit 79 (Pontiac Rd.) east one mile to University Dr. (313) 370-3140. Self-guided tours year-round Sun 1-4. Guided tours in July & August, Mon-Sat 10:15-3:45. Closed holidays. $5, seniors $4, children 5-12 $3 . Also open daily in early Dec; call.

Holocaust Memorial Center

Grim and disturbing, this outstanding museum illuminates what led to the mass murder of Jews.

The murder of 6 million Jews by Hitler's Nazis during World War II is documented in a chilling, almost low-key manner in this multifaceted, superbly designed museum. Visitors to the $7 million center begin the self-guided tour hearing the sweet, haunting voice of a mother singing a Jewish lullaby. You enter a darkened, ominous-looking tunnel and pass a video of Hitler bombastically shouting to a throng of Germans his racist message and world view. Displays put into historical context Germany's suffering after World War I and the punishing peace imposed by the French. It becomes clear how humiliation and economic distress led many Germans to turn upon their Jewish fellow Germans as scapegoats.

Displays use a sophisticated combination of historical artifacts, photos, dioramas, and film footage, so that no visitor can escape the Holocaust's horror. What comes across is the almost incredible act of the systematic extermination of millions of men, women, and children by an industrialized, Western society quite similar to our own. The Nazis' blatant sadism is also evident. These victims not only died but experienced extraordinary suffering before death.

This obviously isn't a pleasant place to visit. Children under 14 aren't advised to come. But the Holocaust museum exposes us to sad truths about what the human race is capable of.

6602 W. Maple in West Bloomfield Township, 2 miles west of Orchard Lake Rd. In the Jewish Community Center across from Henry Ford Hospital. From I-696, take Orchard Lake Rd. exit 3 miles north to Maple, turn left. (313) 661-0840. Sun-Thurs 10-3:30. 1^1/$_2$ public tour Sun 1 p.m. No admission charge.

Plymouth

This attractive suburb, birthplace of Daisy Air Rifle, has two interesting districts of shops.

What makes this small, attractive suburb worth a visit are its two increasingly interesting commercial districts. They contain a variety of noteworthy shops and a couple of exceptional places to eat.

Most towns of 10,000 don't come close to the vitality of Plymouth's downtown and Old Village. For years, because it was home of the Daisy Air Rifle Company, Plymouth was known far and wide as the air rifle capital of the world. Daisy was initially the Plymouth Windmill Company, but when sales declined, the firm decided to make and give away an all-metal air rifle to any farmer who would buy its windmill. The air rifle sold briskly while windmill sales languished. So the company stopped making windmills and changed its name to the Daisy Manufacturing Company in 1895. It moved to Arkansas in 1958.

Highlights of Plymouth are:

◆**Kellogg Park.** A shady triangular downtown park that creates a pleasant center to the city. It was donated by John Kellogg, who arrived in 1832 with a chest full of gold coins, having just sold a hotel and warehouse on the Erie Canal in Palmyra, New York. Opposite the park on Penniman is the **Farmer's Market**, where fresh produce is sold Saturdays from 8 a.m. to 1 p.m., May through October. At the **Penn Theatre**, not-quite-first-run movies are shown, usually at 7 and 9, for $2. (313) 453-0870.

◆ **Penniman Street.** This pleasant block just west of Kellogg Park between Harvey and Main streets is home of the **Folkways Trading Company**, a delightful gift shop where you can buy anything from a 75¢ whistle to gleaming Turkish copper pots. Across the street is the exquisite **Penniman Showcase of Arts & Crafts**, where the work of some 150 American craftsmen in porcelain, stoneware, fibers, and jewelry is attractively displayed. The richly colorful blown display of blown glass is a special treat. Prices range from $20 to $500. A block away at 880 W. Ann Arbor Trail is **Maggie & Me**, a well-regarded women's clothing store where two-thirds of the clothes are designed in-house by Maggie. Lace mixed with menswear fabrics, sometimes even heavy suiting, is her trademark, and she also uses a lot of hand-dyed silk ribbon and roses. Everything is in natural fibers, and one size fits all.

◆ **Old Village.** An interesting, eclectic commercial district dating from the simultaneous arrival of two railroad lines to Plymouth in 1871. It became a busy railroad area, with as many as 18 passenger trains arriving a day. What you find here now, and in houses along Starkweather and Mill, are a number of funky resale and antique shops. The antique shops, mostly on the old brick commercial block of Liberty, are especially worth a visit. At the northernmost part of the district is the highly regarded **Sweet Afton Tea Room**. (See 000). Also, the **Plymouth Antique Mall** at 900 N. Mill has an good collection of dealers. *Open 11-7 daily.* **LaDonna's** at 638 Starkweather carries previously owned ladies' designer clothing sold for a third or a fourth of its original price. Dresses run $30 and up. **Born Again Resale** at 900 Starkweather is strongest in women's and children's clothing. *The Old Village is between Starkweather, Pearl, Mill, and Spring Streets in north Plymouth, towards Northville.*

The Daisy Air Rifle's depiction of "An American Boy's Bill of Rights" includes the right to learn to shoot a gun.

◆ **Plymouth Historical Museum.** A highlight here is the BB-gun room displaying the locally manufactured Daisy and Markham BB guns and fascinating advertising for them. One 1910 Daisy Air Rifle ad proclaims, "Boy, you ought to have a gun this summer. Make up your mind to get one, and learn to shoot straight." In the basement is a wonderful model of the countryside along the Middle Rouge River showing the village industries Henry Ford built. Two bargains in the **gift shop** are a $2 paperback on the history of Daisy Air Rifle and an especially well written hardbound history of Plymouth by Sam Hudson for $8. *155 S. Main St. (313) 455-8940. Wed, Thurs, Sat 1-4, Sun 2-5. Adults $1.50, children 5-17 50¢, families $4.*

Ford Rouge Complex

*An awesome historic symbol of American industry
at its most vibrant and oppressive*

This historic colossus of American industry is, sadly, no
longer open for tours, but you can drive around the complex to take in its awesome magnitude and powerful
visual forms. The Rouge was where Henry Ford put it all
together. It was the world's first vertically integrated factory, an
idea much copied but later discredited as too centralized and
massive. Iron ore came in by ship to Rouge Steel, and cars rolled
out the connected auto assembly plant.

Dredging the shallow River Rouge for three and a half mile up
from its mouth at the Detroit River enabled freighters to deliver
limestone, coal, iron ore, and other raw materials to the 1,100-
acre site. The huge factories Ford built here turned the raw
materials into the steel, plastic, rubber and glass parts, which
were then assembled into Ford automobiles. By the 1920s this
had become the world's biggest manufacturing complex; 10,000
cars a day were made here. The Rouge became a potent symbol
of the machine age. Precisionist painter Charles Sheeler did a
series of famous landscapes here in the 1930s. (Unfortunately,
none hang in the Detroit Institute of Arts.)

Ford's historic Highland Park Plant, where he introduced the assembly line, was only five years old when he started planning for the much bigger Rouge plant in 1914. It was located not far from the Dearborn farm where he grew up. The 1,100 acres were marshy farmland when Ford sent his agents to buy up the component parcels all in a single day. The Rouge's first products were submarine-chasing Eagle boats made at the tail end of World War I. By the late 1920s, 75,000 workers were making Model As here, turning raw materials into completed vehicles in just 33 hours.

It was an extraordinarily bold move for Henry Ford to invest the hundreds of millions of dollars needed to make this giant car-manufacturing complex, including a state-of-the-art steel-making plant. Another Rouge plant turned 210,000 bushels of soybeans a year into paints, plastics, and binders. An electrical power plant added in 1920 was one of the world's largest. One plant made the tires for Ford cars, while another made the glass windshields. Yet another made the famous Ford V-8 engine, Henry Ford's last engineering triumph.

But the Rouge was also the scene of terrible labor strife. The aging Henry Ford lost interest in industrial production. "The Rouge isn't fun any more," he explained, and he turned his interests to Greenfield Village, McGuffey's Readers, and an idealized American past — ironically, the pre-industrial, rural past of Ford's hometown of Dearborn before his own factories transformed it.

As Henry Ford aged, the dark, suspicious side in him grew. It allowed little sympathy for the workers. They were pushed to exhaustion and spied upon. At Ford Motor Company, Henry's capable son, Edsel, was cruelly frustrated, while Henry empowered the notorious Harry Bennett and his security department — virtual thugs and spies who infiltrated many potential organizing meetings. Symptoms of oppressive working conditions were many. Innocent protesters were slaughtered during the 1932 Hunger March. In the 1937 Battle of the Overpass, Walter Reuther and other union organizers passing out leaflets were flagrantly beaten up by Bennett's goons, even though photographers were present. The resulting photographs helped turn public opinion in the union's favor. Finally, a strike in 1941 prompted the company to recognize unionized workers.

Labor difficulties, along with the threat of German bombing attacks at the huge complex, led Ford management to decentralize operations after World War II. The Rouge's equipment grew outdated until its very existence was threatened during the auto depression of the early 1980s. Workers at the complex dwindled to about 15,000.

But a 1983 labor-management agreement prompted the company to invest $500 million to modernize its steel mill, which now makes galvanized (rust-resistant) steel. It's the new blue-colored plant you see at the south end of Schaefer near Dix. Finally it is making a profit, and Ford has sold it. Indeed, the entire Rouge complex seems to be experiencing a renaissance. The soybean and tire plants were scrapped long ago, but the electrical plant still generates enough power to serve a city the size of Boston. Mustangs roll off the assembly line at the rate of one a minute. Each year freighters carry 5 million tons of coal, iron-rich taconite pellets, and limestone to the complex. The blast furnaces can produce over 2 million tons of iron and the steelmaking facilities 3.7 million tons of ingots a year. An engine plant makes 612,000 of the 1.9 liter, four-cylinder engines for Ford Escorts each year.

A DRIVE AROUND THE ROUGE . . . . . Start at the north. Take Miller from Michigan Avenue, or take the Rotunda Drive exit from I-94 (Exit 209). As Miller Road passes high over the rail lines, a vast panorama of this awesome industrial complex opens up. Unfortunately, it's almost impossible to park near here and take in the view. A little farther on, by Gate 4, the main gate, you can pull over to look at the Dearborn Historical Society's marker — which neglects to mention the historic Battle of the Overpass that took place on a bridge near here. That bridge is gone, but it looked like the current overpass you see leading to the employee parking lot.

Turn west onto Dix Avenue just as it passes over the River Rouge. The drawbridge here raises to let big freighters come in from the Great Lakes. The once-meandering river is now dredged straight and so polluted with chemicals that it never freezes in the winter. In the distance you can often see freighters unloading at the huge steel foundry to the north.

Along Dix west of here is an ugly, striking landscape created by piles of raw materials and byproducts of industry. Firms like a refinery and Detroit Tarpaulin are mixed in with factory-gate bars and junkyards advertising for wrecked cars. At this point you may want to turn around and head back on Dix into Dearborn's south end, the working-class neighborhood at the factory gates. Or you can continue onto Schaefer Drive and back to I-94 or Michigan Avenue.

A SNACK OR MEAL IN THE NEARBY MIDDLE EAST. . . . . Directly in front of this American industrial legend is a bit of the Middle East, not five miles from Greenfield Village. There you can buy delicious, healthy breads, meat pies, meals, and ingredients for Middle Eastern cooking. The **Red Sea** Yemeni restaurant serves huge portions of good food in pleasant surroundings (p. 232).

❶ Greenfield Village. Henry Ford's extraordinary collection of important American buildings brings history to life.

❷ Henry Ford Museum. Stunning displays of recent technological eras & many famous items like car Kennedy was shot in.

❸ Fair Lane. Henry Ford's final home, built on picturesque spot of River Rouge, complete with massive water-powered electrical plant.

❹ Rouge Plant. Awesome auto complex where 100,000 once worked. Iron ore came in ships; Fords rolled out.

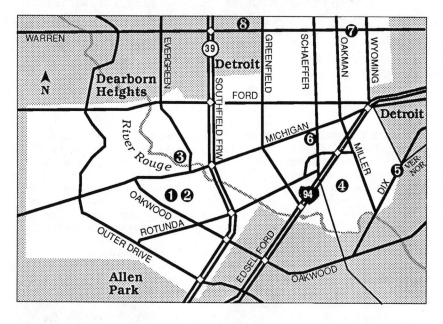

❺ Southend Arab shops. Port of entry for Arabs. Nice Arab museum. Good Yemeni restaurant, Lebanese bakery.

❻ Alcamo's Market. Outstanding Italian grocery with hard-to-find cheeses, sausage, imported pastas.

❼ Arab shops on W. Warren. Thousands of Arab immigrants have created good bakeries, restaurants, groceries.

❽ Judy's Cafe. Great, cheap food in homey atmosphere. Everything from spaghetti to Cuban black bean soup.

Highlights of
Dearborn

0   1   2
miles

Two Arab neighborhoods in Dearborn

Exceptional bakeries, good, cheap fresh fruit, and Arab hospitality in an exotic setting

THE SOUTH END

Today Dearborn's South End is as exotic as anyplace in the U.S. The working-class neighborhood near the Ford Rouge factory gates is the point of entry for Dearborn's large (20,000) and growing Islamic Arab community. Here head scarves are common among women, and Yemeni men wear traditional skullcaps. The call to prayer can be heard from the mosque five times a day. Storekeepers uncover small prayer rugs on their counters and pray.

People from around much of the world came to work in Detroit during its 1920s boom years. The first mosque in the U.S., in fact, was near Ford's Highland Park plant. Dearborn's South End residential neighborhood grew up quickly in the early 1920s around the factory gates of the famous Ford Rouge plant, which once employed over 90,000 workers. The South End was a true American melting pot of dozens of nationalities working at Ford, until well after World War II. Today newly arrived Arab immigrants have replaced the older-generation autoworkers who have moved to better housing elsewhere.

Now that the South End is Arab and Islamic, its dozens of bars have disappeared. Arab bakeries, groceries, hair salons, and meat markets have blossomed in their place. These serve neighborhood residents, plus the larger Islamic community which attends the big Sunni Moslem Mosque on Vernor at Dix.

The Muslim autoworkers who started building the mosque in 1939 have mostly moved on "into business" — the second stage of Arabs' preferred career pattern that ends up, one or two generations after immigration, in "the professions," especially law. Now the South End is the reception area for a continuing stream of immigrants. When they can afford it, they'll likely move to the middle-class part of east Dearborn around Warren and Schaefer, where roomy brick houses were originally built for Ford foremen and craftsmen. The Lebanese and West Bank Palestinians, escaping wars at home, have come to America as families. Yemeni men usually come alone. They frequent the South End's coffeehouses, intended for Arab men only. Yemenis in America long dreamed of saving enough money to return and live comfortably with their families in their beloved but impoverished homeland. Now, finally, they're resigned to a life across the ocean in America.

To learn more about the positive aspects of Arab culture over the centuries, plan a visit to the excellent **Arab-American Community Center for Economic and Social Services** (better known as ACCESS), open weekdays 9-5. Outstanding displays of interesting artifacts, photos, and text feature Islamic contributions to science, coffee-drinking, beautiful embroidered garments, architecture, and calligraphy. Look for music and local Arab history exhibits in the library, which contains a comprehensive collection of books and videos on the Arab world, open to the general public. *Take Dix east of Miller 7 blocks, turn north (left) onto Saulino Court. Call (313) 842-7010 to schedule weekend group tours.*

South End stores are on Dix and Vernor just east of Miller. Take Miller south from I-94 or Michigan Avenue. *Many stores are open from 9 a.m. to 9 p.m., 7 days a week.* Two shops that stand out are:

◆ **Arabian Village Bakery.** There's no display case at this homestyle bakery, so you have to ask for what's just come out of the oven. For a dollar each, there are meat pies and baked kibbee (cracked wheat) stuffed with lamb. You can warm them up in the oven for healthy fast-food meals, or fry them. (For takeout eating on the run, the clerk will microwave them and squirt on a hummus sauce.) *Zahtar* are delicious flat breads flavored with oregano, sumac, and sesame. *Kaak*(3/$1) are spice cookies attractively stamped with decorative molds. *10045 W. Vernor at Dix.*

◆ **Arabian Gulf Market.** At Middle Eastern groceries like this, you'll find many kinds of rice — in bulk (mostly 50¢ a pound) or in huge bags, imported olives at $1.29 a pound, unusual baked goods and candies, chunks of pressed tobacco, exotic tins of olive oils and fruits, and other staples, along with brass coffee boilers for making Turkish coffee. *1001 W. Vernor near Dix.*

WEST WARREN BETWEEN SCHAEFER AND MILLER

Arab culture, with its long tradition of trading, dovetails with the American dream of success through entrepreneurial energy and hard work. Storefronts of West Warren, largely empty 15 years ago, are bursting with immigrant energy. Signs are in Arabic and English, giving the ordinary 1920s shopping strip an oddly exotic air.

Arabs set great store by fresh fruit, good breads, and pastries. Prices are often astonishingly low. "Shopping is a social event," says an Arab woman, "and the price is always questioned." Bargaining is never considered rude.

Competition is fierce, and most Arab restaurants here are good, with similar menus. Many are quite popular with non-Arab customers, who enjoy the healthy food and hospitable service. The restaurant scene here is in constant flux. New ones are opening all the time, ownership changes frequently — the restaurant business lacks status among Arabs — and some restaurants that still have good reputations among outsiders have gone way down hill.

From the car, everything blurs together on this busy street. The area is best enjoyed on foot — window-shopping, buying food, stopping for pastry or coffee. Gift shops featuring fashions, coffee sets, and games are becoming more common. Many stores stay open late, so you can shop after dinner. For restaurants, see p. 232. Here is a selection of noteworthy shops:

◆ **Eastborn Fruit Market.** Arabs eat prodigious quantities of fresh fruit, and Dearborn produce markets offer low prices and unusual things like fresh figs and crunchy, tart-sweet fresh dates in season. This popular new store, deliberately taking a cue from West Dearborn's popular Westborn Market on Michigan at Oakwood, is the area's first Arab produce store that's modern and even a little slick. It also carries imported oils, rice, and other grains. *7431 Wyoming north of Warren. 8 a.m.-8 p.m.*

◆ **Bon Juice.** Snazzy juice bar with tables offers fresh fruit juices and concoctions like Kashta (sweetened milk curds; $2) and the Energizer (a refreshing combination of bananas, strawberries, milk, and honey; $1.50). *10621 W. Warren. Open 'til 9 p.m.*

◆ **Afrah Pastry.** Small shop well thought of by locals. Afrah offers beautiful honey-filo-nut pastries, and some French pastries, at lower prices. The bird's nest with pistachios (60¢) is excellent. Tables make this a nice place to stop in an interesting area. *12741 W. Warren. Daily 8 a.m.-11 p.m.*

◆ **Express Jewelry.** Middle Eastern jewelry and gold. In the fluid, war-torn Arab world, gold jewelry is as esteemed as a portable form of wealth as it is for display and status. *12817 Warren at Appoline.*

◆ **Coffee and Nut Gallery.** The smells of coffee beans and spices in this tiny grocery are wonderful. *13029 W. Warren next to the Cedarland Restaurant.*

◆ **New Yasmeen Bakery.** Some feel the Syrian pita bread here is so good, it's worth the trip to Dearborn — but now it's distributed much more widely. A local says the spinach pies here are "the best in the world." *13728 W. Warren. Daily 5 a.m.-6 p.m.*

◆ **Joe and Ed's Schaefer Market.** Larger than most convenience stores, Joe and Ed's has a big selection of Middle Eastern food, from produce and breads to canned goods, bulk rice, and beans. *5635 Schaefer near Ford Rd. (313) 846-5725. 9:30 a.m.-1 a.m.*

◆ **El-Masri Bakery.** Founded in Palestine shortly after the turn of the century, and recently moved to Dearborn. Known for *kanify,* a Palestinian delicacy something like a pizza made with sweet, soft cheese — sold by the slice or by the pie. Also on hand: an extensive variety of traditional honey-nut-filo pastries and beautifully decorated French pastries (actually lighter and less buttery) with whipped cream, at incredibly low prices like 60¢. Tables let you sit, eat, drink coffee, and watch people. El-Masri has fast become a very popular local gathering spot. Generous hospitality and entertaining at home are hallmarks of Arab culture. Strong Turkish coffee (flavored with cardamom) and delicious pastries are indispensable, and trips to pastry shops are frequent. *5125 Schaefer 1 block north of Michigan. (313) 584-3500. Daily 9 a.m.-10 p.m.*

OTHER GOOD ETHNIC FOOD SHOPS IN THE VICINITY . . . . . When you walk in the door of **Alcamo's Market,** East Dearborn's celebrated Italian specialty store, you're overwhelmed by the beguiling fragrances of spicy salamis, garlic, cheeses, coffee beans, and breads. There are two aisles of imported pastas in this spiffily updated old-time grocery, along with Italian specialties like fava beans, imported Italian cookies, crackers, appetizers, and sauces. Produce is gorgeous. There's some Greek food, too. *4423 Schaefer, 2 blocks south of Michigan in downtown East Dearborn. (313) 584-3010. Mon-Sat 9-6, Fri 'til 7. Easy to miss. Look for the red awning. Park in lot on Schaefer and Osborn.* . . . . In the stable Polish neighborhood in a part of Detroit's west side wedged between East Dearborn and Dearborn Heights, two longtime retail neighbors have combined. **Kowalski Sausage** sells takeout Polish favorites like stuffed cabbage, in addition to its well-known kielbasa and such. At the **West Warren Bakery** good pumpernickel and rye breads are well under a dollar a loaf. There are Polish specialties like angel wings and jelly donuts, and a very good sourdough French bread, great for toast, also baked as submarine rolls that are served next door at the highly regarded Judy's Cafe. They're chewy, with a crunchy crust that holds in the juice from tomatoes, and only a quarter apiece. Order ahead to be sure of availability. *15708 W. Warren at Montrose, 2 blocks west of Greenfield and about a mile east of the Southfield Freeway in Detroit. (313) 584-2610. Mon-Sat 5 a.m.-7 p.m.*

Greenfield Village

A product of Henry Ford's great interest
in American history is a major U.S. sight.

This famous outdoor museum is a direct outgrowth of Henry Ford's desire to show how technology has changed the lives of ordinary Americans. As Ford entered his sixties, he developed a passionate interest in the tangible manifestations of American history. Ford had a different collecting agenda from most of his wealthy contemporaries who sought out the pinnacles of achievement in the arts and crafts. In the Henry Ford Museum and Greenfield Village, Ford wanted mainly to document the ordinary life of the past, that of farmers and shopkeepers and artisans, the more common people. He focused on America's industrial transformation in the late 19th and early 20th centuries.

Not only did Ford spend millions to obtain the many buildings and artifacts assembled here, but he also personally spent months actively seeking them out. He supervised their placement here, and would spend hours in these historic places — often alone — savoring their connection with the past. In layout and landscaping, no real village ever resembled Greenfield Village. It is simply a collection of historic buildings. Some were idealized and upgraded when they were "restored."

Village highlights include:

◆ **Wright Cycle Shop.** Here, in the famed birthplace of aviation, Orville and Wilbur Wright built kites, gliders, and ultimately the world's first successful flying machine. By 1903, the American bicycle craze of the 1890s was on the wane. The Wrights eked out a living selling bicycles and bicycling paraphernalia from the store and repairing bikes in the room behind it. In the very back, they built their flying machines. Moved from Dayton, Ohio, in 1936, the building has been restored to look much as it did in 1903, the year of their first motorized flight.

◆ **Susquehanna Plantation.** Redone and reopened in 1988, this Maryland plantation house is interpreted as it would have existed in 1860. It illuminates the economic and social basis of slavery — who the slaves and masters were, their various roles, and the relationships among them.

◆ **Glass, pottery, printing, tinsmithing, and textile demonstrations.** Using 19th-century techniques, craftspeople show how these important products were made.

◆ **Ford's birthplace.** This simple Greek Revival farmhouse was built on Ford Road in Dearborn by Henry's father William in 1861. Widespread fascination with Henry Ford makes this exhibit popular.

◆ **Bagley Avenue Shed.** A replica of the shed in which Henry Ford and his associates built their first car, the Quadricycle, in 1896. The cluttered scene enables you to appreciate Ford's ingenuity in building a car from scratch.

◆ **Ford Mack Avenue Factory.** In 1903 the first production-model Fords were manufactured in the original of this building. This factory turned out up to 18 cars a day and quickly made Henry wealthy. The 4 horsepower vehicles started at $800 apiece.

◆ **Mrs. Cohen's millinery shop.** A Detroit widow ran this shop at the turn of the century to support her family. Visitors enjoy seeing hats made and trying them on.

◆ **Armington & Sims Machine Shop.** Many visitors are unexpectedly fascinated by the awesome turn-of-the-century steam engines demonstrated here.

◆ **Edison's Menlo Park Compound.** In this complex of six plain New Jersey buildings, one can relive one of the most extraordinary phenomena in American history. Thomas Edison's 1880 laboratories were the world's first commercial research and development center. Edison gathered chemists, machinists, craftsmen, glass blowers, and other specialists and gave them a wide assortment of tools and materials. The results were spectacular. In just 10 years, 420 of Edison's 1,093 patents came from here, including the electric light bulb, phonograph, and electric sewing machine.

◆ **Plympton House.** This small, rude, one-room house from Massachusetts nicely reveals how a typical colonial New England family lived in the 1600s. It was the home of Thomas Plympton, his wife, and seven children. A recorded discussion among family members reveals the strikingly different dialect of that time.

◆ **Noah Webster House.** Here Noah Webster completed his famous dictionary. An upstairs room displays the extraordinary number of his accomplishments, from founding Amherst College to serving in the state legislature.

Henry Ford's Dearborn birthplace, now in Greenfield Village.

◆ **Cotswold Buildings.** This 17th-century stone cottage and barn was brought from southwestern England — 175 tons in all.

◆ **Eagle Tavern.** Transported from Clinton, Michigan, this 19th century tavern is complete with ladies' parlor, sitting room, and bar. Here you can buy weak versions of authentic drinks from the 1850s such as a "Jersey Lightning" ($1.75). In back, a restaurant serves huge, reasonably-priced meals from recipes of the era such as stewed rabbit ($7.95) and pork loin.

◆ **Elias Brown General Store.** This is one of the very best reconstructions of a classic American 19th-century general store to be found. The store building was moved from Waterford, Michigan, in Oakland County; the contents, dating from about 1860, came from a store in Minaville, New York. Note the paper bags above the counter, an innovation introduced in 1864.

Several eateries, a bakery, and a restaurant are scattered throughout the village. The food is far from great, but it is palatable, and sometimes pretty good. The best things are the bakery's brownies and coffee. The **Greenfield Village Store** gift shop has many toys and games for children, in addition to reproductions of antiques and jewelry in the collection here, handcrafts made in the village, and an outstanding book store like that in the Henry Ford Museum.

Greenfield Village's mammoth size is a strength and a weakness. The quality of interpretation is uneven. You may only want to see half of the big complex at one visit. Visitors can break up their walking tour with a **train ride** on the village's splendid steam locomotive that circles the entire complex. $2 gives you unlimited rides for the day. Or you can take a horse-driven **carriage ride** ($4 per person) or **bus ride** ($3 per person); both last 30 to 35 minutes. All three rides provide an ongoing description of what you pass.

*Greenfield Village is in West Dearborn. From Michigan Avenue, turn south onto Oakwood at the green-roofed Westborn Market. From I-94, take the Southfield Freeway north and follow signs for the Village. (313) 271-1620. For 24-hour taped info, call (313) 271-1976. **Open** daily 9-5. Buildings are closed Jan-mid-March, but the exteriors can be viewed for free with a ticket to Henry Ford Museum. **Admission:** adults $10.50, seniors $9.50, youths 5-12 $5.25, under 5 free. 2-day unlimited-admission ticket to Museum and Village $9 youths, $18 adults. The Museum/Village **annual pass** ($22 adults, $11 youths) makes frequent visits affordable.*

Henry Ford Museum

*A world-famous collection of American products
along with remarkable exhibits*

Henry Ford's squadrons of pickers spread over the Midwest and New England to come up with an astounding array of artifacts for this vast (12 acres) indoor museum next to Greenfield Village. The museum's dignified exterior is an exact copy of Philadelphia's Independence Hall. Inside is one colossal collection after another. There's the world's greatest collection of 19th-century farm and kitchen implements. The exhibit on the history of lighting, from candles through electric bulbs, is immense enough to comprise a substantial museum in itself. The same could be said for the large collection of airplanes and cars. Nowhere will you find a more complete historical collection of American tractors.

Over the years the museum staff has worked to give shape to this huge, at times bewildering, hoard of items. The evolution of the auto industry is brilliantly elucidated by using a sequence of TV monitors showing short historical film clips with the autos of the period as a backdrop.

A crowd favorite is the grandiose exhibit called **The Automobile in American Life**, a lavish series of full-scale displays nostalgically showing the car's effect on American landscapes. There's a vintage McDonald's sign, complete with oversized golden arches, a Holiday Inn guest room, and a diner plucked from Marlboro, Massachusetts, lovingly refurbished to its pristine state in 1946, when an egg salad sandwich cost 15¢. At a gleaming green and white 1940 Texaco service station, you can even peer

Part of "The Automobile and American Life" exhibit.

into the garage and see the tools used at the time.

In counterpoint to these mammoth display areas, the museum also holds an assortment of fascinating isolated items. There's the 1961 Lincoln limousine in which John F. Kennedy was shot, and the rocking chair in which Lincoln was murdered. You can see the huge, 600-ton 1941 "Allegheny" steam locomotive, one of the last and largest of a proud era. A Lunar Roving Vehicle, one made by NASA to transport astronauts on the moon is in the concourse.

At the supervised **Activities Center** children can operate an assembly line, pedal a high-wheel bike, and do other hands-on things. At the end of the walk from the entrance, the **American Cafe** and soda fountain is open 9-4:30, year around. No museum ticket is required. Here the hot dogs cost a hefty $1.70 but the $5.25 beef stew lunch is hearty and filling. Visitors can also bring bag lunches to eat at the Corner Cupboard within the museum. The **Plaza Store** within the museum sells handcrafts (many made in Greenfield Village) and a wide range of toys for children and adults.

See Greenfield Village above for directions, phone, and prices.

A GREAT MUSEUM STORE . . . . . . You don't have to have a museum ticket to shop at Henry Ford Museum's **Museum Store** (open 9-5 daily). Its outstanding book section is especially strong on automobiles and roadside architecture, Henry Ford and Ford Motor, antiques, crafts, Detroit history, and inexpensive Dover paper toys and coloring books.Many of the dolls, crystal, china, and other gift items reproduce objects in the Museum's collections.

Henry Ford's Fair Lane

His final resting place is disappointing
as an auto baron mansion, but the grounds are grand.

By the time his estate was completed in 1914, Henry Ford's interests and activities were already expanding beyond manufacturing cars. His wife Clara and son Edsel moved into Fair Lane without him in December while he was taking his peace ship to Europe in a quixotic attempt to stop World War I.

The mansion is disappointing architecturally. It's a strange amalgam of Frank Lloyd Wright's naturalistic Prairie Style and the medieval-influenced Scottish baronial style. Ford changed architects in midstream, and it shows.

The Ford heirs auctioned off most of the original furniture after Henry and Clara died, and University of Michigan-Dearborn offices occupy 30% of the mansion. So you won't see how the Fords really lived here.

The home seems a bad fit for Henry Ford's down-to-earth tastes. Not surprisingly, a favorite room was the rustic Field Room. Its raw-timbered ambience is unlike the ornate interiors in the rest of the house.

Ford applied his restless, creative energy not to the house but to its huge hydroelectric power plant. It occupies a separate structure and is connected by a long underground tunnel with the mansion. Ford teamed up with friend Thomas Edison to create an extraordinary 110-kilowatt electric system — quite a feat, given the small size of the River Rouge. Almost half of the 1 1/2-hour tour is devoted to this plant. Visitors learn perhaps more than they ever wanted to know about its design. The independence provided by having his own power plant must have fulfilled a deep-seated need in Ford; he went on to build another 20 hydroelectric plants on small rivers in southeastern Michigan.

The grounds are the high point of a visit to Fair Lane. The mansion overlooks a beautiful, wooded portion of the River Rouge at the point of a delightful small waterfall. After seeing garbage floating past his mansion, Henry Ford was personally responsible for getting the upstream towns of Plymouth and Northville upstream to stop dumping raw sewage in the river.

The surrounding 1,600 acres were transformed by the famous landscape architect Jens Jensen into a series of naturalistic meadows and forests. With the aid of a well-designed $1 map of the grounds, you can take your own tour of this vast area. The map is available at the gift shop or reception desk inside Fair Lane.

Nature was one of Ford's many passions. An avid bird-watcher, he installed hundreds of birdhouses — eight heated in winter! Almost 600 deer roamed the woods and fields. Clara Ford's taste was for more formal English gardens. She appropriated one of Jensen's meadows to create a fantastic rose garden that gained national attention in its day. Today you can see its ruins, for it would cost $400,000 a year to maintain.

It's worth having lunch at **The Pool**, a restaurant in the dramatically illuminated space which was initially the mansion's swimming pool. It's open weekdays from 11 to 2. A variety of sandwiches is under $5, and homemade soup and a trip to the salad bar is only $3.95.

In west Dearborn, west off Evergreen between Michigan Ave. and Ford Rd. From I-94 or I-96, take the Southfield Freeway (M-39) to Michigan Ave. in Dearborn, go west to Evergreen, north to Fair Lane. Park at the Visitors' Center. (313) 593-5590. Jan-April wekdays, one tour daily. Sundays 1-4:30 p.m. on the half hour. $6/adult, $5/seniors and students, 5 and under free.

Recommended Restaurants & Lodgings
Metro Detroit

Regional map p. 128.

American Coney Island. *114 W. Lafayette between Griswold & Shelby. (313) 961-7758. Open 24 hours, 7 days. Beer. No credit cards.* Beloved institution with egalitarian mystique. It and neighboring Lafayette Coney Island, run by cousins, serve an extraordinary cross-section of humanity, from bums to super-rich. Hot dogs $1.45, loose hamburger $1.67, chili fries w/cheese $2, chili $. Soups. Desserts (pies, rice pudding, baklava) $1.

Summit Steak House. *In RenCen on 71st floor. E. Jefferson at Brush on Detroit River. (313) 568-8600. Full bar. Major credit cards. Lunch: Mon-Sat 11:30 -2:30 Dinner: Sun-Thurs 5:30-10, Fri-Sat 5:30-11. Sun brunch 10-2:30: $18, kids 3-10 $8.* Lounge w/ snacks on 73rd floor. Amazing, map-like view in clear weather. Low lunch prices for such a spectacle: $5 for soup and 1/2 sandwich, $8.50 for good prime rib sandwich, $12 for charco-broiled NY strip. Dinners ($25-$46) come w/ bucket of shrimp in shell, salad; steak or seafood broiled on cart. Prime rib $32, 14 oz. filet mignon $36.

Epicurean Cafe. *In Penobscot Building, Griswold at Fort, lower level. (313) 965-4998. Mon-Fri 6:30 a.m.-4 p.m. No alcohol or credit cards.* Big, bustling cafeteria in a top 1920s skyscraper. Entrees $4 (spaghetti)-$7 (prime rib). Moussaka a favorite. Big on pies ($1.55), many unusual juices. Daily specials.

London Chop House. *155 W. Congress between Sh~~ ~~ Griswold. (313) 962-0277 ~~ ~~ -Fri 11:30 - 3. Dinner ~~ ~~ 1, Fri-Sat 5-1. F~~ ~~ edit cards.* A la carte ~~ ~~ nch entrees $10-$16, dinne ~~ ~~ 20-$30. Detroit's version of

CLOSED

21. Fabled power lunches in men's club setting. Bailed out, spruced up by loyalists who kept traditional frog legs, prime rib; updated oysters, lobster, clams. Popular picks: Poncho burger ($9), lobster club sandwich ($13) at lunch, perfect Caesar salad. Famous desserts like chocolate ravioli $5-$7. Top 40 dance band Sat evenings. May become catering-only; call to confirm.

GREEKTOWN

The Blue Nile. *InTrappers Alley (Monroe at Beaubien), 2nd floor). (313) 964-6699. Daily 5-10. Full bar. Major credit cards.* Superb Ethiopian restaurant. Diners sit on low goatskin-cushioned chairs, eat "Ethiopian feast" with hands from communal platter covered with bread, torn off to scoop up fragrant meat and vegetable stews. Some are bland, some spicy. Wash hands with steaming cloths. $15/person for meat feast, $12 vegetarian. A second Blue Nile is on Braun Ct. in Ann Arbor's Kerrytown.

Greektown. *Monroe Street between St. Antoine and Beaubien. Most restaurants are open 11 a.m.-2 a.m. or later, 7 days/week. All have full bars, accept most major credit cards. Park in city structure to the east, entered off Monroe or Macomb.* Food at these popular restaurants is mostly similar and reasonably priced. $7 buys a typical entree, with salad and bread. Downtown workers come here. So do visitors here for sagnaki (flaming kasseri cheese) presented with "Opa!" and a festive flourish. A native Greek who's knowledgeable about food rates **The Laikon** (569 Monroe, 313-963-7058) "most authentic." He loves their home-style bean soup and pan-fried cod with garlic sauce. Owners run the kitchen; vegetables like okra and beans are likely fresh. **Pegasus Taverna** (558 Monroe, 313-964-6800) has OK food in a big, busy, theatrical setting some people really like. Its successful owners now control much prime Greektown property, including Trappers Alley. **Lindos Taverna** (511 Monroe, 313-961-2070) offers less common homestyle dishes in a whitewashed, Greek countryside setting.

Fishbone's Rhythm Kitchen.
Monroe at Brush. (313) 965-4600. Sun-Thurs 11-midnight, Fri & Sat 11-2 a.m. Full bar. AmEx, Visa, MC, Diners. Lunch entrees $6-$9, dinner $9-$14 w/ rice, veg.. Big, noisy, spirited New Orleans-style place from owners of Pegasus. Approximation of genuine creole cooking is pretty good. A standout: crawfish etouffee ($14 at dinner). Lunch hit: whisky ribs ($9). Shrimp or chicken jambalaya w/ sausage is $8 at lunch/$12 at dinner.

THEATER DISTRICT

🍽

Tres Vite. *Next to Fox Theater on Woodward just e. of Fisher Freeway. (313) 964-4144. Lunch Mon-Fri 11:30-2. Light menu (pizza, salad, soup) 2 until closing. Dinner Tues-Sat 5-11. Opens Sun-Mon before shows at Fox. Full bar. Visa, MC, AmEx. Reservations advised for show nights.* Glamorous cafe showcases famed chef Jimmy Schmidt's modern American cuisine - at moderate prices! Sandwiches are $4-$6. Menu changes daily. Good at lunch: soups $2-$4.25, Caesar salad $3.25, 1-person cracker-crust pizzas $5. Dinner picks: spicy BBQ ribs ($14), thin-pounded chicken w/ wild mushroom-artichoke salsa ($10). All entrees include appropriate side. Fabulous desserts like white chocolate ravioli w/ hazelnut creme anglaise ($5).

America's Pizza Cafe. *(Next to Fox Theater on Woodward, 2 blocks n.w. of Grand Circus Park. (313) 964-3122. Mon-Thurs 11-9:30, Fri 11-12, Sat 12-12, Sun 12-9:30. May stay open later for show at Fox. Full bar. Visa, MC, AmEx.* Upscale pizzeria format of Fox owner Mike Ilitch's Little Caesar's chain. 9" round, thin-crust, 1-person pizzas only. 23 kinds ($5.25-$9), 20 pastas ($5-$9), 8 salads ($5-$7). You can get pizzas w/ goat cheese, spinach, and artichokes, but Detroit's picks are BBQ chicken pizza ($7), Coney Island pizza ($6), Mexican Burrito pizza ($7.50). $5 lunch specials.

Elwood Bar & Grill. *Woodward at Elizabeth, across from the Fox. (313) 961-7485. Mon 11-4, Tues-Thurs 11-12, Fri 11-2, Sat 12-2 a.m. (Open Sun-Mon nights for Fox shows.) Full bar. MC, Visa.* Sandwiches (around $5), appetizers, dinner menu all day to 9; light menu thereafter. High-energy Yuppie diner/bar in new-old Art Deco spot. Good, updated diner fare. Veal featured in meat loaf ($6.75 at dinner), stew. Dinner entrees come w/ appropriate side. Other favorites: chicken & dumplings ($8), Louisiana seafood gumbo ($9). Noteworthy desserts.

VICINITY OF TIGER STADIUM

🍽

Maxie's Leftfield Deli. *Michigan at Trumbull, across from Tiger Stadium. (313) 961-7968. Mon-Sat 7:30-3. No alcohol or credit cards.* Judges and bums come here for good soup ($1.25-$2/bowl) and good cheer, dispensed by gregarious octogenarian Max Silk. Former boxer, bar owner, bookie, pal of priests, a true philanthropist. Wednesday means potato pancakes, Fridays seafood chowder (both $2.50) Fans love wild omelets, corned beef sandwiches. Mostly $4 and under.

O'Leary's Tea Room. *1411 Brooklyn in Corktown. From Michigan Ave. at Tiger Stadium, go east 3 blocks on Brooklyn. (313) 964-0936. Mon-Fri 9-4, Sat 10-2, Sun 10:30-3. Dinner: Fri-Sat 6-10. Visa, MC, checks. No alcohol.* Homey, personal, very popular. Irish bric a brac for sale. (Corktown, founded by Irish, revived by their descendants, is city's oldest neighborhood.) Known for homemade soups, scones, bread pudding w/ Irish whiskey sauce ($2.50). Several kinds of pasties ($6.50 w/salad), tuna-avocado melt on toasted crumpet ($5.75). New weekend dinners: $11 for Delmonico in Guiness, $12 poached salmon or lamb chops w/ wild rice dressing, chutney. Includes salad, potato, veggies. Tea reader Tues & Thurs 2-4

Xochimilco. *3409 Bagley at 23rd St., just west of I-75 exit 47B. From Tiger*

Stadium/downtown, take Vernor across I-75, turn left on 23rd. (313) 843-0179. Full bar. All major credit cards. Open daily 11 -4 a.m. Most popular, highly regarded of Mexican Town's restaurants. Goofy murals in upstairs lounge. Known for botanas ($6.75) that feed 4: corn chips w/refried beans, tomatoes, and chorizo. Mexican standards $3.75-$5.75, steaks $7.50.

RIVERTOWN/EAST SIDE

Woodbridge Tavern. *289 St. Aubin at Woodbridge. (313) 259-0578. Mon-Sat 11 -2 a.m., Sun noon-10. Full bar. Major credit cards.* Old Belgian waterfront grocery and speakeasy retains beat-up, utterly plain character as popular meeting place. Back grape arbor, side deck are delightful on a summer's night. Big menu, good service for a bar: soup, chili, meal-size salads with and without meat ($4-$6), 1/3 lb. burgers ($3.25 and up), healthy sandwiches like grilled chicken/hummus/tomato on pita bread ($5), lake perch dinners ($12). Deep-dish pizza ($6, $8, and $13) a favorite. Classic rock Fri & Sat plus summer Sundays. Karaoke machine Thursdays.

Roma Cafe. *3401 Riopelle at Erskine, a few blocks n.w. of Eastern Market. From Gratiot, turn n. onto Russell, right onto Erskine. From I-75, take Mack exit e. to Russell, s. 2 blocks to Eerskine, left to Riopelle. (313) 831-5940. Mon-Fri 11-10:30, Sat 11-1 a.m. Full bar. Major credit cards. A la carte entrees: lunch $5.50-$11, dinner $12-$19.* Detroit's oldest (over 100) and probably most popular Italian restaurant. Not a trend in sight. Veal a specialty. Veal parmesan $16. 25 at dinner, veal tosa $12. Shrimp scampi $28. Salad $1 extra, soup is $2. People rave over $14.50 Monday-night pasta buffet. Check out old photos of 1920s pushcarts at nearby Eastern Market.

Joe Muer's. *2000 Gratiot at St. Aubin, 1 1/2 mi. n.e. of downtown. Take I-75 to Gratiot exit, turn left, 1/4 mi. on right. (313) 567-1088. Mon-Thurs 11:15-10, Fri 11:15 -10:30, Sat 5-*

11. *Reservations for large groups only.* Long Detroit's best for seafood. Utterly traditional. Top ingredients — 30 kinds of fish and seafood — simply fixed, served with the likes of boiled potatoes, creamed spinach, slaw. Specialities: flounder stuffed w/ crabmeat $24, Lake Superior whitefish $18 with soup, salad, vegetable. Lunch entrees $6-$12. New dessert menu.

Rattlesnake Club. *Stroh River Place at foot of Joseph Campau. Take E. Jefferson 1 mi. from RenCen, turn s. on Jos. Campau just past Doctors' Hospital. (313) 567-4400. Mon-Thurs 11:30-10 Fri 11:30 -11, Sat 5:30-11. Full bar. Major credit cards. Valet parking.* Celebrated chef Jimmy Schmidt's $3 million riverview spot is bright, contemporary, sophisticated showplace for understated little luxuries AND fresh, seasonal food. Expect award-winning dishes like persillade swordfish with citrus sauce and ginger on the changing menu, but there's still porterhouse steak ($24) for traditionalists, and pastas ($13 or so) for the impecunious. All entrees include appropriate starch,vegetable. $20 prix fixe menu includes appetizer, entree, dessert. Lunches from $6 (personal, thin-crust pizzas) and $8 (sandwiches, salads) to $14 entrees. Pleasant patio.

New Detroiter. *7339 E. Jefferson at Sheridan, 2 blocks east of Belle Isle bridge. Park in front or rear. (313) 822-2642. Sun-Thurs 7 a.m.-1 a.m., Fri & Sat 7 a.m.-4 a.m. No alcohol. Visa, MC, Disc. Same menu all day.* Simple, delilcious soul food — Southern home cooking. Good view of Belle Isle bridge. Recommended: catfish chunks in cornmeal batter , pit BBQ chicken or 6 ribs, all $9 with salad, cornbread, two sides. Or make a meal of the $1 sides: mac & cheese, yams, pintos, greens, green beans, etc. , all cooked from scratch. Weekly specials $6-$7. Sandwiches $1.80-$5.50.

VanDyke Place. *649 Van Dyke, 3 buildings north of Jefferson. (313) 821-2620. Tues-Thurs 6-9:30, Fri & Sat 5-11. Full bar. Major credit cards. Reservations accepted. Prix fixe dinner $39:*

appetizer, entree, dessert. Beautifully restored West Village mansion now geared to regional Great Lakes cuisine. Fresh, updated atmosphere. Specialties: rack of lamb w/ garlic, salmon in potato envelope.

GROSSE POINTE

🍴

Sparky Herbert's. *15117 Kercheval near Wayburn in Grosse Pointe Park. (313) 822-0266. Mon-Sat 11:30-12, Sun brunch 10:30-2:30, dinner 3:30-10. Full bar, extensive wine list. Major credit cards. Sandwich menu ($5-$7) all day. Lunch $5-$10 w/ veg., starch; dinner $10-$21 w/ veg., salad, starch.* Eclectic place: part pub, part fine dining, part wine bar, with much whimsy. Key Lime Pie ($3.75), Sparkyburger on homemade roll, Texas chili ($2/$2.60) may be best-known, but appetizers like pesto escargots, vegetarian pierogis, and new Mediterranean paellas and bouillabaisse also win raves. Changing regular menu. Diverse clientele, casual to dressy.

Janet's Lunch. *Kercheval at Wayburn, Grosse Pointe Park. (313) 331-5776. Mon-Fri 6 -6 , Sat 'til 2 p.m. No credit cards or alcohol.* Classic, ungentrified lunch counter with incredibly diverse, loyal clientele. Most breakfasts $3.25 and less. Lunch favorite: pork or beef sandwich ($4.60).

Cafe Le Chat. *672 Notre Dame at Kercheval, behind Merry Mouse gourmet shop. (313) 884-9077. Lunch Mon-Sat 11:30-3, dinner Wed-Sat 5-9:30. Bistro menu starts at 6, regular menu at 6. Sun brunch 11-2:30. Cocktails & wine w/food only. Lunch (w/ side garnish) $5-$12. Dinners (a la carte w/ garnish) from $10 (bistro menu) to $29 sampler.* Tiny, personal country French spot gets better and better as its menu expands. Romantic mood at dinner, when adjoining store is closed. Current highlight on changing menu: chicken strudel ($7 at lunch), veal Zurich w/mushroom sauce, pasta ($16 at dinner). New sidewalk cafe. Rich desserts $4.

Original Pancake House. *Mack at Lochmoor, Grosse Pointe Woods. (313) 884-4144. Daily 7 a.m.-9 p.m. No credit cards or alcohol.* Breakfast all day. The perfect breakfast all day long: fresh OJ, super coffee, homemade syrups, good service. Wonderfully light buttermilk pancakes from $2.75 (plain) to $3.85 (blueberry), omelets $4.25 to $5.75, crepes, waffles. Big Apple (crispy, oven-baked cinnamon pancake over apple mountain; $5.69) wins raves.

Cadieux Cafe. *4300 Cadieux at Waveny, between Mack and Warren in Detroit, behind Grosse Pointe. (313) 882-8560. Mon-Thurs 4-11, Fri & Sat to 12, Sun 4-10. Visa, MC.* Among Detroit's less evident ethnic groups: more Belgians than anywhere outside of Belgium. (Eastsiders, they started out mostly in the building trades circa 1910.) They meet at this tidy corner tavern, vintage 1950s, for the Belgian sports of bicycling, pigeon racing, and feather bowling in the adjacent dirt alleys. Contests get underway by 7 or 8 Thurs-Sat. You can sit and watch, or play if the alley is unreserved. Dinners of good fried perch ($9.50), steak, pickerel, come w/ 2 sides, but steamed mussels ($12/bucket, $7 1/2 bucket) are the big draw. Get them Belgian-style and you get carrots, celery, onions; sop up the soup with bread. Other Belgian specialties: mashed potatoes w/ spinach & nutmeg, roast rabbit ($9) on Sundays.

WAYNE STATE/ CULTURAL CENTER

🍴

Cosmic Cafe. *87 W. Palmer near Cass at the n.w. edge of Wayne campus. (313) 832-0001. Mon-Fri 8-8, Sat 11-4, shorter hours in summer. No credit cards, checks, alcohol, or smoking.* Vegetarian throwback to simple, serene counterculture aesthetic of the 1970s. Terrific bulletin board and freebies table spotlight cuturally vibrant Wayne area. Specialities: omelets and scrambles (tomato-Gouda-basil omelet, $3.45 w/fruit); sweet & sout tofu w/veggies on brown rice w/ salad ($6), avacodo melt ($4.25), and Mr. Natural-burger ($4). $2.25 desserts come sinful or healthy. Poetry 3rd Wed of month.

Traffic Jam & Snug. *511 W. Canfield at Second, 2 blocks s. of Wayne State campus. Lighted, patrolled parking. (313) 831-9470. Mon 11-3 p.m., Tues-Thurs 11-10:30, Fri 11-12, Sat 5-12. Full bar. MC, Visa. Same menu all day.* Entrees $7-$9, sandwiches $5.50-$7; salads $2.25-$6.75. Famous desserts: Itty Bitty $3.35-Carlotta Chocolate Ice Cream Cheese Cake $5.95. Extraordinary eclectic food & customers — sort of a hippie hangout that grew and changed with the times. Changing menu. many vegetarian selections. Full of surprises, beginning with terrific bread basket. Dairy, bakery on premises; brewery hoped for. Outstanding wine selection, values.

The Whitney. *4221 Woodward at Canfield, between Orchestra Hall and DIA. (313) 832-5700. Lunch Mon-Fri 11-2 , dinner Mon-Thurs 6-9, Fri & Sat 5-12, 4-course Sun brunch 11-3 (cost $20); dinner 5-8. Full bar, extensive wine list. Major credit cards. A la carte entrees: lunch $9-$22, dinner $18-$29.* Food lives up to setting in super-spectacular lumber baron's 1894 chateau, lavish w/ stained glass, turrets, ornament. American classics (oysters Rockefeller, Dover sole) with thoughtful garnishes. Example: $29 rack of lamb has garlic-mustard crust, potato noisette garnish. Budget-conscious diners welcome to make a meal of soup ($5-6), salad ($5-$10), or come for coffee and desserts ($5-$8). Much-praised chicken pot pie or warm scallop sandwich between potato pancakes are $9 at lunch. Light menu (salads, appetizers) at 3rd floor Winter Garden bar, w/ pianist & singer Tues-Sat 9-1.

HAMTRAMCK AREA

Polonia. *2934 Yemans, just e. of Joseph Campau. (313) 873-8432. Tues-Thurs 11-7, Fri & Sat 11-8, Sun 12-7. Lunches and dinners: $4-$7. Full bar. Visa, MC.* Hamtramck restaurants can't be beat for value: good home cooked meals under $10 complete. Here the 1930s Detroit Workingman's Co-op has been transformed into a Polish countryside arbor peopled with costumed peasants. The FDR portrait is still over the counter.You can't go wrong with the $6.55 combination plate: terrific stuffed cabbage, homemade sausage, dumplings, a crepe, mashed potatoes , sauerkraut. Homemade tortes are $1.50. Other Hamtramck restaurants worth a visit: Under the Eagle, 9000 Joseph Campau 3 blocks s. of Holbrook (closed Wed); The Golden Duckling, 9711 Conant (Wed-Sat only).

Buddy's Pizza. *17125 Conant at 6 Mile, in Detroit just n. of Hamtramck's n.e. line. (313) 892-9001. Mon-Thurs 11-11, Fri-Sat 11-12, Sun 12-10. Full bar. Major credit cards.* The original Buddy's that spawned Detroit's top-rated pizza chain. A plain, lively, unpretentious neighborhood bar with *bocce,* much favored by locals who grew up in and around Hamtramck. This is square pizza (one size only, $11.80 w/ two ingredients) with a thick, chewy crust, loaded with pepperoni, cheese, onions. Pitchers of beer $(5), soft drink ($4). Good salads to share or make a meal of: antipasto ($3.80/$5.88/$8.27), Greek.

DETROIT HOTELS

Westin Hotel. *(313) 568-8300. In Renaissance Center, E. Jefferson at Brush downtown.* 1400 floors on 73 floors. $145-$200. Higher floors cost more.the rates. $99 weekend package includes $25 restaurant credit. Cable TV. Indoor pool, health club, Nautilus, jogging track, masseuse. 3 restaurants. *Spectacular views from upper floors at one of the world's tallest hotels*

Radisson Hotel Pontchartrain. *(313) 965-0200. Washington Blvd. at Jefferson downtown.* 412 rooms on 26 floors. $125-$135,$75 weekends. Weekend package: $95 1st night w/ breakfast, drinks, $55 2nd night. Cable TV. Outdoor pool, health club,

whirlpool, sauna. Comp. limo service. 3 restaurants, bar.
River view, good Cobo Hall location in downtown's most elegant hotel

Omni International Hotel.
(313) 222-7700. 333 W. Jefferson at Randolph. 254 rooms on 21 floors. $170, weekend specials from $88. Cable TV. Olympic-size indoor pool, health club, valet parking. Fitness center & sauna $5 extra. Restaurant, bar. Some views of river or downtown. People Mover stop in building.
Olympic-size indoor pool, good downtown location near Greektown

Holiday Inn Windsor. *(519) 253-4411. 480 Riverside Dr. on river.* 238 rooms on 4 floors. $102 Canadian. Cable TV. Outdoor pool. Restaurant, bar w/weekend entertainment. Riverside rooms have balconies over water.
Best views of ships, Detroit skyline

Shorecrest Motor Inn. *(313) 568-3000. 1316 E.Jefferson 2 blocks e. of RenCen.* 54 rooms on 2 floors. $46-$68, suites avail. Satellite TV, refrigerators. Restaurant. Convenient Rivertown location. 3 blocks to People Mover. Clean, well managed.
Convenient budget downtown choice

Hotel St. Regis. *(313) 873-3000. W. Grand at 2nd Ave.* 233 rooms on 6 floors. $130, w/jacuzzi $150. Weekend packages, suites. Morning coffee & muffins. Cable TV. Free shuttle service, exercise room. Restaurant, bar. Upkeep could be better.
New Center location next to Fisher Theater, mall, GM, near art museum

Blanche House B&B. *(313) 882-7090. 506 Parkview 1 1/4 mi. e. of Belle Isle Bridge.* 8 rooms w/ baths on 3 floors. $60-$105. Full breakfast, cable TV, phones. Circa 1900 mansion near mayor's residence. Big, attractive rooms restored by friendly, knowledgeable Detroit native and family. River access via canal. Adjoining *Castle*, former boys' school w/ 5 rooms, is partly restored.
Friendly B&B in elegant mansion near Indian Village

River Place Inn. *(313) 259-2500. Stroh River Place at Jos. Campau, 3 blks s. of Jefferson.* 108 rooms on 5 floors. $160. $85/night for Fri +Sat, $125 for room and dinner. Cable TV. Indoor pool, fitness center. Outstanding River Room restaurant run by Jimmy Schmidt. Former Parke-Davis HQ developed as Stroh Brewery HQ, apts. Rooms overlook river or gardens. Croquet.
European-style luxury on the river between downtown and Belle Isle

Parkcrest Inn. *(313) 884-8800. On Harper (service dr.), Allard exit off I-94 between 7 & 8 Mile in Harper Woods.* 49 rooms on 2 floors. $61-$66. 3 efficiencies $78. Cable TV. Restaurant/bar.
Closest to the Pointes, outdoor pool, in residential area

ROYAL OAK

Inn Season. *500 E. Fourth, 3 blocks e. of Main. (313) 547-7916. Mon-Sat 11-10. Closes at 9 Mon-Thurs in fall & winter. Major credit cards. No alcohol or smoking. Lunch entrees average $7-$8. Full dinners $11-$15.* Attractive, friendly spot w/ creative, flavorful vegetarian approach influenced by Greek owner's training in India. 4-7 popular daily fish dishes like whitefish w/ sesame-dijon sauce ($12, less at lunch). Pizzas with 3 special crusts from $10 for med. w/ 3 options. Mexican dishes, 4th St. Burger (lentils, oats, rice, herbs; $5) have fans. 7 house salad dressings. Caesar-style w/o eggs, Ligurian pasta salad $5.

Les Auteurs. *222 Sherman in Washington Square. 2 blocks s. of 11 Mile; 2 blocks w. of Main. (313) 544-2887. Lunch Mon-Sat 11:30-2:30; dinner Mon-Thurs 5:30-10:30, Fri & Sat 6-11:30, Sun 5:30-9:30. Reservations suggested. Closed 1st week in July. Entrees: $4-$10 (lunch); $12-$20 (dinner). Full bar. Visa, MC, AmEx .* Founding owner Keith Famie got ahead of the trend to casual chic & bistro dining here. Now he's into a spicy rotisserie chicken takeout chain. New chef Jeff Gabriel (said to have the only perfect score on his master chef exam) runs the kitchen. Menu changes often. Favorites: black bean cake with smoked chicken and fresh tomato salsa, thin-crusted California pizza with sun-dried tomato, goat cheese, roast garlic, fresh basil (each $4.75 as dinner appetizer, $7 as lunch entree). Good herbed bread sticks on the house; small salad w/ lunch entrees. See pastries made from dining area, sidewalk.

BIRMINGHAM/SOUTHFIELD

Golden Mushroom/Mushroom Cellar. *W. 10 Mile at Southfield Rd. (e. side of city of Southfield) next to gas station. (313) 559-4230. Lunch Mon-Thurs 11:30-4. Dinner Mon-Thurs 5-11, Fri-Sat 5-12. Full bar. Major credit cards. A la carte entrees: lunch $9-$20, dinner $19-$30.* Luxurious setting and fare; wild game a specialty. Most desserts $5.50. Coffee, soft drinks $1-$1.25. Chef Milos Cihelka has trained many of area's best young chefs. Casual Mushroom Cellar serves sandwiches ($5-$6.50) at lunch, at dinner, pizza, burgers, some items on upstairs menu for less $ ($8-$10/entree).

Sweet Lorraine's Cafe. *29101 Greenfield n. of 12 Mile (n.e. edge of Southfield s. of Beaumont Hospital). (313) 559-5985. Mon-Thurs 11-10:30. Fri-Sat 11-12. Full bar, wines by glass, imported beers. Major credit cards.* Cheerful Art Deco bistro w/creative kitchen, changing menu. Keeps getting better. Old favorites: pecan chicken w/ mustard sauce, Jamaican steak ($12/$14). Many fish dishes. All entrees come w/ starch, garnish, terrific bread basket; soup or salad $1.50 extra. Picks from dessert menu ($2.50-$4.25): Scottish country pudding, white chocolate cheesecake.

Phoenicia. *588 S. Woodward, on s. edge of downtown Birmingham. (313) 644-3122. Mon-Thurs 11-10, Fri-Sat 11-11. Full bar. Major credit cards. Entrees (including salad) lunch $7-$9, dinner $7.25-$22.* Serene, sophisti-cated Lebanese restaurant, perhaps the best in a town blessed with good Middle Eastern food. Standouts: shish tawook (marinated chicken breast; $7/lunch, $12/dinner), shawarma (marinated lamb w/ hummus, onions, sumac; $8/$14) rack of lamb ($19at dinner). Or order excellent appetizers Chinese-style: tabooli, baba ganoush, stuffed eggplant, $5.50 each. Bird's nest filo-honey-nut dessert ($2.50) great w/ Arabic coffee.

Pike Street Restaurant. *18 W. Pike St., s. of Huron & n. of Orchard Lake Rd. in downtown Pontiac. (313) 334-7878. Lunch Mon-Fri 11-3; dinner Tues-Thurs 5-10, Fri-Sa 5-11. Full bar, outstanding wine list. Major credit cards. Entrees $6-$11 (lunch, inc. salad); $17-$25 (dinner).* "Remarkably affordable" offerings from "one of the most talented chefs in town," says the *Free Press's* Molly Abraham. Chef Brian Polcyn combines flair, classic training, love of Polish home cooking. Delicious food attuned to Michigan ingredients, seasons. For May: whitetail venison ($24.50) served w/ apple-sage stuffing, wild leeks, fiddlehead ferns, stuffed morels. Wild mushroom among excellent soups ($3.50-$4.25 lunch, $4.50-$5 dinner). All-day sandwich menu in piano bar. Pianist Thurs-Sat at 8 & for Piston home games. Old brick building handsomely renovated by former GM exec to help revive downtown Pontiac. New venture across the street: Chimayo, area's 1st southwestern restaurant.

Barclay Inn. *(800) 541-9742, (313) 646-7300. S.e. corner of Maple & Hunter, downtown Birmingham.* 125 rooms on 5 floors. $75-$85 weekdays, $59-$69 weekends. Cable TV. Refrigerators. Birmingham Theater packages. Upper floors have good downtown views.
Good downtown Birmingham location

Townsend Hotel. *(313) 642-7900. 100 Townsend.* 87 rooms on 4 floors. $165-$175, suites $195-$205. Luxury packageavail. Cable TV. Health club facilities nearby. Rugby Grill restau-

rant, bar. English tea in beautiful
lobby ($10). Some rooms look onto
Shain Park. On quiet downtown street.
*Elegant, European-style hotel
in the heart of Birmingham*

Birmingham Village Inn. *(313)*
*642-6200. 300 N. Hunter, downtown
Birmingham.* 64 rooms on 4 floors.
$67-$75 weekdeys, $49-$59 weekends.
Cont. breakfast, cable TV. Balconies
on some rooms overlook city.
*Birmingham's best weekend rates,
downtown location*

Holiday Inn of Bloomfield Hills.
*(313) 334-2444. 1801 S. Telegraph just
s. of Orchard Lake Rd. on busy strip.* 42
rooms on 2 floors. $65-$75. Cable TV.
Outdoor pool. Restaurant, bar. Usually
booked up well in advance in summer.
Pleasant interior courtyard, pool

Kingsley Inn. *(800) 544-6835. 1495
N. Woodward just s. of Long Lake Rd. in
Bloomfield Hills.* 220 rooms on 3
floors. $84-$89 weekdays, $69 week-
ends. Suites avail. Cable TV. Indoor
pool, whirlpool, exercise room. Restaurant, coffee shop. Bar w/enter-
tainment.
*Attractive weekend rates
for Bloomfield Hills, indoor pool*

St. Christopher Hotel. *(313)*
*647-1800. 3915 Telegraph at Long
Lake, 3 mi. n. of Maple in W. Bloomfield Twp.* 22 rooms, 1 floor. $35-$40.
Best value at clean, older family motel

PLYMOUTH

Sweet Afton Tearoom. *985 N.
Mill St., 3 blocks n. of Plymouth Rd. in
Old Village. (313) 454-0777. Tues-Sat
11-5. Reservations required between
noon and 2. No credit cards or alcohol.*
The best of Britain in a tiny spot w/
frilly, feminine Victorian atmosphere.
Perfect execution of details , from
homemade lemon curd to Devon
cream, individually brewed Fortnum
& Mason tea. Scones, nibbles (desserts
average $2), cutout tea sandwiches (6
for $4, with pickles), milk served in tea

pot for children. Only serve salads in
summer; winter brings flaky Wellington meat pie ($6), Ploughman's Lunch
($5): chunk of white cheddar, thick
slice of warm bread, pickled onions,
cup of hot soup.

Knights Inn Detroit West. *(313)*
*981-5000. On Ford Rd. I-275 exit 25. On
busy strip, Canton.* 105 rooms on 1
floor. $40. Cable TV. Cont. breakfast.
Outdoor pool. 11 efficiencies.
*Budget choice near Plymouth,
beautiful Rouge Parkway*

Plymouth Radisson. *(313)*
*459-4500. 14707 Northville Rd. at 5
Mile.* 195 rooms on 5 floors. $64-$68.
Weekend packages: $59 w/ cont. break-
fast, $86 with $30 fun money, 2 comedy club tickets. Cable TV. Indoor pool,
whirlpool, sauna, game room, exercise
room, jungle gym for kids. Restaurant,
bar. Comedy club.
*Lost of activities, on Rouge Parkway
between Plymouth & Northville*

Mayflower Hotel. *(313) 453-1620.
Ann Arbor Trail at Main.* 100 rooms
on 3 floors. $73.50, jacuzzi suites w/
champagne: $125 &$150. Cable TV.
Breakfast. Whirlpool rooms avail.
Weekend packages. 3 restaurants &
pub. Some views of Kellogg Park. *Renovated downtown Plymouth hotel*

NORTHVILLE/NOVI

MacKinnon's. *126 E. Main St.
(downtown Northville). (313)
348-1991. Lunch: Mon-Fri 11-5, Sat
11:30-4. Dinner: Mon-Thur s5-10,
Fri-Sat 5-11. Full bar. Major credit
cards.* Food and decor of inconspicuous storefront feature game —
with excellent results. Noteworthy at
dinner: wild turkey tenderloin broil
w/ spiced berry sauce, poppyseed
bread timbale ($16), charcoal duck
with raspberry sauce ($17), grilled
scallops Santa Fe ($17). All w/ salad,
starch. Lunch picks: crab pasta du
chef or baked chicken strudel ($7),
each with soup or salad.

Novi Hilton. *(313) 349-4000. 21111 Haggerty Rd near 8 Mile exit of I-275. 3 mi. from Northville.* 237 rooms on 7 floors. $129. Weekends: $65. Romance packages, luxury suites. Cable TV. Glass-domed pool, hot tub, sauna, exercise room. Restaurants, nightclub w/ band & dancing 6 nights/week, amateur star search on Sun. w/ karaoke machine. *Entertainment, activities near metro Detroit's top mall, 12 Oaks*

Atchison House B&B. *(313) 349-3340. 501 W. Dunlap on quiet Northville street of historic homes. Walk downtown.* 5 rooms w/ baths. $70-$120. Reduced weekday business rates. A/C, phones avail. Full breakfast. Cable TV in common area. No smoking. 1882 Italianate house beautifully restored, furnished with antiques. Evening refreshments. *Nice hosts, beautiful setting*

DEARBORN

Red Sea Restaurant. *10307 Dix at Salina, South End.* (313) 843-8211. 24 hrs daily. Meals $6-$12 w/ rice, salad. No alcohol or credit cards. Standard Middle Eastern dishes *plus* Yemeni specialties like gullabah, lamb stew with onions, peppers, Indian spices ($8). Half orders available; eat for days on a full portion. Thick, cardamom-flavored Arabic coffee a nice finish with rice pudding ($1.50).

Giovanni's. *330 S. Oakwood just w. of Fort, just s. of Ford Rouge. Actually in Detroit. Take I-75, Springwells exit s. or I-94 Oakwood exit e.* (313) 841-0122. Tues-Thurs 11-9, Fri to 10, Sat 4-11. Full bar, big Italian wine list. Lunch $7-$10, dinner $9-$19, both w/ appetizer, soup or salad. Major credit cards. Serious but unpretentious Italian homestyle cooking in friendly, family spot. Lots for vegetarians. Excellent homemade pasta. Standouts: gnocchi verde Alfredo (spinach dumplings in cheese sauce) and capelletti (baby ravioli stuffed with meat) — each $10.50 at dinner. Veal dishes

around $13.50, fresh fish $18. "Roman Feast": 12 family-style courses, $26/person.

Dearborn Inn. *20301 Oakwood Blvd. 1 mi. s. of Michigan, 1/2 mi. n. of Rotunda Dr.* (313) 271-2700. Lunch Mon-Sat 11-2; dinner Tues-Thurs 6-10, Fri-Sat to 11; Sun brunch 10-2. Full bar. Major credit cards. Entree, starch, veg.: lunch $8.50-$15, dinner $15-$26. Updated Early American Room still a tribute to founder Henry Ford's vision of America. Comfortable elegance, good service. Favorites from updated menu: grilled pork loin or seafood fettucini ($15), prime rib ($20), wild Michigan pheasant ($22), lamb ($23). Desserts from own pastry kitchen ($4-$7). Appetizers ($4-$9) include housemade pasta dishes like whole wheat angelhair pasta w/ smoked chicken & ham. Harpist Fri & Sat plus Sun brunch.

Judy's Cafe. *15714 W. Warren at Montrose in Detroit, just w. of East Dearborn. 2 1/2 blocks w. of Greenfield, less than 1 mi. e. of Southfield Frwy. Look for striped awning.* (313) 581-8185. Tues-Fri 11-8, Sat 8-2 summer (8-4 winter). Closed for long holiday weekends, Xmas week, middle of Aug. No alcohol or credit cards. Like dropping in on a neighbor's plain, homey kitchen and being surprised with a fabulous meal, not fancy but uniformly excellent. Loyal following drives miles to eat here. Eclectic menu varies daily. Entrees under $6: potato pancakes, salmon patties, Chinese pork & broccoli, variety of Italian dishes w/homemade pasta. Hot sandwich w/ soup $4.25, salad & soup $5.50.

Cedarland Restaurant. *13027 W. Warren near Appoline, between Schaefer and Miller.* (313) 582-4849. Daily 9 a.m.-midnight. No alcohol. MC/Visa. Most of the many Arab restaurants on W. Warren are pretty good. This family-oriented spot is our favorite. Super-hospitable wait staff. Pretty, tasty Arabic salad ($2.50). Daily special ($5.50). Middle Eastern standards run $6-$7: parsley tabooli, lamb shishkebab, shwarma(shaved seared meat like gyros), felafel (spiced chickpea patties), hummus (spread of chickpeas, sesame paste, garlic). A good idea: sharing combination plate ($14). Large complimentary appetizer. Dessert idea: stroll to nearby Afrah pastry (p. 000).

🛏️

Village Inn of Dearborn. *(313) 565-8511. 21725 Michigan e. of Oak-wood.* 30 rooms on 2 floors. Summer $45-$48, winter $40. Cable TV. Walk to famous Westborn Fruit Market, down-town West Dearborn.
Convenient budget choice

Ritz Carlton Dearborn. *(313) 441-2000. In Fairlane Town Center mall.* 308 units on 11 floors. $140-$160, luxury club w/ snacks, drinks $180. Weekend packages from $95. . Cable TV. Indoor pool, sauna, jacuzzi, fitness center. Good views of down-town Detroit, Ambassador Bridge, Windsor from upper floors. Luxurious decor. Daily afternoon tea. 2 restau-rants. Mobil 4 Star rating.
Michigan's most elegant, English, and pretentious hotel

Dearborn Inn. *(313) 271-2700. On Oakwood Blvd., 2 mi. w. of Southfield Frwy. (M-39).* 222 rooms, inc. 20 suites, on 4 floors. $79 weekend, $130-$145

midweek. Suites $149 weekend, $165-$190 midweek. Cable TV. Outdoor pool, 2 exercise rooms. 2 restaurants. On 23 acres close to Ford Motor HQ & Green-field Village. Built by Henry Ford in 1931, recently renovated by Marriott. Replicas of famous American homes, added behind the hotel in 1936-7, in-clude the Edgar Allen Poe cottage ($250 a night) and 4 others divided into suites, $175.
Henry Ford's Early American vision of American history

Best Western Greenfield Inn. *(313) 271-1600. At I-94 & Oakwood 2 mi. s. of Greenfield Village.* 210 rooms on 3 floors. $60 weekend w/breakfast, $69 weekdays. Sun free w/Fri. & Sat. Cable TV, refrigerator, mini TV in bath. Indoor pool, whirlpool, sauna, exercise room. Restaurant, sports bar. New Victorian style.
Mid-priced luxury, good location

Holiday Inn Fairlane. *(313) 336-3340. Just n. of Southfield Frwy & Ford Rd.* 347 rooms on 6 floors. $65 weekend, $84 weekday. Jacuzzi suites $165. Cable TV. Indoor & outdoor pools, whirlpool, sauna, exercise room, tennis court, basketball. 2 restaurants, bar.
Great exercise and sports facilities by Fairlane Mall

Chapter 5
Saginaw Valley & the Thumb

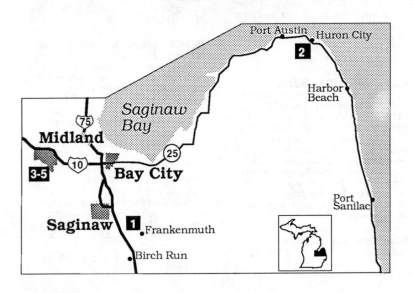

HIGHLIGHTS

Frankenmuth

An insider's guide to the real Frankenmuth —
and the best things to do there

Surprisingly, this former German farm town of 4,400 has become Michigan's top tourist draw. Visitors flock to its Bavarian-themed street of gift shops, now two miles long. Two mammoth restaurants anchor the bustling pedestrian strip. Zehnder's and the Bavarian Inn rank among the 10 biggest-volume restaurants in the U.S., serving up to 10,000 guests on a weekend. The entire commercial area is dolled up in a relentless Alpine manner: chalet-type buildings with cutout wood balconies and wavy trim on the eaves. Geraniums are everywhere in warm weather; the streets and sidewalks are Disneyland-clean.

People seem to love it. Frankenmuth accounts for some three million visits a year, over twice as many as Michigan's second-biggest destination, Greenfield Village. Frankenmuth's fame began with chicken dinners at several hotels that took advantage of their convenient location between Detroit, Flint, and Saginaw. These all-you-can-eat dinners drew traveling salesmen at first and then, in the 1920s and 1930s, when auto touring was a novelty, families out for a drive. During the 1950s, the Christmas decorating business and gift shop begun as a sideline of Wally Bronner's sign shop quickly grew into a famous institution advertised on billboards as far away as Pennsylvania and Florida. Gift shops by the score followed suit, building on the reputation long established by Frankenmuth breweries, sausagemakers, and cheesemakers. Today, with Michigan's largest discount shopping mall at the nearest I-75 exit in Birch Run, seven miles away, the Frankenmuth phenomenon still seems to be gaining momentum.

The old downtown buildings are part of a historic district. But what with the Alpine-style signage and such, little still resembles the town before it became a tourist mecca. It was a plain, sober Lutheran farm town like many others in the Saginaw Valley and the Thumb today. Although the town is still populated by Lutherans from Franconia, it adopted the more familiar Alpine architecture of southern Bavaria to attract tourists. Within Germany, Franconia isn't considered Bavarian at all, even though the region has been part of Bavaria since Napoleon reorganized his conquests in 1803. Real Bavarians are Catholic, notably easygoing and fun-loving, while the Germans who settled Frankenmuth in 1845 were devout Lutherans, serious and extremely hard-working, just like their descendants today.

A band of 14 young Lutherans from the town of Neudettelsau near Nuremberg followed their pastor's call to become missionaries in America to minister to the many Germans already in the Saginaw Valley and to the area's Chippewa Indians. Not surprisingly, the settlers failed in their efforts to Germanize local Indians.

The interstate highway program of the 1950s was what caused Alpine Bavarian architecture to be taken up with such enthusiasm in Frankenmuth. The new I-75 missed Frankenmuth by eight miles. Worried that their big chicken-dinner restaurants might be bypassed, the Zehnder family decided upon a dramatic theme to help business. They remodeled their Fischer Hotel in the picturesque Bavarian style. As the new Bavarian Inn, it offered waitresses dressed in dirndls, and German specialties like sauerbraten and schnitzel. (Zehnder's, the family's first restaurant styled after Mount Vernon, retains its Early American decor and emphasis on fried chicken.)

The contrived Bavarian trappings notwithstanding, Frankenmuth remains very German and very much a community. It's much more genuine than you might think. Everybody knows everybody else, and quite a bit about their family history, too. You can meet locals as young as 40 who speak English with a slight German accent even though their ancestors have been in Michigan well over a hundred years — because they didn't learn English until school. Cleanliness and local pride are pervasive. Even the bank president can be seen picking up stray trash on his way to work; it's bad form in Frankenmuth to ignore litter. The unassuming Zehnder brothers, who own Zehnder's and the Bavarian Inn, live right in town on the main tourist drag. They are hands-on managers, and everybody seems to like them.

Certainly Frankenmuth today is in the great American tradition of too much of everything. Nevertheless, you can have a wonderful time here, and come home with some excellent made-in-Frankenmuth products. The secret is in sticking to a short list of sights and not allowing yourself to drift into too many, too-similar shops.

Park in the big lots behind the Bavarian Inn or Zehnder's. (Overflow parking is across the wooden bridge.) At the Bavarian-style **Visitor's Information Center** north of the Bavarian Inn, pick up a helpful map and well-organized advertising **guide**. Take a snack and rest break in the park at Main and Tuscola, at the Main Street Tavern, or the Riverboat Cruise. Finish with a trip to Bronner's to see the lights. Remarkably, **all visitor attractions in Frankenmuth are handicapped-accessible** except for the second floor of Schoolhaus Square.

MUST-SEE SIGHTS

◆ **Zeesenagel Italian Alpine Village.** This wonderful diorama and
the simple Christmas legend told with it is alone worth a trip to
Frankenmuth. Interior designers David Zeese and Don Nagel were
so inspired by the 18th-century *presepio* or nativity scene they
saw in a Roman church 25 years ago, they decided to create figures for a permanent one of their own. Traditional *presepio*, commissioned by wealthy nobles, often included representations of
entire villages or estates, with realistic individual portraits of loyal
retainers or productive farmers they wished to honor.

Zeesenagel's 1/6 scale scenes have come to fill six vignettes of
10 to 20 feet each with 500 realistic figures. Their Alpine village
includes all segments of society — dignitaries with their noses in
the air, beggars (a reminder to others to share), and a fool,
ignored by all, who in the end delivers the moral. Colorful scenes
of Italian street life are everywhere — a customer sniffing a fish-
monger's wares, a fruit vendor arguing with a customer, a puppet
theater, a lacemaker. A delight in itself is the eclectic Zeesenagel
gift shop of international Christmas figures and crafts, from dollar
novelties to costly Lladro porcelain and beautiful Greek icons. *780
Mill, at the bottom of the hill south of Zehnder's. (517)
652-2591. May 1-Jan. 6: open daily 10-6. Otherwise: weekdays
12-5, weekends 10-6. Tours ($2 adults, $1 12 and under) on the
half-hour between 10:30 and 5:30 (last tour). Winter tours only on
weekends.*

◆ **Bronner's CHRISTmas Wonderland.** For years it's been the
world's largest Christmas store, and now it's twice as big —
200,000 square feet in all, including warehousing. The new part
recreates a German Christkindlmarkt (a traditional outdoor
Christmas market) with colorful small booths.

Bronner's is a phenomenon. The year-round illuminated **outdoor display** is eye-popping. Indoors there are 260 decorated
Christmas trees and 800 animated figures. In many categories —
Advent calendars, nutcrackers, 6,000 kinds of glass ornaments,
500 styles of Nativity scenes from 75 countries — Bronner's selection is stupendous. Much is from Germany (German craftspeople have always done Christmas best), but Bronner's emphasizes the international aspect of Christmas, and keeps the focus
on Christ, as their name indicates. Bibles come in 33 languages,
and ornaments and banners in 70. Children's books and Christmas stories in world languages are on hand. Bronner's is not a
discount store, and high quality standards are apparent. But it
imports in such quantity that some prices — for instance, on glass
ornaments ordered direct from German factories — are very
attractive.

Not quite everything relates to Christmas. Decorations for other seasons and holidays are on hand, and collectibles like Hummel and Precious Moments attract post-Christmas shoppers. The place is so big — with one and a third football fields of sales and display area — it's easy to become disoriented. Refer to the store directory to find what you're especially interested in. And break up your visit by going to the new **refreshment area,** or by seeing **"The World of Bronner's,"** an 18-minute, multi-projector slide show that tells the Bronner's story. It's shown every hour or so, from 10 or 11 until 4 or 7 (more frequent showings over a longer time period from June through December). *On S. Main at Weiss on the south end of Frankenmuth. Events line: 1-800-ALL-YEAR. Open 361 days. June-Dec. 24: Mon-Fri 9-9, Sat 9-7, Sun 12-7. Dec. 26-May 31: Mon-Sat 9-5:30, Fri until 9, Sun 1-5:30.*

CRAFTS AND MANUFACTURING DEMOS & TOURS

Fudgemaking, cheesemaking, woodcarving, wool-carding, milling, beermaking, taffypulling — a visit to Frankenmuth has become a great place to see a variety of free crafts demonstrations. Now the city has started a new Agriculture Tourism Park on Weiss Street behind Bronner's. Only agricultural production facilities can locate there, and only if they offer public tours of the entire manufacting process.

The following demonstrations and tours stand out:

◆ **Frankenmuth Brewery.** Now that Heileman's has closed its big Frankenmuth brewery, this new microbrewery is the state's largest brewery and one of only two remaining. Breweries under 15,000 are classified as micros; last year Frankenmuth Brewery, in the remodeled old Geyer's Brewery, produced 7,500 barrels. Its German brewmaster makes distinctive, flavorful German-style beers using state-of-the-art German equipment. Frankenmuth Dark and Frankenmuth Bock (a dark, rich, beer traditionally brewed only in springtime) have won awards. There's also a lighter, more American pilsner, a new lite beer, and Old Detroit ale. They sell for $5.39 a six-pack at Meijer. Free half-hour tours, given each hour, include a video on brewing and a short tour of the tanks and bottling line, followed by two beers of your choice in the hospitality room. *425 S. Main, just south of Tuscola. (517) 652-6183. Jan-March: Thurs-Mon noon-5. April-May: Mon-Sat noon-5. June-Dec: Mon-Sat 10-5 (until 6 in summer), Sun 12-5. Last tour an hour before closing.*

◆ **St. Julian Winery.** This facility includes not only a free tasting room for the many noteworthy wines and sparkling fruit juices from the mid-range St. Julian Winery (Michigan's largest), but an actual small winery where solera cream sherry is aged from wine started in the main winery in Paw Paw. *127 S. Main, 1 block north of School Haus Square. (517) 652-3281. Tasting room open Mon-Sat 10-6, Sunday 12-6, closes at 5 daily Jan thru April. Free winery tours weekends at 1 and 3.*

◆ **Frankenmuth Woodcarving Studio.** You can watch noted German sculptor Georg Keilhofer execute commissions for churches and individuals. Instruction in wood-carving is offered, along with a large selection of tools and supplies — and a large selection of wood carvings. *976 S. Main, south of the river but north of Jefferson. (517) 652-2975.*

◆ **Zeilinger Wool Company.** For over 80 years Zeilinger's has processed raw wool, straight off the sheep, and used it as batting in custom comforters. A self-guided tour shows visitors all steps of the process, from washing and air-drying wool to carding it and making hand-stitched quilts and comforters. On weekends, however, manufacturing employees are off. Quilting supplies and fabrics are here, too. *1130 Weiss (north of Bronner's). (517) 652-2920. Mon-Sat 9-5:30, Sun 12-5.*

◆ **Frankenmuth's Historic Woolen Mill.** Today this old mill is more of an upscale sweater store, though you can see wool-filled comforters being made in a large workroom, and see how wool is processed — right on Frankenmuth's main pedestrian drag. *570 S. Main between Cass and Tuscola. (517) 652-8121. Open daily. Jan-mid-April: 9-6. Mem.-Labor Day: 9-9. Otherwise: 9-8.*

FRANKENMUTH HISTORY

◆ **Frankenmuth Historical Museum.** At this superior local-history museum light is shed on everything from chicken dinners to Frankenmuth's origins near Nuremberg. Strong visuals and lots of letters convey the immigration experience, the life left behind in Franconia, and the unusually strong ethnic community they created here. New hands-on exhibits include the Immigration Game, in which chance and choice determine a young man's fate: he could stay in Germany and be drafted, or emigrate and perhaps earn enough to buy land. One gallery is for special exhibits that change yearly. *613 S. Main. (517) 652-9701. May-Dec: Mon-Sat 10:30-5, Sun 12:30-5. Jan-March: weekends only. April: Wed-Sun. Admission by donation.*

◆ **St. Lorenz Church and Log Cabin Church.** This much-enlarged 1880 brick Gothic-style church houses the largest congregation east of the Mississippi — 4,300 strong — in the conservative Missouri Synod of the Lutheran Church. You can stop in any weekday for a self-guided tour of the sanctuary, where splendid contemporary stained-glass windows show scenes of Lutheran history, from St. Paul to Luther to Frankenmuth's missionary ministers on horseback. If you call in advance, volunteer Sharon Bickell will give you a most interesting look back at the settlement's early days. You'll visit a reconstruction of the original log church and parsonage, complete with packing-case pulpit. St. Lorenz still holds a German-language service with hymns each Sunday at 9:15 and on Wednesdays in Lent and Advent at 9:30. *On Tuscola at Mayer, about a mile west of downtown. Park in rear and go in back door. Call (517) 652-6141 for tour.*

PLACES TO TAKE A REST

◆ **Willkommen Park.** A pleasant, shady spot on downtown Frankenmuth's main intersection at Main and Tuscola. Benches, drinking fountain, but no restrooms. Carryout food from Willi's, Main Street Tavern, or Satow's.

◆ **Tiffany Biergarten** (p. 259), **Main Street Tavern** (p. 259), or the **Riverview Cafe,** 445 S. Main are nice places to sit and rest. The cafe has shady decks going down to the Cass River.

◆ **Frankenmuth Riverboat Tour.** Festive Dixieland music and informative commentary by a Frankenmuth native make this 45-minute cruise up the pretty Cass River especially enjoyable. The boat is a diesel-powered, two-deck paddle wheeler. A fine way to rest your feet while learning more about Frankenmuth. *Leaves from the Riverview Cafe, 445 S. Main. (517) 652-8844. Runs May thru Oct. Leaves at 12:30, 2:30, 4:30, 7 (6 in May, Sept & Oct). $5/adult, $2.50 12 & under. Tip: buy tickets early. $10 cocktail cruise July & August includes minstrel, hors d'oeuvres.*

◆ **Fischer Platz.** This pretty, popular Bavarian-style "town square" with many benches was created as part of the Bavarian theme campaign circa 1960. The Pied Piper tale is enacted on the Glockenspiel several times a day (check sign in front) but it's a disappointment compared to the wonderful antique German moving clocks it was modeled on. Restrooms, visitor information kiosks. *Just north of the Bavarian Inn, next to the Visitors' Center.*

◆ **Picnic facilities in public parks.** Picnic tables and barbeque grills are in tip-top shape at both convenient city parks. **Heritage Park** at the north end of Weiss has long, scenic frontage along the Cass River, and more playground equipment. **Memorial Park** on East Tuscola, 1/4 mile east of downtown, is a hilly area with a creek running through it. (Tobogganing here is the best around.) Amenities include a **swimming pool** open to all, **rose gardens**, and an **exercise trail**. Get good bratwurst and franks, rolls, potato salad, and cole slaw at Willi's Sausage Haus (p. 241).

OLD FRANKENMUTH

Beneath the thick icing of tourism, there's still a very German small town in downtown Frankenmuth. Here's where to find it.

◆ **Satow's Drug Store.** The lunch counter is a popular local hangout where you can get an earful of German, and of the distinctive Frankenmuth dialect of English, in which "just" may be "chust" and nearly every sentence sounds like a question. The soups are homemade, and the prices can't be beat; lunch specials are $3 and under. *308 S. Main, just north of Tuscola. Mon-Fri 8-9, Sat until 7, Sun until 4.*

◆ **Main Street Tavern.** An utterly plain German-American gasthaus where the food's as important as the beer. Owner Keith Boesnecker, who was Zehnder's baker for years, spotlights local products whenever possible. And he makes all the bread and buns on the premises. That all makes for bar food of the highest quality — at terrific prices. The $2.10 quarter-pound cheeseburger is made from local beef and cheese. Willi's next door supplies the excellent bratwurst ($2.50) and the beef stix and Italian sausage used on the Willi Pizza. (Square pizzas are a house specialty.) Frankenmuth Pilsner and Dark are $1.25 on draft, while Carling's (still a local favorite even if no longer locally made) is 75¢, or 50¢ on darts night (Wednesday). *310 S. Main, just north of Tuscola. (517) 652-2222. Mon-Sat 9 a.m.-2 a.m., Sun noon-2 a.m.*

◆ **Willi's Sausage Haus.** As soon as you walk in the door, the smell and the plain, super-clean appearance tell you how German Willi's is. A master sausagemaker, he turns out sausages, hams, and bacon — 95 items in all — here in his shop and smokehouse, and in his new wholesale plant in Vassar. Locals shop here for their traditional favorites — from bratwurst and weisswurst to head cheese and a famous beef jerky made from carefully trimmed top round. Non-traditonal innovations include many turkey products, made without fatty skin, such as turkey pepper loaf and smoked turkey bratwurst. Prices compare favorably with suburban delis.

Willi will grill a sausage of your choice to eat at his Schnellimbiss stand-up counter or in the park across the street. A line of imported German specialties is on hand: chocolates, mustards, cookies (good holiday gifts) and Rudolph's excellent rye bread from Toronto. Small-group tours may be arranged. *316 S. Main, just north of Tuscola. (517) 652-9041. Mon-Sat 8-6, Sun 11-5.*

◆ **Star of the West Milling Company.** Michigan's wheat fields once made it a breadbasket of America, but Michigan wheat has been relegated to niche markets since Minneapolis became America's milling center at the turn of the century. That niche is strong, because Michigan soft winter wheat has the lowest protein of any east of the Rockies. Low protein means low viscosity, and a flour that's good for cookies and pie crust. The Star of the West is one of only six commercial mills left in Michigan, all enormous. Its big silos are right downtown. Customers include commercial bakers and Battle Creek's cereal makers, who buy bran. At its interesting store across the street, 25-pound sacks of Nightengale brand pastry-type flour — white, graham, wheat germ, and bran — are sold for under $5/bag. This is also a sporty work clothes shop, and a garden shop with bird feeders, seed, and the like and a farm-supply store where you can get (among other things) numbers to put on cows' ears. *121 E. Tuscola. (517) 652-9971. Mon-Fri 7-5, open Sat mainly in spring.*

GIFT AND SPECIALTY SHOPS

Competition has made for a very broad market. Many shops focus on high-ticket collectible lines, character dolls, wood carvings, German beer steins and cuckoo clocks. There's some good stuff here, if you focus on finding what really interests you. Here are some highlights:

◆ **Rau's Country Store.** A rambling, appealing mix of many gift categories and price levels. Hard candies, tin boxes, reproduction Victorian lamps and glassware carry out the old-fashioned country store theme up front, but there's lots more further back and downstairs, including cassettes of polkas and German folk songs, a nice selection of Chinese baskets, die-cast toys, oak shelves, miniature cottages, and, in the basement, loads of inexpensive scrapbook cutouts. **Doll house miniatures,** displayed in well over a hundred room settings, are fabulous. (Pinocchio's across the street may be even better, and it has a mail-order catalog.) *656 S. Main. (517) 652-8388. Mon-Fri 10-8, Sat 9-10, Sun 12-7. Longer summer hours.*

◆ **Kite Kraft.** It's mostly kites — over 100 kinds, plus windsocks and other flying toys — but it's also activity-oriented toys, from Brio trains to funny wind-ups and cheap, entertaining novelties like the $1.25 balloonocopter (helicopter blades powered by balloons) and a $2 blugle (a bright plastic tube that plays different notes when you swing it). Toys are demonstrated all the time. The owner, a longtime elementary teacher, follows up customers' suggestions. *In School Haus Square, 245 S. Main north of Tuscola. June-Christmas: Mon-Thurs 10-6, Fri & Sat 10-8, Sun 11-6. Otherwise: closes weekdays at 6, Sun at 5.*

COLLECTORS' MUSEUMS

Frankenmuth's huge flow of customer traffic makes possible some wonderful displays of serious collectors' stuff. **Michigan's Own Military Museum** with state veterans' memorabilia (1250

Weiss; 517-652-8005) and **Antique Auto Village** at 576 S. Main appeal to special interests. Of more general interest are:

◆ **Rau's Country Store.** In a basement gallery is a really charming collection of 19th-century **German souvenir glassware** — mementoes of stays at spas and resorts. Some glasses are painted, most are cut in two-layered cranberry glass. (See p. 242.) *Free.*

◆ **Memory Lane Arcade.** Test Your Strength, Kiss-O-Meter, The Egyptian Mummy Answers Your Question — here are favorite coin-operated games and music from amusement parks and saloons going back 90 years. They're playable, though you don't always get enough time for your quarter. Still, it's magical to go back in time and play all these cheesily evocative devices: Klassy Kinescope, Play Golf, the Mystic Swami, nickelodeons, pinball games. The fabulous Arburo Dance Organ from the 1930s includes an accordion, drums, and 170 organ pipes; it can sound like a marching band, a jazz combo, a church organ, and a dance band. There's a big, coin-operated Lionel layout, and current video games. *626 S. Main. (517) 652-8881. Open daily 12-9 in summer, until dark in fall, after Xmas weekends only, weather permitting. Free admission.*

◆ **Main Street Tavern.** (See p. 259). Collection of **breweriana** about Frankenmuth beers, plus a history written by the owner.

DISCOUNT SHOPPING AT BIRCH RUN . . . . . Before 1986 it was an obscure village at the I-75 Frankenmuth exit. Now Birch Run is Michigan's discount shopping capital. With 85 stores, its **Manufacturers Market Place** is bigger than its sister malls at Holland, Monroe, and Traverse City. Now it has been joined by **Village Shops at Birch Run,** with 34 designer outlets.

Manufacturers Market Place features mostly brand-name outlets, including Gitano, Oshkosh, Bugle Boy, Van Heusen, Corning, and American Tourister. It has a multi-outlet food court. Village Shops at Birch Run's roster of designer outlets includes Liz Claiborne, Anne Klein, Evan-Picone, Capezio, J. Crew, Adolfo II, and Villeroy & Boch. It has a food vendor outside in good weather and umbrellaed tables on a terrace. Its indoor "relaxation room" offers TVs with sports events (to placate male companions of relentless shoppers), vending machines, tables, even couches for naps. Both malls deal mostly in manufacturers' overruns not bought by non-discount retailers. Fashions typically show up six to eight weeks later than in department stores, though some are last year's models. Prices range from 20% to 70% off, which often can be beat by special sales at department stores, but the selection of discounted goods in one place is so far unparalleled in Michigan. *At I-75 exit 136; go west on Birch Run Rd. Village Shops are just west of Manufacturers Market Place. Both malls have similar hours. From April thru Dec: Mon-Sat 10-9, Sun 11-6. Jan-March: Mon-Thurs 10-6, Fri & Sat 10-9, Sun 12-6.*

Historic Huron City

A look at the civilized, relaxed summer life of Yale's Billy Phelps, "America's favorite college professor"

Time moves slowly in Michigan's Thumb. The landscape is utterly flat, and the Lake Huron scenery is pleasant but unspectacular, no match for the Grand Traverse region or West Michigan's sand dunes. So even vacation development is blessedly low-key. In the absence of pressure to sell and develop property, old households have often survived intact, with all their everyday furnishings. They are natural museums maintained by heirs over the decades, until they emerge as organized museums with public hours. Examples are the Sanilac Historical Museum in Port Sanilac (which includes the local doctor's home, furnishings, records, and library) and the Harbor Beach law office of Frank Murphy, Michigan's most illustrious leader of the Depression era.

But the **House of the Seven Gables** in the historic **Huron City** museum village is the most wonderful survivor of all. The big, comfortable Italianate house built by lumberman Langdon Phelps sits behind a picket fence atop a long hill overlooking Lake Huron. When you enter this informal house and walk into the cozy, memento-filled library, the tea cart by the fire is set for afternoon tea. Books are piled on the center table waiting to be read and reviewed by Hubbard's son-in-law, William Lyon Phelps, called "America's favorite college professor" in a 1930s *Life* magazine feature. Classic Adirondack chairs look out across to the lake. It's easy to imagine that it's 1932 and Billy Phelps is about to come back from his afternoon game of golf.

Visitors immediately feel that this interior is no historical reconstruction. It's simply an old house that has been lived in by the same family ever since it was built in 1881 — and a very interesting family at that, sure of themselves and unconcerned with fashion. Langdon Hubbard had come to Michigan from Connecticut as a young, high-minded, and ambitious young man hoping to make his fortune in the West. He bought 29,000 acres of timberland and an old sawmill, which he developed into a lake port with a half mile-long dock.

By 1880 Hubbard's two sawmills produced 20,000 feet of lumber a day. But the great Thumb fire of 1881 burned up the area's remaining timber. Such fires were common in logging regions. Loggers left treetops in the woods; dried out, they caught fire easily. The fire hastened the growth of inland towns like Bad Axe and Sandusky, as burned-over forests here proved excellent for growing navy beans, potatoes, and later sugar beets. Old lumber ports like Huron City, however, were destined to languish except as modest resorts. In this area brine wells and salt-making had been a byproduct of lumbering, and the process ended up contaminating well water with salt. The only sources of fresh water for port communities were Lake Huron and shallow, easily polluted wells. That limited their development.

After the fire, Hubbard rebuilt his big Italianate house and sold off his timberland to prospective German and Polish farmers. He didn't rebuild his sawmills, which could have salvaged the dead trees and provided some local employment. A general store, inn, church, and school were built for the farm village Hubbard hoped would prosper on the site. Today they survive, fully furnished, as components of Historic Huron City. Hubbard provided unusual amenities for villagers — a social parlor in the inn, a roller rink near the store and books from his personal library to borrow. But by 1883 Huron City had less than two dozen residents, down from 1,500 before the fire.

Huron City did prove an ideal summer retreat for the Hubbard descendants, who moved to Grosse Pointe, and their friends. The daughter, Annabel, married William Lyon Phelps, a phenomenally popular English professor at Yale. He was Billy Phelps to generations of Yale students who flocked to his interesting, easy-to-take lectures. Phelps was also an American Baptist preacher and a prolific writer of book reviews and literary appreciations for the general reading public. He and Anabel summered in the House of the Seven Gables. So many vacationers showed up at his non-denominational, Sunday-afternoon sermons that the little church was expanded to hold 600. Seven Gables remained in use through the death of the Phelps's heir in 1987.

Physical evidence of the Hubbards' and Phelps's affluent, civilized, and relaxed lifestyle is everywhere. There's an ornate 1886 pool table in the double parlors, and above it a print of a Raphael Madonna. Parlor amusements range from a music box with huge discs, circa 1885, to Mah-Jong tiles from that craze. There are portraits of favorite dogs and cats, and racks of croquet mallets and tennis rackets in the study. The ladies' fancy work, seed pictures, twig shelves, and Anabel Phelps's almost Expressionistic landscape paintings are all interesting. The books and magazines in Phelps's large, airy upstairs study give a good idea of the literary fare of well-read people in the 1920s and 1930s.

A house like this required an upstairs maid and a parlor maid. Also, a cook and a kitchen maid worked in a cheerful, practical kitchen, state-of-the-art in 1915 and hardly changed since. Enthusiasts for period decor won't be disappointed.

The genial Phelps stuck to a productive daily routine, beginning with calisthentics at six a.m. (All guests were awakened to
join in.) Phelps retired to his study to write until noon. After
lunch, he played golf. Grazing sheep clipped the golf course between the house and Lake Huron, but were rounded up at game
time and herded under the old roller rink. Edgar Guest, The
Detroit Free Press columnist famed for his light verse, was a frequent golfing buddy, and eventually built a summer cottage in
nearby Pointe aux Barques.

After Billy and Annabel Phelps's deaths, the property came into
the hands of Annabel's niece, Carolyn Hubbard Parcells Lucas. The
dynamic personality of Billy Phelps and the public's great interest
in him inspired her to furnish and preserve Huron City's church,
inn, and general store, and to build a trim brick **museum building**
to house exhibits on local history and Phelps's career. All the
buildings are simple and attractive, painted white with green
trim, giving them a neat New England look.

Huron City's buildings are more fully and authentically furnished than most museums', a result of local people's long memories and many contributions. Much of the merchandise in the
general store was left over from Langdon Hubbard's stock. The
original **post office** and **lumbering office** remain in back of the
store, while a large room is given over to displays of tools for
lumbering and cutting ice. In a **lifesaving station** moved onto the
site, a breeches buoy and other lifesaving equipment can be seen,
along with displays on local marine history. Teenage tour guides
are pleasant and competent.

Seen alone, Huron City is impressive. But it is overwhelmed by
the compelling intimacy of the House of the Seven Gables, which
seems too real to be a museum. If you visit Seven Gables in August, your tour guides will likely be the Proberts, old family
friends of the Phelpses and their niece, and you will get a fascinating, first-hand blend of tour and reminiscence. If you do take
both tours on the same day, bring a snack or lunch to eat at a
picnic table. No refreshments except soft drinks are nearby, and
each tour lasts 1 1/2 hours.

Huron City is on M-25 8 miles south of Port Austin and 8 miles
north of Port Hope. (517) 428-4123. Open July 1-Labor Day, ev-
ery day but Tuesday, 10-5. Group tours available in June through
Sept. Admission to each tour (Huron City or Seven Gables):
$4/adult, $3.50 seniors, $3 12-18, under 12 free. $1 discount if
you take both tours.

ANOTHER TRIP BACK IN TIME TO THE 1920s AND 1930s. . . . . is the **Frank Murphy Birthplace** in Harbor Beach. Murphy was the Michigan governor who refused to use the National Guard to quash the 1937 Flint Sit-Down Strike. By initiating collective bargaining, he paved the way for the UAW. This is a very simple frame house, to which the storefront law office of Murphy's father is attached. Walk in and you feel like you're in 1910, what with the potbelly stove and plain wood chairs. Murphy's father made enough money to move into the impressive Gothic Revival house next door, where the children grew up. His famous son, a true labor hero, started his career in Detroit, became mayor (no Depression-era mayor did more to alleviate hunger among the jobless), governor (1936-38), U.S. Attorney General, and U.S. Supreme Court judge (1940 to his death in 1949). Murphy seems to have used the little house as a home base and repository for books and gifts, souvenirs and snapshots. The houses are treasure troves of interesting historical objects. They're due to become a state-operated historic site when fund-raising is complete. For now, you can learn a lot about Murphy's character from the things he left here, and from talking to the UAW retirees who, as true keepers of the flame, run the museum. Inspirational books, pairs of riding boots, and crucifixes and religious statues, countless autographed photos of Murphy with celebrities and labor leaders — all add up to a picture of his political ambition and concern for achievement and high principles, his Catholic faith, and his love of challenge and hard work. While governor of the Philippines from 1933 to 1935, he received some most unusual gifts displayed here. *142 S. Huron in central Harbor Beach, across from Norm's Place. (517) 479-9664. Open mid-June-Labor Day, Mon-Sat 10-5:30, Sun 11-5. Free admission; donations welcome.*

A NICE PLACE TO LINGER AND WATCH BOATS. . . . . is shady **Harbor Park** overlooking the busy transient marina at Port Sanilac (population 650), some 40 miles south of Huron City on M-25. To get the feeling of being out on Lake Huron, you can walk out to the long **breakwater** past the pretty, prim Victorian **lighthouse** and the **Old Bark Shanty** (a favorite local landmark from pioneer days, not open to the public). Mornings and evenings it's usually well populated by fishermen, and for the October salmon run it's packed.

THE FINE ITALIANATE HOME OF A PIONEER DOCTOR . . . . . and most all his things, from a massive curio case full of bird's nests, Indian pipes, and coral specimens to medical books and his original medicines, and apothecary bottles make the **Sanilac Historical Museum** special. The doctor's grandson and only heir became a ship's captain, and never threw anything out or modernized much, since he only stayed here occasionally. Some rooms are given over to museum displays: a first-rate **quilt collection**, a Victorian display of stuffed birds with a painted backdrop, a good **marine history room** about the area's famous shipwrecks, and odd donations like a Mexican bullfrog mariachi band of stuffed bullfrogs wearing sombreros. There's a lot of high-quality stuff to see here (carriages, old log cabin, a little dairy museum — Sanilac is Michigan's #1 milk-producing county). Pleasant **picnic area** and grounds, too. *On the west side of M-25 at the south edge of Sanilac. (616) 622-9946. Open from Mem. to Labor Day, Thurs-Sun noon-4:30. Modest admission fee.*

Dow Chemical Visitor Center & Tour, H.H. Dow Historical Museum

Top-notch industrial history at a rude brine well and a sprawling modern chemical complex

Good museums of industrial history are a new and unusual phenomenon, and industrial tours of any kind have become increasingly rare because of widespread concern for industrial espionage. Visitors to Midland can be treated to not one but *two* exceptionally interesting looks at Dow Chemical, the world's sixth-biggest chemical firm. Dow was founded here in 1897, and out-of-the-way Midland (population 38,000) remains its headquarters today.

The new **H. H. Dow Museum** tells the dramatic story of Dow's origins at a replica of the simple old grist mill and brine well where founder Herbert Dow started out in 1890. **Dow's plant tour** shows visitors parts of its Michigan Division, one of the world's largest and most diversified chemical plants. That 19,000-acre complex along the Tittabawassee River just east of downtown Midland employs 5,400, including Dow's world-wide research and development staff. Finally, there's the Dow Visitor Center, open weekdays, which shows interested visitors an overview of Dow consumer products and an interesting illustrated summary of its history.

These are probably the most intelligent exhibits of corporate industrial history in Michigan. They're made even more interesting by exploring the character and motivation of its remarkably persistent, independent, and creative founder. Herbert Dow was more than a good scientist and collaborator with others. As a hard-headed businessman, he was able to break the lock German cartels had on the American market for chemicals, thus paving the way for a strong American chemical industry.

Still, you won't get the *whole* Dow story at the museum or visitor center. There's little official mention of "Crazy Dow." That's what skeptical Midlanders called 24-year-old Herbert Dow shortly after he arrived in town with a suitcase, a few hundred dollars, and an idea for extracting the valuable chemical bromine from the bromine-rich brine deposits under Midland. His studies at the

Case School of Applied Science in Cleveland had convinced him that he could use electricity to extract commercial quantities of bromine from such salt deposits. Its use in photo processing and pharmaceuticals had made bromine valuable.

Nor are visitors reminded of the numerous campus protests against Dow in the 1960s and 1970s for making napalm for the U.S. military to use against Vietnamese troops and villagers. There's no mention of a much-publicized chemical spill in nearby Freeland (people left their homes for a week, according to rigorous emergency guidelines, but no one was hurt). Or of the controversial plans for the ill-fated Midland nuclear power plant. Or of how Greenpeace environmental activists in canoes plugged the plant's outlets into the Tittabawassee River to dramatize the environmental impact of Dow discharges. Or how irate Dow administrators had activists spied on for years.

You *do* hear a lot on the tour about good walleye fishing in the Tittabawassee River and about Dow's ingenious uses for turning waste into new products, its advanced methods of waste treatment, and its generally outstanding safety and occupational health record.

◆ **Dow Chemical Tours.** Dow's Midland operation, like many chemical facilities, is an amazing-looking labyrinth of buildings, industrial equipment, and pipes. Just driving by is impressive. Seventy independent plants, each with its own production facility, quality control analysis lab, and warehouse, are joined by a network of insulated overhead pipes that carry steam, water, and raw materials to each individual plant. This open-air plant design differs from conventional plants enclosed in huge buildings. It allows for good ventilation, easy maintenance access, and great flexibility. Buildings and equipment are constantly being changed. Aerial views would provide a lot of detailed information about operations that Dow would prefer to keep from its competitors; the firm has arranged to prohibit overflights by any aircraft.

Visitors who make tour reservations are driven through this interesting complex in a van for an up-close (if selective) view of operations. Your guide is an amiable, well-informed veteran foreman. He displays the upbeat enthusiasm and faith in better living through chemistry that marks Dow's corporate culture.

Tour stops include the Saran wrap plant and a state-of-the-art analytical lab. If everything is presented with an ideal, picture-perfect glow, down to happy-looking workers viewed on break in a snack room with a giant, deer-in-forest photo mural — well, that's more or less the way working at Dow really is, to hear most locals talk about it. Layoffs are unheard of. Dow workers are well paid. Its big research staff gives Midland the educational and income demographics and international population of a university town. Midland residents enjoy fabulous sports and cultural facilities. (Shopping is rotten, however.) And Midland is one of a dwindling number of places where good jobs are still available to high school graduates. No other company town we've seen in Michigan — not Ann Arbor or Battle Creek, Dearborn or Flint — thinks anywhere near as highly of its reigning presence. *Reservations required for free public tours, held Mon 9:30-11:30. (517) 636-8658. Call early; availability limited, especially for spring and summer tours.*

◆ **Dow Visitors Center.** Many of the 500 products made in Midland are displayed here — including Saran Wrap (introduced in 1953), Ziploc bags (1972), Spray 'n' Wash (1970), Cepacol mouthwash, Dursban insecticide, and Styrofoam (along with lots of free ideas for holiday crafts using it). To move away from producing mainly bulk chemicals with lower profit margins and big price swings, Dow is increasingly stressing consumer products, with new research or acquisitions in personal care products and pharmaceuticals.

Engineering models of the award-winning Salzburg hazardous waste landfill cell and the Midland aspirin plant, which makes a third of the aspirin used in the U.S., will appeal mainly to the technical-minded, as will many free educational publications. But the interesting panels of photographs and text on company history are of considerable general interest. *500 E. Lyon Rd. at Bayliss, in the Dow complex just east of downtown Midland. From I-75, take U.S. 10 into town. After you've passed much of the Dow complex, look for Bayliss and turn left. Center is in 1 block. (517) 636-8658. Open Mon-Fri 8-4:30. Call to see if museum room is closed for Dow group meetings.*

◆ **H. H. Dow Historical Museum.** The life and accomplishments of Herbert Dow are engagingly presented in rough wood replicas of the buildings where he launched Dow Chemical. These include a primitive grist mill, brine well and derrick with handmade wooden pumping machinery, and pegged wood brine storage tank. The museum, owned and operated by the Midland Historical Society, uses some slick presentational techniques — voiceovers of actors who play family members and associates, a worthwhile 12-minute film on Midland shown in a nifty little 1890s theater, and a spectral image of Dow himself, fancifully revisiting Midland 60 years after his death and talking about his challenges and satisfactions. (Family members say it sounds like Dow, informal and down-to-earth.)

This isn't the pompous puffery you might expect, and it's not only for chemists and engineers, though they will be especially interested in the big display on steam engines (they fascinated Dow from a very early age) and the reconstructed 1890 lab/ manufacturing plant showing the bromine-extracting process on which Dow Chemical was built. There is a recreation of the workshop where, in his youth, Dow happily spent hours working on the inventions and projects of his mentor father, who was a master mechanic for a Cleveland shovel works. In a ghostly life-size tableau, early Dow scientists, recruited by Herbert Dow from his old alma mater, Case, sit around in shirtsleeves late at night brainstorming to solve a problem. *From downtown Midland, take Main Street west about 1 1/4 miles to Cook Road, turn left, and you're there. (517) 832-5319. Wed-Sat 10-4, Sun 1-5. $2 admission.*

CANOEING ON MIDLAND'S THREE RIVERS . . . . . is made easy with the **City of Midland canoe livery** (517-832-8438). It's at the foot of Ashman, which crosses Main in the very center of downtown Midland. You can paddle up the Chippewa to the Chippewa Nature Center, and from there up the Pine and back. They flow into the Tittabawassee, which is lined by city parks and golf courses northwest of downtown and by Dow Chemical to the southeast. But don't think you can get a duck's-eye view of the giant chemical complex. Canoeists will be met by Dow security who will transport them and their canoe around the plant and deposit them by the Mapleton boat launch to the east.

TUBING DOWN THE RIVER . . . . . is a popular recreation in these parts. Mount Pleasant, 30 miles west of Midland, has so little industry and such a modern sewage treatment plant that Central Michigan students like to float on inner tubes all the way through town. Tube and canoe rentals and transportation are available thorugh **Chippewa Valley Canoe Livery and Campground** 13 miles west of Midland. (800) 686-2447.

Chippewa Nature Center

*Michigan's best all-around nature center
has a good natural history museum, interpreted trails,
and an authentic 1870s log homestead.*

Midland's Chippewa Nature Center clearly stands out from the rest of Michigan's many fine nature centers. First, it has a fabulous classroom and museum building. A comfortable lounge, shaped like a riverboat pilot house, seems suspended over the Pine River with long views upstream and down to the nearby confluence of the Pine and Chippewa. Using the birdwatchers' telescope provided, you can look out and see birds patrolling the river, hoping to catch a fish. The Center's architect, Midland's creative Alden Dow (see p. 248), learned from his teacher, Frank Lloyd Wright, how to design buildings that, when you're inside, seem to melt into the living world around them.

Displays, trails, and programs are all intelligently planned and user-friendly, with good signage to help you understand what you're looking at. Finally, Chippewa offers an unusually rich mix of things to do and see, including an authentic log homestead and displays of items as old as 7,000 years from on-site archaeological digs. Other nature centers have more interesting sites than this flat riverside bottomland of second-growth woods. But Chippewa provides the best all-around introduction to the natural history of its area, outdoors and in, and man's use of the environment.

Highlights include:

◆ **Outstanding indoor wildlife observation areas** that look out onto feeders, shrubs, and flowers busy with birds and chipmunks. Bright annuals attract hummingbirds to the river window. The museum's wildlife window is busy year-round. Even the most infirm visitors could sit here and enjoy nature for hours.

◆ **A museum of colorful, well-done dioramas showing geological time periods and scenes from Saginaw Valley Indian cultures** of different eras. The geology exhibits nicely illustrate the notion that, seen in geological cross-section, Michigan is like a set of nesting bowls formed during different eras, mostly overlaid by a heavy layer of glacial till. Shown with each diorama are rocks or artifacts that go with that geological age. Unusually vivid displays on Indian cultures show scenes from everyday life in the Saginaw Valley at different periods, together with objects excavated from the nature center site and the archaeological methods used to uncover and identify them. The Saginaw River system, abundant with game and fish, has been one of Michigan's most important centers of Indian life.

The museum displays are intelligent and clear but dense and best absorbed a little at a time. Easier to enjoy are Indian naturalist Smokey Joe Jackson's wonderful painted carvings of birds and animals, and a scene with a giant beaver. Just after the last ice age, Michigan was home to beavers 3 1/2 feet tall.

◆ **"The Naturalist's Challenge,"** a nifty exercise in slowing down and making observations of natural objects. It starts with an indoor hands-on display, followed up with outdoor observations made with the help of a borrowed bird whistle, magnifying glass, and bug box. Parents are well advised to try this out first to get the hang of it.

◆ A good **museum shop** is focused on books and projects about nature appreciation, not decorative gift items with natural motifs.

◆ **A 12-mile trail system** on flat terrain often parallels the Chippewa River. Highlights are the .4 mile **Arbury Trail**, handicapped-accessible and planned for blind people, and a wooded, fern-filled **oxbow** where nesting waterfowl and muskrats can be seen from a wildlife blind. In winter the trails are used for cross-country skiing and hiking; they're ungroomed and sometimes rough.

◆ **An 1870s log homestead** from Midland County. The house is well crafted, not a temporary cabin, and authentically furnished. (The nature center staff includes an historian.) Other log buildings moved to the site include a barn, a log schoolhouse, and a sugarhouse used every weekend in March for very popular maple syrup-making demonstrations. *The homestead buildings are open for special events and on Sunday afternoons, 1-4, May through October. Walkers are otherwise welcome to look in the windows.*

◆ **Weekend programs**, usually free and geared to families, are usually on Saturday and Sunday afternoons. Early October's **Fall Harvest Festival** and March's **Maple Syrup Festival** are big annual events. *Southwest of downtown Midland on Badour Rd. at the Chippewa River. From downtown, take Poseyville Rd. across bridge, turn right immediately onto St. Charles, turn left onto Whitman. In 3 miles, turn right at sign for nature center. (517) 631-0830. Mon-Fri 8-5, Sat 9-5, Sun 1-5. Free.*

Dow Gardens

A place of year-round beauty and harmony,
it fosters exploring and playful creativity
and shows what's possible in your own yard.

As soon as you enter the Dow Gardens, you're aware of how unusual they are. Signs and brochures invite you to explore the gardens by walking anywhere, including the grass. (But don't climb rocks and waterfalls.) One of the first things you see are not flower beds or a striking vista but a stand of tall pines with remarkable chunky bark — a clear hint that texture, form, and contrasts are as important here as more obvious displays of colorful blooms. Some staffers like the gardens best of all in winter, after a fresh snow.

The design of the place beckons and draws you in, to explore an unfolding array of environments. Past the pine grove, the trail squeezes between massive boulders crossed by a splashing waterfall, then opens out to the annual flower beds and rose garden on your left. To your right is a maze formed by viburnums. Beyond that, an Oriental-looking red bridge draws your eye up a meandering creek.

In the rarefied ranks of great American gardens, the Dow Gardens are *most* unusual — fresh and creative. They owe little to the European gardens imitated by wealthy American industrialists who built Italian palazzi, Tudor mansions, or Norman French castles and installed gardens to go with them.

Visitors often call the Dow Gardens Japanese or Oriental because of the striking red bridge, the emphasis on textures and rocks, and the design principle of inviting you to explore without showing an overview of the entire place. Director Doug Chapman bristles at the idea that these gardens are Japanese. He wastes no time in explaining that these are *American* gardens and nothing else. Japanese gardens are small and very, very controlled miniature environments of highly selected plant materials. They are fussily maintained, pruned, and raked down to the last detail.

The Dow Gardens are big — 66 acres altogether, quite enormous when compared with gardens that seem large but are really just half a dozen acres. Yet the staff of gardeners here is quite small. Maintenance is relaxed. Occasional weeds are allowed to invade the lawn. Sprays and pruning are minimized. This is no minimal, sparse, symbolic landscape like a Japanese garden. The

famous red bridge here is red because red is the natural complement of green, not because it's supposed to look Oriental.

A broad range of plants, not just choice specimens, are allowed
to grow here, but only if they do well in Midland's cold winters
and sandy soils, and only if they help create a sense of balanced
harmony. "There is no such thing as a bad plant, just a bad place"
is an operating principle, illustrated by the presence of a big silver maple, commonly considered a weed tree for its messy habits.

The gardens are really the extended back yard of Dow Chemical
founder Herbert Dow. Creative and questioning by nature, he had
always been interested in shaping his surroundings. When he
arrived at Midland, a landscape of stumps surrounded the declining lumbering town. Beginning in 1899, he landscaped his house
here to show what fellow townspeople could do with their own
yards, and kept the grounds open to the public. Dow's forest
green house, facing West Main, can be seen from the far side of
the gardens.

Dow, an enthusiastic traveler, became friends with a noted
designer of Tokyo parks, who visited Midland frequently and
shared landscaping ideas with Dow and other Midlanders. Lack of
money had early prevented Dow from studying architecture; it
was no surprise when his youngest son, Alden, forsook engineering and a Dow Chemical career for architecture.

**Alden Dow's studio
home overlooks the
Dow Gardens.**

Alden Dow became one of Frank Lloyd Wright's original Taliesin fellows. In his own long (1934-1973) architectural career, based in Midland, he remained absorbed in harmoniously joining architecture and nature — a clear debt to Wright, and to the Japanese. "Gardens never end, and buildings never begin," he liked to say. He found many ways to bring the outdoors inside and extend architecture out, via retaining walls, paving, bridges, and other garden structures. No better example exists than these gardens and **Alden Dow's own studio-home**, one of the most celebrated of all 20th-century houses. You glimpse it from the gardens beyond the red bridge, a long, low house with extending copper-green eaves that seems to float on the pond that surrounds most of it.

Renewing the Dow Gardens, which had fallen into disrepair, and extending them became Alden Dow's retirement project in the 1970s. Working with director Doug Chapman, a former Michigan State University extension horticulturist, he refined favorite design ideas, added over a thousand different trees and shrubs, and built a visitor center and classroom building. The reorganized Gardens extended Herbert Dow's original philosophy of helping and inspiring the backyard gardener. Call (517) 631-2677 for information on one-day **gardening workshops**.

In the gardens Alden Dow developed smaller fantasy environments that bring out the playful child in visitors. (The Dow family — Herbert, Alden, and others — considered creative play an important part of adult life.) Stepping stones cross the creek. A **"jungle walk"** through a hilly thicket leads to a hidden pool and wildflower garden. There's an irregular **maze** through viburnums, and a **land sculpture** of rounded miniature mountains.

Visit the gardens in the gentle, playful spirit of Alden Dow. Follow your instincts and explore. Don't stay on the main path. Don't let the map guide you. And don't pay much attention to the plant labels. Instead, follow the sound of plashing water or the scent of wet pine needles. If a distant object beckons, go there.

If you only have a little time, visit the **sensory trail** (for people who have lost one or more senses) by the main entrance and the nearby **boulders and waterfall**. If you have longer, you can check out the special areas like the **herb garden**, or **All-America display garden** of annual flowers, or the **rose garden** or **perennial garden**. The sizable, attractive **gift shop** emphasizes books on horticulture, garden planning, and nature, with some plant-related gift items and cards.

The Gardens are next to the Midland Center for the Arts on Eastman Rd. (Bus. Rte. 10) at West St. Andrew's, just northwest of downtown Midland. (517) 631-2677. $2 for admission card good all year. Children 5 and under free. Open 7 days a week at 10 a.m.

During Standard Time, closing is at 4:15. After Daylight Savings, closes at 7, gradually lengthening to 8:30 in summer, cutting back to 7 and 6 in fall.

MORE OF ALDEN DOW'S BEST WORKS . . . . . , including Dow's studio, are part of an interesting, worthwhile **Midland Architectural Tour** on cassette tape, meant for your car's tape deck. It may be rented for $5 at the Midland Center for the Arts, right next to the Dow Gardens. (The center is open from 10 a.m. until performances and classes are over at night). The homes Dow designed in the 1930s and 1940s are a must for anyone interested in his teacher, Frank Lloyd Wright. The narrated tour takes you through Midland's most elite neighborhoods and surveys noteworthy historic architecture from the 19th century to a 1957 space-age dome, insulated with Dow Chemical's Styrofoam. The tour takes at least an hour and a half — with options, two hours or more. It's like having a well-informed local resident show you around. An **annual tour of Dow designs** always includes a visit inside his studio-house — a fascinating place, full of playful surprises including a toy train collection and the so-called "Submarine Conference Room." (The pond outside comes up to its windows.) Call 1-800-678-1961 for information.

A LAVISH COMMUNITY CENTER FOR THE ARTS. . . . . is one of Alden Dow's ugliest buildings, the **Midland Center for the Arts,** next to the Dow Gardens. The interior space is much nicer, something like Wright's Guggenheim Museum. It includes a splendid performance space, changing **art and history exhibits** (on the 4th floor), and an attractive **gift shop** with handmade and ethnic gifts and jewelry. The unusual **Hall of Ideas** (levels 1-3) starts with geological eras in Michigan and a Foucault pendulum and ends with *you* and your possibilities for contributing to the future. It's a typically dynamic, Dow approach that joins art and history, business and science in an idiosyncratic synthesis. The hands-on exhibits are unusual and stimulating if you're fresh. (This is serious stuff with a lot of reading, big on science and technology, and overwhelming if you're tired.) *On Eastman Rd. (Bus. Rte. 10) at St. Andrew's, just northwest of downtown Midland. Call (517) 631-5930 for performance and exhibit information. Hall of Ideas open 10-6 weekdays, 1-5 weekends. No fee; donation appreciated.*

PICNICKING . . . . . is encouraged in the **park by the Tridge,** architect Alden Dow's unique three-legged arched footbridge at the confluence of the Chippewa and Tittawabasse rivers in downtown Midland. There are picnic tables and grills, and you can walk across the Tittabawasse to a playground in Chippewassee Park. Take Ashman from Business Route 10 west into the heart of downtown all the way down to the river. The Tridge is right there, along with a lively **farmers' market,** open Wednesdays and Saturdays from spring through fall.

Recommended Restaurants & Lodgings

Saginaw Valley & the Thumb

Regional map p. 234.

PORT AUSTIN

🍴

The Bank. *8646 Lake downtown. (517) 738-5353. Open from late April to mid-Oct. Mem.-Labor Day Tues-Sun, otherwise Thurs-Sun, 5-10. MC, Visa, AmEx. Full bar, select wine list.* Limited menu, choice selections. *N.Y. Times* praised fish cookery. Fresh Lake Superior walleye ($14), whitefish ($12), perch from Sag. Bay ($13). Prime rib ($15-$17), also shrimp scampi ($15), chicken Wellington ($14). All w/ sourdough bread, tossed salad, potato. Thoughtfully chosen appetizers, desserts ($3.75 & under) like pot de creme, fresh fruit pies, choc. truffle torte. Children welcome. In 1884 brick bank.

Chuck & Jane's. *8714 Lake St. Follow M-53 into Port Austin to lake. (517) 738-7111. Thurs-Tues (closed Wed) 6 a.m.-9 p.m. MC, Visa, AmEx. No alcohol. Lunches about $5, dinners $5-$9. Both include beverage.* Locals' top pick for family dining. Dinner favorites: roast beef, fried perch ($9 w/ salad bar). For lunch, 1/4 lb. burger ($2.25), specials. All day: sandwiches, baskets of chicken or shrimp ($5), 21-item salad bar ($2 for 1 trip, $4 unlimited). Homemade pie $1.25/slice.

Garfield Inn. *8544 Lake St. just e. of downtown. (517) 738-5254. Summer hours: Sun for dinner, Mon-Sat (except Tues) 12-2:30 & 5-10. Winter: Fri & Sat 5-10. MC, Visa, AmEx. Full bar.* Ambitious cuisine comes to the Thumb w/ chef who apprenticed at The Lark. His dinner picks: sesame encrusted salmon w/ soy ginger sauce ($19), filet mignon w/ herbed boursin cheese wrapped in smoked beef ($22). Seafood flown in from Boston daily. Mainstream budget choice: 1/2 roast chicken w/ potatoes & giblet gravy ($13). All w/ salad, starch. For lunch: chef's choice of 2-3 entrees $5-$10 w/ appropriate side. Changing seasonal dessert $4-$7. Massive Italianate house w/ fabulous woodwork.

🐖

The Castaways. *(517) 738-5101. 1404 Port Austin Rd. on Lake Huron, 3 mi. w. of Port Austin.* 36 rooms on 2 floors. Open all year. $45 (w/ lake view), $35. Mem.-Labor Day: $60, $55. Cable TV. Kitchenettes avail. 10 cottages sleep 8, $325-$428/week. Horseshoes, bonfires, picnic tables & grills, playground, volleyball, supervised children's activities in summer. Sunset views. Restaurant w/ dinner music, dancing Thurs-Sat in summer.
Many activities, beach, moderate rates

Lake Vista Motel & Cottages. *(517) 738-8612. 168 W. Spring on Lake Huron, 2 blocks w. of M-53 on w. edge of town.* 18 units on 1 floor. June 15-Sept 15: $50 midweek, $54 weekend. Off-season $39. Horseshoes, picnic grills, playground. Snack bar. Sell bait, fishing supplies.
Trim, cute older motel, in-town lakefront location

PORT SANILAC

🍴

Wayside Inn. *4250 N. Lakeshore Rd. 8 1/2 mi. n. of Port Sanilac on M-25. (313) 376-4148. Mon-Thurs 10-8, Fri-Sat 10-9:30, Sun 12-7 (closed Mon in winter). Visa, MC. Full bar.* Lunches under $5 w/ slaw. Dinners $7.25-$14. Casual, simple family spot praised by locals. Known for prime rib (8 oz, $9.25, 14 oz. $11).

Mary's Diner. *14 N. Ridge (M-25) downtown. (313) 622-9377. Mon-Thurs 7 a.m.-8 p.m., Fri-Sat to 9, Sun 7-7. Shorter winter hours. No credit cards or alcohol. Same menu al day.* Totally unpretentious, wildly popular for good food, low prices. Busy on weekends; reservations recommended.

Daily breakfast special $3.25. 1/3 lb. burger $2. Lunch special $3.50. Known for fresh fish. Perch or whitefish dinners $8 w/ soup, salad, starch or w/ terrific weekend salad bar of unusually good homemade salads ($3.25 alone). Desserts $1-$2.25 include hot cream puffs, strawberry shortcake.

🐕 Raymond House Inn. (313) 622-8800. 111 S. Ridge (M-25) on s. edge of downtown. 7 large roomw w/ baths in antique-filled, comfortable 1871 brick house. Walk downtown, to pretty park, marina. Full breakfast, pleasant yard. Innkeeper's pottery studio in back. *B&B with history, comfort, good location, genial hosts*

FRANKENMUTH
🍴

Bavarian Inn.(517) 652-9941. 713 S. Main, downtown. Open daily, 10 a.m.-9 p.m. or later. Visa, MC, AmEx. Full bar. Of the Zehnder family's 2 huge fried chicken restaurants, this one went German-theme in Alpine decor, dirndl-clad waitresses, German specialties ($11 sausage plate, $16 family-style 5-meat dinner). Of course there's fried chicken $11-$12 w/ soup, salad, potato, 3 relishes, ice cream. At lunch, soups ($1-$2), sandwiches. Lots of food, good value, OK food.

Zehnder's. 730 S. Main St. (517) 652-9925. Daily 11-9:30, coffee shop 8-9. Visa, MC, Disc, AmEx. Home of the famous Frankenmuth family-style chicken dinners ($11.50): unfussy country cooking, lots of food (dinner includes refills, lots of sides, beverage, ice cream), good service, so-so quality (after all, the two Zehnder family restaurants are among the 10 biggest U.S. restaurants). Early American theme. Lunches (Mon-Sat) $6.25-$9, dinners (w/soup, salad, potato, vegetable) to $17 for steaks, seafood. Known for Black forest torte and apple pie ($2.25-$3). Basement coffee shop serves breakfast ($4.50-$5), sandwiches, lunch-type entrees.

Main Street Tavern. See p. 241. The real Frankenmuth. Plain, not a bit cute. Simple, excellent food, almost all locally produced. Great value.

Gepetto's. 281 Heinlein Strasse, directly behind Bronner's. Take Weiss St. off M-83 to Heinlein St. (517) 652-6060. Open 7 days 11-10 (closes earlier in winter) MC, Visa, Disc, AmEx, Diners. Full bar. Updated Italian in mood, better-than-average food — something different for Frankenmuth. Diners look onto central bar on main floor and from 2nd-floor balconies. Butcher paper-topped tables supplied with crayons. All entrees include homemade bread, salad or slaw, vegetables. Lunch $6-$11. Dinner from $7.50 (linguine w/ marinara sauce) to $15 (prime rib or specialty fish). BBQ or garlic-broiled shrimp $12, BBQ ribs $9-$14. 12" cheese pizza $7 + .50 per item. Desserts (Sanders hot fudge treats, apple mountain) $1.75-$3.

Tiffany Biergarten. 656 S. Main, 3 doors n. of Zehnder's. (616) 652-6881. 7 days 11-11. Visa, MC. Full bar. Convenient location on main pedestrian drag, good food, great, authentic atmosphere in old hotel with intact turn-of-the-century bar in lumberman's baroque, complete with lots of stained glass, elaborate murals, and tile cuspidor trough at bar's base. Family atmposphere. Takeout available. Menu same all day. Sandwiches from $3 (pizza sub or bratwurst) to $5 (chargrilled chicken breast). Round and Sicilian pizzas from $7 to $10 plus extras. Housemade pasta, steaks.

🐎 Bavarian Inn Lodge. (517) 652-2651. 1 block e. behind Bavarian Inn restaurant. 198 rooms on 4 floors. $79-$89 for 1-4 people. Suites & packages avail. Cable TV. 2 indoor pools, 2 whirlpools, game room, exercise room, play area, pool tables, snack bar. Restaurant, bar w/ entertainment. *Family fun center*

Zehnder's Bavarian Haus Motel.
*(517) 652-6144. 1365 S. Main St., near
Bronner's.* 114 rooms on 2 floors.
Summer $69-$78. Off-season $60. Jan-
Apr weekdey special $59 includes 2
chicken dinners at Zehnder's. Satel-
lite TV. Outdoor pool (indoor by winter
1991), sauna, jacuzzi, exercise equip.
Coffee shop.
Outstanding spring values

BRIDGEPORT

Garten Haus Inn. *(517) 777-2582.
6361 Dixie Hwy., exit 144 B off I-75.*
111 rooms on 1 floor. May-Nov: $38-
$53. Dec-May: $27. Cable TV.
*New, pleasant budget choice 8 miles
from Frankenmuth*

Heidelberg Inn Motel. *(517)
777-2195. 6815 Dixie Hwy., 8 mi. n .of
Frankenmuth.* 14 rooms on 1 floor.
Summer $42, lower off-season. Cable
TV.
Budget choice close to Frankenmuth

SAGINAW

Montague Inn. *1581 S. Washington
(M-13) across from Hoyt Park just s. of
downtown. 1/4 mi. n. of Rust (M-46).
(517) 752-3939. Tues-Sat 11:30-2 &
510.* AmEx, MC, Visa. Full bar. Lunch
$6.25-$9.75, dinner $14.50-$24, both
include salad, appropriate side dish.
Elegant dining in impressive Georgian
mansion, park-like setting. Uniformly good food, from house-made bread
basket to coffee, desserts ($3.50). Nor-
wegian salmon ($18.50), other fresh
seafood popular on widely varied
seasonal menu. Wide variety of dishes,
menu changes 3 times a year.

El Farolito. *1346 N. Washington
across from massive GMC Grey Iron
Foundry 2 mi. n. of downtown. Easy
stop from I-75: Take exit 153 s. about 1
mi. (517) 771-9460. Mon-Thurs 10-9,
Fri -Sat 10-3:30 a.m., Sun 10-7.* MC,
Visa. Beer, wine, margaritas. Saginaw's east side is home to many Mexi-
can-Americans, originally drawn by
work for railroads, sugar beet refiner-

ies. This modest spot is considered
most authentic of many Mexican restaurants. Popular standards (tacos,
tamales) at great prices: $3.25 for any
2 plus beans, rice, salsa $3.25. What's
unusual are old Mexican dishes: chich-
arrone (pork rind) con chile, lengua
(beef tongue) en salsa, menudo (tripe
soup w/hominy). Breakfast all day
$3.75-$5 , Mex. or American style.
Steak fajita dinner tops menu: $8.50
w/ fries, beans, rice, salad.

Casa Chapa. *1319 E. Genesee at Hoyt.
1 1/2 mi. s.e. of downtown. (517) 752-
9381. 7 days 9-8.* Mexican bakery -
grocery (takeout only). Try simple
cookies ($3/dozen) if you like sweets
that aren't rich. From the deli, weekends, make your own sandwich. BBQ
beef, deep-fried pord $4.25/lb. Wrap in
tortillas, eat in Hoyt Park (good
children's zoo). Huge pieces of chichar-
rones (fried pork rinds) $5.50 lb.

Montague Inn. *(517) 752-3939. 1581
S. Washington, M-13, across from
Hoyt Park. 1 1/2 mi. s. of downtown.*
18 rooms (16 w/ baths), 13 in 3-story
1928 Georgian mansion, 5 in guest
house. 18th-c. English antique repro
furniture. $60-$130. Big, good cont.
breakfast. A/C, TV. Library; parlor
sometimes used by outside parties.
Outstanding restaurant for lunch, dinner. On 8 park-like acres. Original
owner made fortune developing hand
lotion & cleanser from area sugar
beets, selling out to Jergens.
*Elegant getaway near antiquing,
Japanese tea house*

Holiday Inn. *(517) 755-0461. I-75 &
M-46 on busy strip east of Saginaw.*
158 rooms on 4 floors. $57-$73. Cable
TV. Holidome: indoor pool, whirlpool,
sauna, exercise room, rec. area, 1
racquet ball court. Restaurant, bar
w/wknd entertainment.
Holidome near Frankenmuth

Knights Inn South. *(517) 754-
9200. 1403 S. Outer Dr at I-75 & M-46
on busy strip east of Saginaw.* 109
rooms on 1 floor. $41, less in winter..
Cable TV. Outdoor pool.
Near Frankenmuth, reasonable rates

Sheraton Fashion Square Inn.
(517) 790-5050. At I-675 & Tittaba-wasee on busy strip n. of downtown. 156 rooms on 6 floors. $92. Packages avail. Cable TV. Indoor pool, whirl-pool, sauna, hot tub, game room. Restaurant, bar w/ entertainment. Next to Fashion Square Mall, movies. *Luxury choice with lots of activities*

BAY CITY

Krzysiak's House.
1605 Michigan just s. of Cass about 2 mi. s. e. of downtown. (From I-75, go n. on M- 13 to edge of town, east on Cass 1/2 mi. (517) 894-5531. Open daily 6:30 a.m. -9 p.m., except Sun clising at 8, Fri & Sat to 10. AmEx, Visa, MC. Full bar.
Amazing unlimited buffet at bustling, pleasant Polish restaurant w/ Polish groceries for sale, own butcher shop nearby. Very good food , especially considering the hard-to-believe prices. Buffet changes w/ day. At lunch we had pasta salads, delicious deboned BBQ ribs, meatballs, pierogi, kraut, spicy cabbage roll, more for $5 (11-2). Dinner (4-8 p.m.) includes walleye, chicken, BBQ ($4.59 Tues, $5.79 Wed & Thurs), $13 Fri & Sat — with unlimited NY strip & prime rib. Also very good: Polish combination platter ($5 at lunch). A great rest stop on I-75 trips!

Terry & Jerry's O Sole Mio.
1005 Saginaw, downtown. From I-75 exit 162A, take B.R. 75/M-25 e. 2 mi. to downtown (e. side of river), left onto Saginaw. Lunch Tues-Fri 11-2. Dinner: Tues-Thurs 5-10, Fri & Sat to 10:30, Sun 4-10. Visa, AmEx, BanA, MC.
Since 1951. Warm and casual (pine paneling, paintings on walls), draws locals & travelers alike. Big menu w/ many specialties, mostly prepared in classic Italian manner: veal (around $16), steaks, tenderloin prepared w/ several Italian sauces (about $20-$26), fresh fish in season ($13-$15). Wonderful spaghetti (from $8 to $12 w/ shrimp). All the old favorites, too: chicken cacciatore ($11.65), meat ball diner ($9), ravioli ($8.55).

William Clements Inn.
(517) 894-4600.1712 Center (M-25) in area of lumbermen's big houses, about 1 mi. from downtown. 6 rooms w/ baths (2 w/ fireplaces) on 2nd floor. $59-$89. Full breakfast. A/C. TV, phones. Big 1886 home built by lumberman-crane mfr. Wm. Clements. Organ & piano for guests' use. Elaborate woodwork, gas lights intact.
B&B in memorable historic area; band concerts in nearby park

Euclid Motel.
(517) 684-9455. 809 N. Euclid, 2 mi. w. of downtown on busy strip. From I-75 exit 162A, take M-25 e. about 2 mi. , n. on Euclid. 3 6 units on 1 floor. $31-$40. Cable TV. Outdoor pool, playground, basketball. *Outdoor sports, low rates, easy I-75 access*

BAY CITY TO MIDLAND

Shari at the Willard Hilton.
W. Beaver at 11 Mile in what used to be Willard, about 9 mi. n.e. of Midland. From I-75, take Beaver Rd. exit w. 4 mi. (517) 662-6621. Mon-Sat 6-10, closes earlier in winter. Group lunches arranged for 10 or more. Old country tavern w/ improbably creative and affordable cuisine from Culinary Institute alum Shari Smith. Four stars from Molly Abraham. Attention lavished on everything from complimentary appetizer, soups, terrific pastas, classic Caesar salad, to house-made ice creams, French custard creme desserts ($3.50-$5.50). Bistro menu ($9-$13), dinner menu ($11-$21, many grilled meats w/ interesting sauces) both served w/ appropriate sides. Entree salads $7-$11. A perennial standout: seafood strudel ($9) in phyllo dough w/ orange butter sauce.

Bay Valley Hotel & Resort.
(517) 686-3500. 2470 Old Bridge Rd. (M-84) , 1/4 mi. s.w. of I-75, M-84 exit 160. 151 rooms on 3 floors. Summer: $95-$108. Winter: $69-$105. Suites, packages

avail. Cable TV. Indoor/outdoor pool, sauna, whirlpool, exercise equip. Fees for 12 tennis courts (6 indoor, 6 clay outdoor), 18 hole championship golf course. Rentals: paddle boats, canoes, bikes. X-c ski trails & equip, skating rink. Summer rec. & childrens' programs. Restaurant, bar w/ weekend entertainment.
Full-scale resort w/ golf, many activities & rentals; close to all Tri-Cities attractions

MIDLAND

Cafe Edward. *5010 Bay City Rd., 1/4 mi. w. of U.S. 10 exit on e. side of Midland. From I-75, take U.S. 10, 10 mi. w. (517) 496-3012. Mon-Sat 5-10. AmEx, MC, Visa. Full bar; extensive wine list.* Wonderful food, incredible value; 3-course meal (appetizer, entree, dessert) for $9 to $21. The sumptuous meals at Justine's (same chef, same place) drew raves from Detroit-area diners but couldn't make it in tight-fisted Midland. Cafe Edward is less involved, country European. Feast on the likes of snails in a herbed tarte, scallop and vegetable salad, warm chicken livers (appetizers), tart lemon pie or rich chocolate marquise for dessert. Entrees from $9 (duck or venison sausage w/ red cabbage, spaetzle) to $20 (country roast — amy be lamb, veal, beef). Cooking from scratch, own meat-cutting, fresh fish flown in. Famed for service. Linens, formal but comfortable room.

Valley Plaza Inn. *(800) 825-2700, (517) 496-2700. 5221 Bay City Rd. just w. off U.S. 10 on e. edge of Midland. From I-75, take U.S. 10 10 mi. w., exit at Bay City Rd.* .237 rooms on 2 floors. $73 2-5 people. Packages avail. Cable TV. Indoor pool, whirlpool, sauna, game room. Lake w/sandy beach, 40-lane bowling center, health club, 3-screen movie theater. Campground. 2 restaurants. 2 bars. On busy freeway interchange. Cafe Edward across road.
Multi-faceted year-round resort

Holiday Inn. *(517) 631-4220. Eastman Rd. exit off U.S. 10., n. w. side of Midland on busy strip.* 220 rooms on 2 floors. $77. Satellite TV. Holidome: indoor pool, whirlpool, sauna, game & exercise rooms. Racquetball avail. Restaurant, lounge w/ video bar.
Holidome; convenient to Dow Gardens

The Bramble House B&B. *(517) 832-5082. 4309 Brambleridge in elite residential neighborhood, 2 mi. from U.S. 10 Eastman exit.* 3 rooms, 1 w/ private bath, 2 share bath. $70-$80. A/C. TV optional, phone avail. Full breakfast, soup on arrival. Use of entire house; family room w/ fireplace & TV, library w/ fireplace, living and dining rooms, big porch.
Luxurious living in large contemporary house, beautiful area

Chapter 6
Mid-Michigan

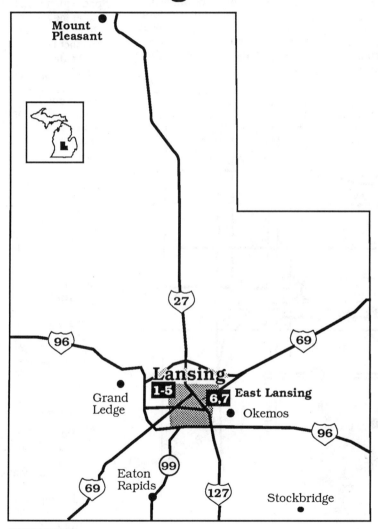

❶ State Capitol. Masterpiece of Victorian decorating. See politicians in action Tuesday through Thursday.

❷ Michigan Historical Museum. Fine visuals present history with flair. Lumbering, mining, & prehistory stand out.

❸ Washington Street. Daytime-only downtown. Architecture and a few good shops make it worth a look.

❹ Riverfront Park and River Trail. 5 1/2 mile pedestrian/bike path along the Grand and Red Cedar rivers connect lively destinations

❺ City Market. Fresh produce, baked goods, cheese, meat, and more, sold indoors year-round.

❻ Elderly Instruments. America's headquarters for folk recordings & instruments is a category killer with amazing selection and savvy staff.

❼ Three unusual museums. Impressions 5: Michigan's best hands-on museum. A car museum featuring Lansing's Ransom Olds. Plus the only U.S. surveying museum.

❽ Potter Park and Zoo. Riverside picnic grove, playground, canoe rentals. Pleasant small zoo perfect for brief visits. (Map shows entrance only. Park is to east.)

Highlights of
Lansing

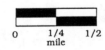

0   1/4   1/2
mile

Michigan State Capitol

*A tour de force of rich Victorian decorating
that's intense with political energy*

Michigan's state capitol is an exciting place to visit for the
spectacle it presents of seeing lawmakers in action in a
richly decorated Victorian setting. The high-domed
exterior looks like a state capitol ought to look: formal and impressive. Finished in 1879, it was the first state capitol modeled
after the nation's Capitol, which had itself been remodeled during
the Civil War. Lincoln insisted that capitol construction continue
despite the war because the Capitol stood for the union. The tall
central dome was made possible by using cast iron, a new and
relatively inexpensive building material. A Michigan soldier's letters home mentioned that the unfinished dome was the first
thing he saw coming into Washington to join the fight, and that
the finished dome was the last thing he saw leaving Washington
finally to return home. The capitol with the finished dome, he
said, represented everything he had fought for.

Before Michigan's capitol was built, state capitols had come in
many styles, including Greek temples and Gothic castles. Michigan's use of the national Capitol as a model established that
building form as the very symbol of the democratic form of government: the central dome standing for the executive branch and
the balanced wings for the senate and house of representatives.
This form set the standard for virtually all state capitols to come.

Even on the exterior, details like the oval windows in the dome hint that this building is no stern exercise in Roman dignity, but a product of the Gilded Age. The interior is rich in vivid colors, contrasting decorative textures and patterns (including plaster swirled like tight waves, and lots of gold leaf), and ornamental details like chandeliers embellished with stags. It was a tour de force for its cost-conscious architect, Elijah Myers, who called for very little marble, expensive stone, or cabinet-grade wood. Most of the opulent effect was achieved with elaborate painted designs on plaster, and with pine grained to resemble walnut. Myers' success with Michigan's capitol enabled him to win later commissions for capitols in Texas. Idaho, and Colorado.

A careful restoration, begun in 1987, has now finished renewing beautiful painted wall decorations and an elaborate ceiling in the Senate and House chambers. The Senate walls, no longer a cautious, conservative forest green, have returned to their original colors, predominantly a rich Prussian blue with trim of the elaborate plasterwork in several shades of warm yellows, gold, and rose. An electronic display board is concealed in the wall until the board's lights are turned on. It shows proposed legislation and records the legislators' votes on it. Ceiling panels of ruby glass etched with seals of all the states can again be seen — a favorite with visitors. The House has received a similar treatment in its original color scheme: vibrant corals, teals, and metallic silver, bronze, copper, and pewter.

However, the rotunda will be filled with scaffolding through 1991 at least, and the walls of main hallways and stairways are being worked on. It's interesting to be able to look at the work in progress, by the noted painting restorer Darla Olson and her team. By 1992 the governors' portraits and the flags carried by Michigan's Civil War regiments in battle will be back. You can then again get the spectacular full effect of looking up at the richly patterned dome with its starry inner eye, and down to the floor below from the fourth-story gallery.

The capitol building is merely a magnificent stage set for the drama of everyday government. Controversies are played out and laws are made right here. When important legislation is being voted on, the entrance lobbies to the house and senate chambers really are filled with lobbyists — so-called because they must wait in lobbies. Barred from the legislative floor, they send messages to legislators via pages and confer with them in the lobby.

The capitol and all its public meeting rooms are open to all Michigan citizens; as the colorful tour guide, Tony Dodos, repeatedly points out, "Everyone here — the governor, your representative, me — works for *you.* You pay us every time you pay a state tax." Some retirees attend legislative sessions regularly and keep scorecards of the proceedings as if they were at a ball game.

Here's what you need to know to be able to observe the legislature in action and figure out what's going on:

◆ Call the **Capitol Tour Guide and Information Service** at (517) 335-1483 to find out if the legislature is in session and to find out who your representatives are if you don't know. Normally the legislature is in session Tuesdays through Thursdays (occasionally well on into the evening and early morning). Breaks are at Christmas (3-4 weeks), Easter (2 weeks), and summer (from June or July into September).

◆ Your representative will be happy to phone or mail you information on what's happening on a given day, or when action is scheduled on particular bills, or the dates of hearings on subjects that concern you.

◆ Bring your binoculars. Otherwise you probably won't be able to read the nameplates on each legislator's desk.

◆ If at all possible, go on a free **capitol tour** when the legislature is in session. Tours leave every half hour from the tour desk in the ground floor, east (front) wing. Call (517) 335-1483 for groups of 10 or more. From March through May, you'll probably be with an elementary school group, but you'll still learn a lot you didn't know. When the tour group is on the balcony, your guide can show you how to figure out what's going on.

Tours generally last about half an hour, but if you request guide Tony Dodos, you'll be treated to a longer, more personal introduction to state government that's both inspirational and irreverently humorous. Dodos loves the political process, and it shows. Unlike most guides, he knows the place and its people from the inside out, having served as a capitol page and intern.

◆ Stop by your senator or representative's office for a look around and to pick up interesting free material, including a capitol walking tour, a coloring book for kids, and an introduction to state government. Especially helpful for your visit and for having input on legislation is *A Citizen's Guide to State Government*, with lobbying tips and legislators' photos and addresses.

◆ At the ground-floor tour guide desk in the east (front) wing, get a map. The printed journal of yesterday's legislative proceedings and today's agenda can be had for no charge at the Documents Room in the ground floor north wing, off Ottawa Street. (You can also ask for copies of any state laws.)

◆ Visitors are free to sit in the balconies in the rear of the senate or house, and in the senate and house fourth-floor conference rooms during any public proceedings. In the senate, speakers' voices come over a p.a. system, so it's hard to tell who's talking. Look for the microphones on the side aisles, where senators come to speak. A light goes on by the speaker's microphone. What's being considered on the floor is displayed on the electronic display board; refer to your agenda to learn more about it.

On Capitol at the head of Michigan Avenue in downtown Lansing. From I-496, take Grand or Walnut exits and go north. The capitol is open weekdays from 8 to 5 (first tour at 8:20, last tour at 4); Sat 10-4 (tours on the hour; last tour at 3); and Sun 12-4 (tours at 1, 2, and 3). Free admission. For group tours and questions on state government, contact the Capitol Tour Guide and Information Service, ground floor, north (front) wing, (517) 335-1483. Convenient parking is in structures at S. Capitol and Allegan (just south of the Capitol), at Capitol and Kalamazoo, and at Grand north of Ottawa.

BEFORE YOUR GROUP VISIT TO THE CAPITOL . . . . . you can see an outstanding **video** about its construction, history, and the renovation process. The Michigan Capitol Committee will mail it to you free of charge. Sign up early, especially in spring. Call (517) 373-5527, or write the committee in care of L.S.B., 124 W. Allegan, Box 30036, Lansing, MI 48909.

THE PLEASURES OF DOWNTOWN LANSING . . . . . aren't exactly obvious. Urban renewal in the 1960s accelerated the loss of retailing. Today downtown is geared to weekday office workers, with lots of quick lunch spots, card shops, and a good Woolworth's. It's pretty much dead on evenings and Sundays. But a stroll down Washington from Michigan Avenue has its high points, starting with the **Manufacturers Bank** on that corner. The elaborate sculptures on the pilasters of the Romanesque portal incorporate Lansing products (including a Reo auto) and institutions. The splendid original 1932 interior is worth a a look. **The Peanut Shop** at 117 S. Washington is an old-fashioned nut shop (candies, too) which has an ancient peanut-shaped nut roaster. You can get a nifty Mr. Peanut bank for under $3. **Michigania** at 212 S. Washington specializes in Michigan-made foods, souvenirs, books, and crafts.

When you come to the Italian Renaissance facade of the 1921 **Michigan Theater**, now converted to office, look inside. It still has its original interior arcade and rear grand staircase to the balcony, where beautiful floral stained glass casts a gentle golden glow. Some real deals are to be found at the **Junior League Cedar Chest**, an unusually well organized resale shop at 221 S. Washington. **Kilimanjaro**, 237 S. Washington at Washtenaw, offers an unusual mix of jewelry, beads, scarves, accessories, and artifacts from around the world, especially from Africa. Michigan's most futuristic Art Deco building is the 1937 J. W. Knapp department store, now **Knapp's Office Center**, on Washington at Washtenaw. It's a sleek, streamlined affair of glass block and bright blue and yellow enamel panels. "Futuristic nostalgia," including clever T-shirts and consciously kitschy novelties, is the stock in trade of **Ma-Ahs**, on Washington at Kalamazoo. *Stores open weekdays and Saturday daytime only.*

Michigan Historical Museum

Michigan history through the 19th century,
told with visual pizzazz and architectural drama

After a century of being relegated to makeshift quarters, the state historical museum now enjoys a stunning new space and has become a major Michigan tourist destination. The combined museum/state library/archives complex, opened in 1989, is a real architectural and artistic show-stopper. Detroit architect William Kessler brilliantly played off contrasts between polished and rough surfaces and natural elements associated with Michigan, including limestone, copper, granite, and a 60-foot white pine, Michigan's state tree, carefully planted in the central court. In the museum entrance foyer, tall, narrow, light-filled spaces make you tilt your head back, look up, and understand just how tall the realistic fiberglass replicas of white pines in front of you really are.

The museum only covers up to 1900. The 20th-century exhibits are to be installed in the third floor. Many of the expensive, expertly made displays are memorable: an Indian canoe pulled into stretch of marsh and cattails in front of a realistic diorama of a lake; a lumberman's big wheel, 12 feet in diameter, used to move logs easily out of stump-filled forests; a two-story replica of the front part of Muskegon lumber baron Charles Hackley's elaborate Queen Anne home (see West Michigan chapter). Don't miss **"Growing Up in Michigan: 1880-1895"** in the mezzanine, which is entered up the house's stairs (opens November, 1991).

The historical narrative itself is honest and intelligent. No punches are pulled. Within a few generations of contact with Europeans, it says, Native American culture was nearly destroyed and their self-sufficient way of life had become dependent on manufactured goods. "Give the least to get the most" was the business motto of John Jacob Astor, whose fur empire drove the Michigan wilderness's economy in the first part of the 19th century.

For those who take the time to read and look, many basics — especially in geology, Indian cultures, and mining — are clearly explained and interestingly illustrated. The mining exhibit is especially detailed and satisfying (better than anything found in Copper Country today), down to specifics and samples of rock types and diagrams of the mining and smelting process. Visitors walk through a life-size passage of a **copper mine**, supported by leaning timbers, to see miners and carts and hear the boom of a distant blast. Interesting **video shows on lumbering and mining** by the state Bureau of History illuminate life in camps. Small sit-down theaters give your feet a rest.

What's disappointing here is the lack of labels identifying the locations of many photographs on display. The chief shapers of Michigan never come to life as the fascinating people they were. However, helpful volunteer **docents** are on hand to field visitors' questions and expand on exhibits. And the enlarged museum staff is collecting surveys and visitor feedback to improve the forth-coming exhibits after 1900.

On the lower level there's an **exhibit gallery** for changing shows, a large **snack area** with sandwiches (weekdays only) and vending machines, and an attractive small **museum shop** (closed Mondays) with books and gifts mostly about the exhibits.

The center is between Washtenaw and Allegan southwest of the capitol and east of Logan. See p. 264 for directional map. Park (free on weekends) just south of the building. (517) 373-3559. To schedule free tours of the Library and Historical Center for 10 or more, call (517) 335-1483. Mon-Fri 9-4:30, Sat 10-4, Sun 1-5. Free admission.

WHILE YOU'RE IN THE LIBRARY AND HISTORICAL CENTER . . . . pick up a pam-phlet about the striking, unusually powerful **art works** in the building, and take a look around. . . . . **Michigan residents** can easily get **library cards** for the Library **of Michigan,** Michigan's version of the Library of Congress, in the west wing. (Materials may be checked out for a month and mailed back.) Collections of this beautiful and very user-friendly library focus on all areas of government, from social services to highways and sewers, and on local history and Michigan authors. *(517) 373-5400. Mon-Fri 8-6, Sat 9-5, Sun 1-5, closed state holidays.*

LUNCH WHERE THE MOVERS AND SHAKERS HANG OUT. . . . . at the **Parthenon** restaurant (p. 287) at 227 S. Washington in downtown Lansing. The food — Greek and American, meat and vegetarian — is pretty good, and at the noon hour the place is packed with politicians and state employees. Political meetings and receptions are often held here, too.

Riverfront Park and Trail

A 5 1/2-mile riverside path through Lansing
connects museums and market, fishing spots and zoo.

Lansing is one of those cities that puts its worst foot forward. Casual visitors see its less attractive side right away.
Porn shops line two blocks of the Michigan Avenue vista
crowned by the capitol dome. Parking structures and empty
spaces dominate much of a downtown that comes to life only at
weekday lunch hours.

Lansing's real beauty spots are a
number of distinctive parks along the
Red Cedar and Grand rivers, which
join in Lansing. These places are so
hidden away, you have to already
know about them to see them. Riverfront Park, an award-winning linear
park along the Grand, is a marvelous
rarity in the Midwest: an urban park
and pathway that both dramatizes a
beautiful natural feature and connects
interesting destinations. Landscaping
features encourage walkers, joggers, fishermen, bicycles, and canoeists. The path is
so well used, night and day, that the park
has been virtually crime-free since it opened in 1976.

Here, as in most American cities, rivers attracted early industries and railroads. They became sewers and dumps. Warehouses
and factories blocked them from public view as long as industrial
activity remained centered downtown. The notion of an urban
greenway in Lansing, discussed since the 1920s, was finally realized as a Bicentennial project in 1976.

You could start the walk near Michigan Avenue. Parking by the
museums or city market is easiest to find and usually plentiful.
(Sometimes it's completely full in nice weather when there are
events.) But it's a more dramatic walk to start by the north end at
the dam and head toward the market and city center, with
Lansing's surprisingly impressive skyline ahead of you. A vivid
landscape really comes together here. There's the wide river and,
behind it, the skyline, dominated by the capitol dome, some new
glass buildings, and the warm orange and yellow bricks of two
fine Art Deco buildings, the Michigan National Bank tower and

the Board of Water and Light, Lansing's city-owned utility, with its landmark stack. Though many old warehouses were demolished for the park, enough industrial relics remain to give the walk some character. There are coal silos by the dam and the frame and girders of the old salt sheds by Lansing Community College.

North of Shiawassee Street the Grand's riverbanks haven't been artificially straightened and channelized. Here they have grown up wild with small, moisture-loving poplars, willows, and maples. This accidental landscaping softens the urban views and creates some lovely seasonal effects that look wonderful against the river's sparkling surface on sunny days: the spring-green of buds, bright yellows in fall, snow-traced branches in winter.

Highlights along the 5 1/2 mile riverwalk include:

◆ **The North Lansing dam, canoe and fishing platform, and fish ladder.** Some fishermen can nearly always be found at this beautiful spot, where a water-level platform provides easy access for canoeists and fishermen. The Grand's natural species here include catfish, suckers, carp, bass, bluegill, and perch. Walleye, coho, and steelhead have been planted. Fine organic sediments in runoff makes for water that's typically murky, but the Department of Natural Resources says without reservations that fish caught here are edible. **Grand River Bait and Tackle** (517-482-4461) is a block away at 123 E. Grand River by the bridge.

Off to one side, by the stone generator built to power Lansing's street lights, is an elaborate sculptural **fish ladder** on the very site of the cabin and dam built by Lansing's first settler in 1843. During the fall salmon run from late September to mid or late October, it's usually crowded with people scrutinizing the roiling waters of the fish ladder steps to get a glimpse of a big fish heroically struggling upstream to return to where she was hatched and deposit her eggs. **Benches and picnic tables** make this a nice place to linger. Park off of Race, which goes south off Grand River Avenue just east of the river itself.

◆ The fabled **Elderly Instruments** (p. 277) makes a good destination if you're walking north along the park from the market and museum area. It's just west of the river on Washington just south of Grand River Avenue. For a return trip downtown through what was Lansing's most elegant neighborhood circa 1900, go south on Washington.

◆ **A pedestrian and train bridge** are just south of the Saginaw Street bridge, near the tennis courts. Here you can cross the river to the busy **Lansing Community College campus** and the outdoor performing space by the salt sheds. For upcoming LCC **performances, lectures, and exhibits,** call 517-483-1880 weekdays.

◆ For delicious, spicy, quick **Thai food**, eat in or take out from

Bangkok House, on the south side of Saginaw in Riverfront Mall just east of the park. Benches (but no tables) overlook the river.

◆ The **Lansing City Market** occupies two enclosed market halls built in 1938. A smaller, enclosed version of Detroit's fabled Eastern market, it also continues the tradition of big-city markets as places where a broad spectrum of social classes and ethnic groups come together to shop. The market operates year-round, so even in winter there's fresh produce brought in from the south, along with locally produced maple syrup, eggs, apples, root vegetables, baked goods, and such. A cheese shop, meat market, and florist are more like stores than stalls. A good bakery features cookies, breads, and a number of meat, vegetable, and cheese pies for $2, and there's a snack bar with coffee. Sit down and eat at indoor picnic tables or the **picnic/restroom/playground area** by the river across the parking lot.

From spring through fall, the colors and smells of the plants and produce are wonderful. Here as at many markets, there are fewer farmers-producers and more purveyors of crafts and manufactured trinkets. Women from Lansing's Hmong community of Laotian refugees sometimes sell their intricate geometric and storytelling embroideries and appliques here usually around Christmas and in summer. *On Cedar (one-way southbound) at Shiawassee. From Michigan Avenue, go north on Larch, and west on Shiawassee, then south on Cedar. (517) 483-4300. Free parking on market days. Tues-Sat 8-5:30.*

◆ **A picnic area and small playground** are between the market and the river. For takeout food, try the market itself or Roma Bakery and Imported Foods, a longtime Italian grocery at 428 North Cedar across from the market.

◆ **The new Lansing Center** convention facility has been built between the market and Michigan Avenue. The path squeezes alongside it by the river to get to the museums. Walkers can cross the river to the Radisson Hotel and Grand parking garage on a handy skywalk, reached by stairs or elevator in the Lansing Center parking garage.

◆ **Impressions 5, the REO Museum, and the Michigan Museum of Surveying** — see p. 275 for all three — are just off the riverwalk south of the Michigan Avenue bridge. This cluster ends the intensely developed section of the riverwalk with many destinations. Stop in at the upper foyer of Impressions 5 for no charge and see a delightful soft-sculpture underwater scene of the Grand River, complete with channel catfish, a school of shiners, and an old tire.

◆ **Potter Park** (see p. 274), $1^1/_2$ miles southeast of downtown along the riverwalk, has a big playground, a picnic area and nifty small **zoo** (see p. 274) in a grove of large oaks, and canoeing on the river.

◆ **Rental canoes and information on canoeing** can be obtained from the Potter Park canoe livery (517-374-1022). As they flow through Lansing, the Red Cedar and Grand are good beginner's rivers, shallow enough that most adults could stand up in them. You lose sight of the city along much of the waterway. Fall color along the riverbanks is good. *Riverfront Park's current **northern terminus** is at the Fish Ladder and dam. Park in the lot off Race or Factory just south of Grand River Ave. and east of the river. In the **market area**, park at the market, the Lansing Center lot ($2/ all day) or in the Grand garage just west of the river and north of the Radisson. The riverwalk enters **Potter Park** at Pennsylvania Avenue south of the Olds Freeway and the Grand Trunk tracks and goes all the way to the East Lansing city limits at Clippert, for 5 1/2 miles of paved riverfront bike path separate from streets.*

CAPITOL CITY RIVERFEST . . . . . over the Labor Day weekend is a wonderful, free four-day event held on both sides of Riverfront Park between the City Market and Lansing Community College. On the river's east bank is a **carnival midway** and beverage tent with entertainment; on the west side there's an **international food court** and "kids korral" activity area, and various waterskiing, fishing, and canoeing contests and river exhibits. One stage features rock, jazzy, country, and gospel music; another stage has acoustic folk music, including dulcimers. A Gus Macker 3-on-3 **basketball tournament**, a Sunday-night lighted **pontoon parade**, and Monday-night **fireworks** round out the schedule. (517) 483-4499.

A NIFTY STOP ON AN OUTING WITH KIDS . . . . . is Lansing's **Potter Park** and its fine small zoo. They're a perfect place for a picnic lunch and letting off steam. The park's pleasant setting is in a large grove of big oaks alongside the Red Cedar River. There's plenty of **playground equipment** and space for games, along with **picnic tables** and grills. **Canoes** can be rented here, too (517-374-1022).

The **Potter Park Zoo** has a tropical bird house, many monkeys and larger primates, big cats that look comfortable in natural-looking outdoor displays, and a farmyard. (Kids can take camel and pony rides and go in a big enclosure and feed friendly goats. There are 400 animals in all, enough variety to please most kids, and admission is free once you've paid the $1 parking fee. Especially fun to watch are the penguins in their pool, many playful, cat-like lemurs with long, ringed tails, or raccoon-like red pandas, or spider monkeys. Somehow the animals look happier under the leafy canopy, with chipmunks and squirrels scampering around. Pick up a self-guided tour and map (25¢) at the Zoovenir shop. *Park entrance is on Pennsylvania just north of the Red Cedar River north of Mt. Hope Rd. From the Olds Freeway (U.S. 27) or Michigan Ave., take Pennsylvania south. (517) 483-4222. Zoo open 9-7 during daylight time, 9-5 standard time. $1/car parking for park & zoo.*

Museum Drive

The state's best hands-on museum is next to two other interesting museums, all on the Grand River.

On a bank of the Grand River just east of the state capitol and downtown Lansing are three noteworthy museums all in a row. This was an old warehouse district, and the museums have made use of the spacious old brick buildings to house their displays. Visitors can also embark on the interesting riverwalk from here (see p. 271).

◆ **Impressions 5.** Hands-on museums are difficult to do well. Especially when the emphasis is science, as is the case here, the tendency is to allow corporate benefactors to influence the displays and activities, too often destroying the interest value for kids. Impressions 5 has successfully blended meaningful instruction with absorbing activities.

There's a lot of space here — 40,000 square feet, and it's full of interesting, informative things to do. There are classics found in many hands-on museums such as the giant soap bubble maker and a bicycle wheel gyroscope, along with uniquely ambitious projects. A room-sized electronic circuit lets kids plug in various components to create different effects. A professional-looking chemistry lab allows kids to make slime and other concoctions. Big satellite dishes allow one person to communicate by whispers with another person 50 feet away. A "touch tunnel" leads kids into a darkened world where they experience tactile qualities more vividly. Some of the exhibits, like pulleys lifting 30-lb. weights, demonstrate important principles with elegant simplicity. Others, such as one on fiber optics, are much more complex but still engaging. *200 Museum Drive, south off Michigan Ave. just east of the Grand River and downtown. (517) 485-8116. Mon-Sat 10-5, Sun 12-5. Adults $3.50, children 4-18 $2.50.*

◆ **R.E. Olds Transportation Museum.** Not many people realize that Lansing native Ransom E. Olds was one of the towering pioneers of the auto industry. His curved-dash runabout was the world's first mass-produced car. From 1901 to 1907, it sold more than all other models combined. Although Olds is responsible for Oldsmobile's headquarters remaining in Lansing to this day, he left after disagreements in 1904 and formed the Reo Motor Car Company, also in Lansing. The Reo proved fabulously successful, too, but succumbed during the Depression.

In this small museum, the cars Ransom Olds manufactured are lined up in chronological order along the outer walls, beginning with the world's oldest Oldsmobile, built in 1897. There are three classic curved-dash Oldsmobiles, with their famous sleigh-like front. Three brass-era Reos from 1906 to 1919 show the early evolution of that important model. You can also see a jaunty yellow Reo Speedwagon truck, viewed here once by the popular rock group which had not originally known the source for its name. In the center of the room are seven Packards from 1933 to 1955. *240 Museum Drive. (517) 372-0422. Tues-Sat 10-5, Sun 12-5. Adults $2.50, students $1.50.*

◆ **Michigan Museum of Surveying.** This, the only surveying museum in the country, shows what a feat it was to survey Michigan by foot in the 19th century. From 1815 to 1857, surveyors plotted out the state's 1,900 townships, each 36 square miles. At the museum is the rock which marked the spot southeast of Lansing from which all other measurements for the state are taken. Surveyors back then were paid $3 a day, with which they had to buy equipment and supplies and pay a field cook, hunter, rod man, chain man, and a brush cutter. Historical photos show some of these intrepid men, who had to push straight through dense swamps to follow lines.

Michigan had a famous surveyor, William Burt, whose compass deflections first alerted him to the presence of huge iron lodes in the U.P. His solar compass, invented in 1835, is on display here. It was a revolutionary improvement in the accuracy of field surveying, allowing much more accurate meridian measurements just by sighting the sun. *220 Museum Drive. (517) 484-6605. Mon-Fri 10-3. $1.*

Elderly Instruments

*America's mail-order center for traditional music
is the retail hub of a lively local folk scene.*

The square brick Oddfellows' Hall in North Lansing has
been reborn as a folkies' heaven — 14,000 square feet
where you can find obscure recordings of bluegrass,
blues, country, folk, jazz, and music with traditional roots from
many countries and cultures. There's Tex-Mex and Celtic, African
and Arab, and many more. Even more remarkable is the fact that
musicians can try out almost any kind of acoustic instrument that
exists, from the complete line of legendary Martin guitars to
pennywhistles and concertinas, zydeco washboards and musical
saws, simple rhythm instruments and kazoos. Gift items include
postcards, rubber stamps, trading cards, musical toys, dozens of
T-shirts featuring blues masters, and bumper stickers with say-
ings like "String band music is a social disease" and "Hammer
dulcimists never fret." The repair department is run by an internationally known instrument maker.

Bulletin boards and literature racks in the front hall put you in
touch with folk-related festivals and workshops throughout the
region. Early evenings the place is busy with lessons.

Some customers drive a long way just
to visit Elderly. It may seem improbable
to find the world's largest dealer in
stringed instruments in a medium-sized
Midwestern city. In fact, much of Elderly's business comes from catalog sales.
Its four plump catalogs (recordings,
acoustic instruments and accessories,
books and videos, and amplified instruments) are themselves full of interesting
reading on such topics as recommended
recordings or ukeleles (billed as the instrument of the 90s). A more frequent
publication lists Elderly's current supply
of used instruments, their prices, and
descriptions. Ask for the latest catalogs
by calling (517) 372-4161.

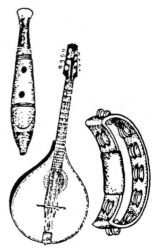

The idea for this extraordinary institution occurred in Ann Arbor, at the
open-mike nights at The Ark, the now-

legendary folk-music coffeehouse. There Sharon McIntruff met graduate student and banjo player Stan Werbin. A chance purchase of a guitar at a yard sale prompted them to think about starting a business selling used acoustic instruments (hence the "Elderly" name). But a store already occupied that niche in Ann Arbor, so they moved to East Lansing and set up shop in a tiny space across from the Michigan State University campus. They couldn't afford to stock much, but they would order anything — and at a discount. Werbin hailed from the aggressive business environment of New York City, so discounts were natural to him.

The folk music revival was already on the wane in Greenwich Village and Harvard Square. But it hadn't really arrived in East Lansing, so it was still fresh and potentially exciting. Sally Rogers, an M.S.U. undergraduate who has gone on to become a well-known folk singer, inspired enthusiasm by teaching at Elderly and performing on campus. Without a big local market, members of Lansing's growing folk community had to organize for themselves volunteer-run coffeehouses in churches and campus performing spaces. Thus developed an active folk community, less vulnerable to shifting mass-market taste than passive consumers of big trends in entertainment.

Interest in folk music increased in the Lansing area as the boom ceased nationally. Elderly grew in its own grassroots way. By 1975, the big folk-oriented music stores were fading, and Elderly was well positioned to introduce a memorable mail-order catalog and become a dominant force in the shrunken field of folk.

1110 N. Washington one block south of Grand River and a mile north of downtown Lansing. (517) 372-7880. Mail order phone (mon-Fri 9-5): (517) 372-7890. Store hours: Mon-Wed 11-7, Thurs 11-9, Fri & Sat 10-6.

ANOTHER ENTREE TO LANSING'S LIVELY ALTERNATIVE CULTURE . . . . . can be found at some of the shops on the friendly block of **East Michigan Avenue between Clemens and Fairview**, about 1 1/2 miles east of the capitol. In the early 20th century, these small storefronts were geared around a streetcar stop on the busy car line between Lansing and East Lansing. Today their attractive off-campus rents and convenient location have attracted an interesting variety of stores oriented to M.S.U. students and ex-students. They make for great browsing. Many are open daily, including Sundays, and evenings: the Hearthstone Community Bakery/restaurant (see p. 287), Wolf Moon Food Co-op, the delightfully old-fashioned Gnome Sweet Shoppe, and Capital City Comics and Books (good prices on good books). Stores with shorter hours include several worthwhile resale shops, Raupp Campfitters, and a women's bookstore.

Beal Garden and M.S.U. campus plantings

At America's first college of scientific agriculture, a gorgeous campus combines beauty and learning in a demonstration landscape.

Curving drives and Collegiate Gothic buildings in a parklike setting full of stately trees and flowering shrubs — the older part of Michigan State University's campus fits the ideal image of a college. Huge beeches and some gnarled white oaks over 200 years old are between the Union and Beaumont Tower, just south of Grand River Avenue along West Circle Drive. Students walk to class through what has become a true arboretum over the years, with some 8,000 varieties of woody plants. Among M.S.U.'s huge, 42,000-student undergraduate population, appreciation of the gardens, the majestic trees, and the beautiful displays of lilacs, azaleas, and viburnum is surprisingly widespread — partly because the tucked-away nooks of the Beal Botanical Garden and the paths along the Red Cedar River winding through campus are popular trysting spots.

Campus plantings here have been a central part of the institution's mission for well over a hundred years. Michigan State started in 1857 as the first U.S. agricultural college to teach scientific agriculture. The campus has long been regarded as a great outdoor laboratory for teaching, research, and observation. Horticulture, botany, and landscape architecture classes take advantage of the campus display of the widest possible variety of trees, shrubs, and woody vines suited to this climate. Very few planted environments in the Middle West have enjoyed such sustained commitment by faculty and staff.

Highlights of campus plantings include:

◆ **The Beal Botanical Garden**, an outdoor museum of living plants arranged by family and by use. Plants used for dyes, flavorings, and perfumes can be found here, along with flowering plants good for honeybees, and select landscaping and vegetable species.

Look for the entrance **gazebo** by the IM Sports Building on West Circle Drive, not too far from the Beal Entrance off Michigan Avenue. A box along the walk usually contains a **free brochure** about the gardens, with map and botanical lists. Exotic flowering landscape specimens have been planted on descending slopes from which brick clay was dug for the campus's first buildings. Below is a flat, sunken area where specimen plants and signs march like columns of soldiers in rows of regular squares of soil. The signs, well written and informative, are a big part of what makes visiting the garden so enjoyable.

Some plants are common weeds — weeds that invade field crops, and plants that foul up agricultural machinery, even poison ivy, neatly staked and marked with a red sign of warning. There are plants used in modern pharmaceuticals; cotton, flax, hemp, and other fiber plants; and plants used as food by Indians — all described as to origin, use, and culture.

By a charming **goldfish pond** around behind the library, there are benches and a plaque commemorating botany professor William James Beal, his 50 years of service to Michigan Agricultural College, and his pioneering experiments in hybridizing corn. In 1873 Beal established this garden. According to the staff, the Beal Garden is "the oldest continuously operating botanical garden" in the U.S.

◆ **The azalea and rhododendron garden,** by the music school just north of the Beal Garden across West Circle Drive, has soil adapted to acid-loving plants. Its displays are spectacular from late April through May and even into June.

◆ **Landscaping groupings and collections of dogwoods, viburnums, and clematis** are behind and alongside the IM Sports Building just west of the Beal Garden. These beautiful paths with their secret nooks show the lush, sensuous effects that can be achieved with screens and ground covers in narrow, shady spaces. The display of spring bulbs and early-blooming woody plants begins in March and gets into high gear from mid-April through May and early June.

◆ **The old Horticulture Gardens** on East Circle Drive at the northern end of Farm Lane are still gorgeous in spring because of all the lilacs and flowering crabs around the pool. But the expanding Horticulture Department has moved everything else to a new location (see below) that's nearly three times as large.

◆ **The new Horticulture Gardens** are south of the Plant & Soil Science Building on Bogue Street just south of Wilson Avenue and east of Farm Lane. The rose garden and perennial garden are complete but not mature. Greatly expanded annual beds are well underway in 1991. It takes years for new gardens to look settled-in; the grand re-opening is set for July, 1993. But the All-America trial gardens (in which All-America flower selections from U.S. seed companies are grown and tested) and rose gardens are already worth a look. A complete **student-run flower shop** in the Plant & Soil Science Building is open weekdays during the school

❶ Beal Gardens. Outdoor museum of plants used in dyes, drugs, food. Landscaping demo area full of ideas for gardeners. Fascinating signs.

❷ M.S.U. Museums. Michigan folk culture, international displays, rich tableaux on Michigan history plus outstanding life-size dioramas of North American ecosystems.

❸ Kresge Art Museum. Small size, intelligent presentation perfect for quick, stimulating visit. Much African art.

❹ Abrams Planetarium. Top technical equipment, enthusiastic presentations make weekend sky shows popular.

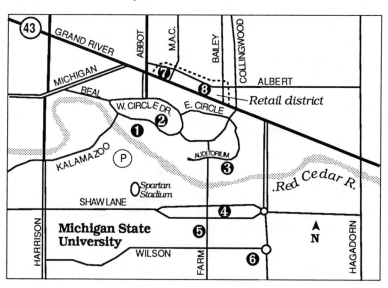

❺ The Dairy Store. Student-run dairy known for huge ice cream cones, yogurt, chocolate cheese.

❻ New Horticultural Gardens. Still under development. More perennial & annual flowers. Shop run by floriculture students.

❼ Pinball Pete's. State's premiere video game arcade, plus pinball, billiards, served up with declasseé panache.

❽ Jocundry's Books. New location has performing area, frequent events, free coffee, places to sit. Three times bigger.

Highlights of
East Lansing

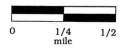

0   1/4   1/2
       mile

year from 11-5:30. Student-raised Easter lilies, mums, poinsettias, and annuals are sold at attractive prices. *Park off Bogue by the Grand Trunk tracks. $1 weekdays, otherwise free.*

The campus has been planted to be attractive at all seasons, and it is. Early bulbs and flowering witch hazel are out in March, followed by a panoply of flowering shrubs and vines, plus annuals, that extend the season up to frost. Fall color and winter bark textures and branch forms are important considerations in plant selection.

Plant-lovers could get a good horticultural education just by studying campus plantings on several fine days throughout the year. Many campus plants are labeled; some have excellent explanatory signs for gardeners about which varieties to choose and what plant materials go well together. **"Campus Plantings,"** a map and complete guide to 15 shrub and tree collections and 200 individual specimens, is available from Campus Park and Planning, 412 Olds Hall, M.S.U., East Lansing, MI 48824.

Michigan State has such a splendid campus because it has long been one of the nation's premiere colleges of agriculture. Credit goes to the enlightened Michigan farmers who in 1849 began lobbying for a state college to promote modern agriculture. The University of Michigan in Ann Arbor and Michigan Normal in Ypsilanti both wanted the new agriculture school, but its farmer backers insisted on an autonomous college. They chose as its site 677 acres of forest five miles east of the new state capital in Lansing, conveniently located just south of the old plank road to Detroit (now Grand River Avenue).

Michigan's agriculture leaders became important backers of the 1862 Morrill Act. It established land-grant colleges to be funded by sales of federal lands and geared toward broad-based, practical education and public service for all levels of society. Michigan State and Pennsylvania State share honors as the first land-grant colleges.

For many decades, manual labor, three hours a day, was expected of all students — part of the hands-on laboratory approach which also enabled poor students to afford a college education.

A BEAUTIFUL, LEAFY PATH . . . . . for walking, biking, and jogging runs along the south side of the Red Cedar River almost the entire length of the campus, from the Kellogg Center on Harrison Road past the statue of "Sparty" the M.S.U. Spartan, to Hagadorn Road.

Michigan State University museums and more

Reaching out to the general public
with intelligence and enthusiasm

Compared with universities that have had over a century's worth of archaeological and natural history expeditions, Michigan State hasn't received the rare artifacts, unusual specimens, donations of art, or bequests that build up the most prestigious museum collections over generations. Up through World War II, Michigan State's alumni body was made up mainly of farmers, teachers, and such — not lines of work likely to result in gifts of magnificent buildings or choice libraries of rare books to the old alma mater.

But what M.S.U.'s museums lack in accumulations of rare and costly possessions, they usually make up in spirit — a real excitement about teaching and an enthusiasm for reaching out and connecting up with the everyday experience of the general public. M.S.U. museums are unusually well suited for family outings with children.

◆ **Michigan State University Museum** is M.S.U.'s many-sided museum of natural science, history, folk life, paleontology, and anthropology, founded in 1857. Some of its 1 1/2 million objects and specimens are stored in an entire sub-basement beneath Spartan Stadium, while the museum building itself is relatively small. Museum exhibits are rigorously selected and thought out to pack a lot of interesting material into a compact space. No other museum in Michigan has quite its knack for choosing themes and details that put visitors in touch with who we are in Michigan, where we are in the world, and where we come from.

On the first floor, **Heritage Hall** has small dioramas of Michigan logging camps and locks, a fishing wharf, forts and copper mines, along with appealing, authentically detailed life-sized recreations of a country kitchen, a general store, and a fur-trading post. A shed houses a 1904 Oldsmobile curved-dash runabout, the world's first popular-priced car, which turned Lansing into a center of the auto industry. The interesting **Special Exhibits Gallery** generally highlights folk culture: the likes of African-American quilts, or Finnish saunas, or duck blinds and decoys. There's a good, small **gift shop**.

Upstairs, seven North American habitats, from forests to grass-
lands, tropics to tundra, are wonderfully represented in huge dioramas in **Habitat Hall**. Sweeping scenes, large animal specimens,
and tiny insects and plants on the ground make it fun to examine
these in detail. The hall's central area has two complete skeletons of the North American dinosaurs, allosaurus and stegosaurus.
Displays in the compact, well-thought-out **Artisans Hall** — American pottery, a violin-maker's shop, the evolution of the ax, styles
of log house construction, and fashionable bonnets, among others
— provide many insights gleaned in a day at Greenfield Village in
a fraction of the time and space. Changing exhibits in the **West
Gallery** are always worth checking out.

On the lower level, the **Discovery Theater** offers well-chosen
films, often on nature or Michigan history. **The Hall of Life** does a
good job of illustrating every geological time period with scenes
and samples of animal and plant fossils formed in that time. **The
Hall of World Cultures** has colorful, interesting displays of artifacts
from different cultures: shadow puppets from Java, swords from
many cultures, the ritual uses of African masks, and South American clothing. The **Great Lakes Indians Hall** combines dioramas of
periods in Indian history with how-to exhibits of basketry, stone-
cutting, bone and feather decoration, pottery, beadwork, and
pipes. Artists and craftspeople will find much of interest on this
floor. *See map, p. 281. Call (517) 355-2370 for information on
classes, activities, exhibits. Open Mon-Fri 9-5, Thurs until 9, Sat
10-5 (except for home football Sat), Sun 9-1. Free; donations
welcome. Metered visitor parking in front, sometimes scarce.*

◆ **The Kresge Art Museum,** select and intimate, makes up in
clever presentation what its collection lacks in depth. Highlights
are wide-ranging: Zurbaran's dramatic "Vision of St. Anthony," G.
Mennen and Nancy Williams' collection of African art, and a gigantic 1967 color-field canvas by Morris Louis. The introductory
gallery of Greek through medieval art has a wonderful way of
getting you to really look at individual small objects. *See map, p.
281. Call (517) 355-7631 for **changing exhibits, special events.**
School-year hours: weekdays except Thurs 9:30-4:30, Thurs 12-
8, weekends 1-4. Summer hours: weekdays 11-4, weekends 1-4.
Closed Thanksgiving vacation, mid-Dec.-early Jan., Easter, Mem.
Day and July 4 weekend, and mid-Aug. through 3rd wk. in Sept.
Free admission, donations appreciated. Limited visitor parking in
front of museum.*

◆ **Abrams Planetarium.** Enthusiastic presenters and top-notch
projectors in the 250-seat auditorium make planetarium shows a
popular form of entertainment for area families. Astronomy exhibits in the black light gallery are open weekdays (8:30-4:30 with

an hour at noon), and before regular weekend shows. Call (517) 355-4672 for this week's program. *Show times: Fri & Sat 8 p.m., Sun 4 p.m. Special shows for children at 2:30 Sun. Adults $2.50, students $2, kids 12 and under $1.50.* **Starline** *(star-gazing info on this week's skies): (517) 332-STAR.*

◆ **The Dairy Store.** The M.S.U. dairy program manufactures and sells its own ice cream, yogurt, and cheeses right here. If you come by at the right time, you can look through the plate-glass window and watch. Students love the generous cones of rich ice cream; black cherry is a special favorite. Wierdest item: chocolate cheese (it's something like a dairy-based fudge), developed for kids who won't drink their milk. *On the west side of Farm Lane just south of Shaw Lane and the Abrams Planetarium. (517) 355-4676. Mon-Wed 10-5, Thurs & Fri 10-8, Sat on special occasions.*

FIRST SUNDAYS IN EAST LANSING . . . . . are something of an **arts open house** at various stores, museums, and restaurants. It's featured in a handy monthly **cultural calendar** available at Jocundry's, Brother Gambit, and elsewhere.

CANOE THE RED CEDAR THROUGH CAMPUS . . . . . and up to the dam at Okemos or (if you portage around a dam) down to Potter Park. The **M.S.U. canoe livery,** also known as the Red Cedar Yacht Club, is behind Bessey Hall at Farm Lane. (517) 355-3397.

VISITOR PARKING ON CAMPUS. . . . . . is easy if you're willing to walk from two convenient **visitor lots** just south of the Red Cedar River. The Spartan Stadium lot at the very east end of Kalamazoo Street has a manned booth. It's a short, pretty walk to the Beal Garden across a foot bridge or the Kalamazoo Street bridge. Another lot is on Farm Lane at Shaw, in front of the Planetarium. On weekends, spaces along the circle drives can often be found.

GOOD BOOKS, FINE CRAFTS, AND GREAT PINBALL . . . . . are in downtown East Lansing across from Michigan State University, along Grand River and Albert, one block behind it, M.A.C. Avenue (it stands for "Michigan Agricultural College") is a connecting spine. Though still overwhelmingly oriented to undergraduates, with the predictable record stores, fast food and ice cream shops, and casual clothing stores, downtown is much more broadly interesting than it was even five years ago. In comparison with hubs of sophistication like Birmingham and Ann Arbor, there's a "we try harder" friendliness about East Lansing that's refreshing.

Retail standouts along M.A.C. include **Brother Gambit** (leather and wood crafts and jewelry), **Campbell's Smoke Shop** (an old-fashioned tobacco shop with candy, knives, and gadgets, too), **Prints Ancient and Modern** (a new gallery of antique and contemporary prints), the original **Pinball Pete's** (Michigan's biggest and best games arcade, also with lovingly maintained pinball machines and bargain pop; the entrance is around the corner on Albert), and **Mackerel Sky Gallery of Contemporary Craft** in the diagonal row of stores facing Albert.

Jocundry's Books, after years of running a virtual cultural center in extremely cramped quarters on M.A.C., has finished a new store triple the size. It incorporates a Dragon's Cave for kids, a performing area, many more places to sit, a fountain and plaza, more gallery space, bigger bulletin board and info center. Regular **stories and songs for kids** are Saturday mornings at 10:30. *515 East Grand River west of Bailey, by the east end of the M.S.U. campus. Call (517) 332-0856 for readings, book signings, etc. Mon-Sat 10-10, Sun 10-6.*

Just east of M.A.C. in the 300 block of East Grand River, the **Curious Used Book Shop** appealingly blends serious reading, comics, science fiction, sports memorabilia, and all sorts of old magazines and printed emphemera; **Jacobson's** department store has a second-floor restaurant overlooking the campus. *A great deal of attended parking in ramps and lots along Albert means you needn't worry about getting a ticket. Many downtown stores open Sunday afternoons and Thurs & Fri evenings.*

ANIMAL BARNS ARE OPEN TO THE PUBLIC. . . . . Involving the public is a tradition that goes back to M.S.U.'s roots as Michigan Agricultural College and the oldest land-grant college. South of Mount Hope Road, much of the vast campus is devoted to animal husbandry. Visitors are welcome to stop by the barns any day, look at the animals, and ask questions of the staff.

Recommended
Restaurant & Lodging
Mid-Michigan

To locate cities, see regional map,
p. 263.

LANSING

Parthenon Restaurant &
Bakery. *227 S. Washington, down-*
town. (517) 484-0573. Mon-Sat 7 a.m.-
8 p.m. Major credit cards (not Disc).
Full bar. Greek diner has expanded,
evolved into the leading downtown
restaurant, favored by politicians,
govt. workers. Hums at lunch. Vegetarians won't starve. Greek specialties
(gyros, shish-kebob, moussaka, broiled lamb chops, Greek salad, etc.) good
but not great. Combination plate $7.50
at lunch, $11 at dinner. Entrees $6-$7
at lunch, $9-$15 at dinner, all w/
small salad.

Clara's. *637 E. Michigan between*
Pennsylvania & Larch at RR tracks. 6
blocks east of the capitol. (517)
372-7120. Mon-Fri 11-11, Fri-Sat 11-
midnight, Sun 10-10. Sun brunch 10-3
$9 ($3/kids). Major credit cards. Full
bar. Same menu all day. The setting's
the thing: big space in old Michigan
Central train station. 2 levels. Stained
glass windows , interesting stuff
hanging. Fun family dining. As for
food, there's pizza (crusty or pan),
sandiwches ($4-$6), dinners w/potato,
salad bar from $10 (chicken, top sir-
loin) to $15 (steak & shrimp). Ice
cream fountain desserts & more start
at $1.35. Piano for Sun brunch, on
patio Wed evenings.

El Azteco. *1016 W. Saginaw. (517)*
485-4589. Westside Lansing location
of popular East Lansing spot. Full bar.
Visa, MC. For more details, see p. 288.

Hearthstone Community
Bakery. *2003 E. Michigan at*
Fairview, 1 /2 mi. e. of capitol. (517)
485-8600. Mon-Thurs 7:30 a.m.-10
p.m., Fri to midnight, Sat 9 a.m.-

midnight. No alcohol or credit cards.
Cheerful co-op bakery/deli w/ a few
tables, $4.75 vegetarian ethnic dinners
served starting at 4 p.m. until food
runs out. Delicious sweetrolls, coffee.
Some healthy, wholegrain veggie
pizzas, but kids won't like them. Free
coffeehouse w/entertainment Fri &
Sat.

Holiday Inn. *(517) 627-3211. 7501 W.*
Saginaw (M-43), just east of I-96 on
busy strip w. of downtown. 245 rooms
on 3 floors. $69-$75. Cable TV. Holidome: indoor & outdoor pools, sauna,
whirlpool, 2 tennis courts, game &
exercise rooms, arcade, ping pong,
pool. Restaurant, bar w/ weekend
entertainment.
Westside location, lots to do

Radisson Hotel. *(517) 482-0188.*
111 N. Grand at Michigan & Grand
River, downtown. 260 rooms on 11
floors. $85-$90, $59 weekend. Jacuzzi
suites w/kitchenettes. Cable TV.
Indoor pool, whirlpool, sauna, exercise room. Restaurant, bar. Good view.
Indoor pool, great downtown location
on Riverwalk, near kids' museum

EAST LANSING

Beggar's Banquet. *218 Abbot just*
n. of Grand River, downtown. (517)
351-4540. Mon-Fri 11 a.m.-2 a.m., Sat
10 a.m. -2 a.m., Sun 10 a.m. -midnight.
Visa, MC, Disc. Full bar. Pleasantly
odd blend of old hippie bar & gourmet
restaurant. Beat-up booths, fresh flowers on table. Wildly eclectic menu
includes salmon mousse ($6 appetizer),
excellent London broilf Famous chili
w/ fresh jalapenos ($2.75/bowl, draft
beer 35$ extra), any time. Chicken Kiev
at top of dinner menu ($15), most in
$7-$9 range, like chicken parmigiane,
manicotti. All dinners w/ salad, veg.).
Daily soups from scratch, specials:
lunch soup & sand. $4.50, entree $7; at
dinner from $11-$17. All-day sandwich menu $4-$6, w/ fries or pasta
salad. Always good, sometimes outstanding. Kitchen closes at midnight.

Said to be Gov. Engler's favorite spot (!) — he gets private booth.

El Azteco. *203 M.A.C. (downstairs); after fall 1991, 225 Ann at Albert just w. of M.A.C. Mon-Thurs 11-midnight, Fri & Sat 11-2 a.m., Sun 12-10. Same menu all day. Cash only. Beer, wine, margaritas.* Favorite campus hangout in new above-ground home w/natural light. Good Mexican food in ample portions. Goes beyond ordinary standards with chile rellenos (stuffed peppers), menudo (trip soup). Most meals are $5. A generation of busy people on budgets have survived on the $6.75 Topopo salad — beans, cheese, meat on a mountain of greens & veggies; feeds 2.

Kellogg Center, State Room.
On M.S.U. campus, Harrison Rd. just n. of Red Cedar River. Take U.S. 127 Trowbridge exit e. to Harrison, turn left on Harrison. (517) 332-6571. Mon-Sat breakfast 7-10, lunch 11:30-2, dinner 5:30-8:30. Sun breakfast 8-10, brunch/dinner 11-3. AmEx, Visa, Diners, MC. No alcohol. Culinary flagship of institutional food system, restaurant school that takes pride in its mass-feeding savvy. Known for cashew chicken $7, chicken salad plate $7.45 (slightly less at lunch). Lunch: sandwiches $4.25-$6, entrees $5-$9. Top of the line: $15 steak w/ soup or salad, potato. Nothing exciting, but competent. Nice setting, good service.

Holiday Inn. *(517) 337-4440. M.A.C. at Albert, downtown.* 181 rooms on 7 floors. $90 except graduation & MSU home football games ($105 w/2-night min.). Cable TV. Indoor pool, whirlpool, sauna, exercise room.Restaurant. *Indoor pool, best location: near campus, good restaurants*

Harley Hotel. *(517) 351-7600. I-496 (U.S. 127) & Jolly Rd exit s.w. of East Lansing. Not on on a strip.* 150 rooms on 2 floors. $44-$85, suites & weekend packages avail. Cable TV. Large indoor & outdoor pools, whirlpool, putting green, 2 lighted tennis courts, playground, game room, exercise room,

basketball court. Restaurant, bar w/entertainment.
Huge indoor pool, many activities. Quick access to both M.S.U. & downtown Lansing

Kellogg Center. *(517) 355-9313. S. Harrison Rd. n. of Red Cedar River on M.S.U. campus.* 165 rooms on 6 floors. $59 double, suites avail. Cable TV. Recently remodeled. All M.S.U. sports facilities avail. Excellent dining room & cafeteria run by M.S. U. hotel school. May be booked up with conferences. *Good food, good campus location, chance to use M.S.U. sports facilities.*

Park Inn International. *(517) 351-5500. 1100 Trowbridge, East Lansing. 1/2 mi. e. of I-496 (U.S. 127) at Trowbridge exit, next to shopping center at the edge of M.S.U. campus next.* 168 rooms on 2 floors. $42 double, $55 suites. Kitchenettes avail. Cable TV. Small outdoor pool. Restaurant, bar (jazz lounge). Next to good Korean restaurant, fast food spots. *Attractive, convenient budget choice*

OKEMOS

Travelers Club International Restaurant & Tuba Museum.
Hamilton Rd. at Okemos Rd. 2 blocks s. of Grand River, 1 1/2 mi. e. of East Lansing. From I-96, take Okemos Rd. exit 110, go 2 1/4 mi. n. (517) 349-1701. Mon-Fri 7 a.m.-9 p.m., Sat & Sun 9-9. No credit cards; trying for liquor license. International home cooking — part diner (corner fountain was once a Miller's ice cream & sandwich shop), part exotic restaurant. Wall decor: 1 owner's tuba collection, 1 owner's ethnic textiles. Eclectic menu features old-fashioned fountain treats, hot dogs and $2.75 burgers (but buffalo burgers), vegetarian standbys like tabooli, salad bar ($2/bowl, $3.75 w/ soup), stir-fries ($5-$6), $5 gyros plate. Popular breakfasts. Unique attraction: revolving international menu (Jan. & Feb. are Asia, March India & Sri Lanka, etc.) with rotating meat entrees and coordinated side dishes (around $10), vegetarian sampler

platter ($9). Always worth trying! Erratic service; food can be great. Ethnic music night: f1st Fri., 7-10 p.m. $2 cover. Call for ethnic banquets.

EATON RAPIDS

Dusty's English Inn. *728 Michigan (M-99) on n. side of Eaton Rapids. From I-96 exit 101, go s. on M-99 8 miles. Look for Tudor house on e. side of road. (517) 663-2500. Mon-Sat 11:30-1:30 & 5:30-8:30. Full bar. Visa, MC.* Limited menu of well-prepared continental cuisine served in paneled living room of spectacular Tudor mansion. Beautiful gardens, backs up on Grand River. For lunch, sandwiches and salads ($7-$9). Dinners from $11 (pasta in cream sauce w/ ham & broccoli) to $18 (baked salmon w/ herbs), all w/ salad, vegetables, redskins.

Dusty's English Inn. *(517) 663-2500. See above.* 6 large rooms w/ baths, $75-$130. Outstanding collection of English antiques, art. Guests can use sitting room, garden, canoes. TVs avail. Beautiful grounds.

MT. PLEASANT

The Embers. *1217 S. Mission St. 1 1/2 mi. s. of downtown on U.S. 27 bus. rte. (517) 773-5007. Mon-Thurs 5-9, Fri-Sat 5-10, Sun 10-7. Lounge open Mon-Fri 11:30-10. All major credit cards. Full bar. Sun brunch 11-2 $10.* Middle-American food prepared and served to perfection, geared to big appetites. Famous 1 lb. pork chop ($16) better than it sounds— marinated, complex. Other favorites: lasagna ($14), chicken Vesuvio on rice ($15), fresh catch of the day. Entrees come w/ 7 compartment relish tray (including famous peas and peanut salad), bread, cheeses, salad. Sandwiches ($5-$7), salads ($6-$8), smaller meals like 1/2 lb. pork chop w/ salad, potatoes, veggies ($8) or shrimp & scallop stir fry ($9) served all day Mon-fri at **The Tease** lounge.

Chippewa Motel. *(517) 772-1751. 5662 E. Picard Ave. at U.S. 27 & M-20 east.* 29 rooms on 2 floors. $35-$50, 22 bdrm units $60. Cable TV. *Convenient stopover, reasonable rates*

Chapter 7
West Michigan

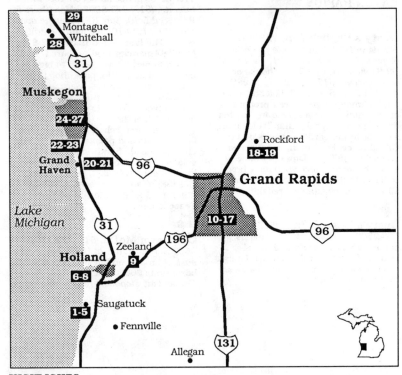

HIGHLIGHTS

Gerald R. Ford Museum

*This superb museum vividly shows
the highs and lows of the short, eventful presidency
of Grand Rapids' native son.*

One of Michigan's very most interesting museums, this presidential museum also has a striking setting — on the western bank of the wide Grand River across from downtown Grand Rapids. The building is effectively monumental. The many permanent displays about Ford are outstanding. They're visually arresting, informative without being taxing.

Gerald Ford was only president for two and a half years, but he enjoyed a rich political career and confronted a number of important challenges as president. The display on Ford's fateful 1974 decision to pardon Nixon includes some of the many letters of outrage Ford subsequently received. Another fine exhibit uses once-classified intelligence reports to give a detailed account of the dramatic Mayaguez incident, during which Ford ordered Marines to recapture a pirated U.S. vessel. Ford's 1976 loss to

Quonset hut headquarters for Jerry Ford's 1948 Congressional campaign, when he ran as a reform candidate against the Grand Rapids Republican machine.

Jimmy Carter, when he came from 20 percentage points behind and almost beat the Georgia governor, is colorfully documented. Betty Ford's courage and candor as First Lady is also nicely captured on a wall filled with photos, text, and memorabilia.

The museum's most popular display is the full-size **replica of the Oval Office** in the White House, just as it looked while Ford was president. It effectively gives the visitor a sense of what it's like to be in that room, known to intimidate even seasoned politicians. Just as arresting are the **showcases of gifts** from visiting dignitaries. There are big, brightly painted floor vases from the Chinese, a diamond-crested bird of solid gold on a silver tree from the Sultan of Oman, a dazzling ivory and gold bejeweled sword from General Suharto of Indonesia, and many more.

Every hour, a **28-minute film** on Gerald Ford's life and presidency is presented in the comfortable auditorium. A small **gift shop** is tightly focused on presidential items, including real campaign buttons ($3 each, both parties), postcards of past presidents and their wives, lots of inexpensive souvenirs for kids, and many books (some autographed) by and about Ford.

North side of Pearl Street on the west bank of the Grand River; another entrance is off Bridge. From U.S. 131, take Pearl St exit 31B. Less than 1/2 mile by foot from downtown via a pedestrian bridge behind Welsh Auditorium and the Amway Grand Plaza. By car, take the Pearl Street bridge west and turn right, or take the Michigan Ave./ Bridge St. bridge and turn left. (616) 456-2675. Mon-Sat 9-4:45; Sun 12-4:45. adults $2, seniors and children 6-15 $1.50, 5 and under free.

NEAR THE FORD MUSEUM . . . . . Ah-Nab-Awen Bicentennial Park in front of the Gerald Ford Museum is pleasantly open to the sky and cityscape. It's studded with interesting landscape features and sculptures, including a fountain and a giant button children can climb through. The interconnected, curved walkways are favored by strollers, dog-walkers, and joggers. A **pedestrian bridge** lets you cross the Grand in leisure, look down at the water, and walk over to downtown and the Riverwalk behind the Grand Center complex. The bridge is a remodeled interurban trestle. A **visitor information kiosk** by the parking lot and bridge is open Memorial Day to Labor Day. *Along the west bank of the Grand from Bridge St. to Pearl. Park in Ford Museum's Pearl St. parking lot. .*

TAKEOUT FOR A PICNIC in Ah-Nab-Awen or John Ball parks . . . . . Get sandwiches and soups from the Choo-Choo Grill, Plainfield at Leonard (see p. 349), fried fish and coleslaw from the Flying Bridge fish store across Leonard, or Mexican sandwiches from Maggie's Kitchen (p. 349).

❶ Gerald Ford Museum. Lavish, superbly executed tribute to Grand Rapids' native son. One of the Midwest's top historical museums.

❷ Amway Grand Plaza. Posh union of old and new, West Michigan's top hotel has several excellent restaurants, two floors of fine shops.

❸ John Ball Zoo. Dramatic hilly setting gives this splendid zoo an inviting atmosphere. See mirthful otters, monkey hill seen from above.

❹ Ed's Breads. Marvelous East European breads. Stands out in a state with many good ethnic bakeries.

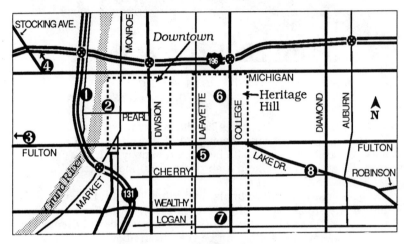

❺ Public Museum. Sprawling city museum has remarkable life-size recreations of Indian life, realistic 1890s Grand Rapids street scene, interesting costume displays.

❻ Heritage Hill. Grand Rapids' elite residential area from 1840s to 1920s. Many architectural styles and detailing for the city's style- and craftsmanship-conscious business leaders.

❼ Meyer May House. Frank Lloyd Wright architecture at its best. Meticulous restoration makes this spot alone worth a trip to Grand Rapids.

❽ Gaia Coffeehouse. The real thing, where the spirit of the counterculture lives on. Nearby **Heartwood antiques** has select furniture from Arts & Crafts and 1940s-1950s modernist eras.

Highlights of
Grand Rapids

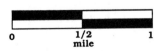

0   1/2   1
mile

John Ball Zoo & Park

A gem of a zoo with a lush setting
and wonderful views of playful otters and monkeys

What it lacks in size this splendid zoo makes up in atmosphere. It's built on a dramatic hill, the valley wall of the Grand River, and it sits beneath a canopy of trees. On a hot summer day this feels like a lush oasis. A 60-foot waterfall in the center adds to the effect.

The zoo has over 600 animals, including lions and tigers in depressingly small cages. There are black bears and zebras and exotic birds. Two sights stand out. There's a wonderful **display of otters** whose playful antics can be seen from above and below water, thanks to a glass-walled tank. At **Monkey Island,** an elevated **boardwalk** gives a spectacular view down onto a rocky hill over which a big band of monkeys cavorts.

The darkened **herpetarium** lets you see nocturnal animals like foxes, jungle cats, and bushbabies, under conditions in which they are naturally active. In the **penguin room** you can view the birds in their refrigerated swimming pool.

John Ball, pioneer, legislator, and lawyer, was one of the many people who came west to Michigan in the last century to speculate in land. A delightful bronze statue at the zoo entrance shows him as an old man with children at his knees. It commemorates his gift of 40 acres to the city for a park. Today the **park** part of the 100-acre complex is a large, shady, flat expanse with **picnic facilities**, ball diamonds, playground, tennis courts, and some playful contemporary sculptures.

Fulton St. and Valley Ave., 1¹/₄ miles west of the Grand. (616) 776-2590 (recording); (616) 776-2591 (office). Open daily 10 a.m.-4 p.m. ('til 6 in summer), year-round, including holidays. Adults $2, children and seniors $1, under 5 free. Strollers and wheelchairs available.

Ed's Breads

*In a state with many good ethnic bakeries,
this one stands out.*

Ed's outstanding traditional East European breads are
dense and flavorful, especially the sourer doughs, like the
fabulous Latvian rye. At $1.50 to $2.25 for a big loaf, the
breads here are a terrific value, and very good. So are the cookies, sweet-rolls, and rolls. Basics here, baked daily, are the huge,
2 1/4-pound loaf of Polish rye ($2), a staple with the German,
Polish, and Lithuanian westsiders, and a 2 1/2-pound whole
wheat loaf, popular with the co-op buyers. These are heavy,
nutritious breads, truly the staff of life. A loaf of Ed's Bread
"passes the bam test," we were told with pride. "You lay it down
on the counter and it goes, 'Bam!'"

Customers from all walks of life, from all over Grand Rapids
and as far as Muskegon and Holland, come here regularly for
their favorites like cream cheese-raisin bread (baked on Wednesdays in limited quantities) and bacon-onion rolls called bundukies (Saturdays).

Founder Ed Parauka had baked and improved his Lithuanian
and Polish grandmothers' recipes in his basement. When he got
them right, he opened this shop. Eventually a baker's long hours
got to Ed, and he quit for a career installing industrial waste-
water treatment systems. Now his onetime assistant and
successor, Kathryn Kelly, continues and improves on his
tradition. Her hand-rolled loaves are made without preservatives
rolling machines, yeast stabilizers, or any of the modern
inventions that enable bakers to easily turn out consistent
products despite variations in temperature and humidity.
Traditional baking is "more by instinct and experience — more
alchemy," she says cheerfully. It's more time-consuming but
more challenging, almost an art.

Here, for your convenience, is Ed's weekly schedule of specialty breads. Come early in the day for best selection. Load up on
bread for your freezer on your way home. You won't be sorry.

Tuesday: health bread. **Wednesday:** cream cheese-raisin, Latvian rye,
oatmeal-honey, horseshoe rolls. **Thursday:** pumpernickel, sour French,
potato bread. **Friday:** Lithuanian rye, oatmeal-honey, hotdog and
hamburger buns, Parker House rolls. **Saturday:** bundukies, buns,
Parker House rolls.

While you're here, stop in at the clean, well-organized **Tried and True Consignment Shop** next door. It's a fine place to find conservative career clothes and Sunday-best outfits for kids.

1204 Leonard on the west side of Grand Rapids, just west of Garfield and across from Burger King. Leonard is a major east-west artery on the north side. From U.S. 131, take the Leonard St. exit and go west one mile. From downtown, take Division to Leonard, then west. (616) 451-9100. Tues-Fri 8 a.m.-5:30 p.m., Sat 8-noon. (Customers welcome before 8, but all baking may not be finished.)

A TASTE OF EASTERN EUROPE AND OLD MEXICO ON THE WEST SIDE. . . . .
Grand Rapids' working-class, multi-ethnic west side is home to many other worthwhile specialty food shops with authentic ethnic ingredients, superior quality, and attractive prices.

In a plain, inconspicuous neighborhood grocery on Walker at Powers is the **Lewandoski Market**, where butcher-owner Vic Hill makes widely admired sausages, not super-lean but awfully good: smoked kielbasa ($2.39/lb.); delicious, super-spicy pepperoni ($3.99); German-style wieners ($2.49); ring bologna ($2.19); head cheese ($1.99); and kiska (a Polish sausage made of buckwheat, pork, and blood; $1.69). From Ed's, go south on Garfield to Walker (the diagonal street), then left for two blocks.

Continue into town (southeast) on Walker, which turns into Stocking. Where it intersects with Bridge is an aging commercial district busy with small-scale entrepreneurial activity. Turn right onto Bridge and stop at two Mexican markets. **El Matador Mercado,** 642 Bridge, is a small retail outlet of El Matador Tortilla Company, recently moved out of the neighborhood into a new $3 million factory. Its corn chips are sold here in quantity ($3.75 for a 3-pound bag), along with basics like masa (corn meal), salsa, many sizes of canned refried beans, chorizo, and a half-gallon of Picante sauce for $4.95. Hispanics are the fastest-growing segment of Grand Rapids' population, and Hispanic businesses have flourished. El Matador's founding family, Mike and Isabel Navarro, are among a dozen Mexican-American millionaires in the area. They came to western Michigan to pick celery after World War II. At 636 Bridge, **Moctezuma Mexican Food Products** and **Maggie's Kitchen** share a very large, bright space with all the basic Mexican groceries and exotic canned juices. A full line of spices for Mexican cooking in institutional sizes is imported and distributed by the owners. The basement is full of Spanish-language videos and recordings and lots of bright piñatas. Maggie makes to order a range of unusual Mexican sandwiches for $2 and $3. Many are meal-size.

A nerve center of the West Side's huge Polish community is **American Bread**, a popular bakery (good enough, but no equal to Ed's) and lunch counter at 712 Bridge. While you're in the area, you might want to check out the **Bridge Street Antique Center** at 445 Bridge, a pleasant, well-organized mall with 15 to 20 dealers. (Closed Mondays)

Amway Grand Plaza Hotel

A union of elegant old and new, it's a successful
centerpiece of downtown Grand Rapids.

Several outstanding restaurants and some interesting shops
make this striking 682-room hotel worth a visit. It's a
subsidiary of Amway, the direct-sales home products
firm headquartered in nearby Ada, Michigan. The 29-story glass
tower, built in 1983 has been integrated with the historic, ornate
Pantlind Hotel (1913) on Monroe Avenue, once the elegant social
hub of Grand Rapids' big furniture markets. The Pantlind's lobby,
ballroom, and dining room have been restored and embellished
to out-dazzle their former sedate elegance. Lavish accents
include three two-ton chandeliers of Austrian crystal, a gilded
antique sunburst from a Venetian palace, and a 7,000-square-foot
gold leaf ceiling. "The largest gold leaf installation in the United
States!" gushes the informative Amway **walking tour pamphlet**.
You can pick it up at the concierge and make your own worthwhile combination of short walking tours. There's a lot to see: a
seven-story **atrium** with waterfall and reflecting pool, a good view
across the Grand, and lots of accessible art created especially for
the hotel.

Shops cluster on the first and second floors near the Pearl
Street entrance. The **Bergsma Gallery** features 25 artists, mostly
from west Michigan. **Linda's** is a popular, high-fashion women's
wear shop. **Ragamuffins** carries a remarkable array of clothing
and accessories for children. **Cornucopia,** on the ground level
offers an interesting variety of gourmet foods, baked goods,
coffee, and pizza slices.

Main auto entrance on Pearl west of Monroe. just east of the
Grand River in downtown Grand Rapids. The historic Pantlind
entrance is on Monroe Ave. (616) 774-2000. See pp. 350 and
351 for hotel and restaurant information.

Public Museum of Grand Rapids

*A big, diverse museum with fine Indian displays
and a realistic gaslight village*

This interesting history and natural science museum occupies a sprawling, rather confusing labyrinth of spaces. It's filled with exhibits on everything from Michigan butterflies to war relics. The front building from the 1930s is tacked onto a former streetcar barn. Improved new quarters across the river are in the works. The museum's vast holdings, received from a century's worth of donors from this industrious city, include nationally known collections of furniture, clothing, and glass.

Don't miss **The People of the Grand,** a large and ambitious look at the immigration of Indians to North America, with life-size representations of Native American societies who have lived here by the Grand River. It's as unsentimental, vivid, and interesting a history of Indian life as you're likely to find anywhere. **Gaslight Village** is a full-scale reproduction of a downtown cobblestone street at night in the 1890s. Here you can peek in windows and see a realistic drugstore, police station, dry goods emporium, and 14 other shops and offices.

Dolls, Victorian women's underwear, Hopewell Indian pots from the Grand Valley, and Grand Rapids furniture are a few of the many subjects interestingly presented in the sprawling Public Museum.

The museum's great size and profusion of topics makes it important to plan your visit selectively. On the main floor, room after room of nature exhibits give good, close-up views of **Michigan wildlife.** The second floor has a series of rooms, each focused on a topic: war relics, artifacts from the Orient and Pacific Islands, and human anatomy.

Some of the best displays are tucked away upstairs in the East Building beyond Gaslight Village. **Furniture highlights** are presented in 11 period rooms. **Costume displays** are accompanied with irreverent captions. "The Glory of Underwear," "A Plague of Plush," "Art in the Victorian Parlor" are fresh, unstuffy treatments of subjects that can be tiresome. A wonderful, eclectic **doll collection** includes kachinas, Japanese ladies, Haitian voodoo figures, and pre-Disney Snow Whites. Miniature **historical interiors** with dressed dolls are memorable. So are the displays of **ethnic decorative crafts:** Dutch, Latvian, African-American, Mexican, Polish, and German — all nationalities well represented in the city of Grand Rapids.

The Curiosity Shop for children has a fine array of books, educational games, and toys, mostly related to natural history. There's lots for 25¢ to $3; little costs over $20. Michigan products are emphasized.

54 Jefferson SE at Washington, 1 block south of Fulton, on the southeast side of downtown Grand Rapids. (616) 456-3977. Mon-Fri 10-5, Sat & Sun 1-5. Adults $1, seniors and children 5-15 50¢.

SKY SHOWS IN THE MUSEUM . . . . . is the **Roger B. Chaffee Planetarium.** In addition to shows, it has lobby displays on astronomy and the weather, viewable during Public Museum hours. *Daytime entrance: through Public Museum. Evening entrance around the corner on Washington St. (616) 456-3977. 24-hour Skyline: 456-3200. Astronomy shows: Oct. to mid-April Fri and Sat 8 p.m., Sat & Sun 1:30, 2:30, 3:30. Mid-April through August Fri & Sat 8, Sat & Sun 1:30, 2:30, call for weekday afternoon shows. Closed September. $2 adults, $1.50 children 3-15, seniors. Under 3 not admitted. Laser light shows to rock music: Oct., Nov., Jan. through mid-April Fri & Sat 9 & 10 p.m. All seats $3.50.*

Meyer May House

Serene and sublime, it's a remarkably complete example of Frank Lloyd Wright's famous Prairie Style.

Seeing photos of Wright interiors — or seeing objects he designed taken out of context — leaves people unprepared for the emotional impact of the places he designed. Wright was famed for designing total environments, including leaded glass and furniture. He worked with favorite craftspeople and dictated to his clients just what kind of pictures and ceramics his rooms should have.

The May House was designed for the owner of a Grand Rapids menswear store in 1908, the same year as Wright's famous Robie House in Chicago. Famed architectural historian Vincent Scully has called it the most beautifully and completely restored of any of Wright's Prairie houses: serene, and suffused by a gentle unity. "To come suddenly into that interior environment is an overwhelming experience. It is to be wholly caught up and carried along by something rarely experienced: absolute peace, integral order, deep quiet grandeur and calm — all of it achieved in a house of no more than moderate size, ... set in the typical grid pattern of the American town." It's a vivid testament to Wright's originality to see this house in the context of its more conventional Heritage Hill neighbors in their late Queen Anne, Craftsman, and classical revival styles. (Since the completion of the Meyer May House restoration, the much larger, verging-on-opulent Dana House, in Springfield, Illinois, has been renovated and furnished with many pieces of Wright furniture and art glass, not necessarily original to the house.)

The quiet generosity of Steelcase, the big Grand Rapids office furniture manufacturer, made this amazing restoration possible. Except for the kitchen, it almost duplicates the house's 1916 appearance. The ambitious project employed scholars and top local and national conservators and restoration craftsmen in everything from furniture and art glass to pottery and linen. Knowledgeable locals estimate a price tag of $3 million to $6 million. With typical modesty, Steelcase officials don't like to brag or talk about cost. They say the restoration is honoring a debt to Wright. In his celebrated Johnson Wax Administration Building, Wright insisted on designing a total work environment, the beginning of the modern workstation that is the bread and butter of today's office furniture manufacturers centered in and near Grand Rapids. Wright contracted with Steelcase to manufacture desks and chairs for Johnson Wax.

Visitors on the 1 $^1/_2$-hour tour first come to the visitor center in the house next door and watch an interesting video showing the Meyer May house before, during, and after restoration. It focuses on techniques and puts the house in historical context.

The top-notch tour effectively illuminates the rationale for Wright's design idiosyncrasies. He designed each house as a private family refuge. This house has a hidden entrance to the side. The deep balcony overhangs let occupants sit on porches in privacy. The bedroom ceilings, like little tents, worked to promote a settled feeling of enclosed security. In contrast, downstairs ceiling and molding details emphasized the flow from room to room, and a sense of richly expansive vistas.

The perennial flower garden — a striking geometric design in bloom spring through fall — is behind the house off Logan. People are welcome to look at it any time.

450 Madison S.E. at Logan southeast of downtown Grand Rapids in the Heritage Hill historic district. Take Fulton, Cherry or Wealthy to Madison, turn south. (616) 246-4821. Tues & Thurs 10-2 (last tour begins at 1), Sun 1-5. Closed some Sundays; call ahead. Reservations required for groups of 10 or more. Free.

Heritage Hill

Grand Rapids' historic neighborhood
of superbly detailed homes
is probably the richest and most varied in the U.S.

Heritage Hill is one of America's most extraordinary historic districts. It numbers hundreds of uniquely detailed houses in an amazing variety of styles — over 60, from Greek Revival and Gothic Revival of the 1840s to Arts and Crafts and Spanish Revival of the 1920s. As a manufacturing city with many locally owned businesses, Grand Rapids generated considerable wealth and wasn't shy about displaying it. Prominent families, including design-conscious owners of the city's famous furniture factories, built these hillside homes up and away from their factories' smoke.

The historic district is six blocks wide and nearly one and a half miles long. It rises up and along the crest of the hill east of downtown Grand Rapids. Nearly every street presents old-house fans with uncommon and rare things: unusually heavy and ornately detailed Italianate doors and window caps, unaltered Stick Style cottages, rambling Shingle Style lodges, Chauteauesque castles, and a most peculiar Queen Anne house constructed of logs for a rustic effect. The Hill has two **Frank Lloyd Wright houses** and one adapted from one of his *Ladies' Home Journal* plans for small, moderate-priced houses. Wright's Meyer May House (p. 300) is the most authentically furnished Wright design in existence.

From the 1840s into the 1920s, the hill remained Grand Rapids' residential area of choice — a remarkably long period for any prosperous American city. By the time people could afford to build on the prestigious hill, they were already middle-aged and wealthy. Families competed in devising unusual details to distinguish their ample, often monumental residences. Grand Tours in Europe acquainted them with many prototypes, which were seldom literally copied. Especially on the hill's south end, developed after 1885 or so, you can see strange blends of architectural styles.

In the 1920s the Hill was supplanted as Grand Rapids' best address by East Grand Rapids — part of the nation-wide retreat of the upper classes to less public life in the suburbs. By the 1950s the Hill had become an aging neighborhood. The threat to this nationally significant neighborhood prompted the Grand Rapids city council in 1970 to create one of the country's earliest and largest historic districts and a neighborhood support agency. An innovative revolving fund enabled many houses to be renovated and sold without use of any public grant money.

Exploring any Heritage Hill street by foot is rewarding, though south of Wealthy the neighborhood changes for the worse.

Houses of special historic or architectural interest are listed from northeast to southwest. * means you can look inside during business hours.

◆ **Rowe House.** *226 Prospect north of Lyon.* Prairie Style. Built from a 1907 Frank Lloyd Wright *Ladies' Home Journal* design as "A Fireproof House for $5,000."

◆ **230 Fountain** *just west of Lafayette.* 1872, Italianate, with 1894 Classic Revival modifications. The onion-domed garage (visible from Lafayette) shows the kind of detail lavished even on fences and accessory buildings on Heritage Hill. From 1907 to 1964 Edmund Booth of Booth Newspapers fame lived here.

◆ **Holt House.** *50 Lafayette.* 1886. Unusual house in fieldstone and shingles, with many inventive touches. Reminiscent of rambling Shingle Style summer cottages in New England.

◆ **T. Stewart White House.** * *427 E. Fulton.* 1907, Tudor Revival. A lumber baron built this house. It has a gold leaf dining room ceiling by Tiffany's. Three sons became famous: Roderick White as a concert violinist, Gilbert White as a sculptor in Paris, and Stewart Edward White as a nationally known writer. Drawing on his father's experiences, Stewart White chronicled Michigan lumberjacks and the early West. Gilbert painted murals in the house's library with scenes from King Arthur's court, using faces of family members. As Warren Hall, the building now houses Davenport College of Business offices. Call ahead (616-451-3511) if you'd like to look at the murals.

◆ **264 College.** 1889 Queen Anne with eccentric log construction. Built by an architect as his own home.

◆ **Gay House.** *422-426 E. Fulton.* 1883. Built for the co-founder of Berkey & Gay, long Grand Rapids' leading furniture manufacturer, for $50,000 — then an astounding sum.

◆ **Sweet House/Women's City Club.** *254 Fulton.* The cast-iron fence and drooping camperdown elm in front of this 1860 Italian villa-style house were popular Victorian lawn accents. Its builder, lumberman Martin Sweet, long the richest man in town, was ruined in the financial panic of 1893 and died here in near poverty. Later the house became a music school attended by young Arnold Gingrich, who became *Esquire* magazine's brilliant founding editor. He set his 1935 novel, *Cast Down the Laurel,* in this house. Today it's a private women's club.

◆ **Voigt House.** Victorian chateau with original furnishing, p. 305.

◆ **Byrne/Hanchett House.** *125 College.* Circa 1891. Attractive landscaping complements the rose stone and ornate detailing of this beautiful English manor house, built for a single woman. Private chapel has sumptuous stained glass windows.

◆ **The Castle.*** *455 Cherry at College.* 1884. This rugged granite Norman chateau is a neighborhood landmark. It was built by bachelor brothers who got rich selling lumber for railroad ties. **The Castle Gallery,** with paintings, jewelry, sculpture, and dolls by contemporary artists, is usually open Wednesdays and Saturdays 12-7 or by appointment (616-235-1260)

◆ **Sanford House. *** *540 Cherry,* 1847. Greek Revival. This imposing house was once a country estate on the outskirts of town. Now it's a counseling office, and visitors can see the stair hall's splendid handpainted mural of a tropical scene.

◆ **McKay House.** *411 Morris.* 1924. Plain but impressive tile-roofed house built by Republican boss Frank McKay. His control of the state Republican party was finally broken in 1948, when young Gerald Ford defeated his candidate for Congress.

◆ **Amberg House.** *505 College at Logan.* 1910, Prairie Style. Frank Lloyd Wright started design work on it, but Marion Mahoney, his first apprentice, finished after Wright abruptly left his practice in Oak Park and his wife and six children to spend a year in Europe with a client's wife.

◆ **Meyer May House.** *1908.* Most completely furnished and restored Frank Lloyd Wright house in existence. See p. 300.

*See Grand Rapids map. Get a **free walking tour map** from the Heritage Hill Association office, 126 College (in rear) S.E., Grand Rapids 54903. Office open Mon-Fri 9-5. (616) 459-8950.* **Homes tour:** *first full weekend in Oct. $10, $8 in advance.*

Voigt House

*A miraculously preserved Victorian mansion —
from the velvet scarf on the library table
to the pills and tonics in the medicine chest*

Here, remarkably preserved, is a Victorian household in a big, turreted 1895 chateau, complete down to the last fringed piano scarf. It brims with the excess that epitomized Victorian decor. A table with carved lion legs is diagonally draped with a fringed velvet cloth. Antimacassars decorate the tops of every upholstered chair. Oriental carpets rest on parquet floors with elaborate inlaid borders. Doorways and windows are draped or festooned with heavy multi-layered window treatments and portieres. Patterns on patterns are everywhere. Rich reds and greens predominate.

Some visitors love the Voigt House's richness. Others, claustrophobic and stifled, feel like running out into the sunshine and fresh air.

This fascinating place is a monument to family prosperity. It's a gem of a historic house because the authenticity of its furnishings is above suspicion. The two generations of Voigts who lived here until 1971 saved just about everything: letters, receipts, dresses, the entire contents of medicine chests. Everything is here the way it was. Most of the elaborately styled furniture is from Grand Rapids, the conventional best that America's Furniture City had to offer. There's a heavy, masculine library and hallway accented with exotica like an Arab figure holding calling cards, a delicate French parlor, a rather Germanic dining room with loads of Bavarian china, and a comfortable, casual music room. In the basement is the original laundry, fully furnished with soap, along with interesting Voigt flour mill memorabilia.

The German-American Voigts made their fortune milling flour. They were supremely fussy, according to descriptions of a former housekeeper. Cotton wads at the corners of pictures protected the walls. Except for cleaning, servants never used the main staircase, avoiding unnecessary wear on the carpet.

The possessions of Ralph Voigt, the son and heir to the family flour mills, extend the house into more modern times. They include a banjo and a simple bedroom suite with mementoes of his years at Yale. The yard is planted and landscaped with plants of the Victorian era, a rose bower, and an iron geranium stand.

115 College between Fulton and Cherry. (616) 458-2422. Tues 11-3, 2nd and 4th Sundays 1-3. $3 admission.

FOR A MEMORABLE CONTRAST . . . . . plan to visit Frank Lloyd Wright's serene Meyer May house after seeing the Voigt House, an encrusted late Victorian mock-European chateau — just what Wright detested. Both homes are fully furnished — a rare treat. It's hard to believe that they were built and furnished just 11 years apart. They're both open at the same time on Tuesdays and alternate Sundays.

OTHER RECOMMENDED ATTRACTIONS NEAR HERITAGE HILL. . . . Take Fulton or Cherry east to diagonal Lake Street, turn southeast, and you'll soon reach two interesting commercial subdistricts. Turn west onto Diamond and you'll be at the **Gaia Coffeehouse** (p. 350), a pleasantly laid-back counterculture hangout, and the exceptional **Heartwood** antiques, known for its Arts and Crafts, Art Deco, and moderne furniture and accessories. Farther out, at Robinson Road and Wealthy, is **Eastown**, an offbeat collection of snack shops, offbeat shops, and bookstores. Especially worth checking out: the quality hot dogs and amusing soda shoppe atmosphere at **Yesterdog** (1505 Wealthy); **Argos** used books (1405 Robinson just east of Wealthy); **Tim's Pantry** (1507 Wealthy), with fresh-brewed specialty coffee, teas, brewing devices, and such a range of unusual beans that it has a big mail-order business without advertising; the user-friendly **Eastown Co-op** (1450 Wealthy); and **McKendree** hand-crafted jewelry (1443 Wealthy), in a fascinating woodsman's baroque building where Grand Rapids' fabled wood craftsmanship took off on a wildly organic, 1960s bent. Be sure to see the bone-like interior staircase.

Rosie's Diner and The Diner Store

Vintage 1940s diners, moved and restored by a diner fan and ceramics artist, now sell art and updated diner food.

Jerry Berta still marvels at how he, a ceramics artist, has become the savior and owner of two orphaned diners from the 1940s — and a restaurateur to boot. He is the owner of **Rosie's Diner**, now north of Grand Rapids, 700 miles from its first home on Route 46 in Little Ferry, New Jersey. Generations of TV viewers know Rosie's from the Bounty paper towel commercials starring Nancy Walker as Rosie the waitress. Rosie's continues to open early (at 5 a.m.) and to serve classic diner fare: burgers, meat loaf, breakfast all day, and blue plate specials for a change of pace. Next door to the revived Rosie's is another vintage diner. **The Diner Store** is a 1947 diner known for the better part of three decades as Uncle Bob's Diner in Flint . Now it's Berta's ceramics studio and gallery. The original formica counter and booths and the pie shelf now display Berta's porcelain diner night lights ($125 and up), gas stations, salt-and-pepper sets and butter dishes ($35), fantasy diners shaped like hotdogs and hamburgers, and diners with neon "EAT" signs. In a similarly playful vein are patterned teapots and slab vases by Berta's wife, Madeleine Kaczmarczk, neon clocks and signs by his friend, Ian McCartney, and souvenir mugs and pins.

This strange little diner village sits on a busy stretch of M-57 just north of Rockford, 15 minutes north of Grand Rapids and half a mile east of the U.S. 131 superhighway that heads north to Big Rapids and Cadillac.

If you've only seen pictures and video images of diners, it's a thrill to experience the stainless steel sunburst surfaces, cozy booths and counter, and classic accoutrements (thick china mugs, ketchup bottles, menu boards, etc.) of the real thing.

Berta's playful, cartoon-like porcelain pieces of post-World War II Americana have long included diners, tail-finned cars, movie theaters, gas stations, and tiny blue plate specials, worn as pins. The miniature diners are what precipitated Berta's unexpected debut in the restaurant and tourism game. Looking up old diners to study and draw as sources of design details, he came upon Uncle Bob's in Flint, derelict and awaiting destruction. It seemed an ideal studio on account of its unusually large size (74 seats), so Berta bought it for $2,000. He found a highway lot a half a mile from his studio/home in the woods. For another $14,000 he moved the diner's four sections to Rockford. "NO FOOD — JUST ART," proclaims the neon window sign.

When Berta revisited Rosie's in New Jersey and owner Ralph Carrado asked him if he wanted to buy it, Berta was thrilled. Carrado had already sold the lot to a neighbor and had unsuccessfully offered the diner to the Smithsonian. He too was thrilled that the landmark diner would survive in good hands.

Rosie's Farmland Diner, manufactured in 1946, gained its present name after TV stardom. It's an unusually large diner — the long camera angles made it a favorite with ad directors for many products — and in excellent condition. The Paramount Dining Car Company included in this diner most of the design hallmarks of the best of the golden age of diners, that period shortly after World War II when America took to the road and returning GIs found diners attractive investments. Rosie's has curved glass-brick corners, a rounded Pullman-style roof, and an interior full of reflecting stainless steel sunbursts and a jazzy combination of ceramic tile, vintage Formica, and leatherette in red, pink, light blue, and black.

The diners are at 450014 Mile Rd. (M-57) 5 miles north of Rockford. 1/2 mile east of U.S. 131, 1/2 mile west of Beltline. Rosie's is open Mon-Sat 5 a.m.-9 p.m., Sun 6 a.m.-9 p.m. (Call to confirm hours.) (616) 696-FOOD. V, MC. The Diner Store is open at least Tues-Sat 1-5, quite possibly longer. (616) 696-CLAY.

SPECIALTY SHOPPING IN A MOST SCENIC SPOT. . . . . is the big attraction of the **Squires Street Shops** in downtown Rockford, a pleasant place that's the world headquarters of Wolverine Worldwide shoe manufacturers (see p. 310). An old mill, now the **Arnie's Old Mill Restaurant** (one of the popular, upbeat, affordable Grand Rapids chain of Arnie's Bakery Restaurants), is at the center of an informal group of a couple dozen stores, mostly gift shops. Behind the shops by the Rogue River and dam is an attractive little park just east of Squires Street is Rockford's main business block, with a great old hardware store and **The Corner Bar** with its well-known Hot Dog Hall of Fame (see Restaurants, p. 351). Connecting them is Courtland Street. The **post office** there has a WPA mural, "Along the Furrows," with an unusual, cubist-tinged version of Midwestern farm life.

Three Squires Street shops stand out. **Mr. Whisker's Toy Shop** at 25 Squires Street is geared to creative, active toys, not TV fare, but it's no upscale grandparents' toy store. Its well-selected, not terribly expensive toys score high with babies and kids, reports one pleased mom. **The Melting Pot,** 63 Courtland, resembles a fudge, cookware, and gourmet shop like many others, but its owners are commit-

ted to doing things right — and not for maximum profit, either. They're extremely
knowledgeable about coffee. You may see snapshots from their recent trip to a
supplier plantation in Costa Rica, for instance. As a wholesaler, they roast a day's
supply of many kinds of beans fresh each day. (Freshness is paramount for great
coffee.) Retail prices are unusually low — typically $4.75 and $5.75 a pound. Mail-
order (616-866-2900) is available. Good fudge and chocolates are also made fresh
daily, as are bagels — a boon to transplanted urbanites in the area. Open at 8 a.m.

   Baskets in the Belfry at 46 East Bridge has evolved from a basket shop into the
ultimate, all-round feminine gift shop that makes the most of the familiar Vic-
torian-country genre and expands it without ever seeming slavishly imitative or
hackneyed. The romantic tone is set by grapevines and flowers, potpourri and
soaps, lace and cutwork (an outstanding selection, from collars to valences, and
not terribly expensive). But if you take the time to explore the many rooms of this
former print shop, each with its own personality, you'll also find African and
South American stone and wood carvings, nature books, a great all-around garden tool, afghans, an extensive selection of picnic baskets, and many surprises.
*Shops are one block east of Main on Squires between Bridge and Courtland. If
parking's tight, try the lot across from the Factory outlets or the lot off Monroe,
one block east of the principal business block on Main. Typical hours are 10-5
daily, to 8 Fridays, and 12-5 Sundays, with summer weekdays to 8.*

THE ATTRACTIVE ROGUE RIVER DAM . . . . . is where many things come together.
It's a very popular **fishing spot.** Below the dam is busy during spring steelhead
runs and fall salmon runs. Above the dam are pike, bass, and panfish. A big **platform for handicapped fishermen** is on the west bank. The Rogue is clean enough
for swimming and tubing. Canoe and tubing trips can be arranged through AAA
Rogue River Canoe Rentals at 8 West Bridge, (616) 866-9264. (Warning: there's not
much current, and you have to do a lot of paddling even downstream.)

   You can enjoy the scenery and activity from a park bench behind the old mill
and Squires Street shops, or take a cloth for a regular picnic. Takeout recommendations: coffee and bagels from The Melting Pot, or hot dogs or burgers from The
Corner Bar (p. 351). The **Rockford Historical Museum** (open May through October,
Tues-Sun 1:30-3:30) fills the former powerhouse on East Bridge with a more-
interesting-than-usual mix of old stuff.

Wolverine World Wide Tour

*An illuminating factory tour shows
how flat shoe uppers become finished Hush Puppies.*

The factory tour at Hush-Puppy shoes is one of the best in the state. It offers a slice-of-life glimpse of an interesting manufacturing process from start to finish. (Many tours just show the packaging process.) And it's delivered by a veteran employee familiar with all aspects of plant operation. Here you see already-cut shoe uppers being shaped on a last (a form that's sized for different lengths and widths of feet). "Shoes are made with a lot of heat, steam, and pressure," explains personnel director/tour guide Jackie Thompson. Heat softens the leather, steam shapes it on the last, and pressure applies the cement and tacks that hold the shoe together. Then you see the shoes polished, inspected for quality, and packaged.

Wolverine World Wide began as the Krause tannery here in Rockford and remains headquartered here today. It's one of the leading U.S. shoe companies, with factories in the U. S., Puerto Rico, and the Dominican Republic. The firm's big breakthrough came when it invented a new process for getting skin off pigs sent to slaughterhouses. The old method immersed them in boiling water, thereby ruining the pigskin for any other use. "If people were smart, they'd wear pigskin work shoes in summer," Thompson says, because pigskin, with its bristle pores, breathes more than cowhide. Pigskin's extra comfort prompted the Hush-Puppy name and then then well-known logo.

As soon as you walk into this busy, noisy place and see the degree of unautomated hand work in the 14-step shoemaking process, it's clear why so much U.S. shoe manufacturing has been relocated to countries with cheaper labor. Workers in the factory we toured are highly competitive piece-rate workers — "a different breed from hourly workers" — who earn up to $8 an hour. Each worker can perform at least two jobs and knows the procedure on 40 different shoe patterns at a time.

Wolverine World Wide employs a thousand people in Rockford, including 300 in the tannery, one of the world's largest. **Tannery tours** may be arranged for appropriate groups well in advance by calling Jim Wilcox or Kirk Spencer at (616) 866-5500. It's a messy process in which raw pigskins straight from slaughterhouses are tanned and colored — not for the squeamish, and not for children.

Many employees commute from towns like Greenville and Belding, which have been badly hurt by plant closings. It's logical that labor-intensive, relatively low-paying factory work like this could survive in this part of western Michigan, where the cost of living is much lower than in high-wage areas like Detroit.

To schedule a free tour, call Human Resources Director Jackie Thompson at least a few weeks ahead of time, weekdays at (616) 866-5500, ext. 5354. Young children must be very well supervised (2 adults/child).

REAL FACTORY OUTLETS . . . . . occupy the old Wolverine World Wide buildings along Main Street north of downtown Rockford. A large building now contains the Rockford Factory Outlet Mall and Shoe Museum. Now that the huge Manufacturers' Marketplace has opened in Holland, the mall has lost many stores, but bargains aplenty are still to be found. The **Little Red Shoe House** here is enormous, the biggest by far in the chain of WWW's off-price shoe stores. Prices average 25% off suggested retail, and, in the clearance loft to the back, an additional 25% to 50% less. Stock includes seconds, irregulars, overruns, closeouts of discontinued styles, and some regular styles of WWW brands (Hush-Puppies, Town and Country, Brooks) and others (Naturalizer, LA Gear). Special promotions on work shoes, athletic shoes, etc. change frequently. What makes this special are the discounts on all kinds of shoes for men, women, and children. There's an excellent supply of everyday athletic shoes and sandals, plus $15-$20 basic leather handbags. **Winona Knits** has outstanding values on non-gimmicky all-cotton and all-wool sweaters. Thick wool mittens, made of leftover yarn, are regularly on hand for $6. The **Brooks** retail store has discounts on the full line of Brooks athletic shoes. In the north end basement, the **shoe museum** has displays of Wolverine shoes, from 1900 to modern times. Here are big historical photos (one shows flesh being scraped off horsehide in the tannery) and a step-by-step explanation of how shoes are made today. *(616) 866-9100. Hours for Little Red Shoe House & Winona Knits: Mon-Fri 9-8, Sat 9-6, Sun 12-5. Mall hours: 10-7 weekdays, longer in summer, Sat 9-6, Sun 12-5.*

❶ Kirk Park.
Area's best beach combines natural scenery, pretty picnic spots, good playground, splendid beach backed by high dunes and dark beech woods. Bike path from Holland.

❷ Veldheer Tulip Gardens.
Costs $2 in May to enter the formal garden, but the 30-acre tulip field out back is more magical. Visit at dusk, when tulips glow. Next door is only Delftware factory outside Netherlands.

❸ Dekker Huis.
Splendid local museum illuminates lives of impoverished rural Dutch immigrants of 1847. Vivid displays of early austerity, eventual prosperity.

❹ Dutch Village.
Beguiling mix of history, nostalgia, and storybook kitsch. Small theme park; 18th-19th c. village theme. Wonderful antique carnival rides, street organs. klompen dancers.

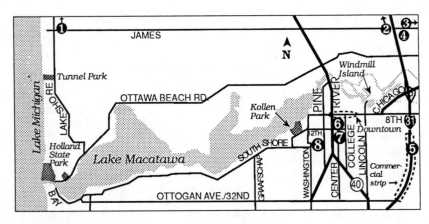

❺ Wooden Shoe Factory.
Fun, old-timey tourist trap has Holland's best demonstrations of wooden shoe making. See antique French sabots and Dutch klompen; sample Dutch sweets and cheese.

❻ Centennial Park. Old-fashioned park with lighted fountain, rock grotto, windmill-shaped flower beds, potted palms from city greenhouse, all beneath canopy of century-old trees.

❼ Netherlands Museum. Dutch bourgeoisie were the Western World's first to create cozy, private homes. See their cheerful 18th-c. sitting rooms, outstanding collections of Delftware, pewter.

❽ Pereddies.
Authentic Italian bakery-deli started by transplants from metro Detroit. Typifies the new Holland: easygoing, pleasant, and multiethnic. Mexican neighborhood just south of here.

Highlights of
Holland

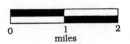

0   1   2
miles

Dutch Village

*The charm and music of an old Dutch street carnival
in a recreated 19th-century village*

If you go to only one tourist sight in Holland, Dutch Village
should be it. This recreation of a 19th-century Dutch village is a beguiling combination of fantasy, nostalgia, education, and gentle kitsch. A private, family-fun attraction that grew
out of a tulip farm, it does a good job of illuminating the 18th- and
19th-century village life Holland's immigrants left behind — better than the city's two municipally owned sights, the Netherlands
Museum and Windmill Island.

The brick buildings that line Dutch Village's four canals look
authentic, with their careful detailing and imported tile roofs.
They are sandwiched between truck-filled U.S. 31 (noise buffers
would be a nice improvement) and the 65-store Manufacturers'
Marketplace outlet mall. Despite the busy location, an illusion of
leaving the 20th century behind is effectively created by the big
willows and cheery brick houses.

The best part of Dutch Village is the operating, antique street
carnival, free for the cost of admission to the grounds. There's a
carousel, two splendid, ornately carved Dutch **street organs**, and
the **Zweefmolen**, a swing something like an antique carousel. It's
just scary enough for older kids to want to ride it again and again
— conveniently allowing adults to look longer at interesting
exhibits and shops.

High-kicking, adept **klompen dancers** perform at 10:30, 12, 2,
4, and 6 to waltzes and gallops played on the **Gauen Engel organ**,
an oversize 1880 Amsterdam street organ restored by the famous
Carl Frey in 1960. For organ-lovers, this alone is worth the cost
of admission. Visitors can go behind the organ to see the bellows,
wood pipes, and punched music paper (much like a player piano's) in action. Recordings of street-organ classics are for sale
in one of the gift shops. For little children, there's a wavy **slide**
descending from a wooden-shoe house. **Ducks** can be fed on the
pond, and **goats** and **sheep** in the half-scale barn.

Attached to the barn is a typical 18th-century **farmhouse**, realistically furnished, with an alcove bed in the stairwell, and a root
cellar down below. The nearby garden area has a European-style
grape arbor, roses, loads of tulips in season, and a giant stork
holding a diaper. Visitors can sit and pose for photos — one of
many such planned photo opportunities.

Tucked away and easy to miss are displays of **Dutch regional costumes** and a well-done **windmill diorama** in a building across the way, along with a **cheese-making exhibit**. Next to it, in a grisly allusion to medieval superstitions that survived in 17th-century Holland, is a scale where suspected witches were weighed. If they were unusually light, they were suspected of being able to fly. Near the entrance, the **Bioskoop** (movie theater) shows a free movie on the Netherlands.

The gift shops at Dutch Village cover an enormous range. The **Souvenir Shop** covers the low end, including the usual Dutchware plus costume dolls, God Bless Our Camper plaques, and some attractive tulip posters. The **Arts and Crafts Building** goes way upscale with lead crystal, Dutch lace valences, a lot of pricey English and French collectibles (interesting carved figures, quaint porcelain villages), beer steins, Delft-trimmed Dutch copper and brass cookware, and cases of stunning Royal Delft, including a $900 plate after a Rembrandt painting. In the same building is a small **wooden shoe factory** (for demonstration only) and shop.

Imported cheeses, Belgian chocolates, Dutch cookies, and jams are for sale in the **Gourmet Food Shop** and **terrace** overlooking the Manufacturers' Marketplace pond.

Holland's only restaurant serving Dutch food is the attached **Queen's Inn** (see p. 354). Don't miss the section of real thatched roof. It comes down to near eye-level so you can see just how thick and tight-bundled it is.

*James at U.S. 31, 2 miles northeast of downtown Holland. (616) 396-1475. **Shops** open year-round 9-5:30, in summer until 8. Free admission when grounds are closed. **Grounds** are open from the last weekend of April through September. Gates open at 9 a.m. and close at 6. Admission: $4 adults, $2 children 3-11.*

BEST WOODEN-SHOEMAKING DEMONSTRATIONS. . . . . The only American member of the Dutch guild of klompenmakers works in a sawdusty, sneezy wood shop at the **Wooden Shoe Factory**, a giant, old-timey tourist trap that's lots of fun. The specialized wood-turning equipment used here in making wooden shoes was manufactured in the Netherlands and France at the turn of the century. An interesting display shows many kind of wooden shoes worn in low-lying areas of France, Holland, and Belgium. *On U.S. 31 just south of 16th St. 8 a.m.-6 p.m. daily. Demonstrations run from 8 a.m. to 4:30 daily except Sunday.*

Veldheer Tulip Gardens/ DeKlomp Wooden Shoe & Delftware Factory

The acres of spring tulip fields are spectacular, especially when the sun is low.

Veldheer's spectacular mass of tulips attracts throngs of tourists in May. The longtime Holland tulip-grower has a very pleasant formal garden, complete with drawbridges and the inevitable ornamental windmills, which are also sold in the adjoining garden shop. (The large windmill is an authentic copy of a traditional Dutch drainage windmill.) In summer the gardens are filled with new varieties of lilies, peonies, and Dutch iris that Veldheer's is introducing.

But the truly spectacular sight is the 30-acre tulip field behind the warehouses. Evenings, when the tour buses are gone, the locals come out after work to enjoy the tulips. At dusk, the sweeping masses of flowers, almost as far as you can see, seem to glow and shimmer with their own light, especially on overcast days.

Beds in the formal gardens are numbered to correspond with mail-order catalogs, so you can place orders for fall bulbs after seeing the real thing in bloom (about April 20 through May). Veldheer claims to grow the world's largest selection of tulips, 76 varieties in all, plus various daffodils, hyacinths, crocus, fritillaria, and the new peonies and lilies. Prices: $5 to $6.70 for 10 tulip bulbs.

Next door, under the same ownership and management, is the **DeKlomp wooden shoe and delftware factory.** It's the only place outside the Netherlands where earthenware is hand-painted in the Dutch style using genuine Delft glaze. In the 17th-century, during the short but glorious time of Dutch dominance at sea, blue-and-white Delft imitating expensive Chinese porcelains was manufactured for middle-class Hollanders. Painters here are happy to answer questions and explain the difference between real, handpainted Delft and much cheaper lookalikes with printed decal transfers. Popular items include personalized wedding and retirement plates ($80 and up when completely handpainted), tiny shoes and figurines ($8), house portraits, and wedding or baby tiles.

De Klomp also has a **wooden shoe demonstration workshop** with picture windows. The large stock of plain and decorated wooden shoes ("klompen" in Dutch, "sabots" in French) is made in the Netherlands; prices here ($16.45 for a women's size 7) are somewhat cheaper than at other outlets. The usual Dutch sweets and souvenirs are also for sale.

On Quincy just east of U.S. 31, 4 miles north of Holland. Clearly visible from the highway. (616) 399-1900. Open year-round. May: daily 8-dusk. June through Oct: daily 8-6. Nov-April: 8-5. Admission for formal gardens (May only), $2 adults, $1 children 6-16.

WORTHWHILE IF YOU LIKE OLD CARS. . . . . An unpretentious museum with an interesting assortment of vintage American vehicles, the **Poll Museum of Transportation** was started by a retired tool-and-die manufacturer. His collection is continually being upgraded. Favorites include a rare 1904 Cadillac, 1908 and 1910 Buicks, a 1931 Packard, and the big, wood-sided 1948 Chrysler Town and Country convertible in mint condition. Collections of toy trucks, model trains, seashells, and bottles, plus a large gift shop, broaden the appeal. *On U.S. 31 at New Holland Rd., a mile north of Veldheer's. Open Mon-Sat May 1-Labor Day. Adults $1, children 10-12 50¢, under 10 free.*

BEST BEACH NEAR HOLLAND. . . . . Holland State Park is the busy, treeless beach most tourists head for, but if you want a beautiful natural setting, Ottawa County's **Kirk Park** is far superior. There's a nifty playground near the entrance, a food wagon in summer, a picnic area, and a lovely trail past a deeply shady dune to a lake overlook platform and the 800-foot beach. *From Dutch Village, go 10 miles north on U. S. 31, turn west onto Fillmore and go 2 miles. Turn right (north) onto Lake Shore and you'll be there. $2/car.*

Netherlands Museum

A visual feast of homey ornament:
Delftware and local costumes,
pewter and lace, cottage sitting rooms with tile ovens

Interesting decorative objects are the strength of this unusual museum, the only one in the U. S. to focus broadly on Dutch culture in the old and new worlds. We recommend it with qualifications. If you aren't interested in decorative objects, you'll likely be bored.

Throughout history Dutch life has been centered on the home. Every nook and cranny of a Dutch household was typically embellished with affection. Indeed, it was bourgeois Dutch in the 17th century who invented the concept of cozy, comfortable, private domestic life. A Dutch housewife's kitchen, centered on an elaborately decorated tile oven, was as beautiful as the parlor. In middle-class French and English homes, where servants did all the work, kitchens were plain and dark.

All sorts of wonderful ornament make this museum's collections a visual feast: lots of Delftware, carved furniture, pewter, and Leerdam glassware. A dollhouse

Sitting room of a Dutch cottage in the 19th century, about the time of the migrations to Michigan.

is furnished down to inkwells and cookie cutters. Cheerful period sitting rooms of an 18th-century fisherman's home and a Zeeland farmhouse have lots of lace and blue and white plates and tiles, and cupboard beds to keep out damp drafts. Many colorful provincial costumes are displayed in the basement.

A few stories are told well here — the hardships and disease of Holland's first winter and the fire of 1871. But most of these displays fail to use things to tell stories and convey ideas. For concepts applied to the human experience of Dutch immigrants, Dekker Huis in Zeeland (p. 319) does a much better job. Look for major changes when the Netherlands Museum leaves its big brick house for much larger quarters in the renovated post office.

12th St. at Central Ave., kitty-corner from Centennial Park. (616) 392-9084. April-Dec.: Mon-Sat 9-5, Sun (mid-May to Sept.) 11:30-5. Jan.-March: Thurs-Sat 1-4 and by appointment. $1/adults, children 12 and under free with adults.

FOR TWO WALKING TOURS OF OLD HOLLAND. . . . . Go down 12th to River and stop in at the Herrick Public Library. One tour includes Holland's unusually handsome **downtown**, centered on 8th, and nearby Hope College. The other covers the beautiful **historic neighborhood** around 12th between Pine and Washington, just west of River Avenue. . . . . Both tours start at **Centennial Park**, the sweetly old-fashioned, shady downtown square across the street. Its landscaping has a 19th-century picturesque, European air — rock grottoes, a circular fountain (illuminated at night) palm trees and tropical flowering plants brought out each summer from the city's own greenhouse, "carpet beds" of flowers shaped like a windmill and wooden shoe.

THE ONLY WORKING ANTIQUE WINDMILL OUTSIDE HOLLAND. . . . . De Zwaan ('the swan") is the centerpiece of Holland's **Windmill Island Municipal Park**. You can see the mill grind flour, but only when flour supplies sold at the park are low and the wind is between 15 and 20 knots. The rest of the park is disappointing, despite some nice touches like the handmade folk-art model of a Dutch canal town in 1847 and a canal-side terrace and carousel. We recommend Dutch Village as a better value and more interesting Dutch-theme tourist attraction. De Zwaan is in some ways more majestic when viewed in the distance from the walkway in the Window on the Waterfront Park, where River Street crosses the Black River. *Windmill Island is on 7th at Lincoln, northeast of downtown. Open daily, May-Oct. (616) 396-5433. Adults $3.50, children $1.75.*

Dekker Huis

Where Dutch immigrants' faith, early poverty,
and hard-won success come to life.

When it comes to conveying the life experiences of ordinary people, this small museum, run by the Zeeland Historical Society, is one of the very best around. The historical society members who show visitors around are apt to be lifelong Zeelanders who are part of the history themselves. Their museum brilliantly uses objects to convey ideas. There's a trunk — a very small trunk — displayed with everything the typical Zeeland pioneering immigrant family took to America. These Dutch Secessionists were simple country people, among the poorest of all the American emigrants from Northern Europe. When they first arrived in western Michigan, they lived very simply indeed.

The museum consists of a furnished house built by a grocer next to his store and, in the store, exhibit space including a gallery for **changing shows.** The founders of Zeeland all belonged to the same Secessionist congregation in the Zeeland farm town of Goes (pronounced "Hoos") in Zeeland, a northern province of the Netherlands. They emigrated as a group in 1847. They left their cozy Dutch kitchens for a harsh environment on the Michigan frontier, where, for awhile, the whole village shared a single hand-made shovel. (It's here in the museum.)

When you step inside the grocer's small but comfortable dining room and parlor, furnished roughly as it was about 1920, you experience the material success the immigrants were so proud of, and the bourgeois domesticity for which the Dutch are famous. Lace curtains, dark wood trim, imitation Oriental carpets — it feels cozy but a little stuffy, like the living rooms of millions of Americans' grandmothers' houses. So does the master bedroom, with its made-in-Zeeland bedroom suite and blue-and-white linoleum imitating tile. The laundry is set up for wash day on the house's side porch — complete with washtubs, mops in the corner, underwear drying, and blueing in a jar.

37 E. Main in Zeeland, about half a block west of the downtown business district. (616) 772-4079. Thurs 10-4, Sat 10-1. Closed Nov.-early March.

ALSO RECOMMENDED . . . . . A brief look at the rest of **Zeeland,** a most distinctive American town that bans the sale of liquor, shuts down on Sunday, and has more jobs (7,000) than people (5,400). It is still almost entirely Dutch, the way nearby Holland used to be. The **Zeeland Bakery** on Main Street bakes Dutch butter cookies and Holland rusk, which locals eat soaked in milk.

Nowhere is the vaunted Dutch-American work ethic more pronounced than in Zeeland, the headquarters of three large and famous home-grown industries: Bil Mar Foods ("Mr. Turkey"), Herman Miller furniture (a leader in functional design with one of the most admired corporate cultures in America), and Howard Miller clocks. (The latter two are seen east of town out Main.) Poultry farming and vegetable-raising, two traditional occupations, are still in evidence. **DeBruyn Produce** on Washington at Chicago sells many varieties of bulk vegetable seeds to growers (and the general public). On **Church Street**, one street south of Main, are huge Dutch Reformed churches, impressive homes from the early 20th century, and old-fashioned corner parks at Church and Central. The street's air of well-built solidity suggests the Calvinist attitude that worldly prosperity is a natural sign of devout Christian faith. Paul de Kruif, Dutch rebel, science popularizer, and author of *Microbe Hunters*, grew up in the Queen Anne house just east of the largest park.

Saugatuck

*One of the state's most picturesque resorts,
with interesting shops, outstanding bed & breakfasts,
great views from Mt. Baldhead, and a popular beach*

Saugatuck is one of the state's jewels, a town blessed with a combination of natural and man-made beauty. Too small to handle large crowds gracefully, it can strike a dissonant note when jammed with tourists on summer weekends. On less crowded days and in the off-season, it is relaxed and pleasant.

The town is nestled along the Kalamazoo River on a half-mile-long plain between hills and dunes to both east and west. Because Saugatuck was largely bypassed by railroads and late-19th-century commerce, it has the quaint look of pre-industrial New England. There's a lovely old village green. Small-scale clapboard buildings are often embellished with Victorian gingerbread trim. Paths lead to tucked-away shops, patios, and balconies set back from the sidewalk activity. The public gardens and parks are delightful.

Here is probably the densest concentration of top-notch bed-and-breakfast inns in Michigan, ranging from elegant to country relaxed. The community has been invigorated by gays and other talented urban refugees, even as Saugatuck's reputation as an art colony diminishes.

Saugatuck is unusual in having a town common, deeded by town founder William Gay Butler, a Connecticut Yankee. Today these three corner parks on Butler at Main continue to have a small-scale New England charm. The temple-like facade of the Christian Science church is an attractive backdrop for the delightful little garden in the southwest park. A bronze statue of a girl with a puppet commemorates Saugatuck summer resident Burr Tillstrom, creator of 1950s TV puppets "Kukla, Fran and Ollie." Across Main Street is a pleasant children's playground. **Tennis courts,** a **basketball court,** and a gaily painted **restroom** building are on the other side of Butler.

Peaceful **Wicks Park,** on Water Street at Main, offers some lovely views over the river and across to the old cottage colony clustered around Mount Baldhead. **Riverside benches,** away from the summer crowds in downtown Saugatuck, make this a nice spot for a takeout picnic. Daytime **art lessons** and evenings of **romantic dancing** or **concerts** take place around the **gazebo.**

On the Kalamazoo River in downtown Saugatuck is the **Coral**

Gables, a vast, rambling dance hall/restaurant, reminiscent of the big old nightspots up and down the coast built to attract thousands of Chicagoans. The hottest action is at the **Crow Bar**, a rock 'n' roll dance hall featuring live bands. Friday and Saturday nights from 8 to 2, it packs in a young crowd of hundreds. In the **Rathskeller** below, a trio entertains a more sedate, smaller crowd of dancers. The **El Forno** dining room (lunch and dinner) has the best water view. **The Bootlegger** bar features shrimp and oysters.

Art has made Saugatuck nationally known. **Ox-Bow**, a summer school of art connected with the Chicago Institute of Art, operates at the picturesque remote tip of the peninsula across the river from downtown. It opened back in 1910 and still attracts serious students of art. The town's most visible artistic presence today are its unusually interesting art galleries.

Saugatuck scenes by the late Gerritt Beverwyk can be seen at the Cain Gallery.

Saugatuck's downtown on Butler and Water streets has a strong mix of gift shops, resortwear, and traditional casual clothing. **Saugatuck Drugs** on Butler at Mason is a town hub — a vast old drugstore with soda fountain and video arcade.

Here are some shopping highlights :

◆ **Water Street Galleries.** A quality gallery, showing name artists from all over the U.S. Paintings by William Aiken of San Francisco, prints by Tony Saladino of Texas, bronze sculpture by Jean Jacques Porret of Chicago, and glass by Craig Campbell of Minnesota. *403 Water. (616) 857-8485. Daily 10-5:30. Closed Tues. from Sept. through April.*

◆ **Polka Gallery.** Genial, European-trained oil painter John Polka has been a Saugatuck fixture since 1964. In his studio/gallery you can see him at work on his own dreamily romantic, impressionist paintings of flowers, landscapes, and figures ($100 to $5,000). Many scenes are local. Polka also does commission portraits and teaches classes in his studio. *731 Water. Year-round, daily 10-9.*

◆ **Cain Gallery.** The summer home of a gallery in suburban Oak Park, Illinois, Cain shows paintings and prints, jewelry, sculpture, and art glass by living artists with national reputations. *322 Butler. Open Mother's Day thru color season. June 1 through Labor Day: 11-5 daily. Weekends only in May and fall.*

◆ **Singapore Bank Bookstore.** Saugatuck's biggest bookstore, a cozy, personal place run by an avid sailor, is located in the old Singapore Bank building. Moving the structure here saved it from entombment by dune sands. *317 Butler (2nd floor). May through Dec: Sun-Thurs 10-6. Fri & Sat 10-8. Winter: may close Tues-Thurs. Call first.*

◆ **East of the Sun.** Rambling gift shop has several talented buyers, so the selection is interestingly varied. There are a number of rooms (including some upstairs) to mosey through. Lamps, home accessories, whimsical gifts, garden accessories, prints, Christmas ornaments, and lots more. *252 Butler. Mon-Sat 10-5:30, Sun 11-5. Closed Tues-Thurs in Feb. & March.*

◆ **The Design Shop.** Interior design studio with a relaxed mix of interesting accessories: antique prints (botanicals and birds), afghans, colorful Italian pitchers, unusual baskets, and posters. *133 Main at Butler, behind the village green. Summer hours: Mon-Sat 10-5, Sun 12-5. Otherwise closed Tues & Wed, except for Jan (weekends only) and Feb & March (closed).*

◆ **Hoopdee Scootee.** This outrageous, amusing shop does a booming business in unisex clothing, Art Deco reproductions, T-shirts, sculpture, and adult cards. Custom-designed neon sells for $150 to $400. The checkout counter is made out of the front of a 1 1/2 ton truck. A car door shields the dressing room. *133 Mason, around the corner from Butler. (616) 857-4141. Open April 15- Halloween.*

◆ **Good Goods.** "Global art and artifacts" from traditional ethnic craftspeople and American artists. Everything from $5 Chinese papercuttings to fine contemporary gold and silver jewelry and handblown glass perfume bottles and lamps. . Handmade clothing includes chenille scarves ($30-$50), felted *samii* mittens and caps with a Lapllander look ($20-$30), and elegantly draped ikat silk swing coats ($650). Unusual musical instruments: African stringed instruments and drums ($5-$200), pottery flutes and ocarinas. *106 Mason. (616) 857-1557. Mid-April & May, and Labor Day-Xmas: open 10-6 daily. Mid-June-Labor Day: open daily 10-10. Jan-March: open Fri-Mon 10-6.*

◆ **Joyce Petter Gallery.** Often humorous or richly decorative, this art is easy to live with. Eclectic, accessible, and interesting, the Petter Gallery showcases 50 high-quality American painters, printmakers, sculptors, glassmakers, and ceramicists in an intriguing series of spaces. Prices range from $85 to $7,000. *134 Butler. (616) 857-7861. Mon-Sat 10-5:30, Sun noon-5:30. Closed Jan & Feb. May move; call to confirm location.*

◆ **The Butler Pantry.** A kitchen accessory shop of unusual quality, the Pantry was created by ex-Chicagoans Fritz Helman and Ron Aure. Upstairs the owners have fashioned a beguiling little **mini-mall** looking out onto a delightful alleyway courtyard and arranged around a **deli-cafe** (see Restaurants) where they make their own jams and jellies. *121 Butler. (616) 857-4875. Open year around. Sun-Thurs 10-5, Fri & Sat until 6.*

◆ **Tuck's of Saugatuck.** Delightful shop devoted to fine Christmas ornaments and accessories, many designed especially for the shop. Each year Tuck dramatically changes the decor, which alone is worth a look. *249 Culver. Open all year. May-Dec.; open daily 11-5, in summer 10-8. Jan-April: Sat & Sun only, 11-5.*

◆ **Button Galleries.** The site alone is so attractive, it's worth the drive to Douglas's leafy area of summer homes along Lake Michigan. Visitors can walk through the garden filled with rhododendrons and azaleas. Features contemporary oils and water colors by national and regional artists. *955 Center in Douglas, one block east of Lake Michigan. Turn west from Blue Star Hwy. onto Center at the light, proceed toward lake. (616) 857-2175. Usually open daily 11-5 between mid-May and mid-Oct. Call first.* One of the state's finest galleries.

❶ Saugatuck Dunes State Park. Wild, pristine dune country, 2 mi. of uncrowded beach, 14 mi. of hiking trails. Dune tops offer nice lake views.

❷ Downtown Saugatuck. Lively mix of quality galleries, gift & clothing shops along with delightful town common and gardens.

❸ Queen of Saugatuck. Informative cruise on fake steamboat highlights marine geography of Kalamazoo Lake and Lake Michigan shoreline.

❹ Wicks Park & boardwalk. Civilized little park with benches looks across river to Mt. Baldhead. Evening concerts with dance orchestra in gazebo.

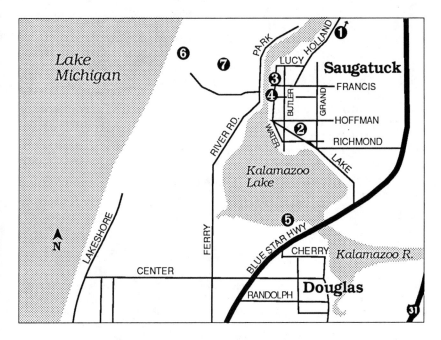

❺ S.S. Keewatin. Bygone glories of elegant Great Lakes cruise ships live on in this 336-foot steamship, now a museum.

❻ Oval Beach. Costs $5 a car on weekends to join the crowd at this popular beach. Well-stocked concession stand.

❼ Mt. Baldhead. Reward of short but strenuous climb is splendid views of city and lakes. Pleasant picnic site below on river.

Bed and breakfast inns. Outstanding quality & variety; over 12 in area, from elegant to casual.

Highlights of
Saugatuck

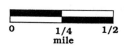

Queen of Saugatuck

One of the very best Lake Michigan boat rides

Interestingly varied scenery make this an enjoyable 1 1/2-hour voyage. The 67-foot, 82-passenger boat goes out on Lake Michigan when the waves aren't too high. The informative guide comments colorfully on passing sights. He explains how the little flags on charter fishing boats tell how many fish were caught on the last outing, how the Lake Michigan shoreline has eroded 300 feet over the past 88 years, how the soft-sounding foghorn at the end of the channel going into Lake Michigan sounds much louder in a fog. It's best to take this pleasant voyage when it isn't too windy and the boat can safely make it out into Lake Michigan. In general, the earlier in the day, the calmer the water. Restrooms, food and drinks, beer, and wine, on board.

716 Water near Spear next to Gleason's Party Store, on the Kalamazoo River. (616) 857-4261. Daily early May thru 3rd week of Sept; weekends thru Oct. weather permitting. $6 adults, $3 children.

THE SAUGATUCK DUNE RIDES . . . . plunge you through shifting sands in a converted 3/4 ton Dodge pickup. The 35-minute ride emphasizes amusement, not nature appreciation. Roaring up and down steep slopes, the driver is likely to suddenly shout things like, "No brakes! We've lost the brakes!" Even without the histrionics, the journey is rather harrowing. The 16-seat open-air vehicles have no rollbars. *Blue Star Highway, 1/2 mile west of I-196 on exit 41, 1 mile northeast of Saugatuck. (616) 857-2253. Open May 1 through mid-October. Through September Mon-Sat 10-6, Sun 12-6. In July & Aug. open until 8. In October weekends only. $8 adults; $5 children ten and under.*

Mt. Baldhead & Oval Beach

*A fine panorama, a great picnic spot, dune trails,
and a well-equipped beach*

Named for its sandy crown before trees were planted on top,
this 262-foot dune is the tallest in the region. It provides a
superb view of Saugatuck, Lake Kalamazoo, and Douglas.
The climb by wooden stairway is short but steep.

You can easily get here from downtown Saugatuck by taking the
chain ferry, which runs from Mary and Water in downtown Saugatuck to Ferry Street, across the Kalamazoo River. *Mem.- Labor Day
9-9. Adults $1; children 50¢ one way.*

For a **delightful car-free picnic,** pick up tasty sandwiches at The
Butler Pantry Deli, 121 Butler. Take the chain ferry across the
river and head north along Park Street to the foot of Mt. Baldhead. You can picnic either on the top or on the pleasant deck
overlooking the river and downtown Saugatuck across the river.

On top of Mt. Baldhead is a radar dome, installed in 1957 as
part of the DEW line stretching across northern America to warn
of Soviet attack from the north. Shut down years ago, the dome
now holds a ship-to-shore antenna. From the top, two interesting
trails, one to the north and one to the south, lead to scenic views
of the lake and forested surroundings.

The popular city-owned **Oval Beach** is on the west side of Mt.
Baldhead. There are restrooms, changing rooms, a snack stand
(chili is $2 a bowl), a game arcade, a big parking lot, and a place
to buy beach paraphernalia. You can rent **giant tubes** for $1 an
hour, and also chairs and cabanas.

Just above the beach, signs point to some quite nice **walks up
on the dunes.** The one heading north along the ridge is especially
recommended for its view over the lake.

*To climb Mt. Baldhead, park across the Kalamazoo River from
downtown. Reach it on foot from downtown Saugatuck by the
chain ferry or arrive by car through Douglas. Oval Beach (616)
857-1121. $3 per car weekdays, $5 weekends. Walk-ins free.*

S.S. Keewatin ship museum

A huge steamer evokes the era of elegantly appointed ships which cruised the Great Lakes.

The 336-foot *Keewatin*, permanently moored here, is a rare vestige of the wonderful era of Great Lakes steamship travel. It was one of the last of the big boats, in service until 1965. The *Keewatin* sailed from eastern Lake Huron to Thunder Bay on western Lake Superior. The six-day round trip cost $30 in 1908, including meals.

An admirably knowledgeable tour guide gives a thorough look at the Scottish-built vessel: the ornately carved mahogany interiors, the compact staterooms, the forward lounge for female passengers only, and the Edwardian dining room. The spartan galley had Chinese chefs. (The original French cooks drank too much.) On top is the great 50-foot funnel. Powered by coal, the boat's 3,300 horsepower engine took 150 tons of coal a week. Alongside the *Keewatin* is the last of the coal-powered Great Lakes steam tugs, the *Reiss.*.

See map. (616) 857-2107. Guided tours 10-4:30 daily, Mem. Day-Labor Day. Adults $3, children 6-12 $1.50.

A MOST NATURAL AND PEACEFUL BEACH SOUTH OF MUSKEGON . . . . . the **Saugatuck Dunes State Park** is protected from hoards of beachgoers by its remote location. It's one of western Michigan's most beautiful yet uncrowded nature spots. The 1,100 acres include over two miles of Lake Michigan **beach** and 14 miles of **hiking trails** through the wild, pristine dune country to wonderful dune-top views of the lake. The parking lot is a mile from the beach, and the sandy, hilly path makes it seem even longer. *3 1/2 miles north of Saugatuck. Take Blue Star Highway to 64th St., go north 1 1/2 miles to 138th Ave., west 1 mile to park. (616) 399-9390. 8 a.m.-10 p.m. daily. $3/car/day, $15 annual state park sticker.* **No camping.**

Grand Haven's Boardwalk

*A two-mile riverfront stroll takes you by
an extraordinary variety of interesting sights.*

Boaters, strollers and joggers visit this interesting walkway from early morning until late evening. It stretches about two miles from a lighthouse on Lake Michigan all the way along the Grand River past downtown to Linear Park next to the huge municipal power plant. Active boat traffic on this part of the Grand ranges from large freighters to million-dollar yachts.

Many highlights accent this pleasant walk:

◆ A striking **historic railroad display** near the east end of the Boardwalk includes a huge concrete coaling tower, and a 1941 steam locomotive, with tender and two old cabooses.

◆ The **farmers' market** is off North Harbor just east of Chinook Pier, open Wednesdays and Saturdays from 8 a.m. to 2 p.m. from June through October, plus Mondays 3-7 p.m. in July and Aug.

◆ **Chinook Pier**, two blocks north of Washington, is home of a large charter fishing fleet (616-842-2229) and the departure point for two summer sightseeing tours, one by bus and the other by boat. The bus tour is far more interesting; it leaves on the half hour. Alongside popular Marina Mike's convenience store are shops selling cookies and ice cream, resortwear and T-shirts.

◆ The famous **Musical Fountain** across the Grand River is seen from a viewing stands at the foot of Washington downtown. It attracts hundreds at dusk, daily from mid-May through Labor Day, for a coordinated half-hour concert of recorded music (12,000 watts worth) and changing colored lights beamed on changing sprays of water. The often sizable crowd that gathers nightly is as much a part of the spectacle as the fountain. Pleasure boats crowd together in the river to view the event.

◆ **Downtown Grand Haven** has some of West Michigan's best specialty shopping. Closest to the boardwalk is **Harbourfront Place,** a shopping/restaurant/office complex in a big 1906 piano factory. At the foot of Washington is the popular **Kirby Grill**, a superior bistro-type restaurant that turns into a boisterous, convivial drinking spot at night. The town's top gourmet shop for good wines, cheeses, fancy foods, and freshly roasted peanuts, is **Fortino's**, 114 Washington. Next door, the **Mackinaw Kite Company** has an awesome selection of kites and other wind toys, from indoor versions to traditional Chinese kites to stunt kites and power kites that pick the flier off the ground. The **Michigan Rag Company** at 121 Washington sells colorful, sturdy beach and and boating wear designed and manufactured in Grand Haven by the same firm. An exceptional gift shop, **Ad Lib**, 218 Washington, carries quite a mix of contemporary crafts, Mexican painted earthenware, crystal and silver, paisley, inexpensive folk jewelry, and funny wind-up toys.

◆ The **Tri-Cities Historical Museum**, is on the river at the head of Washington Street in the old Grand Trunk Depot. It has a wonderfully rich assortment of local artifacts illuminating the area's colorful past, from trapping, lumbering, and shipping to manufacturing, railroading, and the Coast Guard past. *Open daily except Mon. in summer 10 a.m. until 9:30 (12 to 6 Sun.). Open weekend afternoons Sept-May. Adults $1, children free.*

◆ The **Brass River Display,** between the Chamber of Commerce and the historical museum, is a wonderful brass sidewalk map, 50 feet wide, of all the rivers and creeks which feed into the Grand River. This splendid brass map vividly shows how the immense catchment area of the mighty Grand River extends all the way to the Irish Hills south of Jackson. It was made with volunteer help by employees of the local Grand Haven Brass Foundry.

◆ The striking **South Pier** with its **catwalk** and **lighthouse** is at the end of the boardwalk. The outer light dates from 1875. The long pier's catwalk, once used to get out to the lights during storms, has great nostalgic value to locals, who pitched in to restore it. The pier is a great place to stroll — except during storms, when it is dangerous. It's also popular with perch fishermen.

ON LAKE MICHIGAN AT THE END OF THE BOARDWALK . . . . The long, sandy beaches of **Grand Haven State Park** and the city of Grand Haven are among the most popular in Michigan. They're busy with stunt kites, teens, and jet skis on weekends, but families frequent them, too. There's little in the way of nature to shade the asphalt and sand. Most of the 182 campsites are booked up months in advance. (616) 842-6020.

❶ North Beach Park. Nice, less crowded beach and terrific dune to climb, with splendid view of town and lake.

❷ Arboreal Inn. Out of the way, but worth the drive. Good food, great atmosphere in quaint, rustic setting.

❸ Boardwalk. Lively and scenic, with lots of boats, views, strollers, snacks, Snug Harbor Restaurant.

❹ South Pier. Dramatic walk out to two old lighthouses. As popular with strollers as fishermen.

❺ Lake Michigan beaches. Trees are scarce, but these beachside parks are packed with swimmers, kites, and RVs.

❻ Highland Park. Haunting Victorian summer colony in wooded dunes. Scenic boardwalk winds through it.

❼ Lake Forest Cemetery & Duncan Park. Beautiful 19th-century setting with hills, dales, majestic beeches.

❽ Idyllic drive along the Grand to historic Eastmanville, Lamont, mid-19th-century river villages.

Highlights of
Grand Haven

0   1/4   1/2
mile

Highland Park

*Grand Haven's enchanting 19th-century
cottage colony has magical boardwalks
through steep, forested hills and shady valleys.*

T his haunting summer colony of a hundred cottages sits among dunes overlooking Lake Michigan. Highland Park has long been a summer retreat for well-to-do families from as far away as St. Louis and Louisville, as well as Chicago and Grand Rapids. Today these cottages command fancy prices — from $100,000 to $250,000. Many longtime family cottages retain a rather austere simplicity that hasn't changed for decades. What's special here are the quaint narrow roads, the striking dune environment with steep hills and shady valleys, and the old beech and maple forests.

The best look at Highland Park is from the rambling **boardwalks** that go back and dip through the steep, heavily wooded back dunes. It's dark and cool here, a nice respite from too much sun on the beach. The dunes drop off so dramatically, the boardwalks seem suspended in the treetops as they pass by the cottages' ample porches. From them you can look down on wild flowers and scampering chipmunks. The quainter cottages are back away from the lake, some approachable only via the boardwalk and numerous steps.

The leisurely atmosphere of plain, rustic summer retreats survives at Highland park's Khardomah Lodge.

Finding Highland Park's boardwalks can be a trick. If you are on the beach, look for the stairs climbing the bluff just south of Lake Avenue. They lead to an overlook with benches, a popular place for viewing sunsets, in front of the pink Highland Park Hotel. Walk briefly back along Lake Avenue; behind the hotel, you'll see Lover's Lane. Go down it a ways, and a little to your left you'll see the white painted railing to stairs that look like a private cottage entrance. This is actually part of the boardwalk, maintained by the Highland Park Association. The boardwalk winds around among the cottages, sometimes ending on a road. (The roads themselves, are oriented to parking, not views, and much less interesting.)

To more fully experience the beauty of Highland Park, you may want to stay either in the **Khardomah Lodge**, which dates from 1873, or the **Highland Park Hotel**, a bed and breakfast. See **Lodgings** for details.

Along and off of Highland Rd., south of Lake Ave., overlooking Lake Michigan. Just east of the Bil Mar Restaurant, which is at 1223 S. Harbor.

BEHIND HIGHLAND PARK . . . . . Duncan Park is a dark and mysterious-looking beech-maple climax forest on the back dunes about half a mile from Lake Michigan. It's for walking, cross-country skiing in winter, and picnicking. Just west of the park's Lake Drive entrance, entered off Lake, is **Lake Forest Cemetery**, established in 1872 among the hills and dales of the forested back dunes. Few cemeteries can approach this one for the combination of beautiful setting, interesting plants and monuments, and varied strands of local history and American immigrants' experience represented in the dates and birthplaces of people buried here: Yankee, Scotch, and Irish pioneers, soon followed by numerous Dutch. The deep shade of majestic beeches contrasts with the play of light on their elephant-smooth trunks. The great trees anchor the winding paths and are effective natural foils to the elaborate post-Civil War monuments. To get a splendid map and history of Lake Forest Cemetery, complete with 35 identified sites, ask at the Tri-Cities Historical Museum (p. 330).

Hoffmaster State Park and Gillette Visitors' Center

An inspired nature center expands your enjoyment of Lake Michigan's splendid dunes.

Part of the magic of the dunes is their contrast of sun and sand with deep, dark shade. The beach and foredunes are sunny and windswept, with only dune grass and occasional shrubs and scrawny trees. The back dunes are dark and cool, mysterious beneath the canopy of huge maples and ancient, elephant-barked beeches. Hoffmaster State Park, more than most Lake Michigan parks, gets you interested in the complete dune environment, not just the beach and foredunes.

What makes Hoffmaster so very special is the top-notch nature center at the **Gillette Visitors' Center**. It provides one of the best views of Lake Michigan's dunes, which are the longest stretch of freshwater dunes in the world. And it tells their story in an unusually compelling way that makes you respect their fragile ecology and grandeur.

The best part of the story is told outdoors, on the dunes themselves, through excellent diagrams and explanations geared to the very view you are seeing. A **boardwalk** and 200-step **dune stairway** lead visitors up through a beech maple forest so towering, dark, and shady that it seems to have been there forever. There are frequent seats for resting and looking down on the trees. At the summit is a spectacular 180-foot-high overlook with a bird's-eye view of a vast landscape. To the west and north you see Lake Michigan and the two lines of dunes paralleling it. East you see sandy, low-lying blueberry farms and pretty Little Black Lake.

On the walk up the stairway and back down and out to the beach, you see how the back dunes vary from desert-like conditions on their west-facing slopes to virtual rain forests of perpetual dampness in the troughs and east slopes, where moist winds off the lake drop their moisture as they hit land. These diverse biologic zones fascinate naturalists; the basic principles of plant succession were, in fact, based on observations of Lake Michigan sand dunes by University of Chicago biologists.

The nature center here is one of the two or three best in Michigan. If you're short on time, pass over the elaborate but jargon-filled displays of the Exhibit Hall, prepared by an outside firm of museum professionals. Opt instead for the outstanding multi-image slide shop, **"Michigan Sand Dunes and Hoffmaster State Park,"** shown in the comfortable, 82-seat theater. Written and produced by the center's own talented naturalists, it tells Lake Michigan's sand dune story from their formation by prevailing westerlies, through the 19th-century logging and resort eras, up into the present time. Every hour on the hour, a second beautifully photographed slide show features seasonal wildflowers or other natural subjects in the park.

Downstairs, the well-thought-out **hands-on classroom** is a great rainy-day destination. Here are numerous live animals and fish to watch. Kids seem fascinated cuddling a stuffed owl to see how soft and plumped-up its layers of feathers are. Visitors can request to see videos on shoreline erosion and on moose, loons, and bluebirds — all species at risk due to increased development of their natural habitats.

The Mother's Day Trillium Festival celebrates Hoffmaster's spectacular wildflower display in the wooded back dunes.

The excellent **bookstore,** run by an enthusiastic volunteer organization, focuses on nature publications for all ages. It has an interesting array of posters, notecards, and nature-related gifts, too.

Spring wildflower displays in backdune forests like these are spectacular. On Mother's Day each year the **Trillium Festival** offers many guided walks and more. Call (616) 798-3573 for a schedule of **nature walks and talks** at Gillette; group tours are by appointment.

Adjoining the visitors' center are 10 miles of wonderful **hiking trails** through beech-maple forests, up dunes and down onto fairly remote beaches. In winter, three miles of intermediate cross-country **ski trails** through the forests begin by the picnic shelter at the end of the drive past the Visitors' Center.

Hoffmaster has 2 1/2 miles of **beach** with beautiful dunes as a backdrop. It's most crowded by the concession stand and bath-house, close to large parking lots and an unshaded **picnic area.** But if you walk south down the beach, in 10 minutes you can be away from the crowds, and close to the beautiful boardwalk that leads back to the spectacular dune overlook connected to the Gillette Visitors' Center. Much nicer **picnic areas,** deeply shaded and relatively private, are along the main road past the beach turnoff.

The 333-space modern **campground** is one of the nicest in Michigan, despite its large size. It's in a separate part of the park, off Lake Harbor Road, beneath a shady canopy of pines and hard-woods. Its beautiful setting and proximity to a campers-only beach make it quite popular. Half the spaces are reservable, and reservations are advised on all summer weekends. Weekdays there's usually space except during special events. The campground is open all year, but water and showers are turned off from mid-October through mid-April.

See map for location of Hoffmaster State Park. It's 6 miles south of Muskegon and 7 miles north of Grand Haven. From U.S. 31, take the Pontaluna Rd. exit and go west. (616) 798-3711. State park sticker required: $3/day, $15/year. Gillette Visitor Center: (616) 798-3573. Open all year 10-5 daily, closed Mon. No extra fee.

Pleasure Island Water Park

Scary plunges are a big hit with kids.

This attractive, water amusement park is built around three lagoons and a stretch of shoreline on Little Black Lake. The waterslides range from the long (410 feet), gentle corkscrew (it starts from Michigan's tallest slide tower) to the rather terrifying Black Hole. In the latter, a green translucent tube goes through the side of a hill and make several harrowing loops before depositing its victims at high speed into a bank of water. Almost as scary is the Rampage water slide, which hurtles you in a small sled steeply down a slide and sends you skidding across a pond.

The bumper boats are a change of pace. You have your own little rubber boat, complete with small outboard motor. For five minutes you can bash into the other boats in the pond to your heart's content. Calmer activities include 18 holes of miniature golf, a kiddie water play area, pedal boats, and a sandy beach for picnicking and swimming.

Warning: this place is a good deal if you visit early in the morning or after 4:30 on a weekday. On weekends in the past, you could spend most of your time waiting in lines.

Pontaluna Rd. at Martin Rd. on Little Black Lake, 7 miles south of downtown Muskegon. From U.S. 31, take Pontaluna Rd. exit, go 1 1/2 miles west. (616) 798-7857. Open daily Mem. Day-Labor Day, Weekdays 10-4 first half of June, 10-6 weekends. Thereafter, it closes at 9 p.m. $11.95 admission and all rides for anyone over 48" tall. $8.95 for kids 2-4 or under 48". Spectator: $4.95. Discounts after 4:30: $6.95, or $5.95 for kids 2-4.

ANOTHER THRILL PARK NEAR MUSKEGON . . . . . Michigan Adventure is a small amusement park with 2 roller coasters and exceptional bump 'em cars. There is a big new water park, with a wave pool and other attractions. *8 miles north of Muskegon; take Russell Rd. exit from U.S.-31. (616) 766-3377. Open weekends in May, daily from June 1 thru 2nd week of Sept. 11 a.m.-7 p.m. (8 p.m. after late June). $14/person. Weekday special: $4 off with a can of Vernor's or Dr. Pepper. $9/person in pre-arranged groups of 25 or more. $12 admission.*

❶ Muskegon S.P./Scenic Dr. Beautiful park, uncrowded 3 miles of beach, dunes, inland beach & campgrounds.

❷ Winter Sports Complex. Learn to use 40 mph sled. Scenic lighted x-c ski trails, warming lodge. In beautiful state park.

❸ Museum of Art. Outstanding small museum geared to a refreshingly broad public. Don't miss Curry's "Tornado over Kansas."

❹ Hackley House. Exuberant, spare-no-expense Queen Anne fantasy built by Muskegon's great benefactor.

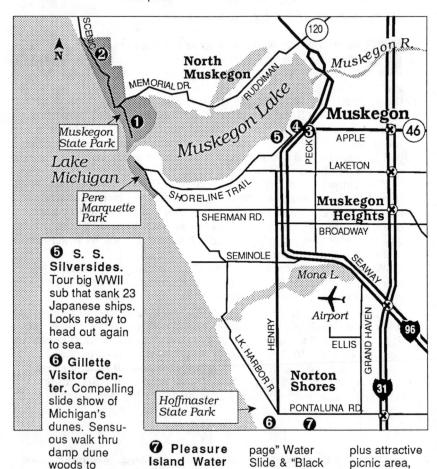

❺ S. S. Silversides. Tour big WWII sub that sank 23 Japanese ships. Looks ready to head out again to sea.

❻ Gillette Visitor Center. Compelling slide show of Michigan's dunes. Sensuous walk thru damp dune woods to spectacular overlook.

❼ Pleasure Island Water Fun Park. Scary "Ram page" Water Slide & "Black Hole"; kiddie water play area; plus attractive picnic area, sandy beach.

Highlights of
Muskegon

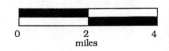

0   2   4
miles

U. S. S. Silversides

*Tour one of World War II's fightingest subs,
which looks much as it did back then.*

For anyone interested in the World War II or naval warfare,
this is a major attraction in western Michigan. Military
equipment that survives a war has usually seen little
action, but this big sub was a Pacific workhorse. Completed just
after the attack on Pearl Harbor in 1942, the Silversides went on
to sink 23 ships. It went on 14 patrols in all, losing only one man
while sinking over 90,000 tons. During one reconnaissance mission, crew members even watched a Japanese horse race by
periscope.

The excellent condition of the boat and its near-complete furnishings makes the tour worthwhile. As you go below and walk
from bow to stern, it looks very much as it did during World War
II, with the same bunks, sonar equipment, brass torpedo doors,
radios, and charting table. The tour gives a good feel of what it
was like in those very cramped spaces to go out on a 45-day tour
deep into enemy territory.

*740 W. Western Ave at foot of 9th St., just east of Heritage Land-
ing and west of downtown Muskegon on Muskegon Lake.. Ticket
booth (616) 755-1230; curator (616) 744-9117. April-Oct 10-
5:30; May & Sept weekdays 1-5:30; Jun-Aug daily 10-5:30. Adults
$3.50, children 5-11 $1.50. Group overnights may be arranged.*

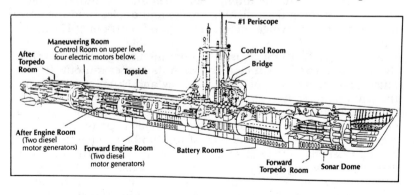

Hackley & Hume
Historic Site

A gem of Victorian architecture —
the exuberant legacy of Muskegon's
richest and most generous lumber baron

Victorian love of ornament may have reached a new height in the 1888 home of Muskegon's great benefactor and richest lumber baron, Charles Hackley. It shares an elaborate carriage house with the impressive but more modest next door home of his partner, Thomas Hume. The three buildings form a remarkable urban ensemble, almost Oriental in their rich colors and textures and many-turreted silhouette. Twenty-eight shades of paint were used to duplicate the rich, complex Victorian paint scheme of the Hackley House exterior. Inside it is almost completely restored and fully furnished, often with the Hackleys' own furniture. Noted architectural historian Wayne Andrews called the Hackley and Hume houses "peerless specimens of the flamboyant style" and devoted nine pages to them in *Architecture in Michigan.*

Houses of this size and splendor were usually made of brick or stone, but Hackley and Hume built in wood, the material that made their fortunes. Surfaces are alive with carved and tiled ornament. Stained glass filters outside light for a dreamy interior look. Highlights are the dining room tiles and woodwork, replete with deer, hunting dogs, fishing creels, and apples, and the entry hall's glass and carvings, including caryatid portraits of Hackley and the architect.

Hackley (1837-1905) refused to take his money and run from the stump-scarred north country when its timber ran out. In Muskegon's boom year of 1886, Hackley and Hume were among the few who already realized that Michigan's timber would soon run out. To perpetuate their fortune, they acquired vast acreages of timberland in the West and South. Hackley apparently regarded his great wealth as a trust fund to be administered for society's benefit — though some small-town cynics attributed his generosity to vanity and a wish to rename Muskegon "Hackleyville." At any rate, Hackley decided to invest in Muskegon and try to develop it as a modern, enlightened industrial city.

A retiring and enigmatic personality, Hackley often deferred to the advice of a trusted circle of friends. He started by giving the city a superb library, park, hospital, and new industrial arts school, then promoted the city as a superior place to live and do business. He and his friends used those model institutions to attract industrial companies that could, and did, turn Muskegon into an important industrial city, the biggest on Lake Michigan's eastern shore. Modern-day Muskegon's leading employers Sealed Power (now SPX), Brunswick bowling, S. D. Warren paper, and Shaw-Walker office furniture — all originally located in Muskegon because of the Muskegon Improvement Company started by Hackley and his friends.

In all, Hackley's gifts to Muskegon between 1888 and 1912 totalled nearly $6 million — a stunning testimony to the wealth of successful capitalists before income tax. In appreciation, Muskegon has celebrated Hackley Day (May 25) as a school and city holiday since 1888. Hackley's monumental legacies dominate central Muskegon.

The volunteer Hackley Heritage Association conducts friendly, well-informed tours of the houses where Hackley and Hume spent the rest of their lives. The houses are being slowly and meticulously restored, thanks to a local millage. The surprisingly comfortable Hume House has been furnished with rooms typical of the period when the Hume family lived there, from 1888 to 1942.

484 W. Webster at Sixth, downtown, 2 blocks southwest of Hackley Park. From U. S. 31, take Bus. U.S. 31 (Seaway) to Sixth, turn left and go 2 blocks. (616) 722-7578. Open mid-May through September, Wed, Sat & Sun 1-4. Group tours by appt. other times. $2/adults, $1 students, 12 and under free.

FOR MUSKEGON'S FASCINATING LUMBERING HISTORY. . . . . . go to the worthwhile but uneven **Muskegon County Museum**. In the Lumber Queen gallery, first request to see the outstanding half-hour tape/slide show. It clearly conveys the lumber barons' business strategy, along with the colorful, dangerous life in lumber camps. Then look at the dioramas of lumbering scenes in Muskegon. Other museum highlights: the poignant display on the extinct **passenger pigeons** that once darkened the skies here along the Lake Michigan shore. A dramatic, oversized painting by folk artist Lewis Cross of nearby Spring Lake shows a swirl of the docile birds being shot at by farmers. Also, Victor Casenelli's 19 dreamily impressionistic **murals of Muskegon's history**, done for Lumberman's Bank in 1929, and a competent **hands-on gallery of the human body** and how it works. *430 W. Clay at Fourth in downtown Muskegon, 1 block west of Hackley Park. (616) 722-0278. Mon-Fri 9:30-4:30, Sat & Sun 12:30-4:30. Free.*

Muskegon Museum of Art

Western Michigan's top art museum —
small, stimulating, geared to a broad audience

Thanks to the beneficence of museum founder Charles Hackley (p. 340) and two astute early directors, Muskegon has long had the finest art museum in western Michigan. It's a very pleasant, easily managed place, accessible and stimulating. The Hackley Gallery contains the permanent collection, strong on realistic paintings that are interesting and complex. The Walker Gallery is a big, open space well suited to changing shows, sometimes very large in scale and quite powerful.

Some choice paintings are here, mostly purchased many decades ago. The best-known is the dramatic "Tornado over Kansas" by John Steuart Curry, a prominent proponent of the regionalism that dominated American art in the 1930s. Whistler's famous "A Study in Rose and Brown," a simplified, unpretty portrait of a young woman, created such a controversy in Muskegon that the museum's talented first director, Raymond Wyer, quit in a huff. He then went to Worcester, Massachusetts, and developed its museum to attain national prominence. The extraordinary "Tea Time," by Whistler's contemporary William Merritt Chase, was also avant-garde in its day. Edward Hopper, N. C. Wyeth, and Winslow Homer are among the other prominent American painters represented here.

The European holdings, not as extensive, also include some choice works. The most important is "St. Jerome in Penitence," painted circa 1516 by Joos Van Cleve. The saint, in a fascinating, vivid landscape, is surrounded by symbolic and anthropormorphic forms. Don't miss another important Dutch painting, Jan van der Heyden's haunting "The Moat of a Castle with Drawbridge." Portraits of Martin Luther and his wife, Katharina von Bora, were painted by their friend, Cranach the Elder.

"We've always been a cutting-edge, open museum, geared to a broader public but ahead of the crowd," says director Al Kochka with pride. Some two dozen **changing exhibits** a year cover topics from printmaking to floral watercolors to porcelain and cross-fertilization between Asian and Western art; they make it worthwhile to stop in whenever you're in the vicinity. (Access and parking are easy.) The basement **gift shop** has a nice selection of notecards, books, posters, jewelry, and inexpensive gifts for children.

On West Webster just east of Third and Hackley Park in downtown Muskegon. Park alongside the towered building on Third. (616) 722-2600. Tues-Fri 10-5, Sat & Sun 12-5. Free; donations appreciated.

FABULOUS VICTORIANA AND A CURIOUS DOWNTOWN MALL . . . are within easy walking distance of the museum. Right next door on Webster at Third is the first and most splendid of all Charles Hackley's gifts to Muskegon, the **Hackley Public Library**, a Romanesque Revival castle from 1890. Don't miss the impressive main reading room sparkling with leaded glass; the huge oil painting of the library's dedication (a hundred deft portraits of Muskegon society at the twilight of the lumbering era); four stone fireplaces with Art Nouveau touches; and the upstairs children's room mural of a parade of colorful literary characters from around the world. . . . . Across Webster is the **Torrent House**, a massive stone chateau built in 1892 for the then-astonishing sum of $250,000. Lumberman and mayor John Torrent located his magnificent pile here to show up his rival, Hackley. Visitors are welcome to look in. . . . . At Webster and Third is shady **Hackley Park**, Hackley's entry in the competition among aspiring cities of the late 19th century to erect monumental public sculptures honoring the veterans who served their country. At the corners, bronze figures of Lincoln, Grant, Sherman, and Admiral David Farragut were radical for their day because of their realistic poses. Popular **Parties in the Park** with live music, food, and beer are held here Fridays from 5 to 9, from early June through early September. . . . A block down Third at Clay is one of the nation's most unusual malls. In the 1970s **Muskegon Mall** put a roof over four principal downtown retail blocks. It incorporated several large office buildings and the stately old Century Club and tore down 96 surrounding buildings to provide free parking in the heart of downtown. The only trouble is, there's not much of downtown left except for parking lots and large institutional buildings. It was a dramatic — or desperate — solution for a depressed industrial city. Unlike many such cities, downtown Muskegon is not deserted at night. Nearby frontage along Muskegon Lake has finally been developed for recreation and entertainment, and the mall is being expanded to stay competitive.

ANOTHER STOP FOR ART-LOVERS . . . . . Interesting photography, prints, and illustration — media with few exhibition outlets in western Michigan— are showcased at **Deborah's Choice**. Its one-, two-, and three-person shows often feature unusual techniques. Deborah Socol has moved her gallery/frame shop into a big space overlooking Muskegon's once-bustling Romanesque train station and docks. It's on the second floor of the monumental old Amazon knitting factory on Western Avenue in downtown Muskegon. What with 14' ceilings and open, mill construction, it has the atmosphere of Soho galleries. Some former neighbors from the Muskegon Mall's demolished gallery row have joined Socol. There's jewelry and other crafts and art from area contributors to the Wren Gallery, and Corky Corcoran, whose gallery was one of the most respected in the Midwest, guest curates two shows a year. *Entrance is at 1010 Mart, a short side street off Western between Fifth and Sixth, back toward the Mart dock. (616) 726-4747. Open Tues-Fri 12-5, Sat 10-3.*

Muskegon Winter Sports Park & State Park

A quarter-mile of Olympic sledding thrills,
delightful cross-country skiing at night,
and wonderfully uncrowded beaches

Centerpieces of the beautiful Muskegon Winter Sports Complex in Muskegon State Park are a **luge run** (one of only two or three luges in the U.S.) and some of the longest lighted cross-country ski trails in Michigan. The luge (pronounced LOOzh, it's French for sled) is an Olympic sport in which a small, one-person sled of wood, metal, and canvas is steered down an iced chute that has wood walls. The side walls are contoured with snowy slush, and the luge run is iced nightly after each day's use with a mix of snow and water, then misted for a slick, even surface.

The helmeted driver lies down facing up on the sled and steers it by bending one flexible front wood runner support and raising the opposite shoulder. Everything goes by in a blur. On the Muskegon course, sleds can go up to 40 m.p.h. And that seems even faster when you're four inches from the ground. Anybody can experience the thrill of luging. Some people do have more of a knack for steering to achieve the maximum possible speed, without costly overcorrections on turns. A teenage girl who luges here regularly is the leading local Olympic hopeful.

A volunteer group of outdoors enthusiasts started this facility, remarkably attractive and inexpensive for users, in order to develop interest in the sport in the Midwest. They hope to feed lugers to the U.S. Olympic team training in Lake Placid.

Anyone can get introductory lessons for $10 a day, including all equipment. Within the same season, beginners can go up to 40 m.p.h. You don't need reservations for these open clinics. Just show up in lightweight shoes or boots, gloves, and clothes that are warm but not fancy. First-timers are fully supervised; they start at the base of the starting ramp of the shorter, slower lower run, so they can become accustomed to the sensation and gradually build up speed without being terrified. Careful volunteer coaches observe and instruct all lugers and decide when they can advance to a higher level. Waits are not long. By the end of the day beginners will be completing the entire lower run in 10 seconds, a speed of about 25 m.p.h. The faster (40 m.p.h.), twisting upper run has far more turns and banks.

Reliable lake-effect snowfall and beautiful, forested scenery make Muskegon State Park ideal for winter sports. It commonly has at least some snow when most of southern Michigan is completely snowless. In a dark, snowy evergreen forest, the golden glow of dots from the lights and the big golden beacon from the warming house's big windows are enchanting. Plans call for maintaining a family-oriented ice rink, weather cooperating.

The **ski trails** were laid out specifically for skiing. Many state park ski trails are really hiking trails, with turns too sudden for all but the best skiers. These are ideal for novices, because they combine easy turns and interesting scenery. The 2 1/2 kilometer trail is flat to rolling; the 5k trail has three hills that provide a challenge for better skiers. (A bypass lets less skillful skiers avoid the short, steep hill.) Trails are tracked for both ski-skaters and conventional skiers, except that the 2.5k trail has two sets of conventional two-tracks on weekends. Sheltering pines protect skiers from the wind and preserve the snow from the sun. **Ski rentals** are available ($5/ 2 hours) for adults and children.

The Winter Sports Park is at the north end of Muskegon State Park, off Scenic Dr. across from the Lakeshore Campground, around the curve north of the landmark blockhouse. (616) 744-9629. Season from mid-Dec. to mid-March, depending on weather. Park hours: Mon-Fri 3-10 p.m., Sat & Sun 10-10. Luge open hours: Thurs & Fri 5-9, Sat & Sun 2-9. Competitions and meets held on Sat. a.m.; public welcome. State park sticker required: $3/day, $15/year. Ski trail fee: $2/person. Luge fee (including equipment rental): $10/first day, $7 other days.

BEAUTIFUL BEACHES THAT ARE NEVER CROWDED . . . . . are what **Muskegon State Park** is known for. When Holland and Grand Haven are packed, this is the place to reliably find waves, sand, and solitude. There's three miles of Lake Michigan beach along Scenic Drive, plus **Snug Harbor,** a pleasant, quiet bay of Muskegon Lake, with warmer water. Off Memorial Drive, it's a perfect place for small children to swim, swing, and fish. The 177-site, modern **Muskegon Lake Campground** by the boat launch on the channel's Muskegon Lake side is favored by boaters and fishermen. The 180-site **Lake Michigan Campground** (also modern) is among the most scenic state park campgrounds, nestled in a grove of towering maples and beaches, an easy walk across the dunes from a campers-only beach. Campgrounds fill on summer weekends, often by Wednesday night.*On the north side of the Muskegon Lake channel. From U.S. 31, take M-120 southwest and follow the signs through North Muskegon onto Memorial Drive (the park's south entrance). Or take Scenic Dr. from Whitehall. (616) 744-3480. State park sticker required: $3/day, $15/year.*

White River Lighthouse Museum

An unspoiled and picturesque setting — like the relaxed, old-fashioned resort life of the White Lake area

Tucked away behind huge beech trees at the channel from Lake Michigan to White Lake, this old limestone and brick lighthouse looks so simple and homey, it seems the lighthouse-keeper could still be there. Today this delightful little museum owned by Fruitland Township is still a home. The curator lives here. Low-key displays include photographs and maps about White Lake's maritime history. First it was related to furs and fishing, then to logging, followed by the resort era beginning in the 1880s, when big steamers brought summer people from Chicago, Indiana, and St. Louis to White Lake's summer hotels and cottages. Boaters will enjoy the museum's nautical artifacts and navigational devices, a ship's helm, and the station's original Fresnel lens, which reflected and magnified the tower light.

Tightly spiraled in the narrow tower is a beautiful wrought iron stairway. After a somewhat spooky, claustrophobic ascent, it leads you to a fine view of Lake Michigan.

Year-round, people come to the lighthouse to walk along the channel wall and get to Lake Michigan. (The beach up past the water line is privately owned.) This "Government Channel" was created in 1876, during the lumber boom. Lumber schooners leaving Lake Michigan's lumber ports had become so numerous that the federal government financed many navigational improvements, including this lighthouse.

The direct channel here bypassed the White River's circuitous old channel north of here. Today the **Old Channel Trail** leading west and north from Montague makes for an exceptionally scenic drive. To get to little **Medbury Park** and beach across the channel from the lighthouse here, take Old Channel Trail, but turn west at Lau Road when the main road turns north.

The lighthouse is at the south side of the White Lake channel, at the end of Murray Rd. Murray Rd. goes west from the junction of Scenic Dr. (along Lake Michigan from Muskegon) and South Shore Rd. (along White Lake from Whitehall). Or come from U.S. 31 via Duck Lake State Park (see below). (616) 894-8265.
***Museum** open Mem. Day through Labor Day Tues-Fri 11-5, Sat &*

Sun noon-6. In Sept.: weekends only. 50¢ admission 12 and over.
Tours of museum and dune ecology available by arrangement.
*Grounds and channel walk are a **public park** open year-round.*

A SCENIC DRIVE AND NICE BEACHES . . . . . Civilized simplicity still sets the
tone for White Lake resort life, which feels far away from the 1980s and harried,
big-spending Yuppies. Cottages here are likely painted classic white with green
trim, *never* mauve and pink. Trees and green are everywhere. These charms are
showcased on drives to the lighthouse. . . . . . South Shore Drive along White Lake
from Whitehall is pleasant. To get to the beaches, go south along the aptly named
Scenic Drive to **Duck Lake State Park**, an old scout camp. It has beach frontage
on both Lake Michigan (park along Scenic) and on pretty Duck Lake, unspoiled
by development and good for fishing Take Michillinda Road to the main park
entrance. The picnic area is beneath big oaks. For a pretty, winding way to
Muskegon, continue south on Scenic through the wooded dunes of Muskegon
State Park into the beautiful lakefront suburb of North Muskegon. *To get to Duck
Lake State Park from U.S. 31,, take the Lakewood Club exit 10 miles north of
Muskegon and follow signs. (616) 744-3480. No camping.*

THE LOW-KEY CHARMS OF WHITEHALL AND MONTAGUE. . . . . Friendly and
unfussy, the twin towns at the head of White Lake offer two rival weathervane
manufacturers (both on Water Street in Montague), two drugstores with soda
fountains (**Lipka's** and the bustling **Todd Pharmacy**), both on Ferry in Montague,
and two good eat-in bakeries, both in Whitehall. **Morat's Bakery** on North Mears
overlooking the White River marsh, and **Robinson's Bakery** at 1019 S. Mears
makes outstanding, authentic Swedish breads and cookies.

There's the weird, wonderful **Montague Historical Museum**, a community attic
in a church on Meade and Church up the hill in Montague. It's open summer
weekends 1-5. Also worth checking out in central Whitehall: a rambling,
satisfying antique shop, the **Pack Rat**, at 116 W. Slocum (closed Sun. & Mon.), the
Timekeepers' Clock Shop, 303 S. Mears, with refurbished antique clocks at, and,
inside the First of America Muskegon Bank at 119 S. Mears, the remarkable,
accurate **paintings chronicling White Lake's lumbering industry**, done from life
by an area signpainter in the 1870s.

The local claim to fame, the **world's largest weather vane**, is less appealing
than its setting on the **causeway** between Whitehall and Montague that separates
White Lake from the sweeping marsh of the White River. Take in the views and
the marsh's many swans from the asphalt boardwalk or the Dog and Suds
parking lot. And stop by the **Chamber of Commerce**, in the old depot on the
causeway, for more information about this attractive, unspoiled resort area.

White River Canoeing

*One of the state's most scenic and underrated
canoeing rivers is just north of Muskegon.*

Famous as a logging river, the White River today is a hidden treasure for canoeists. It is less canoed, less fished, and more remote in feel than some better-known, longer rivers up north. A quiet river trip here puts you in touch with wildlife that usually flees at the sound of hikers. Especially in the early morning and late afternoon, you can see blue heron, sandhill cranes, many kinds of ducks, and occasionally beaver.

The narrow White winds through the Manistee National Forest across a floodplain that's a half-mile to a mile wide. Sometimes it's up against a steep, forested bank. Sometimes it's surrounded by marshy flats. Other times it flows through forest that hasn't been logged in this century. It's a designated wild-scenic river, which means that timber on the floodplain can't be cut. The mixed conifer and deciduous forest is what grew up after the late 19th-century logging boom cleared the virgin forests of white pine and hardwoods. Fishing is good for bass, northern pike, and salmon and steelhead runs.

In *Canoeing Michigan Rivers,* Jerry Dennis and Craig Date say the lower part of the White is fine for beginners and for families with small children, except when water is high. The canoeable part begins at the Hesperia Dam at Hesperia. The first 8 1/2 miles are shallow, with riffles — sometimes so shallow they can't be canoed. There aren't many public access points to the river. By far the easiest way to canoe it is to use the **Happy Mohawk Canoe Livery**, which rents canoes, tubes, rafts, and kayaks. Sample prices, including all equipment and transportation: $11.25/person for a canoe trip of four hours paddling time; $7/person for a 2-3 hour tubing expedition.

The Happy Mohawk owners also own and operate the exceptionally picturesque **White River Campground**. It's in the heavily wooded valley of pretty little Sand Creek where it joins the White River.

*735 E. Fruitvale Rd., 5 miles east of U.S. 31 northeast of Montague. From U.S. 31, take Fruitvale Rd. exit, go 5 miles east.
(616) 894-4209. Campground open May through October.*

Recommended Restaurants & Lodgings
West Michigan

To locate cities, see regional map, p. 290.

IONIA

The Union Hill Inn. *(616) 527-0955. 306 Union, 2 blks from downtown.* 5 rooms w/2 baths. $55-$65. Full breakfast. A/C, TV. 2 phones avail. 1860s Italianate mansion, living room w/ piano, dining room, huge veranda. Garden & large lawn. *Victorian hillside mansion in attractive town with state's most impressive Italianate architecture*

GRAND RAPIDS

Little Mexico Cafe. *401 Stocking at Bridge 1/4 mi. w. of Grand River & downtown. (616) 774-8822. Open daily, noon- 2 a.m. Visa, MC.* Full bar. Mexican restaurant with fascinating Olmec and Mayan-inspired contemporary interior, by well-known designer Bill Bowsma, honoring colorful owner's Indian ancestry. Like a Gaudi creation in plastic. Big menu goes beyond standards. Two favorites: wet burritos w/ choice of meat ($5.20/lunch, $5.80/dinner), meal-size Martin's special w/ beef tips, vegetables ($5.65/$6.25).

Vitale's Italian Ristorante. *834 E. Leonard. From U..S. 131, take Leonard St. exit 87 e. From I-196, take College St. exit 78 n., then e. on Leonard. (616) 458-8368. Mon-Thurs 11-11, Fri 11-12, Sat 4:30-12, Sun 4:30-11. Visa, AmEx, MC.* Full bar. Grand Rapids' most popular pizzeria also serves more elaborate food in this fascinating warren of rooms, each dramatically decorated in a different style (grape arbor, Roman forum, etc.) by the owner. Lunch sausage, pastas, etc. run $5-7. Veal dishes at dinner ($14) are excellent. Small salad comes w/ all meals. Good

meatballs, plenty of red sauce — nothing trendy, just the basics.

Maggie's Kitchen. *636 Bridge just west of Stocking. Inside Moctezuma Food Products, across from Little Mexico Cafe. (616) 458-8583. Tues-Sat 9-7, Sun 9-4.* Large Mexican grocery. Takeout kitchen features unusual Mexican sandwiches and barbecue (BBQ) in addition to standard burritos and such — large, very tasty, priced under $2 and $3. Pick up a fruit juice, and enjoy al fresco meal in riverside Ab-Nab-Awen Park by Ford Museum.

Choo-Choo Grill. *1209 Plainfield just n.w. of Leonard, 1 mi. n. of downtown & just east of river. From U.S. 131, take Leonard St. exit east. (616) 774-8652. Mon-Fri 6:30-4, Sat 7-2.* No credit cards or alcohol. Vintage diner with flair, very good food. Breakfasts $2.50-$4, sandwiches $2-$3.75, good homemade soup & chile $1.79. Neat booths and counter; terrific neon sign. Eat in or take out; pretty Riverside Park is 1 mi. n. on Monroe.

Flying Bridge Fish Market. *1171 Plainfield at s.w. corner of Leonard. See directions for Choo-Choo above. (616) 458-6566. Mon-Thurs 11-8, Fri to 11, Sat to 9.* No alcohol or credit cards. Fish market sells fresh & deep-fried fish, mostly to go. Dinners w/ fried: smelt $3.80, cod $4.25, shrimp $8. Also by the pound: $3.80 for smelt, $12.99 for shrimp. A few tables, no atmosphere. Convenient to parks, freeway; ask for directions to fish ladder.

1913 Room. *In Amway Grand Plaza, Pearl & Monroe , downtown. (616) 776-6426. Mon-Fri 11:30-2, Mon-Sat 5:30-10, Sun brunch (call to confirm)11-2:30. Major credit cards.* Full bar. Elegant Old World setting evokes 1913, when historic part of hotel was built. Food wins raves. Specialties: 1913 French onion soup, Caesar salad. Sandwiches $7-$8. Lunch entrees $8-$11, dinners from $16 (roast chicken) to $24 (sauteed lobster in port); all w/ vegetable, salad.

Cottage Bar. *18 LaGrave just s. of Fulton between Jefferson & Division, downtown. (616) 454-9088. Mon-Sat 11 a.m.-2:30 a.m. (kitchen closes at 12:30). Full bar. No credit cards.* Since 1927. Much expanded, but still visually a warm, wonderful period piece: Art Deco mahogany bar, lots of varnished wood, booths. Lively crowd, well-organized staff, exceptional burgers. Mexican menu: wet burrito, chicken chimichanga, taco salad, super nachos, all under $5. Some salads, lots of sandwiches, even a steak sizzler ($6), but standouts are homemade soups ($1.30/$1.60); white, 3-alarm, 4-alarm chilis ((mostly $2/$2.50 w/ tortilla chips); famous Cottage Burger ($3.50): 1/4 lb. beef patty on rye bun w/ bacon, garnish, 2 cheeses, olives, hickory dressing. Super-busy at mealtime; come early or wait. Neat little alley terrace.

Schnitzelbank. *342 Jefferson just s. of downtown. (616) 459-9527. Mon-Thurs 11-8, Fri 11-9, Sat 5-9. AmEx, Visa, MC. Full bar.* Big German restaurant from 1930s drips with atmosphere. Good, hearty German specialties like sauerbraten w/spaetzle, $11 at dinner. You can also eat light — Reuben sandwich at dinner is $6.25. Lunch entrees: $4-$7 w/ side dishes.

Gaia Coffeehouse. *209 S. Diamond at the intersection of Cherry & Lake. About 1/2 mi. s.e. of Fulton on Lake. (616) 454-6233. Tues-Fri 8-2 & 5:30-9, Sat 9-2 & 5:30-9. Sun 9-2. No alcohol or credit cards.* Delightfully simple and serene organic-vegetarian cafe with heart. Omelets, veggie hash, potatoes are big at breakfast ($3.25-$4.75). Stir-fries, brown rice at lunch. Deluxe skillet pizza w/ whole wheat crust: $8.25. Not only for the truly committed; good food, pleasant atmosphere appeal to many types. Changing art exhibits; open poetry readings 1 Friday night/month.

Yesterdog. *1505 Wealthy just w. of Lake in Eastown. No phone. Mon-Sat 10:30 a.m. to 2:30 a.m.* Super-limited menu: chili dogs (90¢) w/fixings, soup in cold weather. Hot dogs, under $1, Everything's good, but the atmosphere

is what people talk about: a tiny old soda shoppe, encrusted with local history and advertising memorabilia. One of the very few places in town where black and white, suburban and urban, mix.

Gibson's. *1033 Lake Dr. SE just south of Eastown. Take I-96 to Fuller south on Fuller 1 1/2 mi to Lake. (616) 774-8535. Mon-Fri 11:30-2, Mon-Sat 5:30-11. AmEx, Visa, MC, Diners. Full bar.* Beautiful Victorian mansion between East Grand Rapids and Eastown houses Gibson's (formal) and The Grapevine (informal). Known for prime rib, but menus are wide-ranging (chicken dijonaise, fish, roasts) and the food is excellent. Gibson's meals include potato, vegetable; smaller portions at Grapevine also include salad. Lunches there are $6-$10. Known for prime rib: $14/$9.

Fountain Hill B&B. *(616) 458-6621. 222 Fountain, Heritage Hill.* 2 rooms w/ baths 1 w/ jacuzzi). $65. Cont. breakfast. A/C, cable TV, phone. 3 common rooms, enc. sun porch (up), porch(down). Bold, elegant decor. Hosts knowledgeable about GR. *1874 Italianate home overlooking downtown*

B&B of Grand Rapids. *(616) 451-4849.* 3 homes each with 2 guest rooms, cont. breakfasts. $55. Heald-Lear House is 1893 Shingle Style house w\solarium, private baths. Brayton House is 1889 Georgian Revival with circular stairway mural, shared bath. Barber House is 1908 Arts & Crafts, private baths. *Splendid homes on Heritage Hill; perfect HQ for museums, antiquing*

Amway Grand Plaza. *(616) 774-2000. Pearl at Monroe, downtown on Grand River.* 682 rooms, 27 floors. $110-$135. Packages start at $79. Some suites, luxury level. Views surprisingly unsatisfying. Cable TV. Small indoor pool, whirlpool, sauna, exercise room, 2 lighted tennis courts, racquetball, squash. Several very good, expensive restaurants, bars.

Downtown resort on riverwalk, near park , walk to museums

President's Inn. *(800) 445-5004, (616) 363-0800. 3221 Plainfield Ave, N.E. off I-96 (exit 33) on busy strip .* 135 rooms on 3 floors. $40-$43. Cont. breakfast. Cable TV. Indoor pool, game room. 5 min. to downtown.
Good value, indoor pool & game room, close to Rockford

President Suites. *(800) 441-9628, (616) 940-8100. On 28th just east of I-96 exit 43B next to Home Design Center.* 121 suites on 3 floors. $71. A/C, cable TVs. Cont. breakfast. Suites have living area, kitchenette, bedroom. Ample indoor pool, whirlpool, exercise room.
Outstanding family value on upscale part of busy 28th St. strip

Howard Johnson. *(616) 452-5141. 35 28th St. S.W., 2 blocks e. of US. 131, exit 81. Older part of busy strip.* 104 rooms on 2 floors. $38-$45. TV w/ Showtime. Indoor pool, whirlpool. 24 hr.-restaurant.
28th St. family budget choice with indoor pool

Days Inn Downtown. *(616) 235-7611. 310 Pearl at US. 131, downtown just w. of river.* 175 rooms on 8 floors. $64.50. Cable TV. Indoor pool, whirlpool, exercise equip. Restaurant.
New, indoor pool, good downtown location near nice park, Ford Museum.

ROCKFORD

The Corner Bar. *31 N. Main s. of Court, downtown Rockford. (616) 866-9866. Mon-sat 10 a.m.-2 a.m., Sun noon-8.* Full bar. Visa, MC. Big family tavern is *the* place to eat among locals and visitors drawn by the Hot Dog Hall of Fame. Eat 12 chili dogs (they're 85¢, 3 for $2.50) and your name joins the hundreds (or thousands?) hanging on the wall. Current record-holder: a petite dental hygienist who's eaten 42. Hot dogs eclipse the wide-ranging menu of sandwiches, salads, lunch specials, Mexican favorites, din-

ners.Examples: big chef salad ($4.20), wet burritos ($4.25/$5.25), fried perch or smelt, 1/3 lb. buffalo burger ($3.50 alone, or $5 w/ spicy, curly fried, slaw).

SAUGATUCK

Marro's Pizza. *147 Water (across from the Coral Gables). (616) 857-4248.* Open last weekend April through last weekend Oct. Mon-Thurs 5 p.m.-12, Fri 5-1, Sat & Sun noon-1 a.m. No deliveries. Thin-crust pizza with regional reputation. Top sausage, pepperoni, and mushroom pizza: $13 large, $7 small. Many veggie items. 24 entrees from pasta ($7) to Italian-style fisherman's platter ($17).

Butler Pantry Restaurant & Deli. *121 Butler (upstairs). (616) 857-1635. Summer: Sun-Thurs 10-6, Fri & Sat 10-9. Closes at 5 in winter.* Pleasant little spot overlooking arty courtyard. Good food for lunch, takeout to Wicks Park. Popular items: chicken salad & meat loaf sandwiches ($4.50), 3-cheese spinach quiche ($6), Fritz's artichoke frittata ($6), pasta salad. Local Fenn Valley wine $1.50/glass.

Chequers. *220 Culver (1/2 block east of Butler). Mon-Thurs 11:30-9, Fri-Sat 11:30-10, Sun noon-9. Stays open 1 hour later in summer.* Comfortable English-style pub with convivial atmosphere, fish and chips, imported beers (Watneys' on tap) and pub-style menu with things like shepherd's pie ($7), English trifle ($3) for dessert. Sandwiches all day, dinners w/ vegetable, appetizer, from $6 to $14. Small and very popular; come early or wait. Toulouse, a new sister restaurant, , 3 doors east on Culver, features French Provençal food (hearty soups, salad, thick bread) at similar prices: $4-$8 at lunch, dinners around $12.

Goshorn Lake Resort. *(616) 857-4808. Just n. of Blue Star Hwy. n. of Saugatuck and w. of dune rides. Follow signs.* 12 rustic wood cabins w/ kitchens, screen porches. Open May-

Oct. Cabins rent by week in July & Aug. $275 sleeps 2-4, $325 sleeps 4-6. By day May, June, Sept & Oct. $55-$65. Bring sheets, towels, toaster, coffee maker, etc., or rent linens. Hodge-podge of old furniture. Adj. 400 ft. sandy beach & dock on Goshorn Lake. Boat & bike rentals, fishing, shuffleboard, swings, horseshoes, grills.
Scenic, quiet resort setting in dunes — a budget find

Timberline Motel. *(616) 857-2147. 3353 Blue Star Hwy., between exits 36 & 41 off I-196 outside Saugatuck.* 28 rooms on 1 floor. May-Sept 10: $55-$85. Sept. 11-Apr.: $40-$65. Cable TV, morning coffee. Heated pool, playground. Unusually well-maintained family-run motel.
Super-pleasant, moderate rates

Twin Gables Country Inn. *(616) 857-4346. 900 Lake St. overlooking Kalamazoo Lake, 10-min. walk to downtown Saugatuck.* B&B. 14 rooms w/ baths. A/C, cont. breakfast. May-Oct: $49-$64 weekdays, $69-$94 weekends. Nov-April: $44-$54 weekdays, $53-$68 weekends. Country & antique decor. More casual than many Saugatuck B&B's. Built in 1865, hotel since 1900. Large dining & common areas. w/ TV, phone. Indoor hot tub, outdoor pool. Big front porch, beautiful sunsets on Kalamazoo Lake. 3 cottages.
Casual B&B with pool, moderate weekday rates

Kemah Guest House. *(616) 857-2919. 633 Pleasant, 3 blocks from downtown, on hill in quieter residential area.* 6 rooms w/shared baths. May-Oct: $75-$95. Nov-April: $65-$85. 1900 mansion, remodeled in 1920s with Germanic Art Deco flavor. 2-acre hilltop site w/ cave, quiet spots with view of river. TV & phone in library. Guests can use parlor w/ baby grand, solarium, sun porch, dining room, beamed rathskeller & game room.
Most unusual, romantic house of any Saugatuck B&B

Wickwood Inn. *(616) 857-1097. 510 Butler at Mary, 2 blocks from Saugatuck's retail district.* 11 rooms with baths. Cont. breakfast, Sun brunch, hors d'oeuvres at teatime. A/C. TV & phone in common areas. May-Dec: $90-$127. Jan-April: $70-$111. Big living room, garden-game room, library-bar. Screened gazebo. Sophisticated, cheerful decor w/ family & area antiques. Perhaps the very nicest bed & breakfast in a town with many fine ones.
B&B with comfortable elegance, good location

Ship 'n' Shore Motel. *(616) 857-2194. 528 Water on the river at downtown's edge.* 40 units on 2 floors. All but 4 overlook river. Open April to mid-Oct. $110, $69-$89 before Mem. Day & after Labor Day. Cable TV. Heated pool, jacuzzi. Great location if you like boating activity, party atmosphere. Veranda, much landscaping.
Only Saugatuck lodging on water

DOUGLAS

Rosemont Inn. *(616) 857-2637. 83 Lakeshore Dr. in Douglas.* 14 rooms w/ baths, 9 w/ fireplaces. Main section is Queen Anne house w/ large parlor. Garden room overlooks outdoor pool. 8 rooms in new addition. Cont. breakfast. A/C. Cable TV & phone in common area. Douglas Beach across road. Must drive for meals. Attractive but spare decor w/ antique reproductions.
On quiet shady, shore drive of Douglas

PIER COVE

The Porches. *(616) 543-4162. 2297 70th St. (Lakeshore Dr.), 1/2 mi. s. of M-89 in Pier Cove.* 5 rooms w/ baths. Open May -Oct. $55 weekdays, $64 weekends (Thurs-Sun). Huge wrap-around porches, upstairs & down, look out to Lake Michigan. Beach access across street. Big common area, fireplace. Sunken side garden, ravine with hiking trails on 70 acres. Comfy, slightly musty cottagey atmosphere,

slightly musty cottagey atmosphere,
castoff furniture of many styles.
*Idyllic, quiet location,
authentic, unfussy cottage atmosphere*

FENNVILLE

Crane's Orchards and Pie Pantry Restaurant. *(616)*
*561-2297. On M-89, 2 mi. w. of Fen-
nville and 3 1/2 mi. e. of I-196 exit 34.
Open all year. Mother's Day-Oct: Mon-
Sat 9 -7 , Sun 11-7. Nov-March: Tues-
Sat 10-5, Sun 11-5. April-Mother's
Day: weekends only. MC, Visa.* Exceptionally interesting, individualistic
family farm turned into visitor destination. 5th- generation fruit farmers
grow all the fruit they sell and make
into very good pies, dumplings, crisps
($1.75/portion), cider (10¢ glass). Good
soups ($1.85), ham, beef, and turkey
sandwiches ($2.50-$3) on dense, flavorful homemade buns. New: grill for
burgers. Restaurant, in lower level of
old barn, is a cheerful, clever melange
of interesting old things. Can have cup
of coffee, cider, donuts, muffins. U-
pick fruit, or buy picked fruit + cider.

Su Casa Restaurant/Supermer-cado Mexico. *306 Main, just w. of
downtown Fennville, next to Shell
convenience store. Daily 8:30 a.m.-10
p.m.* Restaurant is tucked behind
Mexican grocery store, packed with
big containers of pinto beans, chiles,
huge pieces of fried pork rind. Serves
big community of Mexican-American
fruit workers at breakfast, lunch.
Outstanding food brings Anglos at
night. Mexican music on jukebox.
Free before meals: delicious dark corn
chips, bowls of hot guacamole and
salsa. Recommended for dinner: carne
asada (skirt steak with salad , guacamole; around $6;), shrimp in hot
sauce (around $8), combination #1
(broiled beef, taco, enchilada, soup;
around $7).

The Crane House. *(616) 561-6931.
On M-89 2 1/2 mi. w. of Fennville.* 5
rooms, private or shared baths, $60-

$90. Excellent big breakfast. Guests
can use comfortable parlor w/parlor
stove, dining-game room, 2nd-floor
deck. Cranes' 1872 family homestead ,
surrounded by orchards. Run by family, not hired help. Crane's Pie Pantry
restaurant across street. Mix of primitive, farmy antiques, quilts, and
Americana.
*B&B with wonderful farm decor
and atmosphere*

ALLEGAN

Delano Inn.*(616) 673-2609. 302 Cut-
ler. n.w. of downtown.* 6 rooms. $45-
85. A/C, shared baths (1 men's, 1
women's). TV, phone in common area.
Landscaped gardens. Near downtown,
riverwalk. Funny, friendly host cooks
terrific breakfasts.
*Gorgeous 1863 Italianate mansion in
one of state's prettiest small towns*

Sunset Motel Budget Host.
*(616) 673-6622. 1/2 mi. n. of Allegan
on M-89/M-40.* 19 rooms, all but 4 on
ground floor. $30-$60 midweek, $35-
$65 weekends (Fri./Sat.). Cable TV.
*Budget choice near beautiful x-c ski
trails, hiking, swimming in Allegan
State Forest*

HOLLAND

Till Midnight. *208 College Ave.,
half a block south of 8th in downtown
Holland. (616) 392-6883.* Mon-Sat
lunch 11:30-2:30, dinner 5-midnight.
Sat breakfast 8-11:30, Sun brunch 10-
3. Good selection of non-alcoholic
beer & wine. Visa, MC, AmEx. Holland's first creative, late-evening
downtown restaurant. Owner/chef
Spring TenKley is a perfectionist in
every detail, starting w/ 3 breads in
complimentary breadbasket, baked
fresh daily. Menu changes every 6
weeks. Famous for pastas ($10-$12 at
dinner), desserts. Customers screamed
to keep cheese tortellini w/ Italian
sausage ($7 at lunch) on menu. Salads,
sandwiches avail. all day. Standouts:
grilled sea scallop salad ($5.50), ter-

rific grilled chicken breast w/ cheese, sun-dried tomato mayo (under $6). Dinner entrees run $10-$16. For a superb light meal, get bread basket, bowl of soup ($3) — delectable things like creamed acorn squash or asparagus w/ saffron, all made from stock. Wildly popular. Come early or make reservations.

Pereddies. *447 Washington Square between 18th and 19th. (616) 394-3061. Mon-Thurs 10-10, Fri & Sat 10-11. Dinner reservations recommended. Beer and wine. Visa, MC.* Pioneer of casual chic in Holland. Bakery-deli-restaurant in tradition of old Italian neighborhood groceries. Stars are homemade breads, pasta sauces (red or white, w/or without mushrooms or clams), signature meatballs — $5 on a sub at lunch, $8.50-$13 at dinner. (Dinner entrees, from $8.50 to $16.50, come w/ salad, bread.) Pizza after 5: 9" x 13" trays ($14) come w/ custom options like goat cheese. Desserts $3. Great place for takeout to nearby Kollen Park.

The Sandpiper. *2225 South Shore in Macatawa next to Eldean's Marina. From River St. downtown, go s., turn w. onto 16th. It turns into South Shore. (616) 335-5866. Mem Day-Labor Day: lunch 7 days 11:30-2, dinner daily including Sun 5:-9. Off season: lunch Mon-Fri, dinner 7 days. Full bar, many Michigan wines. Visa, MC.* Creative food from Culinary Institute alum is regarded as some of West Michigan's best. Lunch more conventional: $5.25 soup, half sandwich, salad combo is top seller — and soup is excellent. Some picks on current menu: roast duck w/ molasses glaze, raspberry sauce ($15), rosemary-skewered pork, potato cakes, hot pepper vinaigrette ($13.25). Dinners come w/ salad, good, crusty Italian bread, fresh veggie medley. Dessert winner: chocolate ravioli w/ cherries, raspberry sauce ($3.50). Patio for lunch, drinks. View of water is mostly masts in marina. (Point West has wonderful view, erratic food & service.)

Russ'. *3 Holland locations: at 210 N. River on the north side, 1060 Lincoln at U.S. 31 on the south side, and the original Russ' on 361 E. 8th at Chicago. Mon-Sat 7 a.m.-11 p.m. No alcohol or credit cards.* It says a lot about Holland that when you ask about where the oldtimers and insiders go for coffee and talk, the answer is usually Russ'. Started here. Reputation built on burgers (from $1.10 to $3), pies ($1.25-$1.40/slice). Now a growing West Michigan family restaurant chain. Homey decor, friendly efficient service, good value. Dinners (including roll, potato, salad or soup) $4-$6.

Queen's Inn at Dutch Village. *James just east of U.S. 31 (see map). Mon-Sat 11-9, Sun to 8. (616) 393-0310. Full bar. Major credit cards. Lunch menu (all day) $4-$7.50 a la carte. Dinners $4-$11 w/ soup and potato.* Oddly, Dutch cooking hasn't contributed much to the American culinary smorgasbord. Even in Holland, only at this attractive tourist destination can more than 1 or 2 Dutch specialties be found, along w/ standards like steak, perch, burgers, and a salad bar. Recommended: frog legs ($10), Pigs in a Blanket (pork sausage in pastry dough) w/ pea soup and Dutch apple pie ($5, lunch only); mettwurst with hot potato salad and red cabbage ($5.25/$7.25); nasi goreng (Indonesian rice with pork and fried egg; $7 at dinner with salad). Pleasant Old World decor with mottos stencilled on beams. Real thatched roof on part of the exterior; it's close to eye level, so you can see how thick it is.

The Old Schoolhouse. *9354 Port Sheldon Rd., just e. of the center of Borculo, 8 mi. n.e. of Holland. From Zeeland, take State St./96th Ave. 5 mi. n., turn e. onto Pt. Sheldon. From U.S. 31 6 mi. n. of Holland, take Pt. Sheldon Rd. 5 mi. e. (616) 875-7200. Tues-Sat 8-8. No alcohol or credit cards. Out-of-town checks OK.* Eating at this large country schoolhouse, decorated w/ class pictures, teachers' aids, is a little like going to a rural school reunion. Food is quality middle-American basics. Known for BBQ beef ribs ($7.45 full, $5.75 half) , homemade soup ($1.50./bowl), pies ($1.20). Favorite dishes include homemade French toast at breakfast ($2.65 including meat). Amazing prices: lunches from $2.50 to $5.35 w/ potato, salad), $4.75 dinner w/ small portion baked chicken, Swiss steak. Vegetarians could make a meal of the soups, salads, and sides alone. Saturday there's a $7.45 dinner buffet.

Borculo is in the heart of Dutch farming country, historically an important center of poultry production. Ask for directions to nearby Bil - Mar ("Mr. Turkey") Country Store.

Lake Ranch Resort. *(616) 399-9380 (in season). (616) 457-3215 (off season). 226 Ottawa Beach Rd. across from Holland State Park.* Motel condo w/ 29 units in rental pool. Open April 15-Oct. 15. Sample rates: 2 double beds $45 off-season/$65 in-season. 2 rooms (sleeps 4): $63/$91, w/ kitchenette, living room, bedroom. 2 bldgs. of attached, 1-story units face Lake Macatawa, flanking central lawn & activity area w/ heated pool, volleyball, shuffleboard, picnic & BBQ area, marina. Attractive contemporary decor. Fish-cleaning station.
New rooms, activity area, on water, near state park beach, bikeway

Point West Resort. *(616) 335-5894. 2330 S. Shore Dr. in Macatawa, s.w. of downtown Holland.* 60 rooms. Half in 4-floor highrise, each w/ balcony, good water views. Heated outdoor pool, game area. Rates vary from $69-$129. Cable TV. Access to private Lake Michigan beach. 5 tennis courts, fishing, boat slips. Mediocre restaurant, bar w/ entertainment weekends.
Best resort location in Holland area, private beach, many sports

Wooden Shoe Motel. *(616) 392-8521. U.S. 31 at 16th, on busy strip.* 29 rooms on 2 floors. Tulip time: $65-$75. May-Sept: $52-$58. Oct.-April $34-$38. TV w/ 2 PG movies nightly. Outdoor pool, $3 mini golf. Wooden Shoe family restaurant.
Best budget family choice

Blue Mill Inn. *(616) 392-7073. 409 U.S. 31 at 16th, on busy strip.* 81 units on 2 floors. Summer: $42-$47. Winter $37-$43. Some waterbeds. Cable TV, VCR rental. Good sound insulation. Well maintained.
VCR rentals, moderate price

Holiday Inn. *(616) 394-0111. 650 E. 24th at U.S. 31, 3 mi. from downtown, on busy strip.* 168 units on 2 floors. $76-$88. Suites $105. Call for weekend pkgs. Cable TV. Holidome: indoor pool, whirlpool, sauna, indoor rec. area. exercise room. Calypso's restaurant/bar.
Best in Holland for indoor activities

GRAND HAVEN

Official Chicken Co. *In Harbourfront Place on Washington, downtown.* (616) 846-7861. *Tues-Sat 11:30-8, Mon 11:30-5:30, Sun 12-4.* Superior fast-food outlet in food court of renovated piano factory. , Good for picking up a quick picnic to enjoy on the Grand River boardwalk nearby. A good choice: chicken fajita ($3.61), BBQ chicken dinners w/ slaw, fresh fries, (3 pieces $5.50, 6 $9.60, 9 $12.90). Burgers, steak fajitas also available.

Kirby Grill. *Washington at Harbor Dr., downtown.* (616) 846-3299. *Sun-Thurs 11-11. Fri-Sat 11-1 a.m. Closed Mon off season.* Full bar. MC, Visa, AmEx. New spot a smash hit for upbeat, casual chic ambiance & the best food in town. Known for white chili ($3.75/bowl), pasta like pasta primavera in roasted garlic cream sauce ($6.75), BBQ buffalo sandwich ($4.75 w/ onion rings). Entrees at lunch ($6-$7) and dinner ($7-$14) come w/ starch, vegetable. Much fish and seafood — for instance, baked cajun catfish ($12), grilled scallops in mustard-cream sauce ($14). Some booths have river view. Becomes a boisterous, convivial drinking spot by night.

Fricano's Pizza Tavern. *1400 Fulton at Hopkins, 4 blocks east of U.S. 31. (616) 842-8640. Mon-Thurs 5-12, Fri & Sat to 1. Closed Sundays. Full bar. No credit cards.* Notably plain, utterly untrendy spot on industrial east side packs 'em in with a menu that hasn't changed for 40 years: a 12" thin-crusted pizza with distinctive sauce, plus beer. One line forms for front room, another for rear. The pizza is $5 plain, up to $7 w/ all the toppings.

Arboreal Inn. *18191 174th. Take US. 31 n. from Grand Haven to Van Wagoner exit, w. 1 mi. to T, turn right onto 174th. On w. side of road in 1/4 mi. (616) 842-3800. Lunch Mon-Fri 11-2. Dinner Mon-Sat 5-10. A la carte lunch entrees $4-$7. Dinner $12-$26, inc. starch, soup or salad. Full bar, outstanding wine list. MC, Visa, AmEx, Discover.* Classic country inn is one of very most delightful restaurants in west Michigan. Unpretentious good taste in a European vein. Simple menu, excellent ingredients. Fresh whitefish is from inland Canadian lakes. Steaks. Tornedos Oscar ($19) w/ mushrooms, crab in Bernaise sauce. Special dinners like Chateaubriand for 2 w/ 24 hours' notice. For lunch, sandwiches, soups, salads. Evening sandwich menu in bar area on weekday.

Khardomah Lodge. *(616) 842-2990. 1365 Lake Ave. in Highland Park area (p. 332).* 16 small, simple rooms on 2nd floor of old summer hotel Each sleeps 2-4. Some have bunks. Baths at end of hall. In-season: $49/double, $5 extra person. Off-season: $39. Phone avail. Coffee provided; kitchen privileges. Comfortable common areas with ravine view, massive stone fireplace. Big dining area. Owners have preserved authentic cottage atmosphere with bits of nostalgic leftovers: chenille bedspreads, player piano, games. Clean, not musty. 150 yards to beach. *Authentic 1900's lodge with simple rooms, big porches and common areas where guests can spread out or mingle*

Highland Park Hotel. *(616) 846-1473. 1414 Lake Ave. in Highland Park.* 6 rooms w/ baths. May 1-Oct. 1: $80 weeknights, $90 weekends. Off-season $60. Cont. breakfast. Cocktails. A/C, TV in lounge, phone avail. The old annex, all that's left of the Highland Park hotel, has delightful small 2nd floor porch & enclosed lounge for guests, panoramic view of Lake Michigan. Medium-size guest rooms have angled lake view. Cheerful, sophisticated country decor w/antiques. *Convival B&B with lake view in one of Michigan's most enchanting cottage colonies*

Boyden House. *(616) 846-3538. 301 S. Fifth at Lafayette, about 5 blocks to downtown.* 5 rooms w/ baths. Summer: $75-$85. Winter: $65-$85. A/C. full breakfast. TV & phone in common areas. Large guest rooms inc. sitting area; some have fireplaces. Big front porch, back deck, several common rooms, ornate carved woodwork. Walk to downtown, boardwalk, Duncan Park. Innkeepers are outgoing Dutch couple in interior design business. On busy street. *B&B a friendly showplace in odd 1874 lumber baron's mansion*

Holiday Inn. *(616) 846-1000. 940 W. Savidge, Spring Lake, just n.e. of drawbridge.* 121 rooms on 2 floors, 32 w/river view . Slips occasionally avail. ($35-$60). Summer: $75-$95. Winter: $64-$76. Prices vary; call to confirm. Cable TV. Indoor & outdoor pool, health club, whirlpool, steam room, dry sauna. Restaurant, bar w/DJ. Charter fishing at docks. Popular & busy place. Boring view is of the Grand River full of pleasure boats. *Big-time boating scene, lots to do*

Days Inn. *(616) 842-1999. S. Beacon Blvd. (US .31), 2 mi. s. of drawbridge over Grand River on busy strip.* 100 rooms on 2 floors. Summer: $69-$79. Winter $52-$62. Rates vary frequently. Special weekend prices for families in winter. Cable TV. Indoor swimming pool, game room. Adj. restaurant/bar. *Indoor pool, good winter family deals for x-c skiers and lugers*

LAMONT

Riverview B&B. *(616) 677-3921. 4580 Leonard Rd. in Lamont, 20 min. from Grand Haven and Grand Rapids.* 3 rooms share 2 baths baths. $55-$65. A/C. Complete breakfast. TV, phones in common area. 1850 Greek Revival home with a beautiful view of the Grand River. Sunny, big porch/ dining area, living room, large patio for guests. Very large, lushly landscaped yard w/outdoor games & play area. Tasteful country decor w/ antiques. Nearby fishing, boat rentals, golf. *Lovely, relaxing riverside location in quaint village of Lamont*

FRUITPORT

Village Park B&B. *(616) 865-6289. 60 W. Park St.* 6 rooms w/baths. Summer: $60. Off-season: $50. Wellness Wknd pkgs. Closest B&B to Hoffmaster State Park. Fresh, airy old house w/big yard, deck. Quiet town. *Across from park on Spring Lake.*

MUSKEGON

The Hearthstone. *In Cornerhouse Motor Inn just off Bus. 31/Seaway where it turns n. Turn e. onto Norton and immediately right onto Glade. (616) 733-1056. Full bar.* Major credit cards. Mon-Thurs 11-11, Fri & Sat 11-1, Sun 5-11. Same menu all day; sandwiches $4-$6. The practical approach to preparing consistently good food: a limited menu (hearty soups, sandwiches on crusty French rolls, pasta and pasta salads) with lots of surprises. Soups ($2/cup, $4/bowl w/bread) could be any of 100 recipes. Pasta salads ($6.25-$8) may be linguine with pesto, cream, cappicola, walnuts, or brie w/ herbed olive oil, or marinated vegetables, tomato, bacon. Daily lunch specials under $4.

Cobwebs and Rafters. *3006 Lake Shore Dr. going to Pere Marquette Park on s. side of Muskegon Lake. Past paper mill, Lincoln. (616) 755-5305. Mon-Thurs 10-midnight, Fri & Sat to 1, Sun 12-12, shorter hours off-season. Full bar.* Visa, MC. Bright, fun, airy, place in old boathouse & 1930s restaurant overlooks marina & Muskegon Lake. Food from hot dogs ($2), bar food, huge burrito ($6), or $3.95 burgers (a 1/2 lb. burger at build-your-own burger bar is $4) to to seafood, steaks. Popular steak & perch dinner $11. Big deck. Superior live entertainment (vintage rock, blues, jazz) weekends 8:30 to 12:30.

Rafferty's. *601 Terrace Point Blvd., on Muskegon Lake at the end of Apple (M-46). w. of Muskegon Mall. (616) 722-4461. Mon-Thurs 11-10, Fri & Sat to 11, Sun breakfast buffet 9-3. Bar open 2 p.m. to closing.* Visa, MC, AmEx, personal checks. Full bar. Lunch $4.25-$6.45; dinner $9 to $17 — both w salad, potato. Takeout. Fine dining format in swank new waterfront development on giant foundry site symbolizing Muskegon's hopes for transition from rust belt to boating image. Overlooks luxury marina. (HQ of SPX, Fortune 500 mfr. of automotive equipment, is part of Terrace Point.) Known for prime rib ($17), lobster (market price). Specialty: Rafferty boil (steaming pot of shrimp, lobster, mussels, sausage, new potatoes, corn on cob w/garlic bread) for 2, currently $55. Dinner: Large salads ($5-$8) avail. at dinner, sandwiches & salads at lunch. Next to marina; boaters can hire chef for shipboard dinner.

Bear Lake Tavern. *360 Ruddiman at Bear Lake channel in North Muskegon, about 6 mi. from downtown, 2 mi. from Muskegon State Park. (616) 744-1161. Mon-Fri 11:30-10, Fri to 11, Sat 7a.m.-10 p.m., Sun 7a.m.-9p.m. Drinks served later. Full bar.* No credit cards. Out-of-town checks OK. Rustic tavern from the 1920s. Glows with varnished old wood. Overlooks channel between Muskegon and Bear lakes. Service is competent, but it helps to come early at dinner, when fresh fried perch (about $10) packs them in. Good, juicy burger with slaw and fries is around $5 (1/2 lb.) and $4 (1/4 lb.). Perch sandwich is a new introduction.   Dinners start at $9 for grilled or BBQ chicken.

U.S. 31 Barbecue. *151 W. Muskegon (Bus. 31) downtown. (616) 722-3948. Mon-Thurs 11-7, Fri & Sat until 9. Takeout available. No alcohol or credit cards.* 50-year Muskegon landmark serves soup, chili, fries, and 3 BBQ sandwiches: pork, ham or beef ($2), 2 meats ($2.29), all 3 meats ($2.49). Meat — 1,000 pounds a week — is roasted in big brick & glass rotisserie on view in back. Lighter than Southern BBQ, made w/ cabbage relish. Dramatic vintage decor, up-to-the-minute in 1962, hasn't changed a bit since. Extras: old-fashioned milkshakes, pie , carrot cake — $1.50.

Days Inn. *(616) 739-9429. 150 Seaway/Bus. U.S. 31 in Muskegon Hts., 3 mi. s. of downtown Muskegon.* 152 rooms on 2 floors. Summer: $52. Winter: $44. Hot breakfast. Cable TV. Whirlpool. Family restaurant, no alcohol.
Indoor pool, free breakfast, easy freeway access to area sights

Cornerhouse Motor Inn. *(616) 733-2651. 4 mi. s. of downtown on Glade, bus. U.S. 31 & I-96.* 23 units on 2 floors. $34-$39, may vary slightly in summer. Cable TV. Excellent in-house restaurant/bar, Hearthstone.
Best budget choice, good restaurant

Best Western Park Plaza. *(616) 733-2651. 2967 Henry at Summit, 3 mi. s. of downtown. On main commercial strip.* 110 rooms on 4 floors. $67, $53 off-season. Jacuzzi suites avail. Cable TV. Large indoor pool, dry sauna, whirlpool, game room. Limo service. Restaurant. Bar.
Best choice for activities, pool

MONTAGUE/WHITEHALL

Todd Pharmacy. *8744 Ferry 1/2 block n. of Dowling in downtown Montague. (616) 894-4573. Year-round hours: Mon-Fri 8:30-9 p.m., Sat to 7, Sun until 1. No alcohol. Visa, MC, Discover.* Large soda fountain & grill with booths where just about everybody in town shows up. For summer people, nostalgic attraction is malts and sodas ($1.65) and old-fashioned fountain treats like cherry or vanilla phosphates. Soups, salads, sandwiches are served from 10:30 on, after breakfast. Most food is homemade, from potatoes to pies ($1). Incredibly low prices: $1.55 for hamburgers, $1.60 for a chef salad in a soup bowl, $3.10 for hot specials (meat loaf or casserole w/ salad, potato). *wonderful*

Morat's River Walk Cafe and Bakery. *N. Mears overlooking White River marsh, just n. of Colby in downtown Whitehall. (616) 893-5163. Mem. Day-Labor Day: Mon-Sat 6 a.m.-5:30 p.m., Sun 8-1 (but no Sun lunch). Otherwise Mon-Sat 7-5:30.* Busy, full-line bakery w/ pleasant eating area, terrace overlooking marsh, Montague hill. Breakfast hits: French toast ($3), ham/egg/cheese ($3.25). In addition to breakfast rolls, pastries, coffee, there are soups ($2/bowl), chef, chicken, and pasta salads (about $3.75), deli sandwiches on fresh-baked bread ($3.75), and hot dogs. A delightful place to linger on downtown jaunts.

Pekadyll's Ice Cream Parlour. *503 S. Mears, 5 blocks south of downtown Whitehall. (616) 894-9551. Summer hours: 11:30-10 daily. April, May, Sept. hours: 11:30-8. Winter: 11:30-3.* Spiffed-up red-and-white former grocery store. Trim and button-cute without being overdone. Front part is a quintessential ice cream parlor, 1920s-style. Hudsonville ice cream served in cones ($.85 a scoop, or $1.10 w/ homemade cone), splits, parfaits, shakes ($2), sodas, 11 kinds of sundaes. Columbo frozen yogurt, too. You can eat flavorful homemade soups ($2.29/bowl), outstanding subs ($2.50 for 4", $4.50 for 8") on the sun-dappled terrace, beneath big pines, or in the plain, cheery rear rooms. Daily special (soup, sandwich, beverage) $4.

Lakeside Inn. *5700 Scenic Dr. at South Shore, 6 mi. w. of downtown Whitehall overlooking White Lake. (616) 893-8315. In July & Aug: open daily for breakfast 7:30-10 and dinner 6-9. Mother's Day to Labor Day open Fri-Sun for dinner 6-9. Full bar. Visa, MC.* Many people think this resort's public dining room has the area's best food, considering quality and value. Breakfasts are basic. At dinner the inn is known for prime rib ($12.25/ $14.25), shrimp and scallops ($11.25), shrimp or scallops $12.25, and fried perch ($10.25). All w/ salad bar, potato, homemade rolls, muffins. Dining room and patio have nice lake view.

Lakeside Inn. *(616) 893-8315. 5700 N. Scenic Dr at South Shore Dr. on White Lake.* 30 rooms, 1 cottage w/kitchen $45 (older rooms in 2-story lodge)-$70 (large motel units on lake), $5 for extra person. 15 units w/ lake view. Open mid May-mid Oct. Cable TV, private baths, no phones. Outdoor pool, dock, fishing, tennis court, playground. Common rooms for games, gatherings. Good restaurant, bar. Beautiful setting w/ lawn, lake view. Small beach. Reserve ahead. *Not fancy but delightful lakeside resort; an excellent value*

Timekeeper's Inn. *(616) 894-5169. 303 Mears at Slocum, in central Whitehall, across from the Howmet Playhouse.* 4 rooms w/ baths. May-Mid Oct.: $60. Winter rates less. Breakfast. Upstairs kitchenette for guests. Some rooms A/C. TV, phone in sitting

room. 2 blocks to downtown, 1 block to lake. Owners' clock shop in front room. Unusually comfortable. *B&B in solid old house in prettiest part of Whitehall, near summer theater*

Driftwood Resort. *(616) 893-7035. 6180 Murray Rd., the continuation of South Shore almost to the channel.* 13 rooms w/baths in 3-story summer hotel c. 1900. $50-$55/day. 6 cottages sleep 2-8, $450-$550/week. TV in lounge area. Nice lawn & small beach), short walk to private Lake Michigan beach or lighthouse museum. Wonderful old lobby, dining area. Good restaurant next door. Rooms being renovated; some have ugly paneling. Tennis courts, boat dock, game room. *The best location on White Lake*

Super 8 Motel. *(616) 894-4848. 3080 Holton-Whitehall Rd. between U.S. 31 and Whitehall.* 54 rooms on 3 floors. $35-$77. Whirlpool suites & waterbeds avail. Cable TV, phones, comp. coffee. *New motel on freeway*

WHITE CLOUD

The Shack B&B. *(616) 924-6683. 2263 W. 14th., White Cloud.* 26 rooms on 2 floors. $45-$60. Hot tub rooms: $75-$90. Budget rooms, no phone or TV: $40-$45. A/C. Satellite TV. Breakfast, banana split in evening. Restaurant. Large log structure (part old, part new) overlooks Robinson Lake. Butterflies, macrame hangings, corny plaques: like going to grandma's. *Log lodge at lakeside resort with homey Middle American atmosphere*

Chapter 8
Northern Michigan

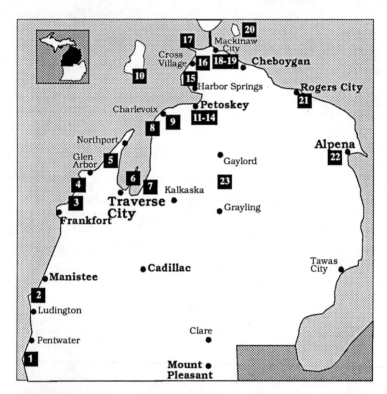

HIGHLIGHTS

Mac Woods' Dune Rides at Silver Lake

Thrills and insight on the ghostly dunes,
with sunset's pinks and purple shadows

This 35-minute ride up and down the sand dunes at Silver Lake offers thrills, hauntingly eerie scenery, and surprisingly intelligent commentary. It's actually worth the money, unlike most of the overpriced go-kart rides, water slides, and family attractions that could make a Silver Lake vacation a thrifty parent's nightmare.

The tour conveys the drama of these unusual dunes west and north of Silver Lake. They are *live* dunes, constantly moved by the wind. On a windy day you can feel the dunes in action as you're peppered with wind-borne sand. When the shoreline timber was logged off in the 19th century, hardy dune grass restabilized most denuded sand dunes enough that new vegetation eventually stopped most wind erosion and created "dead" dunes. But in a few places the dunes were so high and windblown that dune grasses couldn't get established.

Crescent-shaped Silver Lake itself is filling in with windblown sand about four feet a year. It's really "Sliver Lake," the tour guide jokes. Eventually the wind will cut down the high dunes that separate Silver Lake from Lake Michigan to a more typical height. A few sandblasted pine stumps remain from the logging era. Treetops buried by shifting dunes look like bushes. The buried jack pines die, but poplars survive by sending out additional root systems from their trunks. Mostly, though, what you see is a treeless desert, more like the Sahara than normal Michigan dunes with their diverse plant life.

You are driven in trucks with fat tires, modified as long, open-air vehicles. The ride includes some moderately thrilling dips and climbs, stops for picture taking, and a pause to wade in the beach. Towards sunset is by far the best time to go on the ride. The flaming sky and blue lake are dramatic behind the rosy dunes, and the slanting light delineates the dunes' shapes and patterns. Oddly, crowds are smaller at this spectacular time.

Old-fashioned tourism prevails here. The dune rides' gift shop is a classic, genial tourist trap. The Burma-Shave-type signs as you enter the dunes have corny mother-in-law jokes. In the 1930s, resort operator Mac Woods bought a thousand acres of this duneland cheap. When the state of Michigan bought the land as part of an expanded Silver Lake State Park, the dune rides retained concession rights to continue operations. Since the dunes are already actively moving, the rides don't contribute to extra erosion.

On 16th Ave. just south of Silver Lake. From U.S. 31, take Shelby exit, go west on Shelby Rd. 6 1/2 miles, north on 16th about 3 1/2 miles to dune rides. (616) 873-2817. Open mid-May-mid-October. Late June-Labor Day: open daily 9:30-sundown. May, June, Sept. & Oct.: slightly shorter hours, closed Thurs. Adults $7.50, children 3-10 $4.50, under 3 free.

MICHIGAN'S ONLY DESIGNATED OFF-ROAD-VEHICLE AREA . . . . . is at the north end of the dunes at **Silver Lake State Park**. Here the 300-space parking lot is frequently filled as four-wheelers, dune buggies, trucks, and motorcycles from all over the Midwest create a constant whine and roar that's heard for miles. This goes on from April 1 through October 31. Sandy Korners (616-873-5048) offers **ORV rentals** (about $20/hour), lessons, and guided drives.

WALKING THROUGH THE DUNES. . . . . is permitted in a third section of Silver Lake State Park. But the distant roar of off-road vehicles is omnipresent. Wilderness-seekers will prefer the undeveloped **Nordhouse Dunes** north of **Ludington State Park** (p. 362).

THE SILVER LAKE SCENE. . . . . is tacky — commercial tourism of an intensity seldom found in Michigan. Minigolf, go-kart rides, Jellystone Park, waterslides, trout farms, frozen yogurt stands, and such are everywhere, and hardly anything is cheap. But when the sun is low and the sky illuminated, it is lovely to look across the genuinely silver lake to the ghostly bare, dunes. Blue shadows are cast on the pink dunes. **Pontoons, sailboards, jet skis, and more can be rented** from the Silver Lake Sports Shop, (616) 873-5048. . . . . The **Silver Lake State Park beach** along Silver Lake takes advantage of the beautiful dune view and provides an island of some serenity. It's a kempt, suburban little park with grassy lawns. Some good-sized pines provide up-north vacation atmosphere and shade. The lakeshore campground of 102 small lots is typically jammed with campers' boats. The 146-lot campground across the road is roomier and more private. Both have electricity and showers, and both are likely to be full. Reservations are advisable; nearby private campgrounds can handle overflow. *From U.S. 31, take Hart/Mears exit at Polk Rd., go west on Polk through Mears, follow signs to Silver Lake State Park beach. (616) 873-3083. State park sticker required: $3/day $15/year.*

A LOVELY, SECLUDED LAKE MICHIGAN BEACH . . . . . away from the hubbub of Silver Lake, but nearby, is **the Little Point Sable Beach** section of the state park.

(Sable is pronounced "SAH-bel" and means sand.) It's a long beach with an open landscape of poplars, beachgrass, and low dunes, dominated by the tall red brick shaft of the handsome **Little Point Sable Lighthouse**. Get there by taking Scenic Drive along the south shore of Silver Lake. Past the Mac Woods Dune Rides building and many cottages, it becomes Channel Drive. The paved road stops by Silver Creek. Look for the signs and the narrow dirt road at the left. It goes alongside the creek, through a heavily wooded area of surprisingly dramatic cottages, to **Golden Township Park** and then on to Little Point Sable. In the peak summer season plan on arriving by 10 a.m. to find a spot in the smallish lot of this attractive beach. *State park sticker required.*

BIKE THROUGH FIELDS, ORCHARDS, AND SMALL TOWNS . . . . . . from Hart and Silver Lake to Montague without being bothered by passing cars and trucks. A stretch of old C&O railroad bed has become the **Hart-Montague Bicycle Trail State Park**, a 23-mile linear park for bicyclists and horseback riders. (In winter cross-country skiers and snowmobilers share the trail, which is said to be wide enough for both.) The asphalt trail passes across two river valleys, through scenic rolling fields and orchards, which are especially pretty at blossomtime and in late summer. Towards Montague it becomes quite flat. As the train once did, the trail goes right through the small towns of Rothbury, New Era, Shelby, and Mears — simple places which have restaurants and groceries. Shrubby growth and trees along the right of way muffle road noise (a good deal of the trail parallels roads) and provide cover for abundant wildlife.

A chatty, informative **trail guide** with information about motels, camping, restaurants, and bed and breakfasts can be obtained from the chambers of commerce at White Lake (616-893-4585) and Silver Lake (616-873-5048). In addition to camping at Silver Lake State Park west of Mears, there's camping at the **Hart city campground** on Hart Lake. Bicycles can be rented for $2/hour, $12.50/day (including trail fee) at **McKay's Bicycle Rental** on 56th Ave. south of Mears (616-873-4271). *Hart trailhead is just east of the U.S. 31 Polk Rd. exit at the parking lot to Hansen's supermarket. Montague trailhead is on Eilers Rd. just east of Bus. Route 31 at the northeast edge of Montague. Administered by Silver Lake State Park; call (616) 873-3083 for information. Trail pass: $2/day, $10/year, or $5/day, $25/year family pass. 8 a.m.-10 p.m.*

PRETTY PENTWATER . . . . . a resort village of charming clapboard store-fronts and pleasant houses, looks a lot like Saugatuck without so many shops. It's about 15 miles north of Silver Lake, just off U.S. 31. There's a nice **park** for picnics by the marina on Pentwater Lake. The sugar-sand Lake Michigan beach at **Charles Mears State Park** is an easy walk to town. A **double-decker bus** goes to Ludington. For particulars on Pentwater, call (616) 869-4150.

THE LAKE MICHIGAN CARFERRY . . . . . between Ludington and Manitowoc, Wisconsin, proved a hit of 1992's travel season. The four-hour voyage (May-October) leaves Ludington at 7:30 a.m., with an extra evening sailing in peak season. A Ludington native and benefactor has renovated the old *Badger* attractively for passengers' comfort. No more railroad cars on board! It's a civilized alternative to driving through Chicago or across the U.P. One-way rates: $40/car, $30/person, 5-15 $15. Call (800) 841-4243.

Ludington State Park and Nordhouse Dunes

The best-rounded of Michigan's many state parks

Ludington State Park offers the most satisfying mix of natural scenery and popular activities — swimming, boating, hiking, fishing — of any single state park. It has six miles of sandy, dune-backed Lake Michigan beach with a handsome lighthouse, an outstanding fishing lake, an inland beach, a fine nature center, and 18 miles of hiking trails. For people who really want to get away from it all, it joins the 3,400-acre Nordhouse Dunes, where cars are not permitted.

With so many fine outdoor features together in one park, it's no wonder you have to make summer reservations for Ludington State Park's 398 campsites early. But you don't have to camp here to enjoy the park. The town of Ludington has a big variety of motels, and nearby campgrounds don't usually fill up. Backpackers can camp along any of the Nordhouse Dunes' trails.

Of special interest here are:

◆ The park's six-mile **Lake Michigan beach,** backed by low to high dunes, is longer than any other in Michigan's state park system. The designated swimming area stands out because of a handsome shingle **bathhouse** and **concession** building built by the Civilian Conservation Corps during the Depression. Beachgoers can pull over, park anywhere along the 3 1/2-mile main entry road and walk over to the beach, or walk another mile and a half up the beach from the bath house to the beautiful Point Sable Lighthouse.

◆ An **inland beach,** good for swimming on days when the big lake's too cool, is by the dam at the west end of Hamlin Lake.

◆ The mile-long **Big Sable River** joins Hamlin Lake and Lake Michigan right at the main swimming beach. It's shallow and clear, ideal for **tubing.** A **bike and jogging path** parallels it and the road to Hamlin Lake. A pretty **picnic area** is midway.

◆ **Hamlin Lake** is a 4,000-acre lake, 10 miles long, with excellent **fishing** (panfish, some walleye and pike), with lots of coves and inlets that make for interesting boating, too. During the fall salmon run, snagging is permitted below the dam.

◆ **Canoes and boats** can be rented at Hamlin Beach.

◆ The **trail system** is one of the very best in the state parks system. It's long — 18 miles altogether. It's varied, passing through dunes, by Hamlin Lake, and the river. Interconnected trails go to all the park's major activity centers, for hikes of 1 to 8 hours. Trails are dotted with occasional scenic lookouts, shelters, and toilets. Sixteen miles are designated cross-country ski trails.

◆ The attractive small **nature center** is tucked between deeply shady back dunes and the south bank of the Big Sable River, behind the windswept entry area of scrubby jack pines. Its highlight is an outstanding multi-screen **slide/tape show** that puts Ludington State Park and Michigan's sand dunes (the world's longest freshwater dunes) into geological and historical perspective, from the dunes' formation some 3,000 years ago to logging and tourism in the late 19th century. If you see the sand dune show, you will look at Lake Michigan's lakeshore in a new, more comprehending way.

Exhibits include live snakes (kids come regularly to play with them) and detailed three-dimensional maps of the bottoms of all the Great Lakes, of special interest to sailors. The one-mile **Skyline Loop** starts with a dune stair by the parking area and climbs the dune ridge for views clear to the Ludington light and down into the treetops below. A small **gift shop** is well-stocked with nature books. Call for times of scheduled **nature walks.** *Easy to miss; look for the sign three miles into the park, shortly before you come to the river. Typically open May-Sept, daily 10-5:30. Call to confirm spring & fall hours.*

◆ **398 modern campsites,** on three mostly shady campgrounds, offer little privacy but are always full in July and August. *Ludington State Park is 7 mi. n. of Ludington on M-116. (616) 843-8671. State park sticker required: $3/day, $15/year.*

A DUNELAND WILDERNESS . . . . . where wheeled vehicles are forbidden is the 4,300-acre **Nordhouse Dunes**, just north of Ludington State Park. Naturalists appreciate dune country for its many kinds of habitats, from damp to desert-like. Ten miles of trails here go through areas rich in wildlife and wildflowers. A long, sandy beach is fine for swimming. Backcountry camping is permitted along the trails. The **Lake Michigan Recreation Area** operated by the U.S. Forest Service has 100 of the nicest campsites in the U.S.: very large, shady, and close to the beach. No electricity or showers; two of the four loops have flush toilets. $7/night. Reserve well in advance for peak summer season, or plan on staying in overflow space until a spot opens up. *Lake Mich. Rec. Area and the trailhead for Nordhouse Dunes trails are about 10 mi. s. of Manistee, then west off U.S. 31. Lake Mich. Rec. Area Rd. leads to campground in about 12 miles. Call (616) 723-6716 or (616) 723-2211 for information on the dunes and recreation area. Call 1 3(800) 283-CAMP for reservations.*

Gwen Frostic Prints

*At this fanciful studio, see prints being made
in a beautiful natural setting.*

The setting is what's unique about this place. A whimsical, rambling stone studio is romantically set in an idyllic 280-acre nature preserve east of Frankfort. Big windows in the relaxing library provide a splendid view of a pond. Free-form rock pillars add to the fanciful atmosphere.

Gwen Frostic's simple prints of natural subjects are widely distributed and enduringly popular. They illustrate books and decorate note cards and napkins. The octogenarian artist moved here in 1955. A prolific printmaker and engagingly direct personality, she has built her out-of-the-way business to employ a 30 full-time workers — a remarkably large number.

From another set of large windows visitors can look down on 13 old Heidelberg presses. The air is filled with the smell of ink as the sheet-fed presses print reproductions of Frostic's original etchings of nature scenes.

River Rd, 2 miles west of U.S. 31 between Benzonia and Frankfurt. Drive down to studio is just west of Higgins Rd. intersection. Open daily from 1st Sun of May to 1st Sun of Nov, 9-5:30. Otherwise open Mon-Sat 9-4:30. (616) 882-5505.

A CITY UPON THE HILL . . . . . in the Biblical sense of a holy place elevated above crass trading and sensuality. That's what the idealistic Congregational founders of **Benzonia** hoped to build. Their plans to develop Northern Michigan's version of Oberlin College failed, however, as famed Civil War historian Bruce Catton described in *Waiting for the Morning Train,* his compelling personal history of his hometown and region at the end of the lumber boom. The college and its successor failed to flourish. Today Benzonia is a backwater compared with Leelanau County resorts not far to the north. The charming cluster of art galleries and a good bakery, just west of U.S. 31 by the main four corners, is worth a visit. Benzonia's history is told in the **museum** that now occupies the large old Congregational Church across from the onetime college campus.

Sleeping Bear Dunes National Lakeshore

*Beaches and trails with splendid views,
maritime and lumbering history,
and two uninhabited islands to explore.*

Centerpiece of this sprawling national park is the most
famous of Great Lakes dunes, Sleeping Bear. It towers
above Lake Michigan and is a popular climb for many of
the 1.25 million who visit here annually. The national park is a
varied 35-mile stretch of scenic shoreline extending some two
miles inland. It includes a scenic drive, a dozen hiking trails to
many outstanding overlooks, smaller lakes, rivers, and beaches,
an attractively woodsy rustic campground and a modern one to
open in 1992, and two large islands, North and South Manitou.

The area offers a hard-to-match blend of outstanding natural
areas and civilized amenities. No matter how crowded the towns
are, there's plenty of room to spread out in the national park. To
acquaint yourself with the area, start with the following:

◆ Begin your visit with a stop at the **Sleeping Bear Dunes Visitor
Center** just outside the village of Empire. Its **book shop** is excellent. The array of **free literature** includes several pamphlets well
worth reading carefully to kick off your stay here. "Sleeping Bear
Dunes," "The Story of the Sand Dunes" (a fine introduction to
local geology), "Sleeping Bear Point Coast Guard Station," and
pieces on North and South Manitou Islands and Pierce Stocking
Scenic Drive. "Hiking Trails" summarizes all 12 trails. The free
hiking trail maps don't give elevations; to really know what hills
you're in for, buy a topo map ($2.50/area) at the visitor center.
Visitor maps from the Empire and Glen Lake chambers of commerce include a lot of helpful information. *Off M-72 at M-22 just
east of Empire. (616) 326-5134. Open daily except Thanksgiving
and Christmas, at least from 9:30 to 4. June-Sept: 9-6. Free.*

◆ Next, take a short, marvelous hike along the **Empire Bluff Trail.**
This highly recommended 1 1/2-mile round trip goes up into a
deeply shady beech-maple climax forest, out into the high,
perched dunes, and to an observation platform some 400 feet
above the lake below. The **trail guide**, free from the visitors' center, makes it even more enjoyable. Your reward is a view that
includes two-thirds of the entire National Lakeshore, from Platte

Bay on the south to Sleeping Bear itself on the north, out to South Manitou Island. *From M-22 about 1 1/2 miles south of Empire, turn northwest onto Wilco Road and look for the sign.*

◆ A third good introduction is the 7.4-mile-long **Pierce Stocking Scenic Drive**, named after the area lumberman who developed it as a private visitor attraction in the 1960s. An excellent interpretive brochure is available at the entrance. The first dune overlook and picnic spot looks down on Glen Lake and a three-mile stretch of duneland leading up to Sleeping Bear itself. The second and third overlook/picnic areas offer a closer look at the vanishing big dune, a mile away; the second Lake Michigan Overlook, also has a fine view of the shoreline down to the Empire Bluffs and Platte Bay. *From M-22 2 miles north of Empire, turn north onto M-109. Drive entrance is in 1 mile. Open 9 a.m. to 1 hour after sunset. For early-morning walks, park by the entrance. Free.*

Here are highlights of the Sleeping Bear Dunes area. All noteworthy attractions are arranged by activity category.

BEACHES

◆ **Empire Beach.** Pleasant village beach with grassy lawns and a fine view of Sleeping Bear, the Manitou Islands, and passing freighters. Sandy beach frontage on both Lake Michigan and South Bar Lake — a nice cool-weather swimming alternative. Picnic area with grills, gazebo, restrooms, volleyball net, basketball court, and playgrounds on both beachfront areas. Boat launch. Shore fishing. Historical marker fills you in on Empire's boom years as a lumbering center, 1873-1917. *From the west end of Front Street in downtown Empire (the westward extension of M-72), turn north onto Lake to reach the beach. No charge. Beach parking can fill up on nice summer days; come by noon.*

◆ **Glen Lake Beach.** Sandy beach with fine view of Little Glen Lake, hills in the background, and the dune climb across the road. Picnic tables, grills, changing house. *Take M-109 from M-22 at either central Glen Arbor or 3 miles north of Empire. Beach is about 4 miles from either end. Free.*

◆ **Glen Haven Beach.** Extremely simple little Lake Michigan beach by the now-deserted piers of the Glen Lake Canning Company. Good swimming. Nice views of the Manitou Islands. Picnic tables, pit toilets. The entire village of Glen Haven is now boarded up, awaiting possible future restoration by the National Parks Service. *From central Glen Arbor, take M-109 west to Glen Haven, turn in by the parking area by the old cannery. Free.*

◆ **Good Harbor Beach.** Very simple, uncrowded beach with lots of surrounding natural vegetation and striking views of the bluffs of Pyramid Point and North Manitou Island. *Take M-22 about 8 miles northeast of Glen Arbor or 9 miles southwest of the intersection with M-204. Turn north at County Road 669 (you'll see the sign to Cedar; go in the opposite direction). When you get to the lake, turn right. Free.*

ADVENTURES

◆ **Dune Climb.** Sleeping Bear today is a live dune. As the wind cuts down its top, sand spills over the back here. This 150-foot wall of sand is a strenuous climb, more so for adults than lightweight kids, but they are rewarded with a view of the surrounding countryside. To see the lake from the top of Sleeping Bear, it's a two-mile walk across hot sand, and two miles back. Water, hats, and sun protection are advised. Picnic tables and a refreshment and souvenir stand are by the road at the dune climb's base.

Sleeping Bear once was larger, looming 600 feet above Lake Michigan. Topped by trees, the dune did look like a bear. It sat back from the shore, protected by a peninsula of sand. But dunes and shorelines are marked by alternating periods of stability and change. Since the early part of this century, wave action has devoured the sand peninsula and begun to erode the glacial plateau beneath Sleeping Bear itself. Its front is now a bluff sliding into Lake Michigan, while winds, having destroyed the plant cover on top, send sands sailing over to the Dune Slide, an area so volatile that human footsteps can do no additional harm. By 1980 Sleeping Bear was down to 400 feet. *Take M-109 from M-22 at either central Glen Arbor or 3 miles north of Empire. Dune climb is about 4 miles from either end. Free.*

◆ **South Manitou Island.** In the early days of Great Lakes shipping, this small island (about 3 1/2 by 3 1/2 miles) bustled with activity. Woodcutters supplied fuel for steamers. (On each trip through the Great Lakes a ship consumed from 100 to 300 cords of wood). South Manitou farms supplied provisions for ship crews. The island had a village with stores, a busy harbor, and a lighthouse to mark the entrance to the Manitou Passage, a much-used but potentially dangerous shortcut. By 1960 the last farms were gone and the Coast Guard station had been closed. Abandoned farm buildings, a school, and a cemetery remain as evocative testimony to changing times.

As part of the National Lakeshore, the island has been open since 1970 to primitive, low-impact campers, to hikers, to boaters (who must anchor offshore and come in by dinghy), and to day-trippers who take the 1 1/2-hour voyage over, spend three hours on the island, and return to Leland. Highlights include **perched dunes** on the west, low dunes and a dwindling **nesting colony of gulls** on the east, a battered **shipwreck** just off the shore, and a grove of **virgin white cedars** with the world record-holder, 17 1/5 feet in circumference. Parks rangers give talks about the lighthouse and shipping (currently at 1 p.m.) that include a trip up the unusually tall, 100-foot tower. The **Visitor Center** in the old village post office tells the island's natural and human history. A 1 1/2 hour **island tour** in an open-air vehicle can be customized to special interests; sign up on the boat from Leland. *($5/adult, $2/children)*. No food is available; bring your own.

Camping is permitted at three main **campgrounds** (from one to four miles from the dock; campers hike there), at scattered **backcountry campsites** for up to 6 people, and at a few larger group campsites. No reservations taken; get a permit at the visitor center. Ten miles of marked **hiking trails** go through dense, mature forests and old fields. Some forests, far from the harbor, have never been cut. Wildflower colonies there have grown undisturbed, so you can see jack-in-the-pulpit and trillium of enormous size. Sandy **beaches** are plentiful; the protected east bay is especially popular. The island's small size makes it hard to get lost for long; South Manitou is a good place for families' first big backpacking adventure. Careful planning and disposal of waste is imperative, to avoid trashing the island. *Manitou Island Transit leaves from Fishtown in downtown Leland. Daily service June thru August; no Tues. or Thurs. trips in May, Sept., Oct. 9:30 a.m. check-in, 10 a.m. departure. Reservations recommended. (616) 256-9061 or (616) 271-4217. Day trip: $14 adults, $10 children 12 and under. Campers add $2.*

◆ **North Manitou Island.** Logging, farming, cherry-raising, and the Coast Guard have all vanished from North Manitou, where two towns once were. All that remains are abandoned and ruined buildings, a few private camps, and a small visitor staging area in the east village with a ranger station for emergency assistance. Most of the island was a private hunting preserve; seven deer introduced in 1927 have proliferated into a herd of two thousand at one point. Their overbrowsing destroys young trees and shrubs and makes the island look like a park — pretty now, but ultimately ruinous, since there are no young trees to replace ones that die. Topography varies from low, open dunes to rugged bluffs.

Since the National Parks Service bought the hunting preserve in 1984, it is managing the island as "a primitive experience emphasizing solitude, a feeling of self-reliance, and a sense of exploration." That means: no cars or wheeled vehicles, water at only one place, two outhouses, one campground, fires only at two fire rings. Low-impact camping (burying human waste, packing out trash) is required. Thirty miles of marked trails make three interconnecting loops around the island. To go elsewhere, a compass is essential. Campers are free to choose backcountry sites under certain limitations. Annual deer hunts are held to reduce the deer population, currently down to around 600. *Manitou Island Transit leaves Leland at 10 on Sunday, Wednesday, and Friday, June thru August and returns immediately, without a layover. Call (616) 256-9061 or (616) 271-4217 for other times and for hunting information. Round-trip fares: $16 adults, $12 children 12 and under.*

◆ **Canoeing on the Platte River.** A delightful, easy 1 1/2-hour trip through hardwood forests, wetlands, sand dunes, and Loon Lake. Much animal and bird life can be seen if you go before noon or after 6. The gentle current of this shallow river makes it ideal for canoeing novices; the wildlife makes it attractive to veteran naturalists. Start by the M-22 bridge at the Platte River between Empire and Frankfort. **Canoe rentals** from the Riverside Canoe Livery (same location), (616) 325-5622.

◆ **Hiking.** The 12 hiking trails lead through distinctive environments to scenic overlooks. The Parks Service's "Hiking Trails" brochure summarizes the special features of each trail; separate hiking and cross-country skiing maps are available for each. Three trails are especially recommended. The 1 1/2-mile **Empire Bluffs Trail** (p. 368) gives the best overview of the entire shoreline. The 4-mile Otter Creek loop of the 15-mile **Platte Plains Trail** goes alongside a stream full of wildlife, including beavers, and through a fragrant cedar swamp. The **Dunes Trail**, a strenuous 2.8 mile loop, starts near the Glen Haven Maritime Museum. It explores the spooky, desolate dunescape atop Sleeping Bear, including a ghost forest of trees that flourished before being buried in sand. Wind-sculpted patterns in the sand are striking. (Water, a hat, sunscreen, and shoes are recommended for hot dune hikes.)

Two easy, 1 1/2-mile, one-hour hikes come with interpretive brochures to put you in touch with sand dune ecology (**Cottonwood Trail**) and the rich variety of species found where forests meet fields (**Windy Moraine Trail**).

INDOOR ACTIVITIES

◆ **Empire Area Historical Museum.** An energetic group of Empire natives (a mix of Belgians, Frenchmen, and Norwegians recruited by logging companies) and summer folk have built up a vast collection of

interesting things. These include antique vehicles, a nifty model of the big Empire Lumber Company where the public beach now is, and a turkey feather Christmas tree. Centerpiece of the museum is the splendid back and front bar from Andrew Roen's saloon that flourished during Empire's logging heyday, along with a coin-operated music box and horse race game. Headlines from newspapers across the nation tell the story of the discovery, after the old man died, of $125,000 in cash, plus this disassembled bar, and "a lot of great stuff that belonged in Empire," according to the museum's founder, a wrecker operator. Many unusually interesting old photos of everyday life in these parts help make this a fine place to spend a rainy day. An inexpensive **gift shop** features local history and reproductions of antique books and cardboard ornaments. *On M-22 at the intersection of La Core and Salisbury, on the north edge of Empire. (616) 326-5314 or (616) 326-5316. Mem. Day thru June: open Fri-Mon 1-4. July & August: daily except Wednesday 10-4. Fall weekend hours a possibility. Also open by appt. Free admission; donations welcome.*

◆ **Sleeping Bear Point Coast Guard Station Maritime Museum.** Worth a visit for the beautiful setting alone. The interesting brochure available at the Visitor Center (p. 367) makes better reading than the exhibit text. "The [Coast Guard] surfmen became folk heroes, greatly respected for their courage and skill," it points out. "Neighbors often came by to watch their drills." You can see a video of the breeches buoy drill and relive the crew's rigorous weekly schedule. The **Manitou Passage** off Sleeping Bear was a favorite shipping shortcut, deep but narrow and therefore the scene of many wrecks, recounted here. The big historic photos and spartan quarters of the lifesaving crew and keeper are dramatic. There's no hint of the personal lives of these self-sacrificing men except the intriguing audio reminiscence of a

Coast Guard admiral whose father was a lighthouse keeper. Don't miss the boathouse, restored to about 1905, with a beach cart, surf boats, and other rescue items. *West of Glen Haven. Take M-109 to Glen Haven, 2 1/2 miles west of Glen Arbor, and follow signs to the Museum on Sleeping Bear Point. (616) 326-5134. Open April through mid-October. May 15-June 30 and Sept. 1 thru mid-October: weekends 10:30-5, Mon-Fri 1-4:30. July & August: daily 10-5. April and early May: weekends 10:30-5. Free.*

♦ **Shopping in Glen Arbor.** The best shops in the Leelanau Peninsula are those that reflect the creative spirits of the area's many urban refugees. Glen Arbor is becoming something of a center for year-round artists. Here artistic energy is making a stand against a rising tide of more ordinarily trendy upscale gift shops. Especially recommended: contemporary crafts at **Glen Arbor City Limits** on M-109 towards Glen Haven; souvenir Leelanau photographs at **Ken Scott Photography** nearby; the **Glen Lake Artists' Gallery** in the **Arbor Lights**, a charmingly spare old country store and dance hall on Lake Street off M-22; handpainted furniture in interestingly accessorized room settings at **Leelanau Interiors** on M-109 just west of M-22 in Glen Arbor; and the pretty rock-bordered perennial garden at **Wildflowers**, on M-22 just south of town.

The National Parks Service will mail you requested information. Call (616) 326-5134 or write: Sleeping Bear Dunes National Lakeshore, National Parks Service, Box 277, Empire, Michigan 49630. For visitor center hours and location, see p. 367.

BEST STOPS FOR PICNIC FIXINGS . . . . . In Empire, **Deering's Market** on Front at La Rue has a big meat counter and produce section and its own smokehouse. . . . . In Glen Arbor, **Steffen's IGA** at M-22 and M-109 has the best selection and prices on groceries and meats. . . . . . Both are open year-round.

A TIME-TESTED BICYCLING GUIDE . . . . . to 6 counties from Leelanau and Benzie to the Straits is available for $5 from Monstrey's General Store (see p. 377) and bike shops in Traverse City and Petoskey. Scenic back roads make for outstanding cycling, mostly fairly challenging, with some flat, easy shoreline routes.

Leelanau Peninsula

A landscape of lakes and hills with long vistas,
accented by pretty villages and cherry orchards,
lighthouses, and barns

T he little finger of lower Michigan's mitten, the Leelanau
Peninsula extends 30 miles into Lake Michigan, forming
the west side of Grand Traverse Bay. Here history and
geology have combined to create a most delightful landscape.
Here the most recent glacier, as it retreated north, formed long,
streamlined hills called drumlins, bordered by long parallel
inland lakes or valleys, or by Lake Michigan. "From every
hillcrest, a panorama of carefully tilled farmlands and wooded
slopes unfolds before the visitor's eye, with the ever present lake
waters as a background," described the Michigan W.P.A. guide of
1940. "Off the western shore of the peninsula, the Manitou
Islands rise, hazy green, above the horizon." Cherry orchards,
joined more recently by a few vineyards, create a beautiful,
orderly, highly cultivated landscape, dotted with nine pleasant
villages unmarred by industry.

Visitors remember Leelanau County's Glen Lake and the dunes
around Sleeping Bear. But the interior's striking hilly landforms
are just as important an element of its special beauty, reminiscent
of upper New England. It's lovely at every time of year. Fruit trees
blossom in the early green of spring. Winter reveals the shapes of
trees and buildings with great clarity. In fall, long views of distant
barns and lakes are framed in hills glowing with color, with
enough evergreens to set off the color. Summer, when the area is
most crowded with visitors, may well be the least interesting season, when the landscape is reduced to vacation basics: lots of
green, blue water, and sand. But the blue itself can be stunning —
on sunny days a vivid turquoise, created by light reflecting from
the white, sandy bottom of Grand Traverse Bay.

The area's diverse economic activities from the 1850s into the
early 20th century created a variety of towns and attracted a variety of peoples that today make the peninsula more interesting
and varied than many other areas dominated by resorts. The
peninsula's first settlements were three separate Indian missions
founded south of Northport around Omena between 1849 and
1852. Protestant missionaries came from Holland, Cross Village
(north of present-day Harbor Springs), and the Old Mission

Peninsula (north of Traverse City) — areas then being impinged upon by encroaching settlement. They brought some of their Indian congregations here because they hoped (in vain) that the isolated area would remain free of white settlers, and away from the corrupting influence of alcohol. Intermarried offspring of these Chippewa and Ottawa bands remain here today, largely in the reservation at Peshawbestown, between Suttons Bay and Omena.

Leland (the county seat) and Northport developed as ports for commercial fishermen and provisioners of Great Lakes vessels. Supplying cordwood and food to ships was the original livelihood for many remote places on the water. Suttons Bay first prospered with sawmills, then became a fruit-processing center. Many nationalities — including Bohemians, Norwegians, Belgians, and Poles — were recruited to work in lumber camps and mills, of which the Empire Lumber Company in Empire was by far the largest. The Polish town of Cedar is locally famous for its sausage and its Polish Festival each August.

What accounts for much of the peninsula's visual charm is the area's economic paralysis since 1910 in every sector but tourism and agriculture. The only non-agricultural industry was 19th-century charcoal iron smelting in Leland and sawmills now long gone. The transition to tourism occurred when Chicagoans, whose city was built by the destruction of Northern Michigan's forests, came north to escape the pressures of city life and find cool weather and solace in many of those very logged-over places that helped build their homes. Summer resorts were developed by associations of city businessmen, beginning in 1868 at Omena. Resort development was in full swing by 1890, well before the lumber ran out.

For most of the 20th century, Leelanau enjoyed a successful balance between local people and nature-loving cottagers and vacationers from big cities, who provided incomes for old Leelenau families. The 1970s saw a new influx of outsiders — urbanites seeking a simple life in tune with nature, including numerous artists and writers. At the same time, the seeds of change were planted that now disrupt the old balance. Second homes — long an important part of the local mix — began to change in character from leisurely summer cottages to condos for people driving up for the weekend, mostly from metro Detroit. These so-called "trunk-slammers" don't have the old-time cottage-owners' concern and commitment to the area, engendered by years of personal ties. The resort economy, which had been on a ma-and-pa level, started attracting big-time developers with large projects like The Homestead and Sugar Loaf resorts and condo complexes. Establishing the Sleeping Bear Dunes National

Lakeshore in 1970 helped promote the change to more intense development. So did the booms in downhill skiing and boating.

Today Suttons Bay, with easy access to Traverse City via M-22, has become a virtual suburb. Leland, long an attractive mix of pleasant but modest houses and old summer homes, has become so slicked up and gentrified, with so many shops geared to traditional decor and upscale resortwear, that many year-round Leelanau residents consider it ruined and avoid it altogether, especially in summer. Zoning policies as far away as Northport are now set by exurbanites intent on fending off threats of development, with the ironic result that cherry farmers attempting to survive by running produce stands are thwarted by strict regulation of signs.

To the casual visitor, the results of all this development are mixed. There are a lot more shops everywhere, and some are quite interesting. Most cater to visitors and second homeowners. (Everybody else depends on a weekly trip to Traverse City.) Leland, Suttons Bay, and Glen Arbor are outstanding places to see the latest ingenious trends in interior design for second homes. Artists' studio-shops are now plentiful; pick up a free copy of *Arts and Crafts Trails in Northern Michigan*, a listing and map of various studios. There are two fabulous restaurants — Hattie's in Suttons Bay and La Becasse in tiny Burdickville — and numerous good ones, all fairly expensive.

The negatives are the traffic in towns and on much of M-22 in summer, and the anger and depressed resignation you encounter among people who love this place. Pick up a copy of the interesting *Leelanau Enterprise*, and you'll realize how intense the local political battles are. It's full of letters by concerned local residents, including novelist Jim Harrison, a persistent critic, about the perils brought by development and tourism to a precious, vulnerable rural way of life.

You can enjoy the Leelanau's beauty without the crowds and unmellow aspects of tourism by seeking out less convenient beaches (see below), by hiking, by biking on scenic roads in the morning, and — perhaps best of all — by planning a visit in May or June, or October or January. An enjoyable, insightful book about the people and worlds that converge on the Leelanau Peninsula today is *Letters from the Leelanau: Essays of People and Place*, by Kathleen Stocking. A native who returned after living in New York, she's part of many circles.

Travel brochures that suggest a 93-mile driving tour of Leelanau to be done in a day (or a half day!) miss the charms of the area entirely. This is a special blend of nature and simple man-made diversions, best enjoyed slowly — lingering and walking, swimming and bicycling.

Here are some of the peninsula's highlights, arranged along M-22 from Traverse City up to Northport and south to Empire:

♦ **Monstrey's General Store and Sport Shop.** Ideal first stop for lots of free printed information and advice on the area. Bicyclists will find a $5 **bicycling guide** to six counties of northwestern Michigan invaluable. Just finding this shop is an adventure that gets you off the beaten path of M-22 and into the hilly, scenic interior overlooking Lake Leelanau. Rentals of bike, tandem bikes, bike carts for small children, sailboards, and tubes. Amish furniture and classic toys, books on the region and on adventure travel, plus groceries. *8332 Bingham Rd. (618). From M-22, about 10 mi. n. of Traverse City, turn w. on 618. Store is between 633 and 641. (616) 946-0018. Summer hours: Mon-Sat 10-7, Sun 12-5. Closed Mon & Tues in fall & spring. Completely closed from Jan to mid-March.*

♦ **L. Mawby Vineyards.** Unpretentious, highly regarded small winery where the owner-vintner-publicist-poet will give you a personal tour. Larry Mawby, an original in all respects, believes that the eventual reputation of this wine region, still in the experimental early stage, will rest on blends of the French hybrid grapes found best suited to the soil, and its own vignoles — wine made from that specific type of white hybrid grape. Mawby is known for rich, full-bodied dry vignoles, fermented and aged in oak, like all his wines, and the fanciful proprietary names of his blends, like Chard O'Neigh (a red chardonnay blend) and P.J.W. Pun. Lately he's also excited about his newer sparkling wines. Striking wine labels, prints and poems, printed on his own press, are also for sale at the tasting room. *4519 Elm Valley Rd. 5 miles s. of Suttons Bay. From M-22 2 mi. n. of 618, turn w. on Hill Top Rd., then n. on Elm Valley. (616) 271-3522. Tastings and tours from May through October, Thurs-Sat 1-6 and by appointment.*

♦ **Suttons Bay.** This village of 560 was not so long ago considered the slummier part of the toney Leelanau Peninsula. Here is where migrant cherry-pickers, who arrived each summer, would hang out evenings. Then mechanical pickers displaced the migrants, and Suttons Bay became gentrified to the point where it is now a fashionable address. The quaintly refurbished row of main street storefronts looks like "a set from a Hollywood movie," as one shopkeeper puts it. Professionals appreciate the convenient commute to Traverse City. But locals who decry the transformation of Leland into "the most pretentious kind of tourist trap" still consider Suttons Bay a nice, friendly town. Don't miss the big old trees and substantial Victorian houses in the picturesque neighborhood just west of downtown on St. Mary's and Lincoln avenues. The **municipal beach** is north of downtown.

Inter-Arts Studio, the first of some two dozen gift and interiors shops in Suttons Bay, remains by far the most interesting. Owner Ken Krantz, an architect by training and admittedly fussy, sells his own drawings of Leelanau scenes along with only things he likes: colorful Polish rugs, many other area rugs, glassware, lots of bedspreads and fabrics (including hard-to-find India print bedspreads, those cheap, multipurpose classics of the 1960s), and other classics of contemporary design. It's on St. Joseph, across from the Total station. **Danbury Antiques** at 305 St. Joseph is widely known for English "smalls": boxes, candlesticks, brass, and porcelain, purchased by the owner in England. It anchors an interesting cluster of shops.

Enerdyne Nature and Science Playthings, owned and run by a former teacher, is based on the premise that science is fun — and that educational toys aren't just for children. This large store has bird houses and feeders, bug boxes, water rockets, butterfly nets, unpolished rocks and rock tumblers, good nature books, woodstoves, and much more. It's between Bahle's department store and the **The Bay Theater** (616-271-3772) on St. Joseph. Its fare is first-run and foreign/art films, and occasional concerts. A popular gathering place for coffee and baked goods is **Suttons Bay-kery**, in a funny storefront by the bridge north of downtown. (See p. 435.) *Suttons Bay shops are open from 10 to 6, Mon-Sat and on Sun 12-4 between July 4 and Labor Day.*

◆ **County Road 637.** For scenic interior drive with less traffic and wonderful vistas, turn west on 204 from Suttons Bay. In about two miles turn north onto 637. You see fieldstone houses and cherry orchards, especially delightful in blossomtime in mid-May and in late June and early July when the fruit is ripening. 637 rejoins M-22 at the popular Happy Hour Tavern.

◆ **Leelanau Sands Casino and Super Bingo Palace.** A 1991 expansion makes this the largest of Michigan's casinos on Indian reservations, with space for 500. The Grand Traverse band runs it to create jobs, fund tribal government, and promote economic development. It advertises "Las Vegas-style gambling." But don't expect bright lights and glamorous shows. This is pretty sedate stuff, geared to conservative Midwestern tourists. The right to gamble on Indian reservations is based on tribal rights to self-government. *On M-22 in Peshawbestown, about 4 mi. n. of Suttons Bay. 1-800-962-4646. Open 7 days a week, year-round.*

◆ **Omena.** This small hamlet at the head of Omena Bay was first settled in 1852. The name means "Is it so?" in Indian, a phrase often used by an early white settler when talking with the local Indians. Steamers made use of the bay to take on cordwood, potatoes, beans and apples from the region. The first dock was built in 1868. Later, hotels and resorts, long since gone, were built to accommodate vacationers.

The **Tamarack Craftsmen Gallery** occupies the old Omena general store, perched on a hill surveying the beach and bay. The building was what inspired owners David and Sally Viskochil to start their extraordinary gallery of American crafts 20 years ago when they got out of the Peace Corps. They are committed to displaying work by artists they believe in. Much of it is interestingly strange. The place has a vivid, imaginative look, with lots of handblown glass. They were the first to show the boldly painted furniture of Craig and Judy Carey. Dewey Blocksma, who is gaining a national reputation for his outsider art, is another longtime artist. So is Catherine Baldwin, the last quill basket-maker in the area. Though prices go into the thousands of dollars, there are plenty of little things like earrings and mugs for $20 and under. *On M-22 in Omena. (616) 386-5529. Mem.-Labor Day: Mon-Sat 10-6, Sun 12-6. Otherwise: Tues-Sat 11-5, Sun 12-5.*

◆ **Northport.** This pretty village has long attracted interesting summer people. Its small business district has an increasing number of galleries and antique shops, mostly seasonal, and two unusually attractive picnic spots. **Bay Front Park**, a couple of blocks away from the commercial district, is right on Grand Traverse Bay, with a good view of tiny Bellow Island in the distance. It has a pleasant beach and playground. The adjacent marina is lined with pleasure boats and charter boats. Northport is where Great Lakes sport trolling was pioneered in the early 1920s by George Ruff. Methods he and his wife developed for catching trout and other gamefish set the pattern for other charter services. A few blocks north up from downtown at Third Street and Fourth is a serene, picturesque **mill pond and park**, shaded by a big old apple tree. A picnic table and short footpath are here. Beyond the pond is the picturesque Old Mill Pond Inn (p. 435).

Tucked in a neighborhood north of the town center, **Joppich's Bay Street Gallery** has been focussing on Michigan artists long before regional art became a popular cause. Owner Edee Joppich, a painter herself, travels throughout the state during the off season searching out 50 artists to participate in the coming year's exhibit. Most have never been shown here before. Typically a third of the participants are on college faculties. Each show tends to highlight a few areas of the state. There can be quite a mix of media here, from oil paintings to porcelain dolls and painted sneakers. Works from $20 to $10,000 are shown together in three small rooms of this house, for an effect completely unlike most galleries. *109 N. Rose (also called Bay), one street over from*

*M-201, Northport's main street, and a block north of the marina.
(616) 386-7428. Open from 11-6, weekends in June and Sept
thru mid-Oct, daily from July 4 weekend thru Aug.*

Just north of town on M-201, **North Country Gardens** offers
over 70 species of perennials, often in many varieties. Prices
range from $1.25 to $7, depending on size of pot. A move into
the center of town, to the northeast corner of Nagonaba and Mill
(M-201), is planned for early 1992. It will bring an expanded
inventory of annuals, outdoor furniture from Honduras, trees and
shrubs, an improved kitchen shop and a Christmas shop. *Summer
hours: Mon-Thurs 9-6, Fri & Sat 8-6, Sun 9-4. Fall and spring
hours: Mon-Sat 9-5, Sun 10-3. Call (616) 386-5031 to confirm.*

◆ **Leelanau State Park.** At the tip of the Leelanau Peninsula, this
1,200-acre state park offers some of the most picturesque **campsites** in the entire state parks system. You can get a relatively
secluded spot overlooking Grand Traverse Bay and a rocky beach
(unpleasant for swimming or wading unless you bring wading
shoes). The 52 campsites are rustic (pit toilets, no showers) but
so beautiful that they're always full in good weather from July to
Labor Day. Over half are reservable, and some vacancies open up
daily, especially in mid-week. They are assigned on a first-come,
first-serve basis.

A beautiful **picnic area** with a playground is by the large lighthouse at the peninsula's very northernmost point. A former lightkeeper's son, who grew up here, is now a retiree who's the curator of the new **lighthouse museum.** *(Open Fri-Sun from 12-5 from
Mem. Day thru mid-Oct.; from July 4 to Labor Day it's open Wed-
Sun.)* From the tower you can see across to the tip of the Old
Mission Peninsula and out to the Manitou and Fox islands. The
curator's father made some of the remarkable **pebble lawn ornaments,** which include an elaborate flower bed in the shape of a
crown and a miniature lighthouse that's a purple martin house.

Eight miles of trails for hiking and cross-country skiing go
through low, wooded dunes along Cathead Bay. After a mile walk
from the parking area, you can reach a wide, sandy beach that's
sure not to be crowded. The **Manitou Overlook** spur of this same
Lake Michigan Trail has an observation deck with a splendid view
of the Fox and Manitou islands. *The lighthouse and campground
are at the end of Country Road 629, 8 mi. n. of Northport. To
trailheads of the southern section, turn w. onto Densmore Rd. 4
mi. out of town. (616) 386-5422. State park sticker required;
$3/day, $15/year.*

◆ **Kilcherman's Christmas Cove Farm.** Third-generation fruit
farmer John Kilcherman has become intensely interested in the
history of old apple varieties. He grows 170 varieties of antique

apples on his farm and sells many of them at this attractive farm stand. For special occasions he makes up sampler boxes of antique apples, complete with a brochure he has written. His wife, Phyllis, sells objects decorated with Scandinavian *rosemaling* — folk art flowers and such. It's a pretty place to stop and sample good apples that aren't grown commercially, and to hear about the travails of fruit farming. *On Christmas Cove Rd. (also called De Long Rd.) off 201 n. of Northport. (616) 386-5637. Call before making a special trip.*

◆ **Peterson Park.** A remote, pretty park — a big, grassy area on a bluff, from which the Manitou and Fox islands can be seen. An amazingly large maple is the park's focal point; there are picnic tables, a small play area, and restrooms tucked away in a woods. Stairs lead down a long ways to a stony **beach.** *From 201 in Northport, take either the North or South Peterson Park Rd. No fee.*

◆ **Woodland Herb Farm.** A delightful enclosed garden and a first-rate herb shop are the attractions of Jon and Pat Bourdo's simple farm, the oldest of a number of herb growers in northern Michigan. The small fragrance garden, enclosed in high shrubbery, includes a tiny pool and a fountain surrounded by plants. Visitors are welcome to sit on a bench and take in this serene scene. On one side is a wonderfully weather-worn shed. Inside the crowded shop are products made with over 200 varieties of herbs grown on the premises — potpourris and sachets, pesto mixes, and unusual vinegars, dressings, relishes, chilis, and chutneys. Advice and recipes based on Pat's long involvement in herb cookery are available in *Herbs and Spices*, for people interested in flavorings as a way to cut back on salt, and *The Woodland Herb Farm and Condiment Cookbook. 7741 North Manitou Trail (M-22), a mile or so west of Northport. (616) 386-5081. Open May-November, Monday through Saturday 11-5.*

Woodland
Herb Farm

◆ **Leland.** Fishtown is a picturesque group of weathered old fishermen's shanties on a Lake Michigan dock. Its development into tourist shops is what laid the way for the transformation of this pretty resort village into a tourist shopping hub. With enough old boats, fishnets, and fishy smells to seem authentic, **Fishtown** is still an interesting place without the crush of crowds. People come to fish by a dramatic little waterfall and dam right at Fishtown, by the river connecting Lake Leelanau with Lake Michigan. Some commercial fishing continues. (Its peak was during the first three decades of the 20th century.) Carlson's Fishery sells smoked whitefish for about $4.50 a pound, and fresh whitefish fillets for $5. The harbor is a lively place, what with a charter fleet and Manitou Transit's boats to the Manitou Islands. The municipal beach is just north of the harbor.

Among the shops, several in the Leland Courtyard on the 100 block of Main Street stand out: Mexican imports and silver at **Tampico** and pottery, glassware, and other crafts with a Scandinavian, close-to-nature feel at **Inland Passage.**

For many, the highlight of Leland may well be the displays on fishing at the **Leelanau Historical Museum.** An old ice shanty here shows what it's like to peer down within the darkened chamber into the hole in the ice and see the painted decoy floating nearby, waiting for a big sturgeon, pike, or muskie. There are cases full of these splendid decoy fish, colorfully painted in an extraordinary variety of ways so they look as much like folk art as a useful tool. Each year there's a special exhibit on some aspect of Leelanau history — 100 years of cherry-growing for 1991. *203 E. Cedar just off Main (M-22). (616) 256-7475. Open Fri-Mon 1-4, longer in summer. $1 admission.*

◆ **Good Harbor Vineyards.** If you show up at the tasting room for the instructive self-guided tour of this small winery, you may be talking to the owner and winemaker, Bruce Simpson, himself. His Trillium, a semi-dry mix of seyval, vignoles, and vidal grapes, is Michigan's most successful blended, proprietary wine. *On M-22, 1/2 mi. s. of the intersection with 204. On a hill behind Manitou Market. (616) 256-7165. Open mid-May thru Oct., Mon-Sat 11-6, Sun 12-6 and by appt.*

◆ **Sleeping Bear Dunes National Lakeshore.** See chapter beginning p. 367.

Old Mission Peninsula

Perfectly suited for growing cherries,
Old Mission is one of the most scenic areas in the state.

This thin, 18-mile-long peninsula bisecting Grand Traverse Bay is more intimate than its neighbor, the bigger, more famous Leelanau Peninsula. The scenery on a drive to the tip is wonderful. The hilly land is some of the finest in the country for growing cherries and grapes. The bay moderates temperatures and prevents early spring warming that endangers fruit buds. So suitable is the soil and climate for cherries that once there was no denser concentration of cherry trees in the country.

The orchards and vineyards are a pleasant foreground for the hilltop vistas of the bay to the east and west. A white sandy bottom makes the water so turquoise that it would seem artificially enhanced if you'd see it in a photograph. The roads hugging the east shore — East Shore Road, Bluff Road, and Smokey Hollow Road — are less developed and more scenic than those on the western shore. Highway M-37 follows the central spine to the northern tip and provides plenty of spectacular panoramas.

The peninsula is named for the first settlement in the Grand Traverse region, a Presbyterian mission started in a log cabin in 1839. A replica of the cabin is now a small museum (see below).

The peninsula is experiencing a fierce, drawn-out struggle between developers and those who want to preserve the rural landscape here. Cherries have been the major crop for well over a century, but depressed cherry prices have made the orchards' economic viability tenuous. Every year over 50 new homes are built on the peninsula, and the population has jumped to over 4,500 from just over 2,500 in 1970.

Recommended stops on the peninsula, arranged from south to north, include:

◆ **Underwood Orchards Country Store.** A cherry and apple orchard's retail outlet. Underwood's has good fresh-baked cinnamon rolls, homemade pies (apple, pumpkin, blueberry, apricot, cherry), apple and cherry-apple cider, fresh doughnuts, and lots of apples (10-12 varieties) which can be bought by the bushel. *From M-37 about 3 miles north of U.S. 31, turn east at McKinley Rd. Open June 15-Dec 23. (616) 947-8799.*

◆ **Chateau Grand Traverse.** This 80-acre winery makes some of

When mechanized cherry-picking machines became prevalent in the 1960s, it spelled an end to the many Mexican migrant pickers who came up to the Old Mission Peninsula and lived in huts along the road.

the finest domestic Rieslings to be found. Owner Ed O'Keefe was for many years the only Michigan vintner to grow exclusively vinifera grapes — prestigious Old World varieties that are more susceptible to frost and disease than hybrid or native grapes. Current wines include five Rieslings (from $8 to $14/bottle), two Chardonnays, three red wines (Zinfandel, Merlot, and Pinot Noir), Pinot Grigio, and a blush blend ($4.50). Chateau Grand Traverse is now sold in 23 states. 300 cases were recently shipped to San Francisco! Try some at their tasting room. The vineyard's much-praised cherry wines ($4.50-$5) are a tasty novelty and good Michigan gift item. Spicy cherry makes a good hot winter drink; the new cherry Riesling is a terrific picnic wine. 25-minute winery tours are held on the hour from June through Christmas. Complimentary tastings are year-round. Call to schedule large groups. Mail order available. *M-37 at Island View Rd. 8 miles out of Traverse City. (616) 223-7355; 1 (800) 283-0247. Open regularly April-Dec. April & May: 10-5. June-Dec: 10-6. No Sunday sales before noon.*

◆ **Bowers Harbor.** Midway up the western shore of the peninsula, Neah-Ta-Wanta Point creates this well-protected harbor. One of the best restaurants in the Traverse City area, the Bowers Harbor Inn, is here (see p. 437). There's also a public beach, a marina, a picnic area, and general store. The old summer hotel at the point is now a bed and breakfast (see p. 437). *Reached by Peninsula Dr. on the west shore, or turn west off M-37 at Devil's Dive Rd., then right onto Peninsula.*

◆ **Old Mission Church.** This little historical museum is a replica of a church built in 1839 by a Presbyterian missionary to the Chippewa Indians. Its original bell is in this belfry. The informative historical displays inside were done by the Old Mission Women's Club — another example of how enthusiastic amateurs can often outdo professional museum curators.

Visitors learn here that until 1900, many residents of the peninsula's eastern shore would get two or three months' provisions at a time by boating across the bay to Elk Rapids. A brief history of local cherry farming points out that because the soil here is so perfect for cherries, that's what everyone grew. So when an early frost occasionally wiped out the cherry crop, the peninsula was thrown into a profound depression. Another disadvantage of a single-crop economy was from having to pick all the cherries at the same time, straining the available labor supply. At first Indians were used as pickers, then Jamaicans, then Japanese, then Mexicans. First the Mexican migrants lived in old cars and tents, then in permanent huts along the roadside. By 1965 cherry-picking machines were becoming widespread and migrants were no longer needed. *On Old Mission Rd. in the hamlet of Old Mission.18 miles out on M-37, turn right onto Old Mission Rd. Open daily (long hours) Mem. Day through October.*

◆ **Haserot Beach.** One local calls this 250-foot public beach the best swimming in northern Michigan. The water remains shallow, not over chest high, for some way out. A lifeguard is provided by township. The beach is protected from chilly winds by the cove. *North of Old Mission. From M-37, take Swaney Rd. east to shore.*

◆ **Old Mission Point and Light.** This quaint old lighthouse dates from 1870. The original frame lightkeeper's dwelling remains. The 45th parallel of latitude intersects here, halfway from the North Pole to the Equator. At the peninsula's point is a swimming beach, a simple, pretty spot. There's a fine view across to Omena on the Leelanau Peninsula and to Eastport at the outlet of Torch Lake. The state has acquired the surrounding 513 acres, but it will remain a day-use facility with no camping.

🌲🌳🌲

The Music House

From music boxes to Nickelodeons and giant organs,
take in the nostalgic sounds and visual glamor
of mechanical music-makers at a top-notch museum.

The story of the automation of music, from the elaborate music boxes of the 1870s to the Victrola and talking movies of 1929, is told — and better yet, played — in this impressive, intelligent museum created by two collectors. The one-and-one-half-hour guided tour includes satisfying demonstrations of music on 12 instruments. The giant Regina music box has interchangeable punched metal discs and a delicate, tinkling sound. There's a reproducing player piano, briefly popular in the 1920s. Its piano roll was punched to exactly recreate, for example, George Gershwin performing *Rhapsody in Blue*. Musicologists come here to hear just how Grieg and Rachmaninoff really played the music they wrote.

It's a thrill to see and hear these instruments in action. Many are lavish with carved ornament and gilt. The music conjures up scenes in shoebox theaters, saloons, and dance halls. Some of the music is meant to blow you away with a throbbing bass and penetrating, clear melody. It's fascinating to watch the inner workings of these clever mechanical devices, with their bellows and hammers.

The magnificent and rare Amaryllis organ — a great, gilded confection of pipes, carved foliage, and moving louvers — imitates a dance orchestra and vibrates the floor with its bass notes. Built for a big Belgian dance hall, it looks like it belongs in an 18th-century Rococco church. A similar instrument in a less elaborate case was once strategically positioned on a rooftop at an amusement park in New Jersey to provide background music throughout the park.

One museum co-founder is an architect interested mainly in the instruments' cases. He has recreated antique room settings for some instruments. The electric player piano (known by many names, including nickelodeon) is in an elaborate ice cream parlor from the 1890s, all mahogany and mirrors. The tiny, make-believe Little Lyric Theater showcases a Reproduco piano-organ combination, used as a popular and inexpensive accompaniment for silent movies.

Restoration of additional instruments is ongoing. Work is

underway on a Wurlitzer room with a dozen jukeboxes. Before or after the tour, visitors can examine extensive **displays on the evolution of the Victrola, the radio, and early TVs.** (No audio demonstrations go with them.) The **gift shop** carries many tapes of music played on music boxes, chapel bells, and player pianos, and street organs.

The Music House occupies the hay barn and granary of the cherry and dairy farm where a co-founder grew up. That's been the story of Grand Traverse, he points out — cherries and agriculture replaced by tourism, condos, and golf.

This museum isn't perfect. It feels a little slick, and the young tour guide (who also restores instruments) may talk *at* you, relying on a memorized script, rather than *to* you. But if you persist in asking questions and interacting, he will prove quite knowledgeable and able to explain things.

The Music House is in a complex of barns on the west side of U.S. 31 about 8 miles northeast of Traverse City and 1/2 miles north of M-72. (616) 938-9300. Open May through October, Mon-Sat 10 a.m.-4 p.m., Sun 1-5. $5/person, children under 6 free. Allow 1 1/2 hours per tour.

🌲🌳🌲

THE BEST CHERRY ORCHARD TOUR. . . . . is just north of the Music House at **Amon's Orchards and U-Pick.** Here in the center of U.S. tart cherry production, overproduction perennially depresses wholesale cherry prices. To stay profitable, orchards have had to turn to marketing their cherries and cherry products direct to visitors. Amon's has reoriented itself to tourism while retaining a pleasantly farmy flavor. It's family-run, and less slick than other heavily advertised orchards. Half-hour horse-drawn wagon **tours** by knowledgeable employees cover area cherry history and how cherries are grown and marketed. There's also a **petting zoo** of common farm animals kids can feed. In the sales room and bakery, you can buy sweet and tart cherries, apples, and plums. Plenty of knowledgeable people are around to field questions about cherry cookery and cherry agriculture. Amon's offers **free samples** of some fairly exotic cherry products like cherry pepper meat sauce and cherry barbecue sauce. Cherry-fudge sauce is the best-seller, and cherry cider is awfully good, too. Splendid views of the East Arm of Grand Traverse Bay make this an outstanding place for an afternoon of cherry-picking. *On the east side of U.S. 41, 2 1/2 miles north of M-72. (616) 938-9160. Call for tour times; $4 adult, $2/child, no more than $10/family. Open year-round. May 1-Oct. 31: open daily from 10-6. Nov. & Dec.: weekends 10-5. Jan.-April: open Sat. 10-5. Free admission to orchards and sales room.*

❶ Fisherman's Island State Park. Outstanding scenery along 5-mile rocky beach, good for finding Petoskey stones. Sandy swimming area. 90 idyllic rustic campsites in pines, some right on lake.

❷ Brumm Showroom. Huge variety of nature-related jewelry and gifts by Norman & Judith Brumm and others. Big area with drawers of specimen shells, polished rocks for collectors and craftsmen.

❸❹ Earl Young gnome homes. Inspired, eccentric rustic architecture. Smurf-like roofs, huge stones, fascinating details. Self-taught architect/ realtor Young built clusters in Boulder Park (❸) & on Park. (❹).

❺ Channel walkway. Very pleasant path leads from busy Bridge St. to Michigan Ave. Beach. Wooded park and Earl Young homes above it. Good for viewing boats, drawbridge, sunsets.

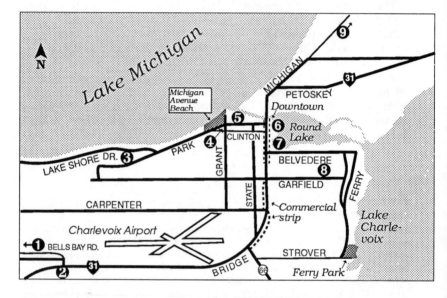

❻ East Park/ City Dock. Colorfully diverse harbor. See Beaver Island ferries, Coast Guard cutter *Acacia*, commercial fishing boats, many sailboats, power boats, big yachts.

❼ John Cross Fisheries. Picturesque landmark famed for good fresh and smoked whitefish, trout, perch, salmon, all locally caught. Fishing boats dock here.

❽ Belvedere Club. Stately row of Victorian cottages on Ferry St. overlook Lake Charlevoix and Yacht Club. Impeccable old resort. Interior closed to public in summer.

❾ Mount Mc-Sauba. Highest dune in area. Scenic downhill and cross-country skiing. Hiking trails, viewing platforms, wonderful beach with wild, natural, open feel.

Highlights of
Charlevoix

0

1/2
mile

Fisherman's Island State Park

An uncrowded up-north Eden

This new and little-developed state park is a stunning bit of pure, unmessed-with natural beauty that occupies a prime spot along six miles of Lake Michigan shore south of Charlevoix. Yet it manages to be uncrowded. Of the 90 rustic campsites, 14 directly overlook the beach. The others are across a road but a very short walk to the beach.

As at many beaches in the Charlevoix-Petoskey area, stretches of rocky piles of limestone gravel here alternate with pockets and little bays of sand. Rocky limestone outcrops make for a more rugged shoreline than vacationers expect. Occasional boulders are dramatic accents. This area south of Charlevoix is actually better for finding **Petoskey stones** than the Petoskey area itself. (Hint: the distinctive markings only show up when the stones are held under water.)

What you gain in scenery and privacy, you give up in convenience. What keeps away the hordes in this popular vacation area is the lack of plumbing (pit toilets are the rule), no showers, and no bathhouse. There isn't much of an official trail system, either. But in from the shore there are plenty of paths through the dense woods of birch and aspen, along with spruce, balsam fir, occasional hardwoods. The many low, swampy areas are full of tamaracks and fragrant cedars.

The main day-use beach and **designated swimming area** is at the end of a two-mile drive past the two campgrounds; its parking area is very seldom full. People are welcome to pull over anywhere along the road and get out and swim. The park's accessible northern section off Bell's Bay Road contains the two sections of campsites and a simple **scenic overlook** near the entrance. The southern part is a secret treasure, completely undeveloped and not even marked by signs. Everywhere here are the simple, beautiful basics conveyed in the romantic image of northern Michigan: the big blue lake and long beaches, accented with birches, aspens, and pines. You have it all to yourself, the way it would have been in Hemingway's time — actually better, since then the North Country had been recently logged over. The trees are much taller today. Twenty miles of unmarked paths wind through the forest, and alongside fragrant cedar swamps.

It's a trick to reach the southern part. Thirteen miles south-west of downtown Charlevoix on U.S. 31, go west on Barnard Road until you get to the Norwood Township Park in the village of Norwood. The two-track road behind the park goes north along the shore. Conditions are rough at best; check ahead at the park office. You may be able to drive 2.3 miles north along the beach to Whiskey Creek. Or you may want to pull over and walk the rest of the way. In his *Michigan State and National Parks* guide, outdoorsman Tom Powers says this lovely, isolated stretch of creek and beach is among his very favorite places in all of northern Michigan. He suggests planning on spending at least the better part of a day here. If you're very lucky, you may come upon what was perhaps the Woodland Indians' most important source of chert stone, used in weapons and tools. The quarry, consisting of holes the size of bushel baskets, is almost impossible to find in the heavy forest with its fern-covered floor.

The main entrance to Fisherman's Island State Park is off Bell's Bay Road, which joins U.S. 31 two miles south of Charlevoix, almost across from the Brumm Showroom (616) 547-6641. State parks sticker required: $3/day or $15/year. Park open May 1 to Dec. 1. 90 rustic campsites (no electricity or running water) fill up on weekends and occasional weekdays in season (mid-June through late August), when reservations are advised.

ARTS AND CRAFTS FROM NATURAL MATERIALS. . . . . are the focus of the **Norman & Judith Brumm Showroom** on U. S. 31 southwest of Charlevoix. The Brumms are well known for their copper enamel bird and wildflower sculptures, and their suncatchers made of sliced agate in black metal frames, often shaped like birds. The large and handsome store also carries a very wide range of jewelry, notecards, prints, baskets, pottery, and other decorative gift items, all with natural themes. Generally simple and good-looking, occasionally they verge on the cute. Even people who aren't drawn to the gift items may well enjoy looking through drawers upon drawers of mineral and shell specimens plus books and drawings on natural subjects. It's like nature's dime store — kids and craftspeople can get a lot of treasures for little money. *On U.S. 31 at Bells Bay Rd., 2 miles west of Charlevoix. Open daily, April through Christmas 9:30-5:30, until 9 Fri. (616) 547-4084.*

Earl Young Houses

Charlevoix's "Mushroom Houses"
look like they were designed by gnomes or Smurfs.

It has been called "Charlevoix the Beautiful" ever since the
dawn of Charlevoix's resort era in 1879, when the humble
lumber port of Pine River was renamed to honor a Jesuit
priest. Rampant overdevelopment has spoiled the nice little
resort town on three beautiful lakes. Today it's condo city along
many stretches of central waterfront. Downtown is such a zoo in
summer that locals and longtime summer people try to avoid it
altogether.

Fortunately, the look of Charlevoix's leisurely, lovely past survives in places. The private Belvedere Club occupies a prominent
hill at the southwest edge of Lake Charlevoix. Its old-fashioned
Victorian houses are ample and gracious. The winding paths along
immaculately trimmed lawns and trees make it special. Summer
colonies like this seem untouched by the hectic, hurried lifestyle
ushered in after World War II; so does the Grey Gables restaurant
in a big Victorian house nearby. You can drive along Ferry on the
colony's west edge any time, but the interior grounds are closed
to the public in July and August.

What makes
Charlevoix worth
a trip today are
the wonderfully
strange stone
homes designed
by Earl Young, a
real estate
broker and self-
taught architect,
He built them
from the 1920s
through the
1950s. These are
the most
surprising of all
the wonderful
northwoods
architecture

302 Park Ave.

Irene Young

inspired by northern Michigan's natural beauty and encouraged by the 1920s' relentless quest for the picturesque.

Young used natural materials — mostly different kinds of stone, with cedar shake roofs. Rather than relying on variations of typical rustic style — log hunting lodges, for instance, or Shingle Style blends — he took popular vernacular styles of the day and fitted them so ingeniously and organically to the materials and sites that they look like they grew of their own accord, following rules devised by gnomes and elves.

Irregularly curving roofs mark all Young's homes. He must have had accomplished craftsmen — maybe boatbuilders accustomed to curving hulls — to make these amazing roofs. The smallish, medievally picturesque 1920s houses in Boulder Park (off Park Avenue along Lake Michigan on the west edge of town) are made of oversized rose and gray fieldstone boulders, sometimes fully three and four feet long. The stones' great size gives the houses a fairytale, dollhouse look. Don't miss the tiny bungalows along Park at Clinton, across from the beautiful woods of a shady park.

By the entrance to Boulder Park are two much later ranch houses, faced with long, thin pieces of local white limestone. Young's flowing roofs and sinuous retaining walls give them a sensuous, romantic appeal that's rare in ranch houses.

To appreciate the details — the roofs, the playful chimneys, the quaint doorways, the inventive retaining walls — plan on parking your car and walking by each group of houses.

Young's only public buildings are the **Appletree** gift shop at 224 Bridge (next to the movie theater), with an unusual stone interior, and two hotels overlooking the Pine River Channel — the **Weathervane Terrace** and **The Lodge**. The lobby interiors are worth a look for their almost incredibly massive fireplaces, but they lack the intimate charm of the house interiors.

For a **free map and brochure** on many of Earl Young's homes, stop at the **Charlevoix Chamber of Commerce** at 408 Bridge, corner of Belvedere; or call (616) 547-2101. The most magical houses of all aren't indicated. Here's how to discover them for yourself. Go north on Bridge Street (U.S. 131) across the channel, At the Y, stay left onto Michigan, a settled old residential street that backs up to Lake Michigan. In about 2 1/2 blocks, look for a small, wooded pullover that goes down by the public walkway to the beach. Park there. Two delightful houses are tucked in the woods to your right. A third, with a crazily constructed gatehouse that confounds conventional building methods, is away from the lake around the corner on Burns.

A CONVENIENT LAKE MICHIGAN BEACH AND SCENIC WALKWAY . . . . . is the
Lake Michigan Beach on Grant north of Park. The beach has changing rooms, a
concession stand, playground, picnic area. No fee. Plenty of parking. The hillside
park behind it provides a lovely backdrop of pine woods, nice for a stroll or picnic. A waterside **walkway** curves around along the channel for a good view of the
busy boat traffic. Best enjoyed at sunset.

ONE OF LAKE MICHIGAN'S LAST FISHERIES. . . . . . is the **John Cross Fishery.**
This simple, highly regarded Charlevoix landmark gives an idea of what fishing
was like in the days before World War II, when Northern Michigan's economy was
more balanced with non-tourist enterprises like commercial fishing. Overfishing
and then alewives brought an end to most commercial fishing, except for Indian
fishing boats permitted by treaty. Indians own and operate the tugs docked here.
They catch the fish that John Cross supplies to leading area restaurants. Smoked
whitefish or whitefish paté and crackers make a nice picnic on a beach or at the
nearby city park off Bridge Street overlooking the busy harbor. Get soup and deli
salads at the Wharfside Deli, 330 Bridge. Prices are reasonable. *John Cross Fishery is down off a drive at 209 Belvedere just east of Bridge. (616) 547-2532. Summer hours: daily 9-5. Winter hours vary with availability; call.*

OF CHARLEVOIX'S MANY SHOPS. . . . . . only the Koucky Gallery can't be found
elsewhere. (Most shops here have branches in other northern Michigan resorts:
Mettler's upscale, updated traditional clothing; **Tom's Mom's Cookies**; the
worthwhile **Rocking Horse Toy Company**; too many fudge shops; and a host of
other stores.) The **Koucky Gallery** features decorative art — mostly playful, fun,
and accessible — from some 300 artists and craftspeople — ceramics, sculpture,
weaving, furniture, jewelry, painting, and prints. About a third of them live
around Charlevoix, which has long been a favorite base for artists who do the circuit of better art fairs. Some pieces here are huge, like local favorite Todd
Warner's earthy four-foot llamas and chickens. Many pieces use odd materials
and techniques, like jewelry made of rubber and glass beads. These are things you
don't see everywhere, and not necessarily expensive. Jewelry and mugs begin at
$20. *The Koucky Gallery is at 319 Bridge in downtown Charlevoix. Open Mon-Sat
9:30-5:30, Sun 10-4. In summer open until 9.*

Beaver Island

A two-hour ferry ride from the mainland,
life here is still pure and simple.

O f all Michigan's permanently inhabited islands, Beaver Island (53 square miles, population 400) is the only one that's over five miles from the mainland. Eighteen miles from the nearest coast, it has much more of an island feeling than islands connected by a bridge or a short ferry ride. It's completely different from summertime Mackinac Island with its huge and stylish Victorian summer "cottages" and hotels, though both are inhabited largely by the descendants of Irish fisherfolk.

How you feel about Beaver Island depends a lot on how you feel about the pace and huge variety of choices of contemporary life — how much you like things slowed down, kept at a distance, and simplified. Beaver Island has cars, but not very many. It costs $75 to take them over and back on the ferry. There's TV, but few stations and no cable. You have to plan ahead to get here. The ferry from Charlevoix takes two hours and costs $22 round-trip. The plane is $25 one-way and only flies in decent weather. The ferry vibrates and sometimes tosses unpleasantly. From late December through March it doesn't run at all.

Beaver Island is occasionally promoted as something of a natural wonder on account of its isolation. But really it's a plain, pleasant piece of Michigan's north country — flat and sandy, covered with second-growth pines and hardwoods, rimmed with sandy beaches. Only in the past 30 years have the beaches gained the inevitable rim of cottages, and those are mostly quite simple, more like Upper Peninsula "camps" than the stylish waterfront second homes on the Leelanau and Old Mission Peninsulas and near Harbor Springs.

What you see when you finally arrive at St. James, Beaver Island's port and only town, is a collection of very plain, small buildings — either clapboard houses and storefronts built over the years by

BEAVER ISLANDER

the descendants of Irish fishermen who first settled in the 1840s, or a few aluminum-sided motels and ranch houses of the 1960s. That's when the man who had been buying property at tax sales over the years divided some of it into vacation lots and sold them.

All that's left of the island's brief, bizarre period as the only kingdom in the United States — the self-proclaimed kingdom of breakaway Mormon leader King James Jesse Strang — are a few old frame buildings (the Mormons' print shop is the local museum) and the name St. James, after Strang himself. Most of the names you see — Erin Motel, O'Donough Grocery, Donegal Bay on the island's northwest end — reflect the island's strongly Irish past and present.

Beaver Island is a subtle place that needs a personal guide, an insider who knows the little, everyday things that make island living special, not just the island's geography and exotic history. Nothing you visit is in any way amazing in and of itself — not the scenery, not the architecture, not the island's few summertime restaurants, shops, and resorts. (Only the sizable, modern supermarket and the Shamrock Tavern are open year-round.)

First-time visitors are lucky to have such a guide in Jim Willis, a crusty but amiable retiree. He is the only full-time employee of Beaver Island Tours. He'll meet you at the dock and take you to all the major sights: the Old Mormon Print Shop and Marine Museum, the lighthouse, the old convent, Barney's Lake, the fateful dock former Tiger star Norm Cash fell off of after a night of drinking and drowned. He'll fill you in on Beaver Island's bizarre history, about how the charismatic Strang (by all accounts a gifted and intelligent leader) moved his band of some 2,000 followers to Beaver Island in the 1850s. The Mormons soon took over the fledgling county government by virtue of their numbers, moved the county seat to St. James, and drove off the Irish fishermen from their "kingdom" before Strang was killed by a rebel of his own group. Later you can make longer, more leisurely expeditions to those places that interest you the most.

Best of all, Willis tells you, in a laconic, philosophical sing-song, about island life today. How the bank is open from 9 to 1 Tuesday mornings, except during the summer season. How Charlevoix County won't give the two island townships a full-time deputy sheriff, so islanders have to make up a living wage for him by paying him to mow the lawns of the two township campgrounds. "The current deputy comes from Battle Crick," Willis says. "Likes it quite well here — and he should. There's no crime here. Most of his problems come when someone has too much to drink at the Shamrock Bar."

Beaver Island was long the center of northern Lake Michigan's profitable fishery, Willis explains, but overfishing and alewives killed off the industry, and the island's population dropped dramatically. A declining population is always a concern in isolated small communities. If it drops too low, important institutions (school, church, having a doctor) are threatened. Beaver Island lost its doctor, and when its resident nurse practitioner left for Operation Desert Storm, it made national headlines. Today building vacation homes keeps the island economy going. Development battles are intensifying between "islanders" (natives who grew up here and who need jobs to stay) and "off-islanders" (people from somewhere else, who usually favor limiting development to preserve the island's natural environment). The islanders have the majority vote in St. James and the northern fourth of the island, but in the southern three-fourths, Peaine Township, off-islanders now outnumber islanders.

Don't plan to come to Beaver Island unless you want to relax. There's very little in the way of entertainment. Transportation for visitors consists of a few taxis, bikes, and their feet. Summer people bring their old cars to the island, but in the off-season, cars aren't a common sight. With so few cars, it looks like the 1930s.

If you just want to look around Beaver Island, you can make a $22 day trip and have 7 1/2 hours on the island. But spending four hours on the ferry to see a few low-key sights on the run doesn't really add up. You're better off to stay a few days, or at least overnight, and unwind. Any of the island's half dozen lodgings or its rental houses are pleasant if simple. You can bring a bike on the ferry for $6, or rent one from Beaver Island Sports (616-448-2266). Then you can explore the island at your leisure. It's about 14 miles long and almost seven miles wide. The west shore is rugged, rocky, and picturesque; the interior is a mix of second-growth forest and a pretty rural landscape of log farms and abandoned barns, with seven inland lakes. Fishing on them isn't too good, but it's awfully pretty. Hiking trails crisscross the interior. There are two sandy swimming beaches and a nine-hole golf course. Sailboards and fishing boats can also be rented at Beaver Island Sports. Local history becomes an avocation for many summer people; the grocery store, museums, and attractive island library (donated by the summer resident who owns the Lands End mail-order company) have many books on the island. Browsing in shops could last a couple of hours, if you stretched it. Boats to smaller islands in the Beaver Archipelago can be chartered. There are enough restaurants to be interesting (the Shamrock has good BBQ, and the Circle M, in the old convent outside town, is a pretty place to spend an evening. (Call and management will provide transportation.)

The two **museums** of the Beaver Island Historical Society do a good job of illuminating the island's history and the lives of the people who have lived on the island — Indians, fishermen, Mormons, and "interesting characters who have sought seclusion," like a beloved Russian refugee physician. Historical society members have tracked down descendants of the Mormons who lived here and invited them back to reunions; their stories are part of Old Mormon Print Shop museum. The Marine Museum offers many displays about fishing and boat-building on the island. *The museums are open from mid-June to Labor Day daily from 11-4, Sundays 12-3. Combined admission: $1.50/adult, 75¢/children.*

Whatever you do, don't leave the island without visiting the **Beaver Island Toy Museum and Store,** overlooking Paradise Bay a little past the Marine Museum. Inside this simple bungalow, the golden age of dime stores lives on. You'll find charms like tiny coppery baseball mitts, tiny plastic ballerinas, magic tricks, cowboy stuff — it's like returning to the 1950s, with bits of the 1960s and 1930s thrown in. Most things are for sale, but some are for display only. The deadly categorizing of the typical serious collector is altogether absent. The owner has managed to avoid any sense of real-world monetary value and make her cache of warehouse finds into a fantasy realm, at fantasy prices. Explore the little creations that line the outdoor paths and gardens, and you may be tempted to create some backyard fantasies of your own. *Open in season, 11-4 daily except Monday. Inquire next door in the off-season.*

PLANNING A STAY AT BEAVER ISLAND . . . . . The **Chamber of Commerce** is an excellent clearinghouse for any inquiries, including cottage rentals. (616) 448-2505. Box 5, St. James, Beaver Island, MI 49782. Get a free map when you get off the boat; the complete $4 map is worthwhile if you intend to bike or hike. . . . . For the ferry schedule and reservations, call the **Beaver Island Boat Company,** (616) 547-2311. From late June through August boats leave Charlevoix at 8:30 a.m. and 2:30 p.m. at least. Inquire about the very attractive fall package (about $60/person for a night's lodging, ferry, breakfast, and dinner). . . . . . **Island Airways** makes frequent, non-scheduled flights from Charlevoix. Call (616) 448-2326). . . . . . **Beaver Island Tours'** excellent 1-hour tour is available daily at the dock as the ferry disembarks. $6/adult, $3/children 5-12. Package tours and custom tours are also available. Arranged through Beaver Island Boat Company.

❶ Gaslight District. Over 75 mostly upper-end resort shops in attractive old storefronts. Watch famous American Spoon kitchen in action.

❷ Bayfront Park. Lively waterfront park with marina, refreshments. West of the museum is a historic mineral spring, scenic Bear River valley & iron bridge.

❸ Little Traverse Museum. Handsome depot now home of stimulating historical museum. Splendid display on passenger pigeons, Ottawa quill boxes.

❹ Crafts shops One mile west on U.S. 31 is cluster of crafts shops, fine bay view. Quality affordable crafts at Artisans, charming studio/galleries nearby.

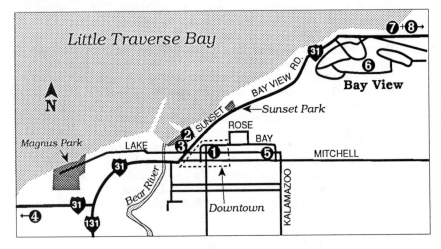

❺ Perry Hotel. 81-room, 1899 brick hotel/restaurant, jazzed up Victorian-style by famed innkeeper Stafford Smith. Long, old-fashioned porch, great Gaslight District location.

❻ Bay View. Peaceful, well-preserved 1875 Methodist summer retreat for relaxation and moral uplift. Wonderful old cottages. Eat and stay at Bay View Inn or Terrace Inn.

❼ Petoskey State Park. Delightful view of bay from 1.25-mile beach with occasional Petoskey stones at south end. Scenic campsites and picnic sites among pines, boardwalk atop wooded dunes.

❽ Indian Hills Trading Co. Choice array of Indian crafts. Southwest, Eskimo, plus local Ottawa specialties like sweet grass boxes and hot pads, quality quill boxes & ash baskets. 1681 Harbor Springs Rd.

Highlights of
Petoskey

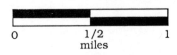

0   1/2   1
          miles

Little Traverse Historical Museum

In a Petoskey landmark by the bay, some fascinating glimpses of the area's rich past.

This large, interesting local museum is in the handsome and impressive 1892 Chicago & West Michigan railroad station right on Little Traverse Bay. The Shingle Style depot, with its massive tower, is an eye-catching sight in its own right, a reminder of the importance of railroads in developing Petoskey as a fashionable summer resort for wealthy Midwesterners. It's just south of the city marina, protected by a large earthen berm from the traffic of U.S. 31.

In the mid-1870s, as the timber on which the local economy depended was running out, railroads teamed up with lumbermen and local business leaders to promote the Little Traverse area as a resort. The museum commemorates Petoskey's railroad era by a reconstructed railroad station manager's office, complete with clicking telegraph key.

Virtually all the giant white pines in the region were logged. A museum display suggests their grandeur with a cross section of a 225-year-old tree that's almost four feet across. A 300-pound Petoskey stone, one of the largest known, is here. Beautifully patterned when polished, it

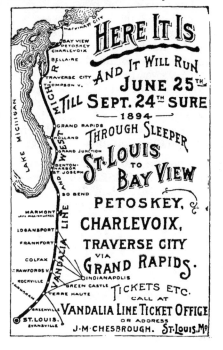

1894 advertisement. Railroads played an essential and active part in developing major Midwestern resorts like Petoskey.

is fossilized coral, a remnant of the Devonian seas that covered Michigan some 250 million years ago.

A vivid old mural depicts passenger pigeon hunting, so popular and lucrative here before the turn of the century that farmers neglected their crops to pursue it. The meat was a delicacy in fancy big-city restaurants, and the feathers were used to make pillows and mattresses. An estimated three billion to five billion of these plump birds were here before settlers arrived. One flock was 240 miles long and a mile wide. The birds were so docile that hunters simply clubbed them to death. By 1878 whole boatloads were being shipped from Petoskey. The last flock was seen in 1900. The last passenger pigeon died in 1914 in a Cincinnati zoo.

Probably the most important collection here is the Ottawa quill boxes made by area craftsmen over a hundred years ago. These small boxes of birchbark are completely covered with beautiful patterns and images of animals and flowers, made of dyed porcupine quills punched into the bark. Boxes of this quality predate the era of commercial Indian crafts made for tourists. It took an immense amount of time to make them (one small box uses ten porcupines' worth of quills), and they were bestowed as important gifts for people the makers especially wished to honor.

But what draws the most visitors here is an extensive collection of material on Ernest Hemingway, who spent all of his first 18 summers at his family's cottage on Walloon Lake south of town. He and his family arrived from Chicago at this station. Later, after Hemingway was wounded as an ambulance driver in World War I, he spent the winter in Petoskey, writing *The Torrents of Spring* and collecting materials for the famous Nick Adams stories that appeared in *In Our Time*. Hemingway met his first wife, St. Louisan Hadley Richardson, in this area; they were married in the little church in Horton Bay. An interesting **gift shop** with many good regional books adds to visitors' enjoyment of the area.

Located on the waterfront of downtown Petoskey, west of the marina. (616) 347-2620. Ample parking by museum. Open from May through December, Tues-Sat 10-4. $1 donation. Research material available in winter by appointment.

A PLEASANT STROLL ON THE WATERFRONT . . . . . extends from the **marina and park** by U.S. 31 to picturesque **Mineral Well Park** by the outlet to Bear River, just west of the Little Traverse Historical Museum. Both parks have picnic tables, but their moods are very different: the sunny, open marina area (also busy with nearby softball games) vs. the secluded, shady, old-fashioned gazebo built so health-conscious Victorian resorters could take in the foul-smelling sulphur waters.

Gaslight District

*Michigan's premiere resort-area shopping
is in historic downtown Petoskey.*

For people who choose to spend their vacation time doing resort-area shopping, the Gaslight District in downtown Petoskey is the best in the state. It stands out for its size (almost 80 stores in a six-block area geared to visitors), for setting (well preserved two-story Victorian brick storefronts and a pleasant park), and for tradition. The area has catered to the Midwest's wealthiest resorters since the turn of the century, when steamers took Harbor Springs summer people across the bay to be fitted for fall suits and dresses. You don't see as many independent boutiques with "Petoskey and Naples" on their signs as you might have 20 years ago, and there's more ordinary gifty stuff, but a good deal of the old flavor remains. Fudge shops haven't taken over.

The Gaslight District is a concentration of shops still oriented to well-heeled summer people and those who want to look and live like them. The area is geared to browsing. Prices are high because rents are high and the season is short, but there are some terrific markdowns at the end of the season in October. Shops now stay open year-round. This is a good place to find fashionable skiwear and after-ski wear, as well as other sports gear and clothing.

Antique shops are clustered around Bay at Howard, at the district's north (bayside) end. Interior furnishings are more likely to be looser and more contemporary, sometimes in a folkish vein, in keeping with a relaxed, summer cottage feel. Updated traditional clothes for women (somewhat less so for men) are the area's strength, in shops like **Mettler's, Hilda's of Iceland**, and **Pappagallo**. This is where to find things like oiled thornproof country jackets imported from England ($260) and top-quality blue blazers for small boys ($150), in addition to handknit sweaters, print sundresses, polo shirts, Benetton, Ralph Lauren, etc. Gifts and collectibles are on the upswing, especially if they have ducks and fish on them, or if they have an Up North flavor (Petoskey stones, moccasins, birch boxes). For toys and novelties, **Games Imported** (206 Howard), **The Rocking Horse Toy Company** (125 E. Bay), and **Grandpa Shorter's** (301 E. Lake) all carry things you're not likely to find at your local mall.

Note: the famous cherry berry pie at Jesperson's Restaurant on

Howard Street, which Hemingway is said to have liked, is overpriced and over-rated (too sweet). The restaurant began in 1903
but lacks any historic charm.

A handy Gaslight shopping guide is available at the helpful
Chamber of Commerce in the little office with columns on the
corner of Mitchell and Howard. Or call (616) 347-4150 for a
visitor packet.

Stores worth worth special mention include:

◆ **Grandpa Shorter's.** The consummate, old-fashioned Northern
Michigan souvenir shop: big selection of moccasins, Petoskey
stones, rubber tomahawks for kids — all the classics, plus well-
chosen new novelties and some quality gifts. Lots of inexpensive
toys and games for kids. Incorporates junk without being junky.
All the fun of a good old-time dime store. *301 E. Lake at Petoskey.*

◆ **Ward & Eis Gallery.** Works by top leather craftspeople from
across the U.S., from practical, moderate-priced sheepskin hats,
beautiful handbags, and many kinds of calendars and organizers to
amazing decorative masks that could also be worn to parties. The
one store in Petoskey not to miss. Beautiful bay view from rear
window. *315 E. Lake.*

◆ **Gattles.** Custom linens for the carriage trade — for instance,
here you could have pillowcases embroidered to match your wallpaper. Big mail-order clientele for unusual merchandise and services. *331 E. Lake.*

◆ **Chandler's Wildlife Gallery.** See finely detailed prize-winning
duck decoys and other handcrafted wildlife art. Non-collectors
may enjoy things like scrimshaw tie tacks and $20 carved wood
earrings that very much resemble real feathers. *217 Howard
(back behind patio).*

◆ **Great Lakes Design.** Geared to informal summer residences. A
good deal of hand-decorated furniture. Each year a changing array
of unusual accents hand-painted in Mexico in folk art styles is featured such as colorful flower and fruit designs on large plates,
blue and white bathroom ceramics in a loose, informal pattern,
from a $20 toothbrush and towel holders to a lavatory basin. *406
Bay (also in Harbor Springs).*

◆ **American Spoon Foods.** Justin Rashid's highly regarded company is Michigan's biggest culinary success story. Its nationally
famed fruit preserves and all-fruit, no-sugar spreads concentrate
the natural-fruit taste by using top ingredients (all from Michigan)
and minimizing sugar. It's on the pricey side ($4.25 a 12-oz. jar),
but it's a souvenir gift with cachet. This small storefront kitchen
and sales room is where all American Spoon products come from.
A big window behind the counter shows visitors where the cook-

ing is done, in four big copper vats. The aroma is strong and enticing. On the counter: an array of opened jars, with spoons and crackers for sampling. Most popular: sugar-free sour cherry spoon fruit. Other big sellers: dried cherries, cherry-fudge sauce. Also for sale: pretty birchbark gift baskets, evocative prints of Northern Michigan scenes by artist Kristin Hurlin. *411 E. Lake, almost at Park Avenue.*

♦ **Northern Possessions.** Bright, often primitive-sophisticated or whimsical American crafts — cabinets painted with bears and fishes, $300 soft suede boots, colorfully embroidered, looking like something a Cossack might wear, furniture, lots of jewelry. Looks more original if you haven't checked out the Chicago gallery scene. *222 Park Ave.*

To get to the Gaslight District, follow signs from U.S. 31 to downtown. Large parking lots are at the foot of Bay Street and between Bay and Lake just east of the tracks. But come by 10 in summer for easy parking. Later, look for a uniformed teen to direct you to long-term parking or a free 1/2 hour space. Shops are open 9:30 to 5, Mon-Sat. Only 20 or so shops stay open summer evenings and Sundays.

FOR A PLEASANT LUNCH BREAK . . . . . treat yourself to a meal in the elegant bay-view dining room of the **Perry Hotel** on Bay at Lewis. The big old brick building, directly across from the old train station and the tracks, has been beautifully restored by area restaurateur Stafford Smith. . . . . . Or you could make up a picnic lunch from the imported cheeses, deli items, and fresh-baked muffins and sourdough bread at **Symons General Store,** Lake at Howard. This charmingly cluttered old storefront with high tin ceilings has supplied the likes of choice caviar ($200 for seven ounces), wine, and dried morels to wealthy summer people for over 30 years. . . . . Picnic spots: the **waterfront park** (get there safely by finding the tunnel under U.S. 31 down from the intersection of Bay and Petoskey streets) or **Pennsylvania Park** (see below).

A SHADY DOWNTOWN PARK . . . . . is alongside the railroad tracks that define the Gaslight District's eastern edge. **Pennsylvania Park** runs between Mitchell and Lake. It has benches, picnic tables, and a gazebo where **summer band concerts** are held Tuesdays and Fridays at 12:15 and 7 p.m. Restrooms and pay phones are across the tracks at the Chamber of Commerce, Mitchell at Howard.

Bay View

*A 19th-century religious resort
that keeps its special atmosphere*

This remarkable colony of 435 cottages and 20 public buildings overlooks Traverse Bay just east of Petoskey. Most of the cottages were built before 1900, and the village, with its big trees and winding lanes, retains the aura of an earlier era. Michigan Methodists organized Bay View in 1875 as a place for summer camp meetings. Initially a tent camp, it grew within 20 years to included elaborate cottages, a hotel, chapel, and eventually a fine library. Famous speakers, including William Jennings Bryan and Booker T. Washington, have given talks here.

The cottages were built on a series of natural terraces — ancient beach lines created by higher lake levels in eras when glacial meltwaters were gradually receding. The founding Methodists were not wealthy people. The first houses were tents and simple 12' by 16' cabins. By the 1890s these cabins were being enlarged in style, with big front additions. The Queen Anne style is dominant, with lots of gingerbread trim on wide porches across the front, and on small second-story porches above. All cottages originally had views of the bay, now blocked by trees. Many of them face away from the drives, so to really experience Bay View, you should get out and walk across the campus. (Parking spaces are plentiful along most drives.) Don't miss the wonderfully complex **Evelyn Hall** from 1891.

"The spiritual atmosphere of Bay View has always been highly moralistic, with a stern interdiction of Demon Rum, cardplaying, dancing, and other fleshly pursuits," wrote the late John Rauch, a longtime observer and chronicler of the area's resort history. Sundays were dedicated to worship and everyone attended three services. . . . As late as 1910, no deliveries in Bay View or other traffic was permitted to disturb the pious Sabbath. There was much hymn singing and prayer meetings on weekday nights."

Today's Bay View is considerably more relaxed. Just about half of the current residents are Methodists, some of them the sixth generation of Bay View summer residents. Members of the Bay View Association have taken great care to preserve the community's Victorian look. Cottage owners are required to get association approval for even minor exterior changes. Residents own their own cottages (costing from $40,000 to $200,000) but lease their land from the association. Bay View is occupied only

Jean Lau

Evelyn Hall in Bay View.

from May through October, although the roads and two inns are open year-round. (It's a beautiful place to cross-country ski.)

Days are filled with courses, sports, lectures, plays, and concerts, just as they were in the colony's early years. A small but select summer school of music attracts gifted musicians from around the country. The 2,000-seat auditorium is where **concerts** are held at 8 p.m Wednesday and Sunday. A **museum** in the two oldest buildings is open beginning in July and August from noon to 1 on Sundays, and 2:30-4:30 Wednesdays.

A popular place for visitors to stay and eat is **Stafford's Bay View Inn** close to Little Traverse Bay. Less fancy, quieter, and more in the original spirit of Bay View is the relatively austere **Terrace Inn**, facing the central campus. (See Restaurants and Lodgings, p. 432.)

The main part of Bay View is just south of U.S. 31 on the east edge of Petoskey. Encampment Drive takes you to the central campus. For information on summer concerts, plays, or events, call the Bay View business office at (616) 347-6225.

Petoskey State Park

Close to upscale resort towns, it has a woodsy setting, scenic beach, dunes, and a wonderful bay view.

Many of Michigan's smaller, older state parks up north don't have much more natural atmosphere than suburbanized lake lots. They have grassy lawns, rows of planted trees, a beach, and boat launch. A lot of the campgrounds resemble miniature subdivisions of RVs.

Petoskey State Park is different. It manages to combine convenience of location and facilities with a wonderful natural atmosphere in only 305 acres. The park enjoys a choice site in and behind the dunes at the funnel-like end of Little Traverse Bay. The mile-long **beach** not only has soft sand but a fabulous view of Harbor Springs and Petoskey in the distance. The shoreline frames the setting sun for spectacular sunsets, followed by the twinkling town lights reflected in the water.

There's a **concession stand, bathhouse,** and **playground.** The parking lot is big enough to handle demand on all but the hottest days of the year. There's plenty of room to walk down the beach and get away from crowds. Wooded dunes provide a natural setting for the beach, unlike some popular parks near resort towns, where the beach environment consists of sand, water, sky, and shimmering row after row of parked cars. The park is gorgeous in fall. A mix of hardwoods makes for especially rich colors contrasting with the conifers' dark green and the white paper bark of birch trees

If you're lucky, you may be able to find a Petoskey stone along the south end of the beach, among the stones and gravel. Sometimes west winds across the funnel-shaped bay concentrate all sorts of floating refuse from boats right here. Parks employees clean up regularly, but it can occasionally be a problem.

A stand of big pines gives the **picnic area** in a hollow behind the dunes its own special aura. It's deeply shady, unlike the open beach, and filled with piney scents and scampering chipmunks.

The two **campgrounds** nestled in wooded dunes behind the beach manage to offer 190 sites with modern amenities (electrical hookups and showers) while retaining a good deal of privacy and a wonderful, woodsy feel. They typically fill up from late June through late August. Reservations for half the sites are taken starting January 1; the other half are first-come, first-serve. They may fill up before noon. You can camp in Petoskey's nearby Magnus Park (on the bay but far less scenic) and take a priority slip that keeps your place in line when the next day's spaces are doled out at 8 a.m.

Petoskey State Park is just off busy M-119, less than 10 miles southeast of Harbor Springs and four miles east of Petoskey. Each resort has bustling, upscale downtowns of charming late 19th-century buildings loaded with all the most refined material diversions of late 20th-century consumerism. Sometimes all that stuff demands an antidote in exercise and nature. Two trail loops start by the campground registration office. At the .7-mile **Old Baldy Trail**, a stairway climbs steeply up into heavily wooded dunes for a spectacular view of the bay through the trees. When you climb the dunewalk stairs into the rustling, dark, cool forest of pines and maples, you feel remote from the traffic along 119's commercial strip half a mile away. The much easier 2.7-mile **Portage Trail** goes through lower dunes to Lake Michigan and a little inland lake. It's recommended for **cross-country skiing** in winter. (The campground stays open in winter, too, but without running water or showers.)

For more of a real wilderness experience, Wilderness State Park (p. 417) and the Bliss Township beach (p. 416) are not too terribly far away — about 35 miles north on county road 81. But for combining natural beauty and convenience to northern Michigan's most attractive old resort communities, Petoskey State Park is tops.

The park is at 2475 Harbor-Petoskey Rd. (U.S. 119) about 1 1/2 miles north of U.S. 31. (616) 347-2311. It's open year-round but running water and flush toilets are shut off between Nov. 1 and May 1. State park sticker required: $3/day or $15/year.

RENT MOUNTAIN BIKES, CROSS COUNTRY SKIS, SNOWSHOES, AND MORE . . . .
at **Adventure Sports**, 1100 Bay View Road east of Bay View. Prices are reasonable ($15/day for a mountain bike and helmet), and the staff can advise you on the many good trails and routes in the area. Open daily in summer and ski season. (616) 347-3041.

❶ Bluff Gardens. Fancy farm market with choice tiny vegetables, jams and jellies & a huge stock of peasanty, gay Quimper earthenware.

❷ East Bluff Drive. Best view of the charming downtown and harbor is from this stairway between the high school on bluff and Spring St. down below.

❸ Downtown shops. Attractive retail area with pricey resortwear and traditional clothing. Creative surprises in crafts and home accessories.

❹ Hoover Flower Shop. Cut flowers, plants, and dried arrangements for stately summer homes come from these colorful fields and greenhouses.

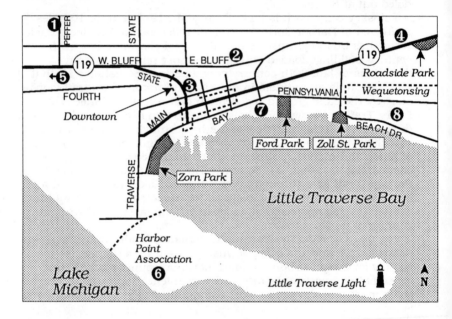

❺ Tunnel of Trees. Twisting highway along Lake Michigan is one of the state's most scenic drives.

❻ Harbor Point. No outsiders allowed at this elite summer colony favored by old Detroit money. Only horses provide summer transportation.

❼ Blackbird Museum. The Indian postmaster built this post office in 1876. Curator Veronica Medicine tells about the traditional life of local Ottawa.

❽ Wequetonsing. Glimpse traditional resort life of the affluent. There's sailing, golf, flowers, drinks on the veranda — at this grand old cottage colony.

Highlights of
Harbor Springs

0   miles   1/4

Harbor Springs

*The Midwest's most exclusive old resort town
has an interesting downtown, lovely resort colonies,
and wonderful views of bay, town, and woods.*

This famous old resort town — "the Newport of the Middle
West" — still manages to hold onto its physical beauty and
small-town charm. This remains true despite the vastly
increased development in the 1970s and 1980s of nearby second
homes, golf and ski resorts and the resulting new intensity of
retail activity. Harbor Springs lacks the disturbing sense of development gone rampant. It has avoided the long, four-story condo
complexes in Charlevoix and the busy fast-food strips abutting Bay
View and Petoskey.

East Bluff Drive still has a stunningly picturesque view. Across a
turn-of-the-century downtown you see a crescent harbor full of
sailboats and, on the point, a leafy, lovely summer cottage colony
and lighthouse. In the century-old resort association of Wequetonsing, a stately parade of large, picture-perfect summer homes
have gracious verandas looking out across flower-bordered lawns
and paths to the sailboats on Little Traverse Bay. There are extensive areas of golf course, woods, and wetlands along the main
entrance to Harbor Springs from Petoskey, buffering the east
edge of town from development.

On a park bench by the harbor it wouldn't be unusual to see an
old Indian man and a retired naval architect sitting together, dis-
cussing fishing and boats. Ottawa Indians moved into the area
between Harbor Springs and Cross Village in the 1700s. Their
large, permanent villages remained here while Indians in the
more desirable farmlands of southern Michigan were forcibly
moved west by the U.S. government. Wealthy Harbor Springs
resorters and tourists actually helped maintain the local Indian
communities by providing an appreciative market for the Ottawas'
famous quillwork and crafts.

At the height of the season in July and August, downtown traffic
and crowds can spoil the tranquil aura of the place. Plan your visit
for the quieter times — midweek in summer or ski season, or in
the lovely spring and fall.

Downtown still has enough old-timey places with character to
maintain the leisurely, civilized sociability of an old resort town.
To see it in action, stop for coffee and doughnuts between 9 and
10 at Mary Ellen's lunch counter and magazine stand on Main

Street. The plywood magazine racks and general ambiance are
straight out of the 1940s. Here you'll witness a congenial coffee
klatsch that includes all spheres of permanent residents, from
natives to "trust-fund babies."

Harbor Springs' identity as the Midwest's premiere resort
community began just five years after the railroad first arrived at
Petoskey in 1873. Lumber, the main freight of Northern Michigan
railroads, was running out, and the railroads aggressively promoted the area's recreational virtues to hayfever sufferers and
wealthy Midwestern families escaping hot summers at home.

The success of nearby Bay View (p. 404) inspired the formation
of two resort associations in Harbor Springs, Harbor Point and
Wequetonsing. (Its local nickname is pronounced WEE-kwee.)
Both were tonier and more fun-loving than earnest, education-
minded Bay View. But both were patterned after the Methodist
colony in that the associations own the land and approve the cottage owners. That control gives resort colonies like these a century-old visual and social continuity that's almost unheard of in
fast-changing American society, where suburbs boom and decline
within a generation.

The old resort families hailed from big Midwestern cities
where technical know-how of German immigrants had combined
with Yankee enterprise to create great manufacturing fortunes in
the decades during and after the Civil War. Townspeople protect
the privacy of the famous old families who come here — they
include some automotive Fords, some glass-making Fords of
Toledo, and the Gambles of Proctor & Gamble — while they readily divulge the presence of newcomers like Detroit Piston Bill
Laimbeer, rock star Bob Seger, and radio personality J. P.
McCarthy, all of whom have homes in the newer areas just outside
Harbor Springs.

Highlights of the Harbor Spring area include:

◆ **Downtown shopping.** (See also Harbor Springs restaurants,
pp. 440-441). The delightful, small-scale historic storefronts and
cottages, combined with the choice merchandise, make for
pleasant browsing in Harbor Springs. Many of the familiar, upper-
end resort retailers in Northern Michigan have shops here. The
1980s boom has also brought a number of fresh, individualistic
new gallery/shops. Several are on North State near the bend at
the bluff. At the nonsensically named **Pooter Olooms** *(339 N.
State; 616-526-6101)*, Scandinavian country antique furniture
form the basis for an inspired and collection of quilts, twig furniture, garden sculpture, jewelry, and folk art, antique and contemporary. Owner Jenny Feldman imports scrubbed pine and
colorfully painted furniture. The folk art, both naive and sophisti-

cated, often has a spiritual, natural aspect and occasionally verges
on the darkly mysterious. It includes Kim Nicolas's odd person-
ages of shells and stones, Kelli Sniveley's muted paintings
incorporating postage stamps like religious icons, and Ivan
Barnett's metal applique assemblages using Indian and animal
motifs. **Boyer Glassworks** *(207 N. State; 616-526-6359)* features
Harry Boyer's handblown glass vases, paperweights, and ornaments, plus less expensive crafts and jewelry. (Boyer's glass
earrings are striking.) Harry Boyer was close to the 1970s
beginnings of the contemporary art glass movement in Toledo.
Visitors can watch him at work.

The **Curtis Gallery** (241 E. Main; 616-526-7313) offers engrav-
ings ranging from pretty, impressionistic landscapes to a spooky
series about the dark side of suburbia called "Unfriendly Neighbors." Nearby, popular *Chicago Tribune* cartoonist **Nancy Drew**
has a shop that makes good use of her bright, kid-style cartoons
about women, mothers, and daughters on her T-shirts, totes,
shirts, and sundresses. Furniture and floors are painted with lots
of zig-zags and squiggles, creating an intensely wacky environment. **Huzza** *(136 E. Main; 616-526-6914)* creates an eclectic
contemporary style that plays off good contemporary design with
antiques in its mix of interior decor, tabletop accessories,
women's clothing, and gifts.

A core of old-line institutions have managed to escape escalat-
ing rents by owning their buildings. **Cassidy Hardware** *(135 E.
Main)* is a classic, with wood fixtures, squeaky floors, and all sorts
of paraphernalia for wild birds. **Hovey's Pharmacy** *(205 E. Main)*
displays interesting historic photos by its entrance. Upstairs
(enter around the corner at 206 Spring) is the **Harbor Springs
Library** (open daily in summer, otherwise most afternoons and
Saturday mornings). This light-filled, comfortable, old-fashioned
space has a fine view of the harbor. There you can browse through
back copies of the *Harbor Light* weekly newspaper, a literate,
leisurely chronicle of town and resort life. It's an all-too-rare
continuation of the tradition of serious small-town journalism.

Mary Ellen's Place at 145 E. Main (formerly Linehan's) is a
newsstand and soda fountain that's the premiere local institution
for keeping up with everyone in town and a fine spot for an
inexpensive snack in this pricey town. Summer residents have
their personal cubbyholes for their hometown papers.

Newer, but in the same relaxed, old-line vein, is the bookstore
across the street, **Between the Covers** (152 E. Main; 616-
526-5591). There's good browsing here, even a backyard terrace
with seats; informed, personal service; and a much broader and
deeper selection than the usual resort bookshop.

Downtown is centered along two blocks of Main St. between

*State and Gardner, with an increasing number of shops on Bay and on the adjoining three blocks of State. **Parking lots** along Third and Bay. **Seasonal hours.** Summer hours: daily 9 or 10 to 5 or 5:30, some stores open evenings. Many stores stay open Sundays through fall color season. Winter hours Mon-Sat 9 or 10 to 5.*

◆ **Holy Childhood Catholic Church and School.** This striking complex — a simple, Gothic clapboard church and adjacent three-story brick school — is the direct descendant of the Catholic Indian mission that was the basis of the first permanent settlement at Harbor Springs. French Catholic missionaries had converted area Indians in the 1700s. In 1823, residents in the nearby Ottawa village of L'Arbre Croche asked the U.S. government to send them a Catholic missionary. By 1833 the mission had become the largest Indian mission in the northern U.S. In 1886 Franciscans took over and built a large school and dormitory for Indian students. Indians today resent such institutions that weakened Indian families. Well into the 20th century services were held in Ottawa and English. *150 W. Main. 616-526-2017. Masses at 8 a.m. weekdays, 5:30 & 7 p.m. Sat., 9:30 and 11 a.m. Sun, year-round.*

◆ **Andrew Blackbird Museum.** Ottawa chief Andrew Blackbird started Harbor Springs' first post office in his kitchen here in 1862. Indians held the paid government jobs in Harbor Springs' early years, but as whites moved in, they took over the Indians' positions. When they claimed Blackbird's house couldn't handle the volume of mail, he built the adjoining storefront. But he lost his job anyway. Blackbird continued his career as a writer and lecturer. His works and some possessions are on display, along with various stone points, baskets, and Indian clothing from here and elsewhere. Recently the local Ottawa tribe took over the museum, and it is in transition.The collection of beautiful Ottawa birchbark boxes covered with dyed porcupine quills is a point of pride. But the best part of a museum visit is listening to its pithy, well-informed curator, Veronica Medicine, talk about the appeal and challenge of living a traditional Indian life. In it, "your people come first, not yourself," she says. *368 E. Main, next to the Shay hexagon house. 616-526-7731. Mem.-Labor Day: Mon-Sat 1-5. Otherwise by appt. Admission $1.*

◆ **Shay House.** This odd hexagonal house with projecting hexagonal wings (1892) illustrates the inventive mind of its owner and designer Ephraim Shay. In 1881 he had invented revolutionary new locomotive. Small and versatile, it enabled narrow-gauge track to be laid easily to remote mines and stands of timber. The Shay locomotive made logging much more efficient — so efficient, in fact, that Northern Michigan's forests, considered so vast they would last a thousand years, were nearly gone by 1910.

In his adopted home town of Harbor Springs, Shay devised an early household water system and experimented with steel-hulled boats. The pleasant, light-filled house, sheathed inside and out with embossed metal in many patterns, is now used as offices. Visitors are welcome in the lobby. *373 E. Main.*

◆ **Wequetonsing.** Unlike many other exclusive summer colonies, Wequetonsing (pronounced WEE-kwee-TON-sing) isn't a gated enclave that's off-limits to the public in summer. It gives you a rare glimpse of the living continuation of a very leisurely, very private, very privileged summer world. Routines for some are generations old. One older banker habitually enjoys a newspaper with breakfast, then spends an hour on the phone with his private secretary back home. Backgammon is at 10, then lunch at the club, followed by golf and bridge, shopping, or a fashion show for his wife. Cocktails on the veranda are followed by dinner, often at the club, and then to bed.

For townspeople and retirees, it can be an education to work for these old guard families, usually so charming and considerate in their private lives. Teams of summer workers start opening the vacation homes in May and June, painting and repairing, grooming the perfect lawns, installing bedding plants. Then eight hectic weeks in the service of the resorters: cleaning, cooking, shopping, and serving. After Labor Day, a deep collective sigh — of relief and regret that the whole magical show is over for another season.

Wequetonsing was laid out on the Bay View plan, with a common activity building (the casino), playgrounds, and tennis courts clustered along Second Avenue between Pennsylvania and Central. The golf course is across the Petoskey Road. The bayside houses grew grand and showy, but simpler places, closely spaced, line the pedestrian walkways that lead back from the water. Just to the west is town. To the east and north are a series of wooded **nature preserves**, open to the public, interlaced with paths and boardwalks.

◆ **Hoover Flower Shop.** Fresh-cut and dried flowers, bedding plants, and shrubs for the carriage trade are supplied from these five greenhouses and five acres of fields. Fields are filled with color in July and August. You can buy dried flowers and grasses by the piece. The color range of dried sweetheart roses (50¢/stem, reduced to 25¢ in spring) may be unequalled. *M-119 (Petoskey Rd.) just east of Harbor Springs. (616) 526-2992. Open May through mid-October and Thanksgiving to Christmas.*

◆ **East Bluff Drive.** This part of Bluff Drive boasts a splendid view of town and bay, along with Harbor Springs' most elaborate non-resort Victorian houses. A stairway descends from the high school up on the bluff down to Spring Street. *State east to Arbor.*

◆ **Bluff Gardens.** A produce stand catering to the entertaining needs of Harbor Point and Wequetonsing resorters has evolved into a purveyor of homemade fancy foods, sold at this glorified farm market and by catalog. There are jams, dressings, and relishes (about $4 an 8-ounce jar). Even the tiny carrots and beets are displayed like jewels in the carpeted sales area. Bluff Gardens' pride is its stock of Quimper, the French earthenware famous for its peasanty motifs in blue, yellow, and red-orange. A dinner plate is $52, but sometimes on sale for $26. *721 W. Lake. From downtown Harbor Springs, take State up the hill to West Bluff (M-119). In about a mile turn right onto Peffer, then left onto Lake. (616) 526-5571.*

◆ **"Tunnel of Trees"** (M-119) to Bliss Township Park and Wilderness State Park. *See p. 416.*

◆ **Thorne Swift Nature Preserve and Beach.** These 30 acres of beautiful beach, dunes, and fragrant cedar swamp have been donated for use as a park and nature center. A dune stair and overlook offer close-up looks at pioneer dune plants, and a panoramic view of the bay. The small swimming beach, seldom crowded, is reached by a 1/4-mile trail. Boardwalks pass shallow-rooted cedars leaning crazily in the swamp for a surreal effect. The wonderful cedar aroma makes this a special destination. So do the outstanding interpretive signs and pamphlets for three short nature trails. Naturalist-rangers give **scheduled guided tours** and are often around to field casual questions. Call to arrange a nature walk anytime in summer. *Lower Shore Dr. 3 1/2 miles west of Harbor Springs. Take M-119 to Lower Shore Dr. (616) 526-6401. Open daily Mem.-Labor Day 10 a.m.-sunset; weekends Sept. & Oct. Call for permission to enter other times. $2/car for non-residents.*

Legs Inn

The pinnacle of rustic folk architecture in Michigan

Northern Michigan is full of inspired folk-art creations. None is more improbable than Legs Inn in Cross Village, 20 miles north of Harbor Springs along the Lake Michigan shore. It's a Polish restaurant and bar created by Stanley Smolak, who came to America as a young man to work in a Detroit auto factory. He got to know the Ottawa Indians in Cross Village, which in the 1920s was still a center of the Ottawa culture. What fascinated him was the Ottawas' close connection with nature, and the intimate linking of the material and spiritual worlds.

In the late 1920s Smolak started work on the inn, which grew in stages to encompass many moods and environments. What's seen from the road verges on ugly. There's no landscaping to soften the busy exterior façade of small, irregular fieldstones, accented by totem poles and a fanciful row of curved upside-down furniture legs on the roof (hence the "Legs" of the name). Hand-painted lettering on piled-up boulders advertises "BEER, LIQUORS, SOUVENIRS, DRiftWOOD."

The interior is far more compelling. The barroom is dark and grotto-like, easy to pass over on your way to the restaurant in the rear. The restaurant's picture windows overlook a beautiful rear terrace, pines, and a flower-filled rock garden. In the distance is Lake Michigan. It's a popular spot on summer evenings at sunset. Children can run around the extensive grounds and play while their parents linger over dinner and dessert.

The restaurant's atmosphere is cheerful and warm. There's a big stone fireplace and interlacing rafters of sticks. Dining areas are separated by screens of intertwined driftwood, glistening with shellac. Here and there primitive, pixyish faces painted on the driftwood peek out.

The food is Polish home cooking, the equal of Hamtramck or Chicago's favorite Polish restaurants. The cabbage rolls are outstanding. Whitefish is also available, along with European dishes like goulash and chicken in wine. Dinners (with soup, salad, and potato) are around $10 to $15, sandwiches and lunch entrees $5 to $6. A world-wide selection of over 50 beers is on hand.

If you time your dinner visit right, you can stroll outside to enjoy the sunset over the lake, and then linger in that amazing grotto of a barroom. After your eyes are acclimated to the dark, you'll make all sorts of discoveries. Phone booths are made of hollowed-out trees. A lacey, tangled lattice of shellacked roots above the balcony disappear into the dark. Faces and figures seem like spirits emerging from branches and roots.

Smolak started Legs Inn in 1930. His Depression-era art is based on found materials, inspiration, persistence, and hard work. "He claims that any man can do what he did if he only keeps his eyes open and his hands busy," stated one appreciative article. "For the world is filled with fine and great wonders, things which people take no notice of because they have eyes yet do not see and hands that lie idle."

After Smolak's death, Legs Inn devolved into something of a dive. Today it has been rejuvenated into a family restaurant and local meeting place that's a refreshing change from the carefully traditional interiors so evident in nearby Harbor Springs and Petoskey. There's live music on weekends — rock and roll/oldies at 10 on Friday and Saturday, a Sunday-afternoon duo in the garden, and the Jelly Roll Blues Band Sunday evenings. Big bands occasionally are booked on weekdays.

Legs Inn is on 119 just north of Levering Road. (616) 526-2281. Open Mem. Day through 3rd wknd Oct. Summer dining-room hours 11-10, Sun. 12-10. Fall hours 12-9. Bar open until 2. Full bar. Visa, MC.

A LOVELY DRIVE TO LEGS INN. . . . . is along the lake, through the celebrated **Tunnel of Trees**, narrow Route 119 that twists above the shoreline. The overarching trees, the glimpses of Lake Michigan from the bluff, the aroma of cedars and pines — all combine to make this very special. Bicyclists favor the drive in morning, but traffic is rarely heavy or fast. Colonies of trillium cover the woods around Memorial Day for a spectacular show. After dark, you're better off avoiding the twists and turns and taking the inland route back to Petoskey. Take 66 (Levering Road) east from Cross Village; in 9 miles turn south at 81. It eventually ends at the Harbor Springs-Petoskey Road.

LEGS INN RENTAL COTTAGES. . . . . are rustic log affairs with two bedrooms (they sleep 6), picnic tables, and an adjacent sandy beach. Rates are $300 a week in July and August, otherwise sometimes by the day for $50 a night.

A DELIGHTFUL BEACH . . . . . with a backdrop of wild-looking dunes, remote from cottage development, is at **Bliss Township Park** on 119 about 10 miles north of Legs Inn on Sturgeon Bay. It's not fancy — amenities consist of two outhouses — but it's a favorite choice of many Petoskey people. From Mackinaw City, take 81 southwest, but keep going west on Lakeview when 81 turns south. See also **Sturgeon Bay Picnic Area** at **Wilderness State Park**, p. 417.

Wilderness State Park

30 miles of unspoiled coast, picturesque cabins,
sandy beaches with no crowds,
and rugged backcountry trails for skiing and hiking

ilderness State Park is a world apart from Mackinaw City's motel-land, yet barely 15 minutes away. It combines a location near major destinations around Petoskey and the Straits with an exceptional expanse of varied natural beauty.

Wilderness Park Road leads from Mackinaw City past the campgrounds and main beach to Waugoshance Point. The shore is accented by five lighthouses, some abandoned, some still functioning. The point and the two long offshore islands near it extend almost five miles out into Lake Michigan, just 15 miles from the Upper Peninsula. It's a fine place for bird-watchers to spot warblers and songbirds. A newly improved gravel road enables you to drive out to the point. You can even walk to the islands in low water.

Lakeshore Campground (150 large modern sites) is an open, suburban-style campground with lake views. Across the road, the 60 large modern sites in the **Pines Campground** are shaded and private. Both fill up in summer. Make reservations, or arrive before 2 p.m. to get a site. Five rustic 4- to 6-person **log cabins** in scenic beach spots are for rent, along with three 24-person cabins near the campgrounds. Reservations needed way ahead.

A sandy beach that's even less crowded and more natural, backed by dunes, is reached at the park's southwest corner, where 119 joins Lakeview Road. Look for the sign to **Sturgeon Bay Picnic Area.** It has grills, tables, and pit toilets.

In the rugged interior backcountry, many paths and old logging roads cross a glacial landscape of wetlands and high hills like Mount Nebo. There are over six miles of groomed **cross-country ski trails** and 12 miles of separate **snowmobile trails.**

Main entrance and booth are on Wilderness Park Rd. (C-81), 12 miles west of Mackinaw City. Write: Wilderness State Park, Carp Lake, MI 49718. (616) 436-5381. State park sticker required: $3/day, $15/year.

Colonial Michilimackinac

Older than any Michigan city,
the fort at the Straits goes back to a time of friction
between Britain and France over control of the fur trade.

Fur-trading in the upper Great Lakes caused competitive friction between France and Great Britain through much of the 18th century. A small fort at the northern tip of Michigan's Lower Peninsula, built here in 1715, was part of France's ongoing efforts to keep the British out of this lucrative trade zone. There was never a big military force here, usually some 20 soldiers, but as the present reconstruction of the old site shows, it was a typical fort of the day, surrounded by an 18-foot-high stockade. As many traders as soldiers lived in the community, which was cut off from the outside world six months a year. The French finally surrendered their northern territories to Great Britain in 1760, and the British occupied Fort Michilimackinac for another 20 years until they built a more defensible fort on Mackinac Island. The most notable event during their stay was the 1763 massacre of most of the fort's British soldiers by the local Indians, part of Chief Pontiac's ultimately unsuccessful plan to repulse the British.

Inside the stockade today, the state Bureau of History has taken care to reconstruct accurately the buildings used both by its French and British occupants. Extensive archaeological digging

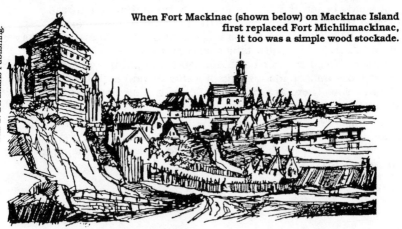

When Fort Mackinac (shown below) on Mackinac Island
first replaced Fort Michilimackinac,
it too was a simple wood stockade.

Reynold Weidenaar, courtesy of
Wm. B. Eerdmans Publishing.

and historical research gives visitors a good sense of what life was really like in the old fort. There's a storehouse, blacksmith shop, barracks, powder magazine, and commanding officer's house, among others. See **cannon firings, musket and drill demonstrations, colonial craftsmen at work,** and well-informed guides in period costumes who answer questions and give talks.

The fort is west of the Mackinac Bridge. East of the bridge is a delightful **nautical museum** in the Old Mackinac Point Lighthouse, part of the same park. In the middle, underneath the bridge approach, is an impressive **Visitor Center** with historical displays and a good **museum store** oriented around the fur-trading era.

Take northbound I-75 to exit 339 just before the bridge. (616) 436-5563. Information pack mailed upon request. Open daily from May to mid-Oct. Hours: June 15-Labor Day 9-7. May 15- 24 10-4. May 25-June 15 9-6. Labor Day- Sept 30 9-5. Oct 1-15 10-4. Adults $6, children 6-12 $3.50, under 6 free. Mackinac State Park combination ticket (for here, fort on island, mill): adults $11, children $6.50.

🌳🌳🌳

TWO OUTSTANDING PRIVATE MUSEUMS IN MACKINAW CITY. . . . . Teysen's **Woodland Indian Museum,** over Teysen's cafeteria restaurant at 416 N. Huron, across from the docks, features gorgeous beaded leather clothing, baskets, and other artifacts in a very interesting, to-the-point display done by Michigan State University museum specialists. It tells you a lot more about Michigan Indian culture than many bigger, more tedious museums. Displays periodically changed, *Open from early May through color season, 7 a.m-9 p.m. $2/adults.* . . . . . The **Mackinac Bridge Museum** was started by an ironworker who helped build the bridge. It's over his pizzeria. The displays aren't professional or slick, but the project has both intelligence and the heart of grassroots history. There are hundreds of workers' personalized hardhats, photos of the ferries and huge lines at the Straits during hunting season, and an excellent half-hour film about designing and building the bridge. Not to be missed. *Over Mama Mia's Pizzeria, 231 E. Central at Henry. Free.*

Mill Creek State Historic Park

A beautiful nature trail
overlooks an 18th-century sawmill.

A reconstructed 18th-century sawmill in an unusually scenic location means that this park is an extraordinary place to visit. The mill was built by a Scottish trader in 1790 to supply lumber for building the British fort on Mackinac Island. It was powered by Mill Creek, which flows into the nearby Straits of Mackinac linking Lake Huron and Lake Michigan.

The mill has been rebuilt to duplicate the original, complete with a big wooden waterwheel. Hourly demonstrations show what noisy, shaking contraptions water-powered mills were. A **visitor center/museum** by the entrance and parking lot puts the site in historical context and displays items uncovered on the site by archaeologists. The excellent **museum shop** features nature-related books, activities, and gifts.

The highlight is a 15-minute walk on **Mill Pond Trail**. It forms a loop from the visitor center to the sawmill and around the mill pond. On the way are two delightful overlooks from which you can look down on the sylvan scene and even see the Straits and Mackinac Island. Another 25-minute trail, also a loop, takes you through a forest along the top of the bluff paralleling the mill stream. An hour-long trail follows the stream farther back to some beaver dams. This point of entry to the natural world of northern Michigan is an excellent complement to the bustle and crowds nearby.

On U.S. 23 1/2 mile southeast of Mackinaw City. (616) 436-7011.
Open mid-May to mid-Oct. Summer hours (June 15-Labor Day)
10-6. Otherwise 10-4. Adults $4, children 6-12 $2.50, 5 & under
free. See p. 419 for information on combination tickets.

Mackinac Island

*World famous, it features historic Fort Mackinac,
the elegant Grand Hotel, striking rock formations,
wonderful bike and carriage rides, and no cars.*

This three-mile-long island, an 18-minute boat ride from
either the Upper or Lower Peninsula, is a major Michigan
highlight for several reasons. Its interestingly rugged
terrain provides many pleasant panoramas and views of striking
limestone formations. The island's military and economic history
is equally colorful. The British built a big fort here in 1781, and
American and British forces fought a battle in 1812. The legendary fur-trading tycoon John Jacob Astor based his central trading
office here. One of America's most renowned hotels, Grand Hotel,
is perched on the side of a hill, visible from the mainland. The
absence of autos and the use of horses and bicycles for transportation give the island the aura of another age. (The decision to
ban autos was made for practical, not aesthetic, reasons in the
1920s, when the potential impact of autos on the island was
becoming apparent.) Even inexperienced cyclists enjoy the
scenic but undemanding trip on the paved road that hugs the
lakeshore all the way around. There's the additional adventure of
having to take one of the many ferries from St. Ignace or Mackinaw City to the island's harbor at its southern end, giving passengers a striking view of the large Victorian summer houses, the big
fort, and the majestic Grand Hotel, all situated on steep limestone slopes.

Because the island is mostly limestone, with only a thin layer of
topsoil, it has been little farmed. The rocky terrain, eroded by
wind and waves, includes many interesting formations such as
Arch Rock, Devil's Kitchen, Sugar Loaf Rock, and Chimney Rock.

The island is thought to have been a popular meeting place for
Indians from different tribes. They called it the great turtle
(Michilimackinac), because of its humped, oval shape. French
missionaries began setting up missions in the Straits area to
convert the Indians in the 17th century. At the same time,
exporting the region's furs to Europe became an increasingly
profitable enterprise, pursued by both the British and French. In
1781 the British moved their mainland fort here, and the island
became a major regional center.

Tourists began visiting the island in 1838. By the 1870s it was
a three-day steamer trip from Detroit and a two-day train trip from
Chicago. Congress made the island the country's second national
park in 1875. Fort Mackinac was closed in 1894, and a year later

Chicago. Congress made the island the country's second national park in 1875. Fort Mackinac was closed in 1894, and a year later over 80% of the island was designated Michigan's first state park.

Under 400 of the island's 2,300 acres remain privately owned. The handsome Victorian summer "cottages" just to the east and west of the harbor now sell for up to $700,000. Even some of the modest workers' homes in Harrisonville, toward the center of the island, sell for over $100,000, forcing some of the 500 year-round residents to leave the island for cheaper housing elsewhere. The biggest issue now facing the island is overdevelopment as new shops and housing have created low water pressure, power outages, and landfill problems.

Some 900,000 "fudgies," the locals' sardonic term for visitors, come to the island each year. Getting off a ferry in the harbor, they are confronted with a bustling street full of carriages and tourists, fudge and souvenir shops.

Highlights for visitors to the island are:

◆ **Carriage tour.** Thirty local families pooled forces over 40 years ago to operate 75 carriages, using some 300 horses, to transport visitors around the island. The most popular tour begins downtown at the two Mackinac Island Carriage booths on Main Street opposite the Arnold and Shepler's ferry docks. It lasts one hour 45 minutes. It's a pleasant, informative, slow-paced drive which takes you by most sights, including Grand Hotel, and stops at Fort Mackinac and Arch Rock to let you get out and enjoy the great views. *Open from May 15 through Oct. Summer hours (June 16-Labor Day) 8:30-5:30. May 15-June 15 9-4. Labor Day-Oct 9-3. Adults $10, children 4-11 $6.*

◆ **Fort Mackinac.** Perched on a bluff overlooking the harbor, this historic fort is well worth visiting. Its views of town and harbor below are delightful. The well-preserved fort has been restored to look as it did in the 1880s. You can see 14 original buildings, including barracks, blockhouses, a canteen, and a post commissary. A short **slide show** is a good introduction to the fort. An enthusiastic and expert costumed guide fires cannons and answers visitors' questions. There's a delightful **tearoom** with a good view within the fort. Its tasty food is prepared in the kitchens of Grand Hotel. The ticket for the fort also allows you to visit some historic and reconstructed buildings in town, including a French-Canadian log house and the Beaumont Memorial, with displays on the startling investigations of the doctor who was the first to observe how the stomach functions, thanks to a gunshot wound of a island resident that never healed. Several crafts demonstrators who have made these summer jobs lifetime avocations are extremely knowledgeable about their subjects.

Same hours, prices as Fort Michilmackinac (p. 418). The helpful visitor center to the fort is below the fort on Main at Fort, opposite the park. It's open 9-7 in summer, to 4 or 5 otherwise.

◆ **Bicycle tour.** Rent either single or tandem bikes for the delightful trip around the rim of the island. Roughly half way around the island on the western shore is **British Landing**, the place where Indians and British soldiers landed in 1812 in their successful surprise attack on Fort Mackinac. You can get a bite to eat at the well-equipped snack shop here. There are also rest rooms, a picnic area, and nature center. The spot also has a good view of the Mackinac Bridge. This is where, during the winter, an ice bridge forms to St. Ignace, allowing year-round residents to snowmobile off the island. If you decide to venture by bike into the island's interior, keep in mind that it's much hillier and therefore a strenuous ride. *Bike rentals by the Arnold docks.*

◆ **Grand Hotel.** This is a living American vestige of the late-19th-century European tradition of elegant summer watering places. When a consortium of railroads and steamship companies finished the hotel in 1887, it became the world's largest summer hotel and the world's largest pine building, with the world's largest porch — 660 feet. It still holds those records today.

The formalities of a bygone era live on here. The hotel still requires dresses or skirts for women and jackets and ties for men at and after dinner. The $5 fee charged non-guests to visit the hotel and grounds is a reasonable cost for spending the better part of a day here, exploring the lovely Victorian gardens, enjoying the lobby and porch with their splendid views of the Straits, and having lunch in the varied restaurants and bars (all top-notch). A swim in the pretty but small pool is $6 extra. But the overpriced ground-floor shops, gussied up with Anglophile status symbols and self-important Grand Hotel souvenirs, with little pertaining to the rest of the island, can leave a bad taste in your mouth. Enter upstairs at the central entrance for a better first impression of the hotel and its busy, courteous desk staff.

Small rooms start at $120/per person, modified American plan, including breakfast and dinner; an extra 18% gratuity is added. To get the most out of a Grand Hotel stay, guests should take advantage of all the special facilities and daily events that were part of resort life in the grand tradition. There's the big breakfast and five-course dinner, the **parlor and porch** (popular for late-afternoon and evening cocktails and just sitting), golf at the **nine-hole course** (it has wonderful views and some challenging holes), **tennis**, swimming in a beautifully landscaped **pool**, a 4 o'clock **tea concert** with champagne, sandwiches, and pastries, **dancing** at dinner, and nightly entertainment in the

intimate **Audubon Bar**, the vintage art deco **Terrace Room**
(dancing with a seven-piece swing orchestra), and the **Cupola Bar**
(dancing to a jazz trio in a rooftop room with a dazzling view).
Grand Hotel has long had a mystique as a summer locus of
fashion, power, and political activity. It hasn't hurt that the Governor's summer mansion is close by. (It's open for public tours on
Wednesdays.) Grand Hotel history is displayed in a two-room
museum on the lower level.

The updated decor of Grand Hotel was created by famed
decorator Carleton Varney, who drew on his own memories of
seaside summers in Massachusetts to emphasize the mood of
Victorian summer resort. He uses motifs like the hotel's signature
red geranium, repeated boldly on black carpets; trellis
wallpapers; and vibrant summer colors for guest rooms: daffodil
yellow, sky blue, deep green, and geranium pink. The effect of all
this clever decorating is cheerful — the interiors feel warm and
lively even on rainy days. Geranium-motif furniture in white, pink,
and green are typical for regular rooms, which are individually
decorated. (Rear rooms without views are a little nicer than
others.) Be forewarned: the old hotel's interior walls are very
thin, and neighbors' voices can be heard clearly, especially in
rooms joined by connecting doors. Also, TVs are not generally
available and must be requested — a shock to some visitors. *(For
reservation information plus information on less expensive places
to stay on the island, see p. 423).*

♦ **Shopping.** Mackinac shopping is improving. Many visitors'
impressions of the island are unfortunately dominated by the
fudge and ice cream shops and generally ordinary souvenir stores
that line Main Street. Sidewalks are crowded in season; service
mostly depends on untrained summer help. For generations,
shopkeepers did well enough appealing to the captive market of
passive day-trippers who visit the fort and Grand Hotel, then
browse in the shops by the ferry docks. Time-honored souvenirs
like rubber tomahawks and moccasins, humorous wood plaques
and souvenir teacups are fun and nostalgic but get tiring fast, as
do suncatchers and T-shirts.

The 1980s' boom in upscale island inns and mainland motels
has brought some new and tony shops, mostly big on updated
traditional clothing and accessories that run heavily in the direction of traditional duck prints and decoys, dolls for collectors,
Victorian-styled luxuries, and fancy soaps. But better stores of this
kind can be found elsewhere in northwest Michigan, especially in
nearby Petoskey and Harbor Springs. The short season and high
rents necessarily tend to increase already high prices. Consider
limiting browsing time in favor of the island's unique scenery and
hiking and bicycling opportunities. *Mostly along Main, with some*

shops on Market.

Four shopping highlights are:

Maeve's Arts & Antiques. Contemporary American handcrafts in a whimsical, folkish vein mix well with funny, cheap toys for kids, a few sweet and sentimental antiques, and colorful imports like Indonesian batik dresses ($70), shirts, and pants ($40 each), grey stoneware decorated with primitive baroque angels in blue, and applique scenes by Hmong tribespeople now living in Michigan. Easily the most surprising store on the island. *Main Street near Astor, between the Arnold and Shepler docks. (906) 847-3755.*

Island Scrimshander. The proprietor is one of three brothers who are the only craftspeople to make a living at the ancient whalers' craft of engraving ivory. Sometimes you can see him at work. *Opposite Maeve's, on Main west of Astor.*

Island Books. Personal, second-story bookstore. A good place to get away from Main Street's crowds and choose from a wide-ranging stock of vacation reading, including many regional titles about Mackinac and much of northern Michigan. *Main near Fort, next to Doud's Mercantile, upstairs.*

Fort Mackinac Museum Shop. One of three very good museum shops of the Mackinac State Park. All go way beyond the usual gift shop in their efforts to illuminate chosen themes and historic periods with a choice selection of books and authentic historic-reproduction artifacts. Specialties here are pre-industrial cooking and crafts, along with military, Civil War, and Indian history and popular culture of the Victorian era, when the fort was still in operation. Out-of-the-ordinary items include replicas of Indian trade silver pendants ($10), tin fifes and harmonicas with instructions, Amish hooked rugs in colorful scenes ($170-$350), $17 tile trivets in quilt block patterns, and tiny birch boxes with quill turtles ($10-$20). Many toys and gifts are $2 and under.

Ferries of three different lines provide transportation to Mackinac Island. They leave from both St. Ignace and Mackinaw City. Service begins about May 1 and continues through Oct. Hourly trips begin from the mainland at about 8 a.m.The last boat leaves the island at 9 p.m. mid-June- Aug, at 6 p.m. before and after that. Round-trip rates: adults $10.50, children $6.50, bikes $3. For more information on what's available on the island, call (906) 847-6418.

❶ Seagull Pt. Nature Area. Picturesque setting on Lake Huron with nature trail and beach.

❷ Gauthier & Spaulding Fisheries. Buy cheap whitefish fresh from Lake Huron at one of the few remaining Great Lakes fisheries.

❸ Plath's Meats. Famous for smoked pork loin, made in the smokehouse back of the 78-year-old German shop.

❹ Historical Museum. Striking old bungalow where presidents of the quarry lived for over 5 decades. 1920s flappers' hats a highlight.

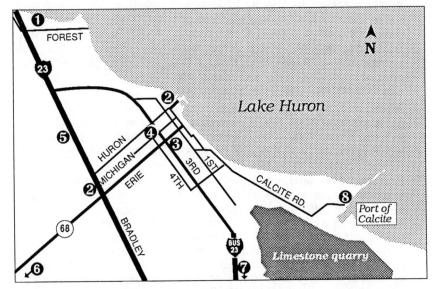

❺ Kortman's Restaurant. Terrific family eatery with good, modestly-priced homemade dishes and plain, down-home atmosphere.

❻ 12 miles to Ocqueoc Falls. Erosion has leveled these waters to a frisky rapids, but it's a pretty picnic site with a 7-mile hiking trail.

❼ Quarry view. 1 mile south. Dramatic bird's-eye view of 5,000-acre, 200-feet-deep limestone quarry, the world's largest. Bring binoculars.

❽ Harbor View. See big freighters load up with limestone at this 5,000-acre quarry. Big brick strcture sorts stones by size.

Highlights of
Rogers City

0   1/2   1
mile

Rogers City

A spectacular quarry, freshly caught whitefish, fabulous smoked pork loin, and miles of uncrowded beaches at this Lake Huron port

This town of 4,000 is home to the largest limestone quarry in the world. Despite the abundance of Lake Huron beaches both in and around the city, few tourists come here compared to the northwestern coast of the Lower Peninsula. The conservative Polish, German, and Italian residents attend the thousand-member-plus Catholic and Lutheran churches in town. Some 300,000 acres of commercially harvested timberlands in the county create the biggest area of employment. German and Polish farmers raise huge quantities of beans. Eight per cent of the country's dark red kidney beans are grown in this county. The cool, moist climate is also excellent for potatoes.

Highlights of Rogers City and vicinity include:

◆ **Michigan Limestone quarry.** It can be viewed from two strategic locations (see map). The viewing stand off Business 23 reveals the vast expanse of the 5,000-acre quarry. Over the decades the company has dug down to 250 feet to mine the almost-pure limestone. View huge shovels scooping up blasted chunks of limestone and loading large dump trucks. From the **harbor view**, open daylight hours, you can better see the screen house, where the chunks are sorted by size, and the harbor, where up to two freighters at a time can be loaded. Some 400 freighter trips haul away the 10 million tons excavated annually. The limestone costs just $3.50 a ton wholesale, less than the cost of shipping. Call (517) 734-2117 to find out when freighters will be in port.

◆ **Gauthier & Spaulding Fisheries.** On the front of G&S's Bradley Highway retail outlet is a colorful painting of the boat used to catch the whitefish sold here. From April to the end of October, the 46-foot *Viking* pulls up a 1,500-foot trapnet from 90 feet of Lake Huron water. A good haul is a ton of fish. Either smoked or fileted, the fish are just $3 a pound.

Third-generation fisherman John Gauthier says northern Lake Huron has the cleanest water in the Great Lakes. On Lake Huron just west of the city harbor is the firm's dock and wholesale office. Around noon daily the *Viking* returns with its haul. Buy fish right off the boat for just $1 pound. Tucked behind their shack-like office loom the decaying remains of the *Catherine*, an old gillnet tug. Looking like a small submarine, these wooden fishing boats were totally enclosed with no deck, so the crew never had to be exposed to the often hazardous, frigid waters of the upper Great Lakes. *103 S. Bradley Hwy (retail outlet). 360 E. Huron Ave. (fishery). (517) 734-3474.*

◆ **Presque Isle County Historical Museum.** This handsome bungalow built in 1914 has occupied by the families of the president of the local limestone quarry company from 1914 until 1957. Some rooms are now furnished with period furniture and accessories. Others have selected local artifacts. Don't miss the flamboyantly colorful 1920s flapper hats discovered decades later in the back of a local clothing shop. In the basement is a beautiful, authentic Indian birchbark canoe. *176 W. Michigan Ave. at Fourth St. Open June through Oct., 12-4 weekdays. (517) 734-4121. No admission charge.*

◆ **Plath's Meats.** A modest-looking meat market on Rogers City's main street, Plath's is famous for the smoked pork loin prepared in the smokehouse behind the retail shop. Third-generation Plaths use the same German recipe for preparing the smoked pork that Emil Plath brought over from Germany in 1913. *116 S. 3rd. (517) 734-2232.*

THE POSEN POTATO FESTIVAL . . . . . **Posen** (population 260), a Polish farming village 15 miles southeast of Rogers City, enjoys a reputation for growing exceptionally tasty potatoes on its rocky limestone soil. On the first weekend after Labor Day each year, it hosts a delightful festival. Polka and country bands play continuously from noon to 1 a.m. Saturday and to 9 p.m. Sunday. As many as 25,000 watch a mile-long parade at 1:30 Sunday. But the big draw is the potato pancake smorgasbord beginning Sunday morning at 10:30. Signs lead visitors to local farmers who sell 100-pound bags of their potatoes for about $7.

"THE LARGEST WATERFALL IN THE LOWER PENINSULA" . . . . . is the title bestowed on **Ocqueoc Falls** — testament to how little competition for the honor there is. It looks more like a rapids than a waterfall, but despite its puny size, it's a fine place for a picnic because of its picturesque site. A seven-mile **hiking and cross-country skiing trail** starts next to the falls. *On M-68 at Ocqueoc Falls Highway, 12 miles west of Rogers City.*

Jesse Besser Museum

*Lavishly funded by an industrialist,
it has remarkable collections of American Indian art,
tools, and weapons.*

One of Michigan's most impressive museums, Besser combines historical, scientific, and art exhibits on two levels. A striking three-story-high Foucault pendulum greets the entering visitor, vividly showing the effect of the earth's rotation.

The museum's highlight is its spectacular collection of Indian artifacts, one of the finest in the country. The 20,000-item Haltiner Collection was gathered beginning in 1912 by a local state highway employee and his son, now a curator at the museum. Their most remarkable discoveries were found right across the street from the museum: copper artifacts dating back 7,000 years made by a still-mysterious people known only as the "copper culture." You can also see one of the finest collections of ceremonial bannerstones and birdstones.

Also notable is the collection of Great Lakes maps, dating from the 1670s to 1874. Children enjoy the 1890s gallery of shops. The **Sky Theater Planetarium** ($1.50 admission) has shows at 2 & 4 p.m. Sundays and 12:30 Wednesdays.

On north edge of Alpena, 1 block east of U.S. 23 north, at 491 Johnson. Open year-round. Mon-Fri 10-5, Thurs to 9, Sat & Sun 12-5. $2/adult, $1/students & seniors, max. $5/family.

ALSO OF INTEREST NEAR ALPENA . . . . . The **Thunder Bay Underwater Preserve** contains 16 shipwrecks in an area of 288 square miles just off Alpena in Lake Huron. The oldest is a 100-foot wooden schooner which sank in 1889. The unusually dense collection of shipwrecks is due to the number of hazardous rock shoals and islands here. In 1981 the state made the area a preserve, prohibiting divers from taking things from the wrecks. Beginners can take a crash 3-day course to learn to dive for $198 at Thunder Bay Divers in Alpena (call 517-356-9336 for reservations). July and August are the best months. From the same place you can rent gear for under $70 a day and for another $55/person one of their boats will take you out to a wreck. A favorite dive is to the 550-foot German freighter Nordmeer in 40 feet of water. It was carrying coiled steel to Chicago when it sank in 1966. Divers can swim through the cabins of the upright wreck. *In Thunder Bay just east of Alpena. between South Point and Middle Island.*

Hartwick Pines State Park

*See a rare, majestic stand of 200-year-old pines,
a remnant of the awesome forests
that once covered a third of the state.*

Before the rush of white settlers to Michigan in the 1830s, over 13 of the state's 38 million acres were covered with white pine. Thriving in poor, sandy soil, these majestic trees grow up to 200 feet tall and could live 500 years. They were prized because the tall, straight trunks make excellent building lumber and are light enough to float down rivers to lumber mills.

It took the white man less than a century to virtually wipe out this enormous tree population. By the 1920s the once-huge forests were cutover fields. One of the very few virgin white pine forests remaining is this 49-acre stand. It was saved by the national panic of 1893, which so depressed demand for lumber that the logging outfit cutting it suspended operations. In 1927 Karen Hartwick purchased 8,236 acres from the Salling Hanson Lumber Company and donated it to the state of for a state park.

The imposing parcel at Hartwick Pines is preserved not as an artificially kempt park but as an authentic white pine forest looking very much like a typical stand half a millennium ago. It's a big enough area to give the visitor a sense what awesome forests covered the state. The white pines are so tall that their wide, dark trunks dominate a walker's view. You have to crane your neck to look high up and see where the trees' branches begin eight or nine stories in the air.

A one-mile **Virgin Pines Foot Trail** takes visitors on a loop

through the woods to a reconstructed **19th-century logging camp** with bunkhouse, sawmill, and dining room. At the parking lot an **interpretive center** illuminates Michigan's logging history and tells about Michigan forests. This park is the best place to learn about Michigan's forests and colorful, important logging era.

Another interesting walk is the nearby three-mile-long **Au Sable River foot trail**. It crosses the east branch of that legendary river twice. Famous for trout fishing, the Au Sable was originally full of grayling until they were fished to extinction in the late 19th century. Stocked trout thrived so well that fishing parties earlier this century readily would catch over 500 fish an outing. Today the river is so heavily canoed that only the upper reaches of its north branch retain the mystique of yesteryear. The foot trail passes a rare forest of virgin hemlock trees 80 to 90 feet tall, saved from the saw by a sudden drop in the price of its bark whichwas used for tanning leather. A **scenic overlook** at the walk's northwest extreme of the walk gives a panoramic view of the area. Another walk, the two-mile **Mertz Grade Nature Trail**, passes through a variety of forests, on part of an old logging railroad grade.

Two especially nice times to visit Hartwick Pines are at the end of September, when the fall color is usually at its peak, and in June when the variety of wild flowers in bloom is greatest. In the winter there is almost always snow on the ground, and a visit then shows what it was like during the logging season.

Hartwick Pines is 7.5 miles northwest of Grayling on M-93. Exit 259 off I-75. Park hours are 8 a.m.-10 p.m. year round. Exhibit buildings open April, May, September & Oct 8-4:30; June-Labor Day 8-7. State parks sticker required; $3/day, $15/year. Campground has 63 campsites, 20 without electricity. Call (517) 348-7068.

🌲🌳🌲

IN NEARBY GAYLORD . . . . a convenient stop is the quarter-century-old **Call of the Wild Museum.** Here you can see dozens of scenes of stuffed wild animals native to the area. Interesting descriptions by each exhibit tell such things as how Michigan's wild turkeys disappeared in 1888 and weren't restocked until the 1950s, or how the American elk was hunted almost to extinction. A large gift shop sells everything from saddles to clothing. *850 S. Wisconsin. Take exit 282 from I-75, east 1/4 mile. (517) 732-4336. June 15-Sept 2: daily 8:30 a.m.-9 p.m. 9:30-6 rest of year. Adults $4, children 5-13 $2.50.*

Recommended Restaurants & Lodgings

Northern Michigan

To locate cities, see regional map, p. 360.

PENTWATER

🍴

Historic Nickerson Inn. *262 W. Lowell (the beach road). From B.R. 31 downtown, follow the signs to Mears State Park.* (616) 869-8241. *Open year-round. Breakfast 8-11, dinner 5-10, closed Tues. Dinner reservations encouraged. Visa, MC, AmEx, Disc, CB. Full bar, long wine list.* New owners of vintage summer hotel on a wooded dune above beach offer best food around. Breakfasts $3-$5 feature Belgian waffles w/ fresh fruit, omelets. Dinner w/salad, vegetable, starch, from $9 (Italian chicken breast over fettucini) to about $20 for filet mignon, Beef Wellington. Completely renovated. Pleasant ambiance. Long veranda overlooks lake.

🐴

The Pentwater Abbey. *(616) 869-4094. 85 W. First.* 4 rooms , 3 share baths. $45-$65. Cable TV in living room. Full breakfast. 1870s house w/ big yard, lawn furniture, between downtown & Mears beach, across street from Pentwater Lake.
B&B in pretty house, nice location

LUDINGTON

🍴

El Jardin. *125 S. James, 1 block s. off Ludington St. (U.S. 10) downtown.* (616) 843-2802. *Open daily, April-Nov. Mem.-Labor Day: 5 a.m.-8 p.m. April-May & Sept-Nov 5-3, Fri-Sat 'til 8. May get liquor license; will stay open year-round. Visa, MC. No alcohol yet).* Unpretentious, pleasant cafe with good Mexican food (also American standards). Breakfast all day. Lunch from $3 (taco w/ rice &

beans) to about $5 for large wet burrito or enchilada. Dinner chicken or steak fajitas w/rice, beans, salad (around $6).

Gibbs Country House. *3951 U.S. 10, e. a block or so at U.S. 31 exit.* (616) 845-0311. *Open late March-Dec 11:30-9. Between May 15-Oct 15 Mon-Sat 11:30-10, Sun from 12. Call for limited winter hrs. AmEx, MC, Visa. Full bar.* Known for a huge soup & salad bar that's like going to a church supper put on by good cooks heavy on the marshmallows and mayo. At lunch (until 4:15) it's $5.50 (and that includes a giant dessert bar with cobblers, brownies, 5 kinds of pie!). Dinner menu, in effect after 4:30 and all day Sunday, includes salad bar, starts at $9 for perch, walleye, offers roast chicken, prime rib, much more. Signature sticky buns served with everything. "Come as you are" family atmosphere, good service.

House of Flavors. *402 W. Ludington Ave. downtown just 3 blocks from Lake Michigan.* (616) 845-5785. *Open 7 days, 6 a.m.-10 p.m., to 11 in summer. No credit cards or alcohol.* Big short-order restaurant that grew as ice cream parlor of dairy in rear. (Old photos by restrooms document the transformation.) Same menu all day. Food's OK and reasonable (the breakfast special w/ 2 eggs, 2 sausage, over-greasy hash browns is $1.60!). Soup & 1/2 sandwich $3. Fried dinner plates to $6. Ice cream treats w/ 20 flavors.

🐴

Ludington House. *(616) 845-7769. 501 E. Ludington Ave. (U.S. 10) e. of downtown.* 9 rooms w/ baths on 3 floors. $55-$75. 1878 house on busy street. A/C. Hot breakfast. Common areas: library w/ VCR, 2 sitting rooms, dining room.
Nicest Ludington B&B on street of grand Victorian homes.

Snyder Shore Line Inn. *(616) 845-1261. 903 W. Ludington at pier, park, Lake Michigan.* 32 rooms on 2 floors. Downstairs rooms (smaller, comfortable country decor) from $62

from mid-June thru Labor day, color weekends, $52 otherwise. Upstairs luxury (i.e., romance) rooms have VCR, refrigerator, microwave, private balcony w/ Lake Mich. view, Jacuzzi bath. $195/$165. More tasteful decor than many such rooms.
Best location on Lake Michigan. Individual decor. By Stearns Park

The Lighthouse Motel. *(616) 845-6117. 710 W. Ludington, 1 1/2 blocks from Lake Mich.* 14 rooms on 1 & 2 floors. Open year-round. July & Aug rates: $50-$60 midweek, $56-$72 weekend. Spring/fall: $30-$45. Winter: $25-$35. Phone in lobby. Attractive, large older rooms. Free coffee.
Reasonable rates; good location near pier, Stearns Park (1/2 mi. beach, playground, shuffleboard)

Nader's Lake Shore Motor Lodge. *(616) 843-8757. 612 N. Lake Shore Dr. a little n. of Stearns Park.* Open May-Oct. 23 rooms, in 1-story motel, cottage-like annex w/ kitchens, & remodeled house. Summer rates: $38-$52. Spring & fall: $30-$36. Big suite w/ hot tub is more. Attractive, unpretentious older resort. Walk to beach, park. Close to golf, Ludington State Park. Cable TV. Small outdoor pool. Shuffleboard. Golf packages.
Private lawn area, good location near beach, reasonable rates

Barothy Lodge. *(616) 898-2340. Off U.S. 10 about 20 mi. e. of Ludington near Walhalla.* Open year-round. 9 chalets w/1-8 bedrooms. $34-$39/ person. Discount for longer stays. Each chalet has kitchen, wood-burning fireplace, 1 bath for every 2 bedrooms, linens provided. Larger chalets have jacuzzi & pool tables. Tennis, canoes, stocked trout ponds, playscape, basketball, volleyball, horseshoes. Swans, ducks, peacocks, pheasants. 5 mi. marked hiking/x-c ski trails in wildlife feeding area. 7 mi. fishing on wild-scenic Pere Marquette River in Manistee National Forest.
Housekeeping chalets by the night, lots of outdoor activities nearby

EMPIRE

Joe's Friendly Tavern. *On Front St. (west continuation of M-72 into downtown Empire). (616) 326-5506. Mon-Sat 7:30 a.m.-11 p.m., Sun to noon. No credit cards; personal checks OK.* Popular pine-paneled North Country family bar. Patronized by locals, also caters to visitors. The original Joe no longer owns it, but it still is friendly. Wide-ranging menu features sandwiches, burgers ($3.40 w/ steak fries), salads (chef salad $4.50), good soups ($1.25/$1.75), wet burritos ($6). Video games. Breakfast served to 11. Pretty good food, reasonable prices (portions go up in off-season).

Lakeshore Inn. *(616) 326-5145. Corner of M-22 & Front in Empire.* 12 rooms on 2 floors. New. Advertises "reasonable rates." Here that means $58 from mid-June to mid-Sept, $48 in fall/spring, $35 in winter. Cable TV. Kitchenettes avail.
Convenient in-town location 3 blocks from beach; good winter rates

GLEN ARBOR AREA

Art's Tavern. *M-22 (Western Ave.) in central Glen Arbor, by Rich's Standard station.* (616) 334-3754. Same menu, same owners as Joe's, and same role as local gathering spot.

Leelanau Country Inn. *149 E. Harbor Hwy (M-22), 8 mi. s. of Leland (616) 228-5060. 7 days 5-9 (Thur-Sun off season).* Visa, MC, AmEx. Full bar, Leelanau Co. wines by glass. Reliably good, made-from-scratch food served in most attractive old country house. Fresh fish flown in daily. Some favorites on changing menu: apple-stuffed chicken w/ cherry glaze ($15.25), whitefish, seafood Alfredo, pork Wellington. Entrees from $10 (veg. stir-fry Cantonese) to $21 (rack of lamb). Price includes salad, vegetable, potato.

The Homestead Resort. *Off M-22 1 mi. n. of Glen Arbor toward Lake Michigan. (616) 334-5000. Five restaurants open during main season (mid-May thru mid-Oct) or ski season. All accept Visa, MC, Disc, personal checks; all with full bar.* OK food in what had been expensive restaurant. Maybe that's why new prices are radically less. The log lodge of the 1920s boys' camp that forms the core of the resort, now known as **The Inn** fine-dining restaurant, is worth a visit for the setting, an elegant version of old wicker and rag rugs. **The Inn** open nightly 6-9 mid June-Labor Day, weekends only from May-mid June & Sept-mid Oct. From $15.50 (pine nut-crusted chicken breast) and $16 (whitefish) to $20. Entrees include salad, vegetable, starch & popovers. Sunset view of Lake Michigan. Its family-dining adjunct, **The Balcony** (dinners $7-$12) , is open nightly throughout the season. The casual **Club Cafe** on the beach of Lake Michigan is open the full season for breakfast ($4.50-$5) and lunch ($4.50 for garden pizza-$8.75 grilled seafood pasta).

The Homestead. *See above. Call (616) 334-5000.* Ski resort of condos, homes on beautiful wooded dunes overlooking Lake Michigan. Built around old camp and private school. Developing hillcrests and wetlands has created a storm of controversies. (Some environmentalists wouldn't want to spend a penny here.) But everyone agrees that the developer did a beautiful job of fitting buildings into a gorgeous natural environment. *Posh resort in prime natural setting*

Sugar Loaf Resort. *(616) 228-5461. Entrance off M-22 s. of Little Traverse Lake, 9 mi. e. of Glen Arbor. From Traverse City, take M-72 w., turn at Co. Rd. 651 at sign.* 150 hotel rooms ($69-$89), 130 condos ($130-$180 1 BR; $145-$230 2 BR, 2-day min.). Rates vary w/ season, weekday or weekend. Ski & golf resort. Spring , fall hotel specials $59. Game room, horseshoes, badminton, volleyball, croquet, tennis. 18 holes championship golf. X-c & downhill skiing. Pizzeria, deli, pub, fine

dining, live entertainment in summer & winter weekends. New tennis & children's programs in summer. *Huge ski & golf resort, 2 mi. from National Lakeshore*

LAKE LEELANAU

Fountain Point. *(616) 256-9800. Off County Rd. 641 on east side of Lake Leelanau. From M-204 just e. of the town of Lake Leelanau, go s. about 1 mi. on 641.* 7 rooms in 1889 frame summer hotel. Open Mem. Day thru color season. $75 w/ lake view, $65; less in fall. Victorian resort w/ big, open lawn, view of distant hills. In same family since 1936. Newly renovated, still very plain & authentic. Ping-pong, billiards, tennis, volleyball, shufflebaord. Mystery library. Big common area, porch on hotel. Canoes. Sandy each. 17 housekeeping cottages w/ heat, bath: $350 + up. Off-season rates after Labor Day. Yarn Basket store sells natural-fiber yarns. *Simple Victorian summer hotel on Lake Leelanau*

LELAND

The Bluebird. *102 River, just e. of Main St. on n. side of river. (616) 256-9081. Open daily in summer, dining room 11:30-3 & 5-10, bar continuously. Off-season: dining room open weekends, dinner only; bar open at 4 Wed-Thurs, noon Fri-Sun. Visa, MC.* Full bar, good selection Michigan wines. Famous for whitefish ($12 at dinner). Big, casual place looks out onto Leland River. Lunch from $3 sandwiches to $6 fish platters. Dinners ($11-$15) inc/ soup or salad bar, vegetable or potato, homemade French bread, celebrated cinnamon rolls.

Leland Lodge. *(616) 256-9848. 565 Pearl.* 18 rooms on 2 floors. June-Labor Day: $95-$135. Off-season weekends: $80-$105. Off-season weekdays: $70-$95. Efficiencies. avail. Cable TV, cont. breakfast. Game room. 18-hole

golf privileges. Restaurant, bar.
*Away from the crush in Leland, but
walking distance to harbor, beach*

NORTHPORT

Fischer's Happy Hour Tavern.
*M-22, midway between Leland &
Northport at the foot of Gills Pier Rd*
(616) 386-9923. *7 days 11-9 (in summer
to 11). Closed major holidays. No
credit cards. Full bar.* Friendly, simple
old tavern, in same family for 50
years, in converted farm house. A favorite local gathering spot; good destination for scenic drive/bike ride.
Burgers ($3 for 1/3 lb.), homemade
soups ($1.50/$2) steal the show. Roast
chicken dinner $7. For dessert, Saun-
ders hot fudge, ice cream, housemade
cream puffs ($3.25).

Stubb's. *115 Waukazoo (M-22), down-
town. (616) 386-7611. Open year-
round. Daily 11-7. No credit cards. Full
bar.* Arty yet unpretentious. A bar, a
local art gallery, a pool hall, a neighborhood cafe patronized by farmers,
artists. Good homemade food with
flair. Pizza ($7.50/14" + 90¢/ item).
Mainly soup & sandwich menu
($1.50/$2.25 for soup, burgers $3,
sandwiches to $5. Dinners (w. salad,
garlic toast, potato) from $ (lasagna,
BBQ half-chicken) to $12 (rainbow
trout stuffed w/seafood). Daily specials. Pies $1.75.

Old Mill Pond Inn. *(616) 386-7341.
202 W. Third , 2 blocks w. of downtown, 3 1/2 blocks from lake.* 5 rooms
on 3 floors share 2 1/2 baths. Mem.
Day-Oct: $60-$75. Off-season $65, or
$50/night for 2 or more nights. Full
breakfast. 1895 summer cottage w/ TV
on large screen porch, wicker; knotty
pine inside. Deck overlooks rose garden. Wandering peacocks, ducks.
Guests use LR, DR, KIT. "Eclectic eccentric" decor of antiques, owners' many
collections. Artists come to sketch,
paint this unique setting.
*Fascinating, picturesque B&B over-
looks beautiful mill pond, park*

Sunrise Landing Motel &
Resort. *(616) 386-5010 or (616)
386-7195. 6530 N. Manitou Trail s. of
Northport.* Motel units in secluded
area on bay. July & Aug. $56-$64/day,
or kitchenettes $420/week. Fall: $46-
$51, $55 for cottages. Separated by
woods from hwy. Sandy beach.
Pretty place on beach in woods

SUTTONS BAY

Sutton's Bay-kery. *318 St. Joseph
(downtown's main street). (616)
271-6540. Tues-Sun 6-6.* Sandwiches
$2.25, breads $1.50-$1.75, pastries .75-
$1 and pies.Uniquely casual setting
with old sofa, mis-matched chairs.
Popular local gathering spot.

Hattie's. *111 St. Joseph downtown.
(616) 271-6222. In season open daily
5:30-as late as 1. Nov-Apr 5:30-8 or 9.
Visa, MC, Disc. Full bar,* extensive
wine list. Critics call it upscale American regional; people here call it "just
good food." Known for pecan-stuffed
pheasant breast w/shiitake mushroom cream sauce ($17.50). Entrees
served w/ house salad, vegetable. Menu
changes monthly, includes fish, vegetarian entree like lasagna (shiitake
mushrooms, spinach, ricotta, house-
made pasta; $14.50). Desserts from in-
house pastry chef $3.50-$4.50.

Open Windows B&B. *(616)
271-4300. 613 St. Mary's just s. of 204.*
3 rooms share 2 baths. Delightful
innkeeper sisters, neat old house w/
view of bay, antiques, wicker on porch,
lost of roses. Guests use living, dining
areas. Comfortable. Near town.
*B&B has cleverly homey, going-to-
grandma's effect without being cute.*

Red Lion Motor Lodge. *(616)
271-6694. M-22 at Fort Rd. s. of Suttons Bay.* 16 rooms, 1 floor. June-Sept:
$55-$80. Otherwise $35-$65. Cont.
breakfast. Phone in office. Away from
road. Pleasant rooms some have bay
view. Beach across street.
Good location, beach, moderate rates

TRAVERSE CITY

🍴

Sleder's Family Tavern. *717 N. Randolph. 1 block off M-37 S. (Division) just s. of U.S. 31. West of downtown.* (616) 947-9213. *Mon-Sat 10-midnight, Sun noon-10.* MC, Visa. Full bar. Tin ceiling, Victorian back bar in Mich.'s oldest continuously operating saloon. Family atmosphere. Light menu all day: bean soup, chili ($2.25), salads $2.25-$5, sandwiches & burgers. Wet burritos (beef, chicken) $4.50. Dinners come w/ starch, salad: smelt or fish & chips $6, chicken $7, BBQ ribs or 8 oz. sizzler $8. $2 kids' menu.

Dill's Olde Town Saloon. *423 S. Union, 3 blocks s. of Front downtown.* (616) 947-7534. *In season open daily 11:30 a.m.-midnight. Otherwise closed Sun.* AmEx, Visa, MC, Disc. Full bar. 100-year-old restaurant is popular local gathering spot. Known for slow-roasted BBQ ribs, marinated in apple juice) w/ regular or cherry BBQ sauce $9.25-$12.25. Entrees w/house salad, roll, vegetable, starch. Deep fried dill pickles another specialty. $6 salad bar. 6 different burgers w/ fries or baked potato $5.25-$9. Golden Garter Revue & dinner by reservation: 3 shows /night, 6 nights in season, weekends off season. Off-season: good music almost nightly.

Oryana Food Co-operative. *601 Randolph at Maple, 1 block s.e. of intersection of U.S.31/37 & M-72 w. of downtown.* (616) 947-0191. Take-out only. Very good salads, sandwiches, fresh breads, trail mixes, produce for picnics on the bay, drives out Leelanau Peninsula. Co-op is the social center for the many health-conscious urban refugees in Grand Traverse area.

The Victoriana. *(616) 929-1009. 622 Washington east of downtown.* Romantically decorated big 1898 house w/ elaborate arch. detail, front porch, gazebo, in beautiful, quiet historic area. 4 rooms w/ baths. May-Oct $55-$70, winter $50-60. A/C. TV in library. 2 parlors. Full breakfast.

In-town B&B in lovely historic area

Park Place Hotel. (616) 946-5000. *300 E. State at Boardman, downtown.* 140 rooms on 9 floors. June-color season: $95-$120 (for concierge floor). Winter: $60-$90. Recently purchased by Rotary and remodeled.Good views of bay, Boardman Lake from upper floors. Cable TV. Indoor pool. Health club. Saunas. 10th floor restaurant. Piano bar. Casual restaurant. Game room. 2 blocks from beach. *Splendid views from 10-story Art Deco hotel in center of town*

Bay Shore Motel. (616) 946-4798. *833 E. Front just e. of Sunset Park.* 30 rooms on 1 floor. July & Aug. $55-$85. Otherwise $28-$58. Older motel & cottages extend back from road to secluded sandy beach on West Arm of bay. Least expensive units have no phone, no A/C. "Another day in paradise," advertise German owners gung-ho on Michigan. Lots of neat touches: Eurobath, coffeepot in room, desk, basketball, picnic grills, rent a rowboat. Clean, tasteful, not fancy. Next to city park w/ tennis, shuffleboard. Walk downtown. Cabins by the week: $150-$350, or $400-$600 in-season. *Terrific little in-town resort w/beach stands out on intense motel strip*

OLD MISSION PENINSULA

🍴

Kelly's Road House Cafe. *14091 Center Rd. (M-37) 11 mi. out on Old Mission peninsula.* (616) 223-7200. *Open year-round Mon-Thurs 11:30-10, Fri-Sat 'til 11, Sun noon-10.* Visa, MC. Full bar with wine list. Family bar w/ beamed ceiling, rustic feel. Panoramic view of both bays. Known for cherrywood smoked ribs ($11), fish, chicken dishes like chicken tarragon w/ spinach fettucini ($9), grilled marinated chicken breast ($7). Entrees come w/ starch, salad. Same menu all day. Sandwiches $4-$6.

Old Mission Tavern. *17015 Center, 14 mi. up Old Mission peninsula.* (616) 223-7280. *May-color season: 7 days 11:30-9:30. Winter Thurs-Sun.*

Visa, MC. Full bar. Cafe and art gallery with works by area artists and craftspeople. Charming setting, touches of gourmet elegance. Lunch can be $3.50 "meal in a bowl" soup to $7 seafood pasta w/ slaw & roll. Dinners from $7 char-broiled sizzler to $13 grilled trout, $15 steak & lobster. Seafood pasta, stuffed fish, chicken breast artichoke are popular. On Thurs: pierogis, kraut cabbage w/spare ribs, polish sausage. Other ethnic specials. Owner/sculptor, Verna Bartnick, has opened art gallery next door.

Bower's Harbor Inn. *13512 Peninsula Dr., 10 mi. out on w. side of Old Mission peninsula just s. of Bowers Harbor. (616) 223-4222. May-Oct: open daily 5-10, to 11 Fri & Sat, Sun breakfast. Closed Sun & Mon Nov-Apr. AmEx, MC, Visa, Disc. Full bar.* A grand neoclassical summer house, 1920s vintage, looks out onto bay, sunset beneath sensuous big trees. Known for fish-in-a-bag ($18). Entrees (w/ salad, vegetable, potato, sorbet) range from chicken ($15) to grilled scallops w/ basil pesto & linguine $20, grilled veal chop $22. Fresh catch daily. Competent food from Grand Rapids chain. More casual dining in coachhouse (no view), **The Bowery**: burgers $5.50, BBQ ribs $13, half $10. (w/ slaw, fries).

Neahtawanta Inn. *(616) 223-7315. On Neahtawanta Rd. (extends west around Bowers Harbor from Peninsula Dr.* 4 rooms share bath ($45-$60) , 2 BR suite w/ bath, own deck ($105-$130). Circa 1900 summer hotel now an inn & center for peace research. Healthy cont. breakfast. Very informal — the common rooms could be called cluttered — w/ books, literature, tapes, etc. Clean.Wonderful spot at foot of heavily wooded hill, on 32-' beach. Sauna. *Peace & quiet, big beach at B&B/ peace research center on wooded point*

ACME

Embers on the Bay. *5055 U.S. 31 in Acme, 6 mi. e. of downtown Traverse. (616) 938-1300. Dinner only,*

Reservations rec. in season. Sun-Thurs 5-10, Fri-Sat 5-11. Sun brunch 10-2. (Closes at 9 off-season.) MC, Visa, Diners, Disc, AmEx. Full bar. Casual dining overlooking bay from the competent Mt. Pleasant Embers people who devised peas-and-peanut salad, one-pound pork chop (interestingly marinated & stuffed, $16). Dinners include: soup & salad bar w/ fresh pecan rolls, potato. Entrees fro $11 (four-cheese pasta) to $18 (filet mignon). Early diner discount Sun-Thurs 5-6.

Trillium. *U.S. 31 at M-72 in Acme. On 16th floor of Grand Traverse Resort Village Hotel (lounge on 17th floor). (616) 938-2100, (800) 748-0303. 7 days 11:30-3 and 6-10. AmEx, CitiBank, Diners, MC, Visa. Full bar.* Fine dining where the view's the thing — Grand Traverse Bay's East Arm. Veal medallions ($20) a specialty. Dinners (inc. salad, starch) from $15 (baked whitefish). Lunch sandwiches, entrees largely $6-$7. Sun brunch from 9:30-2 $14. Entertainment and dancing.

Days Inn. *(616) 941-0208. 420 Munson /U.S. 31 2 mi. e. of downtown Traverse City .* 183 rooms on 2 floors. Mem. Day thru mid-Oct: $80 weekends. Off-season: $48 weekends. Suites, spas to $90. Cont. breakfast. Cable TV. Indoor pool, whirlpool, playground, restaurant adj. *One of Michigan's largest indoor spas*

Grand Traverse Resort. *(616) 938-2100. On U.S. 31/M-72 intersection n. of Traverse in Acme.* 684 rooms, suites, condos on 6-15 floors. May-Oct: $140-$195; condos $110-$275. Oct-Nov: $70-$90; condos $65-$230. Suites avail. Cable TV. 2 indoor pools, 2 outdoor pools, saunas, whirlpools, exercise room w/instr. 9 tennis courts (5 indoor), 3 racquetball cts, jogging path. 2 Championship 18 hole golf courses (inc. Jack Nicklaus', The Bear), fishing, x/c ski trials, ice skating, sleighs, toboggans. Children's program, playground. Ten restaurants, bars w/ entertainment. Mobil 4 Star; AAA, 4 Diamonds. *Home of famous The Bear golf course*

TORCH LAKE AREA

Spencer Creek Landing. *5166 Helena, in Alden at s.e. side of Torch Lake. From Traverse take M-72 east to Rapid city exit, go north to Alden. Right on Torch Lake. (616) 331-6147. Mon-Sat 5:30-9:30 (Tues-Sat in off-season). By reservation only. Visa, MC. Full bar and wine list.* Elegant, relaxed dining in old summer place w/ beautiful lake view. Menu based on fresh ingredients & local fish, changes weekly. Prices from $15 (rainbow trout) to $25 (beef tenderloin). Entrees inc. soup, salad, potatoes, & vegetable.

Tapawingo. *9502 Lake St., 1 mi. e. of Ellsworth on County Rd 48. (616) 588-7971. Dinner only, reservations preferred. July-Aug: daily 6-9. May-June, Sept-Oct: Tues-Sun 6-9. Rest of year Thurs-Sun. Visa, MC. Full bar w/ extensive wine list.* Fabulous food, fabulous setting in onetime summer house overlooking lake. Everything is perfect, from the gorgeous gardens in front. Diners fly in from many states. Harlan "Pete" Peterson, one of many ex-engineer chefs, has become a national culinary star w/ inspired regional cooking. Known for morel dishes. Menu changes frequently. Dinners (inc/ hors d'oeuvre, 1st course, salad, main course) range from $24 (whitefish w/almond & saffron) to $34 (veal forestiere fettucini,made w/ morel mushroom pasta, fresh morel sauce). Fresh fruit and chocolate desserts $5.

CHARLEVOIX AREA

Grey Gables Inn. *308 Belvedere Ave., 3 blocks. e. of U.S. 31, in Charlevoix. (616(547-9261. Open daily 5-11, bar to 2:30 a.m. (Closed Sun & Mon in off -season). MC, Visa. Full bar.* A period piece, from shortly after Scott Fitzgerald's time, w/ a similar preppy, old-money crowd from neighboring Belvedere Club. In a big old house. Clubby, not fancy. Could the wallpaper be 50 years old, or only 30? The food's

OK, the atmosphere's maybe unique. Known for stuffed pork chops $(14.50), whitefish ($13.50). Also lamb chops, prime rib ($14/$16.50), pasta primavera ($8). Early-bird specials before 6:30. Piano jazz at 9 p.m., Wed-Sun (summer).

Great Lakes Whitefish & Chips. *411 Bridge in downtown Charlevoix. (616) 547-4374. Open only Mem.-Labor Day daily 11-9. No credit cards.* No alcohol, but available from adjoining **Villager Pub.** Tremendously popular cafe/carryout. Local whitefish is the main item. Two pieces, w/ fries, slaw $5. When it's closed, the fish basket is available next door at the **Villager Pub** (larger menu, open year-round). 7 days, 11:30-2 a.m. (serves food 'til 9, Fri-Sat 'til 10). Behind the **Pub** is **Terry's Place**, *101 Antrim,* open 7 days in summer, Wed-Sun off-season. More complete dinner menu.

Weathervane Terrace Hotel. *(800) 552-0025, (616) 547-9955. 111 Pine River Lane on w. side of channel downtown.* Some rooms overlook channel or Lake Michigan. 68 rooms & suites on 3 floors. Summer: $85-$165. Late spring & early fall: $45-$95. Ski & fall color seasons: $35-$80. Packages available. Cable TV. Some w/ kitchenettes, living room w/fireplace, jacuzzi. Tower spa w/hot tub. Small outdoor pool, activity room. Stafford's Weathervane Restaurant across street. *Suites with water views in downtown Charlevoix*

Nanny's Motel. *(800)678-0912 (MI only), (616)547-2960. 219 Ferry on Lake Charlevoix, 2 mi. from downtown.* 13 rooms. Summer: $48-$108. Winter: $28. Restaurant, bar.. Cable TV. Next to park, beach, boat ramp. *Low price for Charlevoix, pretty location by lake beach*

Shoreline Motel & Cabins. *(616) 536-2680. 3474 S. M-66 on Lake Charlevoix,1 mi. n of East Jordan.* 10 units. Summer: $53-$63. Winter: $30-$40. Kitchen units & cabins avail. TV. Picnic area, playground, long dock

w/boat slips. Fishing, swimming.
*Trim older motel with beach, dock,
great lake view*

PETOSKEY

Perry Hotel. *Bay & Lewis in
Gaslight District, overlooks bay.* (616)
347-2516, (800) 456-1917. *Open 7 days
8 a.m.-9 p.m.* Visa, MC. Dining in an
elegantly restored old hotel with big
view of bay, from the competent
kitchens of Stafford Smith. Breakfast
($4-$7) includes Michigan cherry-
bread French toast. Lunch $5-$8, dinner $15-$20. Lighter menu in Noggin
Room Pub in basement. Breakfast,
lunch, cocktails on porch in fair
weather. Music on weekends.

The Galley in Gourmet's Port
O'Call. *309 E Lake St. in the Gaslight
District.* (616) 347-7767. Mon-Sat 11-3
(retail store open 10-5). Best pick for a
good, quick bite while shopping.
Mostly take-out (seat 15) Fresh soups,
salads, bread daily. Soup & 1/2 sandwich $3.25. Sandwiches (ham or
turkey salads, veggie, plus more) $3.20;
soups $1.60/$2.60. Salads $3 (pasta or
garden).Fresh-ground coffee 67¢/cup.

Mitchell Street Pub. *426 E.
Mitchell, e. side of downtown.* (616)
347-1801. Mon-Sat 11:30-11 (bar open
'til 2 a.m., closed Sun & holidays).
Visa, MC. Full bar. Family tavern
festooned with all manner of odd stuff;
the more you look, the more you see. A
favorite with locals. Same menu all
day. Daily lunch special (soup & sandwich $4.75). Special might be home-
made cream of potato soup, with open-
face sandwich of turkey & roast beef
w/melted Monterrey jack cheese.
Known for burgers (1/3 lb. $3.50, $4.75
w/fries or onion rings), grilled cheese
(3 cheeses on grilled french bread
w/onion & tomato, $4.25).

Andante. *321 Bay, 2 blocks n. of
Mitchell in Gaslight District.* (616)
348-3321. *Reservations appreciated. In
season open daily 5:30-10 Off season
Tues-Sat 6-9.* Visa, MC, AmEx. Full

bar. Eclectic, creative addition to upscale dining scene. Menu changes frequently. Dinner entrees (inc. salad,
bread) $22 (whitefish in potato &
parsnip crust w/wine sauce) to $31.
(beef tenderloin w/ grilled garlic pol-
enta). Known for desserts ($5) like
chocolate pudding cake w/ caramel/
cognac sauce, lemon curd in pecan
cookie baskets w/ strawberries.
In a pretty old house w/ great bay view.

Stafford's Perry Hotel. (800)
456-1917, (616) 347-4000. *Bay & Lewis,
downtown.* 80 rooms on 3 floors. $59-
$135 (rates vary w/seasons). Package
rates avail. Cable TV. Some rooms
w/balcony, bay view. Hot tub, exercise
equip. Restaurant. Dancing Sat. Pub
w/weekend entertainment.
*Lavishly decorated old hotel
in Petoskey's Gaslight District*

Econo Lodge. (800)748-0417, (616)
348-3324 *1858 U.S. 131 South. On busy
strip at s. edge of Petoskey.* 60 rooms
on 2 floors. $31.50 (1 double bed)-$60
suite. Cont. breakfast. Package rates
avail. TV. Hot tub, outdoor pool, exercise room. Adj. Victory Lanes
w/dining, game room, pool table,
bowling, sports bar.
*Good budget motel with pool,
activities, extras*

Budget Host Inn on the Hill.
(800) 325-3842, (616) 347-4193. *U.S.
131. Busy strip on outskirts of
Petoskey.* 32 rooms on 2 floors. Xmas
mid-March, July-Labor Day: $35-$80.
Off-season: $10-$15 less. Cable TV . 4
kitchenettes. Outdoor pool.
Best economy bet — with pool

Benson House B&B. (616)
347-1338. *618 E. Lake, 2 1/2 blocks to
Gaslight District.* 4 large rooms
w/baths in big Victorian house.$78-
$98. Full breakfast, early evening
snacks. Living room w/phone, TV.
Game room w/board games, puzzles.
Historic hillside neighborhood overlooking downtown and bay. Long,
pleasant porch.
*Attractive B&B in close-in Petoskey
historic neighborhood*

BAY VIEW

Terrace Inn. *216 Fairview, 3 blocks from bay. (616) 347-2410. Mid-June-mid-Oct: open daily 5-8. Jan-March open Thurs-Sat. Visa, MC. No alcohol.* Calm old summer hotel on Bay View's beautiful, leafy interior campus. Specialty is planked whitefish ringed w/ duchess potatoes ($15) — beautiful and delicious. For dessert, brownie bottom pie ($2.25). Dinners, inc. vegetable, starch, salad, roll, start at $10 chicken dishes. Food, setting are both way above average for area.

Stafford's Bay View Inn. *613 Woodland Ave., U.S. 31. 1 mi. north of Petoskey. (616) 347-2771. Visa, MC, AmEx. Non-alcoholic "wine list".* Victorian decor w/costumed staff in gussied-up old inn. Famous Sunday brunch (year round) is quite a feed for $14 — roast turkey, ham, tomato pudding, loads of tiny desserts. Dinner entrees (inc. salad) $15-$18.

Stafford's Bay View Inn. *(616) 347-2771. On busy U.S. 31 in historic Bay View summer colony.* 30 rooms w/private baths on 3 floors. $84 - $128. Package rates avail. Full breakfast in season, cont. breakfast off-season. Open: May 1-mid-Oct, also Xmas week, some winter weekends. No phone or TV in rooms. Restaurant customers seem to dominate inn at times. Large porch w/bay view. Suites w/fireplace, jacuzzi. Walk to small beach. *Famed Victorian inn with busy restaurant, lush decor*

Gingerbread House. *(616) 347-3538. 205 Bluff in Bay View just off U.S. 31.* 5 rooms w/baths. Open Mem. day-October. $50-$90. Cont. breakfast. Access to Bay View Assoc. beach & tennis courts. Open verandas & balconies afford private entry to each suite or room. *B&B in classic Bay View Victorian cottage*

Terrace Inn. *(616) 347-2410. 216*

Fairview, 3 blocks from bay. 44 rooms w/ baths on 3 floors. Open year-round Mid-June thru Oct. & Xmas week: $66-$91. Dec thru Mid-Mar.: $52-$74. Off-off-season: $42-$64. Packages avail. Cont. breakfast. Phone in lobby. Walk to beach, tennis, Sunfish sailing & lessons. Good restaurant & ice cream parlor. In continuous operation since opening in 1911. Large lobby w/ fireplace and tables for games. *Pleasant, somewhat spare inn on beautiful central lawn — most in the authentic Bay View spirit*

HARBOR SPRINGS

Stafford's Pier. *102 Bay St. at the harbor downtown.. (616) 526-6201. Open 7 days 11 a.m.-10 p.m. year-round. Visa, MC, AmEx. Full bar.* Spiffy nautical decor, big windows overlook harbor. Known for whitefish — broiled, baked in parchment, or char-grilled. Dinner entrees (w/ salad, starch) in dress-up Pointer Room from $16.50 (perch)-$22 (rack of lamb), $4-$6 less in casual Chart Room, where you can enjoy the same view for less money, esp. on light menu. Perchwich, chicken oriental, spinach pie, all about $7. Also pheasant, salmon, shrimp jambalaya, smoked trout, charcoal-grilled steak. Cocktails at Wheelhouse lounge, Dudley's Deck.

The New York. *101 State St, downtown on waterfront. (616) 526-6285. Open daily year-round except closed all April. Mem.-Labor Day 8 a.m.-11 p.m. Otherwise 11-9, breakfast weekends & holidays. Visa, MC, AmEx. Full bar, over 125 wines.* "Northern Michigan Bistro" — i.e., eclectic cuisine in looser, less predictable setting. In old Leahys' New York Hotel (est. 1904). Specialties: whitefish chowder ($3.25), Midwest cassoulet (duck, sausage, pork &beans) $12). Breakfast from $3 (continental) to $6 (eggs benedict, omelets). Lunch: burgers $5-$5.50; soup of the day $2.50, French onion $4; seafood & pasta salad or whitefish sauteed w/white wine, capers, parsley $7. Sandwich menu also at dinner, or main course entrees w/salad and appropriate accompaniments, from $11 for roast pork loin stuffed w/rice & cherries or chicken tuscany.

The Harbor Springs Gourmet.
127 State, next to The New York — same owners, too. (616) 526-9607. Open year-round. Mid June-Labor Day :8-8, Sun 8-6. Off-season: Tues-Sat 10-6, Sun 10-4. Visa, MC. Beer & wine. Specialty food store w/gourmet take-out — pick up a picnic for the harbor-side park or Thorne-Swift Beach. Favorites: tarragon chicken salad ($8/lb.), marinated vegetable salad ($6/lb.), lemon chicken breast ($2.75 for a half), gazpacho ($2.50/ bowl). Desserts: mousse $3, cakes $12. Also, fresh fruit flan, tortes, carrot cake).

Juilleret's Family Restaurant.
130 State St. downtown near harbor. (616) 526-2821. Open May-Sept. Mid-June-Labor Day Mon-Fri 10-10, Sat-Sun 9-10. Otherwise Mon-Fri 11-9, Sat-Sun 10-9. Personal checks accepted. No alcohol. Vintage soda shoppe/ restaurant (since 1895, now in 4th generation) caters to kids of each succeeding generation to summer in Harbor Springs. Noise bounces off bare walls. Locally famous for homemade ice cream; said to have originated planked whitefish ($11.50), often featured in media as the best. Breakfast $1.80-$4.60. Lunch (available all day): sandwiches from $1.60 to $7.50 for whitefish or steak w/slaw & fries. Dinner: salad bar $4.50, plate dinners inc. dessert & beverage $7-$8. Full dinner w/soup, salad bar, dessert & beverage $8-$12.

The Arboretum.
7075 S. Lakeshore Dr. (M-119), 3 1/2 mi. nw. of Harbor Springs. (616) 526-6291. Closed April & Nov. May-Oct open daily 5-11. Dec-March Wed-Sat 5-11. Major credit cards. Full bar, extensive wine list. Fine dining in a forest of potted plants, overlooking lake. Elaborate presentations of planked local whitefish ($15), marinated baby rack of lamb ($20). Dinners, served w/appropriate starch & choice of salad, start at $8 for ground sirloin or seafood salad.

Harborside Inn.
(800) 678-9158; (616) 526-6238 E. Main, downtown. 24 suites on 3 floors sleep 4. Mid-June-Labor Day & Xmas week: $130-$155 weekends. Ski season, late spring & fall color: $85-$99 weekends. Off-season weekends: $55-$65. Midweek $10-$30 off. Full kitchen, bar, gas fireplace, TV, phones, whirlpool, shower. Rooftop deck w/ bay view, gas grills, sunning area. Big late 80's intrusion in classic downtown. Infuriated locals.
In-town luxury suites, bay view

Main Street Bed & Breakfast.
(616) 526-7782. 403 E. Main . 4 rooms w/baths. Mem. Day-mid Oct: $70 & $85. Winter: $60 & $70. Gathering room w/TV, VCR, phone. Full breakfast. Nice enclosed porch w/bay view. Pleasant decor.
Homey B&B close to downtown

Harbor Springs Motor Inn.
(616) 526-5431. 145 Zoll St. at Pennsylvania. 20 rooms on 1 floor. In-season (June 21-Sept. 2 & ski season) $65-$75, w/ kitchens $85. Off-season $45-$65. Suite avail. Immaculately maintained. Pretty, large rooms w/ antiques. No phones in room. Nice lobby w/ public phone, nice lawn. Muffins, coffee in season. Bikes, grills, lawn chairs for guests. 1/2 block from Zoll St. Park.
Charming motel, convenient location near beach, downtown, Wequetonsing

CROSS VILLAGE

Legs Inn. See p. 415.

MACKINAW CITY

Darrow's Family Restaurant.
303 Louvigny, s.w. of bridge. Take exit 339. It's 2 blocks s. of the restored fort., 1 block n. of Central. Open early May-end of Oct. Opens at 8 every day, closes at 8 in May, Sept & Oct; at 9 in June, at 10 in July & Aug.. Real home cooking by people who care — the waitresses fix their favorite dishes, some veggies are

from owners' gardens. Knowing about this tucked-away, pleasant, spiffy new spot means you can avoid bad food, crowds, and high prices in town. Homemade soups (w/ homemade noodles) $1.25/$1.55. Good burgers ($2.25). Everything we had was good: stuffed pepper w/ mashed potatoes $4.50), hot turkey & pork sandwich ($5), chef salad ($4.50). Homemade pie $1.60/slice. A dinner treat: fresh whitefish, soup or juice, veg., potato, homemade bread ($9).

Riviera. *(616) 436-5577. 520 N. Huron on the beach.* 24 rooms on 2 floors. Open May-Oct. May $35-$50, June & Sept $40-$55. July-Aug $70-$125. Cable TV, phone in office, portables avail. Outdoor pool. All but 1 room have view of bridge or lake & island, 2 end rooms have panoramic island view. Parks on either side. Well maintained, big rooms.
Choice site by bridge, park

Welcome Inn. *(616) 436-5525. 111 Langlade, across from bakery.* Cable TV, phone in office. Mem. Day-mid Oct $40-$50 (7/4 & Labor Day weekends higher). May & end of Oct $25. Right downtown, close to park, lake, behind old house. Spectacular flower garden.
Neat, homey place in old part of town

Rainbow Motel. *(616) 436-5518, (800) 888-6077. 602 S. Huron Ave., across from Mackinac Island ferries.* 29 rooms on 1 floor. May, June, Sept $26-$42. July-Aug $42-$66. Cable TV, phones. Indoor pool, whirlpool, jacuzzi rooms. Picnic tables, grills, basketball, putting green, playground. Walking distance to town, restaurant 3 doors down.
One of many older facilities w/ big enclosed pool room, many extras

North Star Motel. *(616) 436-5565. 1001 S. Huron, about 1 mi. s. of Center on Lake Huron.* 33 rooms on 1 floor. Open May-3rd week in Oct. Summer (end of June-Labor Day): $55 (1 bed), $66(2 beds), $84 (2 room suite). Spring & fall: $31/$35\$50. Cable TV, free HBO. Deep, large indoor pool. Other good-

value older motels in same beachfront location: Beachcomber (436-8451); Chippewa (436-8661); Mohawk (436-5527).
Own beach, picnic area, indoor pool, view of Mackinac Island, bridge

MACKINAC ISLAND

Eating well on Mackinac Island can be a problem, especially if you're on a budget. In the main summer season, the downtown is packed, and many businesses sell mediocre food at high prices. (Many people prefer to visit the island in spring and fall. Lilac time, ending with a festival the 2nd week in June, is lovely.) In spring and fall, however, most restaurants are closed.

We recommend either choosing a beautiful setting and being willing to pay more, or having a **picnic lunch** in the park below the fort, by the boardwalk below Grand Hotel, on a bike ride, or at some other nice spot. There's a good bakery in Mackinaw City by McDonald's that makes pasties, and a fish market near the docks. On the island, **Doud's Grocery** on Main Street at Fort has $2 sandwiches and deli items. The island's only grocery, it stocks food for everyone from wealthy cottagers to summer help.

Here are some helpful tips. **Grand Hotel** restaurants are always good. Call (906) 847-3331 or ask for a map & brochure of hotel restaurants at main desk. Memorable meals for under $10 may be enjoyed in several hotel lunch spots: outside the main dining room, at the golf course, by the pool, on the lower, garden level (though this is a lot like lunching at a mall). The main dining room at lunch is a buffet used largely by tour groups. Non-guests may enjoy the hotel's sumptuous regular meals — breakfast ($9.50), dinner ($40) plus 18% automatic tip.

Grand Hotel also provides lunch at **Fort Mackinacc**—delicious, hearty soups and bread (about $4) and sandwiches. Terrace nice in good weather, and the walls (about 2 feet thick) are memorable. (Ticket to fort required.)

Insiders recommend taking the earliest possible ferry and enjoying a leisurely breakfast ($5 average) at the

Harbor View in the **Chippewa Hotel**, overlooking the harbor. It's on Main across from Fort, near the yacht dock and state park visitor center. Moderate prices and the view make it a good pick any time.

The **Village Inn** on Hoban Street up from Shepler's dock specializes in reliable good whitefish, served in chowder, smoked, and cooked 3 ways. Dinners typically $15 or less. (Also open at lunch.) Opens earlier, stays open later than many island spots.

For real local color, decent inexpensive burgers, ordinary bar food, try the smoke-filled **Mustang Lounge** on Astor, across from the Arnold docks. Year-round islanders hang out here; after the season is over, they move the pool table back in. Open all winter.

Grand Hotel. *(906) 847-3331; Nov-April call (517) 487-1800.* 317 rooms on 6 floors. $157-$266 per person includes huge full breakfast, dinner, food at tea & cocktail time, mandatory 18% gratuity charge, baggage fee. Luxury rooms themed w/ unusual antiques (Example: T. Roosevelt room w/ horn chair, mounted hunting trophies). NO TIPPING. Food is excellent. No TV except some rentals. Phones. Guests use outdoor pool, whirlpool, sauna, horseshoes, bocce, croquet, volleyball, playground, jogging/exercise trail. Dance bands, floor shows. Fee charged for movies, 9 hole golf, tennis, bikes. Dance music, nightly floor shows during peak season in nightclub. Strict dress code after 6 p.m. Reduced fee packages (include taxes, tip, baggage): spring & fall weekends, Labor Day jazz fest $829/couple, 3 or 4 nights. Special package for AAA members. Summer package July 5-10. 4-night tennis clinic, $1,349/couple.Tour groups take over many public spaces in mid-day. Thin walls. Excellent service.
Remarkable survival of grand Victorian summer resorts

Hotel Iroquois. *(906) 847-3321, (906) 847-6511. At w. end of Main where boardwalk begins.* 47 rooms on 4 floors. Open May-Oct. Early June-Labor Day $98-$216, suites $275-$295. Off-season $62-$170, suites $260-$275. No TV, phone avail. On the beach. Restaurant & bar. Old & new, completely renovated. On swimming beach.
Posh, updated Victorian w/ best waterfront location

Windermere. *(906) 847-3301, 847-3491. West end of Main St., overlooks Straits of Mackinac, close to downtown, Grand Hotel.* 26 rooms w/ baths on 3 floors. Open mid May-mid Oct. Mid June-mid Sept $100-$140. Spring & fall (Sun-Thurs) packages $70-$85. Phone, coffee, donuts, TV in large lobby (several TVs for rent). Big porch. Beach, picnic area across street. Owned by Doud family since 1904.
Best combination of location, true old summer hotel atmosphere

Pontiac Lodge. *(906) 847-3364. Across from Shepler's Ferry, next to Village Inn restaurant. Open all year.* 10 rooms w/ baths on 2nd, 3rd floor. Summer $75-$95, Oct-Spring $50-$65. Continental breakfast. TV, phones, kitchenettes. Some A/C. Restaurant next door open winter weekends.Where business travelers stay.
One of island's best deals; over village stores, own kitchen, nice new rooms

Cloghaun. *(906) 847-3885, off season (313) 885-4547. On Market St.* 7 rooms on 2 floors. 4 w/private baths $75, shared bath $50. Washbasins in all rooms. 1860s house. Owned by descendant of original builder, Irish fisherman/merchant. Not newly decorated; full of antiques that have always been there. Fans, TV & VCR in library, phone avail. Large front porch w/wicker furniture, library, parlor. Large side yard w/flowers & 100 yr old trees.
Peaceful, attractive, affordable inn from earlier tourism era

Metivier Inn. *(906) 847-6234, winter (616) 627-2055. On Market St. 1 block up from Main.* 21 rooms w/ baths on 3 floors. Open May-Oct. July-mid August $115-$165, off-season $88-$145. Cont. breakfast, fans, phone avail. 1 suite w/full kitchen $200. Pretty, large front porch on quieter Market St., 2 dining

areas.
Beautiful B&B w/ lovely porch, yard

Haan's 1830 Inn. *(906) 847-6244.*
*On Huron St. east of the harbor and
adjacent to the gardens of Ste. Anne's
Church.* 7 rooms on 2 floors. Open late
May-mid Oct. $80-$105. Private &
shared baths. Cont. breakfast. Parlor
& dining rooms, 3 porches (1 screened).
*Attractive B&B in pretty residential
area east of retail district*

Mission Point Resort. *(906) 847-
3312, (800) 833-5583. 6-8 blocks e. of
downtown.* 245 rooms ($130-$250) &
suites ($170-$270). TV (cable soon),
fans, phones. Outdoor pool, hot tub,
game & pool room, exercise center,
tennis courts, bike rental. Activities
for adults and children: morning walk,
2 bike tours, volleyball, horseshoes,
storytelling, "kids club."3 restaurants,
bar, entertainment 6 nights a week.
Package weekends from $259-$598/
couple inc. tip, tax, cont. breakfast,
sometimes kids free. At east edge of
intensely developed stretch of island
(quieter than most spots). Built as
conference facility in 1950s by Moral
Rearmament, which started "Up with
People" shows. Unusual contemp./
historic architecture: "old" stone
theater w/ trusses, 16-sided beamed
teepee hall. *Resort w/ tennis, lots to do,
away from crowds, closer to nature*

ROGERS CITY

The Buoy. *530 W. Third overlooking
Lake Huron. (517) 734-4747. Open daily
year-round.* Mid-June-Oct: Mon-Sat
11-10, Sun 9-10. Off-season closes at 9.
Visa, MC, AmEx, Diners. Full bar. Nautical theme w/ big lake view. Some
people dress up. Known for whitefish
($13 at dinner w/ potato, veg., salad; $7
at lunch), prime rib. Daily lunch specials $4-$5. Burgers.

Kortman's. *N. Bradley Hwy. on n.
side of town (see map). (517) 734-3512.
Mon-Fri 6 a.m.-9 p.m., Sat & Sun 6:30-
9. Closes at 8 in off-season. No credit
cards, checks. No alcohol.* Unpreten-

tious diner is popular local hangout.
Outstanding smoked pork loin from
famous Plath's. At dinner it's $6 w/
potato, salad.

Rogers City Motel. *(517) 734-3707.
220 N. Bradley (US. 23).* 12 rooms on 1
floor. June-Nov $31-$34, lower in winter. Cable TV. Fish freezers, boat parking. No phones.
*Good budget choice,
especially for fishermen*

Driftwood Motel. *(517) 734-4777.
540 W. Third, 2 blocks n.w. of town.* 43
rooms on 2 floors. Summer $50-$55.
Fall $45-$50. Winter $44. Cable TV.
Swimming beach, basketball, play &
picnic area. Restaurant. Each room
has own balcony, view of Lake Huron.
*Wonderful place — reasonable, on
beach, good restaurant, play area*

ALPENA

Thunderbird Inn. *1100 State St.
(the in-town extension of U.S. 23) s. of
downtown. (517) 354-8900.* Mon-Sat
11-9 (closed 2-4:30). Visa, MC. Full bar.
The spot in Alpena for destination dining. Big view of Lake Huron. Known for
whitefish ($11 at dinner w/ potato,
salad). Dinners from $8 ·baked cod) to
$15 (NY strip), $20 (2 lobster tails). All-
day light menu, kids' portions. For
budget meals, the **Bird's Nest** (no view)
adjoins. Same menu all day. Soup +
1/2 sandwich $1.79, sizzler steak w/
potato or salad $4.59.

Hunan. *1120 State in front of park by
beach. (517) 356-6461.* Mon-Thurs
11:30-9:30, Fri & Sat to 10:30, Sun 12-
8:30. Visa, MC. Full bar. Excellent
Chinese food, especially at dinner —
surprising in an isolated industrial
place like Alpena. Seafood soup for 2
($3.75) is a big favorite. Dinner dishes
(w. rice) $7-$8 (chicken, beef & pork),
$9-$12 (seafood). Lunch special under
$5 from 11:30-3 p.m. includes soup,
fried rice, crabmeat, beef or shrimp
Rangoon.

Dew Drop Inn. *(517) 356-4414. 2469 French Rd., 1 mi. n. of hospital on U.S. 23.* 14 units on 1 floor. Summer $36-$40, off-season $32-$36. Cable TV. *Good budget choice with picnic area, horseshoes*

Holiday Inn.*(517) 356-2151. 1000 U.S. 23, at northern city limits.* 148 rooms on 2 floors. Open all year. $57-$95. Cable TV. Whirlpool, sauna, putting green, indoor recreation area, game room. Restaurant, bar, live entertainment 7 nights.
Holidome w/ indoor pool, lots to do

GRAYLING

North Country Lodge. *(517) 348-8471. On north I-75 bus. loop off I-75 exit 254.* 24 units. Newer units are on 2 floors. $38-$48. Suites: $80 & $125. Cable TV. Kitchenettes avail. Horseshoes, picnic area. Newly remodeled restaurant adj. Artist-owner has decorated rooms w/her attractive artwork. Near AuSable & Manistee rivers, Hartwick Pines.
Big price range; pleasant, convenient spot

GAYLORD

Sugar Bowl.*216 W. Main Street on M-32 5 blocks e. of I-75.* *(517) 732-5524.* 7 a.m.-11 p.m., Sun to 10 p.m. Visa, MC, AmEx, Disc. Full bar. Big place serving satisfying food began in 1919 as Greek soda shop. Alpine decor (obligatory in Gaylord) . Known for fresh whitefish (around $13.50), Greek specialties on big $8 hot & cold salad bar (in dining room at dinner), fresh raspberry pie in season. Lunch plates (w/ soup or salad and potato) $7 and under, dinners & sandwiches all day in family room, $3.25 to $8, in dining room $8 and up.

Busia's 'A Polish Kitchen.' *Old U.S. 27 S at I-75, exit 279. (517)   732-*

2790. *Mon-Fri 9-9, Sat & Sun 8-9. Visa, MC, AmEx. Full bar.* You can get steak and seafood, but hearty Polish fare is what's special here: czarnina (duck's blood soup), pierogi, potato pancakes, homemade kielbasa, stuffed cabbage. Big sampler plate is $8 at lunch, $10 at dinner; most things are $2 or $3 less. 3 homemade desserts ($2-$3) daily: bread pudding, cobblers, peanut butter pie. Sun breakfast buffet $5, dinner buffet $9. Kids' & seniors' menus.

CADILLAC

Maggie's. *523 N. Mitchell. (616) 775-1810. Visa, MC. Full bar.* Turn-of-century tavern popular w/ local families. Known for subs and burgers on homemade buns: $2.50 for 1/3 lb. burger, $3.25 for 1/2 lb. Original sub $4, "Belly buster" $5. Chili and soup $1.50 cup (Texas chili $2.50). Mexican plate w/ rice, beans lunch $3.75, dinner $5. Also fried cod, shrimp, chicken.

Hermann's European Cafe. *214 N. Mitchell downtown. (616) 775-9563.* Mon-Sat 11 a.m.-10 a.m. *(Winter Mon-Thurs 11-9, Fri-Sat to 10 p.m. MC, Visa. Full bar, extensive wine list.* Known for paper-thin wiener schnitzel ($16 at dinner), apple strudel. Regular menu all day and added 3 lunch special, 3 dinner specials. Dinner entrees (w/ salad, starch, vegetable) from $14.50 (pasta chicken piccata) to $17 (pepper steak). Many available in 1/2 size orders. Desserts change daily $2.50-$4. **Chef's deli** next door. Mon-Sat, 7 a.m.-6 p.m. 24' deli case, 16' bakery counter offer sandwiches, cheese, cold cuts, desserts.

Chapter 9
Upper Peninsula

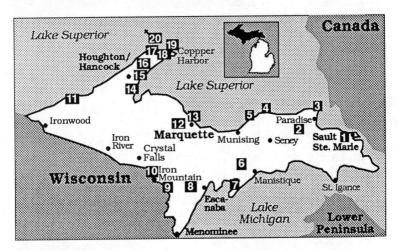

HIGHLIGHTS

Soo Locks

*A key link between the Great Lakes
gives a close-up view of giant freighters.*

Thirteen thousand vessels pass through these locks each year. About 5,000 are huge cargo carriers, some carrying as much as 70,000 tons. Viewing these mammoth boats is so popular that Portage Avenue, which parallels the St. Mary's River, is jammed with souvenir shops. It's a colorful strip, where everything from moccasins to fudge is sold.

The four locks allow the huge freighters to pass between Lake Superior and the rest of the Great Lakes. The principal cargo of the outgoing oceangoing vessels is grain from the American heartland, while Great Lakes freighters are most likely to be carrying iron ore.

The Corps of Engineers, which operates the locks, has built an elaborate **information center** (open 7 a.m.-11 p.m.), including a full-scale model of the locks along with other fancy displays. A sign on the wall tells which freighters are due the next two to three hours. An elevated viewing platform allows you to get a close-up, birds'-eye view of the big boats as they wait the few minutes it takes for a chamber to go 21 feet up to Superior level or 21 feet down to Huron level.

The **Soo Locks Boat Tour**, $10 a ticket, is worth the price. (For details, see end.) Get seats at the front of the boat if possible. The two-hour excursion takes you through the locks up to the level of Lake Superior and a rather surrealistic view of Canada's huge riverfront Algoma Steel Mill, with its 10,000 employees and five blast furnaces. On the wharf are enormous piles of purplish taconite iron pellets from Lake Superior's iron-mining regions. You also pass the quarter-mile-long Edison Sault Electric Company.

It's been a city landmark ever since it was built in 1902 with limestone excavated from the canal that powers it. The 76 water-powered turbines generate 26,000 kilowatts. Across the river, you see downtown Sault Ste. Marie, Canada, and its seaplane station for fighting forest fires. The planes swoop down onto lakes to fill their two water tanks while moving in just seven seconds. The tour boat also passes under the International Bridge to Canada, 2.8 miles long.

Take I-75 to Ashmun Street exit. Dates of opening and closing the locks each year vary with the weather. Usually they open in mid-March and close in mid-December. Corps of Engineers information center open 7 a.m.-11 p.m. daily. Boat tours are from May 15 to Oct 15. (906) 632-6301.

A FREIGHTER AND A MUSEUM . . . . . The **Museum Ship Valley Camp** is an old Great Lakes freighter whose large cargo holds have been converted into a Great Lakes theme museum. In one cavernous space an Edmund Fitzgerald display effectively captures the eeriness with which that huge freighter disappeared suddenly from the view of a trailing freighter. A torn half of one of its lifeboats, one of the few remnants of the wreck to surface, is displayed. Especially interesting is the Valley Camp's pilothouse, which contains one of the lakes' first radar systems. Also on view are the captain's quarters, the quarters of the other officers and crew, the mess hall and galley. *East of the Soo Locks on Water St. Mid-May to mid-Oct. (906) 632-3658. Adults $4.75, children 6-16 $2.75.*

ENTERTAINING AND INFORMATIVE . . . . . but bumpy, the **Soo Locks Tour Trains** take you through both the U.S. and Canadian Sault Ste. Marie. In the U.S. the conveyances are open trailers pulled by a mock-train truck; in Canada it's a double-decker bus. You learn a lot about both cities. The American city (population 15,000) was larger until the turn of the century, but now is dwarfed by its Canadian neighbor (population 82,000). The Canadian guide explains how that country's high taxes on cigarettes, alcohol, and gasoline help pay for the country's universal health insurance and how even a modest home here costs well over $100,000. The Canadian Soo is heavily Italian; Giovanni's is a good Italian restaurant.

Tahquamenon Falls

*Spectacular views of Michigan's
most majestic falls*

Most Michigan waterfalls are scenic but puny affairs compared with the mighty falls of the world. Michigan's one really substantial waterfall is the Upper Falls here at Tahquamenon. The falls are nearly 200 feet across, and as much as 50,000 gallons of water a second plunge 48 feet into a canyon below. The state park has constructed a platform that allows you to stand right at the lip of the fall, taking in the dramatic contrast between the serene meanderings of the Tahquamenon River and the roaring foam at the falls. The river is darkened by the many hemlock trees along its banks, giving the initial spill of water an interesting brownish hue. From this same viewing platform you see, far downstream, the once-again peaceful river as it flows between reddish cliffs another 10 miles towards Lake Superior's Whitefish Bay south of Paradise. Another trail

Lower Tahquamenon Falls, where some even like to swim.

leads to a less spectacular view of the falls from the lower river.

The Lower Falls, four miles downstream, is smaller but, in its own serene way, equally delightful. You can view the series of falls from a high bluff, but for just $1 a person you can rent a rowboat which takes you much closer. A path goes right up to the falls. When it's warm enough, visitors enjoy swimming in the cascading water.

The falls are in 35,000-acre Tahquamenon Falls State Park. Three highly recommended **wilderness trails**, from 3.7 to 13 miles long, enable hikers to get away from the crowds of sightseers at the falls. They pass by many habitats, including pine forests, sandy ridges, and boggy lakes typical of the eastern Upper Peninsula, and a **virgin beech-maple climax forest** some three centuries old. Avoid the swampy areas during black fly season, usually from late June through mid-July. There's a large **visitor center** at the park with a concession stand and gift shop, and four **campgrounds** with 259 modern campsites and 60 rustic sites.

On M-123, 15 miles west of Paradise. Open year-round. State park sticker required; $3/day, or $15/year. (906) 492-3415.

GOOD CANOEING NOT FAR FROM THE FALLS . . . . . The Tahquamenon River is the longest in the eastern U. P., and the 23 miles above the falls is gorgeous, wild country with few signs of man, reachable only by river in most places. But there's no canoe livery. On the nearby Two Hearted River (where Nick Adams fished in Hemingway's stories), **Two Hearted Canoe Trips** can arrange a wonderful, easy four- to six-hour family canoe trip ($20/canoe) to its campground and lodge at the mouth on Lake Superior, or two- and three-day trips for experienced canoeists. (906) 658-3357, or (906) 293-5533 in winter.

HIKE FROM MARQUETTE TO ST. IGNACE . . . . . , over 200 miles, along the completed sections of the **North Country Trail**. It goes from Marquette through the Pictured Rocks and Muskallonge State Park on Lake Superior and the Hiawatha National Forest, passing by the Lower Tahquamenon Falls along the way. For a big brochure, contact the National Parks/National Forest Service visitor center, (906) 387-3700; 400 E. Munising Ave., Munising, MI 49862. Eventually the trail will extend from the Appalachain Trail in New York State to North Dakota.

Great Lakes Shipwreck Historical Museum

*Overlooking treacherous Whitefish Point,
it dramatically illuminates hundreds
of Lake Superior sinkings.*

O n a point of land on Lake Superior's Whitefish Bay, this museum overlooks a patch of water called "the graveyard of the Great Lakes." Shipwrecks were common here because of the relatively congested sea-lanes, high seas from 200 miles of open water to the west, and poor visibility from fog, fires, and snow. Most wrecks are from the 19th century, when over 3,000 commercial vessels plied the lakes, compared with just 200 today. In an 80-mile stretch from Whitefish Point to Pictured Rocks, there have been over 300 shipwrecks, killing 320 sailors. The first to go under was the *Invincible*, a British schooner which went down in an 1816 gale; the last was the *Edmund Fitzgerald* in 1975.

One of the few things to surface from the wreck of the *Edmund Fitgerald* is this battered lifeboat, on display at the Museum Ship Valley Camp in Sault Ste. Marie (see p. 447). The *Fitzgerald* is but one of hundreds of shipwrecks in Whitefish Bay.

The view at the sandy point is beautiful. You can see the Canadian mainland, across water 600 feet deep. Along the beach are countless colored stones worn smooth by water. This was a stopping place for Indians, 17th-century French voyageurs, and Jesuit missionaries. A lighthouse has been in operation here since 1849.

The museum interior uses eerie, somber music and lights to convey the haunting world of underwater shipwrecks. Models of boats which have sunk in Superior are juxtaposed with items brought up form the depths, such as a ship's bell from the schooner *Niagara*, sunk in 1897, or a carved bird from the steamer *Vienna*, sunk in 1892. The centerpiece is a huge, gleaming lighthouse lens with 344 crystal prisms. An adjoining theater shows an entertaining 16-minute film on Great Lakes shipwrecks. *Take M-123 north to the end of Whitefish Rd. past Paradise. (906) 635-1742. Open Memorial Day-Oct. 15, daily 10-6. Adults $3, children $2, families $10.*

MICHIGAN'S BEST BIRDWATCHING FOR BIRDS OF PREY . . . . . is when the hawk migration peaks at **Whitefish Point** during late April and early May. Birds use the point poking out into Lake Superior to minimize flying over open water. Fifteen-to 25 thousand hawks have been counted in a season. Some 7,000 loons come a little later, with ducks and grebes, followed by songbirds through May and early June. The Michigan Audubon Society's **Whitefish Point Bird Observatory** is open next to the old Coast Guard Station from March through June, conducting reseach and banding. In late April and early May, bird-watchers book up area motels for miles around. Almost 300 species of birds in all have been counted here, including bald and golden eagles, merlin and peregrine falcons, and unusual arctic birds. *Call (616) 344-8648 for more information.*

Grand Marais

A tranquil, picturesque refuge on Lake Superior

The quaint little village of Grand Marais sits in splendid isolation on an unusually well protected Lake Superior harbor. West Bay offered such good protection to 17th-century French explorers that they gave it the name "marais," which means "harbor of refuge." The town sits up from the bay, giving most locations a splendid view of the water. This far north, the sun doesn't set until after 10 p.m. in June, and the beautiful afterglow on the lake can last until 11.

Most of Grand Marais' present buildings date from its boom years between 1860 and 1910, when it was an active fishing and lumber port full of saloons and lumber mills. It then lay nearly dormant for over half a century until revived by resorters and tourists attracted to the quiet scenic beauty. For a serene getaway, a place to collect your thoughts and experience a soothing communion with nature, this is an exceptional spot.

Today the village has some 400 year-round residents; its size triples in summer. From any of several downtown lodgings, you can walk a very short distance down to the city park on West Bay. The sand is less rocky in adjacent East Bay, but there aren't many days in the year when most visitors will want to brave the cold Lake Superior water. It's warmest when the wind blows in from the north, piling the warmer top water towards the shoreline.

The short peninsula that forms West Bay leads to a lighthouse and Coast Guard station, home of the Grand Marais **Maritime Museum** *(open weekends 10-6, July through Labor Day)*. Crossing the peninsula takes you to another beach extending miles to the west. This is the famous **agate beach**, where even novices can find the variegated, translucent stones of quartz while strolling along the shoreline looking through the clear water. A one-mile walk down the beach and you're at the mouth of Sable Creek. A short path along the creek leads up to the delightful **Sable Falls**. This is the beginning of the **Sable Banks and Dunes.** Four square miles of dunes rise dramatically 275 feet from the beach at the steep, 35° angle of repose common to all piles of dry sand. They stretch for five miles along Superior, from Grand Marais all the way to the Log Slide (see p. 457). On calm days it is well worth while to rent a canoe or rowboat ($15/day) from the Lakeview Inn in town.

The Sable Falls and Dunes are at the eastern edge of the **Pictured Rocks Natural Lakeshore** (see p. 455). At its **Grand Sable**

Visitor Center, on H-58 about five miles west of Grand Marais, you can find free information on the National Lakeshore, including campgrounds, day hikes, and backcountry camping along the 43-mile **Lakeshore Trail** along the entire shoreline. *Open July through Labor Day, Wednesday through Sunday from 10 to 6.*

You would expect Grand Marais to be at its most tranquil in winter. Ironically, snowmobiles make it a jarring time to visit. The noisy machines converge here some weekends, when local merchants report doing as much business as during the height of the summer season. Winter weekends are the worst; weekdays are likely to be a good deal quieter. One way to be sure to have peace and quite is to rent snowshoes from the Lakeview Inn ($7/day) and hike over the snow either east or west of town.

Along the bluffs either east or west of town are pristine state forests and fine views of Lake Superior. If you head west toward Sable Falls, you'll likely run into sizable herds of nearly tame deer.

The major summertime irritation in this thickly wooded part of the world is bugs. Some days are thick with black flies, house flies, or mosquitoes, especially if the wind is out of the woods. But usually the bug population is moderate to low. Best bug repellent for black flies: Avon Skin So Soft. Nobody knows why it works so well when preparations formulated against bugs fail.

FOR PICNICS ALONG THE SHORE . . . . . you can pick up excellent smoked white-fish sausage, smoked turkey, cheese, and fresh baked bread at **Lefebvre's Fish Market & Bakery** on Harbor Street east of downtown.

CAMPING AT THE NATIONAL LAKESHORE . . . . . is at scenic, rustic camp-grounds. Campfire interpretive programs make them special. Hurricane River and Twelvemile Beach are near Grand Marais, Little Beaver Lake is midway between it and Munising. The 67 spots are available on a first-come, first-serve basis. To get a spot in July and August, come early, wait for someone to leave. Self-registration at the site. $5 fee.

BEAUTIFUL U. P. CAMPGROUNDS WHERE YOU CAN ALWAYS FIND A SPOT . . . . . are the rustic campgrounds on U. S. Forest Service national for-est land. They don't have the amenities (showers, electricity, pump-out sta-tions), but they don't have the crowds, either. $5/night fee; self-registration at the site. Most are on lakes — either Lake Michigan, Lake Superior (by Tahquamenon Bay and also west of Munising), or a smaller lake. The 860,000-acre **Hiawatha National Forest** has 10 campgrounds near St. Ignace and Sault Ste. Marie, and 15 more from Munising and Escanaba to Manistique and Rapid River. For a map of all campgrounds, call (906) 387-3700, write USFS, 400 E. Munising Ave., Munising, MI 49862, or stop by the Park Service/Forest Service visitor center in Munising.

Pictured Rocks National Lakeshore

*Colorful cliffs meet clear, green Superior
in a series of memorable views.*

This extraordinary 43 miles of shoreline, extending from
Munising to Grand Marais, contains some of Michigan's
most remarkable sights. Most famous are the **Pictured
Rocks**, only visible from the water, and best seen toward sunset.
Usually this means taking a three-hour boat cruise from Munising.
Arrive early to get a seat on the top deck, the best place to view
the scenery. The cruise begins by passing 14,600-acre **Grand
Island**, today a primitive (i.e., unimproved) recreation area. A
delightful wooden lighthouse from 1869 is on its eastern shore.

Superior's beautiful green water contrasts strikingly with the
towering cliffs, over 200 feet high. The colors of the sandstone
cliffs are subtle. Blues and greens result from the presence of
copper, the reddish hues from iron. In mid-day on a glary day
they can be washed out; the 5 p.m. cruise in July and August
would be best.

The sandstone cliffs are actually part of the same rock formation which dips like a bowl 1,100 feet below the surface in central Michigan. Wind and water have eroded the cliffs into many
striking formations — arches, pillars, caves and grottoes, beginning with **Miner's Castle** (also reachable by land, with a splendid
view). In June the water is still flowing at nearby Bridal Veil Falls.
If the water is calm enough, the boat actually enters one of the
caves it passes.

Because the scenery is so striking, without equal on the Great
Lakes, Pictured Rocks was designated the first National Lake-

shore in the U.S. in 1966. That means it's administered by the National Park Service. Excellent visitor facilities and printed information is available at visitor centers in Munising and Grand Marais (see logistics at end). Maps to some 16 miles of groomed **cross-country ski trails** are available. A stimulating array of free **guided nature walks and programs** are held daily (often two and times a day and around the campfire at night) from July 1 through Labor Day. Call (906) 387-3700 to time your trip around programs that interest you.

Sights of exceptional interest along the shore, arranged from Munising to Grand Marais, are:

◆ **Munising Falls.** This slender, exceptionally attractive falls has a dramatic five-foot drop into a small, rocky canyon. The pleasant, 800-foot path to the falls actually winds in a loop just *behind* the falls so you can reach out and touch the powerful stream of water. In winter the sight is equally spectacular when the column of water is frozen. The excellent **interpretive center** at the parking lot gives historical perspective on the region's geology and logging history. It's next to the site of an 1868 blast furnace which made 16 tons of pig iron a day. *On H-58 about 2 miles east of downtown Munising and the intersection of M-28 and M-94. Unstaffed center open mid-May through Oct., daily 8-4:30.*

◆ **Sand Point and beach.** From this point of land jutting out toward Grand Island, you get a good view of the island and the city of Munising. In the evening there is a distant view of the Pictured Rocks. (They're shaded in the morning.) The beach just south of the point is one of the warmer swimming spots in Lake Superior. Local swimmers point out that once you get acclimated to the chilly water, you don't feel the cold. *East of Munising a little over a mile on H-58, then left on Washington St. 1/2 mile to Sand Point Rd. North 2 miles.*

◆ **Miners Castle and Falls.** A spectacular view looks down at an emerald-green Lake Superior cove from high upon a majestic, castle-like cliff, a single great stone some nine stories tall. The clearness of the water lets you see the rocky bottom even at considerable depths. Another trail leads to a nice, long beach just north of Miners Castle. Farther inland, on Miners Castle Road, is Miners Falls, one of the Upper Peninsula's larger falls, with a 70-foot drop. Towards the end of the half-mile trail to it is a panoramic view of Lake Superior in the distance. *Take H-58 east from Munising. In about 7 miles, turn north on Miners Castle Rd. for 6 miles to Miners Castle, which is handicap-accessible.*

◆ **Twelvemile Beach.** Long sand and pebble beach is approached from the road through a beautiful white birch forest. Swimming here is awfully cold, but it's fine for picnics and walks along the

Lakeshore Trail. Rustic campsites on a bluff overlook the lake; a two-mile nature trail takes you through the birches. *Take H-58 (unpaved) about 15 miles west of Grand Marais or about 37 miles east of Munising.*

◆ **Log Slide.** This high point of the ridge along Lake Superior is almost 300 feet above the water. In the late 19th century lumbermen rolled and slid logs down a 500-foot slide on the sharp incline, to be loaded on Great Lakes lumber schooners. It is well located for fine views of the Grand Sable Banks and Dunes to the east (p. 453) and the Au Sable Point lighthouse to the west. *Off H-58 about 8 miles west of Grand Marais.*

◆ **Grand Sable Dunes, Sable Falls, Maritime Museum.** See p. 453.

Pictured Rock Boat Cruises leave from downtown Munising between June 1 & October 10. Boats leave at 10 & 2 June 1-June 30 & Sept-Oct 10; at 9, 11, 1, 3 & 5 July through Aug. (906) 387-2379. Adults $17, children under 12 $7, under 5 free. The 37-mile trip takes 2 hours and 40 minutes.

Pictured Rocks National Lakeshore's super-helpful **main visitor center** *is at the junction of M-28 and H-58 in Munising. From late April through October it's open daily 9-4:30 (from 8-6 July thru Labor Day). Otherwise open Tues-Sat only. Call (906) 387-3700 to get a general or backpackers' visitor packet. The* **Grand Sable visitor center** *on H-58 about 3 miles west of Grand Marais is open July thru Labor Day, Wed-Sun 10-6.*

TRIPS TO GRAND ISLAND . . . . . The same cruise service company taking visitors to the Pictured Rocks also provides ferry service to Grand Island. The island is 27 miles in circumference, bigger than Mackinac Island. It has hiking trails, bike trails, places to camp and fish, but few other improvements. It was recently designated a national recreation area, but improvements are still in the planning stages. *2 trips a day in June and September, 3 in July and August. Round-trip fares are $10/adults, $5/children 5-12, under 5/free. Mountain bikes are $3 extra. (906) 387-2379.*

10 MILES SOUTHEAST OF MUNISING . . . . . take a quick **tour of Iverson Snowshoes** in Shingleton. It's one of only two wood-frame snowshoe factories remaining in the U.S. You will see how workers take long strips of white ash, steam them to increase their flexibility, bend them around a form and dry them in a kiln overnight. The labor-intensive job includes hand-lacing with rawhide or neoprene. The handsome pairs cost $65 to $110, including harness. For a bite to eat, try Shingleton's Tanglewood Restaurant, with good homemade soups and pies. *Turn north on Maple St., two blocks west of Shingleton's only blinker.*

Kitch-iti-ki-pi (Big Spring)

*An extraordinary sight: 10,000 gallons of water a minute
bubbling up in a crystal-clear pond*

Few natural sights in Michigan compare with the beauty
and mystique of this enormous, bowl-like spring. Through
a picturebook pine forest, you come upon an amazing,
emerald-green spring, round and jewel-like, 200 feet wide. By
pulling a simple raft, you can get out to the middle and gaze
down through 40 feet of crystal-clear water. Bubbling up from the
bottom is a constant flow of 10,000 gallons of water a minute.
Large trout swim lazily around, their movements readily visible
even at a distance.

The water here stays 45° F. year around, so you can see the
spring in any season. But the best time is during summer, when
this cool glade is a delightful contrast to warm summer days. In
the morning, when mist hangs over the water and turns the
surrounding woods into abstract, mysterious shapes, the effect is
especially powerful. Arrive either before 10 a.m. or after 7 p.m. to
experience the serenity of the place when few others are around.
There's a pleasant **picnic area** and a **concession stand** with
refreshments.

No one knows for sure where this enormous volume of water
comes from. Some say it's from the Seney area. Hydraulic
pressure forces the groundwater to the surface. It empties into a
stream leading to Indian Lake, which in turn empties into the
Manistique River.

*Palms Book State Park s northwest of Manistique. From U.S. 2,
take M-149 8 miles north. (906) 341-2355. State Park sticker
required: $3/day, $15/year.*

CAMPING AND SWIMMING NEARBY . . . . . On the Upper Peninsula's fourth-
biggest lake, **Indian Lake State Park** has two modern campgrounds and beaches,
and good fishing for walleye and perch. South Shore Campground has 157 sites
with little privacy but right on the lake; reserve in advance. The adjacent
Chippewa Trail comes with a brochure about wild foods used by Indians. West
Shore Campground has 144 secluded sites farther from the lake; it's rarely full. *A
few miles west of Manistique. At Thompson, turn north off U. S. 2 onto M-149;
park is in 3 miles. Follow signs to west unit. (906) 341-2355. State Park sticker
required: $3/day, $15/year.*

Fayette Historic Townsite

Once a filthy worksite for iron furnace laborers,
this 19th-century ghost town on the Garden Peninsula
is scenic today.

This picturesque industrial ghost town curves around pretty Snail Shell Harbor, on a bit of land jutting out into northern Lake Michigan. Its heart is the great limestone stacks and beehive charcoal furnaces of a charcoal iron-operation started in the 1860s. The weathered silvery frame buildings and ruins of the stone furnaces have been preserved as ghosts, not repainted and spiffed up as if they were new. A scenic limestone bluff in the background was used as a quarry for stone and for limestone flux which removed impurities in the smelting process. Fayette is a peaceful place today, all green with leaves and grass — a far cry from the mud and dirt and stockpiles of materials during its productive years in the 1870s and 1880s.

Fayette is near the tip of the Garden Peninsula, especially fertile because the moderating waters of Lake Michigan surround it. Isolated and remote, the 21-mile-long peninsula has been such a favorite with marijuana growers that the state carried out its largest-ever eradication program here and on the nearby

Stonington Peninsula.

Demand for high-quality iron escalated during the Civil War. The Jackson Iron Company chose this site for a new blast furnace because it had limestone to purify the molten iron and abundant hardwood forests to fuel the furnaces. A new railroad took iron ore from the Negaunee Range near Marquette to Escanaba, from which it was shipped 25 miles to nearby Fayette.

Fayette set production records during its heyday, but by the mid-1880s, improved methods of making coke iron and steel were making charcoal iron too expensive to produce for its worth. The smelting operation here closed down in 1891. The hotel lived on as a resort for many decades.

You have to plan a visit to Fayette right for it to be a real highlight. The scenery won't automatically carry the day. Lake Michigan is surprisingly seldom seen from most of the Garden Peninsula's roads. And the museum town can be off-putting if you see the wrong things first. Here's what to do:

1. Come early or late in the day when the slanted light is dramatic and there aren't many people. Sometimes a morning mist rising off the harbor gives a soft, romantic, ghostly look to the place. Evening sunsets are spectacular.

2. Get a free townsite map and buy *Fayette: A Visitor's Guide* at the visitors' center front desk for $3. Avoid the misleading visitor center displays, where an unctuous voice in a melodramatic recording proclaims, "It was a nice life" for Fayette's workers, who were "a happy, contented lot." Newer interpretive displays in the village are based on careful historical and archaeological research, and they're much more sophisticated and honest. A visitor's account of Fayette workers' housing in 1870 was of mud, filth, horrible smells, and ragged children — much worse than anything she'd seen in Cleveland slums.

3. Wander around the buildings and look inside. The hotel, town hall and shops, and one supervisor's home are furnished with satisfying period accuracy. Other buildings, like the office, are full of interesting and detailed exhibit panels. Read them, and you'll learn about subjects as diverse as the butcher business, medicine before the acceptance of antiseptics, ladies' entertainments, traveling shows, and labor history. (When orders for iron were slow, workers didn't get paid — sometimes for weeks on end!)

4. After 11 a.m. the village will likely be filling up with tourists. You could take a 25-minute **guided tour** of Fayette's main street. Or take your booklet, sit down on a bench or at the picnic tables at the parking lot's edge, and read through it for a good overview of the charcoal iron-smelting process, the town, and the interesting ongoing archaeological investigations of the area. They are revealing much about the lives of workers and daily activities that hasn't been recorded in surviving letters and diaries.

5. Don't miss the **hiking trail up the limestone bluffs** east of the harbor. Four spots offer beautiful views clear across to the Stonington Peninsula to the west. The state park has **seven miles of hiking trails** in all.

Snail Shell Harbor offers a **transient marina** (there's no pump-out station but a scenic setting for overnights), a **boat ramp**, and **fishing** for perch and smallmouth bass. **Camping** at Fayette is unusually secluded and uncrowded for a state park. Tall trees give each of the 80 campsites unusual privacy, but also block any water view. There's running water, electricity, pit toilets, and no showers, which means the campground fills up only for the park's two special events: the **Blessing of the Fleet** in mid-July and mid-August's **Heritage Days**. The beach is only a quarter-mile walk away.

Fayette State Park is 16 miles down M-183 from Garden Corners and U.S. 2, between Escanaba and Manistique. (906) 644-2603. Open from mid-May through mid-October. Fayette Townsite is open from 8 a.m. to 5 p.m., until 9 in July & August. State park sticker required; $3/day, $15/year.

A 2,000-FOOT WHITE SAND BEACH. . . . . backed by low dunes is about a mile south of Fayette Townsite, in a different part of the state park, reached by another road off M-183. There's a large **picnic area** and a **changing house**. State park sticker required; $3/day, $15/year.

ANOTHER BEACH AND PICNIC AREA . . . . . even less crowded, is the **Sac Bay County Park** off 183 about five miles south of Fayette. Continue south to the end of M-183 and you'll be at **Fairport**, almost at the very tip of the Garden Peninsula. It's **a commercial fishing village**, one of the few left in Michigan. There's no store or restaurant, but you can stop by the fish shed and buy **fresh whitefish to cook out**. Some fishermen are Indians who fish with gill nets, once used by all commercial fishermen. By the 1940s overfishing had greatly reduced Lake Michigan's commercial catch. Laws today favor sport fishermen and prohibit gill nets, except for Indians who are protected by old treaties assuring their traditional means of livelihood.

A LITTLE FARMING AND FISHING VILLAGE. . . . . that's looking more and more like a ghost town itself is **Garden** (population 268), once the peninsula's commercial hub. As small farms and orchards decline, so does its year-round population. Quaint frame storefronts are increasingly empty. Cottagers and retirees bring some life to the place in summer. There's an attractive little crafts gallery and consignment shop, a small, summer-only historical museum, and two popular restaurants with good food.

IXL Museum

At the edge of small U.P. village,
a remarkably well preserved historic office building
lets visitors step back in time.

Few historic sites are preserved so splendidly well as this remote old office of a U.P. hardwood lumber mill. It was here in the 1880s that the machinery to produce hardwood flooring was first perfected. Until then American homes used softer pine for wooden floors. Hardwoods like maple and oak were too difficult to work and tended to warp. Lumber mill manager George Earle perfected a kiln process here to remove the right amount of moisture from hardwood. He also created machinery to make tongue and groove hardwood sections, still the method for laying hardwood floors.

Located just south of Hermansville, the company grounds are in a pristine condition. Except for the absence of a few of the original structures, things are little changed from decades ago. The kiln still operates, although the original company is defunct. The museum building was the business office, built in 1882. Earle's office was here. A medical doctor by training, he used the big table in the middle of his office for amputations and other emergency operations. This building is also where the 600 to 800 IXL workers came to receive their weekly scrip for pay in the company town. (The IXL name is a punning abbreviation for "I excel.")

The interior has not been reconstructed to look like an historic office; it simply has changed little in recent decades. Old Burroughs adding machines and inkwells adorn big oak desks. Dumbwaiters sent messages between the first and second floors. The original old mechanical clocks and crank telephones remain in place, as if the place had suddenly been vacated 75 years ago and left untouched.

Hermansville is on U.S.-2 between Escanaba and Iron Mountain. Turn at the sign for the IXL Museum and go 4 blocks south. (906) 498-2498 or (906) 498-2410. June-Aug, 1-4 daily. Adults $1, students 50¢.

Piers Gorge

Along the Wisconsin border,
the big Menominee River cuts through
a deep trough in a spectacular rush of water.

This beautiful stretch of river is a fine place to frolic in frisky rapids on a hot day. Even on cooler days, you can step across half the wide river using the many large stones and boulders strewn liberally in the riverbed. On its way to Green Bay in Lake Michigan, the Menominee River has cut the dramatically deep gorge, creating powerful rapids. Wisconsin is on the other side.

Several rapids are here. You have to walk well upstream to get to the most dramatic one of all, where the gorge is over 50 feet high. Because this isn't a big tourist spot, the area has kept a natural, isolated appearance. No park signs or steps have been constructed. The riverbanks are loaded with stones of all shapes and sizes, providing plenty of ammunition for stone skippers.

Turn south from U.S. 8, two miles south of Norway. If you reach the river on U.S.8, you've gone too far.

A GOOD MUSEUM IN CASPIAN. . . . . . just south of Iron River, is the notable **Iron County Museum.** Lots of mining exhibits are in the old engine house of the famous Caspian Mine (1903-1937). Over 6 million tons of iron ore were lifted by the giant hoist just east of the engine house. This was among the most productive of the Menominee Range mines. Miniature models of mines show how shafts in the region were as long as one mile. and how huge buckets called "skips" hauled the ore up. A display of beautiful Finnish rag rugs, made by wives of the many Finnish miners, is alone worth a visit.

Lumber had also been important in the area. A large diorama of a lumber camp shows such things as the dining hall, where "The cook made sure that everyone ate and only ate, by standing with a butcher knife and threatening anyone who talked." There are also 3 authentic Indian dugout canoes. Various outbuildings include a 1930s Finnish sauna. *U.S. 2 to exit 424, 2 miles south of Iron River. (906) 265-2617. Open mid-May through October, daily 9-5, Sun 1-5.*

Iron Mountain Iron Mine

*Travel far beneath the earth to see
how difficult and dangerous iron mining really was.*

This journey through 2,600 feet of tunnels 400 feet underground is Michigan's most interesting mine tour. Led by a knowledgeable guide, visitors are transported in the same railway system that took miners to their jobs until the mine closed down in 1945. Visitors experience the gloomy, difficult working conditions in a typical iron mine. There are also spectacular views of large caverns on the 35-minute trip. Drilling demonstrations show how loud, dirty, and dangerous the work was.

When the first tunnel here was dug in 1870, the incredibly rich ore was 85% iron. But it took three men 10 hours to dig by hand just four feet. The highest-paid miner was the blaster, who got 25¢ an hour. Deep shaft mines like this finally became obsolete when huge power shovels made open-pit mining much more economical. Wear a sweater; far underground it stays a constant 43° F. year around.

On U.S. 2 in Vulcan, 10 miles east of Iron Mountain. (906) 563-8077. 35 minute tours June to mid-Oct, daily 9-6. Adults $5, children $4.

ALSO IN IRON MOUNTAIN . . . . . The **Cornish Pump and Mining Museum** has a 725-ton pump, the nation's largest when built in 1890. It lifted 200 tons a minute from the shaft of the Chapin Iron Mine, the largest producer in the Menominee Range. Seeping water is a big problem for deep mines, which have to continuously pump out water to keep operating. It took 11,000 tons of coal a year just to operate the pump. There are also lots of local mining artifacts and photos here, as well as a World War II glider display. The gliders were made in Kingsford, just south of Iron Mountain. . . . . . The **Menominee Range Museum**, located in an old Carnegie library building, has many local historical items, including reconstructions of a dentist's office, trapper's cabin, and a 19th-century kitchen and bedroom. 300 E. Ludington. *(906) 774-4276. Open May-Aug, Mon-Sat 10-4, Sun noon-4. Adults $2.* . . . . . **St. Antoine Park** is a delightful city park on Lake Antoine, just northeast of town. There's a spacious, wooded picnic area and a wonderful swimming beach with a swimmer's dock well out in the lake. A concession stand sells hot dogs, ice cream, popcorn, and camping supplies.

Porcupine Mountains

Huge virgin forests, wonderful waterfalls and views, rugged hiking trails, and wild rivers in a 65,000-acre park overlooking Lake Superior.

This vast and rugged state park in the remote northwestern part of Michigan's Upper Peninsula contains some of the Midwest's most extraordinary natural features. The Porcupine Mountains are often called the region's only true mountains. **Whitewater canoeing** here is the most challenging in Michigan, and downhill skiing is some of the very best in the Midwest. Thirteen slopes have a vertical drop of 600 feet, and the lift ticket fees are bargain-priced. (Kids 12 and under ski free!) Because this area was so inaccessible, an astounding 36,000 acres escaped the lumberman's axe — the largest virgin forest east of the Mississippi. It is a realm of towering hemlocks and hardwoods. There are **85 miles of hiking trails** and dozens of waterfalls.

The **Presque Isle River** is as tumultuous as they come. For many, the highlight of the Porkies is its final half mile before it flows into Lake Superior. You can pull near it by car, then take a half-mile elevated boardwalk up the side of this rollicking river. Multiple waterfalls, powerful rapids, and deep holes make for spectacular scenery and suicidal canoeing here.

In complete contrast is the peaceful scene at **Lake of the Clouds,** one of the state's most famous views. You can look down on it from overlooks near a parking lot, or approach it by footpath another two miles east. The park's most scenic trail is **Escarpment Trail**, four miles long. In addition to a great view of Lake of the Clouds, it reveals interesting rock formations along the dramatic escarpment. Another celebrated panoramic view is from a 40-foot observation tower on Michigan's second-highest point, **Summit Peak**.

Although only the Superior shoreline and southern boundary of the park were ever logged, there was serious copper mining here. Of nine abandoned copper mines, all but one are now capped. The Mead Mine along M-17 allows visitors to enter about 100 feet of the mineshaft . This is also a good place to **picnic;** get supplies at the general store in Silver City.

By all means begin your exploration of the Porcupines with a trip to the **Visitor Center**. Helpful park rangers can give informa

Kristin Hurlin

Lake of the Clouds.

tion about trails, backpacking, canoeing, fishing (for steelhead, salmon, and trout), and more. Call or write, and they'll mail you information. There's a big, detailed relief map of the huge park. Topographical maps are for sale. Displays and a nine-projector **slide show** inform visitors about the area's history and natural features.

Campgrounds range from open modern and semi-modern sites to rustic outposts — 183 sites in all. Reservations are recommended in July and early August. If you reserve one far enough in advance, you can rent a well-equipped, drive-in wilderness cabin, complete (in some cases) with a rowboat to take out on a remote lake.

In winter, the park also features the most exciting place for **downhill skiing** in the Midwest from mid-December through March. Some 10 miles of alpine ski runs include seven intermediate trails, three expert trails, and three novice trails. Current cost of daily lift ticket (likely to go up): $15/day weekends, $13 otherwise, $10/half-day. Ages 13-17: $10/$8/$6. There are also 25 miles of groomed **cross-country ski trails**. A **warming shelter**, **concession**, and **rental facility** serves all skiers.

Headquarters/visitor center is about 4 miles west of Silver City on M-107. Write: Porcupine Mountains Wilderness State Park, 599 M-107, Ontonogan, MI 49953. (906) 885-5275. Visitor center open from late May through mid-October, daily 10-6. Ski season from mid-Dec thru March. State parks sticker required: $3/day, $15/year.

Michigan Iron Industry Museum

Overlooking a picturesque river valley, this superb museum shows the importance of U.P. iron to the nation.

Situated in a rural area that overlooks the Carp River where the first iron forge in the region operated, this impressive museum uses dramatic displays to illuminate an important era in Michigan history. Little remains of that long-abandoned forge, but a pleasant path leads visitors from the museum past the 19th-century site.

Using slide shows, historical artifacts, and enlarged photos, the museum explains the great historical importance of this iron range. The story begins with the 1844 discovery near Negaunee of nearly pure surface iron deposits. This iron had never been excavated, unlike the large deposits of Keweenaw copper which Indians had mined for centuries. The first iron mine opened three miles from the museum. The forge here was used to convert the ore directly into wrought iron for such things as nails, wire, and bolts. It took an acre of hardwoods to make five tons of iron. From this modest beginning blossomed 40 mines in the Marquette Range by 1872. They extracted a million tons a year of the richest iron ore in the world. But by the end of the 1870s the range's rich surface deposits were becoming exhausted and the U.P.'s Menominee and Gegobic Ranges to the west were in the ascendency.

The museum does a good job of showing just how important the U.P.'s iron has been. Almost half of the nation's iron from 1850 to 1900 was mined from here. In the 150 years since 1833, the California gold rush produced less than a billion dollars of minerals. Michigan lumber has produced almost $4.5 million of wood. The Keweenaw copper ranges generated rough twice that amount. But the riches from iron dwarf these, worth some *$48 billion.*

Today none of the miles of U.P. underground iron mine shafts are producing ore. The only two remaining mines are the Tilden and the Empire, both open-pit operations. Today the U.P. iron industry excavates greatly diluted ore in huge, 300-ton blasts. It remains competitive only because of a process that concentrates the ore into 64% pure iron pellets called taconite. These can then be shipped economically from the ports of Marquette and Escanaba to foundries around the Great Lakes.

From U.S. 41, 3 miles east of Negaunee, turn south onto Forge Rd. and go 1 mile. (906) 475-7857. Open daily May-Oct, 9:30-4:30. Free.

HIGH-SPEED SLEDDING IN NEGAUNEE . . . . . The exciting **Lucy Hill Luge Run** is 800 meters long. It's a naturbahn, on an iced track with flat curves, like the old logging roads on which the sport originated in the Alps. The Olympic luge sport is done on a kunstbahn, with banked turns. This steep, ice-slick path, the only U.S. naturbahn, has 29 curves, each named for a local iron mine. For $3 you get use of a sled , helmets, pads, and instructions on how to handle this super-fast run. *From U.S. 41 on the east side of Negaunee, take Bus. Rte. 41 through town, then turn east onto Old M-35 to luge. (906) 475-7792.*

BLACK FLIES, RUSTY CARS, DEER-HUNTING, SEX, SAUNAS, BEER . . . . . and other important aspects of U.P. life have been immortalized in the satirical songs of Da Yoopers of Ishpeming, Mich. "The Second Week of Deer Camp" got nation-wide air play. Simple pleasures are extolled in songs like "Fishin' wit Fred": "It's a perfect day for fishin', drinking beer and telling lies. It's a little bit like Heaven when you're fishin' wit da guys." Da Yoopers have great Yooper accents and a variety of musical styles to suit each topic, from Finnish accordion polkas to heavy metal. Pick up their tapes at Holiday gas stations (*Culture Shock* is our favorite), or at **Da Yooper Shop** on U.S. 41 just west of Ishpeming. (Look for the billboard.) There you can also buy such things as a beer bottle holster or beer gut T-shirt. *Mail-order available. (906) 485-5595. Summer hours: Mon-Fri 9-9, Sat 10-6, Sun 11-4. Winter hours: Mon-Fri 9-5.*

ALSO IN ISHPEMING . . . . . exhibits of antique skis and other skiing equipment plus short biographies of leading U.S. skiers are on display at the **U.S. National Ski Hall of Fame**. Ski-jumping, introduced by the area's numerous Norwegians, got its start in Ishpeming, and the local ski club organized the hall many years ago. *Until 1992, it's on Mather at Poplar. (From U.S. 41, go north up hill at the 76 station, then right on Mather.) Then it occupies a handsome new building on U.S. 41 with a roof shaped like a ski jump. (906) 486-9281. Summer hours: Mon-Fri 9-4, weekends 10-4. Winter: Mon-Fri 9-4, weekends 1-4.*

WINTER SPORTS IN AND AROUND MARQUETTE . . . . . The settings are unusually attractive, the season's from mid-December through March, and it's bonus to be in a lively city with some good restaurants. Al Quaal near Ishpeming features downhill and cross-country skiing and a toboggan run, while Marquette Moun-tain just south of town has a stunning Lake Superior view. There's an 800-meter luge run (iced sledding). And Presque Isle Park is one of many fine places for snowshoeing; equipment can be rented from Johnson's Sport Shop. Call 1-800-544-4321 for brochures on winter sports.

Marquette

*Blessed with beautiful views, imposing buildings,
a wonderful city park, and a delightful downtown*

Compared to the sleepy, depressed look of most Upper
Peninsula towns, this city of 23,000 is an uncommonly
attractive place to visit. Marquette has been an important
port since the 1850s, when the Soo Locks opened up shipping
throughout the Great Lakes. The city rises sharply from the lake,
giving pleasant views of the bay. These are punctuated by dramatic landmarks: the ore docks, the old red lighthouse, and
Presque Isle, a beautiful park jutting out into Lake Superior.
There's more money here than in any other U.P. town and as
much history, so it's not surprising that Marquette has more for
visitors to see and do than anyplace else north of the bridge. It
lives up to its self-description, "Queen City of the North." The
bustling downtown has substantial Victorian buildings of the distinctive reddish and blond sandstone quarried nearby. The
domed county courthouse is made of this sandstone, as is the
striking Catholic cathedral on West Baraga Street.

The billions of tons of iron ore shipped from Marquette since
the 1850s helped pay for many of these fancy buildings. In the
second half of the 19th century, 40% of the world's iron ore
came from here, fueling America's transition from an agricultural
to an industrial society. From April through mid-December, two
to three freighters a day still pick up enormous loads of ore at the
north ore dock just below Presque Isle Park. You can watch the
noisy process from Lakeshore Boulevard or Presque Isle.

Northern Michigan University, with its 8,500 students, gives
economic stability to the city, as does a large regional hospital
complex, the huge K.I. Sawyer Air Force Base just south of here,
and a maximum-security prison. Thanks to its logrolling state
representative Dominic Jacobetti, the university campus now has
the "Yooper Bowl," an 8,500-seat enclosed stadium big enough
for football games.

Highlights include:

♦ **Two spectacular views** of the city. From the south, see the city,
bay, and lake from Mt. Marquette. You can drive to the summit.
From the north, Sugarloaf Mountain offers an equally grand view.
It's a 15- to 20-minute walk to the peak.

♦ **Downtown.** Centered on Washington between Front and Third, this is one of the most pleasing downtowns in the state. There are interesting shops, striking architecture, and nice views down to the bay. **Wattsson & Wattsson Jewelers** (118 W. Washington) has displays on the historic Ropes Gold Mine in nearby Ishpeming as well as jewelry made of that gold. **Michigan Fare** (114 W. Washington) features Michigan products from brass wind chimes to chopping blocks. The old **Vierling Saloon** on the corner of Front and Main streets has a great view of the bay from its back windows(see p. 499). Just south of Washington are the old **County Courthouse** and the impressive **St. Peter's Cathedral.** A block north is the **historical museum.**

◆ **Marquette County Historical Museum** has a huge 1881 bird's-eye drawing of the city showing what a bustling harbor the town had back then. Displays reveal the importance to Marquette of fishing, shipping, logging, and especially William Burt's key discovery of huge deposits of iron nearby in 1844. *213 N. Front near Washington. (906) 226-3571. Mon-Fri 9-4:30, Sat 11-3. Adults $1.50; under 13 free.*

◆ **Fresh fish** from a downtown dock. **Thill's Fish House** is located just north of the downtown ore dock, at the foot of Main. It's the last commercial fishing operation in what was once a thriving fishery. Buy fresh whitefish fillets for $3.65/lb.; smoked whitefish sausage for $3.50/lb.

◆ **Lakeside bike path.** You can rent 5-speed bikes starting at $3 an hour and take a pleasant 12-mile bike ride along a shoreline bike path. It extends 7 miles south of downtown and 5 miles north to Presque Isle. *Rent bikes at Lakeshore Bike and Kite, just west of the lighthouse at 505 Lakeshore Blvd. It's right on the bike path.*

◆ **Maritime Museum.** Located in the big old Water Works Building not far from the lighthouse. Large, colorful ship flags hang from its high ceilings. Outboard engines were first developed in Marquette, and the museum has some very old ones. A typical Finnish fishing shanty has been reconstructed. Photos and exhibits explain how taconite pellets, a condensed form of iron ore, have made it more economical to ship iron. Well-stocked **gift shop** . *E. Ridge at Lakeshore Blvd. just north of downtown. Open Memorial-Labor Day, Tues-Sat. 11 5. (906) 226-2006. $1.50.*

◆ **East Side historic district.** Just north of downtown along Ridge and Arch streets is a neighborhood of impressive 19th-century Victorian mansions built during the iron-mining boom. An informative free pamphlet at the county Historical Museum has a map and details on 23 buildings.

◆ **Presque Isle Park.** This extraordinary 328-acre peninsula just north of town is a wonderful Lake Superior setting for an outing. There's a little **zoo** with deer and other animals, **picnic grounds,** and a **swimming pool.** Paths wind through the park. When the waters aren't too frigid, kids leap off the black rock cliffs into 30 feet of clear Lake Superior water. On Thursday and Sunday evenings in summer there are **city band concerts** in the bandshell.

◆ **Jilbert's Dairy** provides dairy products for much of the U.P. Adjoining the dairy is its popular ice cream shop. A local favorite is "Moosetracks," vanilla with Reese's peanut butter cups mixed in. During daylight hours you can get a tour of the dairy. At any time you can look through glass windows at ice cream being made and milk being processed. *(906) 225-1363. Corner of W. Ridge & Meeske Ave. where U.S. 41 business route splits off the highway.*

◆ **Touch of Finland.** Finns are the dominant group among the U.P.'s diverse ethnic mix. Backyard saunas are a common sight and still regularly used. This shop is so well supplied with Finnish products that Finns come from as far as Chicago to shop here. Sauna supplies such as ladles and scrub brushes are well stocked, along with tapes of Finnish music and more famous Finnish products such as Iittala crystal, Aarikka wooden jewelry, and Pesla wool blankets. *On U.S. 41 west of town (south side of road, across from Westwood Mall. Mon-Fri 9:3-9, Sat 9:30-5:30, Sun 12-5:30.*

◆ **Guided tours of the area.** Marquette native Fred Huffman, owner and operator of Marquette County Tours, takes visitors on informative tours of the city and surrounding countryside. Sunrise and sunset tours of the city are given regularly. Other tours include scenic waterfalls, the historic Marquette Iron Range, and Marquette's rugged north country, Big Bay, and vicinity. The price, vehicle included, is about $20 an hour. *For an appointment, call Fred at (906) 226-6167.*

A SPECTACULAR FALL COLOR TRIP from Marquette to the remote village of **Big Bay** is a circle tour along county road 510 and 550. You'll drive through thick forests and past waterfalls on the 35-mile dirt road. Colors are usually at their peak from late September to mid-October. . . . . . In Big Bay are two of the U.P.'s most famous lodgings: the wonderfully isolated **Big Bay Lighthouse** where you can actually watch Lake Superior storms from the top of the tower, and the historic **Thunder Bay Inn,** once a general store for lumber companies in the region. Henry Ford bought the building in 1943 to use as a hotel for guests. Just down the hill was the lumber mill used to make panels for the famous Ford "woody" station wagons. In 1959 the popular bar here was the setting for parts of "Anatomy of a Murder." Locals still talk about it.

Hanka Homestead

*On a beautiful, remote hillside, take a trip back in time
to a self-sufficient Finnish farm.*

In the western Upper Peninsula, Finns have intermarried
for generations and so colored the regional culture and
accent of the western Upper Peninsula that you can
meet Yoopers (derived from "U.P.") without a drop of Finnish
blood who speak with a strong Finnish accent. Some Finnish
descendants whose families have been in this country for four
generations sound like they learned English as a second language
at the age of nine or ten. Saunas are still commonly seen in back
yards from Marquette to Copper Country. The world's only
Finnish-American college, Suomi College, is in Hancock. Dozens
of co-op stores, a feature of many Finnish agricultural communities, survive in small places. Unfussy Scandinavian cleanliness sets
the norm up here; it's hard to find a Copper Country motel, no
matter how old or primitive, that isn't clean.

While many Finnish things have been incorporated into the
distinctive Yooper culture, pure Finnish survivals are rare. Probably the most remarkable is the Hanka Homestead, a self-sufficient
pioneer farmstead at the base of the Keweenaw Peninsula. Its
farmhouse and nine outbuildings are carefully crafted Scandinavian log construction. The Hanka farm has been restored to the
way it was in its prime in 1920, when Herman Hanka, a disabled
miner, his wife, and their four adult children lived here, continuing their Old World ways they had brought with them to the U.S.

By the time you get to the Hankas' place, you've gone down five
miles of country road off U.S. 41, turned at a fire tower near the
top of a long, high hill, and gone down a rugged gravel road
through a mile of forest. It's quite remote from the outside world,
just as the Finns were who homesteaded here in the 1890s. The
log house, two-story log barn, and smaller outbuildings sit in an
18-acre clearing, surrounded by forest, with the Huron Mountains
blue in the distance across nearby Keweenaw Bay. The scene
looks like something you'd expect to find in a remote hollow of
the Smokey Mountains.

One mainstay of self-sufficient local economies like these was
that neighbors traded and shared harvest work and other skills
and products. The disabled father, Herman, tanned hides and
made shoes for neighbors; his son Jalmar tinkered and fixed
things. The family boarded logging horses, which needed intermit-

tent rest between periods of strenuous work. Jalmar and his brother Nik, the farm manager, worked in logging camps in the winter, where their sister Mary cooked. One neighbor went to town every Saturday to shop for the neighborhood. People raised their own grains and vegetables, kept chickens and sometimes a pig, depended on the Jersey cow and her rich milk for butter and cheese, and hunted rabbits, partridges, and deer. With such a short growing season (85 frost-free days), cold-resistant root crops like turnips, rutabagas, and potatoes were important. Preserving and preparing food took up an immense amount of time. Social life consisted of visiting, playing instruments (Nik played the kantele, a homemade Finnish guitar), occasional dances at a pavilion near where the fire tower is, church, and the weekly Saturday sauna.

Finland's shifting 19th-century economy had transformed many independent farmers into a class of industrial workers and landless tenants without opportunities. Only the oldest son could hope to farm his own land. Finns emigrated to the northern U.S., largely to work in mines. On the edges of U.P. mining towns, miners farmed smaller plots to support their large families. Owning 40 acres under the Homestead Act and becoming a full-time farmer was a big step up from working in the dangerous mines.

Everything changed in the 1920s for farms like the Hankas'. New sanitation policies allowed the sale only of Grade A milk, produced and cooled under super-sanitary, refrigerated conditions. Grade B milk produced at farms like these was sold only as cheese. Phone service in this remote neighborhood, unreliable to begin with, became so expensive that customers dropped it and lines were removed. Forests reclaimed many fields. Sons went into the army, saw a bigger world, and often ended up working in Detroit's auto factories like Mary's son, Arvo. They returned to the U. P. only to retire.

The farm stopped being improved when Nik, an energetic manager, died in 1923. Gradually most of the Hankas died off, but easy-going Jalmar lived on until 1966. His needs were simple and he didn't have the ambition to modernize. The farm pretty much remained in a time capsule.

Scouts from Old World Wisconsin, a museum of ethnic farm buildings near Eagle, Wisconsin, came up here to buy the barn and move it. But they were so impressed with the unaltered condition of the classic Finnish farm that they encouraged a local group to preserve it as a museum. The guide is likely to be descended from nearby Finnish farmers, and thus able to answer many questions and share personal experience. The tour is strong on explaining the how-tos of a subsistence lifestyle: how fish were smoked in the sauna, which was then prepared for the family's bath; how rag rugs were woven on neighborhood looms; how grain and food were stored. The museum group hopes to include actual demonstrations. A satisfying amount of information on the people who lived here is available to the patient reader in a somewhat tedious $6 book.

On U.S. 41 about 10 miles north of Baraga, turn west onto Arnheim Road. As you pass the fire tower, continue straight onto the gravel (the blacktop turns west). Follow the gravel road left (east) to the farm. Open Mem.-Labor Day on weekends noon-6 or by appointment. Probably open daily in summer; call (906) 353-7116 or (906) 334-2590. Admission by donation.

TO EXPERIENCE A WORKING FINNISH DAIRY FARM TODAY . . . . . stay at **Palosaari's Rolling Acres,** a bed and breakfast (p. 501) on a third-generation farm not far from the Hanka Homestead. The 1940s Cape Cod farmhouse is a trim, efficient headquarters of the 200-acre farm. Cliff and Evey Palosaari are no part-time hobby farmers but the real thing — warm, unpretentious hosts who enjoy sharing stories and down-to-earth Finnish philosophizing with their guests. They have seven grown children. One helps run the farm and intends to buy it from his father. The heavily mechanized operation milks three dozen cows; a farm tour explains the equipment, from plows to combines and large round balers. Evy, active in many farm organizations, is also an expert baker well versed in the old Finnish ways.

EXPLORING THE BYWAYS OF THE KEWEENAW COUNTRYSIDE. . . . . is facilitated with a well-organized booklet with maps of driving tours that take you by dairy, beef, goat, and potato farms (many welcome U-pickers and casual visitors), greenhouses, co-ops, nurseries, sugar bushes, and nature walks, plus locally popular restaurants along the way. Visitors are often surprised at the variety and success of agriculture in these far-northern climes. It draws on Finnish traditions of self-sufficiency, small scale, and low debt. Ask for the **Agricultural Guide to the Keweenaw,** and send a $1.50 check to the Keweenaw Peninsula Chamber of Commerce, Box 336, Houghton, Michigan 49931. Or stop by the office in the transit center at 326 Sheldon in downtown Houghton (next to True Value Hardware).

FRUIT, FLOWERS, AND A FIRST-RATE PETTING ZOO. . . . . are at the **Keweenaw Berry Farm** on U.S. 41 a few miles south of Chassell. It's the prettiest of all the produce-stands-turned-into-visitor-attractions we've seen. To get the full effect, you have to walk behind the big retail building through the grounds, colorful with flowers. There's no admission charge to the big, landscaped area for small animals — a delightful spot, not a depressing series of sun-baked pens. Most farmyard favorites are here: pigs wallowing in the mud, big-eyed Jersey cows, goats, ponies, turkeys, chickens and colorful guinea hens. And there are exotics like llamas, wallabees, and buffalo. Little kids are out in force on weekends, feeding animals apples and chatting away with them. You can pick or buy strawberries (small Keweenaw strawberries are unusually sweet) and raspberries. Bakery with pasties, sandwiches, hamburgers. Ice cream. Cider and doughnuts. *(906) 523-6181. Open May 1-Dec. 31, Mon-Sat 8 a.m.-9 p.m., Sun 10-9.*

PREPARE YOURSELF TO SLOW DOWN AND ENTER THE NATURAL WORLD. . . . . by stopping at the **Sturgeon River Slough Natural Area** alongside U.S. 41 about 18 miles north of Baraga. The gruelling drive to get to the Keweenaw Peninsula can leave you spinning. This is a good spot to start unwinding on the last leg of your trip. There's a lookout tower and picnic tables by the roadside parking area. You could pick up a pasty and fresh fruit at the Keweenaw Berry farm just south of here and have a picnic. The **De Vriendt Nature Trail,** with interesting interpretive signs, makes a 1.75-mile loop through the slough, now a nesting site for Canada geese, mallards, wood ducks, black ducks, and blue-winged teal. The view of sweeping marshland and sky is relaxing. The slough had been pastureland so wet it could only by farmed by horses. Now channelization and flood control structures regulate the Sturgeon River to avoid spring flooding, and the slough of one-time farms is managed as a stopover spot for migrating waterfowl and a nesting spot. The aim is to increase the Upper Peninsula's resident goose population for hunting.

AN EXCEPTIONAL GIFT SHOP AND HERB GREENHOUSE . . . . . where the accent is on nature and regional crafts is **Einerlei** (it means "one and the same" in German) on Route 41 in Chassell. This is a restful, resourceful place that makes you want to slow down, enjoy your home, watch birds, and learn to do something useful and enjoyable like making lampshades or embroidering your own placemats. It has grown into a handsome, rambling series of spaces that feature sweaters that look handknit ($40-$75), vintage clothes and reproductions (the cotton shirts and Victorian nightgowns are wonderful), a tabletop shop, a kitchen shop with fancy foods, and an outstanding, well-stocked crafts room strong on how-to books and supplies, from paints and dyes to ribbons. The tightly planned rear garden of herbs, perennials, and scented geraniums (all for sale) centers on a greenhouse disguised as a summer house. *(906) 523-4612. Look for the green awnings on the west side U.S. 41 in the center of Chassell. Mon-Sat 10-6 (until 5 Jan-April), Sun 12-5.*

Quincy Mine Hoist

A Keweenaw landmark, it shows the great lengths mining companies went to extract copper.

This huge hoist shows what a big-time operation copper mining once was on the Keweenaw Peninsula. It was designed to haul ten tons of ore at a speed of 36 mph from a depth of almost two miles. It only operated during the 1920s and early 1930s, near the end of copper country's heyday. The Quincy Mining Company had the resources to build this largest-ever steam-powered hoist because it had mined one billion pounds of copper since opening in 1856. Enormous profits justified the enormous investment for this hoist. The big drum held 13,000 feet of 1 5/8 inch cable, and mine managers hoped that a much deeper shaft would be dug. But worldwide competition finally made the mile-deep Keweenaw copper too expensive to extract. Much cheaper open-pit mining today supplies worldwide demand. The once booming peninsula began its decline in the early 1920s and is still losing population at a greater rate that any other part of Michigan.

Keweenaw diehards still dream of a day when the demand for copper will rise enough to reopen the mine. Only 10% of the copper has been removed. But the temperature stays an uncomfortable 100° F. so far underground. And the big hoist is no longer operable.

A knowledgeable tour guide and a visit to the adjoining headframe make this a worthwhile trip. The headframe is the tall structure sided with corrugated steel that marks the actual entrance to the mineshaft. It was here that the miners began their workshifts, traveling 30 at a time well over a mile down to their stations. It was also here at the headframe that copper ore — millions of tons — was pulled up and dumped. The ore was then taken downhill by rail car to be purified in a stamping plant at Ripley on the canal. An informative six-minute newsreel-type film shows poignant glimpses of the men as they take their seats to be plunged to a dark, hot, and dangerous place of work. *Located 1 mile north of Hancock on U.S. 41. (906) 482-3101. Mid-June to Labor Day, 9:30-5.*

TWO TOURS OF COPPER MINES . . . . . the **Arcadian Copper Mine** tour takes place in a shaft which failed to link up with an older, formerly productive mine. So this isn't one of the many legendary Keweenaw mines, but its 1/4-mile shaft, at the end of which the temperature is just 40° F., gives an idea of what a copper mine is like. *3-minute drive from the bridge on M-26. Follow signs. Open June to mid-October. Mid-summer tours 8-5:25; otherwise 9-4:25. Adults $4, children $2.* . . . . . . Farther north near Copper Harbor is the **Delaware Copper Mine,** in operation from 1847 to 1887. You descend just 110-feet into the main shaft during the 40-minute tour. You can also see evidence of prehistoric mining pits and the ruins of 19th-century mining buildings. *U.S.-41 to Delaware, 12 miles south of Copper Harbor. (906) 289-4688. May-Oct. Adults $4 children $2.50.*

STOCK UP ON PICNIC SUPPLIES . . . . . at the **Keweenaw Co-op** in Hancock. It's definitely the best specialty grocery on the peninsula, with good produce, cheese, Asian and Middle Eastern ingredients, even wine and a deli section with meat, in addition to the expected natural and bulk foods and gourmet specialty items. Stop by for trail mixes and quality deli items before heading out to Copper Harbor, and you'll be prepared for impromptu picnics. (906) 482-2030. Mon-Sat 9-9, Sun 12-5. *As you drive north out of Hancock, U.S. 41 swings hard right at Santori's Tire. To get to the co-op, don't go right, go straight up onto Ethel. Co-op is in 2 blocks at Ethel and Ingot.*

DISTINCTIVE YOOPER FOODS . . . . . are a mark of strong regional identity, self-sufficient isolation, and the great distance from normal distribution channels. Some groceries and big supermarkets like Fraki's in Calumet (one street north of Fifth) have **"squeaky cheese"** (*nisula,* a pleasantly sweetish, somewhat Jello-y fresh cheese), **saffron rolls** (light dinner rolls, flavored and colored with brilliant yellow saffron with raisins added), and local Vollwerth's sausage. **Thimbleberry jam** is sold at houses along main tourist routes, and **pasties,** that famous Cornish meat-potato-rutabaga pie eaten by miners for lunch, are everywhere. **Trenary toast** is a twice-baked cinnamon toast made in Trenary, south of Marquette, and dunked in coffee.

Calumet and Laurium

The past lives on in multi-ethnic Copper Country —
hardy, poor, and friendly, a nation of its own.

The scene on Calumet's main street in the early 1900s was more like a leading metropolis than a remote mining town. It had brick streets, movie theaters and a grand opera house, frequent trolleys, electric lights, and impressive four-story buildings of brick and sandstone. Evenings were as bright and busy as daytime, what with miners working round-the-clock shifts and plenty of people with money to spend.

The Keweenaw's booming copper mines had recruited workers from most parts of Europe, and a polyglot could be heard on the streets: Finnish, Italian, Croatian, Slovenian, French, Polish, German, Swedish, Gaelic, Norwegian, Greek, English (spoken in Cornish, Irish, and Scottish accents), Welsh, and Yiddish. Each major ethnic group had its saloons, over 70 in all, where outsiders dared not venture as the evening wore on. And virtually every nationality had its church, often magnificent, paid for in part by the Boston-based Calumet and Hecla mining company.

Starting in the 1870s, the copper mines around Calumet proved the most profitable the world has known. Copper was an increasingly vital component used in the booming electrical and plumbing industries of a rapidly modernizing world. And these were the biggest copper mines anywhere in those days.

"Everywhere I saw steeples, steeples for churches," writes a fictitious visitor to Calumet in 1900, created by historian-journalist David Marciniak in *Copper Country History* magazine. "On a door one poster advertised a revival and temperance meeting. Another extolled the virtues of an upcoming mandolin and harp concert. . . . Businesses abounded: a candy kitchen, Madam Buddha — clairvoyant and trance medium straight from the World's Fair. Enameled iron beds, four dollars and up. Fishing tackle, lawn mowers, poultry screen and ice cream freezers. A Chinese laundry. The Bosch Brewing Company. . . ."

The Calumet and Hecla Mining Company was the richest and biggest of them all. Its office, now used by its successor, the **Lake Superior Land Company**, aren't on the regular visitor route. But they are interesting, and open to the public during business hours. They're on Red Jacket Road, just west of U.S. 41 by the turnoff to Calumet, in what looks like an oversize Queen Anne house made of contrasting stones of red and grey.

Despite the changes in ownership, the interior of these once-nationally famous offices, trimmed in varnished wood, remains very much as it must have looked when Calumet and Hecla reigned supreme in these parts: classic oak desks and map cases, cases of mineral specimens, and a big oil portrait of Alexander Agassiz, son of the famed Harvard botanist. Though he would rather have devoted himself full-time to the study of botany, Agassiz was persuaded to spend his most productive decades managing Calumet and Hecla in absentia. The company's Bostonian paternalism was widely resented here as controlling and condescending. East of the office building is a big piece of "float copper," pure copper formed in pocketed created by volcanic bubbles. Nearby is a seated bronze likeness of Agassiz. He has a cold, analytical gaze that changes unsettlingly as you change your point of view.

C&H sold its mines and land to Universal Oil Products, which closed the long-declining mines altogether during a 1968 strike. Later Universal sold its property, which includes most of Keweenaw County, to Lake Superior Land. The firm leases land for mineral rights, logging, and recreation, develops it, and sells it, sometimes in small, affordable lakefront lots.

Today Calumet and its more genteel sister community of Laurium are shadows of what they were in the decade after 1910, when 40,000 people lived in the area. Calumet now numbers 800, Laurium 2,200.

The glorious, boisterous past is felt everywhere, but muted by the years, and by the simple lifestyle of the locals. They're a special breed, composed of people who have hung on after the mines finally shut down in 1968, old-timers come back to retire, grown-up kids who went to school or visited grandparents here, and the nature-lovers and Michigan Tech faculty who have moved to these towns 12 miles north of Houghton.

There is an island atmosphere about this isolated place, akin to the gentle, faded mood of declining mining boom towns of the West — the kind of places populated by old hippies, artists, and retired miners. The splendid red brick and red sandstone buildings of the boom years remain. They have been preserved by local pride and the complete absence of development pressure since Keweenaw copper mining first began to sour after World War I.

The people remain, too, hanging on to memories and to dreams that some day, when the world price of copper rises high enough, the mining companies will drain and reopen the mines — and tunnel further south along the Keweenaw vein where much copper still lies deeply buried and untapped. (The Centennial Mine in nearby Kearsarge did reopen in 1990, but more as an adjunct to the timber industry. Its copper is used in a nearby facility that makes wolmanized lumber.)

In the meantime, Copper Country is a proud backwater. "Living up here is like living in the 1940s," says Lake Linden's dentist, a University of Michigan grad in his late 30s who likes to boast that he has the lowest income and best lifestyle of anyone in his dental school class. "The old values are important. Most people are honest. But you have to make your own activities — there's no entertainment here. A lot of newcomers don't understand that."

It especially helps to have a local map here, because Calumet and Laurium are really collections of smaller communities. Many consist of miners' houses clustered around onetime mine shafts: Tamarack, Centennial, Osceola, Red Jacket. Laurium has neighborhoods of more substantial houses for managers and white-collar workers. A good map is in the current year's edition of the always-interesting *Copper Country History*, a free visitor magazine available at the visitor information center on U.S. 41 and Lake Linden Road south of Calumet. Just north of it U.S. 41/Calumet Road passes by the area schools and the old C & H central facilities.

The **horse-drawn wagon tour** that leaves from Copper Town is a good introduction to Calumet then and now. Great old guys with wonderful Copper Country accents (as in "Dey tink dey're gonna do dat.") take you around their old haunts for half an hour. They'll tell you how Calumet stores sold peppermints by the carload because the local citizenry were "church-loving people who also loved to quench their thirst on Saturday night." They'll show you the Italian Hall park and memorial doorway where a horrible and famous disaster took place in 1913, during a prolonged mining strike. Someone yelled, "Fire!" during a Christmas party. There was no fire, but 73 people, mostly children, were trampled to death.

Tour guides don't shrink from mentioning how tailings dumped by the stamping mills into Torch Lake produced "fish with eyes out to here." Over the past few years, however, toxic sediments have settled and become covered over. Fish caught in the lake no longer have tumors. *Leaves from Red Jacket Road in front of the Copper Town museum, northwest of U.S. 41 near downtown Calumet. In July & August, Mon-Wed-Fri 11-4. Tours leave on half-hour. About $3.*

Noteworthy sights in the area include:

◆ The handsome red sandstone **Calumet Theater,** built at Elm and Sixth in 1900, and paid for by taxes on Calumet's busy saloons. Tours (around $2) are held in July and August. The interior has been faithfully restored to its original rich colors of gilt, red, green, and cream. The old theater still creaks enough to seem truly historic. You get to visit the dizzying upper balcony and antiquated lights still in place. When you get to the backstage dressing room used by Sarah Bernhardt, among others, it's not hard to imagine the gruelling life of train travel that took the likes of John Philip Sousa and Douglas Fairbanks to such remote corners of the country. Today many kinds of events are held here, including local theater, visiting foreign bands and dance troupes; a country music series sponsored by a local radio station; and the Detroit Symphony Orchestra. *Call (906) 337-2610 for information.*

◆ Next to the theater at 322 Sixth, you can stop for soup and sandwiches at **Shute's 1890 Bar**. It still has the magnificent back bar and all the trappings that marked boom town saloons. Shute's bar has a splendid stained-glass canopy with vines; elaborate plaster caryatids frame the raised dance floor.

◆ Two blocks south on Sixth at Portland, the **post office** has a dramatic W.P.A. mural of broad-backed miners at work deep within the earth.

◆ Summer tours of the unusually elaborate **St. Paul the Apostle** church, built by Slovenian Catholics from 1903 to 1908, let you see the beautiful stained glass windows, altar, and paintings. Go north on Eighth from here and you'll be in Calumet's most attractive residential district. *Eighth and Oak. Open from mid-July through mid-September, Monday through Friday, noon to 3. Donations appreciated.*

◆ If you take Oak or Elm to Ninth and go south on Ninth until it turns into Osceola, you'll come to **Swedetown** in three-fourths of a mile. It's one of the little outlying mineshaft hamlets where some miners (especially Scandinavians) kept milk cows and chickens and big gardens out back, to help feed their large families and make ends meet. The mining companies built these standard, six-room houses; today they sell for around $20,000. The **Swedetown Ski Trails**, six miles of cross-country trails, wind through small, rolling hills. They're groomed for traditional cross-country and ski-skating, and they're skiable well into April, after the snow cover has melted on south-facing slopes up here.

◆ Retailing in Calumet isn't much, although the town is the trade center for all of Keweenaw County and the northern part of Houghton County. There's just not much money, or many people, here. **Copper World** and **Copper Art** are two visitor-oriented stores together on Fifth at Portland, as you enter downtown from Red Jacket Road. The selection here is tremendous, and prices on items from copper tea pots, plates, and molds to burnished sailboats and copper jewelry are lower than in Copper Harbor's more tasteful, less overwhelmingly coppery shops.

◆ **Copper Town.** This amateur museum doesn't begin to approach the quality of the State of Michigan's iron-mining museum near Negaunee, but it does focus on copper mining and show how Calumet and Hecla produced usable copper from copper-bearing rock. Lots of mining equipment, old and new: drills, lamps, carts, and much more. *On Red Jacket Rd. between U.S. 41 and Calumet. (906) 337-4354. Open mid-June through Sept. Mon-Sat 10-4. Adults $1.50, 12 & under $50¢.*

◆ Neighboring **Laurium** shows off Copper Country's most gracious side. Time has not been kind to the historic downtown along Hecla. But just east of it, along Tamarack, Pewabic, and Iroquois between Second and Fourth, is a lovely, settled, neighborhood of turn-of-the-century homes, built with style and comfort to compensate mine managers for the hardships of having to live in this remote place. Some houses are quite grand, with rear carriage houses, sweeping stairways, stained-glass windows, and low red sandstone walls along the street; some are merely pleasant. Yards feature flower gardens, very long wood piles, and occasional Italian shrines. Deep maple shade sets this part of Laurium apart from the sparse streetscapes of miners' homes. To get to Laurium from U.S. 41. Turn southeast onto Lake Linden Rd. (M-26) at the visitor center.

Laurium Manor, a bed and breakfast inn in the mansion of mining magnate James Hoatson at 320 Tamarack, is open for tours ($2/person) at 2 p.m. daily. *Call (906) 337-2549.* At Third and Pewabic, there's a corner park with a **band shell,** where Thursday-evening summer concerts take place at 7 o'clock.

You could get a good Jilbert's ice cream cone for your walk at the **Honey Cone,** 224 Hecla at Depot. For a takeout picnic in the park, you could pick up pasties at **Toni's Country Kitchen,** nearby on Third at Kearsarge. It's reputed to have the best pasties around.

◆ **Jukuri's Sauna** is one of three public saunas left in the U.P. (Lots of homes have saunas out back, or inside the main house.) This plain tile building has 12 private, gas-fired saunas that rent for $3 an hour. They're fired up Wednesday and Friday from 2 to 10 and Saturday from 10 to 10. For many families, a relaxing visit to Jukuri's is a Saturday-night tradition, especially in mid-winter. (No one wears swimsuits, but men and women usually bathe separately.) Eating and unwinding is part of the event, and a big selection of junk food is sold in the pine-paneled foyer along with Jukuri's sweatshirts and T-shirts. *Wed & Fri 2-10 p.m., Sat 10-10. 600 Lake Linden Rd. (M-26). (906) 337-4145.*

THE BEST DISPLAY OF COPPER-MINING HISTORY . . . . . . is in Lansing in the **State Historical Museum** (see Mid-Michigan). Its **mining exhibits** include a life-size recreated passage within a copper mine, and currently they cover copper-mining far better than anything you'll find on location. (That will change if Calumet and nearby copper-mining attractions become a national park, as locals have been vigorously lobbying for.)

GOING DOWN TO LAKE LINDEN . . . . . from Laurium on M-26 is a spectacularly steep and scenic drive, because you're descending from the tilted-up edge of volcanic crust that carries the vein of copper. . . . . The **Douglass Houghton Falls** drop over the sheer cliffs of this edge. From M-26 about 1 1/2 miles southeast of the outskirts of Laurium, look for a flat dirt parking area to the left (northeast) side of the road. A path along the hilltop offers splendid views and the pleasant sound of Hammell Creek plashing between grassy banks. Then it disappears. Suddenly, without warning signs, a canyon opens up before you, dangerous and dramatic, and you see the creek rushing over rocks, then down to the canyon floor far below. There's no railing at all; this worthwhile adventure is no jaunt for rambunctious children. . . . . **Lake Linden** is a French-Canadian town built alongside the Calumet and Hecla stamping mills. C&H's great innovation was to develop a process that utilized small amounts of copper deposits carried by much of the area's rock, and not just the pure pockets of "float copper" formed in volcanic gas bubbles. C & H carried quantities of copper-rich rock by narrow-gauge railway down to Lake Linden on Torch Lake. There the rocks were crushed and the metal smelted out of the rock. The onetime C&H office and medical dispensary now house the motley collections of the **Houghton County Historical Museum**, yet another collection of poorly explained local history so common in U.P. mining areas. *On M-26 south of downtown. Open mid-June thru Sept, 10-5 daily. $1.50/adult, $3 family* . . . . . Far more evocative and interesting to the average visitor is the **Lindell Chocolate Shoppe** at 300 Calumet in downtown Lake Linden. It is an elaborate sweet shoppe from the 1920s, the glory days of that restaurant genre. Quick lunch counters and soda fountains like this thrived in newly industrialized areas, where workers had cash for inexpensive treats. Italian and especially Greek immigrants latched onto the sweet shoppe as a business opportunity where the whole family could work, making hand-dipped chocolates and ice cream, and where it didn't matter if their English was rudimentary. Here the Greek owners' names, Grammas and Pallis, are proudly spelled out in tiles on the entryway. Inside, the marble counter on the soda fountain has given way to formica, but the back booths and paneling are perfectly preserved. The interior is all aglow with golden oak, accented with little fringed lamps. The food (p. 502) is ordinary lunch-counter fare.

M-26 from Phoenix to Copper Harbor

*Something like Maine, something like Scandinavia —
great natural beauty without any pretensions*

About 15 miles north of Calumet begins one of the most
idyllic and undeveloped landscapes in the United States.
From Eagle River to Copper Harbor, the Lake Superior
shoreline looks a lot like Maine. Rocky shores and islets are interrupted by occasional crescent bays and beaches — some sandy,
some rocky. Few summer houses block the shoreline view from
M-26; considerations of real estate values and money don't seem
to come into play in this remote northwoods paradise. Frequent
roadside parks have benches, picnic tables, and occasional gazebos. Tidy rustic signs hanging from brown cedar posts point out
historic and scenic highlights. On the opposite side of the road,
trails climb into forests of white pine, balsam, and hardwoods
with ferny floors. Here, and on cutover sunny areas of birch and
aspen, the landscape looks amazingly like Scandinavia. Thimbleberry bushes with velvety, maple-like leaves and bright red berries
border many roads and cover open woods; occasional houses
advertise "THIMBLEBERRY JAM FOR SALE." The intensely-fla-
vored spread is locally prized.

Every few miles a sign points out the path to a waterfall, formed
as short creeks and rivers come cascading down to Lake Superior
from the peninsula's high spine. Past Eagle Harbor, you can
choose to stay along the lovely shore. Or you can take the famous
Brockway Mountain Drive (p. 489) up to a spectacular panoramic
view of the shoreline and inland lakes that leaves you feeling
you're floating above the Earth's surface in a balloon.

When you drive out from Calumet on U.S. 41/M-26, you follow a
high ridge and fault line that forms the spine of the Keweenaw
Peninsula. The ridge is marked by a string of spare, plain mining
settlements that stretch much of the way to Copper Harbor. Here
the ancient, mineral-rich volcanic crust, part of the Canadian
Shield, tilts northwest down into Lake Superior. The ridge is the
crust's edge. At the hamlet of Cliff, it becomes a dramatic, sheer
rocky precipice. It looms over the Eagle River, which cuts
through the Cliff Range at Phoenix and tumbles down to Lake
Superior. At Phoenix M-26 turns northwest off U.S. 41 and takes
the scenic route along the Eagle River and Lake Superior shore to

Copper Harbor.

From here to the Keweenaw's tip at Copper Harbor, copper deposits were closer to the surface, and in smaller amounts. Mining boomed early, in the 1840s, and played out soon. All of Keweenaw County, from Allouez and Mohawk to Copper Harbor, numbers only 1,700 year-round residents.

In 1844, the Cliff Mine became the Keweenaw's first mine to strike it rich and earn big profits. It and nearby mining villages and shipping ports toward the Keweenaw's tip are the oldest settlements in the western Upper Peninsula. Many houses and churches date from well before the Civil War and the ensuing industrial boom; they're simple frame buildings — sometimes you even see log houses — without any of the opulence of late 19th-century buildings in Calumet or Laurium, Houghton, or Marquette, with their sandstone ornament and stained glass.

Here are some interesting stops along M-26 between Calumet and Copper Harbor.

◆ **Superior Crafts** in Ahmeek. Resourceful locals make rustic cedar furniture and lawn swings in the former mine shafthouse of Ahmeek 3 and 4. Fifteen people are now employed in the shafthouse where 300 to 400 miners used to clean up and change clothes. Signs about mine safety precautions are still on the walls.

◆ **Keweenaw Handcrafts Shop** and the **snow gauge** just north of Ahmeek mark the entrance to Keweenaw County. The county is full of charming W.P.A. relief projects from the 1930s like these. Relief projects were widespread because of Keweenaw County's 85% unemployment rate during the Depression. The shop, open from summer through color season, sells things made by 260 craftspeople, mostly senior citizens, in three counties. Among the ordinary dolls and kit crafts are some attractive, reasonably priced traditional crafts like rag rugs ($23 for a 55" rug), folk art whirligigs ($32), and handmade children's sweaters under $20. The much-photographed snow gauge records annual cumulative snowfall, often 250 inches. Because the accumulated snow continually compacts and melts, there's rarely more than five feet at a time, except in drifts. (Snow removal is a major priority of local government. Locals figure they'll never have to wait long for the snow plow to come, but it's understood that all engagements are tentative, depending on the weather.)

◆ In **Phoenix**, stop at the **picnic table** by the **Church of the Assumption** or the general store and take in the view of river valley and rocky cliffs. The simple wood church was built in 1858 to serve miners at the Cliff mines. *Viewable by visitors from mid-June through Sept, daily 12-5. Donations welcome.*

◆ **Eagle River**, founded as a copper-shipping port in 1843, was

named after the many eagles soaring overhead. Now a summer
place with a tiny year-round population, it has several interesting
sights the hurried motorist might miss. On M-26 south of the village, the worn monuments in the rustic **Eagle River Cemetery**
attest to the many dangers and accidents that cut short miners'
lives. As you pass over the bridge across the **Eagle River gorge**,
pull over to the right, go over onto the old iron bridge, and look
upstream for a view of rushing rapids, the ruined dam of the Lake
Superior Fuse Company, and the dramatic wood arches supporting
the new bridge.

Douglass Houghton, Michigan's state geologist, who first drew
attention to the Upper Peninsula's mineral riches, drowned off
the shore of Eagle River after he ignored the recommendations of
his French and Indian guides and continued their canoe expedition in a storm. The **Houghton monument** by M-26 is boring.
Much more interesting is a visit to the **Keweenaw County courthouse**, on the upper road that branches off to the right as you
cross the bridge. It looks like a frame Southern mansion, with
massive columns and portico. Inside, you can get a good **map** of
county highways and byways. Government in this tiny county is an
exercise in small-scale thrift and ingenuity, frustrated by dealing
with bureaucrats in Lansing who impose downstate standards on
this depopulated area. For instance, the jail next door, behind the
sheriff's pleasant frame house, is continually threatened with
closing because it doesn't have a corrections officer on duty at all
times for the occasional drunk incarcerated there. Prisoners eat
good food prepared by the sheriff's wife for family and staff. Still,
the tiny county is urged to pay for transporting prisoners considerable distances and jailing them at approved facilities.

The **beach** at Eagle River is sandy and fairly warm but not as
scenic as others farther north. There's a lively beachfront restaurant, and even condos.

◆ **Sand Dunes Drive** is the name of the beautiful eight-mile
stretch of M-26 between Eagle River and Eagle Harbor. It parallels
the sandy beach of the **Great Sand Bay**. Frequent pullovers encourage motorists to get out and take a swim or walk down the beach.
The tilted shelf of volcanic crust drops off so rapidly under water,
that the bay is up to 1,300 feet deep.

Delightful **Jacob's Falls** cascades right near the road. Next to the
scenic pullout, a quaint little shop is now occupied by **The Jam
Pot**, a bakery/jam shop operated by a fellowship of monks established by men from the Lower Peninsula who live all year up here.

◆ **Eagle Harbor** is a quaint collection of ancient frame houses and
newish cottages. They surround a shallow, protected harbor and
beach that's one of Lake Superior's most reliably warm places to

swim. It's the prettiest village in the northern Keweenaw, with just enough attractions to make it a lazily interesting place to stay: two good, homey restaurants with pie and takeout sandwiches for a picnic (see p. 503), easy access to Brockway Mountain Drive and other excursions, and two delightful local museums run by the Keweenaw Historical Society, an energetic group of old-timers and summer people who have produced some impressive exhibits. The **Eagle Harbor Lighthouse and Museum** surveys the harbor entrance. The red brick lightkeeper's house, built in 1871, is realistically furnished circa 1910-1920 and staffed by local people old enough to go back almost that far themselves. Outside are picnic tables on a sunny, rocky promontory with a fabulous view. You could spend rainy hours looking at all the stuff in the adjoining Exhibit House: a mineral collection, paintings of local scenes, a fine exhibit on the Keweenaw's prehistoric copper culture, and an elaborate ritual costume of the fraternal order of the Knights of Pythias. The Eagle Harbor schoolteacher dreamed up the order here and founded it in 1864. The order's ceremonies, based on the Roman story of the friendship of Damian and Pythias, celebrate the virtues of brotherly friendship and self-sacrifice; the Knights' mock-Roman tunics are decorated with hundreds of metal discs.

A separate maritime museum building to the rear covers shipwrecks and fishing in great detail; another building deals with surveying, smelting, and mining. Many exhibits are dense stuff, too much for casual visitors. But the museum is the best single place on the Keweenaw to assemble an overview of the area's history. *Follow signs from M-26 to lighthouse/museum. Open daily, mid-June thru Sept, 12-5. $1/person, $2.50/family.*

More interesting material on the Knights of Pythias, including some fabulous fake jewels and embroidered satin robes, is in the **Rathbone School House** on a side street southeast of M-26 on the village's west side. *Open daily 12-5, mid-June through September. Donations welcome.*

◆ From **Eagle Harbor to Copper Harbor**, the view along 14 miles of lakeshore drive is the Keweenaw's rockiest and most dramatic stretch of shoreline. Four and a half miles east of Eagle Harbor, a roadside sign indicates **Silver River Falls**. By all means take the easy path through an overarching woods, both leafy and pleasantly piney. You'll hear and soon see the sparkling little river descending from a stone-arched bridge. Alternately it spreads out over rocky terraces and rests in a series of pools.

Across the river, **Brockway Mountain Drive** (p. 489) climbs 600 feet to one of the most spectacular views you're likely to see. Save it for an excursion from Copper Harbor. In half a mile, you'll come to **Esprey Park**, with picnic tables and grills, where stone steps go up to a rocky perch and a rustic gazebo. In five more miles, **Bear Foot Gift Shoppe** *(open daily 10-6, mid-May through October)* offers one of the area's nicest selections of crafts by regional artists and a splendid view from its free indoor **observation tower with telescope** (no admission fee). One mile east of it, **Hebard Park** is another simple little park with picnic tables, grills, out-houses, and wonderful view.

Three more miles and you come to the village of **Copper Harbor**, Keweenaw County's tourism hub.

"ONE CANNOT FEEL HISTORY FROM THE AUTOMOBILE," . . . . . advises a fine lit-tle free historical guide put out by the Keweenaw Historical Society, "so take leisurely walks through our old and abandoned villages, around mine sites and historic landmarks, allowing time to reflect upon those who have gone before. Your visit will be greatly enriched at no cost."

THE LOW-KEY CHARMS OF THE KEWEENAW'S EAST SHORE . . . . . Often when the scenic rugged, west-facing side of the peninsula is cloudy, the lower east side, pro-tected by the high central ridge, is sunny. It's completely flat, and once you get away from the towns along Dollar Bay, there's virtually no traffic, which makes for wonderful, easy bicycling. People from Keweenaw towns and cities have their "camps" for fishing and hunting up here ("cottage" is too sedate a term) but there's little resort activity. From Mohawk, turn east toward Gay. At the **Gay Bar**, a typi-cal Yooper bar, you can get a Gay Bar T-shirt, subtitled "Gay, Mich." The scenic **shore line drive** beginning at Gay passes many marshes, and shore birds are fre-quently seen. Wild blueberries can be picked from the road in most of August. The best swimming is at **Bete Grise** (locals say "BAY duh GREE"), east of Lac La Belle. Shallow depth makes for tolerably warm water for swimming. Eagles nest at Bear Bluff across Bete Grise Bay and are frequently seen. For an even less traveled trip, go south from Lake Linden on Bootjack Road and Dreamland Road to get to **Jacob-sville**, at the entry to the Portage Channel. Big red sandstone cliffs were quarried for many of the area's finest buildings. From the old lighthouse and breakwater, there's a fine view across the Keweenaw Bay to the Huron Mountains.

Brockway Mountain Drive

See glorious sunsets, soaring hawks,
and a splendid view of the Keweenaw's rocky shore.
on the highest highway between the Rockies
and the Alleghenies.

Most spectacular of all Keweenaw County's Depression-era relief projects is this nine-mile road that twists and climbs to one of the peninsula's highest peaks, a thousand feet above Lake Superior. At the windswept **Brockway Mountain Lookout**, you're so high above the Keweenaw Peninsula's rocky shore and islands stretched out below you, that the view seems almost like a living map. You can look down on soaring hawks and, occasionally, eagles.

The mountain's slope west down to Lake Superior is the surface of the Keweenaw's uptilted, copper-bearing volcanic crust. Inland, the broken edge along the north-south fault line here becomes an almost vertical rocky cliff that drops down to the river valley below. Each spring, peaking in mid-April, hawks migrate northeast along the entire Keweenaw Peninsula. They gather by these cliffs to ride the updrafts out to the peninsula's end — a final boost before their long flight across Lake Superior.

The view from the lookout is so riveting, it's easy to forget about all the other remarkable features of this unusual road, the highest between the Alleghenies and the Rockies. The habitat toward the top is actually semi-alpine. The mountain's many varied ecosystems are home to trillium, orchids, wild strawberries, and thimbleberries — over 700 flowers in all, including many rare and endangered species, some found nowhere else in Michigan.

Here and all over the northern Keweenaw, the land seems like a vast park. Actually, most of it is onetime mining land now owned by the Lake Superior Land Company (p. 478). In return for favorable commercial forest taxes, this land is legally open to the public for recreational use, including rock-gathering, mountain-biking, and berry-picking. The drive's stone walls — and the drive itself — are part of a Depression-era make-work project.

Be sure to stop at the **panoramic overlook** down onto Copper Harbor near the drive's eastern end. For maximum enjoyment, devote an hour or two to the drive and stop frequently. Bring binoculars, bug spray, walking shoes, and a compass if you want to hike in the forest. Take a late-afternoon trip, and you'll witness a sunset view that's hard to match. Fall color season is even more glorious. It usually begins the second week of September and lasts into mid-October.

Drive entrances are 5 miles northeast of Eagle Harbor and half a mile south of Copper Harbor. The drive is not plowed in winter. It's open from the first snow-free days of spring (that's usually in late May) up to the first snowfall. No admission fee.

GUIDED FIELD TRIPS NEAR COPPER HARBOR . . . . . may be arranged through Jim Rooks' Keweenaw Bear Track Tours. He was instrumental in saving the **Estivant Pines**, the Upper Peninsula's last stand of virgin white pines. They're one of his popular tour destinations, along with old mine sites, birdwatching expeditions, geology or wildflower walks, cross-country skiing, and more. Not for the impatient — Rooks has lots to say — but a good way to focus on the details of the natural world around you. Fees are $10/person/half day, children $5. Call him in advance (906-289-4813) to arrange a trip tailored to your interestes, or sign up for a regular 9 a.m. or 1 p.m. walk beginning at his wife's **Laughing Loon Handcrafts**. Get information about the Estivant Pines there or at Fort Wilkins. Look for *Walking Paths in Keweenaw*, a guide to the Michigan Nature Association's 11 preserves on the peninsula.

Fort Wilkins
Historic Complex

A remote Army outpost, built in the 1840s
to handle America's first mining rush

The 1843 Keweenaw copper rush, the first mining rush in American history, led to the building of this small fort. For three years the fort was the only source of law and order. The government's greatest concern was friction between native Indians and unruly newcomers, but little hostility actually broke out. By 1846 most of the small-time prospectors had left and large mining companies gave order and stability to the region.

This was a typical 19th-century frontier garrison, the most northern in the U.S., 600 miles from Detroit. The old fort became a favorite picnic spot among outdoor enthusiasts after the army abandoned it in the 1870s. The site is uncommonly picturesque, on beautiful Lake Fanny Hooe (named after a pretty young lady who early visited the fort), surrounded by forests. When the old fort became a state park in 1923, less than half the structures remained. Some buildings were rebuilt.

What you see today is a stockade surrounding 11 buildings: kitchen and mess room, hospital, bakery, company quarters, etc. Some have been restored and authentically furnished by the state's first-rate Bureau of History as they might have been; others have brief, to-the-point displays about military life and the archaeology and natural history of the fort. The lakefront building by the creek has a small **natural history bookstore.** Of the soldiers garrisoned here between 1844 and 1870, we learn that 8% died while in the army, half of natural causes, and 11% deserted. The officers' quarters have fancy lamps and furniture befitting their higher status. Their resident wives were supposed to bring civilization to the frontier.

It's worth beginning your visit by seeing the well-written **tape-slide show** in the visitor center installed in the first building you come to from the parking lot. It provides a fine introduction to the early history of Keweenaw copper-mining. (Just outside the fort is an abandoned mine shaft from the 1840s.) **Living history** can be a real highlight of a visit. When you look in some buildings — for instance, an enlisted man's simple cottage — you come upon a woman in period dress working away. Ask her questions about her life on the fort, and she answers in character — with a surprisingly convincing manner and accent. It's worth overcoming any embarrassment you might feel to come in for a chat; kids can really get interested in these conversations.

Check at the big **gift shop** outside the fort for a schedule of **evening slide shows** and events, and for information on boat tours to the **Copper Harbor lighthouse/museum**, managed by the park. The shop suits all tastes and has numerous nifty activity toys, books, and games for children.

2 1/2 miles east of Copper Harbor on U.S. 41. (906) 289-4215. Park open 8 a.m.-10 p.m. State park sticker required; $3/day, $10/year. Park interpreters and living history on site 10-4:30 daily from mid-June to Labor Day. Buildings open mid-May through mid-October. Park open all year.

CAMPING AT FORT WILKINS . . . . . isn't terribly adventurous, but the location is most convenient. 162 modern sites are on big loops in wooded areas that back up on beautiful Lake Fanny Hooe (good for swimming) and are adjacent to the old fort, camp store, old cemetery, and other nifty sights. You can easily walk across the road and see Lake Superior, and it's not far to the town of Copper Harbor, either. Reserve in advance from July through mid-August, especially Monday through Wednesday.

HEAVEN FOR ROCKHOUNDS . . . . . The public is permitted to visit and gather rocks and berries on the vast land holdings of the Lake Superior Land Company, which includes most of the northern Keweenaw Peninsula. Maps of agate beaches and old mines with rock piles can be purchased at the **New Keweenaw Agate Shop** on U.S. 41 in Copper Harbor. Mineralogist-owner Les Tolen has a splendid collection of mineral specimens (datolite, greenstone, and malachite are native to the area), lots of books on area geology, and rockhounds' tools. *Open daily from Memorial Day through mid-October. He may be away at shows other times; call first. (906) 289-4491.*

Isle Royale

Over 50 miles from the Michigan mainland,
this remote and wild island is a superb place
for hikers or fishermen to get away from it all.

For the person seeking the ultimate Midwestern wilderness experience, this 44-mile-long island is a wonderful candidate. The largest and most remote of all Great Lake islands is a 56-mile boat ride from Copper Harbor and Michigan's Upper Peninsula. The narrow island, only three to nine miles wide, is a series of long ridges culminating in several lava peaks. You can still see some of the hundreds of primitive copper-mining pits dug by Indians hundreds of years ago. The only known villages here were short-lived, set up briefly by copper-mining companies in the late 19th century. A few commercial fishermen have lived here, but for the most part this has remained a pristine natural area. A much-studied timber wolf population which crossed on an ice bridge in 1948 has dwindled to 12. A moose herd which crossed frozen Lake Superior in 1912 now numbers 1,300, the greatest density of moose in the lower 48 states.

Hikers have 166 miles of paths to follow, including the 42-mile **Greenstone Trail** following the island's central ridge. This five- to six-day trek is the most popular. Some hikers start out after taking a seaplane to the southeastern end. The trip's first part is through thickly forested terrain affording few views. **Mount Ojibway** (elevation 1,183 feet) is one of several peaks along the trail that provides splendid views to the Canadian mainland 15 miles away. Small campgrounds are along the trail three to 12 miles apart. There are 36 campgrounds in all, with 253 campsites, but only a few allow fires. Other campers bring their own portable stoves. A water filter is also needed, except in the two campgrounds by the ferries on either end of the island. They have water, fire pits, and showers. Backpacking novices are advised to get in shape, try out equipment beforehand, and plan carefully before embarking on a trip where they may be several days' hike from help. Camping is free. Campers should obtain backcountry permits on the island; sites aren't reservable.

Many come to fish for pike, plentiful in lakes such as Lake Richie. Lake Whittlesey is known for walleye, and huge Siskiwit Lake for brook trout. Because the island's 42 lakes have to be reached by foot, none are heavily fished. Boats and canoes can be brought over from Houghton on the Ranger III. Some camp-grounds are on islands reachable only by water.

For those who aren't into backpacking, a concessionaire runs **Rock Harbor Lodge**. Its 60 rooms cost $76 per person, double occupancy, including meals. It is the headquarters for boat and canoe rentals, sightseeing tours (including a two-hour evening cruise/nature hike), a restaurant, and a store with camping supplies. Free nature walks and nightly auditorium programs are held here, too. Twenty nearby housekeeping cabins rent for $88 a night (no meals) and should be reserved well in advance.

Late August and early September is the best time to visit Isle Royale. By then the sometimes irritating fly population has dwindled, and so have the number of visitors. But the island is never crowded. Typically fewer than 300 people share the 134,000 acres.

The nation's most remote national park, Isle Royale is an improbable part of the state of Michigan. It's just 15 miles from Canada and far closer to Minnesota than Michigan. Legend has it that Benjamin Franklin secured it for the U.S. in negotiations with the British because he thought its copper would be useful in electrical experiments.

Open for visitors mid-April through October. Full services mid-June to Labor Day. Boat service from Copper Harbor (4 1/2 hours one-way), Grand Portage, Minnesota, or Houghton (6 hours; $70-$80 round trip for adults, $40 for children under 12, $27 per canoe). Float plane from Houghton. For more details, write Isle Royale National Park 87 N. Ripley, Houghton, MI 49931. (906) 482-0984. Reservations for Rock Harbor Lodge during off season, (502) 773-2191; in season (906) 337-4993.

Recommended Restaurants & Lodgings
Upper Peninsula

To locate cities, see regional map, p. 446.

SAINT IGNACE

Clyde's Drive-In. *On west U.S. 2, just west of the Bridge. (906) 643-8303.* 7 days, 9 a.m.-midnight. No credit cards, no alcohol. Regionally famous for great burgers , from the 1/8-lb. Junior ($1.10) to the 3/4-lb. "Clyde's Colossal" ($4.50). Malts & shakes $1.10/$1.25. Chicken, steak or shrimp dinners with fries & slaw $4.50-$5. Counter seating.

Best Western Georgian House. *(800) 322-8411, (906) 643-8411. 2 mi. north of St. Ignace on Bus. I-75. Busy strip.* 84 rooms on 3 floors. Cable TV, phones. Some jacuzzis. Mid-July-Aug: $84-$104. Early July: $69-$89. Late June & late Aug: $54-$74. Winter: $52-$74. Late spring: $44-$64. Indoor pool, whirlpool, rec. area, playground, miniature golf, on beach w/grills. Restaurant adj.
Loads of activities, indoor pool, own beach, great views

Wayside Motel. *(906) 643-8944. On Bus. I-75, 1 block from ferries in downtown St. Ignace.* 18 units. Summer: $38-45. Off-season: $28-$32. Cable TV. Basketball court. Restaurants nearby.
Budget rates, near Mackinaw Island ferries

Birchwood Motel. *(906) 643-7738. 1809 Bus. I-75, 2 mi. n. of downtown St. Ignace, 1/4 mi. from Castle Rock.* 10 units on 1 floor. $28-$36, $5 extra for kitchenettes. Open year-round. Playground, access to sandy beach. No phones.
Budget rates, beach access

EPOUFETTE

Wonderland Motel. *(906) 292-5574. 80 W. U.S. 2, 28 miles w. of Mackinac Bridge.* 10 rooms on 1 floor. Late June-late Oct $28-$31. Off-season $26-$29. Satellite TV. Phone in office. Picnic area, across from beach. All rooms have view.
Budget choice on bluff overlooking Lake Michigan beach

SAULT STE. MARIE

Freighters. *240 Portage in the Ojibway Hotel. (800) 654-2929, (906) 632-4108. Sun-Thurs 6 a.m.-9:30 p.m., Fri-Sat to 10. Visa, MC, AmEx, Diners. Full bar.* Good view of locks. Known for seafood (shrimp scampi $8/$17) & steaks. Breakfasts $1.25-$5. Lunch prices: $1.75 burger-$8 shrimp scampi w/starch & veg. Dinner includes starch, vegetable, salad: whitefish or lake perch $14, scampi $17, seafood linguine $19.

The Antlers. *804 E. Portage at end of I-75 bus. spur (Ashmun). (906) 632-3571. Open daily 11-10 (shorter winter hours). AmEx, Diners, MC, Visa. Full bar. Same menu all day.* Locals praise rustic bar decor, goofy atmosphere (whistles and sirens), good food. Large collection of mounted animals, birds, memorabilia. Overflow dining room downstairs, canopied outdoor deck/bar. Big draws: BBQ ribs (big rack $14), 1/2 lb. burgers ($3.55), steaks ($9-$15). Sandwiches ($5.25-$6.25) on homemade bread w/fries. Steamed shrimp $10, whitefish $11 (beer-battered or broiled). Mexican: super tacos ($5.25), nachos ($6-$8), huge wet burrito ($7-8).

Clyde's Drive-In. *On Riverside Dr. (Portage changes to Riverside) at gateway to Sugar Island next to municipal campground. (906) 632-2581. Daily 11-11.* Famous, small U.P. burger chain. See St. Ignace, above.

Ojibway Hotel. *(800) 654-2929, (906) 632-4100. 240 W. Portage adjacent to Soo Locks, Locks Park,* 71 rooms on 6 floors. In season: $85-$95. Off-season: $75. Cable TV. Indoor pool, sauna, whirlpool, Freighters restaurant. Restored 1928 historic hotel. Some rooms have view of locks.
Locals' favorite: updated 1928 hotel w/good restaurant

Sno-White Motel. *(906) 632-7413. 3295 I-75 Bus. spur on busy strip south of downtown.* Open May thru mid-Oct. 14 rooms on 1 floor. $28-$42. Cable TV. No A/C.
Good budget choice

Best Western Colonial Inn. *(906) 632-2170. 581 W. 3 Mile at I-75 exit 392 s. of Sault Ste. Marie.* 58 rooms on 2 floors. Mid-June-Labor Day: $67-$77. Sept-mid-Oct: $55-$60. Off-season: $49-$54. Cont. breakfast. Cable TV. Indoor pool, sauna, game room, picnic tables. Shopping, restaurants within 1/4 mi.
Activities, indoor pool

Days Inn. *(906) 635-5200. I-75 Bus. spur. On busy strip 2 mi. s. of downtown.* 82 rooms on 2 floors. Spring: $58-$73. Summer/fall: $72-$84. Winter: $42-$48. Some w/jacuzzi. Cable TV. Indoor pool, jacuzzi, game room. Restaurant/ lounge.
New; best luxury choice

BLANEY PARK

Blaney Inn. *On M-77, 1 mi. n. of U.S. 2 in Blaney Park. (906) 283-3417.* Open mid May-mid Oct. Tues-Sat 5 p.m.10, Sun at noon, closed Mon. Visa, MC, AmEx. Full bar. Renovated dancehall from 1930s resort. Pleasant atmosphere, good food. Known for seafood fettucini ($13). Complete dinners $10 (whitefish or chicken) to $13. A la carte: Blaney burger & soup $6, pasta marinara or alfredo $7, pasta primavera $9. Children half price. Weekend dinner organ music.

Blaney Camp 9. *(906) 283-3163. Blaney Park, corner of U.S. 2 & M-77.* 12 units in rooms or cottages built for 1930s resort. $40-$55. No phones. Cottages have LR, BR, bath, TV. Country decor. Cont. breakfast served to you. Horseshoes, volleyball, gas grills. No cooking.
Delightful colonial cottages, freshly decorated

Celibeth House. *(906) 283-3409. On M-77 1 mi. n. of U.S. 2.* B&B. 9 rooms w/ baths on the first 2 floors. $40-$50. Cont. brkfst. Phones avail., no TV. Living room, reading room, enc. front porch, back deck. Antique-furnished turn-of-the-century house sits on 85 acres overlooking Lake Anne Louise in logging camp-turned-resort. Shore fishing, nature trails.
Beautiful old house; locally knowledgeable hostess

GARDEN CORNERS

Garden Bay Motel. *(906) 644-2258. 1 mi. s. of U.S. 2 on M-183.* 6 units on 1 floor. All have living room, kitchen, bath (5 have 2 bedrooms). $28-$35. TV. Phone in office. On Big Bay De Noc. Picnic area, beach, fish cleaning house.
Fishermen's special: efficiency suites in pretty spot on bay, very low price

MANISTIQUE

Clyde's Drive Inn. *On Chippewa Ave. (old U.S. 2) 1/2 mi. west of "floating bridge" near new U.S. 2 bypass.* (906) 341-6021. Sun-Thurs 9-10 (midnight in summer), Fri-Sat 9-11 (1 a.m. summer). No credit cards or alcohol. Small U.P. chain with great burgers. See p. 000.

Ramada Inn. *(906) 341-6911. On U.S. 2, 1 1/2 mi. e. of Manistique, overlooking Lake Michigan.* 40 rooms on 2

floors. Mid-May thru mid-June: $65. Mid-June thru Labor Day: $75. Oct thru mid-May: $55. Cable TV. Indoor pool, hot tub, sauna, exercise room, game room, basketball court. 2 restaurants, bar w/ weekend entertainment. 40-space campground.
Indoor pool, lots to do

Holiday Motel. *(906) 341-2710. On U.S. 2, 3 1/2 miles e. of Manistique on busy strip.* 20 rooms on 1 floor. June 15-Labor Day week: $36-$40. Off-season: $26-$28. Cable TV. No A/C. Cordless phones available. Outdoor pool, playground, basketball, volleyball, picnic area. Sandwiches and pizza nearby. Park on Lake Michigan within a mile. Owners raise deer at rear of motel, fenced in and very tame.
Lots of outdoor activities, reasonable rates

GRAND MARAIS

Sportsman's Bar. *On M-77 north (main street). Mem.-Labor Day: kitchen open 7:30 a.m.-10 p.m., to 11 Fri & Sat. Otherwise: closes at 9, 10 weekends.* Full bar. Visa, MC. Old-timey bar is most popular eating place in town. $5.25 basket of delicious fried whitefish with coleslaw, fries feeds 2. Other baskets: chicken ($4), perch $6). Big Mexican menu. Wet burrito ($7) feeds 2. Kids menu. BBQ ribs on weekends, prime rib all the time (8 oz. sandwich, salad bar $9). (The Dunes Bar, for more serious drinkers, has the only pizza in town.)

Lakeview Inn. *(906) 494-2612. Hwy M-77 at H-58, 1st house at bottom of hill, just past edge of business block, 1/2 block from beach.* 4 rooms share 2 baths. $40-$50. Year-round. Big breakfast w/ hot dish, many fresh-baked treats. Overlooks bay. Guests use living room w/ TV, sun porch, sitting room. Rentals: snowshoes, canoes, rowboats.
Convenient location, good food, lots to do

Superior Hotel. *(906) 494-2539. 125*

Lake Ave. at the foot of the hill. 9 rooms on 2nd floor of plain old hotel share 2 baths. $15 ($12 if more than 1 night). Only place in town to get a newspaper.
Clean and extremely simple, with hard-to-believe rates

Alverson's Motel. *(906) 494-2681. 1/2 blk e. of M-77 opposite the harbor.* 15 rooms on 2 floors. $28-$33. TV. Phone in lobby. Rec room w/pool table. Pleasant rooms.
Nice view of bay from large second-floor windows

MUNISING

Days Inn. *(906) 387-2493. On M-28 east in downtown Munising.* 59 rooms on 2 floors. $55-$70. Slightly lower in spring & fall. Kitchenettes avail. Cable TV. Indoor pool, hot tub, sauna, basketball.
Indoor pool. U.P. luxury.

Sunset Resort Motel. *(906) 387-4574. M-58 1 mi. e. of M-28. In quiet residential area.* 16 units on 1 floor. Open May-Oct. June 15-Labor Day week: $39. Off-season: $32. All units face Munising Bay. Small beach, play area, shuffleboard.
Budget motel on beach

Yule Log Resort. *(906) 387-3184. On M-28 in Christmas, 3 mi. w. of Munising.* 8 cabins. Open May-Oct. 2 family cabins on beach: $60. Other cabins $25-$60. All w/TV, kitchen or efficiencies. Swings, badminton, horseshoes, picnic area.
Cottages with kitchens. On beach, with activities

SHINGLETON

Tanglewood Restaurant. *On M-28 in town. Open daily 7 a.m.-8 p.m., earlier closing in spring.* Full bar. MC, Visa, Diners, CB. Good homemade pies, soups, fresh whitefish or trout dinners for $9 including soup, salad bar. Hot beef sandwich ($4 w/ slaw) a lunch hit.

MENOMINEE

Schloegel's. *2720 10th St., 1 mi. n. on U.S. 41 overlooking Green Bay. (906) 863-7888. Mon-Sat 6 a.m.-10 p.m., Sun 8-8. No credit cards or alcohol.* Family restaurant, known for New England style clam chowder, fresh local fish, German dishes. One menu all day. Breakfast $4-$5. Sandwiches $2-$4. Complete dinner: meat loaf $5, braised lamb shank $7. Desserts ($1.60) from own bakery. Patio seating on bay side.

HERMANSVILLE

Wildwood Restaurant. *On U.S. 2. (906) 498-2342. Open daily 6 a.m.-8 p.m. No credit cards or alcohol.* Modest diner w/ big portions, good soups. Same menu all day. Plate lunches w/ fries, slaw from $3.40 (burger) to $6 (fried perch). Good roast chicken dinner under $6.

IRON MOUNTAIN AREA

Brenda's Corner Cafe. *221 East "A" St. in Iron Mountain. (906) 774-4202. Mon-Fri 5:30 -4, Sat 6-2 , Sun 7-12:30. No credit cards or alcohol.* Small-town cafe a popular breakfast spot. 2 eggs & toast $1.85; 3-egg omelets $2.75-$5.75. Lunch includes pasties ($2.50), homemade ravioli ($6), $4.25 specials.

Blind Duck Inn. *On Cowboy Lake, across from Kingsford airport (follow signs to airport). (906) 774-0037. Mon-Sat 11-10, Sun 5-10. Visa, MC, Disc, AmEx. Full bar.* Pleasant spot overlooking lake. Best known for wet burrito $4/$5.25. At lunch, Mexican comb. plates or fried cod w/salad & potato are $5.75, salad, potato, sandwich plate is $4.25. Salads & sandwiches avail. all day. Dinners range from spaghetti ($4.50), taco dinner ($5) to shrimp or steak ($12).

Northern Host Inn. *(906) 774-3400. 2702 N. U.S. 2 at n. edge of Iron Mountain.* 90 rooms on 2 floors. $38-$53 double. Suites, kitchenettes avail. Cable TV. Whirlpool, sauna. Near Lake Antoine beach.
Good location, moderate rates

Pine Mountain Lodge. *(800) 321-6298, (906) 774-2747. N3332 Pine Mt. Rd. 2 mi. n. of Iron Mountain.* Summer: $47-$52. Ski season (Thanksgiving-March): $52 midweek, $55-$65 weekends. (4 people: $8 extra). Cable TV. Indoor pool, whirlpool, game room, golf course, tennis, x-c ski trails, downhill skiing. Restaurant, bar. At base of Pine Mountain ski slopes near Wisconsin border.
Ski resort with loads of activities

Blind Duck Inn. *(906) 774-0037. See restaurants for directions.* 4 rooms on 1 floor. $24. A/C, private bath, cable TV. Phone avail. Docks, lake connects with Menominee river. Public beach across lake. Restaurant.
Low rates, lakeside location

Sportsman's Paradise Resort. *(906) 246-3430. Take M-95 n. of Iron Mountain 10 mi., right on county road ER 569 (G-30) 10 1/2 mi, left on Norway Lake Rd. 5 1/2 mi.* Dec 15-Apr 15: $40-$45. Off-season: $30-$35. (Price inc. rowboat, no motors on lake.) Special rates for 2-week stays. 5 cabins w/2 BR, kitchen, shower-bath. Swimming & picnic areas, fire pit, horseshoes, volleyball.
Inexpensive, ample lakeside cottages

ONTONOGAN AREA

Paul's Supper Club. *M-107 in Silver City, in Best Western Porcupine Mt. Lodge. 3 mi. from Porcupine Mts. State Park. On Lake Superior. (906) 885-5311. 7 days 7 a.m.-9:30 p.m. (dinner only in April & May).* Casual spot overlooking lake. Best known for 1-lb. BBQ pork chops w/glazed Chinese red sauce ($10.50). Dinners inc. salad bar: 1/2 lb.

ground sirloin $7, prime rib $14. Lunch entrees with slaw, fries $4-$7. Sandwiches $2.50-$4.25.

Konteka Supper Club. *At M-64 & Main St. in White Pine. (906) 885-5215. Open year-round 6 a.m.-2 a.m. daily. Major credit cards. Full bar.* Known for Sun breakfast buffet ($6), Fri night seafood buffet ($10). All-day sandwich, salad menu. Breakfast averages $3.50. Dinners w/ salad bar from $8 (half-portion baby back rib, chicken dinner) to $13 (steak & shrimp). Fresh Lake Superior fish. 8-lane bowling alley w/games, pool table.

Konteka Motel. *(906) 885-5215. At M-64 & Main St., Mineral River Plaza. White Pine.* 16 rooms on 1 floor. $47 ($40 weekends Apr-Nov). Cable TV. Restaurant and bowling alley/game room adjacent. Park for tennis, basket ball, track,horseshoes 1 block away. *Near many activities, moderate rates*

Best Western Porcupine Mountain Lodge. *(906) 885-5311. M-107 in Silver City, 3 mi. from Porcupine Mt. State Park. On Lake Superior shore.* 49 rooms on 2 floors. Summer & winter $59, April & Oct.15-Nov 15: $49-$59. Packages, group rates avail. A/C, satellite TV. Indoor pool, sauna, spa, game room. Some in-room hot tubs. Restaurant, bar, live music for dancing on winter weekends. *Moderate prices, lake views, lots to do*

MARQUETTE

Entre Amigos. *142 W. Washington, bus. U.S. 41 west of downtown. 1 block off 3rd across from the Delft Twin Cinema. (906) 228-4531. Sun-Thurs 11-10:30, Fri-Sat 11-11:30. Visa, MC.* Beer, wine, margaritas; full bar in lounge upstairs. Same menu all day. 10-min. lunch specials Mon-Fri $3-$5. Entrees served w/ rice & beans, priced from $6.29 (burrito and enchilada, or chicken filet on Spanish rice with sauce) to $12.50 (shrimp fajitas). Steak or chicken fajitas ($10.50) a specialty.

Papa Paul's Pasties. *447 W. Washington (Bus. U.S. 41) across from the Ramada Inn. (906) 225-0310.. Mon-Sat 10-7 (Sun noon-6, summer only). No credit cards or alcohol.* Carryout only. A candidate for best U.P. pasties, though some would ask how much better can one of these meat-potato-rutabaga-onion pies be from another? Jumbo John $2.19, Papa $1.79, Mama $1.49, Bite $2.99 doz. Vegetable: $1.79. Shipped wholesale to supermarkets in Detroit & Grand Rapids.

Northwoods Supper Club. *On Northwoods, 3 1/2 mi. w. of Marquette on U.S. 41/M-28. (2 blocks off hwy, turn at sign). (906) 228-4343. Open daily 11 a.m.-midnight (close at 10 in winter). AmEx, Diners, MC, Visa. Full bar.* Sprawling place in woodsy setting is *the* white-tablecloth destination restaurant in area. Best known for prime rib (3 cuts $12.45-$16.45) and fresh whitefish and lake trout ($11). Also, Sun. brunch (10:30-2, $7) and Tues. night smorgasbord ($10). Complete lunches $6 (for shrimp & scallop platter) and under. Sandwiches available all day in bar.

The Vierling Saloon & Sample Room. *119 S .Front at Main, downtown. (906) 228-3533. Mon-Sat 8 a.m.-10 p.m. (shorter winter hours). MC, Visa, AmEx. Full bar.* 1883 saloon with elaborate old bar, recently renovated, with history memorabilia. Great view of bay, ore docks from back tables. Everything a la carte. Fresh daily Lake Superior whitefish, fixed 5 ways from fried to blackened to caper-wine-tomato sauce ($8-$10) a specialty. Breakfasts $5 and under. Good salads (Greek salad $2.85, shrimp salad $4.50). Many HeartSmart, lighter dinner entrees: vegetable cheese ravioli ($6.50), chicken stir-fry ($8), also rich things like veal and shrimp in bernaise sauce ($12.50).

Cedar Motor Inn. *(906) 228-2280. U.S. 41 (M-28) 2 mi. w. of downtown. On busy strip between 2 malls.* 37 units on 1st floor, 7 units on 2nd floor. July-Oct: $32-$44. Off-season: $30-

$42. Luxury efficiencies avail. Cable
TV. Indoor pool, hot tub, sauna.
Budget choice with indoor pool

Ramada Inn. *(906) 228-600. 4 blocks
w. on U.S. 41 bus. rt.* 115 rooms on 7
floors. $58-$65. Cable TV. Suites avail.
Indoor pool, whirlpool, sauna, game
room. Restaurant, bar.
*Only downtown motel;
indoor pool and good views*

Holiday Inn. *(906) 225-1351. U.S. 41,
1 3/4 mi. w. of Marquette.* 208 rooms.
$39-$54 for 1-4 people. Packages avail.
Cable TV. Indoor pool, sauna, game
room, exercise room. Restaurant, bar.
Reasonable rates, many activities

BIG BAY

Thunder Bay Inn. *(906) 345-9977.*
Open year-round. 14 rooms. June-Oct
$49-$69, off-season $39-$49. Rooms
over busy bar with music. Not for light
sleepers. Share baths (1 for women, 1
for men). Sinks in rooms. Suites have
private baths. Cont. breakfast. No TV.
Phone in lobby. Pool table, jukebox,
horseshoes. Beach, lifeguard down the
street. Bar (built for 1959 classic movie
"Anatomy of a Murder") has full menu.
Adults only. Large lobby. Antique
decor. Henry Ford turned warehouse/
office into a hotel, recently refurbished. Factory across street made bowling
pins, then sides for Ford "woodies."
*Old-timey hotel from Henry Ford era,
recently refurbished*

Big Bay Point Lighthouse. *(906)
345-9957. In old lighthouse on Big Bay
Pointe, 30 mi. n.w .of Marquette.* Open
year-round. 5 rooms in 2-story house,
1 in base of lighthouse). $95-$135. 2
share bath. 3 have baths. Cont.
breakfast. No A/C. Phone avail.
Sauna. Guests can use kitchen, dining,
living room w/fireplace. 100 acres
along 1 mile of Lake Superior. 2 miles
of groomed trails, 5 acres of lawn.
*Great views from B&B
in isolated lighthouse*

ISHPEMING

Mama Mia's. *207 E. Pearl in downtown Ishpeming. (906) 485-5813.* Mon-
Thurs 11-11, Fri 11 -midnight, Sat
4:30-midnight, Sun 4:30-11. MC, Visa,
Disc. Full bar. Known for lasagna ($7
with salad) and steaks ($7.35). Good
Italian sausage sandwich $(2.85).,

MICHIGAMME

Mt. Shasta Restaurant. *On U.S.
41. (906) 323-6312. Open May-Oct.,
may stay open in winter. Open daily,
noon to 10 p.m. Visa, MC. Full bar.*
Vintage log lodge decorated with stills
from "Anatomy of a Murder." Cast
stayed here; author John Voelker was
friend of owner. Ask to see scrapbook.
Sandwiches ($3.25-$5.75 w/fries &
salad) available all day. Complete
dinners range from $6.50 (liver &
onions, fresh lake trout) to $13.50 (T-
bone steak). Homemade pies.

Michigamme Lake Lodge. *(906)
225-1393 on Lake Michigamme off
U.S. 41.* Open May 1-Oct. B&B. 9 rooms
w/private or shared baths. $100-$125.
Cont. breakfast. Phone avail. Living
room w/huge fireplace, outdoor patio
area. Beautiful site on bluff overlooking lake. Private beach, canoeing,
wooded trails. On bluff surrounded by
birch trees.
B&B in wonderful log lodge from 1930s

BARAGA

Lakeshore Motel. *(906) 353-6256.
U.S. 41, 6 mi. n. of Baraga on Keewee-
naw Bay.* 10 units on 1 floor. $28.
Cable TV. View of bay. Sauna.
*Low rates, bay view,
good adjoining restaurant*

CHASSELL

Chippewa Restaurant. *U.S. 41 next to Chippewa Motel in Chassell. (906) 523-4940. Mon-Thurs 7-7, Fri-Sat to 8, Sun 8 -7 (shorter winter hrs.) MC, Visa, Disc, Diners. No alcohol.* Very popular locally. Own bakery. Middle American quality cooking. View of Portage Lake. Huge breakfast cinnamon rolls. All-day sandwich menu. Complete dinner (w/ salad bar in summer) from $5.25 (spaghetti) to $9 (stuffed whitefish), $14 (porterhouse steak).

Onigaming Supper Club. *3 mi. s. of Houghton on Portage Lake side of U.S. 41. (906) 523-4572. Open May-Oct 5-10 p.m. MC, Visa. Full bar.* Houghton area's leading "fine dining" spot has knotty pine, captain's chairs, big windows looking onto Portage Lake. Fresh broiled Lake Superior trout ($10) is tasty indeed. Entrees come w/appropriate sides. From $7.50 (liver burgundy) to $17 (20 oz. T-bone). Also fish, seafood, lamb chops, BBQ ribs ($13).

Chippewa Motel. *(906)-523-4611. U.S. 41 in Chassell on Portage Lake., strip location.* 15 units on 1 floor. 2 bdrm and kitchenettes avail. May-Oct: $38-$70. Nov-Mar: $36-$64. Cable TV. Phone in lobby. Beach, boat ramp, picnic tables, grills, playground in rear. No water views. A friendly favorite with business travelers. *Big, clean rooms, good restaurant*

Palosaari's Rolling Acres B&B. *(906) 523-4947. On North Entry Rd. 1.3 miles. off U.S. 41, 4 mi. s. of Chassell.* 3 small rooms w/shared bath, $36. Big breakfast. Children welcome. Check or cash only. TV in living room, phone in upstairs hall. Electric sauna. Less than 1 mile from channel for picnics, boat launch w/access to Lake Superior. Dairy farm w/small farm animals. Great for getting a taste of real farm life with delightful hosts. Not for the standoffish. *Homey, inexpensive farm stay B&B*

HOUGHTON

The Library Bar & Restaurant. *62 Isle Royale St. off Bus. U.S. 41 downtown. Turn toward channel, park just beyond restaurant. (906) 482-6211.* Mon-Sat 11:30 a.m.-1 a.m., Sun 5 p.m.-1 a.m. Visa, MC, Diners. Full bar. Bar with offbeat, neo-medieval academic look, interesting glow of stained glass on brick walls. Very casual. Sandwiches come in baskets. Popular with Tech students, faculty families. Live music on weekends. Food takes back seat to atmosphere. All-day sandwich menu around $3.25. Complete dinners from $6 (lasagna) to $13 (steak tenderloin). Liver pate, snails, other surprises for U.P. Desserts, homemade ice cream a specialty.

Los Dos Amigos. *52 N. Huron off Bus. U.S. 41 downtown. Turn down toward channel. (906) 482-1991. Mon-Thurs 11-10, Fri-Sat 11-midnight. No credit cards. Full bar, many beers on tap, non-alcoholic drinks. Same menu all day.* Colorful, Mexican hangings, plants. Good Mexican standards come in chicken, seafood, tenderloin; typically $4-5. Known for chicken & steak fajitas $7, shrimp fajitas $7.50. Taco salad w/seafood or tenderloin $4.25/ $8.50. Respectable salads, guacamole; food is a local standout. Miner's pie ($1.75) a specialty.

Suomi Home Bakery & Restaurant. *54 N. Huron off Bus. U.S. 41 downtown. Turn down toward channel. Under covered street. (906) 482-3220. No credit cards or alcohol. Mon 6-5, Tues-Sat 6-6, Sun 7 a.m.-2 p.m.* Antiseptically plain. Friendly service, constant refills on coffee. Amazing prices (pie $1 a slice). Known for Finnish specialties, pasties ($2.20, 16 oz.) , homestyle cooking. Breakfast all day, under $3.60 inc. coffee. Winners: *pan nukakku* (custardy, oven-baked pancake with fruit sauce, $2.25), huge pancakes, *nisu* toast (cinnamon and cardomom). Daily special $3.30, burgers $1.50, homemade soup $1.25.

Best Western King's Inn. *(906) 482-5000. 215 Sheldon in downtown Houghton.* 68 units on 5 floors. Summer: $61-$71. Winter: $54-$64. Some rooms have view across channel to Hancock. Cable TV. Indoor pool, sauna, whirlpool. Larger rooms can sleep 2 more for extra $6 ea.
Indoor pool, downtown location

College Motel. *(906) 482-2202. 1308 College (U.S. 41), 1/2 mi. e .of downtown Houghton.* Large, pleasant rooms, some with view of lift bridge and Portage canal. July-Oct: $34-$42. Nov-June: $30-$36. Cable TV. Basketball, ping pong & fooze ball.
Near Mich. Tech. campus; best budget choice.

LAKE LINDEN

Lindell Chocolate Shoppe. *Calumet St. downtown. (906) 296-0793. Mon-Sat 6:30- 7 , Fri to 9. No credit cards.* Full bar. The food's not great but the setting's stunning: a 1920 Greek sweet shoppe in all its glory. Tile floor, golden oak booths with little fringed shades. Casual dining. Changing daily specials, like Fri fish fry, $5 and under. Sandwiches from $3. Rice pudding, homemade ice cream, $1.50-$2.50.

CALUMET

Thimbleberry Inn. *(906) 337-1332. 1156 Calumet Ave. (U.S. 41) at Sixth St./Lake Linden Ave. on outskirts of Calumet.* 6 rooms share 2 baths in big house built for mining official, later used as convent. $45-$50. Sink in each room. Nicer inside (original woodwork, airy country decor) than out (ugly asbestos shingles). Full breakfast. Phone, TV in 1 of parlors used by guests. Pleasant porch, yard. Genial innkeeper a native, worked in mines.
Convenient B&B in nice old house with Copper Country innkeepers

LAURIUM

Toni's Country Kitchen. *79 3rd St. next to post office in Laurium. (906) 337-0611.* Closed during January. Hours: 8-5, closed Sun June-Oct; Sun-Mon Nov-May. No credit cards or alcohol. Plain new place with a big reputation for pasties. Cheerful, lively. Bakery for desserts, huge cinnamon rolls. $2.25 ($2 take out). Breakfast $1-$3.25. Pasties $2.25, soups $1.25, sandwiches $1.25-$3. Takeout available.

Laurium Manor Inn B&B. *(906) 337-2549. 320 Tamarack St., 2 blocks from downtown.* 10 rooms on 3 floors. Open year round. $35-$85. Continental breakfast. 4 rooms w/ baths, 6 rooms share baths. TV. Phone on main floor. Huge Southern-style 40-room mansion. Built by mining magnate Thomas Hoatson in 1905 for $50,000. Best fixtures have been stripped by past speculator owners, but murals, grand staircase, mantelpieces remain. Guest rooms are pleasant. Shabby common rooms have been redecorated since our visit.
B&B in mansion in lovely, shady historic neighborhood

Superior Motel. *(906) 337-1104. 341 Hecla. 1/2 mi. e. of U.S. 41 in business section.* 14 rooms on 2 floors. Open year-round. $26-$40. A/C. Cable TV, 3 kitchenettes, phones. Trim, clean, sunny, modern motel at right angles to street. Downtown is plain, quiet. Adjoining neighborhoods are most attractive.
Modern amenities in downtown Laurium

KEARSARGE

The Hut. *On U.S. 41 1 mi. n. of Calumet. (906) 337-1133.* May-Oct, 11:30 a.m.-9 p.m. Tues-Sun. Weekends only in winter. MC, Visa. No alcohol. Amazing setting: massive stone walls, low, angled ceilings with big beams, pool & waterfall. Wright-inspired do-it-yourself project made of local poor rock (rock with no copper in it). Begun as a drive-in, added onto each winter. A local favorite with surprisingly good food, casual atmosphere. Known for steakburgers. Lunch entrees $3-$5 with starch. Complete dinners from $4 (hamburger) to $10. Specials. All-day sandwich menu. Thimbleberry torte (in season) $1.50.

Old Country House. *On U.S. 41 in Kearsarge 2 mi. n. of Calumet. (906) 337-4626. Open year-round. Mon-Sat 11:30-8:30, Sun 11:30-7:30. Visa, MC. Full bar.* Rustic log interior. Very popular locally for huge 40-item salad bar ($5.75 at lunch, $7 at dinner) with shrimp in the shell! — except for Wed. Known for wiener schnitzel ($10.25), fresh lake trout ($10), whitefish ($11). Lunch entrees from $3.50 (BLT) to $7 (stuffed flounder). Dinners inc. soup, salad bar. House-made strudel, cherry torte.

Belknap's Garnet House B&B. *(906) 337-5607. U.S. 41 1 1/2 mi. n. of Calumet, across from The Hut restaurant.* Open mid June thru Sept (or color season, whichever is later). $40-$50. 5 rooms on 2nd floor of impressive house built for mining captain, restored & furnished with circa 1900 antiques by old-house lovers from Flint area. Most rooms share baths. Nice original woodwork, lighting, leaded glass. Full breakfast. Phone in common area. TV in den. Guests use dining room, parlor. Big wooded yard, interesting outbuildings.

MOHAWK

Slim's Cafe. *On U.S. 41 in Mohawk, 7 mi. n. of Calumet. (906) 337-3212. Open year-round, daily 7 a.m.-10 p.m. No credit cards, alcohol.* Recommended for authentic local color; nothing touristy. Breakfasts $3-$4. Sandwiches $1.50-$2. Complete dinners: $4 hot beef sandwich; 2 pork chops $6.50. Homemade pie w/ice cream $1.75.

EAGLE HARBOR

Eagle Harbor Inn. *M-26 at w. end of Eagle Harbor. (906) 289-4435. July 4-mid Aug. open daily 8 a.m.-9 p.m. (Call for off-season hours.) MC, Visa. Full bar.* Known for pizza $5-$12, homemade desserts. Still rustic (that's de rigeur up here) but updated and more ambitious than most spots here. Worth the slightly higher prices. Breakfasts avg. $5. Lunch menu: sandwiches (mostly $4-$5), soup, salads (avail. all day). Dinners include salad & starch. From $9 (teriyaki chicken) and $10 (shrimp scampi or scallops) to $12 (filet mignon).

Shoreline Restaurant. *M-26 on the lakeshore in town.. (906) 289-4441. Open mid May-mid Oct. Mon-Fri 8-2 & 5-8, Sat-Sun 8-8. MC, Visa. No alcohol.* Specialties: homemade pies, soups, pies, Sunday baked chicken. Consistently good, health-conscious food, nurturing atmosphere, makes you yearn for simpler times. Pine paneling. Rocks, U.P. books, copper curios for sale. Rock fireplace, sofa in dining room. Daily special (complete meal, beverage, dessert) around $6-7. All-day sandwich menu about $3.

Shoreline Resort. *(906) 289-4637. M-26 on shallow, warm Eagle Harbor bay.* 8 rooms on 1 floor face sand beach, great view of lighthouse, rocks. Open mid May-mid Oct. $38-$42. Satellite TV, 1 kitchenette. No phones. Simple, small rooms. Clean. No A/C ; can be hot on warm days. No phones. Lawn chairs.Thoughtful amenities. Use of canoe. Good restaurant. Reserve early; many repeat customers book ahead.
Beautiful, simple and homey — the Keweenaw at its best

Eagle Harbor Inn. *(906) 289-4435. M-26 at west end of Eagle Harbor.* 9 rooms on 1 floor. Summer $35-$40, lower rates spring & fall. Closed Apr & Nov. Showers, satellite TV. Phone in restaurant. Very nicely decorated in

simple, nature-loving vein.
Older motel, nicely refurbished; good
restaurant adjoining

COPPER HARBOR

Harbor Haus. *4 blocks east from jct.
U.S. 41 & M-26 on lake shore. (906)
289-4222. Open June-Oct. daily 7 a.m.-
9:30 p.m. Major credit cards. Full bar.*
Same owner as Old Country House, but
more ambitious menu w/ German specialties, wild game, fresh trout &
whitefish ($13 on complete dinner). A
la carte lunch items $4-$8; dinners
from $9 (knockwurst, chicken) to $20
(seafood platter). Pastry chef creates
rich continental tortes (up to $4). Out-
standing view, secluded location, lakeview deck. Dirndl-clad waitresses do a
dance when boat to Isle Royale goes by.
Best food in area, but not consistently
amazing.

Keweenaw Mountain Lodge.
*On U.S. 41 1 mi. s. of Copper Harbor.
(906) 289-4403. Open mid-May to mid-
Oct, 8 a.m.-9 p.m. MC, Visa. Full bar.*
Ordinary food, ample servings. The
draw is the setting, in massive log
lodge built as WPA make-work project
in 1930s. Pleasant grounds. Breakfasts $3-$5. A la carte lunch entrees
$6-$7, complete dinners from $9 (roast
chicken) to $15 (lobster). Dinner salad
bar $5. Prime rib Sat $11.

Mariner North. *On M-26 in Copper
Harbor. (906) 289-4637. Lounge open
year-round, dining room open daily
from Dec. 26-3rd week Oct. Summer:
lunch (in bar) 11-11, dinner (dining
room) 5-11. Winter: brkfst 8-11, lunch
11-4:30, dinner 5-9. Major credit
cards. Full bar.* Keweenaw locals come
for weekend pizza, $5 dinner salad bar
heavy on mayo salads, also good on
fresh fruit, veggies. Loudly convivial
bar scene (live music on weekends)
separated from casual dining room
with occluded harbor view. Sandwiches $3-$5. Dinner with salad bar
from $5.75 (half-lb. burger) and $7.50
(6 oz. steak) to $15 (shrimp or T-bone).
Whitefish, trout $10.50.

Norland Harbor. *(906) 289-4815.
On U.S. 41, 1 1/2 mi. e. of Fort Wilkins.*
11 rooms on 1 floor. Open May-Oct.
May,June & Oct $26-$32. July-Sept
$28-$36. (4 overlook Lake Fanny Hooe,
7 efficiencies) Satellite TV. Phone in
office. Horseshoes, picnic area, grills,
canoes. Walk across road to Lake
Mich. Large site away from road has
many pines, beautiful flowers. Owners
could charge more, but prefer to have
repeat customers. Reserve well ahead.
*Delightful resort setting, beautiful
design, budget rates — a real find*

King Copper Motel. *(906) 289-
4214. On the waterfront on harbor in
town.* 34 rooms on 1 floor. July 4-Sept
(color season) $40-$55, $35-$40 off-
season. Cable TV, phone avail. Picnic
area, grills, beach.
*Biggest motel in town, away from
highway, overlooks harbor*

Keweenaw Mountain Lodge.
*(906) 289-4403. On forested hillside off
U.S. 41 1 mi. south of Copper Harbor.*
Open mid May-mid Oct. 34 log cottages
(1 bdrm $49, 2/3 bdrm $59). Reserve
cottages way in advance. Newer 8-unit
motel (large rooms, little atmosphere)
$46. Satellite TV. Shuffleboard. 9-hole
golf course (fee). Wonderful log lodge,
but porches, common room have been
enclosed for restaurant. Trees block
distant vistas.
*Terrific log cottages, resort setting,
fantastic value*

*Restaurants and lodgings are
listed at the end of each region.*

To find out more

 n excellent state highway map with lots of extra information is one of many useful publications available free of charge from the state of Michigan. Write or call:

Michigan Travel Bureau
Box 30226
Lansing, MI 48909

Toll-free: 1-800-5432-YES
For hearing impaired (Michigan only:
TDD-800-722-8191

The state's 13 Welcome Centers at major freeway entry points and on either side of the Mackinac Bridge are also quitehelpful. The literature they stock varies somewhat with the region, but the staff are almost without exception well informed and good at answering questions..
Additional information can be obtained by contacting:

West Michigan Tourist Association
136 E. Fulton St.
Grand Rapids, MI 49503
(616) 456-8557

Upper Peninsula Travel and Rec. Assn.
618 Stephenson Ave.
Box 400
Iron Mountain, MI 49801
(906) 744-5480

All three sources can provide information on fast-changing areas of travel, such as special events and bed and breakfasts, and specifics about outdoor activities like skiing and golf. (Michigan has more public golf courses than any other state!)